Microeconomics for Business

By the same author

Money Matters: A Keynesian Approach to Monetary Economics, with Sheila C. Dow (Martin Robertson, 1982)

The Economic Imagination: Towards a Behavioural Analysis of Choice (Wheatsheaf Books, 1983)

The Corporate Imagination: How Big Companies Make Mistakes (Wheatsheaf Books, 1984)

Lifestyle Economics: Consumer Behaviour in a Turbulent World (Wheatsheaf Books, 1986)

Psychological Economics: Development, Tensions, Prospects, editor (Kluwer Academic Publishers, 1988)

Behavioural Economics (2 Volumes), editor (Edward Elgar Publishing Limited, 1988)

Monetary Scenarios: A Modern Approach to Financial Systems (Edward Elgar Publishing Limited, 1990)

The Economics of Competitive Enterprise: Selected Essays of P.W.S. Andrews, co-editor with F.S. Lee (Edward Elgar Publishing Limited, 1993)

Microeconomics for Business and Marketing

Lectures, Cases and Worked Essays

Peter E. Earl

Professor of Economics
Lincoln University, Canterbury, New Zealand

EDWARD ELGAR

Published by
Edward Elgar Publishing Limited
Gower House
Croft Road
Aldershot
Hants GU11 3HR
England

Edward Elgar Publishing Company
Old Post Road
Brookfield
Vermont 05036
USA

British Library Cataloguing in Publication Data
Earl, Peter E.
  Microeconomics for Business and Marketing: Lectures,
  Cases and Worked Essays
  I. Title
  338.5

Library of Congress Cataloguing in Publication Data
Earl, Peter E.
  Microeconomics for business and marketing: lectures, cases and
worked essays / Peter E. Earl.
    448 p. 24 cm.
    Includes bibliographical references and index.
    1. Microeconomics. 2. Consumer behavior. 3. Utility theory.
  4. Production (Economic theory)   I. Title.
  HB172.E18   1995
  338.5—dc20   94–45021
                                                                          CIP

ISBN 1 85278 861 5 (cased)
      1 85278 862 3 (paperback)

Printed in Great Britain at the University Press, Cambridge

Contents

List of figures and tables   ix

Preface   xi

1   Introduction: alternative ways of learning about microeconomics   1
1.1   The case for a different intermediate microeconomics text   1
1.2   Coping with contending perspectives in economics   7
1.3   Essay-writing skills   12
1.4   A guide to tackling case studies   16
1.5   The economics of coping with examinations   18
1.6   Post-mortem on a 'warm-up' question for developing critical thinking skills   22

2   Theories of choice: an overview   27
2.1   The role of a theory of choice   27
2.2   Alternative approaches to theory construction   28
2.3   Alternative views of information and choice   29
2.4   Conclusion   33

3   Neoclassical theories of consumer behaviour   34
3.1   Introduction   34
3.2   The axioms of neoclassical preference theory   36
3.3   Constraints and consumer equilibrium   42
3.4   Income and substitution effects   46
3.5   Essay example: Housing policy and poverty   51
3.6   The consumer as a producer   52
3.7   Essay example: The usefulness of neoclassical consumer behaviour theory   62
3.8   Exam post-mortem: Anti-smoking policy   64
3.9   Further questions   65

4   Behavioural perspectives on decision-making   67
4.1   Introduction   67
4.2   Complexity and tests of adequacy   72
4.3   Choice rules and the competitive process   76
4.4   Case study: Executive cars   81
4.5   Essay example: Video cassette recorders   84
4.6   Psychological tradeoffs   88
4.7   Cognitive distortion and weakness of will   90
4.8   Economists' choices   94
4.9   Essay example: Consumer theory's relevance to estate agents and valuers   96

4.10	Exam post-mortem: Usefulness of alternative theories of choice in different contexts	98
4.11	Further questions	100

5	**Risk and uncertainty**	**103**
5.1	Introduction	103
5.2	Expected utility theory	104
5.3	Alternative probabilistic theories	108
5.4	Shackle's potential surprise theory	112
5.5	Exam post-mortem: Shackle's model versus expected utility theory	118
5.6	Scenario planning	119
5.7	Procedural approaches for coping with ignorance and uncertainty	124
5.8	Bargaining	127
5.9	Competitive games	136
5.10	Conclusion	140
5.11	Further questions	142

6	**Theories of firms and markets: an overview**	**144**
6.1	Introduction and suggestions on reading	144
6.2	Comparative static equilibrium analysis versus evolutionary analysis	145
6.3	Optimizing versus satisficing views of decision-making	147
6.4	Price competition in respect of a given set of products versus Schumpeterian technological competition	148
6.5	Representative 'black box' firms versus firms as differentiated organizations	150
6.6	Coordination by price alone versus coordination by price and voice	151
6.7	An emphasis on one-off deals versus an emphasis on relational contracting	152
6.8	A focus on products versus a focus on resources and capabilities	153
6.9	The firm as a simple aggregation of product market activities versus the firm as a set of linked activities	154

7	**Production methods and productivity**	**156**
7.1	Introduction	156
7.2	Production functions and cost curves	159
7.3	Factor substitution	169
7.4	The mix of output	170
7.5	Exam post-mortem: Production, costs and multi-product firms	176
7.6	Learning curves and the economics of product life-cycles	177
7.7	Productivity and technical change	181
7.8	Corporate culture, productivity and quality	184
7.9	Flexible specialization	187
7.10	The behavioural theory of the firm	189
7.11	The notion of efficiency in economics	193
7.12	Essay example: Competitive leadership	199
7.13	Further questions	201

8	Price and output decisions (1): from Marshall to marginalism	203
8.1	Introduction	203
8.2	Marshall's evolutionary analysis of the firm	204
8.3	Perfect competition and the debate over returns to scale	208
8.4	Exam post-mortem: Cost-curve dialogue	213
8.5	Imperfect and monopolistic competition: the same or different?	214
8.6	Technical exercise: Monopoly and perfect competition	221
8.7	Early criticism and defence of marginalism	224
8.8	Kinked demand curves	227
8.9	An alternative view of the economics of price cutting in response to reduced sales	231
8.10	Case study: 'Black Engineering'	233
8.11	Case study: 'The Parker retail gun'	238
8.12	Further questions	245

9	Price and output decisions (2): modern variations on Marshall and marginalism	247
9.1	Introduction and summary of the story so far	247
9.2	Pricing of pioneering products and new brands	249
9.3	Essay example: Cellular phone prices	251
9.4	Sales revenue maximization	255
9.5	Essay example: The case for abandoning the assumption of profit maximization	259
9.6	Normal cost analysis	260
9.7	Contestable markets and idiosyncratic products	272
9.8	Essay example: Generalizations about pricing	275
9.9	Essay example: Retail pricing in theory and practice	278
9.10	Exam post-mortem: The contestability *revolution*?	281
9.11	Price discrimination and product bundling	282
9.12	Exam post-mortem: The pricing of books	288
9.13	Essay example: Pricing and the multi-product firm	290
9.14	Conclusion	293
9.15	Further questions	294

10	The coordination of economic activities	298
10.1	Introduction	298
10.2	General equilibrium analysis	299
10.3	The role of the entrepreneur	301
10.4	Richardson's critique of supply and demand	303
10.5	Essay example: Deregulation in aviation and financial services	305
10.6	The Arrow–Debreu solution	309
10.7	Real-world solutions to the Richardson problem	312
10.8	Exam post-mortem: Investment interdependence	315
10.9	Endgames: quitting versus hanging on	316
10.10	Essay example: Price instability	319
10.11	Problem-solving institutions	322

10.12 The rationale of firms and markets   325
10.13 Limits to corporate growth   334
10.14 Conclusion   336
10.15 Further questions   337

11   Economics of corporate strategy and structure   340
11.1   Introduction   340
11.2   Vertical integration   341
11.3   Essay example: The international removals business   350
11.4   Franchising: a case study of McDonald's economics   352
11.5   Exam post-mortem: Real estate and optometry franchising   357
11.6   Diversification   360
11.7   Internal markets and organizational structure   365
11.8   Exam post-mortem: Shareholders and diversification   372
11.9   Essay example: Conglomerates and competition   373
11.10 Case study: The 1986 Daimler-Benz mergers   376
11.11 Joint ventures and other cooperative strategies   380
11.12 Multinational enterprise   385
11.13 Essay example: Transaction costs and tourism   388
11.14 Case study: The rise and fall of Filofax in Japan   393
11.15 Exam post-mortem: Reasons for multinationals   400
11.16 Conclusion   400
11.17 Further questions   401

Bibliography   404

Index   423

List of figures and tables

Figures

3.1	An indifference map	35
3.2	Convexity without strict convexity	38
3.3	Satiation	39
3.4	Vegetarian preferences under conditions of free disposal	41
3.5	The consumer's feasible set	42
3.6	A piecewise linear budget constraint	43
3.7	The consumer's preferred combination	44
3.8	The price-consumption curve	45
3.9	A corner solution	46
3.10	Income-consumption curve for an inferior good	47
3.11	Income and substitution effects for a normal good	48
3.12	A Giffen good	49
3.13	Marginal cost pricing and consumer welfare	50
3.14	Welfare implications of alternative housing policies	51
3.15	Holiday choices in characteristics space	55
3.16	Income and price changes in characteristics space	57
3.17	A Giffen good in characteristics space	58
3.18	Choices of indivisible products	59
4.1	Priorities and choice	75
4.2	Hierarchical choice and an inferior good	79
5.1	The reservation price of insuring a motor vehicle against theft	107
5.2	An S-shaped value function	109
5.3	The weighting function suggested by Kahneman and Tversky	110
5.4	A potential surprise curve	114
5.5	The ascendancy function	115
5.6	Primary and standardized focus gains and losses	116
5.7	A gambler preference map	117
5.8	A 'two point test' filter for rival potential surprise curves	118
5.9	A neoclassical view of gains from trade	128
5.10	Satisficing and gains from bilateral exchange	129
5.11	An optimizing decision-maker bargaining with a satisficer	130
5.12	Expectations and bargaining strategies	134
7.1	Constant, decreasing and increasing returns to scale	160
7.2	Cost-minimizing technologies: a production function's long-run output expansion path	162

List of figures and tables

7.3	Total, average and marginal products when only one input can be varied	163
7.4	The relationship between the total product function and total variable costs when only one input can be varied	164
7.5	The relationship between total, average and marginal variable costs	165
7.6	Factor substitution in response to a change in relative input prices	169
7.7	Short-run versus long-run factor substitutions	170
7.8	The optimal mix of output	171
7.9	Choice of production mix, subject to linear constraints	173
7.10	An '80 per cent' learning curve	178
7.11	Technological progress and supply conditions in a competitive market	182
7.12	Deadweight losses due to the imposition of a tax	194
7.13	Monopolistic pricing and consumer welfare	195
8.1	Long-run equilibrium of a perfectly competitive firm	209
8.2	Short-run equilibrium of an imperfectly/monopolistically competitive firm	215
8.3	Long-run equilibrium of an imperfectly/monopolistically competitive firm	216
8.4	Chamberlin's equilibrium solution for a member of a 'small' group of oligopolistic competitors	219
8.5	Graphical summary of calculations in monopoly and perfect competition exercise	222
8.6	The kinked demand curves proposed by Hayes (1928)	227
8.7	The kinked demand curve and price stickiness	228
8.8	Unstable equilibrium with a reflex kinked demand curve	229
9.1	Revenue, price and profit implications of alternative managerial goals	257
9.2	The 'normal cost' approach to pricing	262
9.3	A price-discriminating monopolist selling in two markets	284
9.4	Price discrimination as a way of making a firm's market viable	285
10.1	An unstable, explosive 'cobweb' cycle	304
11.1	A U-form (functionally-based) corporate structure	369
11.2	M-Form structure of a hypothetical audio-visual entertainments firm	370

Tables

4.1	Choice matrix for video recorders	85
5.1	Hypothetical expected values of rival university courses	105
5.2	Hypothetical expected utilities of rival university courses	105
7.1	Daily capacities of car- and van-production activities	172
7.2	Profitability of car and van production	174

Preface

And now for something completely different. For many years I lived in the hope that someone would write a book which presented, at a level accessible to students of intermediate microeconomics, a guide to the key ideas of both mainstream neoclassical economics as well as to behavioural and institutional economics. Innovative texts did appear, such as Ricketts (1987) and Frank (1991) but, good though they were at covering what their authors set out to cover, they did not explore the full range of microeconomics that I planned to teach when I next had the chance. In 1991, that opportunity was presented to me when I took up the Chair in Economics at Lincoln University in New Zealand. I had no intention of allowing my coverage of microeconomics to be constrained by the existing supply of textbooks but it was quite clear from the outset that most of my class of over 250 students had no intention of learning by reading widely from a reading list: they wanted a set of lecture notes as their main reference tool, with something akin to a textbook as a back-up. It was also clear that most of the class had very poor analytical and essay-writing skills, and that they expected at all times to be told what the 'right' answers were. Clearer still was the impossibility of my doing any research if each week I might expect to have dozens of students knocking on my door expecting a private tutorial on 'how to do the essay'. I wanted to lead them towards being able to analyse practical business problems in a self-reliant way and be able to write up reports and argue cases with a competence that would reflect well on Lincoln University; and I wanted to train them honestly, in the sense of opening their eyes to the range of thinking that exists in microeconomics rather than ignoring non-mainstream contributions even though these might be perfectly accessible to the class. There was only one thing for it: I was going to have to write a textbook myself, a book in which I presented more than a single paradigm and in which I provided copious amounts of role-model material on strategies for tackling essay and case study problems. There was an interesting irony here: I would eventually be writing about vertical integration and market failure, but I was having to produce the text myself because the textbook market had failed to satisfy my needs.

Three years later, as I completed the final draft, it was obvious why the market had hitherto failed in this way. It was not that there was an insufficient demand for this sort of book: on the contrary, even prior to the publication of the finished work, 'desktop publishing' versions of the text were being used by some like-minded economists teaching in other institutions, in Australia, the United Kingdom and Austria. Though I used the book as an intermediate microeconomics text, others have pointed out that it may also serve as a third-year undergraduate text to be read in parallel with a more technical text of the conventional kind, or on microeconomics courses for MBA students. Some might even want to use it in teaching students at the postgraduate level who have hitherto had an exposure only to neoclassical economics, while many lecturers should find it very useful for getting familiar with non-mainstream microeconomics and seeing how it may be applied to new kinds of business problems. This range of audiences is one of the reasons why the book is presented in a more scholarly manner than traditional texts, with an emphasis on original sources so that more advanced student readers study more effectively.

Many other enterprising academics have probably been alert to these potential markets. They were probably more deterred, as I perhaps should have been, by the scale of the enterprise and the career implications of embarking upon it. The book has been written during a period in which academic audits have become all the rage and, in these audits, textbooks count for nothing, regardless of their potential to contribute towards the production of a new breed of economists. This audit frenzy has, however, merely formalized something that has been evident for many years: anyone who wants to get on in the subject rationally invests time in producing articles for the favoured list of 'core' journals, or a thicker pile of articles for second-tier journals. I had the luxury of not having to worry about this (or so I thought, at the start of the project), but that caused its own problems for me in terms of a scarcity of time to write rather than deal with senior-level administrative work and refereeing processes. The result was that much of the writing was done late at night or over weekends, when I had otherwise hoped to be enjoying the pecuniary and lifestyle fruits of my move to New Zealand. At least I was lucky to be sharing a house with my partner Sharon Axford, who was able to put up with this and who, as a psychologist, would know when I was overdoing it. For the final week of writing, she was even prepared to reconstrue the concept of a skiing holiday as an event which entailed her going skiing at Coronet Peak while I remained in front of the Macintosh in our motel in nearby Arrowtown. In addition to thanking Sharon, yet again, for her support and patience, I would like to record my gratitude to those who have affected the form taken by the book, though they are not to be implicated in any of the errors it may contain. It seems appropriate to list these debts in the order in which they were incurred and at the same time reveal more about the book's origins.

The book is undoubtedly influenced by my experiences as an undergraduate at Cambridge in the mid-1970s. It was there that I found myself having to cope with multi-paradigm teaching of economic principles. In that task I was assisted most of all by Ajit Singh, not only because of his guidance on the art of essay writing but also because he noted my interest in the economics of information at an early stage and steered my reading in the direction of behavioural economics, which received little coverage in lectures. I could not have wished for a better role model of a tutor. As a research student (1977–79), I continued reading in this direction and began incorporating behavioural material into my first ventures into teaching undergraduates. They were as excited as I was about theoretical developments that related to the economics of corporate strategy, so topics such as learning curves, investment coordination and the economics of organizational structure became firmly embedded into my vision of what ought to be included in an intermediate-level training in microeconomics.

In 1979 I moved to the University of Stirling to take up my first lectureship. Chapters 8 and 9 of this book are very strongly influenced by this formative experience. Brian Loasby impressed upon me the worth of looking at classic works in the original, opening my eyes particularly to insights present in Marshall (1890) and Chamberlin (1933) that I had not hitherto noticed. My growing interest in behavioural approaches to consumer choice led to my first opportunity to teach marketing, assisting Susan Shaw and in the process learning about the case study method of teaching. I also picked up the case study method from Richard Shaw in teaching management economics with him and Brian Loasby. It is with pleasure that I am able to include also in this book case study problems devised by Sue and Richard that I have enjoyed using in the classroom. The other Stirling influence in this book comes from Neil Kay, who had been one of that university's first economics graduates, though by that stage he was already teaching elsewhere in Scotland. More than anyone else, Neil has helped me to see the strengths of transaction cost approaches to economics and the limitations of Williamson's (1975, 1985) particular brand of transaction cost economics. Chapter 6 as well as parts of Chapter 10 and much of Chapter 11 have been affected by reading Neil's work and meeting with him at frustratingly infrequent intervals over the past decade and a half.

The Stirling influences might have been greater still, had I not decided to move to Tasmania in 1984: the standard of living was much higher but there was, for me, a considerable culture shock on finding myself in a department where, at that time, I was the only person familiar with behavioural microeconomics and Post Keynesian macroeconomics. Fortunately, in Michael Brooks I found a colleague who also moving in the direction of transaction cost economics via an interest in the economics of law and who was also familiar with subjectivist approaches to economics. Michael was the source of many provocative questions, reading suggestions and insights in the seven years we worked together. My teaching eventually involved more marketing than economics and I found that Chris Lock and Norton Grey were an excellent pair of mature tutors with whom to share ideas: many of the notes on case studies originated during the period working with them and they contributed a lot to my experiments in devising new ways to test the understanding of behavioural theories of consumer choice.

At Lincoln, many students and part-time tutors provided helpful feedback on the book while it was being written, as did some colleagues: of these, I am particularly grateful to Libby Benson, Victoria Benton, Tony Davis, Mark Devlin, Lau Wai Kun, John Mulligan, Karen Robinson and Rod St Hill. I was also pleased to have some very useful comments on earlier drafts from Edward Elgar's referees, Mark Blaug, Michael Dietrich, Huw Dixon and Martin Ricketts. However, my biggest intellectual debt during the past three years is to Neil Fleming, the Director of the Education Centre, for introducing me to the work of William Perry (1970, 1981, 1985) on student learning processes. The initial batch of Lincoln students were shocked to find me exposing ambiguities in economics and demonstrating mistakes in standard texts and they tended to rush to Neil for comforting, rather than coming directly to me. Perry helped me make sense of the situation. The class, Neil and I survived the 1991 version of my course on the basis of my standing in for the lack of any textbook by using every available lecture slot in the unit's timetable block and writing, for the restricted loan collection in the library, summaries on close to sixty lectures and essay workshops. For the 1992 year, a very rough first draft of the text was developed from these materials and others from Tasmania and Stirling, and 400 copies were produced by the University Printery. Morale in the class seemed to improve dramatically. A second, completely restructured draft followed in 1993 after I found out how the students used the first one, with a third draft in 1994.

The ability of the University Printery to turn out good quality paperback editions for a very reasonable rate did occasionally make me think I should have carried the process of internalization a bit further and become my own publisher; but with such short product life-cycles for each draft and highly unpredictable student enrolments, I soon became convinced that my comparative advantage lies in writing books, not in making projections of demand, chasing the bookstore for payment, arranging worldwide distribution, and wondering how on earth the Printery could have lost the master copy of the second draft at a time when a surge in student numbers seemed to imply we needed to produce another batch of copies (the master copy was never found but, much to my relief, the class size that semester settled down to about three hundred instead of the figure of over four hundred that came to the first lectures). There is nothing like a venture into desktop publishing to concentrate one's mind on the economics of coordination and business strategy and the need for transaction cost economists to pay more attention to expectations concerning competence, rather than fears of opportunism, as a key factor shaping many decisions about when to rely upon someone else to get something done. It was good to have the support of Edward Elgar yet again, right from the early stages of writing, as our relational contracting moved into its second decade.

Potential adopters of this text may be interested to know that, as the book became more polished, I ceased lecturing from it and instead requested that the class read particular chunks of it prior to particular lecture slots—which were renamed 'forum sessions'—in which I would attempt to deal with any questions they raised. In this way, the students could study at their own pace and I could concentrate on the bits they found most difficult and know where to pay particular attention when preparing the final draft. The study experience thus became somewhat more like distance learning, combined with lecture hall substitutes for office hour inquiries. This style of teaching seems to work as least as well as the conventional style, though it does require students to discipline their studies rather more than they might be used to doing. However, whilst I would urge adopters of the book to consider trying it for themselves, I would warn them that it is an approach to lecturing which does not fit in nicely with standard course evaluation procedures—for a start, many students have no need to show up to most lectures—and it does require considerable determination to convince students that lectures do not intrinsically have to involve lecturers sticking to a prepared script and overheads, where the main activity of students is transcription rather than the construction of meaning. It seems to have taken far too long for academics in general to notice that the significance of the invention of the printing press for universities was that it opened up the possibility for them to spend their teaching time on presenting things that could not yet be found in published form, and on dealing with problems of interpretation that students were having. This book is radically different from rival texts in microeconomics but I hope it is different in a way that opens up new teaching possibilities and makes microeconomics more exciting and enjoyable for open-minded lecturers and their students.

1 Introduction: alternative ways of learning about microeconomics

This opening chapter should be read both by lecturers who use the book as a recommended text and by the students on their courses. It outlines the thinking behind the book, the benefits that students may achieve from using it and some of the costs that may have to be incurred to achieve these benefits. A failure to read this chapter—perhaps on the presumption that it does not contain any economics that might be of use for passing the course for which the book is being used—could result in an inability to understand why the rest of the book proceeds in the way that it does. It would also mean that one missed the last four sections, which examine techniques for writing essays and examination answers and for tackling case study problems in business and marketing.

1.1 The case for a different intermediate microeconomics text

An economist who sets about writing a text for intermediate-level undergraduate students of microeconomics might be expected to consider carefully the economics of this time-consuming task. With so many texts already available, the wisdom of such a project is questionable: on what basis can the author hope to pick up a share of the market at the expense of established works? It would appear that the market is one in which the product has practically reached 'commodity status' in the sense that genuine product differentiation is hard to discern amongst rival textbooks. Most students' ways of thinking as economists will not be fundamentally dependent on which text their lecturers happen to recommend, for one can read from page to page of rival works and discover that, by and large, what they have to say is basically the same, with only the illustrative examples seeming to differ. Nowadays, it would appear that the sales representatives of most academic publishers believe that the way to win sales is to offer products that are basically the same as those supplied by the opposition in terms of their contents but which offer advantages in terms of their visual appeal (multi-colour type-setting in new, easily read fonts) or in terms of the kinds of back-up resources that are made available (such as instructors' manuals that include master copies of overhead transparencies, computer-based test banks of multiple-choice questions, and so on). This back-up material is nowadays so extensive that it seems to remove the need for lecturers who use it to have expertise in the matters of course design and lecture construction. No doubt it will not be long before economics text packages, like those in marketing, even include sets of video tapes that lecturers may play to their classes. By investing more and more in the production of the product and its back-up resources, the giant academic publishing companies appear to be set on raising entry barriers in the market for textbooks. Given such trends, only those academics who have superstar names in the profession and a good stage presence in front of video cameras would find it worthwhile to sign up to write textbooks.

An alternative strategy for a writer/publisher team is to win sales by radical product innovation, by deliberately opting to go against the grain to produce a work which will make a difference to the ways in which its users think about economics. That is precisely the strategy adopted in the case of the present book, and it comes at a cost in terms of the glossiness and scale of the product package. The higher marketing risks limit the size of the initial print run. Consequently, the publisher's fixed costs of production have to be reduced in order to keep the average costs of finished copies competitive with conventional texts that have already been adopted widely. Thus, for the first edition at least, it does without lavish production methods, coming in black and white straight from camera-ready copy produced by the author with the aid of a Macintosh computer and LaserWriter printer. It comes without any students' or instructors' manuals and related paraphernalia. It does not attempt to make the lecturer redundant or reduce the role of the lecturer to that of someone who reads out a text and flashes appropriate transparencies up on a screen. The package may not be as glossy as that which might be offered by a major multinational publisher, but we nonetheless believe it has more to offer as an educational experience. This is because it has been designed to counter a number of significant failings that can be identified in both mainstream textbooks and conventional approaches to the teaching of microeconomics.

One major objection which might be raised is that economics is typically taught in a very one-sided manner. It is possible to emerge from three years of studying economics with no awareness of the variety of approaches to the subject that exist and which one might have had the intellectual capacity to handle at the undergraduate level. Typical students of microeconomics will probably not realize that all their training has consisted of what is known as 'neoclassical' microeconomics: as far as they will be concerned, what they have studied *is* economics, period. And they will probably have grave doubts about whether anyone might find it particularly useful for dealing with practical problems, however useful it has been as a means of gaining course credits. Limited practical applicability might seem of little concern to economists who practice the one-sided approach to teaching their subject: they might maintain that what they are really doing is training their students to think in more advanced ways, with economics being the vehicle that is used to achieve this training, rather than, say, English Literature or Classics. This may be so, but as economists we should consider possible costs of using this vehicle at the expense of alternative possibilities.

To teach economics in a one-sided way seems to me to be doubly unfortunate. First, it means that students will have no knowledge of alternative approaches to economic analysis that in some contexts may be more useful ways than the mainstream approach for thinking about important problems. Secondly, it does nothing to take students away from the idea that places of learning are what one attends to learn *the truth* and it does nothing, therefore, to open their eyes to the debatable nature of knowledge. The sanitized, cut-and-dried presentation of economics as something unblemished by major disputes about how particular phenomena might best be understood is unlikely to be a very good vehicle for helping students to develop an understanding of how high-level intellectual debates can be conducted, or an ability to communicate with each other in debates amongst themselves. If students believe they are being taught *the* way to do economics, there is likely to seem to be little scope for discussing economic theory (aside from technical details) with each other outside of the classroom. Yet it is in debates in informal social settings—over coffee, or in a

2

college bar—that much of a student's intellectual development can take place.

Those who simultaneously teach a variety of approaches to economics seem likely to promote an interest in and awareness of different ways of thinking, and a recognition that the world is a place where things are debatable—where instead of black and white there are many grey areas—and that often skill in asking questions and raising difficulties is more valuable than an ability swiftly to make claims about what *the* answer might be to a problem. But to be really effective in getting students to think more effectively I feel it is important that a microeconomics text actively focuses upon identifying styles of logic and inference that can be either useful or analytically disastrous. One way of achieving such a focus is to show how economists themselves go about trying to solve problems and sometimes get into a mess because of a failure to grasp the implications of their ways of thinking. As a means of promoting better thinking skills, a study of episodes in the history of economic thought therefore seems invaluable, yet authors of mainstream texts tend to dish up their subject matter with what we might call a 'here it is, *now*' mentality, as if the process of development of economic ideas is something from which nothing can be learned.

Such thinking has led me to attempt to present microeconomics here in a way that highlights alternative ways of looking at things and the processes by which they have evolved. Space limitations mean that I cannot examine all the approaches to microeconomics that are being explored at the moment, or which were once thought worthwhile to pursue, but I shall at least try to compare and contrast the neoclassical approach with an alternative approach—behavioural/institutionalist economics—that is rapidly growing in popularity and which already has two Nobel Laureates in Economics (Herbert Simon, 1978; and Ronald Coase, 1991) amongst its leading personalities.

The choice of this alternative in part reflects my own expertise but it is also related to the second failing that I perceive in the way that economics is normally taught. Academic economists nowadays tend to spend most of their teaching time supplying 'service' inputs to audiences of students who are taking degrees in commerce. These degree programmes involve a strong emphasis on accountancy and, sometimes, on marketing and management. The implication of this is that most 'economics students' are not ones who have opted to take specialized degrees in economics. The majority will probably terminate their studies in economics at the end of an intermediate-level course. Heads of economics departments are well aware that these students generate the resources that enable them to run higher-level courses for a small number of economics specialists. However, few of them try to ensure that microeconomic theory is taught in a way that might be particularly useful to their 'bread and butter' audience and at the same time serve as a valuable foundation for the few who are concentrating on a deeper study of economics. Instead, economics lecturers are often allowed to teach as if the entire class is headed towards a Masters-level course in economic analysis.

The basic ideas of neoclassical economics can be taught in quite a short space of time in a relatively non-technical manner. However, in the typical style of teaching, they are done to death in an abstract way which emphasizes the learning of technical set-pieces instead of the development of skills in practical problem-solving. Neoclassical problem-solving exercises involve well-defined questions in which all the ambiguities of the real world are kept out of the way via heroic assumptions about what is known about the problem area in question: if the techniques are applied correctly a particular answer inevitably drops out. The consequence of this seems to be that economics comes to be seen by a typical commerce student as a set of diagrams to be regurgitated at examination time, not as a training in a way of thinking that will be useful after graduation to the world of business.

To some extent, commerce students are entirely justified in behaving as if the economics they learn will be of no practical use once they have graduated. Compared with the behaviouralist/institutionalist alternative, neoclassical economics is often ill-suited for framing business problems. By teaching, for example, behavioural theories of consumer choice and institutionalist analysis of the economics of corporate strategies, economists may be able simultaneously to attract more students to specialize in their subject and generate a greater commitment to it from those who are taking it purely 'because they have to'.

Now, of course, anyone who has got the basics of economics under control will rightly point out that the inclusion of this additional material must come at the cost of leaving something out unless the length of the book is allowed to expand far beyond that of a conventional text. In a book of the length of this one, neoclassical economics is inevitably going to receive a far more superficial coverage that will require remedial work at a later date. I see no problem with this. For a start, there seems to be an awful lot of repetition of material from one degree year to the next in a typical sequence of economics courses. Instead of getting the basics sorted out before allowing progression to technically more demanding material, instructors in a typical programme teach at a technical level that is 'over the heads' of many of their students. Many of those who pass at the first stage only understand a small fraction of the material that the teachers at the next stage initially take for granted. In the subsequent unit, higher-level techniques end up being taught in the midst of an attempt to remedy the failure to understand the basics. Unfortunately, technical skills gained in this manner do not necessarily enhance abilities to tackle practical problems of resource allocation. Students who score well in tests of their technical skills often perform dismally if required to tackle from scratch a real problem of business or public policy. This appears to happen in many cases because they have not picked up the economic way of thinking: they fail to consider alternative possibilities, different ways of approaching a problem, and the different constraining factors that might affect the wisdom of choosing one strategy over another.

There is certainly a cost in terms of a stunted development of formal technical skills if economics is taught in a way that introduces students to a variety of approaches to the subject and stresses their philosophical similarities and differences. However, the end result is likely to be a class that has a better understanding of how economists think and who can then be taught relevant formal techniques with much less trouble if they opt to take higher-level courses in economics. Lecturers who adopt this text will need to ensure that they coordinate their teaching strategies with colleagues who teach units for which the material serves as a foundation, but the effort should be worthwhile for everybody involved.

In this book, I will be making room for the behavioural/institutionalist material by pruning the exposition of the mainstream neoclassical economics down to the minimum that I have found necessary for normal problem-solving purposes. Those students who desire a stronger technical foundation should find a plethora of suitable expositions in mainstream texts. My favourite ones are Eaton and Eaton (1991) and Frank (1991), both of which come slightly closer than most texts to using the philosophy employed in the present work.

(Student readers who are not used to this method of referencing—which is known as the Harvard system—should note that that details of all works referred to by author and date are to be found in the bibliography at the end of the book.) If I could not presume that my target audience would have access to a large library supply of such books, the present work would have to be much longer, or else I would have to keep the length down by abandoning any attempt to deal with my third area of concern, namely, students' poor skills in reading, writing and dealing with examination questions.

Students who fly through first-year courses in economics with apparent ease are often bought down to earth with a bump when they take the kind of second-year course with which this book is designed to be used. The problem is not that they are insufficiently smart to learn the key ideas but, rather, that they do not initially recognize that they have moved into a new kind of territory. They seem unaware of the differences between: (a) the skills required to cope in an environment of multiple-choice and short-answer types of questions; and (b) the skills they will need to practice if they are to survive in an environment of much more open-ended problem-solving and essay topics that focus upon questions of economic method. Such students look shocked if told that, when preparing assignments, they will be penalized for trying to regurgitate chunks of their textbooks and that they are expected to start making use of primary sources in the libraries. After a diet of words of one syllable and two-clause sentences, they claim that they cannot make sense of material beyond their textbooks. Those who mark the assignments then have often to contend with pieces of work that flit between passages of appalling gibberish and misplaced logic (one dreads what will follow 'therefore'!) and chunks of material copied almost word for word from recommended reading sources.

Most authors of traditional types of economics texts seem not to have seen their role as including the facilitation of advances in their student readers' literary and debating skills. Probably they have presumed that this is what lecturers and tutors do when taking tutorials or marking assignments. In reality, however, few lecturers or tutors have the time to mark essays in great detail or provide examination post-mortem sessions to give individual students the kind of feedback that will enable them to make great improvements in their ways of thinking and hence in their written work and examination techniques. In this book I use a variety of strategies to try to help students make progress in these areas and at the same time reinforce their understanding of economics.

First, the book's style of writing may provide a bridge between the undemanding reading of introductory texts and the rather less plain English of primary sources. At times student readers may have to think through a sentence repeatedly before its meaning becomes clear. This is not to say that such sentences have been written in a deliberately obscure manner but, rather, that they have been crafted with economy in mind. For example, a careful use of punctuation may enable one to say in a compound sentence what could only be said in far more words or with far less ultimate force if it were said as a series of short sentences. Students will also find that jargon phrases (such as 'bounded rationality') are taken for granted and used as forms of short-hand following careful initial explanations. Likewise, once an economist has been introduced as having made a particular contribution, the text proceeds as if the reader is familiar with that fact and is using the economist's name as a kind of mental 'pigeonhole'. In both cases, students who do not yet use such devices for organizing their thinking and economizing on words can use the book's index to chase up the first reference, just like an academic reader would do. If I sound short on empathy on this issue, I would simply say that the student who is used to being spoon-fed and being taught economics with no reference to its heritage is unlikely to develop more advanced ways of thinking unless forced to confront them and to practice using aids such as indexes and bibliographies. I shudder to think how many times students have come to me complaining that a recommended text has nothing in it on a particular topic even though I could find relevant material within a few seconds by using the index.

On a more empathic note, I would highlight three further strategies used in this book for improving analytical skills. One is the provision of many worked essay and case study questions where, in keeping with the book's overall philosophy, I focus on the kinds of answers that might be seen as worth rewarding highly, rather than on *the* answer. A second is the provision of a series of 'post-mortem' reports on examination questions that were set to a class brought up on the material covered in this book: they outline some of the kinds of traps into which students seem prone to fall. Both types of material also provide amplification and applications of what has been said elsewhere in the book, and pointers are provided to give suitable directions. In a sense, therefore, this book combines a text with a study guide and an instructors' manual and does not try to conceal from students effective ways of dealing with the sorts of questions that the text may equip them to answer.

In the first draft of this book, these sets of problem-based notes were grouped separately in four chapters at the end—partly so as not to disrupt the flow of text on theoretical material, and partly because they often drew on material from all manner of different theoretical areas covered in the book. Unfortunately, I found that, despite repeated reminders about the presence of this material towards the end of the book, many users of the trial edition tended only to focus their reading on the theory chapters and failed to look at the worked examples and post-mortem discussions when writing essays during semester. In this edition, therefore, I have placed each worked example or post-mortem discussion within the chapter to which it seems most closely related. I have additionally given pointers to earlier or later sections from which useful ideas can be or could have been gleaned. Pointers are also provided from these sections to discussions of questions that make use of their material. I hope these signals will be followed up, and that readers will start realizing that by occasionally delving back and forwards in the book they are likely to develop a better appreciation of microeconomics than if they attempt to read it in a linear manner, from start to finish. Some of my students have said that they found it easier to get a sense of what was going on in a chapter by reading its problem-based sections first and then going back to study the earlier sections in which the ideas were introduced. This was especially so if they were trying to do an essay from scratch in a hurry: for example, if they were doing question 11 from section 3.9, it was a great help to have read the essay example in section 3.7, whereas those who read in a linear manner stopped their reading at the end of section 3.6 in the mistaken belief that they had gone far enough.

A third feature aimed at making the book more user-friendly is a pair of overview chapters (2 and 6), one on theories of decision-making and consumer behaviour (covered in Chapters 3 to 5) and the other on theories of business behaviour (covered in Chapters 7 to 11). These chapters provide introductions to the different philosophies used by neoclassical and behavioural/institutionalist economists and show how these differences in method affect the kinds of questions that they address and the ways they set about trying to answer them.

Chapters 2 and 6 should thus play a major role in sign-posting what I would like readers to look out for and in assisting them to make sense of the subsequent material. In order for readers to see if they have picked up the main messages that I hoped to convey, they should re-read the relevant overview on reaching the end of each chapter. Sometimes, it may be found that this will help clarify the meanings of the overview chapters themselves.

This remark about re-reading applies, at the level of the book as a whole, to the present chapter, particularly to the next section. In general the message is that often you will not see something unless you are actively trying to observe it, and that without repeated prompts it is easy to forget what one is trying to see. The trouble is, an author can only provide an environment in which attempts are made to *help* readers *to form for themselves* a particular set of pictures of how the author sees the world (in this case, the world of microeconomic theory and areas for its application). At the end of the day, an entirely different set of mental pictures might get constructed by readers. Given that this book presents merely my own personal view of microeconomics, this may sometimes be no bad thing, and I welcome feedback from those who think they can show me a better way of looking at things. Certainly, I am not trying to claim that the book is *the* definitive tool for teaching microeconomics to students of business and marketing: quite apart from the issue of my technical interpretation of the work of other scholars and its applicability to practical problems, there is the obvious point that, for different types of audiences—for example, those who already have an extensive background in essay-writing—it might make sense to offer a rather different product.

1.2   Coping with contending perspectives in economics

My initial experience in teaching economics in the manner embodied in this book was that students reacted in a variety of ways. Some found it very exciting to learn about microeconomics in this manner. Others claimed to find it bewildering and had trouble reaching the sorts of grades they were used to obtaining on other courses. This led me to do some research on what is known about learning processes and its implications for the teaching of economics in this way (see Earl, 1995a, which makes extensive use of the work of Perry, 1970, 1981, 1985). One lesson that I drew from this was that students may cope better with this sort of course in economics if their teachers present to them an outline of why different students may tend to react differently to a given learning experience. At the very least, this gives the teachers a chance to comfort their students by telling them that they are aware of the problems that might be encountered. Such comforting is appropriate, for something akin to a grieving process appears to be involved as part of the transition from one way of thinking to another: people tend to cling anxiously to their established ways of making sense of things, rather than trying actively to be open minded. This book is challenging not so much because the ideas are complicated and technically difficult but, rather, because it asks the reader to get used to trying to construct a variety of ways of looking at things they encounter.

The nature of the book's intellectual challenge may be be restated with reference to the kinds of diagrams that are commonly used in introductory psychology lectures on perception. One classic here is a black shape on a white background which some people see first as a vase viewed from the side, but others see as a silhouette of two faces looking at one another. Another is a very rough sketch of the head of an animal which some people see as a rabbit with raised ears but others view as a duck holding its beak upwards and somewhat open. With prompting most people end up being able to see each of these pictures in both ways, but they find it difficult to see each picture in two ways at the same time. With this book I am asking you to get into the habit of looking out for alternatives: if you see a duck first, don't jump to the conclusion that you are looking at a duck. This will be particularly important when you are thinking about examination questions, or when deciding what your lecturer is up to, or what your role is in a tutorial.

A typical classroom will contain students who think about the world in a variety of different ways, some more sophisticated than others. These ways of looking at the world serve as filters that may prevent some students from seeing things as their lecturers expect them to be seen or as their peers are seeing them. The result of this can be that even some very bright students—taken in this case to mean those who have potentially great capacities for processing information and thinking creatively—may fail to cope very well with a course that is found to be enjoyable and rewarding by, say, older students who would not dream of calling themselves particularly bright. After years of advising students on learning problems, William Perry came to the conclusion that students' ways of looking at the world can usefully be analysed with reference to a sequence of stereotypical thinking styles that different people may use at different stages in their lives and in different parts of their lives. How perplexing this book is going to be will depend very much on how far along the sequence its users have progressed, whether in their university studies or in their thinking about other aspects of the world. I will now outline the sequence of thinking styles (or 'Perry progression' in honour of its discoverer) and ask readers to consider with which stereotype they presently identify the most.

Stage 1 students see themselves rather as if they are 'empty vessels' waiting to be filled with knowledge poured in by their lecturers. These students see their lecturers as people who (a) know what the Truth is in their area of expertise and (b) reward students by counting up the number of facts that the students have put down correctly in answering questions set as assignments or in examinations. Lecturers who cannot promptly give clear-cut answers to questions raised by students may therefore be seen as lacking in expertise. Indeed, it is the duty of the lecturer to be clear enough in lectures and in choosing the wording of assignment topics so that there is no need for students to have to ask questions: a lecture in which students keep asking questions must be a bad one. As far as these students are concerned, their responsibility is to work hard by taking notes in lectures and reading what their lecturers tell them to read; their efforts in these areas will determine how much they learn and hence how good their grades are. They prefer questions that involve definitions or requests to outline, explain or describe. If given questions that ask them to 'discuss' or 'compare and contrast', they will tend to view them as being worded in a deliberately obscure manner as a kind of trick and they will tend to answer by providing definitions, descriptions or outlines. They think discussions among themselves are a waste of time because it is the lecturer who knows what needs to be known; their own opinions count for nothing.

Stage 2 students differ from those at Stage 1 primarily because they have discovered that some lecturers or writers disagree with each other about particular issues. They have tried to make sense of this discovery by seeing some of these authorities as competent and deserving of respect and others as fakes, quacks or charlatans who are not telling the Truth. In other words, these students still believe that there does exist such a thing as an objective Truth 'out there' and they resolve differences in claims about what the Truth is by dividing them into two piles, right and wrong. (This is known as a 'dualistic' style of thinking.) It is thus hardly surprising that these students resent being offered a variety of points of view on a particular issue, for they see it as a waste of their time.

Stage 3 students may well have reached their different way of looking at things as a result of one day seeing a teacher that they have respected as a Good Authority admit that there is an unresolved difficulty in a particular area of inquiry. One way of reacting to this is to revise their existing views about whether or not this teacher is worth taking seriously as an expert, but that may be difficult if it is hard to find anyone who claims to know the truth for sure in both the current problem area and other areas previously investigated: perhaps it is really the case that no one does know. Stage 3 students still seek a 'dualistic' world of black and white truths and they make ambiguity tolerable by seeing it as purely temporary: eventually, it will be possible to resolve each difficulty one way or another with the aid or more sophisticated theories and computers, better experiments, and so on. But awareness of it makes them nervous about the prospect of being marked fairly in their examinations: if they write an answer in a style approved of by one lecturer, what happens if it is marked by someone inclined to another point of view about how the debate will get resolved?

Stage 4 students have realized that there are many areas in which debates have been going on for many years with no sign of resolution being imminent. They believe that some debates may never be resolved, which seems to imply that the truth will never be known. This discovery raises major questions about the worth of their own work: if lecturers disagree with each other about who has got the best theory, then who are the lecturers to criticize the opinions of students as expressed in their work or during tutorials? Everybody should be allowed to 'do their own thing' rather than having to end up looking at issues in the same way as people (whether lecturers, parents or whoever) who claim to be experts in particular areas. By this stage class discussions are coming to seen as worthwhile in so far as they serve as sources of ideas about how things *might* be. Interactive lectures are coming to be expected.

Stage 5 students, like those at Stage 4, have abandoned the idea that they are studying to discover an objective truth from people who know for sure what it is. However, they have noticed that in written work or class discussions they get rewarded for how they argue their points of view—for example, by showing they have examined possible alternatives in relation to their logical consistency, how well ideas fit the facts, where they seem to be misleading, and so on—and that what seems to be a worthwhile argument or theory in one setting may not seem so good in another context. They may have noticed this after seeing that what goes on in an educational environment seems rather like what happens in other areas of life, for example when discussing with their friends the merits of particular sporting teams, films, bands or consumer durables, or when arguing about the likely outcome of an election or sporting event. Alternatively, they may have discovered during their studies that it is possible to set up criteria for judging things and that judgements of quality are context-specific and dependent on personal perspectives. Having made these discoveries, they may have realized that life in general is like this: people who try to make a case for holding their particular point of view on an issue, and try to see where others are coming from, may get on far better than if they simply refuse to engage in discussions, argue merely by asserting 'I believe this' without trying to show why or, worse still, lower themselves to the level of 'Yes it is!' versus 'No it isn't!'. By this stage, they are seeing lecturers as people who point them towards better ways of arguing and as sources of feedback on the limitations of the views they have expressed in written work or tutorial discussions. Criticism becomes seen as something which *opens up opportunities* to get closer to one's goals, not as a something that is intended as a personal attack: even if one thinks the critic has missed one's point, the feedback is useful information, for a different way of making the point may be needed if the critic is to be able to comment effectively on whatever one is trying to say.

Stage 6 students have become more mature in a further sense: they are prepared to make some arguments for particular ways of looking at things not simply because they have seen such arguments constructed by others but because they have themselves thought long and hard about rival points of view before deciding to commit themselves one way or another—possibly to a view that they feel no one else seems to hold and which they have constructed for themselves. Having made these personal commitments (with a capital 'C'), they are prepared to stick to them unless shown what they see as convincing reasons for changing their views: they are now people with integrity.

This book, and the style of teaching it is designed to assist, is very much aimed at promoting the ways of thinking used by people at Stage 5 or Stage 6. Many students will probably be at Stage 2 at the time they start using it. Some might even find that it is this book that helps them open their eyes to the innocence of their Stage 1 ways of thinking about economics and leads them, so to speak, out of the Garden of Eden. We should not be surprised to see students getting angry if they find that their ways of looking at the world, which may have seemed to work well in the past, are being challenged: denial is the first stage in the process of grieving. Stage 2 students will initially tend to complain that the lectures are unclear when a lecturer discusses disputed areas of economics simply by talking about them at length and puts nothing except for diagrams and keywords up on the board or projector screen. They will tend to demand point by point summaries of what they should be learning from the lectures, even though Stage 5 students may be quite willing to decide for themselves what to write down as lecture notes. However, it may actually be counter-productive to provide such summaries: they may merely end up being memorized and regurgitated in the examination as 'answers' to questions that invited discussion or analysis. What the Stage 2 students may benefit from is a willingness to start concentrating on constructing their own interpretations of economic debates and of where different theorists are 'coming from'. The basic difficulty is that teachers cannot force their students to see the world in particular ways; all they can do is to try to move aside barriers to learning to think at a higher level. When a person reads an outline of what a particular style of thinking involves there is no guarantee that it will make any sense at all, let alone that it will be seen in the same way as the writer intended. Meaning is something that we each construct for ourselves.

If you are trying to move towards Stages 5 or 6 you may find it particularly useful to note that people typically try to make sense of things by trying to find something familiar with which to compare them and then looking for parallels and differences. Keep trying to do this in a conscious manner. For example, you may try to see economic theories as if they are *tools* for solving problems. This may be a much more homely image of theories than you get by trying to see them as Gospel Truths: a toolbox may contain a variety of tools that might be used for tackling any given problem and often we are not sure which tool is going to work when we open our toolboxes. Like a golfer deciding which iron to use on a particular shot, we think before opting to use a particular tool. However, unlike the golfer for whom every shot counts, it may not matter a great deal if at first we try a tool that turns out not to be up to the task. Indeed, since we do not wish to be lulled into a mistaken belief that we have successfully solved a problem, we may be wise to choose a couple of different theoretical tools for tackling it and compare the end results. By going through such thought experiments we may learn something about the limitations of our tools and be in a position to warn of potential dangers in conclusions reached by others who have not proceeded so carefully, rather as a mechanic may express alarm on hearing that someone has tried to secure a particular type of nut with a simple spanner rather than a torque wrench. You may also try seeing theories as if they are like cars, which differ in their characteristics. If we only have one car we have to make the best of it in all circumstances (unless we hire another for special occasions): sometimes we wish we had a mini, sometimes a convertible, sometimes a four-wheel drive, sometimes a stretch limousine. If you would not for a moment think of arguing that there is only one kind of all-purpose spanner, golf iron or car that is worth having and that specialist items of equipment have their own special advantages and problems, then you should find it possible to get to grips with this book even if it is your first experience of economics as a subject full of uncertainties and unresolved debates.

Mainstream economists tend to look down upon the work of behaviouralists and institutionalists as lacking elegance and rigour, rather as some motoring journalists tend automatically to look down upon a typical Japanese hatchback as boring. However, I often feel that the theoretical framework they use for their research is something of a Ferrari—wonderful in the artificial environment of a racetrack, but hopeless for driving in everyday conditions. In this book, I offer the economics equivalent of a relatively brief trip in a Ferrari, and spend quite a lot of time trying to demonstrate the capabilities of the economics equivalent of a Toyota Corolla or Mazda 323. After considering these different perspectives, you may well decide to look further afield for other possibilities, or even put together your own approach. After all, this book can itself be traced back to deviant undergraduate reading and thinking. As a second-year student, I felt there were issues that were not being adequately addressed by any of the three kinds of theories of value and distribution (neoclassical/general equilibrium, Marxian and neo-Ricardian) to which I was mainly being exposed. I would not for one moment want to pretend that at *that* stage I did not find it rather bewildering to make sense of what was going on in the economics profession. I was subsequently very glad that my tutor, Ajit Singh, suggested that I might enjoy reading Kornai's (1971) contribution to behavioural economics as a fourth perspective even though it had been savagely criticized by Frank Hahn, my lecturer on general equilibrium economics (see Hahn, 1973a). (A couple of years passed before I discovered the powerful critique of Hahn by Coddington, 1975b.)

1.3 Essay-writing skills

Although this book includes many detailed notes on a wide variety of essay topics, I think it is probably appropriate to offer some general comments at the outset about the writing of essays and case studies. After all, such pieces of work are very likely to be providing the immediate inducement for you to read the book. These comments are very much a personal perspective, and you may find it worthwhile to look also at some of the books on study skills that are readily available in most libraries. If you try to find such books and cannot do so, you probably need to ask library staff for advice on how you may improve your use of the library's index systems. This is a good idea, anyway, as the technology is changing rapidly and it is easy to underestimate just how much time can be saved by using modern CD-ROM-based information storage or indexing systems such as ABI/Inform and BPO (Business Periodicals Ondisc) and on-line services such as Reuters Textline. Via these devices you can find out not merely what is available on the shelves of your library; you may also be able to get summaries (abstracts) of journal articles, or even call up articles on a computer screen, browse, and then print out hard copies if they seem to be useful.

If a book that you are trying to find is listed as being out on loan do not simply go on to the next item on your list. Instead, take down its catalogue number and check out the books that are presently on the shelves immediately adjacent to where the book would have been were it not out on loan. Sometimes you may thereby discover a good substitute. However, bear in mind that books about similar topics may often differ radically in the perspectives they offer, so it may be wise also to try to find another work in the same broad area by the author whose book is unavailable. Many economists who have written books on a particular topic will have presented their key ideas in a shorter form as journal articles a few years earlier: you may be able to track these down with the aid of listings in the *Journal of Economic Literature* or find them republished later in books of collected essays by the same authors. Many of the most influential articles are available in reprint form somewhere or other if you cannot find the original source. Here it should be noted that Edward Elgar Publishing Ltd has produced a large number of works that offer this invaluable service. Once you have spotted one of these—an example is my own (1988a) collection on *Behavioural Economics*, another of relevance here is the (1988) collection by Martin Ricketts on *Neoclassical Microeconomics*, in the same 'Schools of Thought in Economics' series—other Elgar publications are easy to pick out on library shelves because of their distinctive style of spine and the fact that inside their front or end pages they list the other volumes in their series.

You probably will not have time to read in detail all the sources to which you obtain access, so you will need to be selective after taking a careful look at introductions, contents pages, abstracts and conclusions. Most of all when using books, you should look up key words in their indexes. If an essay involves the discussion of a particular author's ideas you may find it useful to consult the Social Science Citation Index to find who has been referring to this author in recent articles though, if your library does not take a hard copy or CD-ROM version of the Index, charges could be incurred for an on-line search. Many leading economists' careers and key economic concepts are explored in *The New Palgrave*, a four-volume dictionary of economics edited by Eatwell, Milgate and Newman (1987) and in the handbooks edited by Hodgson, Samuels and Tool (1994) and Arestis and Sawyer

(1994). A book review is often another useful source: this may save you a great deal of reading and it may offer critical comments to bear in mind when writing about the book or actually reading it at length. Book reviews can be sourced with the aid of book review indexes if your library has them. If not, you can look in the annual indexes of many economics journals (especially the *Economic Journal*, *Economica* and the *Journal of Economic Literature*) in the year of publication of the book you are interested in and the next two or three years after its publication date.

No amount of reading will compensate for a failure to make sense of the question in a way that appeals to the person who is going to mark the essay. In fact, if you do not first look at the question and try to decide what your reading should be aimed at achieving, you will probably waste of lot of reading time and either take too many notes or use your highlighter pen on too much text in the photocopies that you have taken. Here, the discussions in section 1.2 are again relevant. If the essay is set on the implicit presumption that students are Stage 5 thinkers and they are actually operating at, say, Stage 2, they are likely to miss the point. For example, the instruction 'Discuss' does not mean 'Write down all you know about the topic that seems to be the subject of the question'. Rather, it requires you to consider what the statement in question might be taken to mean (which could be several, very different things), the circumstances in which these interpretations might be particularly fruitful, and the important, relevant things that the statement is excluding or glossing over. Likewise, 'Compare and contrast A and B' does not mean 'Describe A, then describe B'. Rather, it is an invitation for you to look for similarities and differences between A and B. If you are not clear on the meaning of any key terms in your essay titles, look them up in a dictionary before thinking about consulting your tutor.

Unless you spend time thinking carefully about what the question might or might not require, you are likely to end up wasting a lot of precious time and space in the answer that you write. For example, I have often suggested to students that in their opening sentence they should explain what they think are the central issues being raised by the question. Unfortunately, weaker students tend to treat this as meaning that they should restate the question, rather than explain succinctly the basis for the claim that is being discussed, or say whether it is controversial or why it might be important. Indeed, redundant material is usually most in evidence in introductions to essays, largely because of a failure to work out a clear picture of what the essay should be about or because an awful lot of time is devoted to defining terms. Students who are really on top of the material will rarely spend time defining terms unless required to do so or unless the meaning of the terms has proved contentious and this fact can be used as a basis for getting the essay started. Rather, such students will use the terms with an air of authority and allow their understandings of them to be checked by the reader from the way that the terms are used.

Despite the time pressure under which essays are often written, many students probably spend too much time reading relative to the time they spend trying to think of different angles on the questions that they are attempting to do. Some find it difficult to organize their notes simply because they have too much to organize. To avoid this problem, try taking notes (key sentences or just short-hand) on index cards, one card per point from each source, noting the source on the relevant card. You can then group the cards into piles which seem to have common themes. If you prefer, write on paper but only on one side; then cut the sheets of paper up at breaks between points and clip related cuttings together. It is often quicker to use these techniques than to use highlighter pens on photocopies of what is being read—unless, or course, you are prepared to chop up your photocopies. (As for myself, I nowadays usually try to take notes directly on to a personal computer, organizing them under various headings as I type them in.) Reading a lot can also prove counter-productive if, as a result of spending time reading a particular work, you find it tempting to try to use material from it in the essay regardless of whether it is really relevant. Remember: an essay will be far more convincing as a chain of interlinked arguments if it flows from one point to another without getting sidetracked. Your rewards should be coming from how well you tackle the question, not from displaying how much you have read.

In order to avoid letting your sunk costs of reading rather than your interpretation of the question determine what you write, you may do well to begin writing without making any reference at all to your notes. After you have spent a reasonable time in research, organize your notes into unifying piles and read them through. Then put them aside and try simply to note down what you think the key issues are. This should give you a set of section headings and you can move on to consider different sequences in which you might explore them: some sequences will make it easier to bridge from one issue to the next. Once you feel you have a sequence that makes sense, you can ask yourself whether you can write a paragraph of about half a dozen sentences on each of these major issues. (An essay of 1250 words—about the length of a 45-minute examination answer—should probably consist of about five or six such paragraphs sandwiched between an introduction and a conclusion.) If your essay looks like it is going to consist of lots of unconnected sentences you have not yet identified what the key issues are. You should only refer back to your notes from your reading once you have a fairly clear idea of what you are going to say and the order in which you are going to say it.

Quotations should be used sparingly, but if they are felt essential they should be fully referenced so that the marker can easily find their original sources and hence check, for example, whether confusion is arising because something is being quoted out of context. In general, you will probably learn more by trying to rewrite in your own words the passages that you feel tempted to quote at length, and then direct the marker to the source of your argument via the style of referencing used in this book. By doing this you may get to see whether your interpretation of what is being said makes sense to the marker as an interpretation of the passage whose source you are noting. You may be unable to express the ideas in as elegant and erudite a manner as the person from whom you are deriving them, but if you simply copy them down it may be very unclear to the marker what you actually understand by them. It is by writing experimentally in your own words that you discover limits to your interpretative skills.

The temptation to use a quotation will be particularly acute if you are trying to explain something about which someone has written in a rather technical or obscure manner. In such a situation it is probably going to be better for yourself and for the marker if you try to make the point plain and understandable by reframing it with the aid of a practical example. Do not shun this technique on the ground that 'If I can say it as simply as that, it must be commonsense, so I must be missing the point'. The ideas that you are exploring are probably ones that have practical applications, so by stating them in such down to earth terms you give the marker an idea of how well you might be able to apply them in new contexts.

Sometimes, the things that you read will seem to make little sense or will seem to be saying things that go against your intuition. When this happens, do not push them aside or try to fudge over the difficulties when you write up your essay. Instead, write about the problem you had during your reading. It may be the case that you *have* misunderstood something, or *have* forgotten/failed to notice a key element in the piece in question. In this case, you make it easy for the marker to show you why you were having trouble. However, it *might* also be the case that you have discovered something that is indeed a flaw in, or significant objection to, what you have read. Do not assume that simply because an idea is set down in print it is an idea that should ultimately deserve to be taken seriously. You may fear being penalized for showing yourself to be confused, but that fear should be tempered by the thoughts that you should be rewarded for trying to be a critic and that you will know, at a later date (such as in the final examination for the course), whether it is wise to try to repeat your arguments on this topic.

Feedback on previous essays is probably the most important key to being able to write good essays in the future. If those who mark your essays award marks without commenting on why the marks were awarded and without giving pointers about where and how things could have been done better, then, by my way of looking at things, they are not doing their jobs properly. In this case, you should arrange to discuss your work with them. (Following Robert M. Pirsig's (1974) *Zen and the Art of Motorcycle Maintenance*—a novel that is well worth reading whilst working with the present book—I would argue that it might be better if essay markers gave detailed comments but gave no clue as to what mark the essay was thought to be worth. This would mean that students would not know if their essays yet reached the standards they were trying to attain, so they would be more likely to try to learn as much from the comments as possible in order to improve their work in future. I suspect, however, that few students would find this uncertainty tolerable.)

Finally, it is interesting to note that some educationalists have suggested that students may end up writing better essays if lecturers require them to write their own assessment of their essays at the end, before handing them in. This requirement may initially sound rather peculiar but it makes sense for three reasons. First, it may encourage students to take more care over what they commit to paper: it may be rather hard to bring oneself to submit an essay at the end of which one has written, say, 'Only worth a C– since it displays no evidence of reading and just regurgitates part of last Friday's lecture'. Secondly, it may encourage students to think carefully about the qualities that may be rewarded: they may then decide to (re)write their essays in keeping with their own criteria of excellence. Thirdly, it enables the person marking the essay to provide feedback about any mismatch between the students' own marking criteria and the criteria being used by the marker, as well as between the essay itself and these sets of criteria. A variation on this approach to learning is for students to be required to have preliminary drafts of their essays 'marked' by other students and then to submit the latter's comments sheets with their final versions, along with a note saying what they have done in response to their peers' assessments of their work. To ensure that all students get actively involved in this process, however, it may be necessary to award marks for the quality of self/peer assessment comments.

1.4 A guide to tackling case studies

Case study work in business and marketing normally involves a real or life-like situation about which a particular policy question is being raised. Case studies may vary in length from just a couple of paragraphs to twenty pages or more (for examples of the latter, see Wheelen and Hunger, 1989). But even short cases often present opportunities for using quite a wide range of economic theories: the key thing is to spot which ones might be relevant and then set about seeing what may be done with them to reach a recommendation on the problem that has been raised. Here, I offer some pointers that may help towards this end. I hope you will not just read this section at the start of your studies in this area, not least of all because some of the terms refer to concepts which will be introduced in later chapters.

1. Remember that *every* piece of information is potentially useful, but that it is up to you to spot creative ways of using it: keep asking, 'What relevance could this have?'. However, beware of being caught out by 'red herrings'—pieces of information that are included to see if you can distinguish core issues from peripheral ones.

2. First look for information about the product on which the case focuses. Ask yourself the following questions about it:

(i)   Is it a complicated product to use or to make? Your answers here should be useful in deciding how easily it can be sold with the aid of agents who handle wide ranges of products; whether it might be copied without too much trouble by another potential supplier; whether skills acquired in making or using it might have potential uses in somewhat related contexts, that the firm, or other firms, might be able to satisfy.

(ii)   Is the product protected by a patent or controls on foreign competition?

(iii)   At what stage is the product in its life-cycle? Even if its sales are declining, ask yourself if you can foresee any new uses for it in the near future.

(iv)   Is the product one which is likely to be sensitive to price competition, or is it one which sells mainly on its non-price merits? In the former case, you should consider to what extent the firm is likely to be strong or weak in the event of a price war. In the latter case, consider how easily these characteristics might be copied (are they technical features, such as quality of finish, or are they features such as delivery reliability, which might be much more easily matched?).

(v)   Is the product sold as part of a range of products? If so, consider the production and sales synergy implications of adding it to/dropping it from the range.

(vi)   Does the product require complementary products? If so, are their supplies assured and are they being sold on reasonable terms?

(vii)   Does its production involve any by-products? If so, what might be done with them?

(viii) Is it essential to sell the entire product? (Perhaps it would be wiser to sell just a replaceable component from it, which the firm is especially able to produce.)

(ix)   Can you think of anything nasty that could happen to undermine the product's position in the foreseeable future? (A useful rule might be to consider possible microchip- or computer-based alternatives, or the possibility of increasingly demanding environmental legislation.)

16

3. Next examine the production process carefully, bearing in mind your earlier thoughts on the complexity of the product. Ask yourself:

(i) To what extent does this product involve the firm in new production skills? Even if the skills seem familiar ones, always consider the possibility that production synergy might not be all it seems.

(ii) If the skills don't all seem familiar ones, what scope is there for subcontracting the unfamiliar part of the production process? Here, bear in mind the possibility that subcontractors might accidentally be given secrets concerning the firm's designs, manufacturing tolerances and so on. Also look out for scope for more devious kinds of behaviour on the part of subcontractors and for genuinely accidental supply disruptions that might be more avoidable if production is handled in-house.

(iii) To the extent that the firm is taking on new equipment and personnel, consider possible problems this could entail: a drain on the firm's liquidity (how vulnerable to shocks do the firm's other activities appear to be?); problems of building an effective managerial team in a hurry; scope for incurring considerable start-up losses due to workers taking time to learn how to make the product.

(iv) Consider to what extent the firm might move down a steep learning curve in respect of the costs of manufacturing this product. If it did, would this give it much of a head start over other producers, not yet in the market?

(v) What scope is there for costs to turn out disappointingly high, measured both internally and relative to one's competitors? To what extent are prices of externally sourced components guaranteed by long-term contracts? Are the components sourced domestically or overseas? (Which way do you think the exchange rate could go?) Are the firm's competitors based domestically or overseas? The effects of rising wages in the domestic market might not be too much of a worry if prices are being marked up generally there, and if the market is insulated from import competition.

(vi) What made the firm decide to get into this market? Was it some kind of corporate imbalance that was resulting in excess capacity somewhere in the organization? If so, then on the one hand this may give the firm a head start because of the costs it has already sunk in earlier, related lines of production, but on the other hand, you should consider whether or not other firms, in similar positions, might run into similar imbalances and see similar scope for entering the market.

(vii) More generally, ask yourself about the contestability of the market: who are the potential producers? How much would they have to incur by way of non-recoverable costs to get into the market? In thinking about who might be potential competitors, don't just suggest other firms that produce sets of products similar to the firm in question. Define the entry requirements more broadly (for example: casting skills, metal fabrication expertise). Look out also for possible entry by totally different kinds of firms, if you have already noted possible alternative technologies.

(viii) What is the age structure of plant that is available to produce the product, and how might this affect the competitive process?

(ix) How easy is it to change the rate of output?

4. Don't take the existing market as given. Questions asked earlier should have encouraged you to think carefully about any sales projections that are supplied in the

case study. If these only relate to a domestic market, consider scope for exports, and barriers to successful exports, such as the costs of building up a distribution network, risks of using agents, linguistic problems.

5. More generally, on the marketing side, consider whether the product can be sold effectively using the firm's established distribution system (does the product have similar characteristics in terms of its target market, its degree of complexity, its bulk, perishability and so on?). Could the product be sold more effectively by another company, even if it would fit not too badly into the firm's existing marketing portfolio? What risks are involved here?

6. If you do numerical calculations about price elasticities needed for price cuts to be viable, don't forget to consider the results in relation to your characterization of the product. Is retaliation going to be profitable for rivals, if an unchallenged price cut would be profitable for the firm in question? (How long could the firm's competitors stand losses, if it tried to drive rivals out of the market? Would the regulatory authorities let it get away with such behaviour, anyway?) Does the firm have enough capacity to cope with possible sales increases? And could its suppliers deliver enough components?

7. Does the venture seem to be consistent with the firm's stated goals and general philosophy/strategy? If not, could a past philosophy cause problems for the success of the venture (for example, in moving up- or down-market in a technologically similar area)? Can you see any other ways of achieving these ends (different products, different contracting arrangements)?

Finally, remember that you are likely to force yourself to engage in more powerful discussions if you try to commit yourself to making a recommendation where one is required, rather than 'sitting on the fence'. Such a recommendation might nonetheless be somewhat contingent in nature, for it would be perfectly in order to show what further information you feel would have been useful for sizing up the nature of the problem.

1.5   The economics of coping with examinations

'You can always tell a weak examinee,' Morris observed. 'First they waste time copying out the question. Then they take out their little rulers and rule *lines* under it' (David Lodge, *Small World*, 1985: 60, emphasis in original).

The 'exam post-mortem' sections in this book—which are offered in the belief that it is possible to learn a lot from the mistakes made by others—are based on notes taken as I marked the essay-based final examination that I set for the 1991 Microeconomics for Business and Marketing class at Lincoln University in New Zealand. This class was the first to be taught for this unit using the material now set out in this book rather than with a focus on standard neoclassical texts. The students had little previous experience of essay-based economics examinations, but had attempted tutorial assignments and a major assignment based on the topics that are here discussed in some of the 'Essay Example' sections. I had also presented essay technique workshops which looked at further questions that are used as examples in this book. The last week of lectures for the course was devoted to a fairly detailed discussion of a mock exam paper consisting of questions similar to those provided at the ends of chapters in this book, including some considered as Essay Examples. However, the class of 1991 did not have the advantage of being taught with reference to Perry's work on stages of learning: they had not been through the ideas discussed in section 1.2 and this may help us understand why some of their answers came as a great disappointment to the examiner.

The post-mortem reports contain elements of both comedy and tragedy, for despite my attempts during the course to cultivate techniques for handling essay-based examination questions many students performed very poorly. This might have been a reflection of three months of incoherent lectures, but given the efficacy with which the top ten per cent of students managed to use lecture material, I do not feel particularly culpable in this regard. Where students did poorly for reasons other than a gross failure to put in a decent effort the feature that struck me most about the weaker answers was not the presence of gross technical errors or bizarre and sometimes highly amusing misattributions of the authorship of particular contributions. Rather, it was the difficulty that their authors had in taking the questions to pieces and inferring what they entailed. The saddest and most extreme manifestation of a complete inability to do anything with the essays was a paper handed in by a student who appeared to have spent three hours writing out the questions time and time again—presumably because, compared with sitting doing nothing or being seen to walk out early, this seemed to the student to be a better way of preserving her social-esteem. It seems appropriate to comment on the likely origins of such tragic failures to realize academic potential. What I have to say should be seen as augmenting the analysis presented in sections 1.2 and 1.3.

Students and those who allocate resources to tertiary education both seem to underestimate the extent to which essay-writing skills depend on considerable practising by students and intensive marking of assignments by tutors. I had the good fortune to acquire these skills whilst still at school by having to prepare several essays a week for my 'A Levels', and then had them strongly reinforced as an undergraduate in Cambridge, doing not merely two or three essays every week but also many warm-up essay questions for my tutors in the weeks immediately prior to the examinations. Unfortunately, many schooling systems and most universities do not have the tutoring resources to develop essay skills adequately, as is evidenced by the popularity of multiple-choice examinations, and students do not make the most of such resources as are actually devoted to this end. I nowadays advise my students to form study groups to practise working out how they might tackle questions provided at the ends of other chapters of this book, even if they do not go so far as to practise writing entire answers and then getting each other to mark them. The minority who take this advice report that it has a big impact on their performance as well as making revision much more enjoyable because of its social dimension.

I certainly would have been unable to cope had even a quarter of my 300-strong 1991 class bothered to take up my suggestion that they should lock themselves away from their notes for three hours, free from any other distractions, and practise writing answers to the mock examination paper and then discuss their answers with me during office hours. In the event, I was disappointed that *none* did so, not even the overseas students whom I had especially advised to practise in this way. The entire class seemed to believe that they would improve their marks more by spending more time 'learning the material'—an activity which seems often to involve the writing of endless summaries of lecture notes—rather than practising using it. They failed to take seriously my warnings that they would be more likely to achieve better scores if they were roughly in command of the material but highly adept at interpreting questions and doing the best with what material they had, than if they knew masses of material 'parrot-fashion' but could not work out when it was relevant and lacked the ability to string a coherent answer together.

Part of the reason for the 'learning by summarizing' strategy being so popular prior to final examinations seems to be that students are not absorbing the material as they go along during the weeks that lectures and tutorials are taking place. Many students do not emerge from their tutorials pretty well in control of the material so far covered and in a position to build on it and apply it in later weeks. Fears about looking ignorant or appearing to be showing off in front of their peers get in the way of participating actively in tutorials, and tutorial groups are often large enough for it to be possible to avoid having to participate. (This is something which is ruled out in the character-building one tutor/two students system of tutorials peculiar to Oxford and Cambridge: the students read their essays out in turn and are examined orally by the tutor at any sign of weakness. In such an environment, memories of what was wrong and why it was wrong persist from the tutorial for years to come. The use of small-group brainstorming discussions during tutorials may be a way of getting more active participation within more conventionally sized tutorials.) The result is that for much of the academic year many students might be characterized less as learning by experimentation and error-correction than as merely storing information on paper for later use. This is often disastrous in the long run but at least it preserves the students' self-esteem in the short run.

Despite what I have just said, I do believe that there is a role for extremely brief summaries of material. I would strongly advise you to learn the contents pages of this book, section numbers included. Then, for each each section, try to work out and remember a couple of lines that summarize just the main message you have picked up. An example might be 'Section 8.8, Kinked demand curves: they may help explain why, in oligopolistic markets, firms may not change prices when their sales or variable costs change'. Then, in the examination, you can mentally scroll up and down the contents list when trying to think what might be relevant to the question you are looking at.

Several dysfunctional strategies were frequently in evidence in the examination with which we are here concerned. First, it seemed ironic that economics students should so frequently ignore the notion of diminishing marginal returns rather than apply it to their efforts in the examination. It is far more productive to write half a dozen paragraphs each of which makes a different point in a succinct manner, than to spend three-quarters of an answer belabouring a single point. In many cases, it will take less than a page to deal with the core issues raised by a question (which is why a grossly uneven allocation of time between questions need not turn out to be catastrophic), so the remaining couple of pages can be spent convincing the examiner of one's ability to see the wider ramifications of the question.

Secondly, it seemed that many students believed that they could answer questions successfully without any reference to material from the lectures or recommended reading. To be sure, it sometimes is possible to get by in an intermediate microeconomics examination on the basis of material covered in a less advanced course, or a course in a related subject area such as finance or marketing. And it is good to see essays which could be *intelligible* to a lay person, for in later life one will often need to prepare briefing documents for people who lack one's own specialized backgrounds. However, it is foolish to hope to be awarded high marks for essays which seem like they could have been *written* by a lay person who had walked into the examination hall without any preparation.

The students should constantly have kept in mind the context in which they were attempting the examination: the examiner could reasonably demand that they tried to tackle the questions with reference to ideas that had been covered during the course, and had set the questions with a view to it being possible to tackle them successfully using these ideas. To put it another way: although the questions typically did not *ask* for particular theories to be explained, this did not mean it was safe to try to tackle them without reference to any of the materials covered on the course. The examiner had chosen the questions precisely because they were problems that might usefully be addressed with the aid of some of the tools covered in the course, but it was up to the examinees to decide which ones to select for their potential and then demonstrate their skills in applying them. Herein perhaps lies the key to understanding why 'lay person-style' answers tend to be produced even where people have worked hard at learning theories from lectures and reading: if you have not tried to develop your skills in fitting the theories to new contexts you may wonder what on earth the examination has to do with the theories you have studied and consequently only be able to answer in lay terms. The essay example sections in this book should be invaluable tools for helping students to develop these skills and emerge better equipped for coping with a world in which problems do not jump out at problem-solvers and say 'Hi, I'm a category X problem to which you need to apply theory Q'.

Thirdly, despite my having dispensed advice of the kind given in section 1.3, much time was simply wasted writing down redundant material. For example, weaker students would waste lengthy introductions on definitions rather than explaining what they thought the key issues were and how they proposed to deal with them. By contrast, top-class students would not bother to define terms and would instead get on with considering issues raised by the question, allowing their knowledge of the meaning of key terms to become apparent by the ways in which they used them.

Fourthly, there seemed to be a tendency to plunge into writing answers without first considering carefully whether there might be other ways of interpreting the questions at hand and then considering which interpretation would be the wisest one to use in the context of the course. Often a dictionary will list several different meanings for a particular word and people will consider the rival possibilities, replacing the troublesome word with them in its context of use and asking themselves which possibility makes the most sense. The same sort of thought process needs to be undertaken in examinations. A question set in a subsequent examination (and now discussed in section 9.13) may be a particularly useful example here: it referred to 'common costs and related demand', and the need to 'take pricing decisions jointly'. Most students who tried it saw it simply as an oligopoly question, concerning firms with similar (common) costs and interdependent (related) demand curves for a single kind of product. They ignored the implied issue, in their interpretation, of the legality of collusive (joint) pricing. An alternative and more subtle interpretation, which does not necessitate talking about oligopolists getting together to decide prices, was that the question was about the pricing of a *single* firm's *range* of products which were produced or sold using shared (common) inputs and were seen by customers as complements or substitutes (related). From this standpoint, it was a question about issues such as the implications of the concept of 'synergy' (discussed in section 7.4) for pricing decisions, though that by no means necessarily excluded it from having an oligopoly dimension.

Finally, there seemed to be a tendency for students to treat all questions as if they tested the same set of skills in different contexts. 'Regurgitation' might work reasonably well on some questions, but it is a doomed technique when used as a means of dealing with a question that requires a student to apply theory *creatively* to an unfamiliar practical problem area. Students who can think quickly on their feet may be very good at such questions even though they have weak debating skills that fall short of the kind that are vital for dealing with 'discuss'-type questions. Time spent considering the different skill requirements of different questions before choosing which ones to attempt would in many cases have been time well spent. A student who *has* to use the regurgitation strategy should not necessarily choose essays on the basis of how much s/he can regurgitate on particular topics. Rather, s/he should consider where this strategy will be relatively less disastrous—for example, the person who regurgitates pure theory on an applied question is definitely not answering the question, whereas there may at least be a chance that the regurgitation of a pair of rival theories *might* just about be adequate as a means for dealing with a 'compare and contrast' sort of question.

1.6 Post-mortem on a 'warm-up' question for developing critical thinking skills

Question
Discuss the adequacy of microeconomic theories covered in your previous training (for example, an Introduction to Economics course taken in the first year of a university degree or in the final years at high school) for making sense of economic aspects of the recorded music business.

Reading suggestion
During 1991–93 the *Economist* newspaper ran many articles on aspects of this industry, including: the 'mega-deals' signed by superstars such as Michael Jackson and Madonna; the demise of the vinyl long-playing record, Richard Branson's sale of his Virgin Records interests; differences between CD prices in the UK and the US; and the impending launch of Digital Compact Cassettes by Philips, and recordable Mini-Discs by Sony. These materials may be tracked down with the aid of the *Economist Index*.

Author's notes
This essay topic was given to students as a first tutorial assignment to be handed in at the end of the first week of their course, after they had been introduced to the ideas in section

1.2. The idea was to show the class what might happen if they tackled what is, in Perry's (1970) terms, essentially a 'Stage 5 or beyond' type of question from the standpoint of a Stage 1 or 2 way of viewing the world. Most of the class failed outright because they took the question as an invitation to show they could regurgitate basic economic ideas they had grasped in earlier studies, using the recorded music industry as a vehicle for doing so. This tended to involve diagrams showing price and quantity determination for CDs or tapes—which showed how a rise in demand for recorded music would result in higher prices—or indifference diagrams and expositions of marginal utility theory with records or different types of music being used as examples. What the vast majority of the class conspicuously failed to do was to focus, right from the outset, on how they would size up the adequacy of their introductory economic analysis in this context. In other words, they did not specify criteria such as (to list just two possibilities): 'Does it offer predictions that fit the facts?' or 'Does it seem plausible enough to use as a means of explaining what is going on in this market?'.

I had chosen this context for a discussion of the adequacy of introductory economic analysis because it is an area where such tools seem likely to offer a rather mixed performance, and because it is an area where how useful these tools are depends on how we try to apply them. In general, because the members of the class were not focusing on appraising theories, they failed to be very critical and failed to ask whether they might be failing to see contexts in which a particular idea might fare better or worse than it did in other contexts.

Take for example the idea of diminishing marginal utility. Where students did recognize this was an essay about theory appraisal, they typically said marginal utility theory was pretty hopeless because nobody would purchase more than one copy of a particular CD in the way that they might, say, eat one cake after another and get less and less extra satisfaction from additional units consumed. A few did have a go at relating the product life-cycle and marginal utility concepts to the consequences of repeated hearings of a given piece of music: people might get sick of current chart sounds if they heard them time and time again. However, hardly anybody at all considered the usefulness of the theory at a different level of abstraction: it might have something rather more to say about how many CDs of various kinds a person might end up buying, possibly predicting that they would buy fewer albums per year as they got older and built up larger collections. If this suggestion were made one might then qualify it by considering whether utility theory as such actually explains what is going on and whether or not the theory actually has a time dimension to it when set out in formal terms (story-style expositions usually involve a succession of acts of consumption, but diagrammatic treatments tend not to do so). It might have been asked why marginal utility (whatever that is!) declines: the theory itself does not say, but we can provide some plausible foundations for it by thinking of the economics of time allocation. Each new CD purchase, if it is played, limits the time that a consumer has for using previously purchased CDs or for pursuing other leisure activities (on the economic implications of limited consumption time, see Linder's classic (1970) book *The Harried Leisure Class*).

Few students bothered to consider some of the peculiarities of recorded music products and consumer behaviour which might relate rather poorly to introductory utility theory. Among them the following might have been noticed:

(a) The idea of a 'fan' seems to suggest someone who is not tending to consider alternatives or suffer from diminishing marginal utility (as with the person who tries to own every single recording by a particular artist, regardless of how similar they are).

(b) Introductory consumer theory tends to treat 'economic man' as an isolated individual with a good idea of what he or she wants. In reality, however, much purchasing of recorded music seems to be dominated by social processes, which result in many albums being bought and played rather as if they were fashion products.

(c) The task of choosing what to buy in a well-stocked record store is a complex one, in principle, because there is just so much between which to choose and it will be difficult to sample many albums whilst in the store. Hence people may end up buying what they buy on the basis of what they have heard from their friends' collections or in the media; or they may choose established artists with whose work they are familiar, completely overlooking many albums which they would have liked a lot if only they had come across them. If introductory economic theory has been taught in a way that leads to the conclusion that consumers are sovereign, there may be reasons to be worried in this context about its accuracy. If music is an 'experience good'—hard to judge before you have consumed it—then the mega-deals signed by superstars may be quite easy to explain at least in part with a familiar feature of introductory economics: the theory of economic rent. In other words, although the consumer theory may not apply in a descriptive sense if consumers are choosing on the basis of past reputations, the consequent tendency to consume a disproportionate number of albums by a limited set of safe, predictably good artists may explain why record companies are so willing to pay a fortune to get these artists signed for their labels. A really impressive discussion here could have pointed out that utility theory might perhaps be rescued with reference to the suggestion that past performance is being used to judge expected utility, and that this view of superstar earnings is potentially different from typical examples of economic rent-based earnings of people such as top brain surgeons which are normally based on skill advantages. Here, we might have situations in which well-known performers earn a lot because they are well-known rather than because they are better than artists who have not been widely heard. Obscure artists might be ones whom the public would adore if only they took the risk and sampled their work, but with CD prices being what they are and well-known performers seeming perfectly OK such a risk may not be taken by people wanting some new music.

Students who tried to relate this problem area to the question of pricing did so with mixed results. It was quite commonly recognized that it was helpful to have the elementary ideas of complementarity and substitutability in mind when thinking about this market: for example, how a reduction in the price of CD players could affect the demand for CDs in a favourable manner and yet be disastrous for sales of record turntables. Some students aired their doubts about whether people would substitute if record companies or retail outlets lowered the prices of products to try to boost sales: those who tended to buy heavy rock might not be prone to switch to buying albums of country yodelling hits even if the latter were marked down to next to nothing.

24

Less perceptive were typical discussions of the relevance of supply and demand theory for explaining prices in this industry. Hardly anybody noticed that prices of particular music albums tend to fall into a few distinct bands, with recently released 'full price' recordings tending to have pretty much the same price regardless of whether they were selling by the million or hardly being noticed at all. Such an observation, once made, should prompt a consideration of whether this is at all problematic for a body of theory based around upward-sloping marginal cost curves and supply curves. Without inside information it would certainly be hard to come to conclusions on costs of producing and marketing different albums, but a number of points might reasonably be raised in relation to introductory economic theory:

(a) The costs of recording and mastering a particular piece of music and of making promotional videos and suchlike are essentially fixed costs: the bigger these are, the bigger sales will need to be at any market price if an album is to break even. But with million-sellers, average fixed costs may be far lower, even if bigger investments are made in studio time and promotion.

(b) Once master disks and tapes have been made, the production and retailing of music seems likely to involve similar materials and processing costs, regardless of the album and its volume. This seems to point towards different albums having similar marginal cost functions that can be represented as straight, horizontal lines, not upward-sloping ones. Perhaps prices of albums with different sales rates are being based on these similar cost curves with some conventional mark-up attached. Recordings by superstars would only tend to have higher marginal costs in so far as higher royalty rates are being paid per recording sold. However, record stores might actually be more prone to use them as a focus for discounts (or be forced to take them with a smaller recommended mark-up) because they are unlikely to sit around in stock for long periods incurring interest costs and because they can be ordered in bulk, thus saving time and paperwork.

(c) Working against implications of horizontal or downward-sloping supply curves that might be inferred from the previous two points is the suggestion that record companies may have limited CD-pressing and tape-duplicating facilities, so the cost of producing an extra album by an obscure artist may be the loss of a chance to sell an extra copy of an album by a superstar, and vice versa. However, the idea that capacity constraints might impose some upward-sloping supply function on a typical record company looks less acceptable once we take note of the brevity of product life-cycles for some products in this industry: if products are in the charts for only a few weeks before getting displaced by more recent releases, it could be unwise for a record company to risk being in a position where it has trouble meeting orders and causes record stores to go out of stock. Spare capacity might well worth having, rather than being a sign of too many firms in the industry, which is how it is prone to be portrayed in introductory texts.

(d) The very idea of stable supply and demand functions might be queried anyway for its usefulness as a tool for approximating what is going on in this market: on the demand

25

side, we might note that people may enter a store planning to buy a particular album, find it not in stock and end up purchasing another that they had not even known about until they saw it there by chance; on the supply side, it may be difficult meaningfully to speak of shifts in supply curves due, say, to cost reductions if the product that has the lower price (for example, a CD player) is a new model. The limited ability of introductory theory to help make sense of why people had switched from vinyl LPs to more expensive CDs might also have been raised, along with the question of how helpful the supply and demand framework is for predicting sudden revivals of interest in artists who seemed to have gone out of fashion (as with the Swedish group ABBA in 1992–93). On the other hand, simple ideas about differences in marginal utility leading to differences in strengths of demand from different customers might help explain why record companies successively repackage recordings to sell at different prices as time passes by (as with two-for-one CD reissues of classic rock albums or the downgrading of full-price classical recordings to mid-price and, ultimately, budget-price as new recordings of the same work are released).

There are many other points that could be made in respect of whether introductory textbook economics helps us make sense of or anticipate events in this industry; the ones I have detailed are all we had time to consider in tutorials based around this essay topic. As a final note, it should be pointed out that many of the points raised in this section by way of criticizing the applicability of introductory economics foreshadow material that will be introduced later in this book, such as in the behavioural analysis of consumer choice in Chapter 4 or theories of pricing discussed in Chapter 9. On that basis perhaps I might have appeared mean for penalizing students due to their failure to consider such issues. However, it should be noted that my discussion of what might have been included is couched in simple, everyday terms, relating to observations that might have been made by anybody who tried to think in a questioning manner about things such as the nature of a 'fan' or the experience of shopping for CDs. In other words, to learn a lot it may be necessary to cultivate skills in asking new questions, rather than focusing on finding answers only to existing questions that other people (or other people's bodies of thought—such as introductory economic theory) have focused upon.

2 Theories of choice: an overview

2.1 The role of a theory of choice

Much confusion can arise in the teaching of the economic analysis of choice due to lecturers and students looking at the role of theories of choice in different ways. It seems that many students initially see theories as tools that consumers and managers might use to reach decisions. They tend to write essays that include such comments as 'If people use X's theory to choose how many units of Y to buy, then first they will...'. Lecturers may find such a perspective quite bizarre. For a start it carries a rather odd vision of the point of studying the economics of choice. It seems to imply that students who have grasped what economists have to say in this area are then equipped with tools for taking decisions themselves, or for teaching others about how they could take decisions. This sounds rather like home economics, where consumers are trained in ways of avoiding wasting their households' resources. But home economics is rarely part of a university curriculum in economics (perhaps this is unfortunate: few graduates, I suspect, would claim to be completely immune from tendencies to make poor quality choices). To see that something else is being attempted in this book, student readers need to think carefully about the standpoint from which they are reading it. They should imagine themselves reading it not as consumers but as people who may be called upon, later in their careers, to advise on business or government policy.

Consider the act of purchasing of a video cassette recorder, which we shall examine in section 4.5. An understanding of material in this book, particularly in Chapter 4, may indeed enable a person who is familiar with it to cope with the task of buying such a complex consumer durable. But the provision of assistance of this kind is not my main goal in presenting theories of choice and then considering their relevance to this context. Rather, the point is to equip a potential policy-maker with tools for analysing the behaviour of consumers in this market: the theories are tools for describing how people may be choosing; for explaining why they may be choosing one brand rather than another; and hence for pointing to practical implications for organizations (such as manufacturers or retailers of VCRs) with an interest in predicting and controlling patterns of buyer behaviour. The person with a training in economics is trying to make sense of what others are doing, with a view to anticipating what may happen to their behaviour if particular changes are made in their choice environments (for example, price changes, a new advertising campaign, or changes to the product). In other words, my expectation in writing this book is not that students should not aim to emerge from studying it with the ability to offer consumers advice on how to buy a VCR but, rather, that they should hope to be able to sum up the sorts of processes that may be unfolding when consumers are buying VCRs. Readers should then be able to say what these processes imply for audiences such as suppliers of VCRs, regulators of the industry and consumers' pressure groups. Without even necessarily communicating with any buyers of VCRs, they should be able to provide these audiences with commentary on the buyers' behaviour which is of greater use than anything the buyers themselves could provide. (This is one reason why examination answers in 'lay person-style' without reference to economic theory are likely to be frowned upon by economics lecturers—cf. section 1.5.) With well-trained eyes, economists can also make sophisticated requests for information with a view to enhancing their (or their colleagues') pictures of what is going on or could be induced to happen.

2.2   Alternative approaches to theory construction

Two contrasting ways of looking at consumer behaviour are considered in this book. One of these is indifference analysis, part of what is known as the 'neoclassical' or 'general equilibrium' research programme in economics. This was developed at the London School of Economics in the 1930s by John Hicks, who was later awarded the Nobel Prize in Economics, and Roy Allen (Hicks, 1939; Hicks and Allen, 1934). This is a highly *deductive* approach to economics: a series of assumptive building blocks ('axioms') are selected; the logical implications of accepting these assumptions are then explored, with a view to discovering testable predictions. Overriding the process of selecting axioms is Occam's Razor—the principle that the fewest possible assumptions are to be made in explaining a particular phenomenon—so in Chapter 3 we begin by exploring the ways in which Hicks and Allen sought to build models of the consumer that were analytically rigorous by keeping them free of any unnecessary baggage that might get in the way, particularly any inputs from psychology. The Hicksian model may seem to entail a long list of simplifying assumptions, but the list would be far longer if complex theories and empirical generalizations from outside economics had been used as foundations.

The other approach comes from a very different research programme known as behavioural economics. This was pioneered in the 1940s and 1950s by another Nobel prizewinner, Herbert Simon of Carnegie-Mellon University in Pittsburgh (Simon, 1957, 1959). Simon's approach mixes economics with other disciplines, particularly psychology and management science. It gets its 'behavioural' tag from working on the principle that, before attempting to construct simplifying models of choice, the analyst should study the kinds of problems that actually confront decision-makers and how they actually behave in coping with them. This is quite close to what philosophers of science call an *inductive* method of theorizing, in which one first gathers a limited set of facts and then constructs more generally applicable theories in the light of them (for example, if a sample of smokers has a higher death-rate from lung cancer than does a sample of non-smokers, then it might be inferred that smoking increases the risk of lung cancer in the population at large). However, there is no such thing as theorizing without having some kind of prior beliefs about cause and effect: behavioural theorists, like any others, have to hypothesize at the outset about which facts they should gather and which potential relationships they should ignore. In contrast to the fascination of Hicks and Allen with equilibrium states that consumers might be thought of as arriving at, behavioural theorists see choice as an ongoing process of problem-solving during which consumers' views of the world and of their wants may undergo considerable evolution.

Most textbooks on intermediate microeconomics only offer discussions of neoclassical consumer theory. For textbook presentations of the behavioural approach it is normally necessary to turn to the sort of consumer behaviour text used on a marketing course (for example, Engel, Blackwell and Miniard, 1986). Here, I offer both approaches because I have found both to be useful as aids to thinking about practical problems. Sometimes, and particularly for discussing matters of public policy, the Hicksian model seems illuminating despite the patent unreality of many of its assumptions and its limited ability to offer testable hypotheses (see sections 3.5 and 3.7). Frequently, if dealing with problems in the area of business and marketing, and sometimes in considering public policy, we may get rather further by putting our behavioural hats on, though to do so may involve us in having to keep rather more ideas in mind at any one moment (see sections 4.4, 4.5 and 4.9; for a pioneering application of behavioural theories in the context of public choice, see Brooks, 1988).

As economists, we obviously face choices rather like those faced by a consumer buying, say, a video cassette recorder: we want models that are neither so complex that we cannot use them effectively, nor so simple in design that we end up with a misleading picture or completely miss the point. In section 4.8 we shall look at economists' choices of theories in the light of the material that has been considered. During Chapters 3–5 it should not be forgotten that, although most of the examples used will concern the consumption of goods and services, the theoretical material concerns choice in general: people do not suddenly acquire greater cognitive capabilities the moment they enter their workplaces. In this sense, material on consumer choice is potentially an important foundation for an understanding of how firms operate.

2.3   Alternative views of information and choice

Questions of information arise frequently in literature on the theory of choice, and they will figure often in this book. The next two chapters are likely to be easier to understand if we note at the outset differences in the informational assumptions that neoclassical and behavioural are inclined to make. A convenient focus here is the view expressed by many behaviouralists that choice can be seen as a process of *problem-solving* which involves the chooser in going through a *decision cycle*. The structures of many consumer theory texts in marketing are based on this concept (for example, Engel *et al.*, 1986: Part 1); for an excellent discussion of decision cycles in the context of managerial behaviour, see Loasby (1976: 88–94). A decision cycle may involve up to six stages of gathering and processing information:

1. *Recognition* that it may be unwise to carry on along the course previously adopted. A problem will only be recognized as an occasion for action if information is received which is taken to suggest that expectations are unlikely to be met or if something happens to prompt the chooser to re-evaluate old information in a new way.

2. *Search* for possible solutions to the problem. The chooser draws up a mental list of strategies, of new courses of action, that might better serve as means towards the desired end.

3. *Evaluation* of these rival schemes of action. In the light of information recalled from memory or freshly gathered, the chooser considers which sets of consequences might be associated with each imagined scheme.

4. *Choice*. The chooser ranks the alternatives in order of preference. If the best option on the agenda seems inadequate as a means for solving the problem, search may be resumed.

5. *Implementation*. The chooser may be driven to think again if her/his preferred course of action cannot be implemented, for example, because a product is out of stock.

6. *Hindsight*. The chooser examines the sequel to the choice and considers whether or not the original problem still exists or a new one has arisen.

Neoclassical economists rarely frame their analyses in these terms. Instead, they seem to proceed as if the chooser has already done all the background work prior to stage four of the choice process. Not only this, but the chooser often seems presumed to have gathered *all* the relevant information about *all* possible pertinent courses of action. A neoclassical economist will normally say 'Let us assume that the consumer knows what he or she wants and knows how to get it'. Although theorists from this school seem inclined to depict choice as the processing of this information, they do not address the question of whether choices might be affected by information-processing difficulties. Only occasionally do they construct models in which choosers do not possess at the outset a complete list of what is available and therefore have to apply principles of economizing to the question of whether it would be worthwhile to search for more information. If consumers have free access to relevant information and do not run into cognitive problems when trying to process it, we say that they enjoy *global rationality*. If people who enjoyed global rationality actually existed, they would at all times know of all the things between which they could choose and they would be experts on the *technology of choice*—on how all these items functioned as means towards particular ends. They would also know immediately of any changes in circumstances that had occurred, affecting the sets of things that they might choose and the technology of choice.

Behavioural economists are uneasy about modelling choosers 'as if' they enjoy global rationality, for they see it as at odds with four informational facts of life, the first of which is known as *Miller's rule*. According to the psychologist George Miller (1956), people typically can only keep 7 ± 2 things in mind at the same time. If the choice environment involves more than between five and nine alternatives and problem dimensions, then we may expect them to start filtering out information, focusing on a subset of problem dimensions or a limited range of possible solutions.

Secondly, like computers, people have a finite rate at which they can process information. In fact, human beings can usually only handle about 8–10 bits of information per second with any accuracy (Marschak, 1968: 12). Some skilled pianists and typists can manage processing rates of up to 25 bits of information per second, usually by 'chunking' individual pieces of information together as chords or words (Franz Liszt, for example, is said to have had no trouble sight-reading piano concertos by Grieg and Mendelssohn when confronted with them for the first time). However, busy consumers on shopping expeditions may have to limit considerably the amount of information that they attempt to process. Once we note that a typical supermarket may have 10 000 or more different products or brands in stock we can begin to see the scale of the problem that faces consumers even if they do not try to compare the offerings of rival supermarkets and speciality stores.

A third problem is that information that choosers perceive as relevant to their choices is not available without cost, if it is available at all. When people have identified problems in their lives and are trying to create for themselves lists of possible solutions, they will have to search around themselves and/or pay for expert advice—for example, by purchasing and reading consumer magazines. Some information is unavailable simply because the future is unknowable, for example, because it depends on decisions that other people have not yet taken. Some information is deliberately kept concealed from buyers: a used-car buyer is likely to know less about a particular vehicle than the person who is trying to sell it, while private buyers are unable to purchase the price guides used by dealers. Consequently, choice often involves a good deal of guesswork and speculation about how and where good value for money is to be obtained. The kinds of choices people make may thus be affected greatly by the strategies they use for coping with ignorance and uncertainty.

The fourth problem is the most subtle: the task of working out what is the best thing to do runs into a difficulty known by philosophers as an 'infinite regress'. This potentially paralysing problem is said to exist when an attempt to deal with a question leads to an answer in which the same sort of question appears once again, so it is impossible to 'get to the bottom' of the problem: the decision-maker just ends up in a never-ending spiral or hierarchy of questions. One common example is where the solution to a problem of choice requires me to know what your choice will be but your optimal choice depends on what I do (cf. section 5.9 on the theory of games, the discussions of oligopolistic pricing in Chapters 8 and 9, and the investment coordination problem discussed in Chapter 10). More fundamental is the problem of answering the question 'How do you know X?' with 'I know X because Y': the obvious question then is 'How do you know Y?'. Another example is on a sweatshirt belonging to one of my friends: it says 'Question Everything!' on the front and 'Why?' on the back. (For a detailed but entertaining exploration of infinite regress problems, see the best-selling book *Godel, Escher, Bach: An Eternal Golden Braid*, by Hofstadter, 1979.) If decision-makers are not sure what is available or what they want, they need to ask 'How shall I choose?'. But that question, in turn, raises the question of how to discover ways of choosing and how to choose between the ways that they discover—for example, should I ask a friend what to do about a problem, or should I turn to the Yellow pages and find an expert to advise me, or should I do something else?

Behavioural economists feel that such facts imply the need for an economics that concentrates on the implications of *bounded rationality*, of decision-making when people have to grapple with information problems: information they might like to have may not be available; information that they do have may be too much for them to process in ways that take account of its full complexity. This idea is explained by Herbert Simon as follows: '*The capacity of the human mind for formulating and solving complex problems is very small compared with the size of the problems whose solution is required for objectively rational behavior in the real world*' (1957: 198, emphasis in original; see also Simon, 1976). People suffering from bounded rationality may be unaware of impending problems in their lives, may be unable to work out clearly what problems they face when they recognize that all is not well, and may not even have the linguistic capacities required to articulate their difficulties to those (such as sales personnel, or teaching staff) who might be available to help them.

If people suffer from bounded rationality, they may be unable to decide what is the optimal course of action to undertake. They may also be incapable of knowing that they have chosen the optimal course of action if they happen to select it. Bounded rationality can also be a barrier to the attainment of long-run equilibrium: problems may continue to arise, and the process of choosing is never finished, because decision-makers can only think a limited way ahead and have to look at the world with a constricted field of vision. According to Simon, the pervasiveness of bounded rationality implies that decision-makers may more usefully be thought of not as 'optimizing agents' but as *satisficers*. This term is best seen as related to 'satisfactory' rather than 'satisfy', for when Simon writes about people engaging in satisficing behaviour he means that he views them as if they decide what sort of a choice might be adequate and then set out to find something that is satisfactory ('OK') in the sense that it seems to meet their chosen criteria (see also sections 4.1 and 7.10). Whether or not such choosers find life is full of problems and decisions to make will depend on the types of standards they set themselves and the methods they use for gathering information. Those who set undemanding criteria may find it easy to come across something satisfactory, but they may fail to develop very far their skills as problem-solvers.

Neoclassical theorists construct models based on assumptions of global rationality because of the bounded rationality from which they themselves suffer, not because they prefer to fantasize. It is so much simpler to presume that choosers have, and can process, all the information necessary for taking the best possible decision, and if one can simplify without getting into a mess, then why not do so? Global rationality may seem a fairly safe approximation to make if we are studying buyers who are experienced in the situation in question, who are quite prepared to take time over sizing up the products that are available (because they recognize, perhaps, that the costs of a mistaken purchase are high as a result of the losses they will suffer if they try to trade in a disappointing purchase against something else), and if there is a relatively small number of alternatives between which to choose. Initially, the buyer might be unclear what was available but after the information-gathering process has come to an end, the choice could be said to be based on full information. It might even be the case that the chooser actually enjoys the time spent in the search and appraisal process, so is quite happy to gather the information (for example, an experienced musician buying a new guitar from one of the few instrument stores in her/his city). By contrast, consider someone who has just arrived in a new country and feels a need to find a new car in a hurry: here, it would probably be most unwise to assume global rationality, for unfamiliar types of vehicle may be available, the range between which to choose may seem overwhelming, and even test-driving may be a traumatic experience because of a lack of familiarity with roads and driving regulations. In such a case, a knowledge of strategies that people use for *coping with* complexity, uncertainty and ignorance—rather than *eliminating* the information problems—could prove invaluable to an economist seeking to anticipate the person's behaviour.

In technical terms, the next two chapters concentrate on developing images of: (a) neoclassical economists tending to think about choice in terms of constrained optimization, with tangencies being found between downward-sloping indifference curves and linear budget constraints, such that changes in behaviour depend upon the relative strength of effects due to changes in real income and the consumer's willingness to make substitutions in response to relative price changes; and (b) behavioural economists tending to think about choice in terms of movable aspirational targets and rules of thumb, downplaying the significance of substitution and emphasizing the roles of search processes, personal principles and habits. At a more philosophical level, we may encapsulate the basic difference between these two approaches to choice with the aid of the following passage by Coddington (1975a: 151):

> Instead of asking how reason can be applied to the knowledge that men can or do have of their economic circumstances, [neoclassical economic theory] asks how reason can be applied to circumstances that are perfectly known. The problems of what can be known and how it can come to be known—problems of ignorance, uncertainty, risk, deception, delusion, perception, conjecture, adaptation and learning—are then tackled as a complication or refinement of the theory.
>
> The existing mainstream of economic theory has developed in a manner which has accommodated these knowledge deficiency problems as refinements to the theory of economic action rather than rudiments of it.

It should be evident from Chapter 4 that behavioural theory, by contrast, treats such problems as analytical rudiments. These philosophical differences will also be much in evidence in Chapter 5 when we explore choice in the face of risk and uncertainty.

2.4   Conclusion

I hope that by offering this introductory overview of neoclassical and behavioural theories of choice I have reduced the risk that less attention will be given to one approach than to the other. It is difficult to compress the entire contents of this book into a single semester course, but unlike Frank (1991) I am not about to encourage instructors to sidestep this difficulty by suggesting that non-mainstream materials warrant less attention than the conventional core. (Frank suggests that his text includes novel material in supplementary chapters written in a 'more discursive style' (Frank, 1991: xxiii) so that students can read them on their own without established lecturing plans having to be rejigged to accommodate them.) To make sense of what a neoclassical economist does, and the limitations of this approach to economics, it seems important to study behavioural economics, and vice versa. Without a knowledge of, for example, the cognitive processes that produce beliefs and behaviour at odds with neoclassical views of how people ought to think and act, we may have little idea of the limitations of neoclassical thinking. Yet, without having experienced the convenience of organizing our ideas about choice in terms of well-defined preferences and constraints, we may have trouble understanding why anybody might want to abstract from the sorts of psychological findings that excite behavioural economists. Those who end up feeling more committed to one school of thought than another should also have an idea of where future battles may be fought over the relevance of each kind of theory and the wisdom of spending time teaching it.

3 Neoclassical theories of consumer behaviour

This chapter should not be read without first reading Chapter 2 for an overview of how neoclassical economists operate, in contrast to the methods of the behavioural school whom we will be examining in Chapter 4. You may also be wise to try to read this chapter in conjunction with the classic original works in this area, namely, Hicks (1939) and Hicks and Allen (1934) and, for section 3.6, Lancaster (1966a, 1966b, 1971). You should find that original contributors tend to be much more candid than standard textbook writers when they set out to explain what they are doing and why they are doing it.

3.1 Introduction

Consumers in neoclassical models of choice are assumed to have a single aim in life: to maximize utility. They are assumed to do this by ranking combinations of goods and services in order of preference and then selecting the most preferred combination from the set of feasible combinations. Rarely is any attempt made in these models to explain what utility might consist of, but this does not trouble a neoclassical economist. For purposes of anticipating behaviour, there is no intrinsic need to know in psychological terms what people get out of consumption, or why they may, say, dislike work. All that has to be knowable is the nature of the consumer's preference system.

The utility maximization philosophy and many of the technical tools shortly to be discussed—such as indifference curves and budget lines—were well established prior to the work of Hicks on the theory of demand. Hicks's breakthrough was to recognize that it is possible to construct an analysis in which there is no need for utility to be quantifiable. Prior to his work, models of consumer behaviour had been set out in cardinal terms, based on the idea of diminishing marginal utility. Hicks proposed instead an ordinal view of preferences based on a new idea: consumers' choices reflect diminishing marginal rates of substitution.

Consider choices between alternative bundles of apples and oranges. A person might rank a bundle A consisting of 19 apples and one orange as equally worth having as a bundle B consisting of 16 apples and three oranges: a loss of three apples can be exactly compensated by a gain of two oranges. If three apples have to be sacrificed for the gain of one orange, this person ranks the new position C as inferior to the original one, whereas s/he would feel better off if s/he could give up three apples and get more than two more oranges in exchange, as in bundle D. The person is displaying a *diminishing marginal rate of substitution* if, in order to part with a further three apples, s/he requires compensation of more than two more oranges to end up feeling neither worse off nor better off, as with bundle E, which consists of 13 apples and six oranges. To give up yet more apples will require compensation at an even greater rate if the person is not to feel worse off.

Hicks was not concerned with the origins of the consumer's willingness to make such tradeoffs or the rates at which the consumer might be prepared to make substitutions in practice, and how rapidly these might diminish. All that mattered was that it did not seem unreasonable to assume that, in principle, a consumer might be induced to articulate such broad sets of rankings of rival combinations. A general idea about the forms taken by preferences was all that he needed in order to discuss the nature of the equilibrium position that a typical consumer might choose.

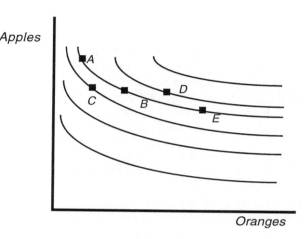

Figure 3.1: An indifference map

In a two-dimensional goods space, such as Figure 3.1, each axis represents amounts of one commodity. If the consumer ranks bundles *A*, *B* and *E* as equally preferable we can think of them as rather like points in geographical space that are the same height above sea level: just as we would represent the latter as points on a particular contour line, so we can represent them as points on a particular line called an indifference curve. Unlike a cardinal contour line (for example, one labelled 1 000 metres above sea level), however, an indifference curve is drawn without any unit representing degree of preference. All we say is that *A*, *B* and *E* are on an indifference curve that is ranked higher than the one on which combination *C* stands and lower than the one on which combination *D* stands. All combinations represented by the latter curve are viewed more favourably by the consumer than combinations such as *A*, *B*, *C* and *E*, that are shown on curves rather nearer to the origin. Although indifference maps such as Figure 3.1 typically show only a handful of indifference curves and are only drawn in terms of two dimensions, a neoclassical economist thinks of consumers as if they have preferences over all possible rival combinations of commodities. This is a point of view that is much easier to handle formally in mathematical terms, as is commonly done in advanced-level treatments. Here, as we use only words and graphs, the all-embracing, *n*-dimensional view of preferences should still be uppermost in our minds.

3.2 The axioms of neoclassical preference theory

Diagrams such as Figure 3.1 turn out to be very convenient for generating unique equilibrium positions of optimal choice, if imagined to be completely covered with smooth, continuous curves. But before they can be drawn a number of simplifying assumptions (or 'preference axioms') have to be taken on board. These are the source of much controversy, not least of all because neoclassical theorists have seen their theory as providing a benchmark for definitions of *rational* behaviour. The rest of this section consists of a discussion of these assumptions.

Consider first *completeness*, the assumption that the consumer can compare any two bundles of goods and say whether s/he is indifferent between them or specify which bundle s/he prefers. This allows that *a* may be preferred to *b*, *or b* may be preferred to *a*, *or* a person may be indifferent between *a and b*, but does not allow a rational person to prefer *a* to *b and* prefer *b* to *a*. This may sound perfectly reasonable if there are only two rival bundles *a* and *b*, but here it is applied to all possible rival combinations of commodities, some almost identical, some wildly different. If we do not make this assumption we are implying that consumers may have holes in their preference maps. If these holes happened to include some bundles that a consumer could afford, it would be unclear how such a consumer could decide what the best course of action would be. I can easily imagine myself in precisely such a position: if I had a sudden major increase in income I would become able seriously to consider choices between bundles that at present I have not even bothered to try to rank. If we are modelling only relatively small change in a consumer's circumstances, the completeness axiom may be less of a worry.

For theoretical purposes we might find it convenient to assume that economic agents are born with complete sets of preferences. However, we would be most unwise to suggest that, if this is not actually the case, people ought to set about discovering how they rate all possible combinations of goods ahead of having to choose between them. When information is costly to gather and process, it may be perfectly rational for individuals to avoid achieving states of complete self-knowledge by considering their attitudes to all possible bundles. Anand (1987: 191–2) notes that a person shopping for just seven items and facing a choice of only two brands for each item is potentially dealing with 91 pairwise combinations. It seems unlikely that the consumer would find it rational to form opinions on the relative merits of all 91 combinations entailed in this relatively short shopping list with a highly restricted range of alternative brands.

Furthermore, there may well be circumstances in which people can only express ambivalence—a pair of opposing attitudes that sum up their present state of mind—towards a particular object and presently feel unable to say one way or the other, whether it is better or worse than a rival. Consider as an example the fact that some people who migrate from the UK to Australia end up feeling very puzzled about where they want to live: when they are in Australia they feel homesick, but the moment they get back to the UK for a visit they know why they migrated. Though they may continue to live Down Under (they have to live somewhere), they never feel settled; their lives are not in equilibrium and might never be until they can make up their minds between the two places or get to live in a third one that seems clearly to dominate over both of them.

Reflexivity is a less controversial axiom: all it involves assuming is that the consumer sees each bundle consisting of a particular set of goods as at least as good as itself. It sounds a trivial axiom at first sight, for how on earth could a consumer not see, say, one bundle containing five apples and three oranges as being at least as good as another bundle containing five apples and three oranges? If we are not including it as another way of saying that we assume preferences are given through time, then the real significance of this axiom is that it forces us to recognize the care with which we need to define the sets of commodities that make up the bundles between which the consumer is trying to choose: objections to assuming reflexivity are likely to arise on the basis that there may be differences in (i) quality (not all apples and oranges are equally desirable), (ii) location (the bundles may be available in different shops, with differences in costs of getting access to them), (iii) the times at which the bundles are available (for example, a shopper might prefer a bundle of fruit from one particular store because it is open later and enables her/him to avoid having to cart it around whilst she is buying other things), or (iv) the state of the world in which the bundles are available (the consumer's circumstances will affect choices, as in the case of a consumer who does not want any fruit today due to an upset stomach but otherwise would have wanted some—see further section 10.6 on contingent commodities). Most of the time 'like' bundles are only compared with themselves at all because the bundles they contain are actually different in one or more of these four ways.

A third axiom is *transitivity*: if a person prefers bundle *a* to bundle *b*, and prefers bundle *b* to bundle *c*, then that person will prefer *a* to *c*. This key axiom rules out the possibility of indifference curves that cross. Its place in prescriptive views of rational behaviour is often justified with reference to what has become known as the 'money pump': to prefer *a* to *b* and *b* to *c* but prefer *c* to *a* would open up the seemingly bizarre possibility that a person would pay a premium to obtain *c* when trading in *a*, follow this act by trading in *c* plus some cash for *b* and then trade in *b* plus some cash to purchase *a* once more—so the person with intransitive preferences would go round in circles all the while getting poorer.

Though the money pump scenario seems odd we may start to think it less peculiar after reflecting on the tendency for intransitive rankings to occur in soccer leagues: Liverpool might beat Manchester United, and Manchester United might beat Everton, and yet Everton might beat Liverpool. This being so, perhaps we might expect a soccer fan in 1991 to drive a Ford Escort, in 1992 a Vauxhall Astra, in 1993 a Volkswagen Golf and in 1994 a Ford Escort once again. Such an intransitivity might be explained with reference to product innovations and information problems, aspects of real life which are also problematic in respect of the axiom of completeness. It is likely that products are changing through time, so a 1994 Escort might be a vastly better car than its 1991 counterpart. As far as the question of insufficient information is concerned, it should be noted that these products are known in marketing as 'experience goods': in other words, it only becomes possible to get a really good idea of what one thinks of them by trying them out over an extended period. (In the case of cars and many other durables it may take quite a while for their reliability and the standard of after-sales service to become apparent and these factors may matter more, ultimately, than many of the qualities that become apparent during a test drive.) In other words, cyclical brand loyalty is not necessarily symptomatic of irrational preferences.

Fourthly, it is assumed that preference sets are *convex*. In fact, diagrams usually seem to be constructed as if preferences are *strictly* convex: this means that if two points on any indifference curve are linked by a straight line, any point on that line (in other words, any linear combination of the two bundles) will be preferred to the pair of points that it links. Figure 3.2 shows convex preferences that are not strictly convex. If all indifference curves on Figure 3.2 were like $I``$ then it would be a case of strict convexity (note that P is preferred to M and N). However, it also includes indifference curve $I`$, consisting of straight-line segments joined together. This implies that the consumer is indifferent between some linear combinations of bundles—for example, S, T and U. As can be seen, this occurs in respect of pairs of bundles on the same segment of such an indifference curve. It means that the marginal rate of substitution between the goods is constant, not diminishing, along that segment: over any portion of such a segment, the neoclassical economist would say that the goods are perfect substitutes. However, if linear combinations of goods were formed from bundles on two different straight-line segments of $I`$, then these would be preferred to the two bundles—examine bundle $V$, which is a linear combination of bundles $R$ and $U$—so overall an indifference curve like $I`$ can be said to be convex even though this does not hold over some ranges.

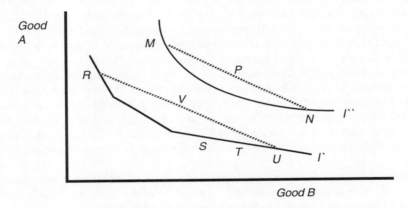

Figure 3.2: Convexity without strict convexity

Strict convexity of preferences tends to get assumed as a consequence of neoclassical economists wanting to study equilibrium situations with reference to the types of adjustments that might be made by consumers in response to small changes in their circumstances. Stability of the systems being investigated may require, fifthly, the axiom of *smoothness*, so that a consumer will only make marginal changes in behaviour in response to marginal changes in circumstances. Preference structures that imply kinked or stepped indifference curves open up the possibility of discontinuous adjustments and are therefore often assumed not to exist. This assumption paves the way for trouble-free applications of calculus to the modelling of the consumer's optimization problem: smoothness of preferences implies utility functions that can be differentiated twice. Psychologists would doubtless be troubled to see this assumption being made, for their experimental work suggests that threshold effects are common: in other words, a small increase in the presence of some feature of the person's environment will not be noticed, but if further increases are successively applied there will eventually come a point at which the person does recognize that things are different (see Drakopoulos, 1992; Kornai, 1971).

Preference sets are assumed, sixthly, to display *monotonicity*: more of a commodity is always preferred to less, other things equal. This ensures that on a two-dimensional diagram indifference curves always slope (monotonously) in the same direction, rather than sloping down and then up, or vice versa. Note that preferences could be convex without exhibiting monotonicity, as in the hypothetical case of a consumer whose preferences implied circular indifference curves. If preferences were monotonic and linear, instead of monotonic and convex, it would be difficult to see why consumers would end up buying a variety of goods, for indifference curves would be downward-sloping straight lines, each stretching from one axis to the other. (See Figure 3.9 below and imagine how the accompanying story would look with straight-line indifference curves, except for the peculiar case where the budget line had the same slope as these curves, implying complete indeterminacy along the budget line.)

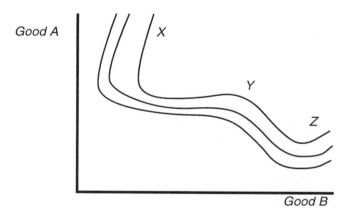

Figure 3.3: Satiation

The assumption of monotonicity rules out the possibility that consumption of more of one commodity might make a person feel worse off even if this is achieved without a need to give up units of any other commodities. Figure 3.3 shows the kinds of indifference curves which would have to be allowed if satiation were recognized as a possibility. Regions X, Y and Z show satiation. In region Z, for example, we can see that the consumer is only willing to accept more units of good 2 if compensated by being given a sufficient amount more of good 1. Although satiation seems quite a reasonable feature to allow, particularly if we are discussing, say, choices of food and drink, it is problematic for Hicks's theory because it opens up the possibility of multiple equilibria. Satiation regions like X and Z on Figure 3.3 are not particularly troublesome in this respect, but indifference curves that were shaped as in the vicinity of Y could imply, in some situations, a consumer who was torn between a pair of best-preferred combinations either side of Y. Hicks (1939: 21–2) drew a parallel between this sort of hesitancy-provoking scenario and the fable of Buridan's ass, which was tethered between two identical bales of hay and starved to death because it could not decide which one to eat. Economists have sometimes tried to justify the assumption of non-satiation by assuming, seventhly, *free disposal*, in other words, that any surfeit of a commodity could be thrown away without cost. In today's world of heightened environmental consciousness such an assumption seems less acceptable.

Eighthly, and finally, in this discussion of key assumptions of neoclassical preference theory, it is most important that we note the axiom of *continuity*: every consumption bundle will be ranked equally with some other consumption bundles. If the consumer can think of no other consumption bundles of equal rank to a particular consumption bundle, then the latter bundle in a sense stands separate from all others and fundamental problems arise for the idea of indifference. What we would be running into is a case where bundle a consisting of a bit less of commodity X cannot be placed on a par with bundle b if attempts are made to remedy the deficiency in a in respect of X by offering compensation in the form of a suitably larger amount of other commodities. Without continuity, we may violate the *Axiom of Archimedes*, also known at the *Principle of Gross Substitution*. In terms of everyday expression this is the assumption that 'Everyone has their price' (see Borch, 1968: 22; Drakopoulos, 1990: 184). An old and somewhat sexist piece of humour is convenient to illustrate an implication of making this assumption, namely, that one may be excluding intolerant behaviour or choices that reflect particular ethical principles and absolute aversions:

He: Will you sleep with me?
She: No.
He: Will you sleep with me for fifty dollars?
She: No, I'm not that kind of woman.
He: How about a hundred dollars?
She: Look, I said I'm not that kind of woman.
He: I'd pay five thousand if I had to.
She: In that case, get out your cheque book!
He: But I can only afford fifty dollars.
She: I did tell you I wasn't that kind of woman.
He: We've just established that you are that kind of woman; now we're just haggling over the price!

In neoclassical consumer theory we do not encounter teetotal, vegetarian, non-smoking consumers who refuse to consume alcohol, meat and cigarettes not because their prices make them unattractive but simply because they prefer not to, period. There is no moral dimension to the theory (cf. Etzioni, 1988). Nor is there room for grief at the loss of a loved one, for rational consumers will have taken out life insurance cover and receive compensation.

It is perfectly possible to represent non-Archimedean preferences in simple diagrammatic terms. Figure 3.4 does so, using the case of how a vegetarian might see alternative bundles of meat and vegetables. News of an opportunity to receive some meat at no sacrifice in terms of vegetables would not make this person feel any better off, regardless of how many or how few vegetables s/he already has. If I had not mentioned conditions of free disposal I should not even be drawing vertical indifference lines on Figure 3.4, for the vegetarian whose preferences are at odds with the axiom of continuity is *only interested in points on the 'vegetables' axis itself*. It is not the case that more meat does not make her/him better off, for a given amount of vegetables. Rather, s/he is simply not interested in having meat. This is why the issue of disposal surfaces once again: how should we view the vegetarian's position in the event—all too common a problem for vegetarians when dining out—that s/he discovers that meat has been *thrust* upon her/him as part of a meal? The chance to sell the meat to someone else might seem to imply that the event is one that enables the consumer to improve her/his welfare. However, many vegetarians would probably feel put out by the unwanted meat and wish that they had not had that meal at all. In this case, their attitudes might better be represented in terms of upward-sloping indifference curves rather than vertical ones, although this does not really capture how they view things when they are choosing freely and knowingly.

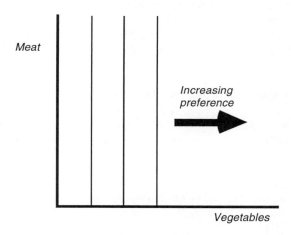

Figure 3.4: Vegetarian preferences under conditions of free disposal

Vegetarianism is an example of a kind of preference system known as a lexicographic preference ordering, after the Greek word for dictionary: to look up a word in a dictionary we have to look at a specific sequence of letters; nothing else will do. Though lexicographic choice receives little attention from neoclassical economists, a considerable literature has grown up on the topic over more than a century (Earl, 1986: 233–9; Drakopoulos, 1994). Much of it raises the possibility that some needs or wants, at least, may be organized in a hierarchical manner. Abraham Maslow (1954), a psychologist, triggered a lot of research by suggesting that human needs take the form of a five-level hierarchy. People who do not have the basics of life in physiological terms will focus exclusively on remedying the deficit, getting enough food first, followed by shelter. The next need is safety and security. If these aspects of life are under control, Maslow predicts that people will start focusing on satisfying a perceived a need to belong, to feel part of society. A concentration on this need will give way to a concern with self- and social-esteem once a satisfactory feeling of belongingness has been achieved. Finally, people experience a need for self-actualization, and if they cannot attend to it adequately they will feel that their lives are not fulfilling. The empirical adequacy of Maslow's views has been questioned (see Lea *et al.*, 1987), though many people would find them easy to relate to, if not in terms of their own experiences then at least with reference to those of people whom they know.

It is easy to see the potential significance of Maslow's thinking in relation to issues such as deforestation in poor nations. People in these nations might ideally wish to behave in ways consistent with ethical concerns over the damage that they could do to the global ecosystem by participating in the logging of rainforests, yet they will act at odds with their ideal view of themselves if this is necessary to meet their basic needs. Solution of the problem may thus depend greatly on consumers in rich nations having environmental consciences and being prepared to limit their overall consumption in order to pay the true costs of producing things. Lux and Lutz (1986: 396) argue that when consumers have reached such a stage, the conventional assumption of maximization subject to a budget constraint is inappropriate: such people are better modelled as 'restrained maximizers'— 'restrained by [their] innermost personal values, articulated by [their] higher-order moral preferences'. On this note, we may turn our attention to the neoclassical analysis of how consumers optimize subject merely to constraints of money and/or time.

3.3   Constraints and consumer equilibrium

In neoclassical economics, the consumer's task when choosing is to work out which is the most desirable combination of commodities from the set of combinations that are feasible given the limitations implied by her/his budget and the prevailing set of prices. On a two-dimensional diagram such as Figure 3.5 a linear budget line may be drawn to mark the boundary between feasible combinations of goods (represented by the shaded area to the left of the line) and combinations that lie beyond the person's purchasing power.

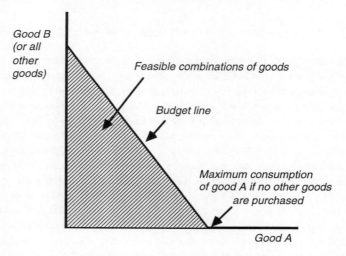

Figure 3.5: The consumer's feasible set

In drawing this line as a clear-cut boundary, we are abstracting from any uncertainty that consumers may feel about what they may actually be able to buy—we are ignoring, for example, the possibility of vagueness in the consumer's view of her/his credit-worthiness.

If we are just discussing choices between consumption items that might be purchased today, we are presuming that a choice has already been made between work and leisure, to generate income, and between consumption today and consumption in the future. Often, however, theorists set up the consumer's optimization problem as if tradeoffs are performed simultaneously on all of these fronts. Note that in cases where choices have to be made between more than two goods the common practice to allow diagrammatic treatment is to lump together all goods bar the one that happens to be of interest. Quite what scale we might have in mind on the vertical axis for 'all other goods' is a puzzle that obviously must be addressed at some stage. If the relative prices of all other goods are constant it is simple to escape questions about how we might aggregate a diverse range of products and achieve a scale for the vertical axis: this axis can simply be said to represent purchasing power/ income available for spending on other items. Such a two-dimensional analysis may seem to capture neatly the idea of a consumer deciding how much to spend on a particular kind of commodity by taking generalized purchasing power as a *simplifying* reference point for what has to be given up, rather than seeing the opportunity cost in terms of specific commodities that the money might have been used to purchase. However, formal neoclassical models are normally set up in *n*-dimensional terms, with no attention being paid to the issue of bounded rationality.

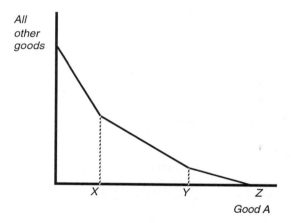

Figure 3.6: A piecewise linear budget constraint

If we draw a linear budget constraint we are assuming that consumers cannot get quantity discounts and do not bid up the price of a product if they try to buy more of it. Quantity discounts are, of course, quite common in practice in various guises. Figure 3.6 illustrates the type of case in which the price charged to the consumer on marginal units falls discontinuously as two purchasing levels, *X* and *Y*, are successively exceeded: it might be that if up to *X* units are purchased, the price per unit is $6.00, but additional units between *X* and *Y* are charged at only $5.00 and units in excess of *Y* are charged at only

$4.00. The resulting budget constraint in this case is a series of linear segments, known technically as a piecewise linear constraint. If the consumer had a budget of $142.00, with X equal to 10 and Y equal to 20, then, at the prices mentioned, Z would have to equal 28: 10 units purchased at $6.00, plus 10 more units purchased at $5.00 leaves $32.00 to spend on 8 additional units at $4.00 each. Other forms of discounting may be envisaged, and some of these may result in non-linear types of budget constraints.

Piecewise budget constraints are commonly encountered in discussions concerning the economics of labour supply and the effects of marginal tax rates on incentives to work (for example, Brown, 1983). However, piecewise and non-linear budget constraints tend to be shunted out of the way in discussions of commodity purchase decisions, for they allow the possibility that consumers could end up with non-unique optimal positions akin to those that might be produced if preferences of the kind shown in Figure 3.3 were confronted with a linear budget constraint. A theorist who is interested in uncovering unique positions of equilibrium for optimizing decision-makers may run into trouble unless dealing with linear budget constraints and preferences that at no point display satiation. Figure 3.7 illustrates such a trouble-free solution.

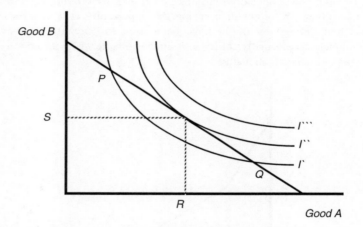

Figure 3.7: The consumer's preferred combination

The best position presently available for the consumer represented in Figure 3.7 is a combination of R units of good A and S units of good B. This enables such a consumer to get on to indifference curve I``, which is tangential to her/his budget line. The consumer would prefer to be at a point on an indifference curve further towards the top right-hand area of the diagram, such as I```, but this is presently impossible given her/his budget and the prices of goods A and B. A tangency between a budget line and an indifference curve represents a situation in which the ratio of relative prices (which determines the slope of the budget line) is equal to the consumer's marginal rate of substitution (which is reflected by the slope of her indifference curves). Points elsewhere on the budget line, such as P and Q, where the budget line is cut by indifference curve I`, are feasible for the consumer but they represent combinations of A and B that the consumer ranks as inferior to the combination implied by the point of tangency. To show the effects of changes in relative prices on preferred combinations, it is necessary to pivot the consumer's budget line on the point where it meets the axis representing the good whose price is being kept constant. Figure 3.8 shows an example of this.

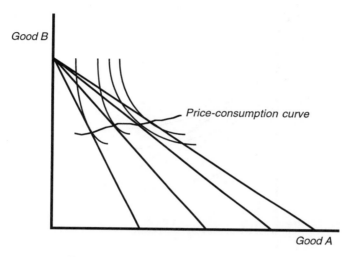

Figure 3.8: The price-consumption curve

Suppose initially the consumer faces the budget line that is furthest to the left on Figure 3.8. Reductions in the price of good A will swing the budget line out to the right. If we superimpose the consumer's set of indifference curves on the map of alternative budget-line scenarios we can find out what the consumer's preferred combination will be at each configuration of relative prices. The line showing the locus of indifference curve/budget line tangencies associated with changes in relative prices is known as the price-consumption curve. In the case shown, reductions in the price of A lead the consumer to purchase more of good A. However, we shall see in the next section that this result is by no means a prediction of the neoclassical framework. It should also be noted that in this example consumption of B rises as A is cheapened: this can arise due to the increase in real income caused by the fall in the price of A or because B is in some way complementary to A.

The examples of equilibrium solutions that I have so far presented involve the consumer purchasing some units of each of the goods. This obviously is not particularly realistic, since there are many goods—or, at least, brands of goods—that a consumer will not be buying. In the previous section, when discussing the Axiom of Archimedes, I discussed types of preference systems that might produce precisely this result (to see this, try superimposing Figure 3.5 on Figure 3.4). The possibility that a consumer will fail to purchase a particular commodity can also be demonstrated in terms of neoclassical types of preferences, so long as the indifference curves are shaped so that they cut one of the axes of the diagram. Figure 3.9 gives an example of this phenomenon, which is known as a corner solution. When the price of A is high, the consumer's budget line has no point of tangency with any of her/his indifference curves. The best choice s/he can make is to purchase only good B, buying K units, where her/his budget line intersects with an indifference curve at the point at which it cuts the B axis. However, a consumer whose preferences can be mapped in this way is not someone who is refusing to buy A on principle. If the price of A is reduced far enough, such a consumer will switch he/his purchasing behaviour in favour of A. The tangency at L illustrates this.

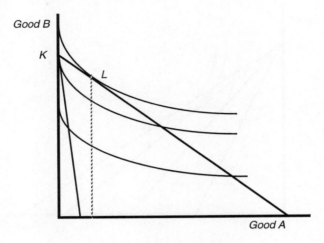

Figure 3.9: A corner solution

An example of how the corner solution framework may help us is in the economics of labour supply, where changes in real wage possibilities may lead people to start trying to get jobs or withdraw from participating in the labour force.

3.4   Income and substitution effects

The examples of consumption equilibria presented in Figures 3.8 and 3.9 show how changes in relative prices may affect the consumer's welfare by tightening or loosening her/his budget constraint. Similar effects can be produced by changes in the consumer's money income, which have the effect of moving the budget line to the right (left), parallel to the initial budget line, if income is increased (reduced). The locus of points of tangency between budget lines and indifference curves in such cases is known as the income-consumption curve (ICC). The slope of this curve will depend on the form of the consumer's preferences.

Figure 3.10 gives an example of a consumer who will buy less of good A as her/his income is increased, as might be the case for people who buy fewer economy-class airline tickets and tend increasingly to travel business-class as their incomes rise. In this case we call A as an 'inferior good'. Products that are inferior goods over part of the ICC (when the curve is downward sloping to the right, if the good in question is on the horizontal axis) may well be 'normal goods' over other parts of the ICC (in other words, the ICC may slope upwards to the right over part of its length). Though economy-class air tickets may come to

46

be disfavoured by the increasingly affluent consumer, we can imagine that they were probably once seen as luxuries, the consumer's consumption of which rose at a faster rate than her/his income. At that stage, rises in income led the consumer to switch in favour of economy-class air travel and away from using the motor car or railways as means of travelling long distances.

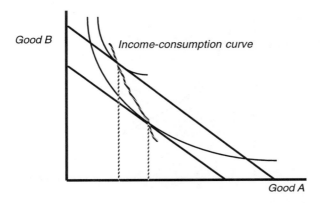

Figure 3.10: Income-consumption curve for an inferior good

If we look back over the analysis of effects of price reductions and income increases it is apparent that they both can serve as means by which consumers may be able to reach higher indifference curves than those to which they have hitherto been constrained. Were we working with cardinal preferences and hence with indifference curves that had some kind of scalar unit attached to them, we would have a ready measure for the percentage change in real income caused for a particular individual by a particular relative price or money income change. Hicks's ordinal analysis of preferences clearly precludes this, but it does at least offer us a way of thinking about the impact that price changes have on real income: as far as the consumer is concerned, there will exist an increase in money income that would be sufficient to make her feel as well off as she would feel if she had instead the chance to take advantage of a particular price reduction.

Consider Figure 3.11. The consumer is initially buying K units of good A, because this gets her/him on to the best indifference curve that s/he can reach, namely $I^{'}$. Suppose the price of good A falls, such that her/his budget line swings from HM to HQ. This would enable her/him to get on to indifference curve $I^{''}$, which entails an increase in consumption of A to N. Another way for the consumer to reach indifference curve $I^{''}$ would be to benefit from increased income, such that her/his budget line were pushed out to the right, parallel to HM, until it became tangential to $I^{''}$. This is the case with budget line JP. If the consumer's budget line were moved to this position, s/he would choose L units of good A.

This line of thinking leads neoclassical economists to decompose the overall 'price effect' of a price change (in this case, the increase of consumption of A from K to N) into an 'income effect' and a 'substitution effect'. The income effect of a fall in the price of A is the impact on the purchasing of A due to the change in real income produced by the price reduction (in this case, an increase from K to L). The substitution effect is the change in consumption of *A* that is due purely to the change in its relative attractiveness produced by the change in its relative price (in this case an increase from *L* to *N*).

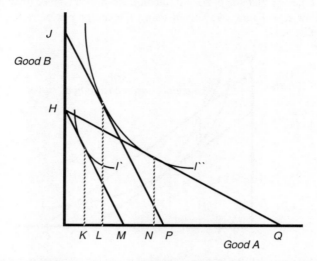

Figure 3.11: Income and substitution effects for a normal good

It should be noted that there are several ways of decomposing price effects into income and substitution effects. They differ in ways that resemble differences between index numbers that use base period quantities as reference points, and those that use current quantities as reference points (for an excellent discussion, see Dobb, 1969: 43–6). The method that I have used here is the 'equivalent variation method' of Hicks. Many texts use Hicks's 'compensating variation method': instead of considering how much of an increase in money income would be required to put the consumer into a position just as good as that permitted by the price reduction, this method considers how much income could be taken away from the consumer while s/he faces the new set of relative prices and yet leave her no worse off than s/he was at the original set of prices.

As a consequence of the assumption that preferences are characterized by a decreasing marginal rate of substitution, substitution effects in neoclassical consumer theory always have a negative sign: a price reduction induces substitution in favour of the good in question. Income effects, by contrast, may have either sign. The case shown in Figure 3.11 concerns a normal good, which means that the income effect is negative: higher real income due to the price reduction leads to a shift in favour of the cheaper good. For inferior goods, the income effect is positive, offsetting to some degree the substitution effect, rather than augmenting it. This leads to an interesting possibility: the price effect may be positive for some inferior goods because the positive income effect is greater than the substitution effect. In this case, we are looking at a hypothetical Giffen good: the reduction in price leads to a reduction in sales, implying a demand curve that has an upward-sloping portion for the consumer in question. Figure 3.12 illustrates this possibility. To cast it into the context of the classic empirical instance in which Giffen identified it—the great Irish potato famine—I have labelled the two axes as meat and potatoes (see Mason, 1989, for a detailed study of Giffen's work).

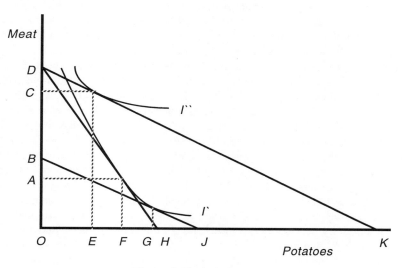

Figure 3.12: A Giffen good

Prior to the famine, the budget line is *DK*. The famine pushes up the price of potatoes sharply, swinging the budget line back to *DH*. The person is thus forced back from indifference curve *I``*, where the consumption bundle was *OC* meat and *OE* potatoes, to indifference curve *I`*, with a consumption bundle of only *OA* meat but an increase in potato consumption to *OF*. This price increase is as disastrous for the consumer as would have been a reduction in income that took the budget line back to *BJ* at the original set of prices. In this case the income effect is positive (amounting to *EG*), that is, the reduction in real income due to the price *increase* leads to an *increase* in potato consumption. The substitution effect is certainly negative, but it is too weak to offset the income effect: the price increase encourages substitution against potatoes which pulls the consumer back from *OG* to *OF*, so overall the price effect is an increase in potato consumption from *OE* to *OF*.

To predict whether or not price or income changes will result in particular kinds of response, let alone to predict quantitative responses to such changes, we need to go beyond the theoretical framework and study the forms actually taken by preferences (see further section 3.7). However, neoclassical economists would argue that even in the absence of knowledge of the precise shapes taken by indifference surfaces it is possible to reach conclusions about the desirability of some policies that may impact upon consumer welfare. The kind of analysis employed to separate income effects from substitution effects— namely, diagrams employing three budget lines, two of which are parallel to each other—is popular as a means for arriving at such pronouncements, and forms the basis of countless exam problems in applied welfare economics.

As an example (see also section 3.5), consider the question of how a university ought to set prices in its student dining hall. Suppose that presently prices are set on the basis of average costs, with the typical student eating 200 meals per year in hall and being charged $4.00 for each meal. Suppose further that the marginal cost of preparing a meal is only $2.00. If meals were priced at marginal cost, losses on overheads would then average $400 per student. An obvious question to consider is whether or not student welfare would be improved by a switch to marginal cost pricing for meals in conjunction with the requirement that each student pays a $400 fixed charge per year towards the kitchen overheads.

Figure 3.13 shows how neoclassical consumer theory can be used to frame an answer to this sort of welfare question. First, show the typical student's initial position via a tangency between a budget line (in this case, *EH*) and an indifference curve (*I`*). The student purchases *OF* meals and *OB* other goods. Next, consider what could happen if meal prices reflected marginal costs rather than average costs. The budget line swings round to the right to *EK*. If the consumer were still to purchase *OF* meals, s/he could now have *OC* other goods. In this case, the university kitchen would be *BC* worse off in cash-equivalent terms. If this sum were charged to the student and meals were charged at marginal cost, the student's budget constraint would now be *DJ*. The university would now be covering its overheads as well as marginal costs on sales of meals. This being so, it would be no worse off than under average cost pricing. However, the student may be able to do better than in the initial situation. By consuming *OG* meals and *OA* other goods, the student can reach the indifference curve *I``*, which previously was not part of her/his feasible set. The student cannot be worse off than before as the original combination of *OF* meals and *OB* other goods is still feasible: it is at this combination that the new budget constraint cuts through indifference curve *I`*.

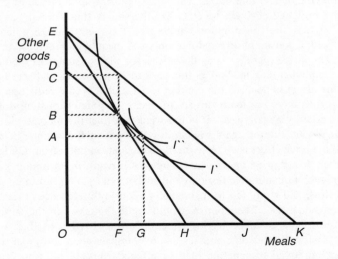

Figure 3.13: Marginal cost pricing and consumer welfare

If this analysis is seen as questionable, the doubts that are raised are likely to be unrelated to worries about the assumptions made to draw the indifference curves. Even if *I`* started sloping upwards beyond *OF* due to satiation, if would appear that the switch to a fixed charge/marginal cost pricing policy could not make the student worse off. Rather, one might expect objections to arise because students are not identical: they may differ in their desires to cook for themselves, to miss some meals or eat off campus. If all are asked to pay the same fixed charge, those who were previously making less than average use of the dining hall would no doubt feel that the situation lacked equity. However, if this problem were recognized and student-specific fixed charges were made on the basis of previous usage rates, the possibility that some students were making dishonest reports of their dining frequencies might be an alternative cause for concern.

3.5   Essay example: Housing policy and poverty

Question
Imagine a situation in which the government wishes to improve the access of the poor to housing. It only wishes to spend a limited sum in this area and wishes to do the best for those at whom its policy is aimed. Would you advise it (i) to use the money to subsidize rents, or (ii) to use the money to increase family income supplements to the poor?

Author's notes
A neoclassical analysis of this sort of problem generally leads to the result that a benefit in cash (in this example, an increase in family income supplements) is always preferable to a benefit in kind (in this example, subsidized rents). The result can be derived with the aid of Figure 3.14, which is drawn to illustrate the preferences and budget constraint faced by a typical poor consumer.

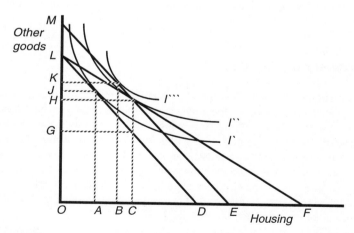

Figure 3.14: Welfare implications of alternative housing policies

Initially the consumer's budget constraint is *LD* and the best attainable position is one on indifference curve *I'* that combines *OA* housing and *OJ* other goods. Suppose the government offers to pay 40 per cent of this consumer's rental costs. The budget line pivots on *L* to become *LF* (*OF* is almost twice *OD*). If housing is not a Giffen good the new optimal position for the consumer will involve an increase in housing consumption, for example, *OC* on indifference curve *I``*. (Note that the labelling of Figure 3.14 dodges the issue of how 'housing' is being quantified: an increase in housing consumption might involve a move to a larger property or a better quality one of the same size, or some combination of these changes.) The rent subsidy thus involves the government in spending as much as it would cost to purchase *GH* of non-housing goods.

If, instead of giving the consumer the rent subsidy, the government gave the consumer enough extra money to purchase *GH* of non-housing goods, the new budget constraint would be *LM* higher (*LM* = *GH*), that is, *ME*. The consumer's preferred position is now shown as involving *OB* housing rather than *OC* or *OA* (housing is not an inferior good in this example), and the consumer is on a higher indifference curve (*I``` * rather than *I``*).

Although the neoclassical framework leads to this conclusion there are several reasons why the government *might* nonetheless be better advised to opt for rent subsidies. First, consumers are not identical in their incomes and preferences, so the other policy implies different income supplements for different consumers, and it may be difficult to obtain honest statements of preference from consumers. Secondly, there are 'merit good' arguments: the income supplement policy leads to less housing being consumed than in the rent subsidy scenario but the government may believe that it is in the best interests of poor consumers to have better housing (and less beer, cigarettes, gambling and so on?). This leads to a third point: the analysis rather fudges between consumers and households without making clear how household indifference curves might be arrived at, or who controls the purse-strings in a household: feminists might want to point out that an increase in general purchasing power might be aimed at improving the welfare of the household in general and yet it might in practice be appropriated by the man of the house and only used to increase his consumption.

3.6   The consumer as a producer

The analysis of consumer behaviour in terms of the toolkit of neoclassical economics has so far been conducted entirely in terms of the goods space: that is to say, each commodity has been depicted as an entity, as something from which consumers might derive satisfaction directly. Not all neoclassical economics portrays the consumer's constrained optimization problem in this way. In this section, I present an alternative approach which is probably more useful for framing business and marketing problems and which is increasingly finding a place in mainstream texts as a 'new' theory even though it comes from a literature that is many decades old. For students of business and marketing, the treatment by Douglas (1987: 86–101) is one of the more useful of those that are available.

As long ago as the 1950s, Houthakker (1952) and Gorman (1956) suggested that it might be a good idea to recognize that consumers often discriminate between goods on the basis of their *characteristics*—the elements/attributes that determine the value for money that they appear to offer—rather than between goods simply as 'wholes'. Given this, it might be instructive to try to build theories in terms of characteristics space rather than goods space. In fact, as Loasby (1978: 3) has pointed out, the idea that consumers are interested in the different qualities of goods as well as their prices is to be found much earlier in the work of Marshall (1920: 86-91); but it has become associated in most economists' minds with the work of Kelvin Lancaster (1966a, 1966b, 1971), who had seen potential in a characteristics framework for making sense of the processes by which new products achieve market share and force others to be discontinued.

Lancaster combined the characteristics idea with another theme (posited almost simultaneously by Becker, 1965, and Muth, 1966): one should see households as being rather akin to firms as they are depicted in neoclassical production theory. Entrepreneurs purchase inputs and use them to produce other goods, from whose sale they hope to realize profits. They have to choose between rival *production technologies*—that is, different mixes of goods that might be used as inputs to produce particular outputs—and between different combinations of outputs. Their prospective profits are maximized when they can see no way of increasing their net revenues by switching to another technology or changing their mix of outputs. Households, likewise, are constrained in their activities by production technologies that limit the outputs of characteristics they can produce using goods inputs, including the scarce time inputs of the household members.

A typical household production technology yields joint products—that is, more than one characteristic output—to which members of the household attach a value. For example, a vacation may be a device that enables a person to relax and participate in new experiences. Likewise, a video cassette recorder enables a person both to make time switches of television programmes and to make use of programme material available in public libraries or from commercial outlets. Changes in relative prices of consumer goods (such as the price of video rentals relative to cinema seats and babysitting charges) have implications for households rather akin to the effects that changes in relative prices of different types of machines and workers have for firms. Likewise, the introduction of new consumption commodities, differentiated by the different characteristics combinations that they can be used to produce, has an obvious parallel with the introduction of new, more cost-effective industrial production techniques.

This starting point enables Lancaster to offer an interpretation of differences in the degrees of substitutability between goods. His analysis rests on the idea that the overall consumption technology that people have to contend with is decomposable into a number of smaller technologies wherein subsets of characteristics can only be produced by particular subsets of commodities. For example, one would not expect much overlap between gardening and oral hygiene technologies: a spade is no use as a toothpick and no one would dream of using toothpaste as a weedkiller. Lancaster (1971: 132–9) is aware that some output characteristics may appeal universally but he argues that imperfect decomposability is not problematic for his analysis so long as subsets of otherwise technologically separate goods yield only a small proportion of the total output of these characteristics. Some evidence that consumers do indeed see goods as intrinsically grouped according to the characteristics with which they are associated is to be found in the work of Pickering *et al.* (1973) and Doyle and Fenwick (1975). This empirical research does not rule out the possibility that people also see their activities as consumers being associated with some fairly universal outputs, both good and bad. For example, many choices may impact upon how busy people feel, how much stress and anxiety they suffer, and on their self- and social-esteem.

Ratchford (1975: 66) welcomes Lancaster's work from the standpoint of marketing theory and suggests that an operational definition of the concept of an industry follows readily from the idea that goods can be sorted into categories on the basis of the characteristics they can help to produce. An economist armed only with Hicks's theory of demand would normally classify products as belonging to particular industries depending on their cross-elasticities of demand. Lancaster's analysis suggests that goods are likely to be close substitutes to the extent that they produce the same characteristics, and complements to the extent that they need to be used together to produce a particular characteristic. Changes in the mix of goods consumed in one technology grouping will not affect the yields of characteristics associated with other technology groupings and may therefore be considered in isolation.

Not all neoclassical economists have been keen to take on board the idea that differences in substitution between goods may reflect differences in the sets of characteristics that they produce. If one prefers not to think of the consumption technology as being nearly-enough decomposable in this sort of way, an alternative approach is to suggest that preferences in terms of goods are separable. This leads to the theory of the 'utility tree' (see Strotz, 1957; Green, 1976: chapter 10) which portrays consumers first as making work/leisure choices, then as budgeting their incomes among broad expenditure categories (food, housing, transport, recreation), and going on to divide these categories up into sub-categories (for example, meat versus dairy products versus vegetables) and sub-sub-categories (chicken versus beef versus lamb), right down to rival brands. Substitution is then not thought of as taking place between items that are not on the same branch: it may be that the consumer allocates funds between meat and cheese, but then thinks separately about substitutions between Cheddar and Camembert cheese and between rival brands of hamburgers. Hamburgers and cheese are not traded directly against each other. Haines (1975: 77–8) and Katzner (1970: 156) both see a hierarchical view of preference systems as enabling neoclassical economists to discuss patterns of cross-elasticities of demand without shifting their formal analysis into characteristics space, and it is interesting to note that Muth's (1966) contribution to the idea of the household as a production system was inspired by the utility tree literature: for much of his paper he writes as if households combine goods to produce other goods (for example, a meal), not characteristics, from which they derive utility.

This debate shows how economists can be reluctant to take on board a new way of thinking even if it makes extensive use of familiar ideas. A more constructive approach is to recognize that the utility tree and characteristics frameworks may be complementary. It may be true that some of the time consumers do think about choices in terms of goods combinations with no conscious reference to characteristics (for example, when budgeting between very different categories of goods), yet it may be difficult to make sense of the branching of a person's utility tree without reference to the characteristics that goods may offer. To distinguish between different goods, people find it necessary to refer to differences and similarities in terms of characteristics, but characteristics only become meaningful as dimensions of choice because goods offer different performances in respect of them. Lancaster himself certainly does seem to have in mind a multi-stage budgeting process, for he normally presumes that the consumer has already allocated a particular sum of money to the production of a particular technologically separable set of characteristics.

Consider the case of a person who has set aside a budget of $2 000 to pay for a vacation with the aim of obtaining both relaxation and new experiences. Different holiday destinations and resorts may provide her with different combinations of these desired outputs. Figure 3.15 shows the kind of diagram that Lancaster devised for depicting the consumer's decision problem and preferred solution. Assume the consumer has four possible destinations in mind. Each resort can be represented diagrammatically as a ray from the origin whose slope depends on the mix of characteristics it offers and whose length shows how much of both characteristics the consumer expects to obtain by spending her/his entire budget on staying at the resort. If s/he spends, say, a fifth of the budget at resort A, s/he will only get a fifth of the way along that resort's technology ray OA. If s/he spends the remaining four-fifths at resort B s/he will in addition get four-fifths of the way along ray OB. The consumer's overall production of the two characteristics for the holiday would then be the combination Y, at the corner of the parallelogram $OXYZ$. Lancaster's model assumes that technologies are linear and open to linear combination, so the technology rays are straight lines and all combinations represented by points on straight lines linking the ends of the technology rays are feasible. Given its present price, resort D is a place that this consumer will not stay at if s/he is only concerned with these two characteristics: it offers both less relaxation and fewer new experiences per dollar than does resort C.

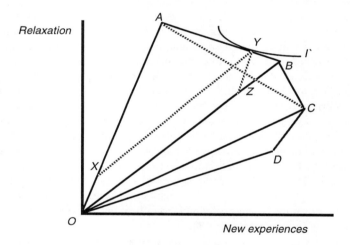

Figure 3.15: Holiday choices in characteristics space

The set of lines linking the outermost points of the undominated rays (in this case ABC) is known as the consumer's efficiency frontier: points to the right of this line are not feasible; points to the left of the line and between the outermost undominated technology rays (in this case, points inside $OABC$)—for example, a combination of time at resorts A and C, leading to an outcome somewhere along the line AC—result in the consumer needlessly forgoing opportunities to obtain these two characteristics. To find the consumer's preferred choice of holiday we superimpose her/his preference map and see which combination will enable the consumer to reach the highest feasible indifference curve. The indifference curves are assumed by Lancaster to have the same form as in standard Hicksian analysis, except that they are, of course, being drawn to reflect the consumer's supposed willingness to make tradeoffs between characteristics. In the case drawn, the consumer's constrained optimum is point Y, which allows her/him to reach indifference curve I. S/he spends a fifth of her/his money staying at resort A, and the rest on staying at resort B. S/he spends no time at all at resorts C or D. To know how long the holiday would last, we would have to specify the expenditure per day at each of resorts A and B.

It should be readily seen that if there are only two characteristics associated with a particular household technology the consumer will pick either a combination of two goods (where one of her/his indifference curves is tangential to the efficiency frontier) or just one of the goods (if the highest ranked indifference curve that is feasible just touches the end of a technology ray and is not cut by a segment of the efficiency frontier). If more than two goods are to be preferred, the consumer must be interested in more than two characteristics. If markets efficiently convey information about products and their prices, a product that is dominated on all dimensions by another product should not pick up any sales at all.

The assumption that consumption technologies are linear turns out to be rather important for ensuring that the hypothetical consumers do not find themselves in states of indecision, each torn between two or more different combinations of products. This possibility was identified by Watts and Gaston (1982). It could arise if, as a result of increasing expenditure on a particular commodity by a particular percentage, the consumer could increase the output of one of the characteristics by a greater percentage. Increasing returns in the production of the characteristic could imply an efficiency frontier which bowed inwards towards the origin, like the consumer's indifference curves, as it sloped downwards to the right (this is the characteristics space equivalent of Figure 3.6). An indifference curve might be tangential to more than one point on such an efficiency frontier. In the case of tourism, we might well expect there to be non-linearities associated with both increasing and decreasing returns to some characteristics: for example, tourists initially may face difficulties in getting to know a new destination, so if they only take a brief stopover it may be a somewhat bewildering experience. However, the longer they stay in a destination the more difficult it will be for them to find new things to do.

A variation on the Watts and Gaston argument was suggested by one of my students, Tony Davis, in a critique of the story told in relation to Figure 3.15. The problem he raised with this vacation example is that it ignores complications caused by the cost of getting from one holiday destination to another. The cost of getting to each resort has to be incurred whether the tourist stays there for a day or for several weeks. We might suppose the end points of the rays drawn for the various resorts to show what the tourist expects to obtain from spending on *staying* at each resort a sum equal to the vacation budget less the cost of getting to the resort. In this way, we can say halving the spending on staying at a resort halves the amounts that the person gets of each of the characteristics associated with the resort. However, if the tourist takes a triangular trip that involves spending time away at two destinations it is likely that the fixed costs of the holiday will be increased. For example, consider the case of someone living in Auckland who decides to spend a week in Sydney followed by a week in Singapore. An Auckland/Sydney/Singapore/Auckland air ticket will cost more than return tickets for either Auckland/Sydney or Auckland/Singapore. Suppose that, on Figure 3.15, OA refers to Sydney and OB refers to Singapore. Having recognized the costs of getting to and between these destinations we can no longer draw an efficiency frontier simply as *AB*. Any holiday that combines both destinations must lie somewhere inside *OAB*.

Price effects, income effects and substitution effects can be readily explored in terms of Lancaster's diagrams, as can the obsolescence of existing products as new ones appear offering better value for money. The only problem is that one is not representing units of consumption of the good in question on any of the axes, so measurement of changes in quantities must be done with reference to changes in the distance the consumer opts to go along the various consumption rays. Linear consumption technologies enable movements along the rays then to be tracked on the characteristics axes in proportional terms. Figure 3.16 shows how the analysis might be started.

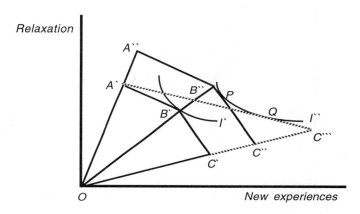

Figure 3.16: Income and price changes in characteristics space

In this example I have continued to consider choices of holiday destinations and have ignored the critical points concerning non-linearities and the fixed costs of travel. We have a consumer thinking about three rival holiday destinations. The consumer's initial budget and set of prices are such as to imply an efficiency frontier of *A`B`C`*. Given the consumer's preferences, the best s/he can do is to choose to stay only at resort *B*, which enables her/him to reach indifference curve *I`*, a corner solution. Now suppose there is a major reduction in the price of staying at resort *C*, such that s/he can get to *C```* by spending the entire budget on a holiday at *C*. In this situation the consumer's efficiency frontier becomes *A`C```* and the best feasible combination is the mix of time spent at resorts *A* and *C* shown by point *Q* on indifference curve *I``*. Resort *B* becomes a dominated alternative in this case, regardless of the consumer's preferences. An alternative way that this consumer might reach indifference curve *I``* would be via a rise in income at the original set of money prices for the resorts, such that her/his efficiency frontier becomes *A``B``C``*. In this case, the preferred position is point *P*, a combination of *B* and *C*.

Lancaster's framework makes it easy to see how Giffen goods might arise, as Lipsey and Rosenbluth (1971) have pointed out. Figure 3.17 presents an example of this possibility. The consumer has a choice between spending money on meat or on vegetables or on combinations of these two goods. Initially, the set of relative prices is such that if s/he buys

57

only meat s/he is on the ray *OM* and gets to point *M*; if s/he buys only vegetables s/he is on ray *OV* but can only get to point *U*. With the initial set of prices the consumer's preferred position is *N* on the efficiency frontier *MU*, which involves a mixture of vegetables (s/he gets as far as point *T* on ray *OV*) and meat (s/he gets as far as point *K* on ray *OM*). If the price of vegetables is reduced sharply it becomes possible for the consumer to get to point *V* if s/he buys only vegetables, or to points along a new efficiency frontier *MV*. Now, her/his favoured position is point *R*, which involves higher meat consumption (s/he moves further along the ray *OM* from *K* to *L*) but a *reduction* in her/his consumption of vegetables (s/he moves back along the ray *OV* from *T* to *S*).

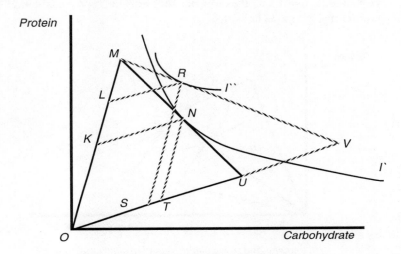

Figure 3.17: A Giffen good in characteristics space

One obvious limitation of Lancaster's framework, examined by Rosen (1974), is that it focuses on the number of units of divisible products that a consumer may decide to buy with a given budget as means of producing particular characteristics. This may be perfectly reasonable for the kinds of goods, such as food, toiletries, beverages, and so on, that fill one's weekly shopping basket in the supermarket, but it looks less satisfactory as a way of framing choices between rival consumer durables. Figure 3.18 is one way of handling indivisibilities.

The idea is that if we are presuming that consumers trade off the various characteristics of a product against each other (and we may not always be wise to make this presumption: see sections 4.2 and 4.3 as well as the earlier discussion in section 3.2 concerning hierarchies of wants), then we can conceive of the consumer as weighing together all of the non-price characteristics that are associated with a particular class of product, to form a particular cardinal rating in non-price terms. The non-price scores of rival products can then be traded off against their prices: in effect, price becomes a further characteristic of a product, for the act of purchasing it produces a hole in the buyer's finances. The line *EE* on Figure 3.18 shows the frontier of efficient products, in other words, the locus of best available non-price performances at each price level. Given the proliferation of brands in many consumer durables markets, it seems not unreasonable to draw this efficiency frontier as an unbroken line, though not necessarily a perfectly smooth one. It seems likely that consumers would perceive the efficiency frontier as sloping upwards at a decreasing rate once a particular point had been passed: after some point, manufacturers may experience diminishing returns in their attempts to achieve improvements to the quality of their products, or may have to spread the costs of achieving them over a smaller and smaller market; by contrast, at the low budget end of the market, there may be increasing returns to spending on product upgrading—recall the maxim 'Don't spoil the ship for a halfpenny-worth of tar'.

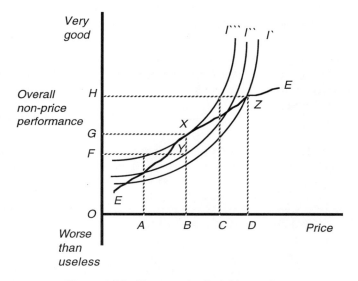

Figure 3.18: Choices of indivisible products

At the present set of prices, product *X* is the consumer's preferred brand. Given the consumer's preference map—which here involves upward-sloping indifference curves, because a higher price is a counter-desired feature of a product—and given her/his views about the relative merits of the products' non-price performances, the highest indifference curve that the consumer can reach is *I*```. Product *Y*, like product *X*, sells for price *B*, but it lies inside the efficiency frontier on account of its inferior non-price performance. If the price of product *Y* were reduced below *A*, the product would then acquire a place on the efficiency frontier and dominate over product *X*: its lower price would be low enough to offset its inferior non-price performance. At the present set of prices, product *Z* would only enable the consumer to reach indifference curve *I*`, despite its superior non-price performance. For *Z* to displace *X* as the consumer's preferred option, its price must be reduced below *C*.

This sort of thinking seems potentially to provide some theoretical foundations for a popular form of empirical work in industrial economics, namely, 'hedonic price analysis'. The 'hedonic' technique, which was actually pioneered over fifty years ago by Court

(1939), involves the use of multiple regression methods to determine functional relationships between the market prices and the non-price characteristics of rival products. The form of the regression is shown in equation (1).

$$P_i = a_0 + a_1 Q_{1i} + a_2 Q_{2i} \ldots + a_k Q_{ki} + e_i \qquad (1)$$

$$i = 1, \ldots N$$

where:

P_i is the price of the ith product (this is often expressed in logarithmic terms).

N is the number of products in the (cross-sectional) sample.

$a_0, a_1, a_2, \ldots, a_k$ are regression-derived weights.

$Q_1, Q_2, \ldots, Q_k$ are the levels of characteristics $1, 2, \ldots, k$ associated with the ith product: if the characteristics do not have a scalar nature (for example, 'sedan' versus 'hatchback'), they will be represented by dichotomous variables (for example, 0 if a saloon, 1 if a hatchback) in the regression.

e_i is an error term.

Once the regression coefficients have been estimated, one can calculate an expected price for each product, given a knowledge of its mix of characteristics. The predicted prices can be expressed as ratios to actual prices: one would expect the ratios to be pretty close to unity in popular parts of the market where competition is strong. This technique has been applied in over fifty studies, which together encompass cars (by far the most popular subject), tractors, washing machines, housing, computers, audio cassette decks, refrigerators and pick-up trucks. However, there has been much debate about precisely what should be read into hedonic equations.

A Lancaster/Rosen type of analysis might be taken as providing theoretical foundations for such work in so far as we see hedonic prices as indicators of how much pleasure typical consumers get from the non-price performances of products, with the weightings reflecting the marginal value placed on individual characteristics. As such, hedonic prices are indicators of willingness to pay on the part of consumers, so we should not expect firms to find it worthwhile to add extra features or otherwise improve the performance of their products if, by doing so, they would push their required price above the hedonic price. Unfortunately, such a view seems to involve assuming that households have identical incomes and preference maps: in reality, consumers are unlikely to have similar marginal rates of substitution between characteristics. Worse still, the linear form of a hedonic equation implies indifference curves that are downward-sloping straight lines so marginal rates of substitution are constant and all equilibria are corner solutions and therefore do not involve equalizing marginal rates of substitution with marginal costs to consumers of changing their mixes of characteristics (see Muellbauer, 1974).

An alternative interpretation of the weightings has been that they indicate the marginal costs to the typical firm of adding particular characteristics to its products. An example of a study along such lines is the work of Fisher *et al.* (1962). This team attempted to assess the cost of providing specification improvements (higher power, automatic transmission, power brakes and so on) to American cars during the 1950s. They found that the cost of model changes since 1949 were running at $5 billion a year, totalling about a quarter of the purchase price per car by the late 1950s. However, consumers seemed prepared to pay this price, for few in the late 1950s were buying base models of modern cars, a strategy which would have enabled them to take advantage of the opportunity that existed to purchase, at significantly lower prices, hedonically similar cars to those they on average purchased ten years before.

To end this discussion of how economists have sought to understand consumer behaviour in terms of production theory and the characteristics space, I feel some remarks are necessary about consumers' perceptions of the characteristics that products have to offer, and how economists measure these properties. Lancaster's (1971: 114–15) view is that characteristics should be defined in terms of the objective properties of goods that consumers find relevant to choice. This is a very different philosophy from that adopted in much of the marketing literature which overlaps with this work (Ratchford, 1975: 74). Different consumers, who see the world through different sets of blinkers, may perceive different characteristics even if they choose between identical goods. Some of these consumers may be faced with uncertainty and attempt to deal with it by rating the prospective characteristics offerings of rival brands according to brand prices. With experience, their perceptions may change. They may see new dimensions of choice and/or rate goods differently in terms of their original repertoires of dimensions. If the technology of consumption has not changed in any 'objective' sense Lancaster would argue that such changes of outlook should be represented as changes in preferences. But as far as consumers themselves are concerned, they may feel that they are facing a new set of technological constraints. It is perhaps unwise, therefore, to leave it to the economic analyst to decide where to draw the dividing line between preferences and constraints.

The subjectivist viewpoint, from which I will be writing in the next chapter, leaves it to consumers to draw the dividing lines between changes in their preferences and constraints. It recognizes that what consumers see in a particular situation may be different from what a researcher sees. The researcher would therefore be wise to undertake market research to uncover consumers' perceptions, instead of presuming that a researcher's personal perceptions are the same as those of the consumers whose behaviour is being studied. Subjectivists advocate the use, wherever possible, of market research methods—such as repertory grid techniques (Stewart and Stewart, 1981; Earl, 1986: 147–54)—that elicit from consumers the brands and characteristics in terms of which they think about their choice problems, rather than forcing them to express their preferences in terms of lists of brands and characteristics supplied by the researcher. Neoclassical economists working on consumer behaviour have preferred to steer well clear of this approach and have normally justified this by professing to have doubts about the wisdom of relying upon consumers to tell the truth to market researchers. Instead, they have tended to confine themselves to studies of choice in relation to characteristics that are easy to measure in supposedly objective terms. In many cases difficulties in obtaining such measurements have driven them to continue to carry out applied demand work purely in the goods space.

3.7 Essay example: The usefulness of neoclassical consumer behaviour theory

Question

'The traditional neoclassical theory of consumer behaviour (the Hicks–Allen theory) is utterly useless because it yields no testable hypotheses.' Discuss.

Author's notes

As with any essay of this kind, it is wise to begin by asking 'What is the question about? Which important analytical issues does it raise?'. The first thing to notice is that the question makes a claim about what renders an economic theory of consumer behaviour utterly useless, namely a failure to yield testable hypotheses. This is just one view of how the dividing line between useful and useless theories might be drawn. There are other views, which can be found discussed in the many books on the methodology of economics that have appeared over the past decade or so, including Blaug (1980), Katouzian (1980), Caldwell (1982), Eichner (ed.) (1983) and Pheby (1988). Blaug's book includes a particularly relevant chapter on problems with consumer theory which would make a good starting point for reading. In the absence of such reading, another logical starting point would be to check what Hicks himself had in mind as the role of his theory. Hicks (1939: 5) actually notes that his interest in consumer theory 'began with the endeavour to supply a needed theoretical foundation for statistical demand studies' and he claimed that it had 'a definite relevance to that field'. However, a theory which predicts that demand curves may slope up *or* down is of rather questionable use to that end.

Many microeconomics texts nowadays offer brief discussions of the distinction between normative economics (which tries to come up with recommendations about what should be done in terms of policy) and positive economics (which is concerned with predicting economic phenomena). In defence of the Hicks–Allen theory it might be argued that the indifference curve/budget line framework is very useful in normative terms, despite its indeterminacy in a predictive sense. The use of the apparatus to analyse marginal cost pricing proposals for a university dining room (see the end of section 3.4) or housing policy (see section 3.5) could both be noted as examples, but the limitations of conclusions drawn in this way could also be pointed out.

The Hicks–Allen theory has provoked much debate about the 'methodology of positive economics' (particularly stirred up by the first essay in a book with that title by Milton Friedman, 1953), owing to its 'unrealistic assumptions'. Every theory is a partial model of the world and involves simplification, so we cannot jump to the conclusion that a theory based on patently unrealistic assumptions is necessarily a bad one. In fact, it might be argued that neoclassical economics is worthy of study because its degree of abstraction is such that precise predictions follow and can be tested to see if they can be refuted. In the area of consumer behaviour, however, predictions of this kind are rather lacking. This essay could probably include some discussion of assumptive realism in relation to the usefulness of the theory: the assumptions of the Hicks–Allen theory may prove convenient for modelling purposes, but it still needs to be considered whether they are grossly misleading rather than helpful to economists seeking to organize their thoughts about policy or trying to *explain* economic phenomena. With material on Lancaster's characteristics-based theory, or from Chapter 4 on the behavioural analysis of choice, one might argue that alternative models of consumer behaviour are much more useful because of their focus on characteristics as well as goods and their recognition of the possible implications of information-processing problems. If the Hicks–Allen theory gets in the way of studying this work then it is perhaps a hindrance rather than merely useless.

A second claim in the statement is that the Hicks–Allen theory yields *no* testable hypotheses. This is something that can be disputed: the theory predicts that the sign of the substitution effect will always be negative. This follows straightforwardly from the Axiom of Archimedes (the Principle of Gross Substitution) that is used in arriving at the familiar continuously downward-sloping indifference curves. But this claim itself leads us back to the question of the usefulness of the theory: counter-examples implying zero substitution effects might be identified. The 'corner solution' possibility might be raised here, in which the consumer starts out purchasing none of the good in question and, over some range at least, continues not to buy it as its price is lowered. But this example ultimately is a matter of having a big enough price change. Eventually the consumer will switch if her/his indifference map has the standard form. A more genuinely problematic example is one involving 'lexicographic preferences', as with consumers who have strong principles (such as vegetarians) or prejudices. It could be argued that the tendency of economists not to question the validity of the principle of gross substitution has been a positive hindrance to policy formation: in other words, the theory is worse than useless. The 'principles and prejudices' theme might be elaborated with the aid of material from Etzioni's (1988) *The Moral Dimension*.

A less dramatic attack on the substitution effect is one that argues on the basis of empirical work that its size is small, that income effects are much more powerful, along with habitual tendencies. The classic empirically-based reference to discuss at this juncture would be Houthakker and Taylor (1970).

Neoclassical economists might try to counter this sort of argument by trying to show how the Hicks–Allen theory can be useful by virtue of its *lack* of testable hypotheses. (Such a paradoxical line of argument would be something of a surprise, given their general inclination to try to make economics a 'hard' science.) A discussion of work/leisure choices and tax reform proposals could be a very effective way of making this point. Right-wing politicians have often claimed that reductions in the marginal rate of income tax for high-income earners, or the reduction of welfare allowances for low earners, would encourage people to work more. This need not be the case: much depends on the shapes of preferences and their implications for the signs and sizes of income effects. The rich might actually work fewer hours if marginal tax rates were reduced: they could enjoy more spare time, up to a point, without losing spending power compared with the original situation. The Hicksian theory sheds light here, even despite its indeterminacy, and guards against simplistic policy recommendations being implemented in advance of appropriate empirical investigations.

A concluding note might follow on from what has just been said and raise the issue of whether we want theories to serve as devices for narrowing the bounds of possibility or for opening our minds to events that otherwise might never have been imagined by us as possibilities (cf. the case for scenario planning, discussed in section 5.6).

3.8   Exam post-mortem: Anti-smoking policy

Question
Consumption of cigarettes imposes on society the burden of paying for their induced health costs. One solution might be to increase taxes on this commodity, and combine this with an income tax rebate of a fixed amount per adult for all citizens. Analyse and comment on the desirability of this solution.

Examiner's notes
This question seemed particularly popular among the weaker students, many of whom attempted to tackle it without any reference at all to material covered on the course. Some examinees spotted that the set of proposals were yet another variation on the 'three budget line' types of questions that had been encountered prior to the examination (as with the meal-pricing example at the end of section 3.4 or the housing policy problem discussed in section 3.5). But few of these were alert or brave enough to point out how difficult it would be to do very much with neoclassical theory in this context. Most of them just floundered around demonstrating nothing in particular beyond the fact that the tax increase would raise cigarette prices (assuming that it were not wholly absorbed by manufacturers or retailers in reduced profit margins) and hence swing the typical consumer's budget line round to the left, pivoting on the point at which it touched the 'all other goods' axis, and that the tax rebate would then produce a rightward shift to a new budget line parallel to the one drawn to show the effect of the tax on cigarettes.

One major difficulty that deserved much more discussion than it received is that consumers differ vastly in the extent to which they smoke, both within and between socio-economic groups. It makes little sense to adopt the usual neoclassical strategy of (a) framing the problem in terms of a representative consumer who consumes a bit of everything and (b) relying on the assumptions of a decreasing marginal rate of substitution and no net change in revenue received by the government, to produce results akin to those derived in sections 3.4 and 3.5. The better attempts included illustrations of non-smokers in lexicographic terms, and used 'corner solution' diagrams to show how a smoker might be prompted to give up smoking altogether; at the other end of the spectrum were answers in which dreadful technical errors included budget lines and demand curves being muddled together. Some students commented on the likelihood that the proposed policy would be highly regressive owing to the incidence of smoking probably being higher amongst the poorer groups in society.

A second peculiarity of this question is that it concerns a product which has addictive properties, so there may be conflict between the desires of smokers to kick the habit and their capacities to do so (for a discussion of the psychological economics of addiction, see Albanese, ed., 1988, chapters 2 and 3). The addiction question was often raised, but no one related it to the economics of self-control associated with Thaler and Elster (cf. section 4.7). Some of those who engaged in a 'three budget line' analysis realized that they could use an assumption of addiction to smoking to show that a rise in cigarette prices would lead to no change in cigarette consumption, with all the burden of adjustment coming in terms of reduced spending on other goods, but they tended not to highlight how odd it was to use the assumption of addiction as a means of locating indifference curves. There were occasional references to nicotine addicts seeking to economize by switching to 'roll your own' cigarettes if the duty changed the relative price of different smoking technologies.

A few students argued that if the increase in duty on cigarettes promoted a major reduction in smoking a fall in tax revenues might occur, so that direct taxation might have to be increased. Unfortunately, they failed to consider what they were saying in relation to the issue of smoking-related expenditure on health care that was mentioned in the question.

Finally, it was disappointing to see how few students tried to consider the costs and benefits of alternative or complementary policies, such as increased anti-smoking propaganda or stricter controls on cigarette advertising and sponsorship of sporting events by tobacco companies. These policies could have been discussed in relation to the question of how tastes for cigarettes are formed—for example, whether or not cigarette advertising only influences brand preferences rather than having a role in determining whether or not people start smoking in the first place.

3.9   Further Questions

1.   In the light of the tendency of patterns of purchases of fashion goods such as hairstyles, clothing and some popular music to 'go round in circles', discuss the wisdom of assuming transitivity in a theory of consumer choice.

2.   How easy is it to relax the assumptions of the neoclassical theory of consumer choice without making it difficult to see how consumers might hypothetically reach equilibrium states that are stable?

3.   Consider the extent to which neoclassical consumer theory can help retail analysts make sense of discontinuous changes in patterns of consumer behaviour sometimes seen in developing countries. In these 'magic moments', masses of people start buying new types of goods, such as radios, packaged goods or bicycles, or start using new kinds of retail outlets. For example, the *Economist* (18 December 1993: 64) reported that 'In 1987, a mere 3% of the Taiwanese population bought groceries in a "modern" shop, such as a supermarket. By 1993 that figure had risen to 50%'.

4.   Consider two individuals, one of whom earns a salary of, say, $30 000 a year, while the other does not participate in the labour force. Suppose there is a rise in average levels of pay in the economy. Analyse the possible effects on market hours worked by these two different individuals.

5.   Imagine that the government is considering abolishing the motor vehicle registration fee and recouping the revenue by an increase in the rate of taxation on petrol. You are invited to discuss the merits of this proposal in the light of relevant microeconomic theory.

6.   'The neoclassical theory of choice shows that a benefit in cash is normally superior to (or in the limiting case is as least as good as) a benefit in kind of the same monetary

value. Yet a large number of government benefits in many countries continue to be paid in kind.' Discuss this conflict between theory and practice.

7. Provide a critical assessment of Kelvin Lancaster's 'characteristics' theory of consumer behaviour. (Note: this essay is best attempted as a revision exercise, after you have read the next chapter.)

8. Examine the likely economic consequences of lowering income tax rates and offsetting the revenue loss from this source by imposing a goods and services tax (or value-added tax) at a uniform rate on all items consumed.

9. In many labour markets the following contract is made: the worker undertakes to work a standard number of hours at a given wage per hour and is promised the opportunity to work 'overtime' when available, at a higher wage per hour. Analyse the effect of this kind of contract on the worker's choice between work and leisure.

10. 'Consumer wants are no longer a matter of individual choice. They are mass produced' (A. Hansen). 'The trouble with traditional consumer theory is that it ignores some of the most basic elements of human motivation, such as altruism, envy and group behaviour.' Discuss these propositions and their implications for the theory of consumer behaviour.

11. 'Lancaster's theory that consumers desire the characteristics embodied in goods rather than the goods themselves is certainly interesting. Yet the predictions yielded by the theory are no different from those yielded by the standard theory.' Discuss.

12. 'Affluent consumers optimize subject to the constraint of their scarce time, not their incomes.' Discuss.

13. Show how the Hicksian analysis of choice may be used to make sense of savings decisions. Consider how a person's saving behaviour may be affected by (a) changes in interest rates and (b) an unexpected promotion at work. Discuss the limitations of the analysis in these contexts.

4 Behavioural perspectives on decision-making

4.1 Introduction

We now change our way of looking at consumers and explore what behavioural economics has to offer in the area of choice. Before you begin to study this new perspective, it is probably wise to take a second look at Chapter 2 and note the idea of the decision cycle and the distinction between bounded and global rationality. It is at this stage that conventional microeconomics texts cease to be of much use as sources of reinforcing reading materials, though Frank (1991) contains some relevant material. Otherwise, one has to consult articles or books by behavioural economists (for example: Baxter, 1993; Etzioni, 1988; Lane, 1991) or marketing theorists (such as Bettman, 1979), and to explore texts designed for consumer behaviour courses in marketing programmes. Much of the latest research in this area by behavioural economists is to be found in specialized journals, including the *Journal of Consumer Research*, the *Journal of Economic Behavior and Organization*, the *Journal of Economic Psychology*, and the *Journal of Socio-Economics* (formerly the *Journal of Behavioral Economics*). There is also a series entitled *Handbook of Behavioral Economics*, the first volumes of which were edited by Gilad and Kaish and appeared in 1986. Many of the articles that I have found especially thought-provoking and useful are reproduced in my (1988a) collection *Behavioural Economics*; and an extended treatment of some of the themes presented in this chapter was presented in my earlier (1983b, 1986) books. Applied essay and case study examples involving the behavioural approach to consumer choice are provided in sections 4.4, 4.5, 4.9 and 4.10.

To grasp the essence of behavioural thinking about choice it is probably useful to know at the outset that Herbert Simon, the most influential contributor to the area, made his mark not as an economist but as a professor of computing science and psychology. In particular, he has been at the forefront of work on artificial intelligence, trying to see whether mental processes can be represented in terms of computer programs. His recent autobiography (Simon, 1992) is an excellent guide to the development of his ideas, as well as to the politics of the academic world and how they affect the acceptance of new bodies of thought—cf. section 4.8 of this chapter. Lying behind all this work seems to be the notion that it is useful to imagine minds as if they function very much like sets of computer programs, which operate according to particular grammatical codes. Life may therefore be seen as the processing of information followed by actions that entail the working through of *procedures* selected from *menus* of possible procedures by the *rules* according to which the information processing has been done. Decision-makers either completely implement their chosen procedures and then bring into play further procedures for deciding what to do next or, if problems are encountered, they switch to other procedures that their information-processing rules deem more suitable for handling the situation.

The processing of information is made more manageable if decision problems are decomposed in hierarchical manner and tackled sequentially, at a variety of distinct levels (Simon, 1969). As decision-makers get deeper into a process of choice, they will normally narrow down the range of possibilities that are being considered, at the same time as increasing the detail in terms of which they consider them. The use of hierarchies is something that we naturally fall into in order to simplify our decision-making. For example, without a hierarchical filing system, a person who has created a large number of computer files may find it very difficult indeed to locate a particular file. Addresses for letters likewise work hierarchically: when we think of where someone lives we don't think in terms of a specific set of coordinates on a map of the world. Multi-stage budgeting, mentioned in section 3.6 in relation to the idea of a utility tree, provides an obvious example of hierarchical decomposition in the context of consumer behaviour.

The programmes that people use for coping with life have been given a variety of names: 'decision heuristics', 'rules of thumb', 'routines' or 'recipes for success'. A few examples might be: 'get three insurance quotations and choose the cheapest'; 'replace the car with the top-selling equivalent model every three years'; 'buy the "best buy" in my budget range in the hi-fi guide'; and finally, some advice I actually received from a colleague, 'if you want to be confident you are buying a bicycle from a shop run by dedicated enthusiasts, see if the staff shave their legs'. Etzioni (1988: chapter 10) provides a detailed discussion which includes further examples. If the consumer's repertoire of rules succeeds as a device for generating decisions, s/he may fail to consider alternative choice procedures that could generate superior outcomes. So long as they seem to generate satisfactory results, there is no sign of a problem requiring a solution: as we noted in Chapter 2, decision-makers in behavioural theory are seen as *satisficers* rather than optimizers. When consumers perceive a particular trigger situation has arisen (for example, the arrival of an insurance renewal notice), they will just bring into play their trusted procedures to match the situation.

It should be noted that often decision-makers would be hard pressed to explain why they believe that particular rules are appropriate in their selected contexts; all that matters is that the rules seem likely to deliver satisfactory outcomes because they have been seen to work in the past—the rule is, if a rule works, don't change it (for an excellent discussion on this theme, see Hoch, 1984). The phrase 'recipes for success' naturally leads one to look to cookery for further clarification: strictly speaking, cookery is applied chemistry, but most people do not approach the task of preparing a meal as if this is so; rather, they simply make a selection from their repertoires of recipes for particular occasions and try to follow the instructions through without error, with little idea of the underlying rationale for many steps in the recipe.

Until fairly recently, there was a tendency for behavioural theorists to write about consumers as if every choice procedure entailed the kind of complexity involved in the idea of the decision cycle, which really entails the working through of a set of interlocking procedures. In marketing, entire texts on consumer behaviour used the decision-cycle concept as a basis for the organization of their chapters. The tendency to treat all choices in this way in consumer theory looked most peculiar from the standpoint of organizational approaches to the theory of the firm where the decision-cycle concept had been pioneered. In the latter context, theorists had been careful to distinguish between *deliberative* choices and *routine* behaviour, and only really meant the decision-cycle concept to apply to the first kind. Much of the credit for getting a shift of focus towards much simpler ways of choosing is probably deserved by Olshavsky and Granbois (1979: 98–9), who took the radical step of suggesting that 'for many purchases a decision process never occurs, not even on the first purchase'. Instead, they argued that

> Purchases can occur out of necessity; they can be derived from culturally mandated lifestyles or from interlocked purchases; they can result from simple conformity to group norms or from the imitation of others; purchases can be made exclusively on recommendations from personal and non-personal sources; they can be made on the bases of surrogates of various types; or they can occur on a random or superficial basis....
>
> [E]ven when purchase behaviour is preceded by a choice it is likely to be very limited, It typically involves evaluation of few alternatives, little external search, few evaluative criteria, and simple evaluation process models. There is little evidence that consumers engage in the very extended types of search and evaluation or product testing that an organization like the Consumers' Union performs routinely.

Following the Olshavsky and Granbois paper, consumer behaviour texts in marketing began to include much more material on ways in which choices might be simplified. A distinction began to be drawn between high- and low-involvement choices. Unfortunately, in moving away from a focus on the decision cycle, some writers tended to assume that the depth of investigations and agonizing prior to choice is always positively related to the consumer's assessment of the importance of the decision. In fact, 'big decisions' may often involve little by way of a decision process because their sheer complexity may present grave information-processing difficulties, especially if the consumer lacks experience in the area in question. In some cases people may be so involved with a particular idea that they fail even to consider alternatives. For example, although there can be few more important decisions in life than those concerning getting married and having children, Richards (1985) found that the majority of couples in her study sample had not considered the possibility of not aiming to marry and raise a family (though many did consider alternative times for having children).

The views of Olshavsky and Granbois are too much for many behaviouralists to stomach in their extreme form, for they seem to run counter to the everyday observation that, at least in some areas of their lives, people are able to express opinions about things that they value or dislike, to advance reasons for these opinions and to adjust them through time. In some of these areas, relatively complex views may have been arrived at via trial and error: people try out different mixes of products and see what they think of the experience. In a stable environment it is conceivable that they may eventually settle on a pretty firm picture of the sorts of tradeoffs that they are willing to make. In this case, perhaps, indifference curves might be reasonably good as a way of approximating their attitudes towards various possibilities, though the behavioural theorist would only want to draw a few, fairly short indifference curves that are fairly close together, for the experience of consumers may be within a rather limited range.

Normally, however, a behavioural economist will try to avoid speaking of consumers as if they possess preference systems. Consider, for example, the work of James March (1988), for many years one of Simon's closest associates. In place of the view that resource allocation involves optimization subject to known technological and resource constraints and given preferences, March offers a picture of the nature of choice that has much in common with that of the 'Personal Construct' school of psychology associated with the work of Kelly (1955): gathering information and making sense of it are the essence of life; choice is an experimental activity, aimed at discovering goals at least as much as for acting on them ('play' is seen by March as a situation in which people temporarily suspend the rules they normally use to manage their lives); people expect their tastes will change through a critical interpretation of outcomes of earlier attempts to deal with their conflicting desires and do not normally expect to develop such consistent views of what they want that they never feel they are taking actions 'against their better judgement'. So, to anticipate a person's choices, the behavioural theorist sets out to discover not indifference maps but, rather, details of the person's system of rules for defining an acceptable course of action and for discovering something that fits into this mould—in other words, the rules that shape the person's satisficing activities. This task is made easier to the extent that individuals adopt rules that involve copying others and adhere to social codes of conduct and the legislative framework (see Etzioni, 1988, and consider as an example the role of traffic codes for facilitating orderly progress on the highways).

While students may feel uncomfortable at the thought of having to think about choice without reference to indifference maps, academic economists have had difficulties in coming to terms with the very idea of satisficing, of choosers seeking merely to find prospects that look like they 'will do' as means of meeting targets. A common misconception is that satisficing behaviour is constrained optimization of the orthodox kind, with an added constraint: the finite computational capacities of the decision-maker. Hence it is suggested that if, for example, people appear to use rules of thumb to deal with their own bounded rationality, then these rules have been chosen as the *optimal* decision-making procedure, not because they are merely judged capable of generating satisfactory outcomes (see Baumol and Quandt, 1964). But this line of thinking seems, to committed behaviouralists, to miss the point.

The basis for the claim that choice is a satisficing activity lies in the logical impossibility of a decision-maker being able to identify an optimal choice even if s/he happens to make one. Problems of infinite regress beset any attempt to avoid satisficing behaviour. In forming their expectations and deciding what to do, people first face the problem that the lists of what they might do, and of what might happen as a result of, or despite, their choices normally are not given but have to be constructed. The task of building up an agenda of possible options and evaluating their properties is not without its costs: for example, if I am trying to widen my agenda, I may be unable to spend much time thinking about the merits of possibilities that I have already discovered. The more information I gather, the more I may be running the risk that I will get confused and process the information poorly. Certainly, on different occasions, different search rules might seem worth trying because the costs of search and of errors differ between types of choice (for an excellent discussion of search strategies, see Hey, 1982). However, it is logically impossible to know in advance the marginal return to marginal outlays on search; one way of searching may improve my choice, but it need not do so and, even if it does, it may not improve it as much as another search strategy might have done. Choices about how to search choices thus involve exactly the same problems of knowledge as the uncertain choices to which they relate. If we use the decision rule 'Question everything', we will be unable even to get started on the business of searching. If we are smart enough to recognize that we are suffering from bounded rationality we are likely to be able to see reasons why we might not do very well if we always adopt the rule 'Do the first thing that comes to mind', to avoid being paralysed in a state of indecision. Yet there is no method of formal reasoning that can tell us what is the best thing to do between these two extremes to enhance the quality of our decisions. Ultimately, we have to rely on intuition (cf. Elster, 1984: 135).

Having selected particular rules for cutting short the infinite regress problem, people may, in the event, find themselves disappointed with the match of outcomes to the aspiration levels that they expected to meet. If so, it is unclear what they should do, just as it is unclear whether outcomes beyond target levels imply that they could regularly be setting higher targets. Simon (1959) presumes that a run of failures will normally provoke search and/or experimentation with new ways of choosing and, if such measures do not halt the run of unsatisfactory results, sights will be lowered. But such adjustments need not be continuous—the idea of a *threshold of response* often seems to make more sense than ongoing adjustments at the margin (Drakopoulos, 1992; Kornai, 1971). Repeated successes may be judged by choosers as implying that they could be raising their targets, or that they may safely take bigger short cuts in the areas in question, thereby leaving themselves with more time for other decisions. It is conceivable that a long bout of experimentation might lead choosers to stumble upon strategies that seemed both sustainable and impossible to improve upon, in which case it might seem reasonable to speak as if satisficing behaviour had converged to marginalism (see Day, 1967). However, there is no guarantee that this will happen, particularly if the choice environment is a turbulent one.

It probably needs to be stressed that the infinite regress issue arises *whenever* a judgement has to be made. When a person says 'I believe this is a good choice for me because...', s/he is saying that this belief depends upon another belief: s/he believes in the grounds for the choice on the basis of yet other grounds. It is necessary to impose an arbitrary foundation—'I believe this because I do'—to be able to form expectations. These unjustified beliefs comprise the cores around which people let their lives revolve. Existing core beliefs may often stand in the way of accepting new methods of forming judgements, but in some cases they may, in effect, stand aside *after* deeming proposed new systems admissible—rather as military dictators sometimes judge that the time has come to hold free elections.

There is a reflexive (self-referencing) dimension in the previous paragraph which should not go unnoticed. The idea that choices and judgements are determined by arbitrary sets of core ways of thinking is part of the core of behavioural thinking. It plays a vital role in preventing the behavioural economist from reaching the conclusion that the goals and perceptions of decision-makers are utterly spontaneous and erratic and that it is impossible to predict behaviour within useful bounds (Earl and Kay, 1985). The assumption that thinking is channelized by a given set of core beliefs is the closest that a behavioural economist is likely to get to the neoclassical assumption that people have given preference orderings. However, we shall see in the next two sections that the kinds of rules that people may judge acceptable as a basis for reaching a decision need not imply behaviour that is consistent with neoclassical axioms.

4.2 Complexity and tests of adequacy

Having noted the role of simplifying procedures for forming expectations and choosing actions, we move on in this section to look at some of the procedures people may employ to rank rival schemes of action in situations in which they actually bother to think about a variety of options in terms of a number of characteristics/attribute dimensions, instead of simply behaving in the manner focused upon by Olshavsky and Granbois. The discussion draws heavily on Tversky (1969, 1972), Ryan and Bonfield (1975), Payne (1976), Lussier and Olshavsky (1979), Hawkins *et al.* (1980), Anand (1982) and Earl (1986); for further readings which stress the difficulties that people face in dealing with decisions involving a moral dimension, see Levi (1986) and Etzioni (1988). Throughout this section, it is important not to lose sight of the information-processing task that a chooser faces. The information set that has to be processed can be represented as a 'choice matrix', one axis of which consists of the rival schemes of action (brands of cars, VCRs, holidays, or whatever) and the other axis of which consists of the characteristics that the consumer sees as relevant to the choice at hand (some of which may have significant psychological or moral connotations). Table 4.1 in section 4.5 is an example of such a matrix in printed form. This may be quite a formidable array of information to handle unless strategies are devised for simplifying it: for example, detailed specifications of vehicles tested in a motoring magazine may include well over 60 pieces of information about each product. These informational issues are given short shrift in neoclassical analysis, and even in marketing texts they tend to be forgotten by those who suggest that consumers rank rival products according to the total scores these achieve in weighted averaging procedures, having chosen their characteristic weights experimentally. Once we recognize the difficulties that consumers face in handling large arrays of information, it no longer seems obvious that such an aggregating, weighted averaging procedure is what consumers in general will use. Life is kept simple for the consumer if s/he has a rule which will either exclude all products except for one, or which will rank products in order of suitability, but it may be unwise to assume that any single procedure will be used.

4.2.1 Compensatory heuristics

In this subsection I consider procedural views of choice that share with Lancaster's analysis the idea that a preferred option may dominate over rivals, even if it is a very poor performer in some respects, so long as it dominates sufficiently in other areas. There are many variations on this 'compensatory' theme, and my discussion of four of them is by no means exhaustive. We begin with the most widely investigated model of all in the non-neoclassical literature on choice: the *Fishbein model of behavioural intentions* (Fishbein and Ajzen, 1975). It is actually specified as a linear equation rather than as a simple rule, but we can nonetheless include it here as a procedure on the basis that a mathematical function is a rule specifying relationships between particular variables. It is better thought of as an 'as if' encapsulation of the process by which a consumer may come to rank rival opportunities, rather than as a description of a rule that is likely to be used in practice. Its empirical standing is the subject of considerable debate, that I have reviewed elsewhere (Earl, 1986: 48–51). Given the appropriate set of data inputs it will generate a set of predicted attitudes towards rival purchasing activities:

$$B \approx BI = \left(\sum_{i=1}^{n} b_i \, e_i\right)W_1 + \left(\sum_{j=1}^{N} NB_j \, MC_j\right)W_2$$

in which: B = overt behaviour, assumed approximately equal to BI; BI = behavioural intentions ('How probable I think it is that I will undertake the activity in question'); W_1 and W_2 are weights that we could estimate using regression techniques; b_i = the consumer's view of the likelihood that performing the activity will result in the consequence i; e_i = the consumer's evaluation of outcome i's goodness/badness; n = the number of salient beliefs the person holds about performing the activity (usually assumed to be 7 ± 2, since people have trouble thinking in any greater detail—cf. Miller's rule); N = the number of other people whose opinions matter to the decision-maker in the context in question; NB_j = the person's assessment of whether referent j thinks s/he should choose to undertake the activity (her 'normative belief'); MC_j = the person's motivation to comply with referent j's opinion.

The model can reduce to the picture of social pressure conjured up by Olshavsky and Granbois: it suggests that if the W_2 weight is relatively large, people *may* undertake activities they basically don't much fancy, because they allow their own opinions to be outweighed by social pressures. In this respect it differs markedly from the neoclassical philosophy of assuming that tastes are not interdependent. Note that it also is unconventional in making no assumption that weightings are attached to the different outcomes associated with a particular activity.

The information-processing burden of deliberating in a compensatory manner can be reduced if a chooser adopts some form of *additive differences* procedure to compare rival schemes. It runs as follows: (a) take a pair of rival products from the list of contenders and compare their anticipated performances, one characteristic at a time; (b) assign values to the differences in their performances and keep a running tally of these difference scores whilst moving on to successive characteristics; (c) use the victor from the original pair as a reference point against a third scheme and repeat the process; (d) use the victor from the second round as a reference point against a fourth scheme, and so on; (e) select the scheme which dominates in the last pairwise comparison. The use of a reference point—the winner of the preceding pairwise test—reduces considerably the memory and information-processing requirements.

Unweighted averaging is a different kind of simplifying strategy sometimes seen in consumer magazines where rival products are scored in marks out of ten for test characteristics and average scores are then computed. This is a somewhat less less rational-sounding procedure since the short cut involves not bothering to ask whether, say, six out of ten on one characteristic is worth more than six out of ten on another characteristic.

A chooser using a *polymorphous* procedure defines a series of aspirational tests (or, for binary characteristics, simple yes/no tests) and ranks products according to the *number* of tests they pass. One might expect the consumer to set a target for the number of tests a product had to pass in order to be deemed satisfactory and to continue to search until she discovers one option which is 'OK' in enough dimensions. Note that this heuristic involves neither a weighted averaging process nor does it take account of whether or not a product fails some tests by small amounts and passes others with a wide margin. The rule's name means 'many forms', as befits a decision-making procedure where the particular set of tests that a product passes seems not to concern the chooser.

4.2.2 Non-compensatory heuristics

The procedures discussed in this subsection are much more controversial. They do not necessarily generate the possibility of substitution in response to changes in relative prices or in particular aspects of non-price performance. Some of them can produce intransitive behaviour. But all have been found to have been employed in practice by some people on some occasions.

Perhaps the most extreme is the *Disjunctive Rule*: choose the product which scores best in respect of *one* particular characteristic, provided that its score reaches a particular target (if not, search for something better, if search seems sufficiently likely to succeed). This sounds, somewhat paradoxically, either like an extremely 'low involvement' procedure or the sort of heuristic that a fanatic might use (for example, the 'hi-fi freak' who wants the best sound system regardless of any of its other characteristics such as bulk, styling and so on). But a fanatic may well be able to break down the dimension with which s/he is obsessed into a number of sub-dimensions (for example, in hi-fi systems, total harmonic distortion, wow and flutter, signal to noise ratio).

Rather less outlandish is the *Conjunctive Rule*: set aspirational targets for each characteristic that one has in mind and reject as unsatisfactory those options that fail to meet any of these targets, regardless of the number of missed targets and the nearness of misses. Consumers who set demanding targets are likely to experience difficulty in finding satisfactory purchases if they habitually use this rule; however, those that make modest demands may tend to find that a conjunctive rule produces tied results.

The difficulties posed by the conjunctive procedure are avoided in *Elimination by Aspects*. This procedure begins with the examination of how each of the rival schemes of action shapes up in respect of the target that has been attached to the first characteristic that comes to mind. Any that fall below the target level are rejected from further consideration, whereas the remainder are tested in respect of the next characteristic to come to mind, and so on, until only one product is left. Note it is assumed that the characteristics targets come to mind in a random order; this is not the case with the remaining two procedures discussed here. A chooser using a *Naive Lexicographic Rule* ranks characteristics in an order of priority; s/he examines all the products on a previously constructed list of possibilities in respect of the top priority characteristic and only moves on to the second priority if there is a tie between two or more products in respect of the first priority, and so on. In the absence of such a tie, this heuristic is rather akin to the disjunctive procedure. A *Behavioural Lexicographic/Characteristic Filtering Rule* differs from a naive lexicographic one in that the chooser sets aspirational targets for characteristics. All products that survive the first test are allowed on to take the second; those that are OK there are allowed on to the third, and so on, until only one product is left. This is not the same as elimination by aspects, since the order of the tests is not random: the consumer has priorities.

If the differences between these last few rules are unclear, attention should be given to Figure 4.1. The diagram should first be seen in terms of a characteristic filtering/behavioural lexicographic approach to choice. Five rival products are shown by points in the two-dimensional characteristics space. *D* and *E* rank first equal, since they meet both priority targets; if the two targets were not prioritized and the consumer were using a conjunctive rule, then these two products would also tie, with the other three being ranked third equal. In the present case, however, *B* ranks third, since it meets the first priority target but fails to meet the second. *A* fails to meet either target but would rank above fifth-placed *C* if a choice had to be made between these products since *A* comes closer to meeting the first priority. If a choice were being made between the same five products in terms of the naive lexicographic rule the ranking would be: first, *E*; second *B* (since *E* and *B* offer the same amount of the first priority, but *B* offers less of the second); third, *D*; fourth *A*; and fifth, *C*.

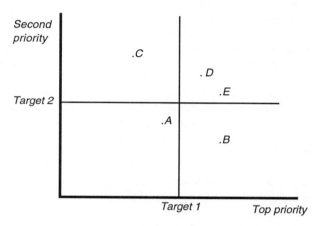

Figure 4.1: Priorities and choice

It should be evident that the information-processing demands that these heuristics place on a consumer are far from identical. One can imagine further refinements to some of them that reduce still further the computational task. For example a consumer might achieve a preliminary choice by starting rather low down a priority listing and then going back to see how adequately the preliminary choice does in terms of the basic criteria that were omitted from the first round of evaluation. If it passes all of these, the consumer has made a successful short cut in terms of the information that s/he has had to process.

4.2.3 Hybrid and contingent rules

Some decision theorists are now coming to recognize that precisely which heuristics are employed to arrive at choices will vary according to the complexity of the information-processing task. One might expect that the greater the number of characteristics and rival products that consumers initially have in mind (in other words, the larger their choice matrices), the more they might be driven to employ simplifying, non-compensatory procedures. Extreme complexity—due to great uncertainty about potential characteristic performances and/or how these impinge on each other—might lead consumers to give up any attempt at high-involvement choice and follow social norms instead, as Olshavsky and Granbois (1979) suggest and as is implied by the Fishbein–Ajzen model.

A further suggestion has been that consumers may not merely employ different kinds of heuristics in different contexts; they may also employ *hybrid* rules or a *contingent set* of heuristics in taking a single decision. An example of a hybrid rule would be where a consumer groups together some of the characteristics s/he has in mind and applies a polymorphous test to them, taking the result as a single test in an elimination by aspects or characteristic filtering procedure (suppose there is a set of ten miscellaneous features: the consumer might be thought of as saying 'I want at least seven of these, though I don't have any preference over which seven').

A contingent heuristics approach to choice is easily illustrated with reference to someone buying a new car. S/he may start out with a data matrix put together from the motoring pages of a motoring magazine. S/he eliminates many of the cars on paper with a simple conjunctive test and then sets about examining the remainder in more detail 'in the flesh'. In doing so, s/he gets a clearer picture of what these cars have to offer. This means that the consumer's data matrix, despite having fewer cars on it, is still pretty formidable. To simplify it once again, s/he might apply a characteristic filtering procedure only to find that several cars still tie (evidently in this case a conjunctive heuristic involving the same set of aspirations would have left her in the same position). To these remaining cars s/he might apply the additive differences procedure, only to end up with a tie between two cars, which s/he then breaks with a disjunctive test, such as 'choose the one with the best fuel economy'. This is only one of the many contingent rule sets that could be employed. We should also note that when consumers find themsleves with a conjunctive tie, they are in a position to raise their aspirations for any of the characteristics in which they are interested: they have acquired information about what is possible, that they did not have at the start of their search/evaluation activities, and they have discovered that they had set their sights too low. Were we speaking in terms of 'preferences' we might thus be rather unwise to presume these are 'given' even during the process of taking a single decision.

All this is clearly something of a headache for an economist who would like to use a single type of heuristic as a basis for analysis, rather than use the contingent heuristics approach as a general framework (or 'meta-theory'). The economist would probably feel that an additive differences procedure might be the best single one to select, but it is by no means obvious that it would be worse to select a non-compensatory procedure such as characteristic filtering. If consumers do not set highly demanding tests in characteristic filtering procedures, they may well end up with choices that do not seem grossly intolerant, even though their procedures reject some products on the basis of single failings. However, a compensatory heuristic is absolutely at a loss to explain situations in which consumers (a) are conspicuously intolerant, (b) refer to rejected possibilities as 'having a fatal flaw' or 'an Achilles heel', or (c) 'single out' a particular characteristic to say why 'in the final analysis' they chose a particular option. With a compensatory heuristic there is no basis for identifying particular characteristics as determinants of choice.

4.3   Choice rules and the competitive process

Some researchers have argued that priority-based decision rules are not fundamentally different from compensatory ones, saying that it is just that the weights are severely skewed according to the priority ordering. Certainly, some buyers might use the phrase 'high priority' to mean the same thing as 'high weighting' but if buyers actually think of priorities as a hierarchy of wants, then it may not be appropriate to treat such comments as merely a case of skewed weights. If a product fails test number one in a characteristic filtering procedure it does not get an awful overall score; it is simply debarred from taking any of the other tests. To put it bluntly, if I see a cake as poisonous, then no amount of decorative icing is going to make me try it, whereas, from a compensatory standpoint, one is driven to suggest that 'low priority' characteristics can contribute to a dominant overall score if their performances are outstanding. If consumers are commonly employing characteristic filtering procedures with roughly identical high priority tests that a firm's product happens to fail, the key thing for the firm to do is either to get consumers to reorder their priorities or modify the product (or at least, the public's perceptions of it) in the high priority dimensions. Adding extra characteristics might help it win a few 'polymorphous' purchasers who otherwise would have shunned it, but will do nothing to make it more acceptable to those with high priority tests that reject it. Improving performances on low priority characteristics is just like adding icing to a cake known to be poisonous.

Where products are closely matched and where a firm's offering has no significant failings, the attention of the firm's management must be devoted to making their product win in tie-break tests or to preventing a tie-break from being necessary in the first place. Here the idea of having extra features that rival brands do not possess makes good sense, so long as including them does not cause the product to fail tests it would otherwise have passed (see the first point in the discussion below on pricing). The 'extra features' strategy helps with compensatory choices as well as with non-compensatory, 'check-list' kinds of heuristics (tie-break situations sound like conjunctive or polymorphous occasions). An alternative approach is to try to use advertisements or sales personnel to get the consumer to focus on the characteristics where one's product—which is otherwise so similar to its rivals in tests of adequacy—is superior, and to suggest that this is precisely the area in which consumers ought to be setting higher standards.

In analyses of choice in terms of compensatory decision rules, the presumption is that if you make something cheap enough people will buy it: the argument is the same as in Figures 3.16 and 3.18 in section 3.6. The role of price in non-compensatory tests is more complex.

First, price may affect the ability to survive a high (top?) priority budget test: 'Is it cheap enough? Does it fit into my budget range?' This is another way of thinking of the idea of an income effect of a price change. Major discontinuities in sales rates may be experienced by firms if they set their prices without giving careful consideration to the budget ranges that would-be customers are using. One response to bounded rationality that is common is to use conventional, rounded numbers in thinking about alternatives. At one point in the late 1980s, for example, the sales of Jaguar cars in New Zealand took a major tumble when their prices were raised beyond the $NZ100 000 figure that was the upper budget that many senior executives were being allowed for their company cars. Until this limit was raised, it made sense to find a way of making Jaguars available for $99 000 or thereabouts. One strategy was to bring in models with lower specifications, with Jaguar's choice of cost savings being made carefully so as to avoid offering a product which would be excluded by many prospective buyers on non-price grounds (one obvious question would be: could a less powerful engine be used without buyers rejecting the product as 'too sluggish'?). It seems easier for this strategy to work at the affluent end of a market where even a somewhat stripped-down entry-level product may still exude quality and carry much of the image of its fully appointed brethren, rather than appearing spartan (note the informational aspects of this comment). At the other end of a market, the 'base model' may be used more as a means for bringing consumers in to see a product which is quite deliberately conceived to appear as a poverty version: the task then is for sales personnel to talk would-be buyers into rethinking the size of their budget ranges. This strategy is likely to be far more effective than what we might tag as the 'Lada strategy' of offering low-budget products that appear to be well endowed with features but achieve their low production costs by failing to get basic design features and quality levels up to the standards set by most buyers. Worse still, for those concerned about the status implications of what they buy, a new Lada gives a far clearer signal about one's budget to non-expert friends than does the purchase of a used car. Again, note the role of information: in a world of fully informed consumers, it would be hard to make any sense of the used-car selling line 'budget-priced prestige' that is often applied to ageing Jaguars, Volvos and BMWs being offered at the price of a new Lada; note also that in the UK a Lada strategy is made rather more effective by the fact that a vehicle's registration plate conveys widely-known information about its age.

Secondly, price may affect consumer perceptions of non-price performances, including snob appeal: consumers may be suspicious of products that look a lot cheaper than those to which they are offered as rivals (see further, Scitovsky, 1945; and Gabor and Granger, 1966). This possibility may combined with the first one to give a third possible role, namely, that price may affect whether or not a product gets examined by consumers who set lower budget limits as well as upper ones. A higher price may mean increased sales if it brings a product into someone's range, making her/him look at it carefully, when otherwise s/he might just have passed it by. For relevant studies, see Taylor and Wills (eds) (1969).

Little empricial work has been done in respect of a fourth issue, related to the idea that choice has a moral dimension: price may affect whether or not the product is seen as a 'rip-off', involving the purchaser in giving a humiliatingly high profit margin to the manufacturer. Some buyers may prefer to make sacrifices of product characteristics than allow themselves to feel they are paying a price that is unduly in excess of production costs.

Last, but probably by no means least, it should be recognized that price may affect the ability of a product to win in a 'choose the cheapest' disjunctive tie-break between products that have survived a conjunctive test or all of a series of characteristic filtering tests. This provides another way of framing the idea of a substitution effect arising from a change in relative prices.

Non-compensatory decision rules lead to some interesting perspectives on the relationship between real income growth and patterns of consumption, and on the origins of product obsolescence, in other words, the 'decline' phase of product life-cycles. For example, the priority framework can be used to make sense of inferior goods in the context of household budgeting decisions concerning divisible products such as foods. Figure 4.2 shows how the phenomenon may arise. Characteristic outputs associated with two products, T and N, are shown as rays extending from the origin, OT and ON. Two aspiration levels, OA and OB, are also depicted, with the consumer's first priority being to reach OA. At low levels of income the consumer will not be able to get very far along either ray, and may be unable to reach either aspiration level. The least bad option will be to purchase only *N*. When the consumer's income reaches such a level that her/his efficiency frontier is moved out to *RL*, s/he can at last meet either priority, but not simultaneously. However, at this stage s/he continues only to purchase *N*. Further increases in income enable movement along the pathway indicated by the bold arrow by spending some of this income on *T*. This behaviour actually involves reducing the consumption of *N*. At point *X*, for example, the consumer is only going to *K* on the *ON* ray, at the same time as moving to *P* on the *OT* ray. This process continues with successive increases of the consumer's income until her/his efficiency frontier is moved out as far as *SM*. Here, s/he can at last satisfy both priorities by cutting consumption of *N*, moving back to *J* on the *ON* ray and advancing to *Q* on the *OT* ray. Further income increases, such as those which would move the efficiency frontier out to *TN*, result in indeterminacy on the diagram: any combination shown by the shaded area is both feasible and sufficient to meet both priorities. If the consumer breaks the tie by considering how the combinations that fall within *UVW* fare in respect of a third priority, it is possible that the inferior good *N* might either suffer a further loss of sales, or that it might now start to come back into favour owing to a superior capacity to help the consumer meet the third priority. Note how consumption of either or both of the first- and second-priority characteristics may be allowed to rise above their target levels if this is a requirement of meeting lower-level aspirations. Note also how the analysis may be extended to include double-sided aspiration levels: the consumer may want neither 'too little' nor 'too much' of some characteristics.

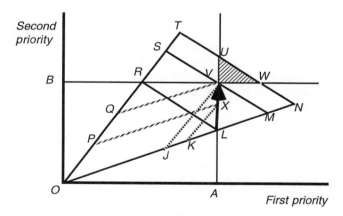

Figure 4.2: Hierarchical choice and an inferior good

The scope that higher incomes give consumers for adding further test criteria to their decision procedures is one obvious non-price source of product obsolescence. The demise of the Model-T Ford at the end of the 1920s may be understood in this way: the American public grew to be able to afford more than basic motorized transportation; they wanted style, protection from the weather, and individuality. In such a situation, Henry Ford could no longer maintain, let alone expand, his market by continuing to cut prices as ways were found to cut the cost of making the Model-T (see section 7.6 on learning curves; for a perspective from General Motors, it is most instructive to read Sloan, 1965, chapter 9). To continue to sell products that have become obsolete due to rising affluence, it may be necessary to look to new markets, possibly by selling the manufacturing rights and tooling to a developing country (the 1980s Ladas were based on 1960s Fiats, whilst cars based on 1950s Fiat and Morris designs were still being made in India in the 1980s).

A second possible cause of product death is the appearance within consumers' budget ranges of innovative products that offer more features without compromising on features that are taken for granted. For example, British motorcycle producers failed to make electric starting a standard feature and lost out to newly imported Japanese models that could offer it without having to be priced at a higher level.

Thirdly, we should note that a lapse in quality or supply disruptions may do irreversible harm to the sales of a product. The temporary problem may lead potential buyers to discover acceptable alternatives that they otherwise would not even have considered. But they might also switch elsewhere in order to meet a priority to have a particular type of product to a particular standard within an acceptable delivery time, even though they might have to sacrifice lower priority targets as a consequence. Experience with other brands may lead to a revision of decision rules in their favour or a more favourable view being taken of what they have to offer. Meanwhile, the distributors of these brands find that the greater rate of sales helps them to establish a more effective dealership and after-sales infrastructure (a classic example is the way that Japanese car-makers built a bridgehead in the UK market in the early 1970s when local manufacturers found it impossible to cope with an unprecedented boom in demand).

Finally, we should note that even if new products offer no new features and no saving in terms of price, they may still hasten the obsolescence of rivals by offering opportunities to meet higher *standards* in some areas without compromises being necessary. So long as such products are priced within the budget ranges of the target market, they may be able to command somewhat higher prices than their rivals if they can be marketed in ways that lead buyers to raise their sights in terms of the non-price dimension where the older designs perform relatively poorly.

Summing up, we may say that if many consumers are believed to be using non-compensatory decision rules then the secret of mass-market success is to offer products in which a surfeit of performance in one dimension is not achieved at the cost of a failure to meet high priority targets or fit into commonly used conjunctive moulds of tolerance. Since the brand which gets furthest down customer priority lists dominates when a filtering rule is being used, products should not only be at least competent in all major respects, they should be made available with all the characteristics offered by rival brands (this strategy works with both behavioural lexicographic procedures and elimination by aspects). In so far as it is not possible to offer all the minor features at a price within the target budget range, the sensible policy is to give consumers as many option combinations as possible. That is to say, consumers should be permitted to create products that fit the moulds of tolerance implied by their personal decision rules; firms should not presume that compulsory characteristics necessarily compensate for absent ones, or that extra characteristics will always justify a higher price.

4.4   Case study: Executive cars

There are many ways of examining how well a student understands the literature on decision rules and its implications. Two rather unusual ones are illustrated in this section and section 4.5. In the question examined in this section, the approach used is rather akin to what decision scientists call 'protocol analysis' (see Waterman and Newell, 1971). Normally the researcher would accompany a decision-maker in the process of reaching a verdict and the decision-maker would be asked to verbalize the thoughts that go through her/his head. The analyst writes them down and then attempts to see what kinds of thought processes can be inferred from the transcript. The question dealt with in section 4.5 gets the student to design some specific choice heuristics and see what kinds of choices would be implied if decision-makers actually used these rules to reach their verdicts. With both questions it is important to realize that it is not necessary to know a lot about the products involved. Students should try to distance themselves from the actual characteristics of these products and think of them merely as elements in the chooser's choice matrix.

Question
Attempt to identify the decision rules used by the journalists who reached the following verdicts in a test of six executive cars with automatic transmissions in *Modern Motor*, March 1985. Explain your reasoning. Do not be afraid to highlight any aspects of their verdicts which make it difficult to decide how the choice was made.

The vehicles tested, their origins and their prices (note: this is an Australian case): Nissan Skyline (imported from Japan) $20 750; Volvo 240GL (Swedish but assembled by Nissan Australia) $23 345; Ford Fairmont Ghia (Australian) $21 472; Holden Calais EI (Australian) $19 701; Peugeot 505 STI (imported from France) $24 600; Toyota Cressida GLXi (imported from Japan) $22 455.

Verdict 1: 'It wasn't until the dying minutes of the test that the Cressida crept in front of the Calais and Fairmont to become my winner. The reason? The Cressida's effortless handling of rough dirt which left some of these cars floundering. The Toyota handled these "real" Australian conditions as competently as it had handled everything else. The Australian cars were good—the Cressida was slightly better. The Volvo is solid but getting old, the Peugeot is comfortable but too underpowered. The Skyline? Its interior is that of an overgrown economy car not a luxury one, its overall ride/handling is poor and its engine can't cope with the high gearing.'

Verdict 2: 'To start at the bottom, although the Skyline manual goes well, this auto was a slug. Its roadholding is actually quite tenacious, though the ride suffers. The interior doesn't reflect the price of this car.
   The Fairmont rated fifth on my list. Whereas other Fairmonts have felt rock-solid and stable on rough and unmade roads, this one lost minor items of trim and the steering column shuddered something fierce. Compared to the Cressida, the Fairmont felt big and clumsy. It's much bigger than it needs to be.
   The Calais was a real surprise, at least in terms of handling. It loped along over rough roads quite happily. Nevertheless, it rated only fourth on my list because of the lack of build quality.
   The Volvo is a funny old car, but it has some admirable qualities. Indeed, quality is one of them. It may fall behind, say, the Peugeot in its dynamics, but it remains an honest car and its

resale value reflects this.

The Peugeot was second on my list of buyables. On fast, open roads its ride and handling were superb. The 2.2-litre four cylinder engine, which works so much better with a five speed manual gearbox, is quite comfortable when wound up, but around town the three-speed auto really takes the edge off it. And the interior, while practical and well laid-out, didn't look particularly opulent.

One would have expected the Cressida, on the other hand, to be a real bells-and-whistles machine [in other words, loaded up with every latest electronic gadget]. But the Japanese have seen the beauty in subtlety. The ride is softish but there's no exaggerated wallow. The Cressida probably sets a new standard for the Japanese ride/handling compromise. The Peugeot is better in both these departments, but doesn't have the Cressida's gutsy 2.8-litre six cylinder engine, its electronic overdrive fourth speed, nor its comprehensive creature comforts. The Cressida came up trumps in this group.'

Verdict 3: 'For two days I tried hard not to believe it, but the Toyota Cressida really does beat the established Aussie and European stars in the $25,000 executive automatic car class. My final rating was Toyota, Holden, Ford, Volvo, Peugeot, Nissan. If the Volvo, Peugeot and Nissan had the manual transmission that suits them so much better—or if the Holden had the V8 engine option and better build quality, or if the Ford had an auto transmission that could rival the Toyota's—it might have been a different story. But the Toyota didn't need any "ifs". The price is right and it delivers the goods—and we didn't ever have to qualify any praise by saying "... for a Japanese car".'

Author's notes

Even before looking at the verdicts there is room for showing the examiner that one is on top of things. It can be pointed out that some initial non-compensatory filtering appears to have occurred: cars with automatic transmissions are the subjects of the test, in the 'executive' part of the market (this may exclude particular kinds of vehicles with the wrong kind of image—sports cars of a roughly similar price, perhaps, or smaller vehicles that have similar prices due to high quality/import duty). Also note that only six have been tested: probably there were others that could have been explored at roughly the same price. Perhaps a budget range is being used to draw up the list of six—between $19 000 and $25 000, for example—though perhaps the unavailability of a test vehicle was also a limiting factor that excluded some possible vehicles. We might thus infer an initial conjunctive screen involving tests for price, type, availability, automatic transmission.

In the first verdict, the phrase 'not until the dying minutes' suggests to me that we are looking at a pretty close-run race, with some form of tie-break criterion being used. Aside from the issue of dirt-road handling, the tester seems to have been ranking the Cressida, the Calais and the Fairmont on an equal footing, without mentioning any failings on their part. The latter fact, coupled with the list of failings of the lower-ranked cars, suggests that a conjunctive rule might have been in use, with the top three cars passing all tests. The dirt-road handling may be taken as a disjunctive tie-break.

Initially I read the text as suggesting that the Cressida actually dominated in other areas just as effectively as it did in dirt-road performance, which was the last thing to be explored. (Consider the logic: if it handled the dirt-roads as competently as everything else but was far superior in its dirt road handling, then it may be construed as not being outperformed by the other two in any area.) This would mean it could also have been in a position to win a compensatory test. However, I now think that the sentence 'The Toyota handled these "real" Australian conditions as competently as it had handled everything else' only refers to the car's handling capabilities (on motorways and urban roads as well as dirt roads in the bush), rather than to the other demands the tester made of the car.

Also going against compensatory kinds of ranking procedures is the 'singling out' of particular failings of the other cars, which suggest a priority ranking for the features in the conjunctive set. Performance adequacy seems to have been ranked very highly, with comfort likewise: the Nissan comes last (if we infer ranking from the order of the comments) by failing on both these counts, but the Peugeot fails only in terms of insufficient power. The Volvo is not recorded as having failed in either of these ways but the impression is given that it is too dated.

You might note that I am suggesting a non-compensatory view despite some of the better points of the lower-ranking cars also being mentioned (the Volvo is solid, the Peugeot comfortable). The tester probably feels obliged to note the better points to give the vehicles a fair go for readers who might have different decision rules. But the lack of an obvious comparison of these three lower-ranking vehicles with the top three and the mentioning of specific problems sounds non-compensatory to me.

The second verdict begins very conveniently for a non-compensatory interpretation such as characteristic filtering. The Skyline comes last because it fails to go well enough ('auto was a slug') and the interior didn't seem good enough value—in other words, these are the two highest-ranking tests that any of the cars failed. The Fairmont didn't seem well enough built and seemed too big, but was not noted as having insufficient performance or too basic an interior. Since the Calais also has poor build quality as a failing but ranks higher than the Fairmont, we might infer one of two things about the tester's decision rules if they are taking a priority-based form: either the 'mustn't be too big or clumsy' characteristic ranks above build quality (clumsiness would then be enough to fail the Fairmont and not the Calais), or, if build quality ranks higher, the failings of the Fairmont in this test were greater than those of the Calais—losing bits of trim is a pretty bad sign as far as quality is concerned! (If build quality ranked above 'unclumsy' and the Calais were worse built than the Fairmont, the Fairmont would have to beat it even if it then failed in terms of clumsiness.)

As we get to the Volvo there are signs that we are witnessing the use of contingent decision rules. Unlike the bottom three, the top three cars are not mentioned as having any particular failings which determine their rankings. So perhaps we should infer that the top three pass the complete set of basic priority tests and that the tester decides between them by switching to an additive differences approach to choice. The Volvo is compared with the Peugeot and loses, whereas the Peugeot loses against the Cressida despite being better in terms of ride and handling. Possibly there is a case for arguing that the switch to the compensatory approach actually comes after the rejection of the Volvo, with the Volvo being rejected in terms of its age and/or oddness.

A really good answer would take note of the fact that the Fairmont was compared with the Cressida and then consider briefly whether this is indicative of an additive differences approach to choice. I would argue against that interpretation, but instead suggest that the Cressida is making the tester rethink his/her ideas about the sorts of test standards that should be set in this market (note also the mention of standards in the last paragraph). If an additive differences procedures were being used throughout the test then the Cressida would also have been compared with the Calais and the Volvo, and we would also have expected to see some comparison of the Fairmont with the Skyline.

Verdict three can be seen as very straightforward: the Cressida is the only car which has no failings whereas none of the others would pass a conjunctive test. Since the also-rans are actually ranked, we can also infer something about how the tester ranks characteristics in priority terms when a conjunctive rule is unworkable. Performance, once again, is a high-ranking feature: it is what the last three cars don't have in large enough measure, though there is not enough information for us to see how the ranking was decided between the last three. The Ford's automatic transmission was its failing, which was seen as worse than the Holden's poor build quality, even though both of these cars were not judged as having failed in terms of performance. On the question of performance: perhaps the mention of a V8-engined Holden is indicative of a disjunctive performance tie-break that would have been used had it been necessary.

An alternative reading of the Holden and Ford comments might be to suggest that they are not listed as being inadequate in terms of the features that are mentioned (the same might be said in respect of the other three as far as performance is concerned), and that what we are really seeing is simply a compensatory way of reaching a decision. What makes me favour the conjunctive story, however, is the phrase 'the Toyota didn't need any "ifs".'

4.5   Essay example: Video cassette recorders

Question
Table 4.1 shows how a sample of twelve video cassette recorders (VCRs) were rated in terms of their characteristics by product testers in a report in New Zealand's *Consumer* magazine in August 1990. In the article from which this matrix of data has been extracted the VCRs were ranked in an order of preference by the testers, but in Table 4.1 the order of the VCRs has been randomized. The key to the features offered by the various VCRs is as follows:

Programming:

R	Remote
V	VCR
L	LCD display on remote control
O	On screen display
B	Bar code reader
12; 24	Clock display hours
D	Records at same time each day
W	Records at same time each week

Other features:

AR	Auto repeat of selected tape section
ISN	Index number search
ISC	Index scan search
IE	Index erase

Other features (continued):

ST	Search ahead a selected time
SO	Search for counter zero
SB	Search for blank tape
R	Reverse play
VS	Variable speed slow motion
HSC	High speed cue/review
QL	Quick look from fast forward
TR	Tape remaining indicator
CVS	Continuously variable speed
C	Child lock
DFF	Digital freeze frame
DTS	Digital still frames of TV
M	Mode display

Table 4.1: Choice matrix for video recorders

	Brand/Model (origin)	Heads	Price	Method	Programing No./Days	Features	Picture Rating	Convenience Rating	Still Rating	Other Features
(a)	JVC HR-D520EA (Japan)	2	$599	V, R	8; 365	L, 24, D, W	Good	Satisfactory	Fair	ISN, ISC, ST,
(b)	Sharp VC-A115NZ (Japan)	2	$599	R	8; 365	D, W, 12	Good	Satisfactory	Good	ISC, ISN, ST, SO, D, CL
(c)	Samsung VB8220 (Korea)	2	$499	V, R	4; 14	L, 12, D	Satisfactory	Satisfactory	Very Good	SO, HSC
(d)	Philips VR6449 79L (Japan)	2	$649	V, R	8; 365	L, 12, D, W	Good	Satisfactory	Good	AR, ISN, ISC (+ Reverse), ST, SO
(e)	Sanyo VHR5300 (Japan)	3	$699	R	6; 365	L, 24, D	Very Good	Good	Very Good	AR, ISN, ISC, IE, ST, SO, SB, VS, TR
(f)	Akai VS-465EA (Japan)	3	$699	R, O	8; 365	24, W	Good	Good	Good	ISN, ISC (+ Reverse), CVS, C (on play), HSC, M
(g)	Hitachi VT528E (Japan)	2	$799	R	8; 365	L, 12, D, W	Good	Good	Fair	AR, ISC, S), DC, C
(h)	Goldstar GHV-1291Z (Korea)	2	$599	V, R, O	8; 365	L, 24, D, W	Satisfactory	Good	Fair	
(i)	Panasonic NV-L20EA (Japan)	3	$699	V, R, B	8; 31	L, D, W, 24	Very Good	Satisfactory	Good	AR (Whole tape only),
(j)	Toshiba DV-90N (Japan)	2	$699	V	4; 21	12, D, W	Good	Satisfactory	Very Good	SO, D, DFF, DTS
(k)	Sony SLV-X10NZ (Japan)	2	$599	V	8; 365	D, 24	Very Good	Good	Satisfactory	AR
(l)	Mitsubishi HS-E11(P) (Japan)	3	$749	R, O	8; 31	D, W, 24	Good	Very Good	Very Good	AR, ISN, ISC (+ Reverse), ST, SO, OL, TR, C, HSC, M

Your task is twofold:

(1) Design six decision rules that VCR buyers might use and show the rankings of the VCRs that each of your hypothetical decision rules would produce.

(2) Suppose that the population of consumers is actually divided up equally into six groups, each of which uses a different one of the six decision rules constructed in the previous question. With the market segmented in this way, which strategies would you advise the producers of poorly ranked VCRs to pursue to improve their competitive positions?

Author's notes

This essay has tended to be construed by some students as requiring them to talk about which product characteristics different types of consumers might be interested to have—for example, the convenience of a machine that records at the same time each day might be of particular interest to someone who works at the time a particular soap opera is on. I certainly would reward students who showed an awareness of the possibility that consumers in different kinds of circumstances might end up using different types of rules, and that their rules may relate to their use of the product as a problem-solving device. However, an interest in recording at the same time each day is not a decision rule—unless it is a kind of disjunctive rule, the only thing the consumer wants—it is merely a single criterion for choice. It does not tell us how the consumer deals with the fact that the products offer different mixes of characteristics. A decision rule is something like, for example, 'I want, first of all, a VCR that costs less than $700, and then it must have three recording heads. If there are several that offer this, I will choose the one with the best picture. If there is a tie here, I will choose the one with the most "other features".' This example is a version of a characteristic filtering rule, though in its fourth test it has a kind of polymorphous procedure. It first excludes brands (g) and (l) as too expensive, and then excludes, from those remaining, all but (e), (f) and (i) because of a failure to offer three heads. Both (e) and (i) offer very good picture quality, but (f) is excluded because it only offers a good picture. Brand (e) dominates over (i) because it has more 'other features'.

Though the wording of the assignment does not exclude an answer framed around six different disjunctive rules, someone who offered such an answer could hardly be said to be displaying a great deal of insight. Rather, when answering this sort of question, it would be wise to show off one's command of more subtle aspects of the decision rules literature. This can be done in two main ways. First, you can choose a range of dissimilar rules, not just a mixture of compensatory and non-compensatory ones but also some contingent and hybrid ones (this may involve deliberately constructing, say, a conjunctive rule whose form is going to produce a tie). Second, you might point out how the information-processing difficulties faced by consumers may relate to the rules that you are discussing. For example, some rules focus on columns in the choice matrix. Others, such as the additive differences types of rules, focus on pairs of rows, while the operation of rules that involve elimination by aspects may depend on which problems and advertising stimuli the consumer has recently noticed.

With the exception of polymorphous rules (in which targets are set for each attribute and victory goes to the brand that meets the most targets), specific examples of compensatory rules can be hard to write down in words with sufficient simplicity to make them seem plausible. One strategy is to write down a compensatory rule as an equation, like a hedonic equation (see section 3.6), suggesting values for the weights for each characteristic. Relative scores of each brand can then be computed. But questions really do need to be raised as to whether such a specification is really in the spirit of the literature on choice heuristics. When some of my students produced quite complex charts of results formed in this way, I was not convinced it was a good approximation to what consumers might do if they were weighing up pros and cons in their heads. The most convincing attempt to capture a relatively complex compensatory rule that I have seen in an answer to this essay involved an unweighted additive differences rule. The student in question suggested that the choice process might begin with the consumer looking at the top two rows in Table 4.1, scanning from left to right to see which brand dominated in each column and then keeping a running tally on which one was ahead. In comparing brands (a) and (b) (JVC and Sharp) it would operate as follows:

(i)   They are initially equal, in terms of the number of heads and their prices.
(ii)   The JVC then moves two tests ahead in programming because it offers alternative methods and more features.
(iii)   The Sharp narrows the gap to one test by offering a better still rating.
(iv)   The Sharp eliminates the gap altogether by having more 'other features'.

With a tie happening to be produced in the first round you are naturally led to consider possible contingent variations on the rule: should the consumer be presumed, say, to compare the Sharp with brand (c) (Samsung) because they are on adjacent rows so eye scanning is easier?; or should the consumer be presumed to be more cautious and compare both the JVC and the Sharp with the Samsung? By my reckoning this unweighted additive differences procedure leads the Sharp and Samsung models to tie with three victories apiece. By contrast, the JVC beats the Samsung by four victories to two. The former result might be assumed to drive the consumer (in a second contingent switch) to use the more cautious contingent rule and thence to a comparison between the JVC model and brand (d), and so on. I found this additive differences rule very thought provoking: it left me wondering just how different the consumer's ranking of the VCRs might be if the order of the rows in Table 4.1 is changed or if the consumer began with the bottom pair of rows and worked upwards. Intransitivity seems to be a possibility that we should look out for when doing this sort of question.

Let us now move to the second part of the question. I have noticed that even students who produce excellent answers to the first part are prone to do badly on the second part as a consequence of not being sufficiently specific in their policy recommendations. It is important to pin down precisely which brands are doing particularly badly in the face of the rules that you have suggested, and then consider which particular modifications can reasonably be suggested as solutions for the manufacturers of these products. For example, take the rule mentioned in the opening paragraph of these notes: brands (g) and (l) are sidelined as too expensive and are falling behind on picture quality, while (g) is only a two head machine. Brand (l) might appeal to other hypothetical consumers who are not worrying about price so much and who want, as a high priority feature, as convenient a machine as possible. However, brand (g) seems to have major problems in terms of value for money which may mean it runs into trouble even with other consumers who set lower targets (or who are using a compensatory method for choosing and attach small weights) in respect of the number of heads or picture quality. The implications of a $150 price cut for (g) might, for example, be tested out in terms of the rules you have designed.

Finally, do not forget to discuss advertising implications of the decision rules that you have proposed, particularly if you have mentioned a rule that involves elimination by aspects with no particular ordering of characteristics: advertising is a way of making less random the order in which characteristics are examined.

4.6   Psychological tradeoffs

In this section and in section 4.7 my aim is to give a small taste of how aspects of psychology are starting to be incorporated as part of economists' analysis of consumer behaviour. My coverage is deliberately selective and aims to focus on a few contributions that relate closely to things that have already been said in this chapter; for more extensive guides to the kind of work that is being done along these lines, see MacFadyen and MacFadyen (eds) (1986), Hogarth and Reder (eds) (1987), Lea, Tarpy and Webley (1987), Albanese (ed.) (1988), Earl (ed.) (1988b), van Raaij, van Veldhoven and Warneryd (eds) (1988), Grunert and Olander (eds) (1989), Earl (1990), Lane (1991) and Lea, Webley and Young (eds) (1992). For this section, I will focus on the work of Scitovsky (1976, 1986) to whom much of the credit is due for triggering the recent growth of interest in the integration of economics and psychology. His contribution is particularly interesting because it relates both to neoclassical interests in optimization and to the behavioural idea that we can usefully see people as information gatherers, for whom life consists of a series of experiments.

The psychological contribution whose economic implications Scitovsky focuses upon is Berlyne's (1960, 1971) optimal arousal model of behaviour, the empirical robustness of which has been demonstrated in a variety of contexts. The essence of the model is neatly summarized by Middleton (1986: 397), who attempts to follow Scitovsky's lead and even uses it as a basis for econometric work. Middleton notes that the optimal arousal model 'hypothesizes that a certain general type of utility is a function of the degree to which the distribution of events in an experiential "frame" is "new" in the subject's experience. Utility increases with "subjective novelty" up to a point, then decreases, and then is replaced by disutility and anxiety. Subjects prefer intermediate degrees of novelty.' Scitovsky illustrated the economic significance of this hypothesis with reference to a diverse range of examples such as tolerance of types of music and other art forms, theme parks, gambling, fashionable clothing, and even economics texts such as his own which would be ignored if either saying nothing new or being seen as too different from the mainstream.

At any moment, how aroused a person becomes in physiological terms, and how much a person experiences a sensation of excitement, will depend on how much novelty the person sees in the situation that she is confronting. Scitovsky portrays the effects of novelty on arousal as arising in so far as a stimulus is strong enough to threaten or challenge one's position and demand that one acts. He sees uncertainty about one's physical or intellectual capacity for dealing with the new situation as a major precondition for any situation to represent a challenge, whether to one's life, limb, health, economic well-being, prestige, status or self-respect. All this fits in very well with the recent psychology literature on stress (such as Hanson, 1987; Hurrell *et al.*, eds, 1988). Our bodies have limited capacities for dealing with high levels of arousal. Sustained challenges over long periods lead to 'burnout'. On the other hand, people will 'rust out' if they do not choose to place themselves in a sufficiently challenging environment. For people to function most efficiently in physical and mental terms they need to position themselves somewhere between these two extremes. So long as they are not fully constrained by their environments, people can choose how much excitement/arousal/stress to confront.

Scitovsky argues that people in relatively primitive societies did not need to seek out excitement: it was often thrust upon them by difficulties in meeting their basic needs. However, the major uncertainties of life were made bearable by its normally sedate pace and the availability of time to spend engaging in folk art and cultural rituals. In advanced economies, by contrast, people may find it necessary to set out to find excitement in so far as their jobs become boringly repetitive whilst providing them with economic security. They can seek to meet this need for excitement by trying new forms of entertainment; in do-it-yourself or travel; by switching, as many are, from being mere spectators to becoming sports participants or political activists; or by indulging in gambling, violence (whether as participants or by watching it on screen) and drugs. Many of these activities display similarities with work, in that they are both rewarding and onerous. But they vary considerably in their social implications, depending on the kinds of externalities they involve: the differences between participation in adult education classes and other cultural and sporting activities, as opposed to vandalism, violence and coping with addictive forms of stimulation, are so obvious as not to need elaboration.

In addition to varying between societies at different stages of development, preferences in respect of excitement may vary through time for an individual (even an elderly person who normally leads a sedate life may be attracted by a challenge involving a burst of great uncertainty so long as its duration is certain to be short) and between individuals at similar life-cycle stages. The latter possibility arises because the way people feel about a given situation will depend on whether they believe they possess the skills required to cope with it. For example, someone who has grown up in a Swiss mountain village might not be greatly aroused by the prospect of skiing, whereas, to someone who has never tried to ski before, the very idea of a skiing holiday could seem far from ideal as a way of winding down. Choice is thus path-dependent, affected both by past experiences resulting from choices based on the exercise of personal imagination and by the social and informational environment in which the individual comes under pressure to try particular activities and picks up ideas about what may be exciting.

The choice of which *level* arousal to aim for is, in Scitovsky's view, a choice about how *comfortable* one's life is to be. How *pleasurable* it will be is an altogether different matter, for experimental work by neurophysiologists suggests that feelings of pleasure arise as a result of *changes* in one's level of arousal, particularly changes which move the level of arousal toward its optimum. The distinction is a major one for normative purposes: to experience pleasure, one must first have sacrificed comfort (by choice or force of circumstances) and moved temporarily away from one's position of optimal arousal. As he studied the behaviour of Americans in the early 1970s, he reached the conclusion that many of them were ending up feeling that, despite their increasing affluence, their lives were not particularly pleasurable—were joyless—without realizing that this was the result of their having chosen to spend their extra money and time in ways which only involved them in facing as much novelty as was necessary to keep themselves at an optimal level of arousal. They were too reluctant to live dangerously.

The detailed portrayal of the American lifestyle offered by Scitovsky (1976) in *The Joyless Economy* was brilliantly summed up as follows by Peacock (1976: 1278–9) in his review of the book:

> Look around you Yankees and see what a miserable lot you are, wholly inexpert in the art of living, laughing and loving. The normal ambiance for a meal resembles the atmosphere of a filling station—it frequently is a filling station—rather than a pleasant communication of connoisseurs. Speech is for rapidity of communication and not leisurely mind-stretching converse. You have no music in your soul. All that leisure time you have created by labor saving devices is used up in being glued to the TV, and when social pressures demand the allocation of some of it to the European Grand Tour, your cultural background is so exposed in its inadequacy that you seek protection in the encapsulated package deal, only too glad at the end to return to the homelier pleasures of coffee and apple pie. Travel broadens your feet but not your mind. Your lack of faith in the quality of your domestic decision-making drives you into the arms of an array of predators, such as home decorators and psychiatrists. In short, the Puritan Ethic haunts you....

Is is, as Peacock points out, rather misleading to treat all Americans as conforming to this stereotype. But so long as a good number do, then there may be a need in the United States for training in how to enjoy an affluent lifestyle. On Scitovsky's analysis, the consumers who find that increasing affluence makes their lives more satisfying may be either the ones for whom affluence provides the means to increase the amount of novelty in their lives and bring them nearer to their optimal level, or those who use greater affluence as a means of obtaining periods of stimulation in which they depart temporarily from their positions of greatest comfort.

4.7 Cognitive distortion and weakness of will

The quality of consumer decision-making might also be improved if consumers were aware of common psychological traps into which people can fall when choosing and monitoring the quality of past decisions. Papers by Thaler (1980) and Hogarth and Makridakis (1981) offer a catalogue of examples in this area. One of the most unsettling to economists is the way in which attitudes towards differences in relative prices are subject to 'framing effects'. Thaler illustrates this phenomenon by asking his readers to imagine that they are (a) close to buying a cheap radio for $25 when they are told by a friend that they can get the same product for only $20 if they go to another store that is ten minutes away; (b) close to buying a colour television for $500 when they are told by a friend that they can get the same product for $495 if they go to another store that is ten minutes away. The decision about whether the ten minutes extra shopping time is worth a saving of $5 should, in terms of standard consumer theory, be the same in both cases, yet in practice people seem less likely to bother to try to save the small sum of money on the more expensive item. A related study by Tversky and Kahneman (1981) showed that transitivity may not be observed when decisions are framed in different ways: they found that 88 per cent of their subjects said that if they were going to the theatre and discovered they had lost $10 on the way to the box office they would still go ahead and buy a $10 ticket, whereas 54 per cent of subjects said that they would not spend $10 to buy a replacement ticket if they arrived at the theatre and discovered that they had lost a $10 ticket which they had bought in advance. In other words, a good part of the population that were questioned preferred a ticket to $10 *and* preferred $10 to a ticket.

The work of Nisbett and Ross (1980) provides a particularly unsettling account of the traps that people are prone to fall into when sizing up situations, traps which prevent them from seeing things in the way that statisticians and mainstream rational choice theorists would hope that they would see them. For example, there is the problem of 'availability bias' in information processing: recently encountered information that conjures up particularly vivid images may play a disproportionate role in shaping expectations. Nisbett and Ross illustrate this by reporting, amongst other things, the case of a person who abandons a plan to buy a Volvo after attending a party and hearing a horror story about the reliability of a particular Volvo car. The previous research that this consumer had done on possible cars to buy had suggested that Volvo cars had a good reliability performance and yet it was ignored in the face of information about a single rogue vehicle.

Often consumers may be oblivious of the ways in which their choices are affected by all manner of blind spots and preconceived notions they have about particular kinds of products. In many contexts the typical consumer will be choosing with reference to only a fraction of the number of dimensions that connoisseurs might use. Some may being doing so in blissful ignorance; some may do so with an air of nonchalance, knowing they are taking a limited view of their options but not expecting any problems to arise from their choices. Following Elster (1989: chapter VI) we might say that this limit to rationality, like the sorts of shortcomings studied by Nisbett and Ross, is produced by 'cool' mechanisms; beliefs are going wrong 'without any nudging from the passions' (Elster, 1989: 38). Other beliefs may result from the working of 'hot', motivational mechanisms (they may be the subject of heated, passionate arguments when challenged). I will now move on to discuss the latter mechanisms. As I do so it seems appropriate to note that the very idea that some people might enjoy great expertise in choosing seems itself to be quite a 'hot' issue. Consider, for example, the way in which people who profess to be able to discriminate between wines in a complex manner are prone to be ridiculed as pretentious 'wine snobs'. Such dismissive attitudes are predictable defensive responses of systems of judgemental rules when they encounter information that challenges core ideas around which other ideas are being framed.

New pieces of information that might assist a person in coping with life are by no means guaranteed to be welcome. A piece of information which is at odds with beliefs close to the inner core of a person's system for making sense of the world is likely to prove highly unacceptable unless it comes complete with a comprehensive set of new subsidiary beliefs. This is because the acceptance of such a piece of information involves throwing away, or at least modifying, the expectations that depend on these beliefs. If the consequence of changing one's mind is to have no ideas about an area of the world, it may seem better to avoid change, even though that strategy is not without its own difficulties. People have to decide for themselves what to believe and it is common to see them attempting to justify what they presently find it *convenient to believe* in three ways. First, they may try to obtain social corroboration (which may be made easier by careful selection of those with whom they mix). Secondly, they may selectively emphasize negative ideas about alternative views that clash with their own (this is the 'sour grapes' attitude to choices that one is precluded from exercising: see Elster, 1983). Thirdly, they may highlight suggestions that are consistent with the optimistic views that are being held. This is 'wishful thinking' and it is something which those involved in marketing have to guard against themselves, for example, when looking at factors that might affect sales projections—see Steinbruner (1974: chapter 4); Earl (1984: chapter 5). All too often, when people have been warned that they will makes fools of themselves if they do not back away from a course of action, they instead tend on the basis of wishful thinking to *escalate* their commitments and eventually come out far worse off than they might have done (Staw and Ross, 1989).

The selective use of information may be observed when people are 'making up their minds' about what to do. It might be said, following Festinger (1957), to be aimed at the elimination of 'cognitive dissonance', the failure of cognitions to be compatible with each other. Festinger pointed out that people experience cognitive dissonance because they are not in control of the information they receive and because many things tend to be a mixture of contradictions. This led him (1957: 3) to advance a pair of basic hypotheses:

i.   The existence of dissonance, being psychologically uncomfortable, will motivate the person to try to reduce the dissonance and achieve consonance.
ii. When dissonance is present, in addition to trying to reduce it the person will actively avoid situations and information which would increase the dissonance.

Such behaviour will arise even if, at the time of choice, people are able to reduce dissonance by careful choices of combinations of beliefs and products, for they may still feel somewhat uncomfortable; or, even though they felt quite OK at the time of the choice, things may now seem not to be turning out as expected. In fact, unlike some authors such as Elster who have followed his lead, Festinger himself set out his theory only as an account of what happened *after* an initial choice had been made. Nonetheless, it offers important messages about how subsequent choices may be path-dependent (Akerlof and Dickens, 1982; Earl, 1992a).

Though he was writing as a psychologist, many of Festinger's own illustrative scenarios actually concern economic situations, such as car ownership, employment choices, decisions not to give up smoking, or even minor decisions about whether to continue on a picnic expedition as gathering clouds start to raise questions about the likely weather at the destination. His scenarios call into question core assumptions of orthodox theory, for they portray decision-makers as prone to go to great lengths to avoid treating irrecoverable costs as having been mistakenly sunk in situations where they encounter information that questions the wisdom of their decisions. Festinger's theory also suggests that, rather than facing up to the fact that life is full of opportunity costs, choosers often may be expected to try to gather together information that will enable them to rationalize away the sacrifices that they have made as a result of committing themselves to particular courses of action. For example, after opting to buy a particular item, they may devote a great deal of attention to advertisements for it, all the while doing their best to ignore advertisements for and reviews of the alternatives that they rejected. (This last position was modified by Festinger in the light of experimental work which showed that, although people are prone to look at *more* advertisements for what they have just purchased, they nonetheless tend to look at *some* advertisements for rejected possibilities: he recognized that confident people might actively expose themselves to dissonant material in order to demonstrate that they could counter-argue.)

Cognitive dissonance theory seems to suggest that firms may do well to consider a rather understated approach to selling their products: this will reduce the risk of feelings of dissonance after the purchase, so long as the understated campaign does not lose the sale in the first place. It implies a role for advertisements as means for telling previous customers that they have done the right thing by their choices (and hence for generating brand loyalty and re-buys), as well as for attracting new customers. We should also note that the post-choice information-gathering process is likely to affect how the consumer sees the market when next in it as a buyer: if people are desperately looking for ways of avoiding a conclusion that their choices were not justified, they may develop new channels of thinking and, as a result, end up with a rather more elaborate view of what matters. Next time, they will be a rather more sophisticated kind of buyer.

Festinger's work has inconvenient implications for firms such as Volvo or Mercedes-Benz that have been trying to build up their markets partly by offering cars with superior standards of passive safety. Buyers may find it very unsettling to think about accidents and justify not purchasing such brands by pointing to active safety features (such as turbo power for easier overtaking, and four-wheel drive for superior grip in adverse conditions) that might enable them to avoid accidents in the first place and which happen to be offered with the sort of stylish, high performance vehicle that fits in easily with their core views of themselves. (Akerlof and Dickens, 1982, offer some related examples, concerning the relevance of cognitive dissonance theory in relation to safety in the workplace.) It may be easiest to sell safety in markets where products are seen as being closely matched in other respects and safety can then be used as a tie-breaker. Otherwise, the tendency to engage in the 'it couldn't happen to me' line of thinking seems to imply that governments may need to use legislation to raise safety standards, rather than rely on consumers being able to recognize what is in their own interests and then choosing to pay for it.

Having highlighted some of the ways in which choices may be affected by *unconscious* distortions of information, I will end this section by noting that some decision-theorists have been investigating what some people do if they are *aware* of their own personal shortcomings in matters of choice. The area of setting and attaining goals has received particular attention (Thaler, 1980; Thaler and Shefrin, 1981; Elster, 1984; Dunn, 1987). Much of this work is built around the idea that the self is divided up into 'planner' and 'doer' components which will at times pull in opposite directions. For example, a person may recognize that, while the planner in her/him wishes to set a goal for, say, giving up smoking, or saving up enough to retire five years ahead of the conventional time, the doer in her/him will be likely to succumb to the temptation to smoke or spend on consumption activities. The planner may nonetheless win out if it is possible to find a way of restraining the doer. This is precisely what Ulysses was doing when he had himself bound to the mast of his boat so as to ensure he did not fall prey to the tempting Sirens. It amounts to selecting an additional constraint when choosing, instead of merely making a choice subject to given constraints.

Choices aimed at engineering self-control and overcoming weakness of will may work in a variety of ways. Would-be non-smokers may pay to have themselves locked away at health farms, and those who are worried about spending and violating their intentions to save may sign up with contractual savings programmes. Related to the latter are Christmas Club Savings Accounts, which often offer lower rates of interest than a regular savings account despite the latter being available for withdrawals throughout the year. Some people are apparently prepared to forgo potential interest earnings in order to have their money tied up so that they cannot spend it long before the time for buying Christmas presents arrives. In some situations people may achieve self-control by making public promises about what they will do. They may then either feel *duty bound* to deliver the goods, or they may become more committed to reaching the goal because they know there is a risk that people will humiliate them by highlighting their failures—a risk that would not have existed had they not made their goals public.

4.8 Economists' choices

An example of a self-control strategy given by Thaler (1980) is that of the academic who offers to present a paper at a conference in order to force himself to find time to write the paper. This example should do more than illustrate the Ulysses and the Sirens phenomenon; it should also remind us that economists are themselves mere mortals who face questions about how they should allocate their scarce time and other resources. The economics of being an economist have, however, received relatively little attention, even though over the past quarter of a century much has been written on the state of economics and about the failure of economists to agree over how the subject should proceed. Writings on method have typically made an implicit assumption that economists are concerned only with the pursuit of knowledge. Little attention has been given to the incentives they may perceive to pursue knowledge in particular kinds of ways. In this section I try to give a brief taste of my (1983a) examination of the economics of being an economist, which considers how career pressures and bounded rationality may affect the production and acceptance of contributions to economic knowledge (see also Earl, ed., 1988b: chapter 15).

Philosophers of science have tended to write as if rival research programmes (such as neoclassical and behavioural economics) achieve their popularity on the basis of their ability to add to knowledge, seen as their ability to offer extra empirical content by predicting some hitherto unexplained fact (Lakatos, 1970: 118; for attempts to summarize the key features of neoclassical economics in Lakatosian terms, see Latsis, ed., 1976; Remenyi, 1979; and Lavoie, 1992). A research programme is said to be degenerating if it seems to be running into empirical difficulties that cannot be explained away in terms of its core notions without recourse to the introduction of *ad hoc* assumptions. We can see the appeal of this view of battles between alternative ways of conducting a particular science in the case of a discipline such as astronomy: there came a point when the earth-centred view of the universe became simply too difficult to reconcile with accumulating data that the

Copernican view could handle comfortably (cf. Skinner, 1979, who discusses Adam Smith's relatively little-known work on the history of astronomy). Unfortunately, in economics, the empirical resolution of struggles between different approaches to the subject is far more problematic. Different approaches to economics lead to theories that cover different empirical territories and to differences in willingness to accept particular kinds of empirical work. Behavioural economists worry about the possible tendency of neoclassical econometricians to engage in 'data mining', while neoclassical economists worry about whether or not subjects in behavioural research are responding to leading questions or are answering questions in a self-serving manner. Debates can thus persist, unresolved.

Empirical content is insufficient to explain choices between approaches to science even in the physical sciences. There are several reasons for this. First, commitment to a particular style of research logically must precede empirical work of a particular kind. That commitment may often arise due to some form of dissatisfaction with existing ways of thinking in the area in question, such as a tendency for the dominant research programme to degenerate, or (and this seems quite common in economics) a reluctance to accept analyses that have been based on grossly unrealistic assumptions.

Secondly, it may well be the case that the scientist's bounded rationality leads to a preference for using theoretical frameworks in particular contexts because they are more convenient to use there than another framework: this is why Newtonian and quantum mechanics both have a role in physics, and it is, of course, why I am setting out both neoclassical and behavioural economics in this text. Not all scientists feel at ease with the 'horses for courses' philosophy (however, see Caldwell, 1982, for a powerful presentation of the case for pluralism in methodology). It has been noticed over many years that scientists commonly crave theories that are widely applicable (Skinner, 1979), and resist new contributions if they seem, to put it in satisficing terms, insufficiently general.

Thirdly, it would be most unwise to presume that scientists are fully informed about the rival ways that have been proposed for confronting particular problems. Even with the aid of modern abstracting systems and computer databases, researchers stand a good chance of failing to uncover relevant work, or of having insufficient time to read every potentially relevant contribution of whose existence they become aware.

These considerations lead to the view that we might see rival contributions to science as multi-characteristic products between which choices are made, in the face of bounded rationality, on the basis of personal decision rules or preferences. In other words, scientific works are goods whose fates we can seek to understand using theoretical perspectives discussed earlier in this chapter as means for making sense of consumer behaviour. Whether or not economists discover and take seriously a particular contribution to the subject will depend on factors such as (a) the information databases and index systems to which they have access, (b) the extent to which they use such information systems or rely on particular screening rules of their own (such as keeping an eye on new issues of a limited set of journals), (c) whose work they judge worth looking at (which may depend on reputations of authors, on reviews of their work, ways in which they have been cited by others, and on their previous experience of them), and (d) how easy it is to make sense of a particular piece of work. Here, as with everyday consumption activities, it cannot be stressed too highly that choices are being made in the context of social networks and that certain academics may exert considerable influence over their peers through their own choices of literature sources and what they do with them. In other words, 'demonstration effects' may be quite significant, and we should not be surprised to see economists jumping on particular research bandwagons in order to keep abreast of current fashions (cf. Leibenstein, 1976: chapter 4).

Choices of which ideas to adopt and which kinds of research to engage in might be justified publicly with reference to past and/or potential empirical relevance, but it is quite conceivable that such justifications are merely manifestations of processes of dissonance reduction by scholars who are, deep down, concerned with other things. Career pressures along with self-image and lifestyle aspirations may shape the kinds of work that gets done. Without an academic position it is hard to do any research in economics, but it may be hard to obtain such a job if one turns out work that is judged unfavourably by mainstream thinkers on appointments committees (for example, mathematical, equilibrium-oriented economists may tend to dismiss behavioural economics as mere 'economic poetry'). The quantity of publications and their locations may also play a major role in shaping an academic's career pathway: during competition on the tenure track, the message is 'Publish or perish'. The difficulties of gathering data in the field and the tendencies of top-ranking journals to publish mainly pure theory with a mathematical emphasis are likely to bias research in favour of econometric studies based on published data sets (which may often be made to serve as proxies for data that have not been gathered) or exercises in mathematical theory (for evidence, see Leontief's foreword to Eichner, ed., 1983).

4.9   Essay example: Consumer theory's relevance to estate agents and valuers

Question

Imagine that you have been invited to give a presentation to an audience of valuers and estate agents about the usefulness of modern consumer behaviour theories as devices for understanding the demand for particular kinds of homes and the willingness of house owners to sell their homes. Your task for this assignment is to prepare a detailed summary of the presentation that you imagine you would give.

Author's notes

Something akin to the following might provide an adequate basis for a presentation of the kind required:

In the past thirty-odd years a number of new models of consumer behaviour have appeared that seem much more likely to be useful in the real estate market than the 1930s work of Sir John Hicks that still continues to dominate the microeconomics textbooks. A good starting point is the idea of a *decision cycle*. This suggests that consumers are prodded into thinking about changing their behaviour by the *recognition of a problem* of some kind. This leads them to *search* for possible solutions to their problem, which they then *evaluate*. Having sized up what the alternatives have to offer they *choose* between them and set about trying to *implement* their choice. Housing seems to fit into this analysis rather well. Although consumers enjoy housing services every day, they only enter the market as buyers or sellers on a relatively infrequent basis: for example, due to changes in family circumstances (fewer/more children, a need to have a granny flat, a job relocation) or financial circumstances (forced sale due to loss of job, a need to move to a cheaper house to raise money for one's own business). In moving house either geographically or into dearer or cheaper market segments they are moving to areas of the housing market where their knowledge is likely to be rather limited—unless they are habitual readers of property pages and real estate guides. If they start from such a position of ignorance and do not call upon estate agents to help them search for a house, would-be buyers may fail to discover something that meets their needs.

I used the phrase 'something suitable', rather than 'the best, given their budgets', because modern consumer theories often portray consumers as carrying on searching only until they find something that meets their criteria for adequacy—a house that will solve their present problems without causing others to arise (they hope!); or, for sellers, a price that seems high enough offered by a potential buyer who seems sufficiently likely to see the deal through to completion. Search is a costly business, and not merely in terms of time. Too long spent searching may mean that a choice becomes impossible to implement because someone else has bought the preferred house. To hold out for the best possible price may mean a very long wait before someone prepared to pay a much higher figure comes along: the house might instead have been sold earlier to someone else and finance saved in the interim.

It must also be recognized that search processes cannot proceed very far without the consumer getting hopelessly confused. According to the psychologist George Miller, people find it hard to keep in mind more than 7 ± 2 things at once. If you want to make sure buyers don't get confused you will need to limit the number of houses they see, or encourage them to take notes (or draw up a matrix of information) about the relative attractions of the houses they have been looking at. It may also help if estate agents encourage buyers to decide whether the house they have just seen meets their requirements better than the house they were previously ranking number one. In this way they are forced to keep down the number of alternatives they have in mind and focus what they *really* want.

To avoid wasting time showing many unsuitable houses, the initial interview with buyers is important. It can be used to try to prise from them how they evaluate things (what do *they* mean by 'an easy care section') and how they rank houses that offer different attributes (for example, a spa but no pool) or differing amounts of particular attributes (a good view versus a panoramic one). The theories suggest that what you should be looking for are your clients' rules for choice. Many of the newer generation of choice models differed from the work of Hicks only in seeing consumers as being prepared to trade a bit less of one attribute to get a bit more of another, rather than a bit more of one product in place of a bit less of another. The rules for choosing (which economists such as Lancaster would still call preferences) thus concerned the terms on which consumers were prepared to make tradeoffs between product characteristics. In the very popular model proposed by Fishbein consideration was also given to the consumer's own views versus the views of friends and relatives (even estate agents' opinions might matter...). But lately rules that do not involve such tradeoffs have been explored. These may involve house-buyers having a checklist of features and wanting to find something which offers a good enough performance in each area (conjunctive rule).

If the buyer's checklist is a long one (as it will tend to be with more expensive properties), or the performance targets are unrealistically high, an estate agent could waste a lot of time showing 'unsatisfactory' houses to the client. Such a client will not be persuaded by suggestions that a deficiency in one area might be compensated for by a great performance in another respect. S/he will tend to demand to see other houses until, perhaps, a rule limiting the search time forces her/him to consider a way of choosing the least bad of the homes that s/he has seen. This might involve listing the characteristics in a priority order, so that the house which gets bought is the one which passes the most tests in the required order before failing one of them. If an initial interview can discover such a priority listing, a lot of time might be saved.

By contrast, buyers who set relatively undemanding conjunctive tests might be forced to use other rules to break ties after only seeing a few houses: these tie-breakers might be compensatory types of rules which can be implemented more easily if only a few alternatives are being examined.

If you discover that a lot of buyers are using rules that involve intolerant targets, checklists and/or priority rankings, and that their rules tend to be rather similar in their requirements, you can keep these popular decision criteria in mind when you give advice to sellers of houses. It may be much better to get sellers to spend quite a bit on redecorating their houses in 'neutral tones' rather than suggest that they lower their prices if their houses are failing to sell quickly and a lot of would-be buyers are commenting on the garish decor. A much lower price may fail to correct the problem. Indeed, if the seller is unwilling to redecorate, it may be better not to lower the price and instead to wait until someone comes along who is colourblind and prepared to pay the sort of price that might be implied by the other, commonly accepted features of the property.

4.10   Exam post-mortem: Usefulness of alternative theories of choice in different contexts

Question
'Decision-makers in the real world have neither the wit nor the information to behave in a manner even approximating to that suggested in neoclassical indifference analysis.' Discuss this statement and its implications for the modelling of consumer behaviour in the context of (a) the purchase of groceries and (b) the purchase of electrical appliances.

Examiner's report
A couple of catastrophic attempts at tackling this question involved bizarre misattributions of contributions to the theory of consumer behaviour: confusion is going to be hard to avoid when a student remembers that Hicks is a famous neoclassical economist but also thinks that decision rules are part of the Hicksian framework. But at least writers of these answers recognized that decision rules might somehow be relevant, in contrast to those that simply sought to defend indifference analysis without making any reference to rival theoretical approaches that might have more to offer in one or both of these contexts. There were some worrying technical errors in some of these regurgitations of indifference analysis: for example, some students wrote as if, at a given set of prices, only one indifference curve would exist in the mind of the consumer—in other words, they were failing to grasp the

basic idea of a comprehensive ordering of preferences; others suggested that consumers would be indifferent as to which curve they would be on. Technical confusion was even more apparent where indifference analysis was conducted in characteristics space: misunderstandings of the idea of a technology ray in Lancaster's diagrammatic framework were particularly common.

Those who sought to say that indifference analysis could capture the essence of consumer choice often fell into either of two traps in respect of the goods mentioned in the question. Some simply failed to make any reference to the particular goods mentioned. Others presented expositions of neoclassical theory in terms of diagrams which had one axis labelled as groceries and the other labelled as electrical appliances. The latter answers might have got somewhere had they adopted this stance as part of a discussion of budgeting with respect to the 'utility tree' idea, but normally this was not done. All they succeeded in doing was to show that they were not thinking about difficulties that might be involved in aggregating different goods that fall into a common category, or that might arise due to indivisibilities.

In both cases students were ignoring pre-exam advice that they should always think carefully about the products to which a question refers. Here, a couple of points should have been obvious. First, the problem of indivisibility and of households often buying either none or one unit would be acute in the case of electrical appliances, but would be less relevant in respect of groceries, so perhaps a neoclassical approach might be appropriate for groceries but not for electrical appliances, regardless of the informational issues raised in the question.

Secondly, the two categories of product were vastly different in informational terms: the range of groceries in a typical supermarket is huge compared with the range of appliances stocked by an electrical retailer. This may make the indifference framework seem questionable, relative to one based on simple rules of thumb, even in the case of groceries—indeed, in later life, Hicks (1976: 137–8) himself expressed doubts about his own theory's explanatory powers in this sort of context. That the complexity of the two types of goods differs also should be obvious if one bothers to contrast the number of characteristics expected of, say, an apple with the number expected of a video cassette recorder (cf. section 4.5). Thoughts in terms of characteristics could then have led to the question of whether or not Lancaster's model of choice was useful in either of these contexts: the better papers recognized this, with some arguing forcefully that Lancaster was a contributor in the neoclassical tradition who had provided a model that might be particularly useful for modelling grocery choices but would be of more doubtful applicability in the case of complex, indivisible electrical appliances. There was also scope for noting the differences in risk associated with the two types of product: a mistaken purchase of an expensive electrical appliance that performs poorly or is poorly matched to the consumer's needs is expensive to correct, whereas grocery items are purchased frequently and, aside from the costs of domestic embarrassments, switches of brand on an experimental basis can be reversed costlessly when next out shopping should they prove to be a disappointment. Such considerations ought to have pointed in the direction of a discussion of the likely role of brand names in these two contexts as symbols of quality, and to a consideration of whether there is a place for the notion of a brand name within indifference analysis.

I was surprised that those who wanted to agree with the view expressed in the quotation quite commonly also did so without saying anything about alternative theoretical approaches. There were many answers which were little more than regurgitations of lecture material in which I had critically commented on the axioms of neoclassical theory (section 3.2). Sometimes these answers mentioned Miller's rule but then failed to note that the decision-rules framework provided an explanation of how consumers might try to cope with complexity despite having limited cognitive powers. Others who wanted to agree with the statement simply seemed to regurgitate everything they could remember on decision rules (they tended to produce great lists of compensatory and non-compensatory heuristics), without at any point showing why neoclassical theory might founder as an approximate description in situations of uncertainty, ignorance and complexity. These answers typically failed to note the relevance of cognitive biasing processes discussed by authors such as Thaler (1980) (see section 4.7, particularly the discussion of framing effects). Many listings of decision rules at no point attempted to discuss the basic idea of satisficing in relation to the problem of knowing how much search to undertake when it is not clear what one's opportunity set consists of. Nor did they draw the high-/low-involvement distinction in relation to the two classes of goods under consideration—a point which could have been used to argue about different types of decision rules being used in different contexts.

Finally, I think it is worth reporting that quite a few answers displayed great confusion about the role of a theory of consumer behaviour in respect of purchases of groceries and electrical appliances. Some students seemed to think that neoclassical theory was being considered as a possible aid to consumers, rather than as an aid to economists and marketers who might be trying to make sense of or anticipate purchasing behaviour. Along with many of those who concentrated on criticizing the unreality of neoclassical axioms, they seemed not to have grasped the idea of a theory as an abstraction for summing up in a workable manner the essence of a complicated phenomenon (cf. sections 2.1 and 3.7). A sign that this idea had been firmly grasped would have been an attempt to pinpoint what one fails to see as a result of trying to make sense of these kinds of purchasing decisions in terms of indifference analysis—for example, the use of non-compensatory decision rules or habits as means of simplifying the choice process might mean that substitution effects were relatively insignificant even at the market level.

4.11   Further questions

1. Imagine a hypothetical meeting between Professor Kelvin Lancaster and Professor Herbert Simon during which a heated discussion develops: Simon claims that Lancaster's 'characteristics approach to consumer behaviour' does not represent a significant enough departure from the older analysis of consumer behaviour developed by the late Sir John Hicks; Lancaster disagrees and is reluctant to accept Simon's preferred approach. Write out in the form of a conversational dialogue the discussion you imagine that they would have.

2. In his autobiography *Models of My Life* Herbert Simon (1992: 105) recalls as follows a visit to his old friend Jacob Marschak:

We took a long walk together, slowly because he was already frail. We engaged in our usual debate, he expressing his permanent faith in human optimizing rationality and I defending a bounded rationality point of view. We were revisiting old territory, yet he expressed no impatience at my intransigence and listened thoughtfully to my arguments.

Write a dialogue showing how you think this debate between Simon and Marschak might have unfolded.

3. The following table of the relative quality of three retail stores has been compiled by a consumer magazine (the highest attainable score in each column is 10):

	Retail chain		
	Alpha	*Beta*	*Gamma*
Attribute			
Location	9	4	6
Price (high number = low price)	4	8	9
Quality of service	8	9	5
Credit facilities	6	6	5

(i) On the basis of this information, identify the chain that follows a strategy of: (1) overall cost leadership, and (2) product superiority. Explain your answer. (10 per cent)

(ii) Consumers frequently use decision rules (heuristics) to choose between rival suppliers whose offerings differ in terms of their attribute score. Give four specific examples of decision rules applicable to this context and show, using the information above, how consumers' choices of retail chain will depend on which of *these* four rules is employed. (40 per cent)

(iii) Retail outlet Beta has been facing declining sales for three years, as a result of which the directors are considering the introduction of major changes in their operations. Explain how Beta's marketers may use models of consumers' decision rules to formulate marketing policy. (50 per cent)

4. 'Fishbein's model of consumer behaviour is unsatisfactory, for the paradoxical reason that it is too demanding of the consumer and yet too simple.' Discuss.

5. Of what practical use are models of consumer choice in designing marketing strategies for low involvement products?

6. How does consumer behaviour theory help us to explain brand loyalty? What does it imply should be done by rival firms to break such loyalty?

7. Discuss the marketing implications of the fact that in many situations a consumer cannot perform a detailed evaluation of a product until after s/he has purchased it.

8. How can knowledge of the decision rules that consumers might use in a particular context assist a firm in marketing the products selected by use of these decision rules?

9. Examine the implications for welfare economics of recent work on decision-making and rationality.

10. Examine ways in which theories of decision-making may be used to make sense of the processes by which firms hire new staff. Comment on which theory you find most useful in this context and why.

5 Risk and uncertainty

5.1 Introduction

The problems that incomplete knowledge may cause for decision-makers have been a recurrent theme in the material so far covered. People may not know what they want. They may not know where to find something if they have decided that they want it. When they do find something that looks like what they have been trying to find, they may find it very hard to judge how well it will serve them if they select it as a means towards particular ends. Advertisements may help people to avoid ending up being paralysed in a state of indecision, and so may sales personnel. People may also be able to purchase advice from those who specialize in being well informed and claim to be impartial. Manufacturers and retailers can assist them by offering guarantees of quality and no-quibble rights to return purchased items that do not do what buyers expected them to do. Some things can be insured against. However, wherever it is costly to gather information or make life more predictable, there always remains a choice about whether or not to live dangerously: 'big decisions' typically derive their importance not from the initial scale of expenditure involved but from the costs associated with reversing them if a hoped-for outcome does not eventuate. Sometimes, it is simply impossible to go back after discovering that one has got on to an undesirable track: for example, people who switch between jobs may be unable to move back to their former positions even if these become vacant once again, and a firm that makes experienced workers redundant during a recession may not be able to get them back when business recovers.

Much of the uncertainty that decision-makers have to contend with is due to the uncertainty that other people are trying to handle. Investment decisions involve uncertainty on the revenue side because of difficulties of knowing about the intentions of competitors and potential customers, the reliability of distribution systems and future government policy. The costs of delivering a product to a particular standard and at a particular rate are usually uncertain not merely because technological innovations or unreliable processes are involved but also because of the potential for outcomes to be affected by suppliers of inputs, industrial action by union members and resignations of key employees. Spending decisions likewise may seem uncertain acts because the consumers are not sure about their security of employment, about the intentions of other people who matter to them, and whether or not firms are thinking of launching new products. In some situations, decision-makers opt to signal their intentions and take steps to make them seem credible, so that others will then be less hesitant about dealing with them. In other cases, decision-makers are wary of ending up with a needlessly poor deal if they provide information and therefore they choose to risk doing badly (such as, doing no deal at all if others view them with great suspicion) in the hope of benefiting from 'keeping their cards close to their chests'.

In this chapter I examine a variety of perspectives on how people go about reaching decisions when they recognize that more than one outcome is possible or probable in respect of a dimension in terms of which they have a preference. The focus initially is on problems that individuals face in their daily lives, but gradually I concentrate more on examples of uncertainty in business decision-making to help readers prepare for Chapters 6 to 11. In section 5.2 I begin with the basics of Subjective Expected Utility theory, longer discussions of which can be found in most standard texts. Empirical problems with this theory have led to a proliferation of other theories in recent years. Section 5.3 is an introduction to some of these, with a particular focus on Prospect Theory, which is starting to be covered as 'supplementary' material in the more adventurous mainstream texts (a particularly useful exposition is Frank, 1991, Chapter 8.) In the middle of the chapter I examine very different views that have emerged from philosophical objections to the expected utility theory, based on the view that risk is very different from uncertainty and that this distinction matters if decisions cannot be repeated and things either happen or they don't. Finally, I turn my attention to problems that involve interaction between several decision-makers who are trying to guess each other's choices before making up their own minds. Economists call such situations 'games' and lately 'game-theoretic' models have become all the rage in advanced teaching and research, particularly in industrial economics (for example, see Tirole, 1988). I give particular attention to bargaining in this part of the chapter; later in the book, you should see that other kinds of decisions, such as pricing and investment, involve a game dimension.

5.2 Expected utility theory

Consider the dilemma of a student who needs to choose between rival courses and is thinking about her chances in respect of a grading system that runs as follows: 0–40: E, 41–49: D, 50–59: C, 60–69: B, 70–100: A. Her assessments of the likelihood of her marks falling into each of these categories are as shown in Table 5.1. These likelihood ratings are shown as fractions that sum to unity, but the decision-maker might prefer to talk about them in terms of probabilities: for example, a likelihood of 0.05 might be expressed as a one-in-twenty chance. She thinks she has a bigger chance of doing very well if she takes Course 1, but is by no means certain she will score highly. She also thinks there is a small chance she could do really badly if she takes this course. Course 2 is one on which she feels very likely to score a basic pass (almost a two-thirds chance), but she sees no chance of doing really poorly and a rather slim chance of doing really well if she signs up for it. The problem is to decide which one to sign up for, given that neither course clearly dominates over the other.

One approach to solving the problem might be to form a weighted average for each course by taking each grade, multiplying it by its likelihood to form what is known as its expected value and then adding these scores together. The overall expected values can then be compared. On this basis, Course 1 comes out slightly ahead, as Table 5.1 shows, with an overall expected value of 58.75 if the mid-points of each grade range are used to facilitate the calculations. This line of thinking implies that the decision-maker would prefer a course on which it were possible to achieve a score of 59, if such a course were available, for its overall expected value would be simply 59 times one. It also implies that the decision-maker would be indifferent between Course 1 and a course that offered a certain prospect of a score of 58.75, so long as the grade was the only thing that mattered and characteristics such as the interest of the subjects or their career relevance did not count.

Table 5.1: Hypothetical expected values of rival university courses

Grade	Mid-point of grade range	Course 1 grade likelihood	Expected value of Course 1	Course 2 grade likelihood	Expected value of Course 2
E	20	0.05	1.00	0.0	0.00
D	45	0.10	4.50	0.05	2.25
C	55	0.40	22.00	0.65	35.25
B	65	0.35	22.75	0.25	16.25
A	85	0.10	8.50	0.05	4.25
Overall expected value			58.75		56.25

Such a view of risk-taking would be called into question if we observed the student actually opting for Course 2 after saying that she saw the courses as identical in all characteristics except for their likelihoods of leaving her with particular marks. It would also have trouble explaining why a person accepted a 50:50 chance of either winning $100 or losing $100, for such a gamble has an expected value of zero: i.e. $(0.5)(100) + (0.5)(-100) = 0$. Such an opportunity is an example of a 'fair gamble', for the expected value of the gambler's wealth is the same regardless of whether the gamble is accepted or rejected. In the Subjective Expected Utility theory (henceforth SEU), developed by von Neumann and Morgenstern (1944), we can see a way of explaining such observations.

SEU goes beyond the basic idea of imagining that probabilities are used to form weighted averages, by assuming that people do not necessarily attach an *expected utility* rating of $2U$ to an outcome whose expected value is twice that of an outcome to which they attach an expected utility of U. Purely for the sake of example, suppose our student has a utility function whose form makes the utility of an outcome equal to the square root of the size of the outcome. Table 5.2 shows what her expected utilities will be.

Table 5.2: Hypothetical expected utilities of rival university courses

Grade	Mid-point of grade range	Course 1 grade likelihood	Expected utility of Course 1 score times its likelihood	Course 2 grade likelihood	Expected utility value of Course 2 score times its likelihood
E	20	0.05	0.224	0.00	0.000
D	45	0.10	0.671	0.05	0.335
C	55	0.40	2.966	0.65	4.821
B	65	0.35	2.822	0.25	2.016
A	85	0.10	0.922	0.05	0.461
Overall expected utility			7.605		7.633

Now Course 2 is just (only just!) ahead. However, now a certain score of just 58.5 is enough to beat either of these two courses (actually, the certain figure must be just greater than 7.633 squared, which is 58.266). The form of utility function that we have imagined is not a particularly plausible one—one might expect there to be some kind of discontinuity if passing scores are seen rather differently from failing marks—but it does at least provide one possible way of explaining how Course 2 might come to be preferred to Course 1 despite having a lower expected value.

Two features of this SEU perspective should be noted. First: this analysis is built around the idea of a cardinal utility function (we have given numerical values to utilities), whereas in neoclassical indifference analysis as proposed by Hicks (1939) we are just concerned with rankings, that do not have numerical values attached to them (this is ordinal utility: our interest is in whether the consumer is able to get on to a higher indifference curve). Secondly, it appears that the expected values of the outcomes of a set of alternatives need not have the same ranking as the expected utilities of the alternatives. This situation arises because of the nature of the chooser's utility function. In making expected utilities a function of the square root of outcome scores, I have produced a concave utility function: the arc between any pair of points on that function always lies above the chord that one could draw connecting these points. A person whose utility function is concave is said to be *risk-averse*: such a person would always refuse a fair gamble. In the case of our hypothetical risk-averse student, a course with a sure score of 58 will dominate over an uncertain set of outcome possibilities whose expected value is also equal to 58 (which is equivalent to an expected value of 0 in terms of gains on a sure 58). This is exactly what we have already seen: Course 2 actually has an expected value of 58.75 but is beaten in expected utility terms by a course with a certain score of slightly less than 58.5.

It is commonly assumed that people are risk-averse. The ground for doing so is that it seems plausible to assume people have a diminishing marginal utility of wealth. As Frank (1991: 184) puts it: 'Most of us are comfortable with the idea that an extra $100 means more to a person if his total wealth is $4 000 than if his total wealth were $1 million. Note that this intuition is equivalent to saying that the utility function is concave in total wealth—which in turn implies that a given gain in wealth produces a smaller gain in utility than the loss that would be caused by a comparable loss in wealth.' A risk-neutral person, by contrast, would have a linear utility function: such a person would be indifferent between accepting or rejecting a fair gamble. A risk-lover would have a convex utility function in terms of her/his total wealth (in other words, its slope would increase with total wealth).

If we knew the form that a person's utility function took, it would be possible to predict that person's behaviour in respect of a variety of financial risks. For example, consider the case of a young man who likes fast cars and has to contend with a dramatic increase in insurance costs owing to the growth of joy-riding as a criminal activity. His wealth consists to a large extent of a sports car worth £10 000 that is now said by insurance companies to have a one in five chance of being stolen over the coming year and recovered in a wrecked state in which it will be worth only £500 to a scrap dealer. His only other wealth is a bank deposit of £3 000. The best insurance quotation he has so far found against theft of his vehicle is for a premium of £2 300 to cover the coming year. (It is not a 'fair gamble' since some of the premium payments that the insurance company receives will be absorbed in administrative costs: it simply does not pay to offer insurance at £1 900, in other words at a fifth of the likely loss of £9 500 [that is, £10 000 − £500].) Will he find the quotation acceptable? If his utility function can be approximated by $U = 5(\sqrt{W})$, where U is utility and

W is the expected value of his wealth, then the answer turns out to be 'Yes, but only just'. Figure 5.1 may help make clear how this result arises.

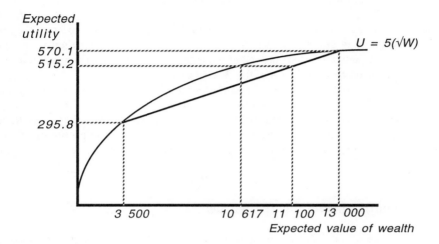

Figure 5.1: The reservation price of insuring a motor vehicle against theft
(scales are approximate on both axes)

If he did not have criminals to worry about, his expected utility would be $(5)(\sqrt{13\ 000})$, which is 570.1. If he were certain that his car would be stolen, then if he did not insure it he would expect to be left with £3 500 after selling the wreck for scrap and his expected utility would be $(5)(\sqrt{3\ 500})$, which is 295.8. However, if he acts on the best available information and accepts that his car has a probability of 0.2 of being taken by joy-riders, then the expected utility of his wealth if he does not take out insurance is 515.2. This is worked out as follows: $U = 0.8(570.1) + 0.2(295.8)$. This is the same level of utility that he would have if he faced a certain prospect that his wealth would be about £10 617, for $(5)(\sqrt{10\ 617}) = 515.2$: so SEU theory labels £10 617 as the 'certainty equivalent value' of taking the gamble and not insuring the car. If he takes out the insurance for £2 300, then he seems to be guaranteed to have wealth of £13 000 − £2 300 = £10 700. This strategy gives him an expected utility of 517.2. If the cheapest available insurance quotation were above £2 383, he would not bother to insure the car, for this figure is the difference between his current wealth and the certainty equivalent value of taking the gamble of not insuring the car. To put it in the jargon of economics, we would say that £2 383 is his 'reservation price' for insurance: if this is the cheapest quotation he can get, then he is indifferent whether he takes out the insurance or gambles that his car will not be stolen if he leaves it uninsured.

One lesson to be drawn from this example is that a person whom an economist would label as a risk-averse decision-maker should *not* be seen as someone 'who always opts for the more certain course of action'—even though in everyday conversation many people seem to mean the latter when they use the expression 'risk-averse'. The decision-maker in the example is risk-averse in the economist's sense: he has a concave utility function since a chord linking any pair of points on it always lies below the function. The expected value of gambling on the car not being stolen if it is not insured is (£13 000)(0.8) + (£3 500)(0.2) = £11 100, a value that lies four-fifths of the way along the distance between $W = £3\,500$ and $W = £13\,000$. This is (rounding errors aside) precisely the value of W at which a line perpendicular to 515.2 on the U axis meets the chord drawn to link the points on the utility function at which W is £13 000 and £3 500. (This can be checked by substituting $U = 515.2$ into $U = 193.75 + 0.0289W$, which is what the equation for the chord can be found to be from a knowledge of the coordinates of the chord's two end points.)

This example could easily be developed further to illustrate how such a motorist might react if faced with a different kind of insurance quotation, such as one involving a smaller fee and an 'excess' that would have to be paid in the event that a claim were made. Another extension would be to cases where the motorist is informed that by fitting a burglar alarm he can expect to reduce the risk of theft by a particular amount and receive a cheaper insurance quotation.

5.3 Alternative probabilistic theories

Despite its simplicity and superficial appeal, the SEU model of choice in the face of risk has come under much criticism. Soon after von Neumann and Morgenstern's book appeared, Allais (1953) discovered in betting experiments that subjects seemed to reverse their preferences between rival gambles if the probabilities of their respective desired outcomes were reduced by identical amounts. This phenomenon has become known as the 'Allais paradox' or 'common consequences effect'. It was replicated in the first pair of experiments in a series conducted by Kahneman and Tversky (1979). In their first experiment, Kahneman and Tversky asked their subjects to choose between A (the chance to receive 2 500 Israeli pounds with a probability of 0.33, 2 400 with a probability of 0.66 and 0 with a probability of 0.01) and B (the opportunity to receive 2 400 with certainty). They found that 18 per cent chose A and 82 per cent chose B. In their second experiment, they asked the same subjects to choose between C (the chance to receive 2 500 with a probability of 0.33 or 0 probability of 0.67) and D (the chance to receive 2 400 with a probability of 0.34 or 0 with a probability of 0.67). According to expected utility theory the second choice is the same as the first except that a 0.66 chance of winning 2 400 has been eliminated from both prospects. But the subjects did not see their choice in these terms: 83 per cent opted for C and 17 per cent opted for D.

Kahneman and Tversky discovered another kind of switch of preferences in a second pair of experiments which were simplified to involve only two-outcome gambles. This one is known as the 'common ratio effect' or the 'certainty effect'. Eighty per cent of subjects preferred a certain 3 000 to an 80 per cent chance of receiving 4 000 and a 20 percent chance of receiving nothing. However, when the probabilities of both gains were reduced by four-fifths, only 35 per cent preferred a 25 per cent chance of receiving 3 000 and a 75 per cent chance of receiving nothing, whereas 65 per cent now preferred a 20 per cent chance of receiving 4 000 and an 80 per cent chance of receiving nothing. Kahneman and Tversky concluded that the preference reversals arose because the subjects in their experiments seemed to over-value outcomes that were certain.

Further pairs of experiments involved giving subjects choices involving similar probability patterns but reversing the gain signs in the first round so that second–round choices involved risks of loss. These mirror-image experiments revealed corresponding reversals of preferences, patterns that Kahneman and Tversky called the 'reflection effect'. In other words, people who were risk-averse when faced with opportunities for gain tended to be risk-lovers when faced with probabilities of losses. However, further experiments seemed to imply that sometimes people seemed to be risk-averse when faced with gambles that involved probabilities of losses and risk-lovers when faced with gambles from which they might benefit. Furthermore, as with their later work on 'framing effects' (see Tversky and Kahneman, 1981, and section 4.7), preferences seemed to depend on the way that problems were presented. Taken together, these results led Kahneman and Tversky (1979) to reject SEU theory and propose an alternative approach, Prospect Theory.

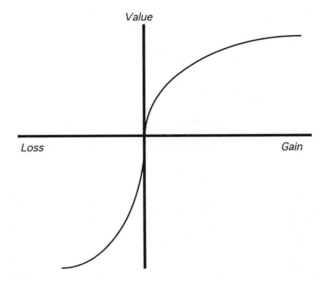

Figure 5.2: An S-shaped value function

Kahneman and Tversky (1979: 279) suggest that a better way of summing up a typical person's value function is not as *either* a concave function (such as in Figure 5.1) *or* as a convex function, but as a combination of the two types of function, plus a reference point in the form of the decision-maker's initial wealth or adaptation level. Their proposed S-shaped function, shown in Figure 5.2, is steepest around the reference point since it is (i) concave for gains and convex for losses, relative to the reference point, and (ii) steeper for losses than for gains. Such a value function makes it very easy to make sense of behaviour that entails a person simultaneously gambling and taking out insurance.

Prospect Theory is complicated, however, by the assumption that when decision-makers weigh up rival outcomes they multiply the gain or loss not by a probability, p, that they (have been advised to) attach to it but by a 'decision weight', $\pi(p)$, which differs from the probability rating in the kind of manner shown by the relationship between the unbroken curve on Figure 5.3 and the broken diagonal line. The curve is deliberately drawn not reaching the vertical axes, as it is assumed not to be well behaved for extreme values: on the one hand, people seem prone to ignore altogether outcomes with *very* low probabilities (such as one in a thousand) even though they also seem to behave as if they are attaching disproportionate significance to relatively low probabilities (such as one in twenty); on the other hand, they seem to neglect *or* exaggerate the difference between certainty and high probability.

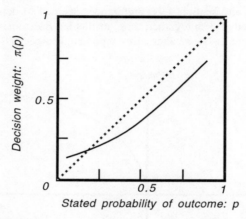

Figure 5.3: The weighting function suggested by Kahneman and Tversky

It was with rather mixed feelings that I chose to include the Kahneman and Tversky (1979) paper in my (1988a) collection *Behavioural Economics*. At first, it appears a piece of work that is very much in the spirit of behavioural economics: it has been inspired by careful empirical investigation of the limitations of the SEU theory and is based explicitly upon knowledge of psychological biases that seem to impinge on decision processes. However, apart from the applications suggested by Thaler (1980), it seems rather distant from the complexities of the kinds of risky choices that are common outside of the laboratory. Two features deserve particular attention. First, it should be noted that, although the value function hypothesized by Kahneman and Tversky involves gains and losses, Prospect Theory was not constructed to make sense of situations in which the decision-maker could come out either better off or worse off as a result of taking a gamble. None of the experiments conducted by Kahneman and Tversky had this form. They all involved gambling about either alternative probable gains with no risk of ending up worse off, or about alternative probable losses with no chance to end up better off. These experiments miss the essence of many of the gambles that we undertake in real life. Often, when we take a chance, we are not choosing merely between different ways of possibly making a gain. Rather, we are also simultaneously choosing between alternative down-side risks. As Ford (1987: 128) observes, Prospect Theory's 'value function might well be appropriate to such situations; but it has never been utilized to handle them'. Secondly, it should also be noted that the kinds of experiments whose results Kahneman and Tversky sought to make sense of with Prospect Theory were very simple lottery experiments. In each of their experiments, subjects were asked which of two fixed-odds bets they preferred. Each bet normally involved only a pair of rival outcomes (at most three outcomes, in the first experiment, one of which was zero gain) to each of which the experimenter had attached a probability. These are very different gambles from the risky choices people often have to take in the world of business, where a number of relevant outcomes, such as sales, profits, reliability rates and so on may be conceived of along scales and where decision-makers have to guess for themselves how likely it is that they might end up at any particular point on each scale. In such situations, bounded rationality may get in the way of attempts to calculate expected utilities (cf. Simon, 1983 and section 5.7) and render debates about the shapes of value functions somewhat pointless.

These two limitations apply equally to Regret Theory, proposed by Loomes and Sugden (1982) as an alternative way of making sense of the experimental results reported by Kahneman and Tversky. Loomes and Sugden agreed that SEU theory seemed to be in need of modification but they felt that Prospect Theory involved a rather more complex and *ad hoc* set of assumptions than they needed for their Regret Theory. Loomes and Sugden suggest that a careful distinction should be drawn between two kinds of utility that people may derive if they find themselves in a particular situation. One kind is *choiceless utility*, how they would feel if they arrived in the situation without having chosen it (for example, due to some natural force or government decree). The other kind they called *modified utility*, which is choiceless utility modified by feelings of regret or rejoicing that arise because of a recognition of the difference between 'what is' and 'what might have been'. Regret is a loss of pleasure due to knowledge that if a different choice had been made a better outcome would have been possible. Rejoicing is extra pleasure due to knowledge that things could have come out worse if the preferred gamble had not been taken. Loomes and Sugden suggest we should think of decision-makers as if they attempt to maximize the expected value of modified utility, and they claim SEU theory has been in error due to focusing on choiceless utilities and ignoring ways in which feelings of expected regret or rejoicing may affect expected utility.

To make this idea clearer, imagine you are facing one of the dilemmas posed by Kahneman and Tversky: either a 0.20 probability of receiving 4 000, or a 0.25 probability of receiving 3 000. Whatever you choose, you cannot be sure what would have happened if you made the reverse choice. Suppose you gamble on getting the 4 000 but are unlucky. Not merely do you get zero; you are also left thinking you *might* instead have gained 3 000. How far you modify the expected value you place on the gamble will depend on what determines your expected feelings of regret. For example, they might depend on both the size of the gain you might instead have got (in this case, 3 000) and on the probability of getting it. Loomes and Sugden themselves use a very simple model of how the degree of regret or rejoicing is worked out—they assume it depends only on the choiceless utility of 'what is' and the choiceless utility of 'what might have been'—but this is enough to enable them to use Regret Theory to make sense of the experimental evidence presented by Kahneman and Tversky.

A third line of constructive criticism of SEU theory has come from Blatt (1983: 253–7), who calls into question the idea that probabilities of very poor attainments can, in principle, always be swamped by suitably large and seemingly probable prospects of good attainments. To illustrate his contention, Blatt considers an illegal gamble—importing heroin into a south-east Asian country—which will result in a death sentence if one is discovered, but which otherwise is very profitable. He then argues that, although it is rare for a would-be criminal to be deterred by a one-in-a-million chance of 'being hanged on the gallows', most such people are deterred when they judge the probability of hanging is *too* high and the probability of survival *too* small 'for the game to be worth the candle'. If they refuse ever-more lucrative offers on this basis, they are violating the Axiom of Archimedes which is one of the key assumptions of SEU theory (as of Hicksian consumer theory: see section 3.2), for they are by implication denying that 'everything has its price'.

The clear implication of this critique is that a fully additive view of risk-taking may be misleading, so Blatt (1983: 279–82) favours following a 'safety first' approach, after Roy (1952). This involves two stages: first, exclude projects with an excessive probability of disaster; second (and here he returns to the additive methodology), rank non-excluded projects in terms of their expected returns. This approach is akin to a characteristic filtering/additive differences hybrid procedure of the kind discussed in section 4.2, except that it all takes place with respect to a single characteristic axis.

5.4   Shackle's potential surprise theory

For many years George Shackle (1949, 1958, 1970, 1979) presented an alternative critique of the SEU model of choice, based on his worries about its philosophical foundations. His main objection was that the probability concept is essentially concerned with relative frequencies of outcomes, whereas choices that are significant—because they are felt likely to make a difference to the unfolding pattern of events—are essentially unique acts. His work overlaps with earlier thinking by Knight (1921) which sought to distinguish between risk and uncertainty. In the aggregate, things may seem to repeat themselves as probabilistic patterns: for example, young males have a predictably higher probability of being involved in motor accidents than do middle-aged women, and 'hot hatchback' motor cars have a higher probability of being stolen than do the low-performance models on which they are based. Such patterns of risk are very much the kind of thing that insurance company actuaries spend their working lives thinking about. However, these probability distributions do not represent uncertainties for the insurance company if the overall environment is not seen as uncertain: insurance company actuaries may not know *who* will have an accident or precisely whose car will be stolen, but they may have a very good idea indeed about *how many* clients of a particular kind *will* have accidents involving particular medical and damage expenses. Matters are different at the level of the individual: things either happen or they do not. For example, one in four motorists in a particular risk category might have a crash in a year, but an individual motorist in this driver category will not have a quarter of a crash, nor will s/he necessarily have one crash every four years or, indeed, any crashes at all within her/his lifetime. The individual faces uncertainty, just as an insurance company faces uncertainty when its customers' environments change and established patterns break down or when it is considering offering a new kind of insurance for which no past records exist. For example, a couple of decades ago, the insurance of satellite launches was a leap into the unknown. It may still be an uncertain business in so far as there have been too few launches of a sufficiently similar kind for patterns to emerge.

Shackle argued that if statistical regularities are seen as irrelevant to one's choice and/or if outcomes are seen simply as mutually exclusive possibilities, then it makes no sense to add up rival outcomes to get an overall expected utility: a bad outcome in prospect will seem no less bad if it is a rival to an imagined good outcome, and its undesirability will not diminish if one suddenly thinks of an even better alternative possible outcome. Yet, in SEU theory, the addition of an extra state of the world with a non-zero probability attached to it will result in a down-grading of the probabilities attached to hitherto-considered future states of the world. The only way this can be avoided is if this extra state of the world is plucked from a category of 'residual hypotheses', comprising 'other unspecified things that I have not yet thought about as possibilities'. Although one might imagine people being able to express the uncertainties they were choosing to shoulder in terms of subjective probabilities, or as equivalent to bets involving particular odds, Shackle preferred instead a theory which was neither additive nor related to a distributional concept. He originally proposed his theory as a descriptive approximation of the kind of thought process people may go through when faced with uncertain choices. It has not been the subject of much empirical investigation: a rare contribution is an experimental study by Hey (1985) who found problems with both Shackle's theory and the conventional probabilistic analysis. However, the critique of probabilistic thinking that it is based on may mean that, even if it does not serve very well as a contribution to positive economics, it still warrants consideration for its normative content, as a device for helping people take better decisions when they face an uncertain future (cf. the discussion of scenario planning in the section 5.6).

In conventional treatments of SEU theory, little attention is given to the possibility of incompleteness in the list of rival possible states of the world that decision-makers have in mind. In SEU theory, history may affect the probabilities that people assign to future events but it does not lead them to change the list of events to which they are assigning probabilities. Shackle, by contrast, noted the scope for lists of possibilities suddenly to be enlarged or contracted by the creative use of the imagination, especially in the light of rumours and the 'state of the news'. He also highlighted the extent to which surprises, both actual and expected, are part of everyday life. (Steinbruner, 1974, has commented rather similarly about the tendency of people often to worry extensively about things that never happen only to find themselves, in the event, faced with situations that they had not even considered as possibilities.) Hence Shackle made the concept of surprise a central feature of his alternative theory.

If the world is full of surprises, it looks rather illogical to think of the idea of a certain prospect, an event with a probability of one. At best we might be able imagine an outcome which seems *perfectly possible*, because, at present, we can think of no potentially insurmountable barriers to its taking place. But perfect possibility must not be confused with certainty: this confusion is most easily avoided if we remember that a person may sometimes think of a number of rival events as perfectly possible (as in 'Things could go either way; I can't see anything to stop either outcome'), whereas a number of rival events cannot logically be assigned probabilities of unity.

If we presently see an event as perfectly possible, we will not expect to be surprised if it actually comes about. But when we can imagine particular outcomes in whose way we envisage potentially insurmountable obstacles, we are thinking of possibilities that we expect would surprise us somewhat if they happened. At the other end of the spectrum there may be some events which seem to have enough potentially lying in their way to make them seem potentially astonishing in prospect: nothing could be more surprising than to see them happen (flying pigs, for example). If we can imagine how surprised we would be to see a particular event actually take place at a particular point in time, then Shackle would say we are in a position to assign a rating of *potential surprise* to that event. He assumes that an event which is seen as perfectly possible has a rating of zero on a potential surprise scale. Maximum potential surprise ratings would be assigned to events that have been imagined but whose taking place would cause astonishment, amazement or a state of complete disbelief. If we say we feel certain that something will occur then, in Shackle's terms, what we are really saying is that we can see no reason why that outcome should not eventuate *and* that we can only imagine alternative outcomes that would cause us complete astonishment if, indeed, we can imagine any alternative outcomes at all.

A set of rival future events and their associated potential surprise ratings can be plotted on a two-dimensional diagram as a 'potential surprise curve'. Shackle was normally writing about investment decisions in which an entrepreneur was thinking about possible gains and losses relative to some safe reference point, *N*. This reference point Shackle called a neutral outcome, and sometimes he likened it to the notion of an aspiration level (for example, see Shackle, 1958: 48–9). In this sort of case, the neutral outcome could refer to a seemingly risk-free strategy in which only one outcome seems possible and there are no reasons to believe it might not occur if the strategy is chosen—for example a strategy of playing safe by leaving the investment funds in a government-guaranteed bank account on a fixed interest deposit. The potential surprise curve for such a strategy would be T-shaped. Figure 5.4 shows how a single scheme's prospects might look to such an entrepreneur. It looks like it *might* turn out better than the neutral outcome, but there are also partially or wholly believable possible losses to think about. If the potential surprise curves for other schemes cross this scheme's potential surprise curve, or if they lie inside it, it is not obvious whether a risk should be taken (if *N* seems perfectly achievable by playing safe) or which seemingly risky venture should be selected.

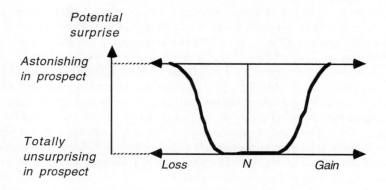

Figure 5.4: A potential surprise curve

The next element in Shackle's theory is the *ascendancy function*, which he constructed after thinking carefully about how people might deal with conflicting possibilities of the kind just raised. He argued that some prospective outcomes will tend to have a greater attention-arresting potential—greater 'ascendancy'—than others. A decision-maker will not be attracted to think at great length about prospective outcomes close to the neutral outcome. Nor will s/he be much interested in very large gains that seem practically unbelievable in prospect. However, s/he will be drawn to consider carefully sizeable prospective gains and losses, the more so the less easy they are to disbelieve. From this line of thinking Shackle postulated an ascendancy function, which can be depicted graphically, as in Figure 5.5, as a set of curves which refer to outcome/potential surprise combinations with identical power to catch the chooser's attention. The iso-ascendancy curves are rather like indifference curves: the most attention-arresting outcomes are those located towards the bottom right and bottom left of the diagram.

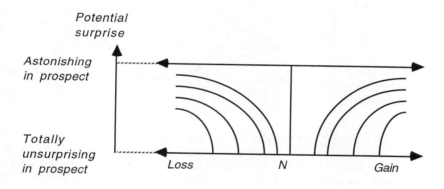

Figure 5.5: The ascendancy function

The ascendancy function and potential surprise curves are all depicted in cardinalist terms, relating to degrees of potential surprise and measurable outcomes. If the potential surprise curves take the kind of shape depicted in Figure 5.4 and are superimposed on the ascendancy function in Figure 5.5, then it will be found that each potential surprise curve has two points of tangency with the iso-ascendancy curves, one on the loss side of N and one on the gain side. Shackle called these the 'primary focus loss' and 'primary focus gain' points for each scheme. These pairs of focus points are the most attention-arresting possibilities imagined for each scheme. There is no reason to expect rival schemes to have identical primary focus outcomes, or for their respective primary focus gains and losses to have identical degrees of potential surprise. This being so, the problem is to compare rival pairs of focus outcomes, but to do so without adding them up (for that would take us back to the kind of philosophy that Shackle was rejecting).

Shackle's first stage in resolving this problem was to note that for each primary focus outcome of a potential surprise curve there exists a hypothetical outcome, off the curve in question but on the gain/loss axis, which would have identical attention-arresting power if it were imagined as a perfectly possible outcome for a rival scheme. Shackle called these types of points 'standardized focus outcomes'. Figure 5.6 shows primary and standardized focus gains and losses for a single scheme of action. Here, *A* represents the primary focus loss, *B* the standardized focus loss, *C* the primary focus gain, and *D* the standardized focus gain. The 'standardization' process means that pairs of attention-grabbing gains and losses can be compared without one having to worry about differences in potential surprise ratings. A somewhat surprising primary focus gain or loss is just as exciting or terrifying in prospect as would be its standardized focus equivalent *if* the latter were imagined as a perfect possibility.

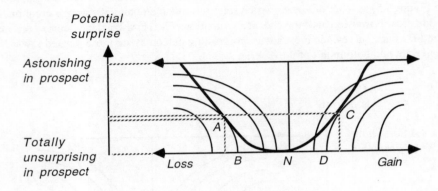

Figure 5.6: Primary and standardized focus gains and losses

Shackle then suggested that we should imagine decision-makers comparing rival pairs of standardized focus outcomes with respect to their *gambler preferences*: their willingness to make tradeoffs between standardized focus gains and standardized focus losses. The curves on Figure 5.7 show how Shackle thought such preferences might be summed up in general terms. The chooser would prefer to be facing schemes whose standardized focus gains and losses implied points on the top left of the diagram. The gambler indifference curves slope upwards to the right because the chooser is assumed to prefer to avoid the prospect of a loss. Each rival scheme's pair of standardized focus outcomes can be represented as a single point on the gambler preference map. The particular gambler preference curve that cuts through the origin on the bottom-left of Figure 5.7 shows gain/loss combinations that would be only as attractive to the chooser as the scheme of action that is seen as the safe ('reference point') scheme for which outcomes less than *N*, the neutral outcome, seem inconceivable. In other words, the scheme whose standardized focus points imply point *U* on this diagram involves taking a risk, but it is rated the same as the reference point scheme. Schemes represented by points on curves to the right of the one that passes through the origin involve gambles that are seen as worse than the neutral scheme. These curves may tend to bunch together on the right-hand side as shown if there is a maximum tolerable prospect of loss that the chooser is prepared knowingly to confront. The scheme which dominates is the scheme whose standardized focus outcomes pairing imply a point on a higher gambler indifference curve than the curves on which any of its rivals' respective points are located.

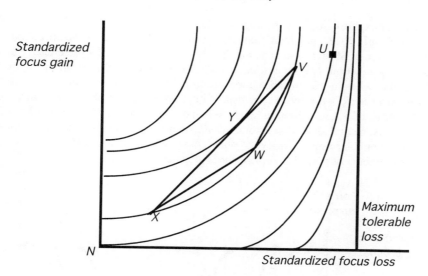

Figure 5.7: A gambler preference map

If several schemes tie for the first place, it may be possible for the chooser to do better in prospect by considering schemes involving combinations of the schemes that have already been considered. This was perfectly feasible with the sorts of portfolio investment schemes that Shackle often considered, for these would normally involve divisible parcels of shares. Shackle assumed that when this was done total focus values of mixed asset choices would be linear combinations of the total focus values of the schemes involving single asset portfolios. In other words, by spending all of his or her money on assets *V*, *W* or *X*, the person might be able to choose between their respective focus pairs *V*, *W* or *X* on Figure 5.7. However, by combining, say, *X* and *W*, points on the chord linking *X* and *W* become feasible. This may be fine until one starts considering how many different assets it might pay to hold at any one time. On the analysis so far presented, the potential surprise model produces the empirically anomalous prediction that people will not hold any more than two types of asset in their portfolios. For example, a combination of *X* and *V* in such proportions as to give point *Y* dominates over any other scheme shown as feasible on the diagram.

Such a peculiar result is one reason why, despite its carefully considered philosophical underpinnings, the Shackle model has had limited success in achieving acceptance as a way of summarizing the process of choice in the face of perceived uncertainty. For my own part, I have felt uneasy about the jump from primary focus gains, via the standardization process, to the gambler preference map. This final section of the model seems to me to conflict with Shackle's desire to avoid reducing uncertain rival prospects to a single value. The process also seems so convoluted as to seem likely to be a poor approximation to the kind of thinking through which a boundedly rational decision-maker might go. Worse still, and despite Shackle's own claims to the contrary, it seems to involve a double-counting of attitudes to gains and losses: the attention-arresting capacity of a particular prospect might be expected to depend on the decision-maker's willingness to forgo prospects for gains in order to avoid imagined scope for making losses.

Such difficulties led my own thinking (Earl, 1983b, 1986) in the direction of a satisficing version of Shackle's model, which does without the gambler preference map and the ascendancy function. My suggestion is very simple and is summed up in Figure 5.8. The idea is that where a person can see reasons to doubt that a scheme of action will lead her/him to meet her/his aspirations in respect of a dimension of choice s/he then starts thinking in terms of a gain aspiration level (*AG*) and a loss-avoidance aspiration level (*AL*) either side of the neutral aspiration level (*AN*) s/he is hoping to attain. S/he also pairs with each of these 'gambler aspiration levels' other constraints, *SAG* and *SAL*, respectively, in respect of the amount of potential surprise she is prepared to embrace.

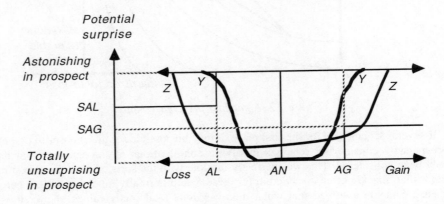

Figure 5.8: A 'two point test' filter for rival potential surprise curves

For a scheme to be deemed an acceptable bet when its outcome is perceived as uncertain it must pass both of the following tests: (a) Would the chooser not feel unduly surprised to see an outcome equal to or in excess of her/his gain aspiration level for the dimension in question? (b) Would the chooser expect to be sufficiently astonished if s/he incurred losses equal to or in excess of her/his loss-avoidance aspiration level? Figure 5.8 shows potential surprise curves for a pair of rival schemes, *YY* and *ZZ*. *ZZ* passes the gain aspiration test, but looks altogether too likely to produce an outcome equal to or worse than the loss-avoidance aspiration. On the other hand, scheme *YY* passes the loss-avoidance test but seems insufficiently promising in respect of the gain aspiration. In this case the decision-maker must either search for something better or consider which failing is the least bad one.

5.5 Exam post-mortem: Shackle's model versus expected utility theory

Question
Does George Shackle's 'potential surprise' model of economic decision-making under uncertainty represent a significant analytical advance on the probabilistic 'expected utility'

models of how people decide which risks to take? Justify your answer.

Examiner's report

This was one of the least popular questions and it was in most cases poorly answered. It was often seen as an opportunity to reproduce Shackle's theory with the main focus being on its graphical elements. Technical errors were quite common, ranging from iso-ascendancy curves that were the wrong way up, to expositions in which the gambler preference map was portrayed as an altogether separate model, unrelated to the potential surprise curves and iso-ascendancy curves. Other students chose to regurgitate expected utility theory, sometimes in terms of a choice-of-universities example taken from Frank (1991: 187) without any great explanation of what was going on and as if the particular form of the utility function used in this example were the form generally required for the theory.

These regurgitationist answers typically failed to address the question head-on by considering what advantages the Shackle model might have and whether or not it had flaws of its own. Those that *did* note that Shackle was rejecting the notion of probability often did not point out the difference between risk and uncertainty or explain its significance (the wording of the question is actually carefully chosen so that Shackle's model is attached to uncertainty and the expected utility model is attached to risk, but this hint was missed). A surprising number claimed that Shackle believed that 'anything is possible'; from such a starting point, coherent explanations of the nature of a potential surprise curve were unlikely to follow.

It would actually have been possible to score very highly on this question without ever drawing any of Shackle's diagrams. Instead, one could simply assume that the examiner was familiar with them and concentrate on the differences between Shackle's model and the conventional one, and the extent to which these represent advances. However, it might be necessary to draw an appropriate gambler preference map to show that one was on top of the difficulty concerning the unfortunate prediction of the potential surprise model that people will select no more than two assets for their portfolios.

Discussions of the adequacy of the predictive powers of either model would have been most welcome, but none were forthcoming, despite discussions of this issue in various items on the subject's reading list (for example, Earl, 1986; Thaler, 1980). More generally, no one bothered to pause to think aloud (the ideal place would have been in their introductions) on the question of how they would differentiate a significant analytical advance from a trivial one or from no advance at all. A set of methodological criteria—such as empirical adequacy, logical coherence, mathematical tractability, assumptive realism, simplicity or philosophical appeal—would have provided the basis for an immediate structure for an answer in the form of a paragraph on each criterion.

5.6 Scenario planning

Uncertainty about the future would be far less of a problem for decision-makers if the commitments they make today could easily be reversed if they seem poorly matched to the state of the world that subsequently materializes. In an ideal world, a mistaken investment decision would be overturned simply by firing or redeploying workers and selling physical assets for their new prices less an amount that reflected their physical depreciation. In the real world, severance payments or retraining costs may have to be incurred and differences between new and secondhand prices are far more marked than physical rates of depreciation might lead one to expect. If many people conclude they have made the same mistake and try to sell simultaneously, they may have great trouble finding anyone who wants to buy what they are selling. However, even when there is not a gross imbalance between supply and demand, mistaken decisions may still be expensive to reverse depending on (i) the degree of specificity and immobility of the item that needs to be sold, (ii) how hard it is for prospective buyers to judge its condition, and (iii) the haste with which one tries to find a buyer (see further, Earl, 1995b). Even if buyers can be found for equipment that is no longer wanted, managers who have come to regret their previous investment decisions may find themselves in a long queue for deliveries of the capital goods they are regretting not ordering in the first place.

As an example of how it pays to be able to foretell the future, consider the profit implications of the following rival types of cost structure for a firm whose managers have to attach a price to its product without knowing how many units they will be able to sell:

Technology A: Fixed costs of $1 000 000 and constant marginal costs (and hence constant average variable costs) of $10 up to a maximum annual capacity of 75 000 units.

Technology B: Fixed costs of $2 000 000 and constant marginal costs (and hence constant average variable costs) of $5 up to a maximum annual capacity of 150 000 units.

Suppose a price of $P = \$25$ per unit is quoted. To find the break-even rate of sales in each case we set total costs equal to total revenue (that is, price multiplied by quantity $= 25Q$) and solve for quantity. Break-even quantities differ markedly:

Technology A: break-even is given by $25Q = 1 000 000 + 10Q$ where $Q = 66 667$

Technology B: break-even is given by $25Q = 2 000 000 + 5Q$ where $Q = 100 000$.

If sales at $25 per unit turn out to be only 70 000, then bottom-line outcomes are:

Technology A gives a profit of $25(70 000) - 1 000 000 - 10(70 000) = \$50 000$

Technology B produces a loss of $25(70 000) - 2 000 000 - 5(70 000) = \$600 000$.

However, if there turns out to be sales potential for 125 000 units, then technology A suffers badly from insufficient capacity, whereas technology B is still inside its maximum rate of output. In this case results are:

Technology A generates profits of only $25(75 000) - 1 000 000 - 10(75 000) = \$125 000$

Technology B generates profits of $25(125 000) - 2 000 000 - 5(125 000) = \$500 000$.

Before a choice of production method is made, it clearly pays to have accurate sales forecasts. It is thus not surprising that many firms hire graduate economists with skills in econometric modelling and expect them to earn their keep by providing forecasts. As yet, relatively few are hired to assist with scenario planning, an activity for improving the quality of decision-making that makes bigger demands of skills in economics than in quantitative methods.

Scenario planning is based on a premise that makes many people uncomfortable, namely, that it is impossible to foretell the future and possibly dangerous to attempt to do so. In the English-speaking world, it is most associated with the Shell International Petroleum Company, some of whose planners have been influenced by Shackle's emphasis on possibility and surprise and his critique of the concept of probability (see Jefferson, 1983; Loasby, 1990b). It is also a technique to which French planners are strongly attracted (for example, Godet, 1987) and which has been employed by some firms in Australasia (see the chapter by Mercer in McKern and Lowenthal, eds, 1985); a useful guide to the practicalities of the technique is to be found in Schoemaker (1991). Both the French and Shackle-inspired scenario-planning enthusiasts stress the role of human action in shaping how events unfold. From their standpoint even the word 'unfold' is rather inappropriate, since they see the future as something which is yet to be *created by people who choose after using their imaginations to think creatively about what to do and what others might do*; the future is not something that could be foretold if only people suffered less from bounded rationality and were more adept at unravelling chains of causality (see Godet, 1987: 5). However, they would not underplay the difficulties that complexity causes for those trying to anticipate events, particularly in so far as they recognize that contributions to modern physics have shown how, in non-linear systems, small events can have major impacts upon the kind of history that subsequently gets constructed (see Buchanan and Vanberg, 1991)

To claim that forecasting is impossible is, of course, a rather extreme way of drawing attention to the frequency with which decision-makers are prone to suffer expensive surprises. It is true that senior managers and corporate planners in most organizations are not constantly being astonished by the way that events unfold. If people actually found it impossible to form bounded conjectures of how the future might unfold, and if events did not normally tend to come out within the expected bounds of possibility, then economic affairs would tend to be very chaotic indeed. Economic activity would rather resemble life in a less-developed country that was suffering from civil war: a place where 'anything might happen'. Scenario planners are thus not the sort of people who are surprised when they wake up in the morning and discover that the sun has risen again and they have not been murdered in their beds overnight. Rather, they are aware that business history is littered with instances of fiascoes that might have been avoided if decision-makers had not tried to predict precisely what would happen and had instead concentrated more on considering the range and implications of possible ways in which the future might unfold.

The extrapolation of trends to generate forecasts is a good example of the kind of behaviour that scenario planners frown upon. A transport economist who used extrapolation as a technique to predict the time at which new runways would be necessary at major city airports in the mid-1960s would probably have overestimated the urgency of beginning construction. Such an economist would have been wise to consider factors that might change the course of the trend line, such as:

(a) Previous trends in demand for air transport might have been reflecting the take-off phase of cheap package holidays, after which growth might be far less spectacular.

(b) On the one hand, the growth of demand for runway space might be limited by the advent of wide-body jets (such as the Boeing 747) which may or may not already be undergoing development; on the other hand, perhaps such jets might cut air transport costs so much that passenger numbers might increase at an even faster rate and lead to more flights in total despite the greater capacity of wide-body jets.

(c) The development of less noisy jet engines might affect the hours that aircraft could be allowed to use airports where noise regulations were in force.

(d) Improvements in air traffic control technologies might enable more aircraft to be stacked safely in the sky at any one time whilst waiting to land.

(e) There might be changes in airport landing fees to ration scarce landing space.

(f) There might be significant changes in the cost of aviation fuel and in the costs of providing security to passengers.

(g) There might be an increase in the use made of smaller towns' airports, facilitated by the development of less noisy jets with shorter runway requirements.

(h) Demand for airport services into and out of the city in question might depend on the capacity of airports at destination and departure cities.

In the case of air traffic into and out of London, extrapolation led some to argue in the 1960s that it was imperative to begin construction of a third airport; thirty years later, however, London is still getting by without a new airport having been constructed. The cost of having public inquiries into a possible third London airport may have seemed high at the time, but it was small beside the cost of building an airport unnecessarily.

A scenario is a carefully argued narrative about a particular way in which the future *might* take shape. It is a story about what could happen if particular assumptions hold true. It is not an attempt to say what *will* happen. Rather, *the idea is to compare its implications with the implications of rival scenarios and then examine the costs of being prepared to cope with the kinds of futures that are being touted as possibilities.* For example, in 1978, while several oil companies were reputedly still planning for the mid-1980s on the basis of specific forecasts for oil prices, in spite of all the obvious unpredictabilities, Shell was thinking of the implications of oil prices ranging from $15 to $50 per barrel. Rival scenarios often have very different implications, as in the numerical example earlier in this section. Sometimes, however, very different stories might produce rather similar implications. An example here might be what could happen to the demand for petrol under high growth and low growth scenarios. High growth might lead more people to upgrade their cars with more modern ones that were more fuel efficient; low growth might limit the number of people who could afford cars and this might hold back overall fuel demand by reducing the growth in the number of vehicles in use even though the average age and fuel efficiency of cars did not fall so rapidly.

The comparison of rival scenarios is not intended immediately to point towards a particular decision but rather to alert the decision-makers both to the kinds of risks they might be running if they choose particular courses of action and to the costs and benefits of choosing between schemes that differ in their degrees of flexibility. This may lead them to dream up further possible courses of action, rather than allowing themselves to be focused on a particular strategy via wishful thinking and dissonance-reducing thoughts and arguments (cf. section 4.7).

When first experimenting with the technique, Shell's strategists tried to come to terms with as many as seven scenarios, but this was soon found to be unworkable due to bounded rationality. Cutting the number to three also proved a failure: there was a tendency to focus on the middle case as if it was the one that would actually eventuate. Scenario planners at Shell were subsequently divided into two teams to explore a pair of very different scenarios (best and worst imaginable) about world developments over the next 15 years in areas of society, politics, economics and technology. These scenarios embrace a wide spectrum of possible developments and combinations of them. They cover five years ahead and are updated annually. They are short on figures and strong on qualitative arguments, presented as starkly contrasting pairs in order to force Shell executives continually to question their assumptions. Neither scenario is expected to be right but, by raising the intellectual level of debate, a comparison of scenarios is likely to lead to the choice of strategies that are resilient or capable of rapid modification in a world of surprises. For example, suppose Shell has tried to ensure that it can adapt relatively easily to the best and worse chains of events that its planners can imagine. If events actually fall outside this range, the managers may be rather surprised but they will be far better placed to stave off disaster or grasp opportunities than they would have been had they tailored their strategy closely around a single, middle-line forecast.

Despite its opposition to extrapolative modelling, the scenario planning philosophy recognizes the potential worth of looking at history as a guide to what could happen. For example, Jefferson (1983: 153, 159) reports how, soon after the 1973 oil crisis, his colleagues at Shell studied how rapidly cartels collapsed: an examination of over thirty historical studies led them to be far less optimistic than many American academics who forecast a rapid demise for OPEC cartel.

Scenario construction requires a certain degree of skill in open-minded and creative thinking: Loasby (1990b) shows how a 'scenarios mentality' is something that firms have to work at, rather than being the natural way of thinking about possible returns to investments. This rather suggests that Shackle's theory of decision-making under uncertainty is best seen as a normative tool rather than as a contribution to positive economics. Even within Shell, perhaps the company whose senior managers are closest to Shackle in their views on uncertainty and choice, scenarios essentially concern events that might occur in the firm's *external* environment and they are worked out prior to the formulation of a potential course of action. Loasby gives the impression that Shell's managers seem to take their firm's environment as outside their control, yet are confident of their ability to produce particular results given a particular environment. They should ideally be asking questions about which outcomes might be produced by the policies they try to implement with the aid of their colleagues and capital equipment: workers and machinery *might* perform better *or* worse than in the past, particularly if placed under greater stress than usual.

To end this section I think it is interesting to note that, in developing their scenario-planning philosophy, senior staff at Shell encountered resistance from colleagues that has much in common with the kind of resistance that students may offer when asked to study economics in the way advocated in this book (cf. the discussion of the work of Perry, 1970, in section 1.2). Shell's top planners had been disturbed by the quality of their own estimates and were beginning, after conducting a lengthy study of how the world might evolve towards the year 2000, to be worried by the possibility of an energy crisis and a generally turbulent corporate environment. They developed the method as a means of learning to cope with a great deal of uncertainty over oil supplies, prices and related issues. As Jefferson (1983) explains, proponents of this philosophy took nearly eight years to convince all the main sectors of the company of the worth of scenario planning. To most people, planning is an activity that should reduce uncertainty rather than increase awareness of it. Managers at all levels tended to crave certainty and hated questioning their key assumptions. They found it very difficult to accept the advice that the world may be like *A* ten or fifteen years from now, or again it may be like *B*, entirely different. Even with the number of scenarios cut to two there remained a tendency for uncertainty-avoiding managers still to try to produce single-line forecasts by drawing a line up the middle of the wide spectrum. In the end, top management's attempts to get scenario planning accepted were helped by some expensive investment failures (including a £300 million loss in a joint venture with Gulf Oil over a high temperature reactor, and a £25 million failure with a polyethylene plant near Manchester) and by upheavals in Iran which eventually toppled the Shah. These upheavals had been part of an 'accident' scenario for 18 months before they occurred: the uncertain element (and the reason for the 'accident' label) applied not to whether the troubles would occur in Iran, but when.

5.7 Procedural approaches for coping with ignorance and uncertainty

The decision-making methods discussed so far in this chapter all presume that it is possible for decision-makers to assign some boundaries to the knowledge problems that confront them. Sometimes, however, decision-makers may feel that they 'haven't got a clue' or 'simply do not know' about the decision environment in which they may find themselves at some point in the future. This feeling of overwhelming uncertainty may arise for two opposing reasons. One is that all the scenarios that come to mind may seem perfectly possible and yet these scenarios may differ in terms of their implications for preparatory actions. The other case is where people are utterly unable to imagine any scenarios at all: they cannot conceive what might happen if they place themselves in a particular situation. A particularly obvious instance of potentially overwhelming uncertainty may be the problem of preparing for an examination. Some students may be able imagine a huge array of possible questions but know that they can only prepare adequately for a limited number of them; others may have no idea of the sorts of things they might be asked. When anxious students such as these set out for the exam hall they may have prepared not merely via last-minute reading of course materials but also by taking precautions such as:

(a) seeing what their 'stars' have to offer by way of advice;
(b) making sure that they get out of bed from the 'right side';
(c) making sure that they have not forgotten the 'lucky mascot' that accompanied them on their past successes;
(d) desperately spending many hours not in revision but in attempting to spot, on the basis of past 'patterns', the questions that *will* eventuate, even though their examiners may

have warned them that topics would be selected at random from amongst those on the syllabus.

The stakes may be high, but the preparatory procedures are essentially *superstitious* in nature: the examinees in these cases are relying on beliefs that particular events are causally linked even though they would find it very difficult to explain precisely how.

Now, one might hope that people might grow out of such 'unscientific' modes of behaviour once they have graduated (as many will, even after wasting their time on 'question spotting' and so on). But Gimpl and Dakin (1984: 125) have argued that, in the turbulent and unpredictable world of business,

> management's enchantment with the magical rites of long-range planning, forecasting, and several other future-oriented techniques is a manifestation of anxiety-relieving superstitious behaviour, and ... forecasting and planning have the same function that magical rites have. Anthropologists and psychologists have long argued that magical rites and superstitious behaviour serve very important functions: they make the world seem more deterministic and give us confidence in our ability to cope; they unite the managerial tribe, and they induce us to take action, at least when the omens are favourable.

Maital (1982: 230) has come to a similar conclusion concerning the means by which people seek to arrange their savings in portfolios of securities which trade in that most random of markets, the stock market. Nowadays it is simple even for quite small savers to obtain returns as good as the stock market index by putting their money in a unit trust based on the market index. Most people seem to find it very hard to accept the idea that the behaviour of share prices displays a random walk and instead they find it very easy to believe that, through careful study, it ought to be possible to develop predictive models of share price behaviour that will provide a way of consistently beating the performance of the index.

This is exactly the same kind of tendency that was evident in binary betting experiments reported by Simon (1959), in which subjects were asked to bet on which of two possible outcomes would eventuate. The experiments were set up so that the outcomes occurred in a ratio of two to one, but in a random sequence. Subjects soon discovered the ratio and started arranging their bets in a systematic manner, in order to try to win more than two-thirds of the time. Their refusal to accept the random aspect of the process meant that they ended up losing needlessly often. In the long run much the same fate awaits those who base their portfolio choices on the reputations of particular financial funds or advisory services. If it really were possible to forecast the behaviour of prices of financial assets, it would make little sense for those who knew how to construct such forecasts to set up in business providing advice to others: they would do far better by concentrating on speculating on their own accounts (cf. McCloskey, 1990). If stock markets are as random as most financial theorists believe them to be, then those investment advisers who claim to have developed forecasting systems, or who claim to be able to see patterns in past records that can be successfully extrapolated to the future ('chartists'), should be seen simply having recently been lucky to beat the market—or as having had access to inside information.

After following superstitious preparatory procedures and trying to force random events into predictable patterns, decision-makers may find that they do indeed 'not have a clue' about what they need to do to cope well in the choice environment that eventuates. Again, procedural responses may be observed. In the case of students who find themselves surprised by the questions for which they had not prepared, the preferred procedures seem to include the following:

(1) flee from the examination hall at the first possible opportunity;
(2) attempt to copy the answers of those at a nearby desk;
(3) write down absolutely everything that comes into their heads and which seems even vaguely related to the questions that they attempt to answer;
(4) attempt questions despite knowing nothing about certain parts of them, and answer as if these parts did not exist at all (often after having impulsively chosen the question in the belief that it will be possible to remember pertinent material before running out of time);
(5) try to avoid specific commitments by being vague when they are not sure;
(6) answer multiple-choice questions with random guesses, or according to some deterministic procedure that relates their ignorance-based answers to their confident answers (for example, the last two were definitely option (a) answers; they wouldn't have set three of these in a row, surely...');
(7) sit and wait for inspiration.

These responses to ignorance or uncertainty can be summed up in procedural terms with phrases such as 'choose impulsively to narrow down the range of things about which it is necessary to worry' (cf. Earl, 1992a), 'hedge, hesitate, or toss a coin' (cf. Carter, 1953: 819), 'ignore things about which one is uncertain, or copy one's reference group in the belief that they are better informed' (cf. Keynes, 1937). These simple decision rules may also be employed when, despite being able to form bounded conjectures, decision-makers nonetheless find it hard to choose (or do not think of choosing) in the manner suggested by any of the theories considered in sections 5.2 to 5.4.

To end this section it is worthwhile to note the role of brand names as devices for assisting people to make decisions when they have little idea how to discriminate between alternative possible courses of action. When Olshavsky and Granbois (1979) refer to choices being 'made on the basis of surrogates of various types' (see section 4.1 for the longer quotation from which this comes), they may well have been thinking of consumers basing choices on brand reputations rather than on any detailed knowledge of what they are buying. Uncertainty may exist in consumers' minds not merely because they do not know what rival products' performances will turn out to be but also because they do not have the experience of that kind of product even to know what they *ought* to want from that kind of product. Retailers may be able to shed some light on the different features offered by rival brands and yet be unable to convince consumers which features they will really find themselves wanting. If previous experience with a product sold under a particular brand name (for example, a Canon camera or printer) seems to imply that the product's manufacturers are good at designing things that serve buyers well, then it might be reasonable to presume that it is quite safe to purchase the same brand when purchasing an unfamiliar but related product for the first time (for example, a Canon fax machine).

5.8 Bargaining

Few texts that are accessible to intermediate-level students provide a useful coverage on the subject of bargaining, despite the fact that it is an accepted aspect of the business of doing a deal in many contexts. A rare exception that provides a stimulating and well-referenced discussion is Casson's (1982) book on entrepreneurship. More recent but less concerned with haggling in business is the contribution of Elster (1989: chapter XIV), whose focus on the role of lawyers in bargaining over divorce settlements serves to highlight the possibility that on some occasions the opposing parties may find themselves bargaining over the sizes of slices of an ever-shrinking pie if they do not reach a settlement swiftly. The neglect of bargaining as a topic for analysis probably has much to do with the difficulties of reaching any clear-cut conclusions. The trouble is that bargaining is a problem of decision-making under uncertainty with an extra twist in the form of uncertainty about the opponent's way of coping with uncertainty. It is a game that involves a sequence of bids and counter bids and as time passes there is scope for the players to observe their opponent's behaviour and revise their expectations about the range within which they might be able to conclude a deal and which strategies and tactics seem particularly likely to help them reach such results.

5.8.1 Room for negotiation

The standard neoclassical tool for beginning investigations of bargaining is known as the Edgeworth Box, after the pioneering analysis of bilateral exchange worked out by F.Y. Edgeworth (1881: 26–9; 1925: 313–19). Edgeworth himself did not actually draw the box diagram that now bears his name but it is implied by his words and his own, rather different diagram. Edgeworth was focusing on scope for gains from trade in a two-person, two-good case and highlighted scope for indeterminacy as far as the ultimate contract is concerned. Figure 5.9 gives an example of an Edgeworth Box. Its size is determined by the amounts of the two goods, A and B, initially possessed by the two parties. He has an initial endowment of *AEH* of good A and *BEH* of good B, measured from the lower-left origin *OH*. She initially is endowed with *AES* and *BES*, measured from the upper-right origin *OS*. His preferences are shown as indifference curves sloping in the conventional way, convex to *OH*. Her preferences are shown as inverted indifference curves, convex to *OS*. Initially, the two decision-makers are at point X on their respective indifference curves that cut through each other at this point. (Point X is where a pair of lines drawn from perpendicular to the arrowheads on the axes would intersect.) Both would be better off if they could agree to any exchange of A and B that left the two parties somewhere in the speckled eliptical zone bounded by the pair of indifference curves. If he were fully informed about her preferences he would realize that the best outcome that he could achieve is point Y, where one of his higher-ranked indifference curves is tangential to the indifference curve that she is on initially. A move from X to Y, in which he gives up some of his A in exchange for some of her B, would be what is known as a 'Pareto improvement in economic efficiency': someone becomes better off without anyone else becoming worse off. But it is difficult here to see why she would bother to participate in such a deal unless for reasons of altruism. (Note the word 'bother' here: once bargaining costs are taken into account, it is possible a move from X to Y is not a Pareto improvement.) As far as she would be concerned, if she were fully informed of his preferences, then the best outcome would be Z, which leaves him no better off than at the start but is an improvement in her welfare which she cannot go beyond without him becoming worse off.

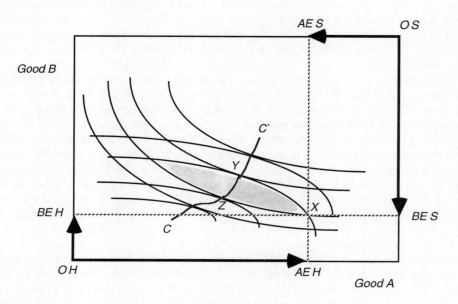

Figure 5.9: A neoclassical view of gains from trade

One of Edgeworth's key insights in exploring such possibilities was his conclusion that the deal ultimately concluded would lie somewhere between the points here labelled as Y and Z on the line CC', which he called the *contract-curve*. The contract-curve is found by joining together all the points at which her indifference curves are tangential to his indifference curves. Points on the contract-curve are nowadays described as Pareto-efficient allocations: he cannot make himself better off without making her worse off, and vice versa. If the two parties initially agree to a point that lies in the speckled elliptical area but is not on the contract curve, then they must be on indifference curves that intersect, just as did the indifference curves they were on at the starting point in our analysis, point X. There must now be a smaller elliptical area within which they could arrange to be by making a further exchange and, in so doing, they would both become better off. This logic would hold until they reached a point on the contract curve. But we have no means of saying how many stages might be involved or whether the final outcome would lie nearer to Y or to Z.

The Edgeworth Box has been adapted for the behavioural framework by Brooks (1988: 171–7), who uses his analysis to examine problems in the area of public economics. Instead of focusing on opposing sets of indifference curves, the Brooks box is based on the assumption that both decision-makers have aspiration levels in respect of the goods in question. Figure 5.10 depicts a pair of decision-makers with the same initial endowments as those depicted in Figure 5.9 but instead they set targets in respect of goods A and B rather than having preferences of a neoclassical kind. He presently has AEH of good A, but only

128

requires at least *ATH*, whereas she has *AES*, rather less than her target of *ATS*. She presently has *BES* of good *B*, much more than her requirement of *BTS*, whereas he has only *BEH* and wants *BTH*. Thus they both have reasons to begin bargaining.

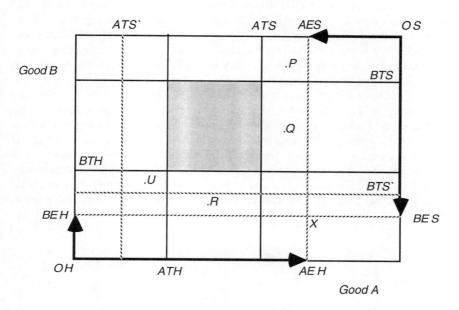

Figure 5.10: Satisficing and gains from bilateral exchange

Any outcome within the shaded area bounded by *ATH, BTH, ATS* and *BTS* will be perfectly satisfactory to both parties. However, other outcomes are conceivable if we allow that one or both parties might accept an outcome that is at least an improvement on the initial endowment even if it is not perfectly satisfactory. This could arise if they judged that the other party were not prepared to make a less demanding bid in order to prevent the deal from collapsing completely. For example, consider outcomes *P* and *Q*. Both of these would be perfectly satisfactory to him, for either would enable him to meet both his targets *ATH* and *BTH*. As far as she is concerned, whether *P* and/or *Q* are improvements on *X* will depend on how she ranks her targets in order of priority. Suppose she ranks *ATS* above *BTS*: both *P* and *Q* are closer to meeting *ATS* than her endowment was but only *Q* achieves this improvement without compromising her target *BTS*. Even so, in lexicographic terms, *P* is still an improvement on the initial endowment *X* for her first priority is to get to *ATS*, at least cost in terms of moving away from *BTS*. Thus if he suggests *P* as a deal, she might accept if she does not believe she can get a better deal at his expense. If she ranked *BTS* above *ATS*, then she would not accept *P* in preference to *X* since to do so would involve breaching her first priority in order to get closer to meeting her second one. However, once again *Q* would be preferred to the original endowment *X*. On this line of thinking, it seems possible for bargaining to take place and lead to mutually acceptable conclusions even where the aspirations of the two parties exceed the available amounts of the goods over which they are bargaining. For example, suppose she actually has much higher targets, *ATS`* and *BTS`*: here, *ATS`* + *ATH* > *AEH* + *AES* and *BTS`* + *BTH* > *BEH* + *BES*. It is impossible for both parties to meet both their targets. However, they might settle on an outcome such as *R*, for this gets him closer to meeting *BTH* without going below *ATH* and it gets her closer to meeting *ATS`* without going below *BTS`*. If he ranked *BTH* above *ATH* and she ranked *ATS`* above *BTS`*, they might settle on a point such as *U*: both would be falling short of their second priorities rather than meeting them as they had with their initial endowments, but both are closer to meeting their first priorities.

It would be perfectly possible to combine elements of both the Edgeworth and Brooks diagrams to construct a hybrid model of why a pair of decision-makers may end up bargaining and of the boundaries within which they might strike a deal from which both benefit. Figure 5.11 gives an illustration of this. The decision-maker whose origin is labelled as *OT* is imagined as having preferences that could be represented in terms of indifference curves, while the other, whose origin is labelled as *OS*, is imagined to choose with reference to aspiration levels, *STA* for good *A* and *STB* for good *B*. The initial allocation of goods between the two choosers is shown by the bold arrows and point *L* inside the box.

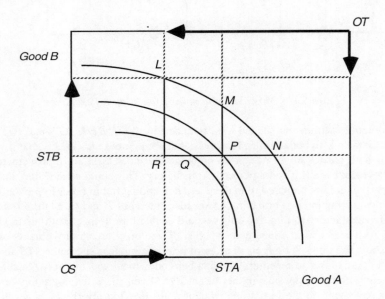

Figure 5.11: An optimizing decision-maker bargaining with a satisficer

The ultimate outcome will fall somewhere in the area bounded by the indifference curve between *L* and *N* and the straight lines *LR* and *NR*. If chooser *S* is to meet both targets then *P* is the best allocation that chooser *T* can hope to achieve, regardless of the slope of *T*'s indifference curves. Any outcome in the area bounded by *MNP* is both satisfactory for chooser S and an improvement for chooser T. However, whether such an outcome will eventuate is uncertain. It is conceivable that the final deal could involve the neoclassical chooser ending up on a superior indifference curve to the one that cuts through point P. For example, suppose chooser T suggests allocation Q: chooser S might eventually accept this since it takes her/him closer to meeting STA without causing a failure to meet STB. S/he might suggest allocation P but find that chooser T refuses to budge. It may seem better to accept Q rather than risk being unable to move from L as might happen if s/he, too, bluffs by refusing to accept anything less than P and then chooser T refuses to negotiate any further. At the start of their negotiations, both parties may be unclear whether their opponents have preferences closer to the neoclassical or behavioural stereotypes. During the course of negotiations, it *may* be possible to infer that one's opponent is thinking in terms of one or more targets below which s/he will not make concessions. But this is by no means guaranteed, for what can be discovered about an opponent's preferences or decision rules will depend very much on the sequence of bids and responses that are made during the negotiations.

5.8.2 *Bargaining procedures*

The focus of the Edgeworth Box on scope for bargaining in respect of alternative bundles of two types of goods has made it very popular for framing negotiations over international trade policy or bargaining between management and trade unions over pay and employment or conditions of work. However, much of what is written in bargaining theory about how a deal is arrived at is cast in terms of haggling between a buyer and a seller over how much money will be paid for one kind of good, or between an aggrieved party and a guilty party over how much compensation will be paid by the latter to the former. Whether the negotiations concern bundles of goods or a single good/money, the essence of the bargaining process seems, in the light of the work of Shackle (1949: chapter VI) and Elster (1989: chapter XIV) to involve each party in making four kinds of decisions:

(a) *What will be my opening bid?* In other words, what is my gambit price, g? The opening gambit must not be so high as to deter a potential trading partner from taking the trouble to see what sort of deal can be worked out. The phrase 'taking the trouble' is important, for bargaining takes up scarce time and may need to be preceded by time spent examining the object of the potential deal. A would-be buyer may not even look at a potential purchase whose asking price seems too high relative to that being asked by competing sellers of similar-sounding products. But if an opening offer is made at what seems a derisory level, the seller may think it is not worth responding with a counter bid. A dilemma arises if I am an expert on, say, antiques and think I have spotted a bargain because you are offering me an antique piece of furniture at a price way below the price at which such an item normally would be sold: perhaps you are so poorly informed that the price can be talked down even further, yet perhaps if the haggling goes on too long another expert will appear on the scene. If I make a low gambit bid and you accept it, I may wonder whether my analysis of the product is correct after all (perhaps it is a fake). But if my first offer is little different from your gambit, then you may realize that something is amiss and realize I am trying to preempt other bids (see Elster, 1989: 142).

(b) *What are the worst terms I am prepare to accept?* In other words, what is my reservation price, *r*? Guesswork is likely to be involved in setting *r*, because if a deal collapses today there is often uncertainty about when it will be possible to conclude a deal at *r* or on better terms (cf. Earl, 1995b).

(c) *What is my strategy for making concessions?* The rate at which a person gives in is significant for two reasons: first, if the person initially seems quite willing to climb down, then that may encourage the other party to respond by adopting a strategy of climbing down very slowly, if at all, during present negotiations; secondly, a person who bargains weakly in a deal today may have to bargain with the same party over another transaction in future, or with someone who observed how willingly concessions were made during the first act of bargaining. Those who establish reputations for being difficult may be rewarded subsequently with an easier life.

If the strategy for making concessions involves a very simple rule, it may be possible for the other party to work out an implied reservation price. For example, suppose I am a used car salesman and am employing what is known in the trade as 'the halving rule'. I may have a gambit price of $14 995 (in other words, $15 000) displayed on the windscreen of the car you hope to buy, and also have in mind a reservation price of $12 000. My negotiating margin is thus $3000. If you say the displayed price is too much and suggest $11 000 looks more realistic, my first counter bid under the halving rule is $13 500: I have given a discount of half of my negotiating margin. If you then offer $11 600, my second bid is $12 750. If you then offer $12 000, I will be puzzling to work out if you are following any consistent climb-down rule (perhaps $12 000 is your reservation price?) and I will counter with $12 375 along with comments about the deal not really being worthwhile at that price, even though I am quietly thinking that at least I might make $375 on top of the margin that is already built into my reservation price. If you have been studying my rate of descent, you may be able to deduce that you can expect me to come down to $12 000 eventually, though it might take quite a while to get me there. I, meanwhile, may start trying to cloud the issue by offering to fit some accessories: a radio upgrade that retails at $200 probably costs my dealership rather less than this. Fortunately for such sales personnel, the typical customer is probably neither aware of the popularity of this rule nor able to keep calm enough to discover that it is being used. Also, the time it takes to win every last concession may not be available or seem worth spending (cf. section 4.7 on framing effects) and the customer may not feel comfortable about being so ruthless over the last few hundred dollars.

(d) *How else can I make my demands seem credible and thereby extract concessions from the other party?* A low concession rate coupled with a realistic gambit price may not be all that bargainers can use to build up credibility if they presently lack reputations as being willing to stick to their guns and let a deal collapse rather than make further concessions. Sometimes, there will be other ways to make the other party believe that one really is willing to let negotiations break off rather than make further concessions. It is useful to be able to point to the possibility of going elsewhere to do a deal similar to what one is asking for, the more so the fewer the informational barriers to finding and setting such an alternative transaction in motion (cf. section 9.7). It also helps to be able to show that one can afford to let the deal collapse, for example by pointing out that this has few damaging repercussions. A threat to resign carries different weight depending on whether the person making the threat has large debts and a family to feed; likewise, the power of a union's strike threat may depend on whether or not it has a substantial strike fund. Some signals may be open to being misconstrued by the other party: for example, if a person seems to be taking a long time to come back with an answer, does this mean she is having great trouble working out how to meet the other party's demand, which stands beyond her reservation price, or is she just acting, trying to give this impression? In the case of a person holding out for a better deal on a new car, the theatrical side of the salesperson's response will often be to go and consult with the sales manager, as though the customer really is asking for a deal that would more than exhaust the firm's negotiating margin.

It seems useful, following Cross (1965), to recognize that many bargaining situations involve elements of two extreme cases. One is what Cross calls 'pure bluffing': each party plans to give in as the other makes concessions and both expect they will eventually reach an agreement at some intermediate point. This is bluffing in the sense of demanding better terms than one actually expects to end up with and misrepresenting one's situation. The other extreme is 'pure intransigence': each person's gambit price is the same as their respective reservation price and each expects that the other will make all the concessions. This is a recipe for deadlock if the two gambit prices do not coincide, for in all other cases expectations are incompatible. Most actual instances of bargaining probably involve bluffing that goes beyond mere ritual where both parties accurately forecast each other's moves. Sometimes, the bargaining process may go on long enough for one or both parties to revise their plans for making concessions, after they have inferred that they had misjudged their opponent's strategies. This makes the formal modelling of bargaining rather complicated, particularly if the learning process is ongoing. In Figure 5.12 I attempt to give a summary of a simple bargaining process in which each party makes only one revision of their original concession plans.

We might imagine the case as involving haggling over the price of a house that X is selling and Y hopes to buy. The house has been advertised by X at Xg, but if necessary X is prepared to descend from this gambit price as far as Xr. From what X has inferred about Y, X has decided that Y is most likely to begin with an offer of around Ygx, but then make concessions as shown by the unbroken line sloping up from Ygx. Since X does not know that Y's reservation price is Ye, X has to guess how generous it might be necessary to be to keep the negotiations going if events begin to unfold as expected. X plans to reduce his demands at the rate shown by the unbroken line sloping downwards from Xg, and expects that by time Xt a deal will be reached at price Xe so long as $Xe \leq Yr$. The trouble is, Y has other ideas. Y responds to Xg with a gambit offer of only Yg. Y's expectations about X and how X will respond to the offer of Yg are such that Y adopts a relatively tough concession strategy and expects it will take until time Yt to beat X down to Ye so long as $Ye \geq Xr$. As the initial bids are exchanged X is greatly surprised by Y's initial offer, but only moderately surprised by Y's rate of ascent. By contrast, Y finds that X is descending at a slightly slower rate than she expected. X is the first to revise his strategy, and begins making concessions at a faster rate than before. Y sees that X is adopting a softer stance, but it is still stronger than she had expected, so she steps up her concession rate somewhat. If both X and Y identify each other's strategies accurately and stick to their respective new concession strategies, then they will both end up expecting to reach a deal at price *Pe* by time *Te*.

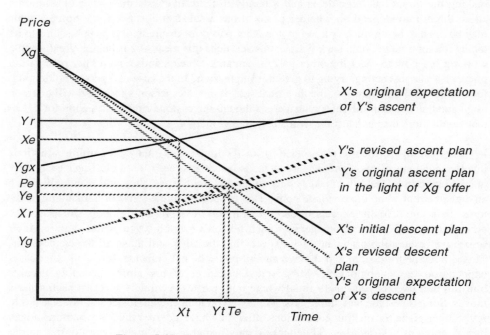

Figure 5.12: Expectations and bargaining strategies

Readers with a tendency to try to link ideas together will probably be somewhat disappointed with Figure 5.12 and its associated discussion. Given what I have said earlier in this chapter, particularly about scenario thinking, such readers will probably be surprised to find that Figure 5.12 is based around single-line expectations. Given the extent of guesswork about the opponent's strategy and where the negotiations might end under different game plans, bargaining seems at first sight to be an area in which it would be natural to want to try to construct extensions of the probabilistic and potential surprise models considered earlier in this chapter. My focus in terms of single-line, 'most likely strategies' was purely to keep the exposition and Figure 5.12 manageable, though we might well pause to consider whether the complexity of a bargaining encounter might drive decision-makers in practice to think in this way rather than in terms of ranges of possible or probable patterns of behaviour. In principle, lines representing imagined most likely strategies could have been replaced by pairs of lines representing ranges of behaviour that are imagined to be perfectly possible. An even messier alternative would be to draw sets of lines linking together imagined bids or counter bids that were seen as having the same degree of potential surprise (or subjective probability) attached to them.

Research on the psychology of negotiation has revealed that some combinations of gambit prices and concession strategies are especially effective because they affect how the other party sees things. An example is where one knowingly makes a highly demanding opening suggestion, follows it rapidly with a sharp climb-down and then stands firm. Here, of course, there is a slim chance of 'making a killing' at the outset, but the normal expectation is to use the extent of the first concession to make the second and subsequent offers *seem* far more attractive than they would have been if they had not been preceded by the outrageously opportunistic opening bid. The speed of the climb-down is necessary to stop the outraged party from walking away from further negotiations. It can be packaged to the outraged party in very apologetic terms as though the original suggestion should not have been made. This is sometimes known as the 'defusing objections' technique (see Pardini and Katzev, 1986). Another intriguing case is what is sometimes known as the 'Chinese' approach to bargaining. Here, the rule is make your initial offer only as low as you judge necessary to ensure it is not rejected out of hand, but then keep refusing to make any concessions at all. This means that all of the climbing down has to be done by the other party. When the other party seems to be resisting, hold out long enough for it to seem like a battle of wills and then make a small concession, giving the impression that you have at last been beaten down. So long as your slightly revised offer is not below the other party's reservation price, then the other party is quite likely to agree to it, worn out by your long refusal to concede and elated at having at last wrung some kind of concession from you.

Finally, I would like to mention a common bargaining strategy that seems paradoxically to involve inverting the idea of a climb-down, in order to extract maximum consumer surplus from a buyer. This is what we might call the 'foot in the door' or 'thin end of the wedge' technique and my remarks about it should be read in conjunction with material from section 9.11 on price discrimination. Here, the initial demand is set to seem low relative to alternatives that the other party might be considering, in order to get the negotiation started. Then, instead of making concessions, one actually asks for more and more, increasing these demands a little at a time, until the other party refuses to give any further ground. But the deal is not packaged like this. The idea is that more may be offered in the form of a better product; however, it comes at a price that involves a higher profit margin. The other person is shown why it could make sense to concede a bit more and at the same time an attempt may be made to show that the previously mentioned deals are no longer available. However, if the other party firmly resists going further, then after some pretence of investigating what can be done, the previous offer will be put back on the table or bargaining of a more conventional kind may be undertaken to see if the superior product can be sold even though concessions may have to be made on the price.

A trusted strategic tool for use with this sort of bargaining strategy is the 'base model' designed to lure people into a showroom but which is rarely to be purchased easily once there. There is the risk that the customer may insist on the base model and nothing else, even though he or she might have been prepared to pay more for a deluxe model with unwanted additional features were the base model not offered. However, if the firm does not at least make a show of offering the stripped-down base model, such a customer may be lost altogether to a rival that claims to have such a model available. Another 'foot in the door' strategy can be seen in some aspects of labour relations: workers may agree to a rather vague employment contract for a particular pecuniary return and then find, once they start on the job, that the employer keeps cranking up the demands made on them, exploiting the vagueness in the written contract.

5.9 Competitive games

We began this chapter by looking at Subjective Expected Utility theory, a view of the process of taking risky decisions that was formalized by von Neumann and Morgenstern (1944). We end the chapter with a brief examination of another contribution associated in its early days with von Neumann and Morgenstern, namely, the theory of games. This is perhaps better described as a collection of theories of interactive decision-making. The bargaining cases just considered obviously come under this heading. They also involve a feature that is central to some other games, namely, scope for using one's choice of move as a means of shaping the beliefs of the other party concerning one's future behaviour. However, some games do not involve a sequence of moves and it is crucial to get the move right first time because there will not be a second time; the trouble is, the right answer depends what the other players are going to do. Some games are zero-sum games: I win, you lose, or vice versa. Other games may involve positive outcomes for all players if particular moves are made or all parties may end up worse off if other moves are made. In this section the aim is merely to introduce readers to some of the types of games most referred to in modern business economics so that later material may be seen from a game-playing perspective. My discussion is quite strongly inspired by the focus on games in John Kay's (1993) recent and highly readable book on the economics of business strategy.

A useful starting point is to note how Morgenstern himself initially recognized that games did not fit in well with the idea of rational choice. Borch (1973: 67) notes that

> As a paradox Morgenstern discusses the problem of Sherlock Holmes who has to escape his enemy Moriarty. Holmes has the choice of taking the train to Dover, or to leave the train at the only stop on the way. In 1928 Morgenstern concluded that the problem had no solution in the conventional sense of the word. Today any undergraduate will recognize the problem as a two-person zero-sum game and he will know that it has a solution only in 'mixed strategies'. Holmes' problem is to keep his enemy guessing and the only certain way of achieving this is to remain guessing himself. Hence the solution is that Holmes should toss a coin and let the outcome decide if he should stay on the train to Dover, or leave at the intermediary stop.

In the Holmes/Moriarty game there is no intermediate outcome: Holmes wins if he gets out at Dover and Moriarty does not, or if he gets out at the earlier stop and Moriarty does not, whereas Moriarty wins if he and Holmes get out of the train at the same station. This is in contrast with many of the games that have attracted attention more recently.

Most famous of these games is the Prisoner's Dilemma, whose structure is as follows. The police have arrested two men whom they believe to be accomplices in a major crime and are trying to make them confess. Unfortunately, the police have no evidence on which to base a prosecution. The men are held in separate cells and told that if they will sign a statement in which they confess and implicate the other person they will be allowed to go free if they are not implicated by the other person, and the other person will very likely go to gaol for ten years. If both confess and implicate each other, then they will both be sent to gaol for seven years. They are also told that if they both refuse to say anything then the police will have them tried on a minor charge, for which good police evidence can be produced, and they will face a two-year gaol term. If the prisoners could count on each other's loyalty then the police would have to go for the minor convictions. However, if the prisoners do not trust each other to keep quiet, the best solution for both is to confess and implicate their accomplice: that way, the worst they can expect is a seven-year gaol sentence and the best they can expect is to go free. By contrast, the keeping quiet strategy has a best payoff of two years in gaol and a worst payoff (if the other party confesses and implicates) of ten years in gaol. In the absence of trust, logic seems to dictate a confession which implicates the other prisoner. If both do not trust each other and follow this logic, the police have an easy time and send both of them to gaol for seven years. The Prisoner's Dilemma game is unusual in having a dominant strategy—the best strategy for me is the best one regardless of what you choose to do—the trouble is, potential gains from cooperation fail to be realized.

An example of a Prisoner's Dilemma in the business world would be where construction companies are submitting tenders for building projects during a period of widespread excess capacity. The customers, who are not sure of the likely quality of the work or the ability of the companies to deliver on time, normally specify that 'the lowest tender, or any tender, might be declined'. If local construction firms are the only ones being invited to submit tenders then these firms will recognize it is in their joint interests that all their bids are only just inside the upper limits of the customers' budgets. If all have rather similar reputations for variability in the service that they provide and if all are equally adept at guessing the customers' upper budget limits, then in probabilistic terms they stand to be offered equal volumes of business if they all pursue the common interest strategy. All may be aware that any firm which tries to grab a very large slice of the market by submitting very low tenders may damage its credibility (the customers may fear that it is so desperate for business that it will not remain solvent long enough to complete the work). However, all may also be aware of the benefits of being the only firm to put in a mid-price tender and hence win a disproportionate share of contracts. If all are afraid that some of the tendering firms will not act in the common interest of the group, all may be inclined to go for mid-price tenders: if any of the rivals does not do this, there is a danger, due to the prevalence of spare capacity, that it would get no business because all the business would be taken by the lower-price firms without them running into capacity constraints. The result is likely to be that everyone bids in the mid-price area and no one makes very much money. From a social point of view it is not obvious that such an outcome is ideal. To be sure, the customers win in the short run, but in the long run relatively low profits may limit investment in this industry and lead future tenders to be made at a higher price. Collusive tendering might actually be socially beneficial in the long run (for a case study of this sort of problem in the heavy electrical engineering industry, see Richardson, 1969).

Prisoner's Dilemma games may take on a rather different complexion if the game is repeated time after time, so long as acts of unilateral cooperation are not catastrophic; or if it is expected that losers may be able to arrange for rough justice to be given to those who did not act in the common interest. If I am playing a repeated Prisoner's Dilemma game and am the only player who acts cooperatively I pay a harsh penalty now but signal my trustworthiness to others. The logic of my position may encourage the others to be more cooperative not just in the future but in the first round in order that they do not signal to me that I should not trust them in future. I may also be able to ensure cooperation by making it clear to other players that I have friends who will be visiting them to voice their displeasure if I end up in gaol because of their noncooperative actions. In a business context, references to longevity (for example, the firm that proudly advertises that it was 'founded in 1897') and offers of comprehensive warranties are commonly employed by firms to signal that they believe they are playing a repeated game and how they play the game relative to the competition.

Kay (1993: 90–92) examines this issue in relation to the problem of quality uncertainty in markets where it costs a manufacturer less to ensure that products are reliable than it costs to fix unreliable products. If the customer is willing to pay extra for reliability but cannot be sure of reliability without experience of a product, it may be difficult to sell high quality products with a premium price. A high price may buy reliability but it may buy a troublesome 'lemon' of a product. On the other hand, a customer might strike it lucky and get a real 'honey' of a cheap product. Given that repair costs *might* be incurred in either case, the customers are prone to presume the worse, pay less and receive poor quality unless the supplier can signal a high-price product's high reliability in a credible way (see also Akerlof, 1970). If a firm puts its well-established reputation at stake, or offers a warranty that it will obviously be expensive to honour if the product is unreliable, then customers may start believing its claims about the quality of what it is trying to sell and believe its premium prices are justified. Businesses within a group of competitors may also be able use threats to ensure that members of the group do not act against the group interest: those whose behaviour threatens the viability of the group may be warned that they will be debarred from membership of the group's trade association: an inability to claim to be a member of such an association may cause difficulties for a firm that is trying to claim that its products offer better value for money than those produced by association members.

Less frequently referred to than Prisoner's Dilemma games, but hardly less relevant to business economics, are games whose structures take the form known as Battle of the Sexes. In its most acute form, a Battle of the Sexes game assumes that the players cannot communicate with each other. A case in point might be where he has met her in the past and they would both like to run into each other again. From the original meeting, he knows she likes going to the opera, whereas she knows he would much prefer to go to the ballet. If he goes to the opera and she goes to the ballet, both will have a dreary evening: they will neither greatly enjoy the entertainment nor bump into each other. If he goes to the opera, he is better off if she goes there too instead of trying to fit in with what she knows of his entertainment preferences: at least he enjoys meeting her there. If they both go to the opera, that is the best outcome for her: she gets her preferred entertainment as well as his company—and vice versa if they both opt to go to the ballet. Even if the couple can communicate and try to work out a joint course of action there is still the risk that they will have great trouble working out what to do if they are both trying to please each other, though they may at least be able to avoid the 'worst of both worlds' kind of outcome.

The most obvious kind of business game that has a Battle of the Sexes structure is a battle to achieve acceptance as the dominant 'standard' in an industry. Standardization often benefits consumers of products that are used in conjunction with complementary products. Obvious examples here are the battles between the Sony Betamax video cassette standard and the JVC-designed VHS standard; between IBM (and makers of IBM-clones) and Apple in the market for personal computers; and between Digital Audio Tapes, Digital Compact Cassettes and Mini-Discs in the market for domestic digital sound recording and playback systems. Once it is commonly believed that a particular system is going to be the victor, the beliefs will tend to be self-fulfilling: developers of complementary products will concentrate on supplying items that fit with this standard in order to increase the size of their potential market and the growth in the market will enable lower prices to be charged; the availability of greater variety of complementary products at lower prices will attract customers to the standard expected to be victorious, giving its manufacturers greater learning advantages and economies of scale (see sections 7.6 and 9.3). Customers will avoid products based on other standards: if Betamax is expected to lose the battle with VHS, then there will be a shrinking range of Betamax videos to rent and, once the Sony Betamax VCR is worn out, the videotapes themselves will be of no use.

If there is little to choose between the products in technical terms, then what matters most for consumer welfare is not *which* standard ultimately wins but that most consumers commit themselves early on to the *same* standard. Therefore, at the start of a standards battle, customers and suppliers of complementary products will be watching each other, waiting for signs about which way the market may go. If the products are finely matched in terms of value for money we have a situation akin to that often encountered in an entrance to a building: 'After you'; 'No, after you!'. Sometimes this can contribute to a complete failure of a market to take off, as in the mid-1970s with quadraphonic record players: when faced with a choice between incompatible systems and limited supplies of quadraphonic albums for the rival systems, hi-fi connoisseurs avoided commitment to either system to such an extent that both fizzled out.

Such 'worst of both worlds' outcomes are often avoided in many social situations via the use of conventions (as with 'Ladies first' to coordinate traffic in a doorway, or 'Give way to traffic approaching from the right' to reduce the incidence of collisions and gridlocks in some countries' road systems), or by the use of some kind of hierarchy (perhaps he always decides what to do in some contexts whereas, in others, it is she who must be obeyed). Firms can try to make the market go their way by basing their promotion campaigns around endorsements of their products by well-known personalities whom a large part of the potential market may see as role models—in other words, by appealing to the hierarchy concept. Otherwise, it appears that participants in Battle of the Sexes games in business tend, sometimes unwittingly, to tip the scales in favour of particular standards by their strategies in respect of technology licensing. IBM's authority in the world of mainframe computers—summed up by the maxim 'Nobody ever got fired for buying IBM'—may have helped contribute to the success of its kind of personal computers in conjunction with the Microsoft DOS operating system, but it seems that Apple in effect shot itself in the foot early on in the battle for the personal computer market by charging overly greedy premium prices for its more user-friendly computers and preventing them from being cloned by other manufacturers. Having pioneered video recording in studio and educational contexts (see Morita, 1987), the Sony corporation probably thought it had the stature to attract household VCR buyers to its Betamax models. However, as Kay (1993: 109) points out, JVC made it easy for other firms to produce VHS VCRs under licence early on in the battle, and the preponderance of VHS models in appliance shops helped ensure that VHS sales quickly overtook Betamax sales.

To end this section, let us consider a game known as 'Chicken', epitomized by an automotive duel sometimes fought by teenagers with tragic consequences. The protagonists drive towards each other at high speed down the middle of a long straight section of road.

Both hope that the other will swerve to avoid colliding with the oncoming car. If neither swerves, both are likely to be killed. If both swerve, both are labelled 'Chicken' by their peers. If one swerves and gets called Chicken, the other lives to enjoy a reputation as someone who should not be called Chicken. Few would wish to play a game of Chicken with someone known to have won previous games by refusing to swerve on every occasion and living to tell the tale, so the game will tend only to be played between parties who have never played before or who have histories of *randomly* choosing to stick or to swerve (cf. the coin toss in the Holmes/Moriarty game). If players wish to avoid random choices between sticking and swerving it must somehow become clear whose role it is to be Chicken. The best way you can convince me that I should swerve to save both of our lives at the cost of my reputation is for you to show me that you *cannot* swerve. This is more difficult in a motoring duel than in the world of business. As regards the former, Kay (1993: 47) notes the fanciful suggestion that one driver might tear off his steering wheel and toss it out of the window when in the sight of the other driver. More realistically, we can note that managers may be able to frighten off their rivals by announcing that they have signed contracts for investment goods necessary for a particular course of action, making it clear that it will be difficult to escape from the contracts without paying huge sums in compensation and that the capital items will be very difficult to re-sell for anything like their purchase prices. Of course, a long war of attrition may be started if several firms make commitments simultaneously and there is insufficient room in the market for all of the schemes to be viable (cf. sections 4.7 and 10.4–10.9).

5.10   Conclusion

We have now completed our exploration of some of the things that economists have written about the nature of decision-making. In the introductory overview in Chapter 2 I sought to draw attention to the ways in which economists differ in the assumptions that they make about the information that decision-makers possess and their capacities for coping with complex problems. The neoclassical models considered in Chapter 3 portrayed choices as if they were made with respect to a given set of information, unhindered by ambiguities or complexity. Complexity began to loom larger as a potential problem as we moved from the basic Hicksian model into expositions of Lancaster's characteristics-based view of decision-making. In the early sections of Chapter 4 we considered how relatively simple decision rules might be used to make manageable the task of choosing between rival products that offer different performances in many different characteristics. At that stage we tended to assume that decision-makers may have undertaken a rather less thorough search for alternatives than might have been possible but that they had a fairly clear idea of what they were looking at in terms of prospective performances along the characteristic axes that they saw as relevant to their choices. Sometimes, however, we conceded that people might simplify the task of choosing in a much more extreme manner, for example by simply copying what their peers did. Towards the end of Chapter 4 a more psychological perspective on choice was introduced, which drew attention to ways in which our minds may edit information or lead us to gather information in a selective manner.

Elements of all these approaches to theorizing about choice have resurfaced in this chapter as we have examined perspectives on how people choose when they are not sure of the consequences of making particular choices. Probabilistic views of choice, such as Subjective Expected Utility (SEU) theory, presume that decision-makers act as if they have a clear idea of the frequency with which particular events tend to occur even if they do not know for sure what will happen to themselves as individuals. In practice, people may be unsure even about the shapes taken by probability distributions. Since probabilistic modes of theorizing tend to presume the past is a good guide to what the future will be like, critics such as scenario planners suggest that these theories are of limited normative use since they fail to face up to the fact that creative acts by individuals make a difference to the path carved out by history. Questions have been asked about the wisdom of assuming for predictive purposes that decision-makers try to add up a multitude of rival outcomes: the SEU model and satisficing versions of Shackle's potential surprise model overlap in philosophy with, respectively, compensatory and non-compensatory analyses of choice between multi-characteristic goods. We have also noted how biased cognitions and an unwillingness to face up to uncertainty may affect the kinds of risks that people are prepared to take on. More often than economists would probably care to admit, people may cope with their ignorance and uncertainty about the consequences of their actions by copying each other or by following simple rules of thumb. Such simple ways of choosing do not lend themselves to expositions in terms of fancy diagrams and yet they may have major significance for policy-makers, for example, because they give producers of well-known brands an advantage over firms whose products are 'unknown quantities'. This should be kept in mind in later chapters as we consider topics such as contestability theory (section 9.7) and franchising (sections 11.4 and 11.5).

The introduction to game theory presented in this chapter should also be revisited during the reading of later chapters, for we shall have much to say about uncertainties concerning the behaviour of other players whose decisions have an impact on the outcomes associated with a particular choice. Readers who compare the treatment of games in this text with treatments elsewhere may notice that other authors delight in making use of two-by-two 'pay-off matrices', which are conspicuous by their absence from section 5.9. Some readers may find it helps to try to construct such diagrams as they take notes from this book, but I would urge them, as they do so, to recognize that they will probably end up defining with undue precision the nature of the game they are looking at. Different players may see a particular situation in different ways and some may try to devise strategies that come as a complete surprise to everyone involved, yet game theorists tend to treat games as if they are played in terms of rules that are well defined and exhaustive: I cannot recall seeing an exposition of the Prisoner's Dilemma in which one of the prisoners opts to astonish the police by confessing and claiming, in an act of altruism, that the other prisoner had nothing at all to do with the crime. Given that there are risks in playing the kinds of games we have considered, we should also keep in mind that theories of risk-taking considered in the first half of the chapter might be applicable for making sense of choices about whether or not to participate in a game in the first place. These choices in turn may be affected in some case by the outcomes of prior attempts to bargain over the terms of the game.

5.11 Further questions

1. Imagine that you have been asked to give a talk to an audience of investment advisers about the relevance of economic theory to understanding how people make their decisions about how to hold their wealth (for example, as bank deposits, in government securities, in superannuation funds, or in real estate or antiques). Prepare a written summary of the talk that you would give.

2. In the winter of 1992, firms and households in New Zealand were asked to economize on their consumption of electricity owing to a lack of water in hydroelectric storage lakes. The electricity supply authorities blamed the crisis on an autumn drought in catchment areas on a scale that only occurred once in a hundred years. What lessons does economic theory have to offer on how such a situation could be allowed to reach crisis proportions and how further electricity crises might be avoided in the future?

3. Ask ten people to write down how they would choose, and the reasons for their choices, if they were offered the opportunity of a free bungey jump or a free trip on a white-water raft. (Tell them they can freely decline both offers if they wish.) Then write a report on how well your sample of potential risk-takers' methods of choosing seems to fit in with what you have read on the theory of choice.

4. Explain what is meant by risk aversion. Suppose a risk-averse individual can either hire himself out as an abalone diver where his wages fluctuate widely or as a commercial diver for a dockyard for a stable wage. You should assume that from all other points of view the two jobs are equivalent. Given that the labour market in diving is competitive, explain using expected utility analysis what sort of relationship you would expect between the expected value of earnings in each occupation.

5. A factory owner is risk-averse and is offered two fire insurance options, the first with no excess, where any claim is met in full but which carries a higher premium than the second which has a lower premium but only pays out above the voluntary excess. Under what circumstances, if any, should the factory owner accept the policy with the voluntary excess?

6. 'Hopes which are mutually exclusive are not additive; fears which are mutually exclusive are not additive. In each case the greatest prevails, and alone determines the power of the attractive or of the deterrent component of the venture's "dual personality". In this last sentence, the word "greatest" is insufficiently precise.... What we mean is the *most powerful element* amongst them' (George Shackle, *Expectation in Economics*, 1949: 38). Discuss.

7. Theories of decision-making in the face of risk and uncertainty are typically set out in the context of one-dimensional choices (for example, profits versus losses). How easily can they be generalized or integrated with other theories of choice so that they can be used to make sense of situations in which decision-makers feel uncertain about a

number of characteristics of the options between which they are trying to choose?

8. In criticizing the 'Edgeworth Box' analysis of bargaining, George Shackle (in *Expectation, Enterprise and Profit*, 1970: 147) argued that the analysis of Edgeworth and many others who have followed him is severely limited due to a concentration on the sole question of what bargainers desire to the exclusion of what they know or believe. To what extent do you agree with Shackle's point of view on this issue? Explain your reasoning.

9. 'Real-world economic actors, peering ahead in time as they must, do not love uncertainty. But on the whole, they accept it rationally as a fact of life and, over time, have invented institutions and precautionary tactics of remarkable ingenuity to shrink it down considerably and otherwise mitigate its negative effects' (David McQueen, in *Challenge* magazine, March/April 1994: 43–4). Discuss.

10. Discuss the possible role of scenario-planning techniques in policy formation with respect to the 'greenhouse effect'.

11. Game theorists often refer to strategies that entail a 'Nash equilibrium', which is defined by John Kay (*Foundations of Corporate Success*, 1993: 374) as 'An outcome in which each player's strategy is best given the strategies adopted by other players'. Discuss the usefulness of the concept of a Nash equilibrium for anticipating the outcomes of interactive decision-making processes in the world of business.

12. 'When firms are fighting for market share in high-technology industries such as computers and consumer electronics, it may be more important for them to possess the capacity to reshape the way that competitive games are played than to have the best technology or cheapest production costs.' Discuss.

13. How can firms establish the credibility of competitive threats that they make against their rivals? What problems may arise if their credibility is in doubt?

6 Theories of firms and markets: an overview

6.1 Introduction and suggestions on reading

This chapter contains a guide to some of the key themes and modes of thought that you will encounter in Chapters 7 to 11 of this book. However, right now, perhaps the best thing to do before going any further is to revisit sections 1.2, 1.4 and 1.6 of Chapter 1, after browsing in the text that formed the basis of your introductory training in the economics of the firm and market processes. The reason that I say this is that we are about to revisit territory over which an introductory training is supposed to help students navigate, but this time around things are going to look very different indeed and that is likely to be quite unsettling. Chapters 8 and 10 will probably be the most troubling ones in this part of the book. Chapter 8 is disconcerting because it reveals how theories of perfect and imperfect/monopolistic competition have been the subjects of major controversy and are not the reliable building blocks for analysing pricing behaviour that introductory textbooks make them out to be. Chapter 10 is downright subversive by comparison even with Chapter 8: it exposes major logical flaws in basic supply and demand theory and shows not only that markets may be rather costly ways of arranging resource allocation but also that in so far as markets work effectively this may often be because of, rather than despite, the presence of features that an introductory training labels as 'market imperfections'. This material could have been covered at the introductory level, for it is not technically demanding and has many user-friendly applications, but if teachers at this level have received a conventional training in economics then many of them are probably utterly unaware of the questionable foundations they are giving their students.

One further strategy that may make it easier to cope with the economics of firms and markets is to read about the theoretical ideas in conjunction with reading in business history or business biography/autobiography. The literature in this area, like many of the books themselves, is huge. I would particularly recommend *My Years with General Motors* by Alfred Sloan (1965) and *Made in Japan: Akio Morita and Sony*, by Akio Morita (1987). The best strategy might be to read Morita fairly early in studying in this area, to get a broad perspective on a high-technology firm expanding in an international environment, and then read Sloan close to the final examination, to give you a chance to see how useful the theories you have covered seem for making sense of what happened during Sloan's long career with General Motors. You should also note that in this part of the book it should often be possible to pick up the essence of parts of the theoretical material by reading the applied essay examples and case study sections first, and then going back to the theory sections: remember that in being explicit about areas of theoretical controversy my aim is to help you develop better skills for making sense of practical problems, rather than to encourage you to study theory for theory's sake. The essay and case study sections in Chapters 7 to 11 may prove useful for helping you to develop your capacities for lateral thinking and integrating ideas from a range of sources.

The rest of this chapter consists of a series of short sections each of which is focused on one main difference between neoclassical and behavioural/institutional views of how to think about firms and market processes. Just as neoclassical and behavioural/institutional economists offer fundamentally different ways of looking at consumer behaviour and decision-making in general, so we shall be seeing marked differences in their perspectives on firms and markets. Many of these contrasts derive from their respective views of decision-making. However, in the chapters that follow I will be using labels such as 'neoclassical' and 'behavioural' somewhat less frequently than in earlier chapters as I discuss the work of particular economists. This is mainly because quite a number of the economists we shall encounter are actually quite problematic to classify since aspects of their work come from both schools of thought. A few notable examples will illustrate this point. Joan Robinson devised the theory of imperfect competition (see section 8.5), which has all the hallmarks of a neoclassical economic model, yet almost all of her other work is critical of neoclassical thinking. Philip Andrews devised his normal cost theory of competitive oligopoly (see section 9.6) as an alternative to Robinson's theory of imperfect competition and normal cost theory, like much of his work, is consistent with behavioural economics. Yet Andrews was a vigorous critic of works such as the behavioural theory of the firm proposed by Cyert and March (1963). Oliver Williamson is a former pupil of Cyert and March who has become famous for his attempts to make sense of the institutions of modern economic systems, such as the internal organization of firms, their choices of activities to undertake inside their legal boundaries, and the contractual linkages between firms (see sections 11.2 and 11.7). Williamson's analysis is based around information problems including bounded rationality and yet he is seen by many behavioural economists as thinking in ways that are often closer to the spirit of neoclassical economics. It should not be surprising that many economists do not seem to be purists in terms of which school of thought their work fits with, given that (a) most economists receive a training in neoclassical economics, (b) old habits of thought are hard to shake off and get in the way of seeing the full implications of alternative ideas, and (c) neoclassical economists have become much more interested in the economics of information in recent years. The question of when a person ceases to be a neoclassical is a bit like the question of when a person can really be said to be a vegetarian. In both cases, not merely is the answer unclear because a variety of intermediate philosophies are possible, but also people may switch between philosophies depending on the context. This should be kept in mind as you read the sections that follow.

6.2 Comparative static equilibrium analysis versus evolutionary analysis

The standard neoclassical approach to analysing changes in economic systems involves three basic stages:

(i) Initially the economist models the decision-making units as if their goal is to maximize the value of some function (for example, a profit function or utility function) and as if they have found in an equilibrium state that is stable in the sense that any accidental deviation from that position would tend to be corrected rather than amplified. A classic example of this in price theory is where a firm is seen as if it chooses to maximize profits by selecting the price and quantity mix at which marginal costs and marginal revenue are equalized, where the marginal cost curve is cut from above by the marginal revenue curve (cf. Figure 8.2 in section 8.5): movements away from this price and quantity mix in either direction both reduce profits; therefore, so long as cost and revenue conditions do not change, managers ought to be able to discover this price and quantity configuration by trial and error even if they cannot actually observe the relevant cost and revenue curves.

(ii) Something of interest to the economic analyst is then assumed to take place unexpectedly—in the neoclassical economist's jargon, 'The system receives a shock'—which changes the coefficients of one of the functions that forms part of the original equilibrium model. For example, the economist might want to explore the implications of change in wage levels, or of entry by new firms which pushes the demand curves of existing firms to the left. The coefficients of the other functions in the models are assumed not to be affected: in other words, the economist assumes *ceteris paribus*, or 'other things equal'.

(iii) The economist then finds the new optimal point of equilibrium and checks it for stability. It is recognized that the system may be temporarily out of equilibrium if decision-makers need to use trial and error to discover the best position. However, the economist concentrates on the end state and ignores possible steps along the way to it on the presumption that it will not be affected by the adjustment process.

This way of analysing change is often said by critics to take place in logical time rather than historical time, owing to its presumption that history is reversible in the sense that, if the 'shock' is reversed, then the decision-making unit will return to the initial position of equilibrium. In the short run, of course, it might not be possible to reverse everything: for example, a change in wages might imply a change in technology; if wages changed back to their original level and there was a big difference between the new and secondhand prices of machinery, a switch back to the original technology might not occur until the machinery wore out (cf. section 7.3).

Behavioural/institutional economists are more interested in how economic *processes* work and are not worried if no equilibrium end *state* is implied by their models. On the contrary, they usually expect changes to continue without apparent end because each time one decision-making unit tries to adapt to a change this tends to cause a change in someone else's decision-making environment. They also note that, in the course of coping with change, people discover new information, so a reversal of a change in their decision-making environments may not lead them to return to their original positions. For example, if a firm experiments with a higher price, some of its customers may purchase from rival suppliers as an experiment and discover that what they get is as good as or better than they had been getting previously. If the firm now reverses its pricing decision they may stick with their new suppliers.

As a result of focusing on both irreversibilities and the linkages between elements of complex economic systems, those who adopt the evolutionary perspective recognize that quite small differences in commitments that people make at one point in history can have very major implications for the patterns of events that subsequently occur. Cumulating processes are enhanced by economies of large-scale production (see Kaldor, 1972) and wherever 'track records' play a major role in determining whether or not suppliers can raise finance or attract customers. Furthermore, 'first-movers'—in other words, those who succeed in winning business at an early stage in the development of a market—often have advantages such as superior knowledge and credibility which makes life difficult for later entrants trying to capture market share from them. Neoclassical economists, by contrast, tend to presume that shocks to an economic system dissipate rather like ripples on a pond.

The idea that small initial differences can be amplified greatly with the passage of time may be illustrated by considering hypothetical consequences of the failure by a firm to win a battle over a technology standard (Sony with Betamax, for example). Though the rival standards may have been close substitutes initially, the consequences of customers opting for one standard at the expense of its rivals has major implications for the producers in terms of the profits that they will have available to plough back into the development of other products; this in turn may affect not merely the outcomes of subsequent standards battles but also whether or not some products even get developed (see further, Arthur, 1989, 1993). The world today might have turned out a very different place in all sorts of ways had the petrol-engined motor car not been selected in preference to the steam car in the early days of motoring: it was by no means a foregone conclusion that this would happen instead of victory going to steam cars or to successors of the electric car that was the first motor vehicle to exceed 60 miles an hour. Once resources have been sunk into a particular technological system and into the intellectual capital that goes with it, it can be very difficult to shake a system out of that particular technological rut. A case in point is the QWERTY typewriter keyboard, which today is seen as ergonomically flawed but which had engineering advantages in the days of mechanical typewriters where collisions between moving parts needed to be kept to a minimum.

6.3 Optimizing versus satisficing views of decision-making

Neoclassical analyses of the firm are very easily mastered if one is on top of Hicksian consumer theory, for they centre on optimization subject to well-defined constraints. The focus is on potential for improving the firm's position through marginal adjustments in the light of changed market circumstances. Equilibrium is found by equating appropriate variables, such as costs and revenues, at the margin. The technical framework is very similar to that outlined in the discussion of neoclassical consumer theory in Chapter 3: instead of a preference ordering, we have a production function which specifies how much of various outputs can be obtained using particular amounts of inputs and from this we get isoquants to confront with isocost lines. The neoclassical analysis is normally set up around the assumption that managers wish to maximize profits, but it lends itself to other maximands, such as maximum turnover, subject to a minimum profits constraint (see section 9.4).

By contrast, the behavioural approach centres on the use of rules of thumb, either in relation to strategic problems (though there is no presumption that all firms engage in strategic planning) or to burning issues of the day, such as a failure of aspirations to be met or the surprise of an unanticipated, devious move by a competitor, supplier or customer. Technological constraints are not seen as given and well known, but as things that the firm struggles to discover and overcome. Productivity and the quality of decision-making depend very much on information flows within the firm, which is seen as a complex organization. The structure of incentives may affect these information flows, for the firm consists of a set of individuals pursuing their own agendas.

Evolutionary extensions of the satisficing theme suggest that, by trial and error, some management teams may succeed in developing sets of strategic themes and tactical routines that match the current environment rather well. Other teams, which experiment with different decision rules, may fail to generate adequate returns. If the business environment changes, we should not presume that a formerly successful organization will come up with—we might say mutate—a new set of procedures that will serve it so well. In a sense, then, we may liken the firm's decision rules to genes, with the environment selecting out some corporate genes and allowing others to survive, not because they are the fittest but because there is sufficient space for them in the competitive market.

6.4 Price competition in respect of a given set of products versus Schumpeterian technological competition

The static/optimizing and evolutionary/satisficing philosophies lead to very different areas of focus as far as competition is concerned. The neoclassical analysis of the firm focuses on the questions of: which products a firm will produce from a given list of products; which of a given set techniques will be used to produce them; how many units of each will be produced; and the prices at which they will be sold. Frequently, this reduces merely to a discussion of the optimal price/output combination of a single, given product, the combination that will result in the firm being in equilibrium. The pricing decision can seem to be little more than a thought experiment: the analysis typically begins by showing the equilibrium combination and then pointing out why any other combination, involving a different point on a given demand curve, would harm the firm's profits position. The ability to move up and down a given demand curve without affecting its position is usually implied in these discussions.

Behavioural economists are much more concerned with the possibility that market conditions are in a continual state of flux. Bounded rationality ensures that firms never completely solve many of the problems that they perceive themselves to be grappling with, and often their perceptions of these problems change as they try to cope with them. The development of better products is a particularly powerful illustration of why managers may base their decisions on simple rules that seem to have worked in the past. For a start, the allocation of resources to research and development ('R&D') involves stepping into unfamiliar territory, so estimates of likely costs and end results are very tenuous (Kay, 1979). Many significant new technologies are discovered by accident during unsuccessful attempts to discover something else. Even when researchers do succeed in developing a

148

technology as initially envisaged they often fail to see its broader applications: for example, Marconi might have been able to raise a lot more money for his research activities had he seen right from the start that radio would have applications beyond just communication between parties for whom wire-based communication was impossible.

When a new or improved product reaches the market, its quality may depend on how long the firm has allowed for the development process as well as on the scale of resources that it allocates to the project. The task is not to produce the perfect product but one that will be good enough for the moment, and research teams will often have a list of things they expect to be able to improve upon in an upgraded version even at the time a product is launched. To launch a product before it has been thoroughly 'debugged' can have disastrous long-run consequences for sales due to the inconvenience that is imposed on customers. However, if managers do not set deadlines for their teams to meet particular objectives, then projects may drag on seemingly without end and more and more sales revenue will be lost forever. Clearly, it is possible to conceive of the general nature of this sort of problem in terms of tradeoffs at the margin, but there is far too much guesswork involved for particular functions to be specified. Hence firms will tend to motivate their research teams by setting priority rankings for the things they want to achieve by particular deadlines. These deadlines will tend to be conventional in nature, for example, dates consistent with the times at which pertinent trade exhibitions (such as the Geneva Motor Show or the Frankfurt Book Fair) are held.

As time passes, attainments in terms of quality and productivity will tend to be raised across all firms that survive in an industry. Difficulties in meeting aspirations can arise on the one hand due to problem-solving activities that lead firms to change their relative competitive positions though internal reorganizations, process innovations, marketing innovation and product innovations—as Schumpeter (1943) emphasized, one firm's way of improving its position tends to be the source of a difficulty for its rivals. On the other hand, buyers are learning too, changing their attitudes to, and awareness of, particular products. Changes in their budget constraints associated with individual life-cycle progressions and changes in the macroeconomic environment keep placing consumers in new 'buying territories', and product innovations and new marketing strategies keep changing the terrain within a given market. This is not to say that price competition may be unimportant, but its significance will vary depending on the stage of development of a market. In early stages in a market life-cycle, buyers may be poorly informed about the point of having the product and concerned about its likely reliability, and whether or not it is likely soon to become obsolete due to design improvements or due to its failure to be accepted as the industry standard. Later on, when the product has become increasingly homogeneous and when information about its design and manufacturing processes has leaked out and become widely known, brand names may count for little as signals of quality and reliability, and price competition may indeed be important. Even at this stage, it may still be questionable whether it makes sense to think of firms as enjoying given demand and cost functions, for changes in income levels may still be going on, and manufacturers of rival product types may be coming up with ways of winning customers back (as with the development of multiplex theatres by cinema chains, in the face of competition from the well-established home video and cable television markets).

For the behaviouralist, price is but one dimension of choice in a world of uncertainty that makes every purchase an opportunity, but not an obligation, to experiment with a new product or a new supplier. In any case, if several suppliers stand equidistant from potential customers and claim to be offering the same product for the same price, the price does not provide a sufficient basis for choice. What may matter much more is what the buyer stands to gain or lose by testing one claim rather than the other. If the information potentially available to buyers were not continually being disrupted by the dynamic aspects of competitive processes, choice might indeed end up being between known, given commodities and be based around the rule of 'choose the cheapest and choose randomly if several tie as cheapest', and brand names would count for little.

6.5   Representative 'black box' firms versus firms as differentiated organizations

To keep their analysis simple and to generate clear-cut equilibrium outcomes, neoclassical economists are inclined to model all firms in a market 'as if' they are identical and 'as if' their behaviour is not dependent on internal factors. The firm is observed from outside in terms of the resources it purchases in the market place and the goods and services it tries to sell on particular terms to other market participants. No attempt is made to model its internal decision processes and there is no suggestion that what it buys and sells in the market is affected by its internal organizational structure. Latsis (1972) calls this approach to theorizing 'situational determinism' or a 'single exit' analysis. By the latter label he means that no role is assigned for individual or collective judgement in shaping how a firm in neoclassical economics responds to a change in market conditions. If the firm is seen simply as a collection of mathematical functions with a particular maximand, then a change in the parameters of one of these functions points as clearly to a new position of equilibrium. This deterministic view can be better appreciated through the metaphor of a room full of people from which there is only one exit. If a fire breaks out in the room, making it difficult to breathe, everyone will try to go out of the same exit: it is the only way out.

Though it is convenient to play down differences between individual firms, behavioural/institutional economists seem to agree with Loasby's (1967: 167) view that 'All firms do not behave in the same way in similar circumstances and a theory which helps to explain why they do not is perhaps to be preferred to one which asserts that they should'. If we return to the burning building metaphor, we can note that in many cases it is not at all clear what to do in a large building when a fire breaks out: on the one hand, the smoke may obscure the exit signs; on the other hand, if the alarm sounds and several exit signs can be seen, it may be unclear which one a person should choose, given that the fire might be raging along some of the exit routes. Managers may not notice a change in the business environment and when they do perceive a possible need to change their behaviour they have to decide for themselves how to interpret the nature of the change that they are facing and what that implies in terms of action. Different managers may thus come to very different conclusions not merely about pricing, output rates, product policy and production methods, but also about the range of activities that should go on inside their firms. For example, if faced with stronger competition, some managers may think it appropriate to retreat to an up-market niche, while others may opt to focus on gaining greater control over their supplies of inputs and/or distribution channels in order to be able to maintain their positions in their existing market territories. Since major decisions are often taken by committees who depend on information supplied from elsewhere in the organization, the kinds of decisions that get taken may depend a great deal on the organizational structure of the firm, its information systems and the composition of the committees. A change in the balance of a committee from engineers towards accountants will probably produce much more technologically conservative corporate policies. Some aspects of corporate behaviour may thus be difficult to predict without a knowledge of a firm's organizational history, structure and politics.

6.6 Coordination by price alone versus coordination by price and voice

The neoclassical view of how resources get allocated focuses on the lure of profits and the repelling effect of losses—that is to say, on differences between revenues and costs. Customers, likewise, simply look at the costs and benefits of rival alternatives and vote with their wallets for some products and against others. If customers buy less of a product, there will be less money to be made by producing it and some firms will thus quit, and vice versa. If managers do not feel workers are performing adequately, they terminate the latter's contracts, and if workers feel they can get a better deal elsewhere they resign and move on. This is the *price mechanism* in essence.

From the behavioural standpoint, this view of resource allocation processes seems somewhat naive in that it ignores the role played by the *voice mechanism*—in other words, actual communication between economic actors (the 'voice' term comes from Hirschman, 1970). Customers for commercial products sometimes advertise, seeking 'expressions of interest', because their needs are so idiosyncratic or novel that the product has to be built to order after a good deal of discussion between the customer and potential suppliers. Dissatisfied customers in some cases do not simply exit in favour of a rival supplier; instead, they complain about lapses of quality, availability or reliability, in an attempt to make their regular supplier raise its standards. This is perfectly rational if switching suppliers involves costs and the risk of 'jumping out of the frying pan and into the fire'. Without such feedback, the supplier would merely observe that sales were falling, not, in the absence of market research, *why* they were falling. Many employers, likewise, do not simply fire employees who perform poorly; rather, they invest management time in discussing the employees' shortcomings and working out strategies by which improvements might be made. Disgruntled employees normally make their dissatisfaction known to their bosses, rather than surprising them with unforeshadowed resignation letters. Both sides of the labour market recognize that it is in their interests to discuss problems rather than terminating contractual arrangements, for it will be costly and risky to put together new contractual arrangements with unfamiliar third parties.

At a more general level of analysis, neoclassical economists could be said to be focusing on relative prices as the sole economic signalling device because they are theorizing 'as if' deals are fully detailed in non-price terms. If that were the case, then changes in relative prices would be the only thing necessary to get someone to undertake or cease performing an activity. However, as Coase (1937) realized, the trouble is that contracts get very costly to draw up if they include a lot of detail, particularly if that detail relates to what will happen in the distant future (see further section 10.11). Employers, suppliers of inputs, and customers often seem to prefer to keep contracts simple, and flexible in the face of potential for surprise, at the cost of leaving obligations within them somewhat vague. For the duration of a vague contract, such as an employment contract, some kind of *hierarchical* arrangement is often used to make clearer the desired outcome and activity required to produce it. In other words, for example, a boss *tells* a subordinate worker to perform a particular task and *does not offer a fresh financial inducement* in order to get the worker to carry out the instruction. Because the boss does not spell out precisely what the task is and is unable to monitor every action undertaken by the worker, the cost of getting something done, in terms of output forgone from other activities, is inherently vague: the worker chooses how, and how far, to try to deliver what has been requested. An employment contract usually lasts through many directives, on the basis of considerable give and take, without its financial terms needing to be renegotiated to stop the parties from parting company. When employer/employee relationships are seen in these terms, the firm starts looking rather like a small command economy, membership of which is voluntary, in contrast to, say, a Stalinist system in which there is no opportunity for workers to exit if they do not like the commands they are given, the conditions of work or the remuneration they receive.

6.7 An emphasis on one-off deals versus an emphasis on relational contracting

The neoclassical portrayal of economic activities tends to treat transactions as if they can all be considered as separate in diachronic terms, as if, that is to say, a deal done today is utterly unconnected with deals done at later dates. For some purposes this is a perfectly acceptable approximation. The market for canned soft drinks may seem a case in point. Suppose I am on holiday in London in a heatwave and I buy a chilled drink from a corner store. This is unlikely to be the first of many purchases I make from the storekeeper, for a heatwave is a rare event in London, as are my visits, and I need refreshing because I am getting hot moving from one part of London to another and just happen to be passing the shop in question. Matters look less simple once it is recognized that the brand of drink that I buy may be one that has global currency, such as Coca Cola. I may not be building up a trading relationship with the corner store, but I may be seeking to buy a can of Coca Cola on the expectation that it will be exactly the same as what I would get if I purchased a can of Coca Cola anywhere else in the world. A good experience with this brand in the past leads me to purchase it in the future: if so, I have built up a kind of relationship with the Coca Cola company and its national franchise operators, just as I have a regular dealing relationship with particular suppliers of professional services (bank, doctor, dentist, lawyer), as well as with firms that supply me with and service particular kinds of consumer durables (cars, electrical, musical and photographic equipment), and so on.

Behavioural economists see relationship-based trading as widespread and as having profound implications for the ways that businesses operate and organize themselves—for example, respectively, firms' choices of price and capacity levels, and whether they participate in trade associations or get involved in franchising systems. By engaging in 'relational contracting' buyers and sellers may hope to increase the quality of the deals they make. A firm that has experience of a customer's background and needs is in a position to provide better service in future to that customer when service is requested and to know which additional services might be marketed to that customer. Such a firm is also more likely to know which services it would be unable to deliver to the customer's satisfaction; by honestly diverting the customer to another, more suitable supplier, it enhances its chances of keeping its trading relationship intact. As far as the customer is concerned, it may seem to pay to return to a supplier who has previously been found to be satisfactory, not merely because of savings in search costs and start-up costs (there is no need to re-supply information that the supplier has stored from the previous occasion), but also because the longer the relationship lasts, the more the supplier will realize that the customer is a valuable source of business for the future and is therefore worth pampering rather than exploiting for short-term gain. Such trading relationships will be particularly important in cases where product quality is initially uncertain and the costs of poor quality are significant, and/or where confidential information is involved. Professional services fit this requirement on all counts, except in so far as professional accreditation systems serve to guarantee quality. Another good example would be the business of supplying electrical components for vehicle manufacturers: poor electrical components may do terrible things to vehicle reliability, and information about product upgrades involving such components would be valuable to competitors. Suppliers will therefore need to demonstrate that they can be relied upon in terms of quality, delivery and confidentiality before they will be given really significant contracts, but they will also require solid indications that they will receive a steady stream of business, before they will be prepared to make investments in items that are specific to serving the needs of particular customers.

6.8 A focus on products versus a focus on resources and capabilities

A neoclassical analysis of firms tends to see them as bodies which purchase inputs in factor markets with a view to making particular products in the most economical manner. In some versions of this, it is assumed that highly specific purchases of factors are made, with what is expected of the factor in terms of product outputs being written down in detail in the purchase contract. But in most versions of the neoclassical theory of the firm the analysis proceeds as if the services of highly substitutable general-purpose workers and capital equipment are being purchased or rented. Previous decisions in this respect are seen as posing a short-run constraint on the achievement of maximum feasible profits in the event that the firm's external environment changes, but they are not portrayed as fundamentally affecting what the firm does in the long run. This style of analysis makes the firm seem able in the long run to move between product markets in a footloose manner, deterred only by technological entry barriers such as the share of market required to reach the minimum efficient scale of production. The neoclassical firm is a firm without a significant history or a mission to operate in particular markets and segments within those markets.

Following the work of Penrose (1959) on the theory of the growth of the firm, behavioural/institutional economists have come to view the set of product markets in which a firm operates as being very much a consequence of the set of resources which the firm has accumulated over the years. Physical and cognitive resources can typically be adapted to more than a single activity, but they suit some activities much better than others. Relatively specific machinery items often have poor secondhand values, particularly if they are physically difficult to move. Hence, if a firm encounters difficulties in selling outputs for which capital items were originally purchased, it is more likely to set about finding an alternative use for these items of capital rather than simply selling them for whatever they will fetch. Difficulties in writing all aspects of an activity down in a contract mean that many operations and much coordination within organizations are based on informal knowledge that people in the organization have built up about it through time and which cannot be transferred costlessly to other organizations. The costs of hiring new staff and integrating them into the firm's style of operations thus militate against repeated hiring and firing of personnel. The upshot of all this is that a firm is typically mobile between product markets but only within a relatively restricted range and it may take a considerable time to effect a successful major change in its focus.

6.9 The firm as a simple aggregation of product market activities versus the firm as a set of linked activities

The differences under this heading are closely related to those we considered under the previous two headings. In neoclassical analysis, it is common for little attention to be given to how corporate choices are affected by complementarities among different activities; the focus is very much on scope for substitution. The firm tends to be treated as if it is either a single-product operation or, if it is actually portrayed as a multi-product business, as nothing more than the sum of a set of separate product market activities. A multi-product neoclassical firm might thus be imagined as a theoretical construct akin to the type of real-world firm known as a 'conglomerate', that is to say, a firm with interests in all manner of different markets, each of which is operated as a separate activity and can be shed at will if the management team believe they can do better by buying into another market.

The behaviouralists, by contrast, argue that we can learn much about the behaviour and relative fortunes of firms if we keep in mind the possibility that their activities are linked to one another (both within an individual firm, and between firms via networks of informal and contractual relationships) with a view to exploiting 'synergy'. This concept appears to have originated in the management literature in the 1960s and has recently been reinvented by neoclassical industrial economists as 'economies of scope'. As we shall see in section 7.4, synergy is usually associated with spill-over effects between activities or the ability to share investments and human resources between activities in ways that result in the corporate whole being greater than the sum of its parts. Most firms grow not merely by investing in producing existing products on a bigger scale but by expanding the scope of what they do, taking on new activities that are in some way related to what they have done well before. The question of how, and how far, activities are linked together thus becomes a major focus for behavioural economists, for though there are often advantages in building strategies around complementarities there are also risks that may result in the whole being less than the sum of the parts. One hazard is that product markets that seem superficially to have much in common may turn out in practice to have fundamental differences. Another is that if a firm's activities are interlinked, problems may arise due to competitive pressure in one area having implications for related activities. Opportunities for achieving synergy also greatly complicate the tasks of designing an organizational structure and of working out which other firms should be cultivated as allies.

An economist who sees a firm as a simple aggregation of product market activities will only be inclined to label some of the firm's activities as 'core' or 'peripheral' depending on whether their direct contributions to its total profits are relatively large or small. By contrast, an economist who looks at a firm as a complex system will also be interested in the extent to which particular activities and resources are vital to the firm's continued existence because other aspects of the firm's operations are dependent on them. In the latter view a firm is rather like a living being: the loss of a finger in an accident may not be catastrophic (except perhaps to a musician), but the failure of an organ such as the heart or liver tends to be fatal in the absence of a transplant.

7 Production methods and productivity

7.1 Introduction

If we are to be able to analyse choices about what to produce and how to produce it, a key requirement may seem to be the ability to identify and measure costs of production. It might seem reasonable to hope that economic theory can make predictions about the kinds of cost structures that we might measure and how managers might be expected to behave in the face of such costs. Unfortunately, there is a fundamental problem which runs throughout most presentations of the economics of the firm without ever being recognized, let alone solved. Having been alerted to this problem via Buchanan and Thirlby (eds) (1973), Littlechild, (1978) and Wiseman and Littlechild (1990), I feel obliged to raise it at the outset, but readers should understand that much of what follows in terms of expositions of mainstream material proceeds as if the problem did not exist. The problem, put simply, is that opportunity costs are subjective phenomena; they cannot be observed.

To open your mind to the difficulty, think back to your first classes in economics which drew your attention to the fact that everything has its opportunity cost. There you should have discovered that the more colourful way economists have for saying this, namely, 'there's no such thing as a free lunch', is often misused by non-economists: the absence of free lunches arises simply because 'you can't have your cake and eat it', not because the person paying for the lunch may be hoping to use it as a means of affecting the recipient's behaviour. The free lunch has a cost in the sense that, by accepting it, the chooser is giving up the opportunity to be doing something else, such as paying for lunch elsewhere, not having lunch at all, continuing to work and having a later lunch, and so on. All this sounds quite innocuous. The trouble is that opportunity costs involve the next best thing that the decision-maker had in mind as a possible course of action but rejected in preference to the action actually selected. If I accept your offer of a free lunch, you cannot see what I would have done instead. If I reject your offer, you may be able to find out what I did instead, but that does not entitle you to infer that your free lunch ranked number two on my list of rival courses of action at the time I made the decision. When I choose, I construct in my mind a list of possible rival courses of action, consider their possible sequels, and then reject all except for one (which might be the decision to keep gathering information about possible courses of action). My choice is based on a set of anticipations, but these, too, only exist in my head. The anticipated consequences of the action I judge to be the least bad alternative to the action I select are my opportunity cost, but these consequences will never be realized. In this sense, cost 'cannot be objective: it refers to a "non-event"' (Wiseman and Littlechild, 1990: 100).

If we see opportunity costs in this way then grave questions arise about the legitimacy of discussing theories of production with reference to 'cost functions' and diagrams that have an axis labelled 'costs'. When a typical objectivist, neoclassical economist draws, say, an 'average total cost curve' what is really being shown are *not costs in the opportunity cost sense but financial outlays*. When an accountant does an audit of 'costs', it is historical outlays that are being examined, not foregone anticipations. When public utility managers are instructed, as they often are, to 'set prices at equal to marginal costs in order to maximize social welfare', their actions cannot be checked by their paymasters with reference to 'costs incurred'. After the event, it is often difficult to prove what would have happened had a different choice been made and, as Littlechild (1978: 53–4) observes,

> [The relevant cost of production] is not the money outlay but the value of some alternative foregone use and this alternative is not 'given' but exists only in the mind of the manager(s). Two managers with different knowledge about available alternatives, or different views about the future, will associate different costs with the very same output. Since the correctness of beliefs about the future cannot be established objectively (at the time), neither can be said to be wrong—each is right given his beliefs.

The moral of all this may be that the theory of costs is at best to be seen as a set of tools for helping potential decision-makers to choose, first, which kinds of information they might want to gather and, then, between rival courses of action, given their perceptions of alternatives. If we want to appraise the quality of managerial decision-making in the past and hence decide whom should be allowed to take particular decisions in the future, perhaps we need to spend time asking managers to give accounts of how they estimated what consumers wanted, which factors of production and production methods were available and which prices it seemed necessary to pay in order to get particular outputs produced. Such accounts might then be examined critically in terms of whether or not the managers in question were prone (a) to have unjustifiably blinkered perceptions of possibilities; (b) to be systematically biased in their assessments; and (c) to use decision rules of doubtful efficacy. Whether or not objectivist theories of costs are useful in getting an idea of what goes on in firms when production decisions are made will depend how well the economist's perspective matches how managers see things in practice.

A second area of difficulty of which it is useful to be aware when studying the economics of the firm is interdependence between production costs and transaction costs. Production costs tend to be seen as payments—note the objectivist view, once again—to human and non-human factors of production which actually produce the output of the firm. These outlays include wages paid to assembly-line workers, lease payments on machinery and the rental of buildings. Transaction costs, which receive a great deal of attention in Chapters 10 and 11, may be said to involve sacrifices incurred in transferring property rights from one legal entity to another and enforcing those property rights—in other words, the costs of doing deals and making sure that one gets no less than one bargained for. An objectivist line of thinking tends to make one give examples of transaction costs in terms of legal bills involved in getting contracts drawn up and signed, advertising and appraisal expenses when new staff are being hired or work put out to tender, and payments to management to ensure that workers' capabilities are used to the best advantage of the firm within the terms of their employment contracts. Subjectivist examples would include, respectively, outcomes that were imagined as possibilities in the event the particular lawyer were not engaged, resources not committed to advertising and appraisal, and what might be forgone if alternative systems of worker motivation, coordination and monitoring were used.

Difficulties in separating the two types of cost arise wherever transaction costs affect production costs or production costs affect transaction costs. An example of the former would be where, as a result of spending more time searching for and evaluating potential employees, the firm ended up with employees who were more professionally capable and committed, more motivated to work without supervision, and who thus produced more for a given wage; or where, as a result of trying to economize on expenditure on managers by giving workers more responsibility over issues such as quality control, output either went up or down for a given employment of line workers. An example of the latter would be where investment in more specialized machinery and tools reduced the incidence of breakdowns and lapses of quality that managers might otherwise be needed to sort out. Once this interdependence is recognized, one can readily see very different strategies of how a firm or public service agency might minimize costs of meeting particular objectives: (a) pay workers well and give them much responsibility to act in a professional manner, and have a lean management structure; and (b) don't trust workers for a moment to know what to do or give a fair day's work for a fair day's pay: instead, pay them as little as possible and spend a lot on management to make sure the job gets done. (As far as workers in public agencies such as universities and hospitals are concerned, I suspect that many would see the first strategy as what prevailed in the 1970s and the second strategy as very much a part of the 1990s.) Unfortunately, the interdependence of production and transaction costs has received little attention.

Much neoclassical work on production and costs ultimately turns out to be focused on specifying the characteristics of an optimal mix of factors of production and rates of output of the items being produced. It makes little reference to transaction costs: the discussion of the equilibrium of the firm centres on showing why a number of variables should be equalized at the margin and how small deviations either side would result in lower levels of profit. The analysis tends to proceed as if the firm is a black box which consists of a set of factors—land, labour and capital items of various kinds—overseen by an entrepreneur who gets to claim what is left over after all the factors of production have been paid from the revenues received by the firm. Because it is often based around assumptions of full information, the neoclassical model of the firm is not amenable to development into anything more than this black box: without information problems, it is hard to see a need for an organizational structure or departments such as sales, finance, and research and development (see Kay, 1984: 34–9). At the other extreme, there is a growing literature on transaction cost economics which tends to focus on the best design of organizational structure, or the best set of decisions about what should be produced within the firm rather than bought from outside suppliers—all as though the optimal technology is given in terms of machines and workers required to perform a particular task and as if the only problem is to devise the best way of motivating them to deliver the goods in the required volumes and standards of quality (cf. Williamson, 1975, 1985). In this chapter, my aim is to begin with an examination of the black box neoclassical perspective on production and costs but then gradually introduce more and more complications associated with problems of knowledge. A lot will be said about transaction costs in the rest of this book but much of this will be in contexts in which deals are done without knowledge of best-practice production technologies.

7.2 Production functions and cost curves

Neoclassical production theory has much in common with neoclassical consumer theory. The technical apparatus is basically the same in both cases, except that, in place of preference orderings depicted graphically as sets of indifference curves, we have production functions depicted as sets of isoquant curves and, instead of budget lines, we have isocost lines. A production function is an engineering relationship between combinations of physical inputs (such as workers with a particular skills background and machines of a particular kind) and physical outputs. One specific example commonly encountered in the economics literature, named after two American economists who used it as a basis for empirical work, is the 'Cobb–Douglas production function':

$$Y = aK^b.L^c$$

For convenience in econometric work aimed at estimating the value of its parameters, it is often written in logarithmic form as:

$$\log Y = \log a + b \log K + c \log L$$

where Y is the maximum possible output of the commodity in question to be obtained using particular amounts of K and L (usually 'capital' and 'labour'). Most introductory books on mathematics for economists give a good range of examples based around this general type of production function, as well as other types that take a more complex form. One thing which should be readily apparent from such a function is that it implies that a given level of output, Y, can be produced in a variety of ways that involve different mixes of the two factors, K and L. If we depict the amounts of the two factors as axes of a two-dimensional diagram, then we can draw on this diagram a set of isoquants, each isoquant showing the alternative mixes of the two factors required to produce a particular output.

A production function such as the one popularized by Cobb and Douglas will generate isoquants that slope downwards to the right at a decreasing rate, just like standard indifference curves. (Indeed, in simple mathematical treatments of neoclassical consumer theory it is common to see a cardinal approach to utility maximization involving a Cobb–Douglas utility function which has exactly the same format as the production function except that Y is replaced by U, for units of utility, and K and L are replaced by two kinds of consumer goods.) Typical production functions are chosen to imply isoquants with a decreasing downward rate of slope on the basis that substitution between one factor of production for another is likely to be imperfect: if one factor is taken as fixed in quantity and additional units of the other factor put to work in conjunction with it there is likely to be a problem of diminishing marginal productivity in respect of the factor that is variable. For example, if the supply of land on a farm is fixed, output may be increased by using more workers to tend the crop, or by applying more fertiliser or machinery. However, more and more units of a variable factor will need to be applied to get a given increment of output. There might even come a point where marginal productivity of a variable factor became negative, implying upward-sloping isoquants: the quality of the crop might suffer from an excess of fertiliser or because workers are getting in each other's way. It is commonly just assumed that marginal products are positive and hence that the slope of isoquants, which is known as (minus) the *marginal rate of technical substitution*, is diminishing. The parallel with diminishing marginal rates of substitution in indifference analysis should be obvious.

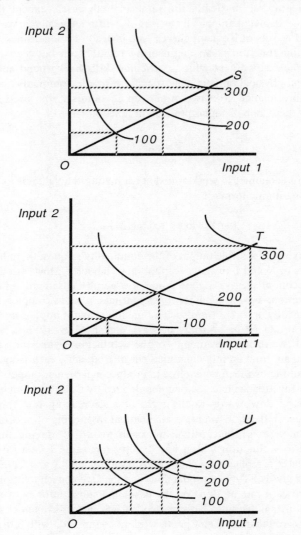

Figure 7.1: Constant, decreasing and increasing returns to scale

It is conventional to speak of a particular ratio of factors of production as a *production technology* and to show an individual technology on an isoquant diagram as a straight-line ray extending from the origin. For example, we might imagine one technology that involves

160

two units of factor K being used with each unit of factor L, and another that involves three units of factor K being used with each unit of factor L: clearly, the two rays will have different slopes, just as with consumption technologies in Lancaster's theory of demand (see section 3.6, but note that in the Lancaster diagrams the axes show the *out*puts of characteristics associated with a particular consumption good or combination of goods). An obvious question of interest is what happens to the volume of output as a technology is scaled up, for this will affect the average cost of producing the product in question. Possible answers are illustrated in the three panels of Figure 7.1 which deal with the issue of returns to scale as it is normally handled in neoclassical economics. Though confined to two dimensions and hence to just a pair of inputs, the thinking outlined in these diagrams could be generalized to more dimensions.

If a doubling of both inputs results in a doubling of output, we have constant returns to scale in engineering terms: technology ray OS may be characterized in this way. If a doubling of both inputs leads to less (more) than twice the output, we have decreasing (increasing) returns to scale, as with technology technology ray OT (OU). If the same kinds of returns to scale are observed along all technology rays on an individual diagram, then the entire production function for the product in question is said to exhibit that kind of returns to scale. As a practice exercise you might try plugging a sample of different values of K and L into a Cobb–Douglas production function and thereby discover whether it exhibits, as a whole, constant, decreasing or increasing returns to scale. What you should find is that if the parameters b and c add up to one the production function as a whole exhibits constant returns to scale, whereas if they add up to more (less) than one, then it exhibits increasing (decreasing) returns to scale.

This way of looking at returns to scale is fine as a formal exercise, but in practice it is difficult to explain the origin of non-constant returns without referring to an indivisibility of some kind. When firms achieve falling average costs as they expand output what typically happens is that rather than a movement further along a particular technology ray, there is a change in the factor mix to a different technology which involves one or all of:

(a) more effective use of an indivisible factor (for example, hooking two personal computers up to a printer that was previously only attached to one and was idle much of the time, or doubling the load carried by a truck but still using only a single driver);

(b) savings in construction or packaging costs due to economies of increased dimensions (for example, an oil tanker that can carry 200 000 deadweight tons of crude oil is only about twice the width, length and depth of one that can carry just 25 000 deadweight tons; and note that a two-metre cube-shaped box has an outside area of 24 square metres and a capacity of 8 cubic metres, whereas the sides of a one metre cube-shaped box have an outside area of 6 square metres even though the box has a capacity of only a single cubic metre);

(c) scope for dividing the tasks up in a more specialized manner, thereby economizing on the time it takes to train each worker to master the operation and reducing time lost switching between tasks (for example, the kind of assembly-line system that Henry Ford developed to manufacture his Model-T car in huge numbers, and which was

161

satirized by Charlie Chaplin in his film *Modern Times*; see also section 7.9).

As far as examples of decreasing returns are concerned, it is commonly noted that if an entrepreneur doubles the scale of her/his operations by building a new factory identical to her/his original one and staffs it in exactly the same way, it might be the case that less than twice the original output is achieved because s/he finds it impossible to be in two places at once to supervise the operations of both factories. The problem is obviously that the entrepreneur is a fixed factor, so in this example we do not have decreasing returns in the precise sense depicted in the middle panel of Figure 7.1 even though it is implied that average costs rise with output.

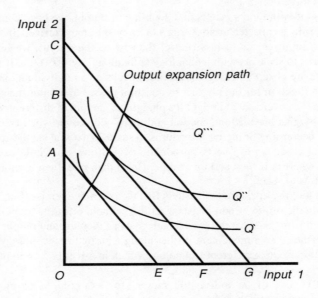

Figure 7.2: Cost-minimizing technologies: a production function's long-run output expansion path

The discussion so far has largely been focusing on physical aspects of the production process with only simple references to changes in average costs of producing each unit associated with scale (dis)economies. Nothing much has been said about the optimal choice of production technology. To understand this, we have to move beyond engineering information and start making reference to the outlays that it will have to incur to hire particular factors of production. Figure 7.2 shows how this may be done in the long-run case where it is possible to vary all the factors of production. In addition to isoquants, $Q`$, $Q``$ and $Q```$, for three levels of output, I have drawn a series of straight lines, *AE*, *BF* and *CG*, parallel to one another. The latter are known as isocost lines, whose slopes reflect the relative prices of the two types of inputs. They show which combinations of factors can be purchased for a particular amount of money, and are thus the production theory equivalent of budget lines in consumer theory. Isocost lines will only be parallel and straight if the relative prices of inputs remain constant whatever the volumes of the inputs that the firm chose to purchase. In practice, of course, it is possible that the firm might find itself bidding up an input price against itself as it purchased more or that it might be in a position to obtain discounts for bulk purchases (cf. sections 8.3 and 9.11). For each isocost line there will be a maximum output that is feasible. Under the standard neoclassical assumptions concerning continuously diminishing marginal technical rates of substitution each isocost line will be tangential with a different isoquant. The line linking these points of tangency is known as the output expansion path for this product at this set of relative prices: it shows the set of expenditure-minimizing bundles of inputs and their associated output levels. It would be simple to turn this information about expenditure and output levels into graphs showing long-run average, total and marginal 'cost' curves.

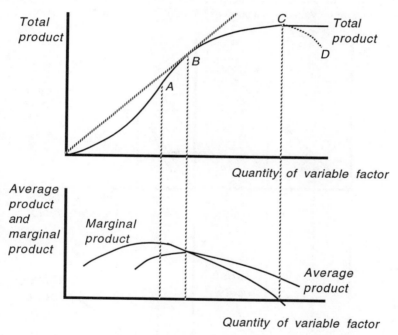

Figure 7.3: Total, average and marginal products when only one input can be varied

Figures 7.3, 7.4 and 7.5 may be studied to see explicitly how engineering information and factor price information can be combined to derive the consequences for output and expenditure of changes in the mix of factors. Unlike Figure 7.2, these diagrams refer to the short run, for I keep things simple by allowing only one input to be variable, with all of the others taken as being in fixed supply. This is easy enough to discuss in theoretical terms but obviously begs some questions about how much scope for substitution there may be in practice: for example, a computer workstation is normally designed for only one keyboard operator, but it may be possible to run extra shifts of workers. With agricultural production

163

it may not be possible, say, to add extra fertiliser without incurring extra labour costs, but existing labour could be diverted away from other activities on the farm and the overall impact on total output could then be investigated.

Neoclassical economists commonly assume that the relationship between total output and the variable factor of production takes the form shown in the upper panel of Figure 7.3. The average product of the variable input is simply total product divided by the number of units of the variable output that are required (along with the given quantity of other inputs) to make it. Average product is indicated by the slope of a straight line from the origin to the total product curve, and in this case it reaches its maximum at point *B* on the total product function. The marginal product of the variable factor is the effect of using an extra units of it on the total product. This is indicated by the slope of the total product function. Initially, as one moves right from the origin, marginal product is assumed to be increasing, hence the increasing slope of the total product function. However, at point *A*, marginal product reaches its maximum value: it is a point of inflexion in the total product curve.

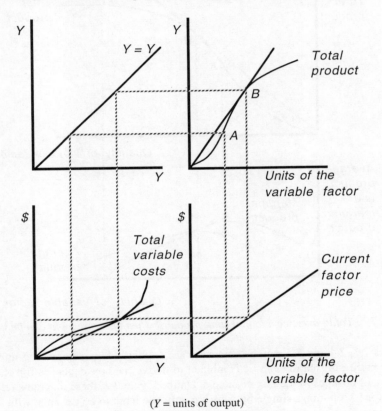

(Y = units of output)

Figure 7.4: The relationship between the total product function and total variable costs when only one input can be varied

Further increases in use of the variable input are accompanied by successively smaller increases in output. An assumption of free disposal (in other words, an unwanted input can be removed from the production process without the firm incurring any cost) ensures that the total product function is *OCE* rather than *OCD*. Otherwise, it could be the case that the the firm ran into a situation in which output fell as more and more units of the variable input were applied: as they say about cases in which the marginal product of labour turns negative, 'too many cooks may spoil the broth'. The lower panel of Figure 7.3 shows the relationships between average product and marginal product for the variable input in question.

The four-panel diagram, Figure 7.4, shows how we can move from a purely physical set of engineering relationships between inputs and outputs to a pecuniary one: if we know the per unit price of the variable input we can infer a total variable cost function for this input while treating other inputs as fixed costs. The relationship between total variable cost, short-run marginal cost and average variable cost is shown below in the two-panel diagram, Figure 7.5. Note the mirror-image relationship between the curves on Figures 7.3 and 7.5.

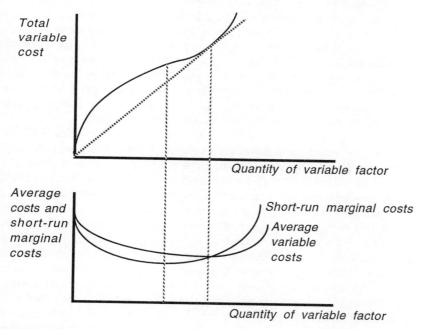

Figure 7.5: The relationship between total, average and marginal variable costs

The neoclassical view of production functions involves a number of simplifying assumptions. First, it presumes that there is a great range of possible techniques of production involving slight variations upon each other, with no discontinuous jumps in output arising due to small changes in the amounts of the factors used, both together or separately. This may not be the case: some products may involve 'fixed proportions production functions', for example, recipes for cooking or making cocktails often require a constant ratio of inputs, and substituting between inputs may produce a totally different kind of end product. (To leave out most of the yeast when making bread and replace it by a great deal more flour may produce loaves of equal volume but they will be more like bricks than bread!) In practice a great range of alternative technologies may not be available between which managers may choose. Technologies have to be invented and brought to production readiness; they are not provided like manna from heaven. But the kinds of technologies that engineers try to develop and find it worthwhile to perfect may be very much dependent upon market incentive structures (see Loasby, 1982: 237, and the discussion of Marshall's work in section 8.2). This point was central to the 'small is beautiful' work of Schumacher (1973), who argued that there was a great gap between technologies suited to rich nations and those that were in use in poor nations: there had been a failure to develop and market what Schumacher called the 'intermediate technologies' that might represent a technological leap forward over, say, harvesting with a scythe and lots of labour time, but which would require less expenditure on capital and use more labour time than a combine harvester.

Second, a production function can only be specified in respect of a limited number of inputs if different inputs of a particular kind can be aggregated in a meaningful way. Many neoclassical economists will happily write about labour and capital without for a moment pausing to think how different types of workers and machinery might be aggregated. Often they simply presume it is safe to add up different types of, say, machines in terms of their market values. Unfortunately, wherever it is possible that changes in the volume of production and/or changes in production methods will affect relative prices in the economy, value-based aggregation runs into various logical problems, whose discovery caused a major debate in economics in the 1950s and 1960s (see Harcourt, 1972).

A particularly contentious area concerned what would happen if the price of labour time fell relative to the rate of return on financial investments in physical capital. Changes in the price of labour will affect the prices of different machines in different ways, because different machines are produced with the aid of different amounts of labour and different production systems have different financial time profiles in terms of outlays and returns. An engineering technique that seems to involve relatively more 'capital' than another at one wages/profit relativity might reverse its ranking as the relative prices of labour and finance changed, but there might even be a switch back to the original ranking if the relative prices were changed further in the same direction. In other words, attempts to speak of increases in capital or labour intensity in response to, respectively, reductions in the rate of interest or falls in real wages could be utterly meaningless if they were intended to relate in some way to changes in aggregate physical quantities of factors. A production process that was once recorded as 'capital intensive' in terms of value of capital per unit of output might have to be relabelled as 'labour intensive', simply because the market price of new replacement machines of the same price had fallen due to changes in wages relative to the rate of interest. This should be kept in mind in section 7.3, which covers the standard analysis of substitution. Purists would prefer to theorize in terms of production functions in which each distinct type of worker or non-human factor of production is thought of as a separate factor, but this rules out the use of convenient two-dimensional diagrams.

Thirdly, the production function framework is essentially static, allowing us to consider alternative logical possibilities that might exist at a point in time. It is tricky to use in respect of changes of technology in response to changes in factor prices that occur as history unfolds. The trouble is that the set of best-practice technologies for particular combinations of spending on different factors of production will change as advances in engineering knowledge occur. Sometimes, it may be possible to incorporate these changes with minor additional expenditure on upgrading equipment and skills, but quite often improved know-how can only be embodied in an economy by replacing old vintages of equipment with brand-new ones and instituting major retraining programmes for workers. The diagrams used in this section to show how neoclassical economists look at the relationship between engineering knowledge and choices of production technique dodged this issue by assuming a given state of knowledge (see, however, section 7.7).

Fourthly, it should be noted that the neoclassical analysis of production proceeds as if all that there is to be known about a particular technique can be written down in an engineering 'blueprint' (neoclassical economists who dislike aggregating labour or capital of different types often describe the state of knowledge about engineering possibilities by using the phrase 'book of blueprints' instead of referring to a production function). It leaves out the human factor in determining how much output one gets from a particular set of machinery and workers. Owing to the limits of language and individual powers of expression—in other words, aspects of bounded rationality—some knowledge may be impossible to write down in this way, and be something that comes only with experience on the job. This kind of knowledge has been labelled 'tacit knowledge' or 'personal knowledge' by Polanyi (1958) (see also Nelson and Winter, 1982: 117–21). An everyday example of this is knowledge of how to swim or ride a bicycle: most of us can undertake these activities but we do so without being able to explain how we manage to do so. Polanyi (1958: 52) had grave doubts about the scope for rigorous scientific study of industrial processes and hence about scope for replicating them or transferring them from one enterprise/plant to another:

> Great industries ... were carrying on their activities in the manner of an art without any clear knowledge of the constituent detailed operations. When modern scientific research was applied to these traditional industries it was faced in the first place with the task of discovering what was actually going on there and how it was that it produced the goods.... [E]ven in the modern industries the indefinable knowledge is still an essential part of technology. I have myself watched in Hungary a new, imported machine for blowing electric lamp bulbs, the exact counterpart of which was operating successfully in Germany, failing for a whole year to produce a single flawless bulb.

Output may thus depend on how much experience the workers have had in using the equipment with which they have been provided (see further, section 7.6). It may also depend on managerial skills: as General Motors discovered through a joint venture in which it allowed Toyota to manage its factory in Fremont, California, a well-run plant using relatively little automation can achieve much lower costs than a state-of-the-art plant managed in a non-Japanese style (see Keller, 1989, and sections 7.8 and 7.11). It is only relatively recently that most economists have woken up to this: for years, many neoclassical studies of economic growth sought to explain productivity differences between nations in terms of differences in the mix and amounts of factors used, rather than in terms of the competence with which they were used.

Whatever we think about the assumptive strategies used by mainstream economists for modelling relationships between inputs and outputs, we may often feel quite relaxed about using the basic idea that there may exist a range of technologies for producing the products in which we are interested. For example, a firm that paints house exteriors may be able to choose between using ladders and scaffolding, between using brushes, rollers and sprays and different types of paint, all of which may involve needs for different amounts of labour time and different degrees of skill on the part of painters. To judge the cheapest way to do a particular job to a required standard may thus involve quite a good deal of expertise, the more so the less standardized the houses happen to be. Even in the process of working out the price to be quoted, the person who works out the firm's estimates may have to choose between different ways of measuring up the house. Likewise, the manager of a transport company will face choices between different ways of getting goods between destinations: time can be saved by substituting more fuel for driver time or even by using aircraft rather than trucks, and different carriage modes may have different chances of being held up due to congestion or bad weather. A behavioural economist would suggest that often the complexity of the problem is such that the decision-maker will fall back on simple rules of thumb rather than try to work out the optimal method of production, but the kind of optimizing analysis involved in the diagrams we are about to explore may not be an unreasonable approximation in situations where the chooser has a great deal of expertise, or can call upon computers for assistance.

An important omission from this discussion of optimal choices of production methods has been any consideration of what it might be optimal to do in an environment where the firm faces fluctuations in its rate of sales. Aside from Stigler (1939), Hart (1940, 1942) and modern-day scenario planners (cf. section 5.6), few economists have devoted much attention to the costs of optimizing a firm's production technique to a particular rate of output. A technology that minimizes costs when sales fall within normal ranges may turn out to be far more expensive to use if production rates have to be moved outside of this normal range. A modular factory that can be closed down or extended in stages may be more costly for any given rate of output, just as a component hi-fi system of a given specification will cost more than an integrated one, yet its flexibility may on some occasions seem worth paying for. There are few easier ways to lose money than to invest in a custom-designed production line which is highly automated and/or involves many individual, specialized job-stations and then have to run it way below full capacity because demand has built up slower than expected or has suffered a setback (cf. Loasby, 1976: 91–2, on Pressed Steel's disastrous attempt to diversify into refrigerator production). It may be very tempting to produce for stock in the hope that soon demand will reach higher levels, but this will not be possible without incurring warehousing costs. If a series of smaller production systems involving fewer, multi-skilled workers is used, costs may be higher for any given rate of output but subsystems can be added or mothballed relatively easily to match output variations. Modular systems—that are, as Simon (1969) puts it, 'decomposable'—also have the advantage that they are less vulnerable to breakdowns: as anyone who works on a computer network knows, the cost of having a central file server and workstations without hard disks is that if the system crashes no one can do any work, whereas if everyone has individual computers running individual software via their own hard disks the failure of a connecting link is far less disruptive.

7.3   Factor substitution

Changes in relative prices of factor inputs will affect the slopes of the isocost lines just as changes in relative prices of consumer goods affect the slope of an individual consumer's budget constraint. The optimal set of production techniques will thus change with changes in relative input prices and we should expect to see substitution between factors. Figure 7.6 shows how a neoclassical economist would analyse factor substitution in response to a relative price change. The analysis here is very similar to typical three-budget line/two-indifference curve exercises in neoclassical consumer theory and welfare economics. Changes in factor prices may affect the firm's preferred rate of output, but to keep the analysis simple we look only at how the cheapening of input 1 affects the cost of producing a given volume of output represented by the isoquant $Q`$, and the optimal technique for producing that volume of output. Initially the firm is using OH units of input 1 and OQ units of input 2, and is spending the amount represented by isocost line SJ. A fall in the relative price of input 1 cause the bottom end of isocost lines to swing to the right, pivoting on their intersections with the vertical axis. SJ thus swings round to become SL. For the same outlay that would previously have been needed to produce $Q`$, the firm can now produce $Q``$. By reducing the use of input 2 from OQ to OP and increasing the use of input 1 from OH to OI, $Q`$ units of output can be achieved at a lower cost than before (on isocost line RK).

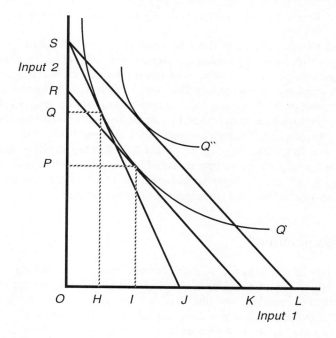

Figure 7.6: Factor substitution in response to a change in relative input prices

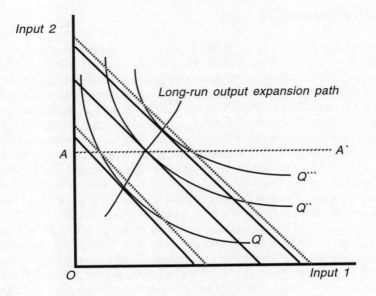

Figure 7.7: Short-run versus long-run factor substitutions

In the short run, however, it will not be possible to vary all factors, so the short-run output expansion path following a change in factor prices will not be the same as the long-run output expansion path for the new set of factor prices (if indeed they persist for long enough for full adaptation to take place). This issue is addressed in Figure 7.7. Here, a firm has committed itself to *OA* of input 2 and it is confined to varying input 1 in the short run. Its short-run output expansion path is thus *AA*`. At the new set of relative prices it is only at output rate *Q*`` that the mix of factors is exactly what the firm would wish to employ in the long run. If it were to produce more (*Q*```) or less (*Q*`) than this it will be able to lower its average costs in the long run by varying its use of both inputs: note the broken isocost lines that cut through the *Q*` and *Q*``` isoquants where they cut *AA*`; these both lie to the right of the solid, parallel isocost lines that are tangential to these isoquants.

7.4   The mix of output

The discussion so far has been focusing on alternative ways of producing a single type of product. To begin to consider choices concerning the optimal mix of a variety of different products, we need to introduce two additional devices: product transformation curves and iso-revenue lines (my discussion here draws on Scitovsky, 1971: 141–3). In Figure 7.8, the three solid curves are hypothetical product transformation curves, which are a variation on the idea of a production possibility frontier presented—often with reference to tradeoff possibilities between outputs of guns and butter—in introductory economics. These curves show the best combinations of outputs that can be produced for financial outlays (or 'costs')

170

of $1.0m, $1.4m or $1.8m. As we move along any one of these curves from its point of intersection with the vertical axis, output of product B has to be given up in order to produce more of A. Formally speaking, we say the curves are concave to the origin. The steepening of the slopes of the curves implies that increasingly large sacrifices of one commodity have to be made to increase the output of the other.

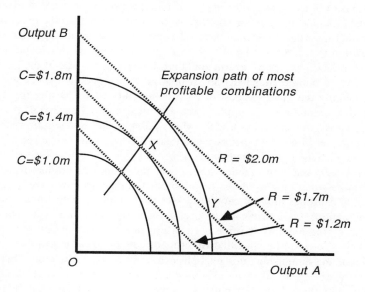

Figure 7.8: The optimal mix of output

The trio of broken straight lines on Figure 7.8 show hypothetical alternative combinations of the two products that could be sold for $1.2m, $1.7m or $2.0m. These iso-revenue lines are linear if the demands for these products are not inter-related. If the market prices of the products are unaffected by the number of units of them that the firm attempts to sell (in other words, if the firm is a price-taker), then the iso-revenue lines will be parallel and the relative revenues that they represent will be reflected by their distances from the origin (a curve involving twice the revenue will be twice as far away). The expansion path of most profitable feasible output combinations is given by the set of tangencies between product transformation curves and iso-revenue curves. Compare combination X and combination Y: both combinations of outputs can be sold for $1.7m, to produce X involves an outlay of only $1.4m and a profit of $0.3m, whereas Y requires an outlay of $1.8m and entails a loss of $0.1m. But we cannot infer which point on the expansion path the firm's managers will choose unless we know what goals they are pursuing.

Concavity of product transformation curves could be explained on the presumption that the marginal cost of producing each type of output rises as the rate of output is increased: constant marginal costs of both commodities would imply linear product transformation curves whose slopes were simply the ratio of the marginal costs of the two commodities. If the production of the two commodities is interconnected in some way, then the

171

transformation curves will be more curved. For example, they may be *joint products* of the same production process: cattle farming may produce meat, milk and hides. Very many production processes involve *by-products*: for example, a major input for the manufacture of acrylic fibre is ammonia, which is produced in vast quantities as a by-product of the ammonium fertiliser industry. (These examples come from a 1982 paper in which Steedman produces dozens of other empirical examples of joint production in order to make the case that economists should treat joint production as the norm rather than the exception. Other examples of interdependence that can have similar effects are discussed at the end of this section in relation to the concept known as 'synergy' or 'economies of scope'.) However, product transformation curves for a firm could be convex to the origin if the production of one commodity is hampered when the firm is also engaged in producing the other commodity, making the marginal cost of each commodity an increasing function of the output of both commodities. Examples here are most easily conceived of where one production process produces a by-product which pollutes the production process for the other commodity, as with a firm that owned a thermal power station that released harmful acid rain over a plantation also owned by the firm.

If attempts were made in practice to discover the shapes of product transformation curves it is unlikely that they would be found to be as smooth as they have been shown in Figure 7.8. Indivisibilities in production processes tend to impose constraints on the set of feasible combinations that a firm can produce, particularly in the short run. The technique known as linear programming is often used in practice for finding optimal solutions to problems where these can be specified in terms of sets of linear constraints rather than constraints involving diminishing marginal physical rates of transformation. This technique would normally be employed in its algebraic form and solutions would be derived in complex cases with the aid of a computer. However, graphical analysis can be used to get the basic idea about how the technique works and Figure 7.9 gives an example of this, based on data shown in Tables 7.1 and Table 7.2.

Table 7.1: Daily capacities of car- and van-production activities

| Activity | | Product | |
Name	Code on Figure 7.9	Cars	Vans
Metal stamping	*AA*	60	40
Engine assembly	*BB*	50	70
Car Assembly	*CC*	45	—
Van assembly	*VV*	—	30

The exposition here, like that in many other texts, is adapted from an example in a classic guide to linear programming by Dorfman, Samuelson and Solow (1958: 133–8). It concerns a hypothetical manufacturer of cars and vans whose operations are limited by four technological constraints arising from investments that the firm has made. First, it has a metal stamping plant which can produce pressings for both cars and vans but not at the same time. The components for the more complex car bodies take one and a half times as long to produce as those for vans: in other words, to produce parts for two car bodies the firm must forgo three van bodies if the pressing plant is working to full capacity. Secondly, the firm has an engine assembly plant and workers there can assemble either car engines or van engines, the latter taking longer per unit. As with the body components stamping process, there are linear tradeoffs between production of car engines and van engines. Whereas engines and body parts are supplied from shared operations, the cars and vans are assembled on separate production lines: cars cannot be assembled on the van line when the car line is working to full capacity, and vice versa.

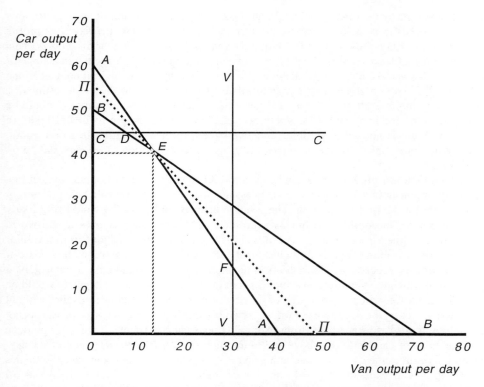

Figure 7.9: Choice of production mix, subject to linear constraints

Taken together, the four linear constraints limit the firm's set of feasible combinations to those on the edges or interior of the polygon *OCDEFV*. To work out which is the most profitable production mix subject to these four constraints we need to know how each car or van that could be produced would contribute to the firm's profits. Table 7.2 gives some hypothetical information on prices at which the products are sold to retailers and the average variable cost of producing each unit.

Table 7.2: Profitability of car and van production

		Cars	Vans
	Ex-factory price	20 000	18 000
less	Average variable costs	18 000	15 800
	Contribution to profits	2 000	2 200

It should be evident from Table 7.2 that if the firm cuts production of vans by 10 units per day, it needs to be able to increase production of cars by 11 units per day if its profits are not to fall, since the gross profit margin on vans is 1.1 times the margin on cars. This information enables a set of iso-profit lines to be drawn on Figure 7.9, each with a slope of minus 1.1. To avoid cluttering the diagram, I have simply drawn the highest attainable one of these, $\Pi\Pi$, which shows that maximum daily profits subject to these constraints are achieved by the feasible mix of cars and vans that generates the same profits as could be obtained from producing either 55 cars or 50 vans, in other words, profits of $110 000. In fact, this figure is not quite possible, since we have a further constraint to worry about, namely the indivisibility of the products: the graph gives a solution of 40 cars and 13.64 vans per day.

Although linear programming can be used to find an optimal mix of output subject to a set of linear constraints, it may be unwise to assume that the solution would be a position of equilibrium for the firm in question. The solution depicted in Figure 7.9 would very likely be seen not as an equilibrium but as a problem if it were generated in a real-world application of linear programming. As Moss (1981: 41–4, 53–5) concludes from a similar example, the situation provides an inducement for a new strategic commitment as part of the evolutionary process by which the firm develops. From the standpoint of managers, a situation in which the van assembly line was running at less than half its capacity would be an inducement for searching for a way of moving some of the constraints to its use, without adversely affecting the operations of the car assembly line. Lowering the price of vans is not a solution in this case since the firm faces binding physical constraints. It can only produce combinations of cars and vans above and to the right of *CDEFV* by increasing efficiency, making new investments or subcontracting some of the work to other companies. Strategies involving new investments in metal stamping or engine assembly will move the *AA* or *BB* constraint lines out to the right, but if such investments come in indivisible lumps then the managers may well find they can solve the problem of excess capacity on its van assembly line only at the cost of leaving themselves with, say, spare capacity in its enlarged engine assembly plant. Managers would set off around the decision cycle yet again.

If the managers find it hard to conceive of ways in which they can make profitable investments aimed solely at relieving the bottlenecks on using their existing plant, then a bit of lateral thinking may yield a different kind of solution. (Certainly, they will have to think of a list of strategies, because such lists are not God-given.) When difficulties in removing excess capacity in one area without causing it to arise elsewhere are due to indivisibilities, the solution often is not to *scale up* all existing operations by different multiples until balance is achieved because all the constraints intersect at the same point. Such a strategy is prone to be thwarted by the markets for the products in question simply being too small to permit such perfect specialization on the existing set of product-markets. Instead, the solution may lie with increasing the *scope* of the firm's operations by taking on new ventures that make the most of advantage of resources into which funds have already been sunk. Such advantages of joint production are usually known nowadays in the economics and business history literatures (for example, Chandler, 1990) as *economies of scope* but they were originally recognized in the management literature under the heading of *synergy* or the '*2 + 2 = 5 effect*'.

Synergy effects are often put forward as the basis for mergers between companies as well as being used to explain the directions in which individual firms opt to expand their activities. The idea is perhaps easier to understand via a merger-based example, and as you think along these lines it might help also to have in mind the economics of marriage or cohabitation and the old expression that 'Two people can live as cheaply as one, so long as one doesn't eat!'. Suppose two firms are merged by synergy-seeking managers, keen to exploit potential linkages between their activities. Various results are possible: one is that there may be no change in the total sales revenue but that total costs are reduced; another is that sales revenues may increase even if no cost savings are achieved. Such improvements can come from a variety of sources. Ansoff (1968), who first propounded the idea, writes of (1) sales synergy (achieved via the use of a common distribution network, brand name, sharing of past reputation, etc.); (2) operating synergy (arising from economies of bulk purchasing, spreading of overheads, higher utilization rates of factors of production); (3) investment synergy (transfer of know-how between products, sharing of research and development [R&D] expertise); and (4) management synergy (transferability of particular skills, such as Just in Time know-how). Positive synergy was the original focus in the business policy literature, but lately attention has been given to adverse spill-over effects (2 + 2 = 3). Negative synergy is easily illustrated with respect to a shared brand name: an unpleasant experience with one brand X item may lead consumers to label all other brand X items as things to avoid.

As an example of a manufacturer apparently investing with an eye to both positive and negative synergy potential we may take the case of Toyota's diversification into luxury cars via the creation of the Lexus brand of products. The creation of the Lexus brand was a gamble based on the belief that a senior executive would find it hard to confess to preferring a Toyota in preference to a Cadillac or Mercedes-Benz. The exclusive Lexus models were distanced in image from normal mass-market Toyotas not merely by their distinctive brand name but also by having them sold and serviced through a separate set of retail franchises. However, many of the technical advances made by Toyota in developing the Lexus models would, in due course, filter down even to more mundane models such as the Toyota Corolla. By having a range covering all market segments, Toyota could spread the fixed costs of making its cars, for example, leaders in refinement over more units than could those of its rivals whose product ranges covered only a limited part of the market.

If we bear in mind the idea of synergy/economies of scope and think again of our linear programming example then we might wish to focus on the following as plausible strategies for dealing with the excess capacity problem:

(a) Keep van production at present levels but adapt the van assembly line so that it can be used to assemble pick-up truck kits supplied by another manufacturer, either on that manufacturer's behalf—just as Nissan Australia once used spare capacity to assemble Volvos for the Australian market—or for sale under the firm's own brand name.

(b) Invest in a larger engine assembly plant, expand van production and use surplus capacity in the engine plant to make engines to sell to other firms—just as Peugeot supplies diesel engines to the Rover Group—or engines for new markets, such as marine engines, lawnmowers or generators; meanwhile, subcontract some of the metal-pressing work so that car production does not have to be cut back in order to make available extra van bodies.

These strategies would make more effective use of the firm's existing pool of resources. However, they differ in their degree of closeness to the firm's previous range of experience. Even if production facilities can be adapted quite easily to produce different types of products, there may be strong grounds for trying to keep any new activities quite close to what one has done before to avoid making a mess of the new venture. Compared with diversification into pick-up truck production, a move into marine engines may involve much more of a departure for an automotive firm that has not previously established a reputation and distribution network in the marine market. But everything has its opportunity cost: strategies involving collaborative deals with competitors may be full of potential difficulties, and though a concentration on area of distinctive competence may enhance competitive strength, that is of little use if some kind of catastrophe wipes out the product market in question. These dilemmas are addressed at length in Chapter 11.

7.5 Exam post-mortem: Production, costs and multi-product firms

Question
What is meant by the term 'production function'? Discuss the relationship between production and cost functions and comment on the particular difficulties which arise in measuring costs of production in a multi-product firm.

Examiner's report
Despite the popularity of the regurgitationist strategy amongst the class and the shortage of debating skills, this set-piece question (which I had set as a potential safety net) was not a popular one. Perhaps the problem was that the relevant diagrams (see section 7.2) were just too complex to learn with any confidence. Certainly there were some remarkable technical errors in the answers that I received, the most memorable of which was a diagram featuring a total cost function which had an inverse U-shape implying that total costs would eventually become zero and then turn negative beyond a particular output rate. At the outset of most attempts there seemed to be a failure to see a production function as an engineering concept relating physical inputs and outputs. This, in turn, naturally led to very confused

statements (from those who tried to get away without drawing the complex diagrams) about the relationship between production functions and cost curves.

Material from later sections of this chapter is also relevant for the first part of the discussion if one wishes to take it beyond mere regurgitation of diagrams so far considered. No one saw the relevance of material on X-efficiency at this stage (section 7.11), but I was pleased to see in one of the better answers an attempt to relate the discussion to material on the effects of Just in Time versus Just in Case stock-control systems, learning by doing, and the costs and benefits of modular production methods (cf. sections 7.6 and 7.9).

Materials from later in the book can be used in answering the second part of the question. Unfortunately, many students did not bother to tackle this part at all. Those that did attempt it usually missed a golden opportunity for discussing the problem of apportioning costs in situations in which a firm was exploiting synergy links between a variety of products. This was an issue which could have been discussed in relation to (a) the problem of designing an organizational structure which would assist in keeping costs down (section 11.7); and (b) the analysis of competitive oligopoly markets in relation to 'normal cost' pricing strategies (sections 9.6, 9.7 and 9.13). A neat way of concluding an answer would have been to note that the question, and much of the textbook literature, seemed to be placing an undue emphasis on manufacturing costs, rather than on costs of research, development and marketing, where problems of jointness could be just as acute.

7.6   Learning curves and the economics of product life-cycles

The neoclassical theory of production is static: it presumes the existence of a given set of technological possibilities without asking how they come to be discovered in practice or how boundedly rational decision-makers might in practice see their firms' opportunity sets. It also proceeds without paying much attention to the rather vague, imperfectly specified nature of employment contracts. Evolutionary economists and management consultants have been taking a rather different view in recent years and paying much attention to dynamics and the effects of attitudes and motivation on productivity. The rest of this chapter considers some of the emerging perspectives. We begin with the notion of the 'learning curve'.

The formal notion of increasing returns to scale was introduced in section 7.2. Strictly speaking this concerns what happens to unit costs of production as all *inputs* are scaled up or down in volume by an identical proportion (constant returns are in evidence if a doubling of all inputs doubles output). In practice, economists often tend to use the term 'economies of scale' in relation to changes in unit costs associated with changes in the scale of *output*, even though this would normally tend to involve a change in the relative mix of factors. Both of these views of the relation between costs and output concern comparisons of alternative *rates* of output per period, and they take as given the state of knowledge about how to use inputs to produce outputs. The learning curve, by contrast, is concerned with what happens to unit costs as a result of an increase in the total number of units that have so far been produced, that is, *accumulated* output. It is a dynamic view of the advantages of producing large runs of a particular product. It is most frequently discussed as having emerged from studies of the aircraft assembly business during the Second World War, but a less formal view of the idea that firms' costs tend to be related to their experience was central to the work of Alfred Marshall in his (1890) *Principles of Economics*. He expected costs, and hence prices, to fall through time, rather than there being a tendency for expansions of output to be limited by rising cost curves (see sections 8.2 and 9.3).

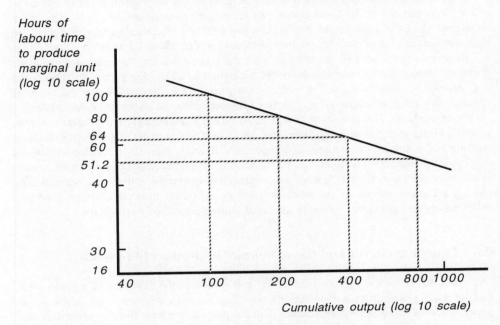

Figure 7.10: An '80 per cent' learning curve

Work on the idea of a learning curve has typically focused on the impact of higher cumulative production volumes on marginal production costs and hence on the average costs of producing additional batches of a particular kind of output. For example, take the case of an '80 per cent learning curve' of the kind typically referred to in the business strategy literature. Suppose the 100th unit of output took 100 hours of labour to make, then, with such a learning rate, the 200th unit would take 80 hours to make, the 400th would take 64 hours, and so on. Figure 7.10 shows how such a learning curve is normally graphed: note the use of logarithmic scales to compress the axes (for a good selection of actual examples, see Department of Prices and Consumer Protection, 1978). By using the mathematical technique known as integration, we can derive a total variable cost function for accumulated output from the learning curve and hence find out how many units can be made in each period. The basic form of a learning curve is

$$f(x) = ax^b$$

where $f(x)$ is the number of labour hours required to produce the marginal unit of output that will bring the total number of units up to x. By rewriting this in terms of logs we can turn it into a linear function of the kind depicted in Figure 7.10:

$$\log f(x) = \log a + b \log x$$

Then, if we know two points on the learning curve, we can discover a and b using elementary methods for finding the slope and constant of a linear equation.

The 80 per cent curve in our example has approximately the following form:

$$f(x) = 440.4x^{-0.322}$$

The constant, a, might be interpreted at the number of hours taken to produce the first unit of output, in this case 440.4. Integration enables us to discover that, for this production situation,

$$\text{total variable costs} = 440.4(x^{0.678})/0.678.$$

If learning by doing does take place at a predictable rate then the effective capacity of a particular manufacturing complex increases in a predictable manner through time: each period's average total cost curve is lower than that of the previous period. Imagine that labour costs are the only variable costs that we are tracking with the learning curve and then suppose, for example, that in each production period in question 10 000 units of labour time are available. This being so, then

$$\text{in the first period, } 10\,000 = 440.4(x^{0.678})/0.678$$

which we can solve to find that $x = 56.4$. But by the end of the second period, when 20 000 units of labour time have been used, cumulated output will have risen to 156.78; in other words, instead of 56.4 being produced with 10 000 units of labour time, 100.38 have been produced. By the end of the third period 285.12 will have been produced, implying that 128.34 were produced with 10 000 units of labour time. By the end of the fourth period production could have totalled 435.8, an increase of 150.68 on the previous cumulative total, and so on.

However, these are merely the upper bounds to output, assuming that the production line is fully absorbing 10 000 units of labour time per period. If orders in the first period are less than 56.4 it will not be possible in the second period to make 100.38 units, as will also be the case if there is a disruption to labour supply in the first period. Suppose for example, that in the first period there are only sufficient orders to employ 8 000 units of labour time. If so, only 40.58 units of output will be produced. In period 2, if there are enough orders to absorb 10 000 units of labour time, cumulated output will reach 134.22, an increase of only 93.64, rather than 100.38. By the end of period 3, and if again 10 000 units of labour time can be absorbed, output will have cumulated to 257.53, an increase of 123.31 rather than 128.34, and so on.

If learning effects have an impact on the effective capacity of the production system these ought to be borne in mind by firms when negotiating with their workers: a supply disruption due to a strike in the present period has flow-on effects in subsequent periods, though these will be smaller the further the firm is into the production run of the product in question. It should also be noted that during a strike there may be some decay of the worker's skills.

Learning effects complicate the kinds of pricing puzzles that we will begin to look at in the next two chapters. This is particularly so if the firm faces an evolving product life-cycle (see sections 9.2 and 9.3). For example, sales in a particular period might be a function not merely of the current price but also of the number of previous sales that have been made. The most commonly drawn product life-cycle diagrams have a bell-shaped profile (time along the horizontal axis, sales on the vertical axis). Initial sales may be ones on which it is possible to charge substantial mark-ups, since customers will be 'pioneers' who have a strong preference for the latest item. However, if these early customers are milked to a large degree, there could be a cost in terms of later sales being supply constrained: in the first period the product will not take off so strongly as with a lower price, so learning effects will be smaller, limiting capacity in later periods. A lower price in the first period opens up the possibility of greater sales later on by promoting greater learning by customers and greater learning on the production line. However, the price-setting strategy must also look far enough ahead to take account of the firm's situation in the late stages of the product life-cycle: rival products may start eating into sales, or, if we are dealing with a durable product, sales may fall to replacement levels even in the absence of changed market conditions. Hence the firm may find itself with a greatly expanded ability to produce but a much reduced ability to sell. As it faces the choice between lowering its price or reducing its rate of production, it might be regretting not investing in a smaller-scale production rig and setting its prices in such a way as to spread out more evenly the willingness of its customers to buy the product.

Various assumptions can be made about the nature of the product life-cycle, in terms of the kind of relation between past and present sales and why the market goes into decline (which will imply differing shapes for the right-hand tail on the typical life-cycle sales profile diagram). But the actual sales profile will depend on the sequence of prices charged, and which prices it makes sense to charge will be affected by capacity considerations. The question thus arises as to whether a rule for a sequence of prices can be formulated, or a rule for a price in a particular period, to maximize the stream of profits over the life of a particular product. The pricing rule could be tailored to include discounting of profits. It could (and should) also include the initial capacity level as a variable.

The question of when learning is most appropriately conducted should also be considered. If firms make too hasty a move to get their new products into production there may follow a disastrous launch: high expectations surrounding the new product are simply not matched by experience; lots of minor details give cause for complaint and as a result goodwill and reputation suffer. An excellent case in point is Ford Australia's 1988 EA-model Falcon. In the three years following the product's launch very many minor improvements were made—an editorial in the May 1991 issue of *Wheels* reported that 'Of the 3 000 major components that comprise a 1991 EA Falcon, around 1 800 are different from those fitted on a 1988 model'—but the company was at that time still struggling to win back from arch-rival General Motors–Holden its leading position in the Australian market, as the 1988 Holden Commodore had been launched with what were then much higher standards of quality. (Within a further year, the EB upgrade model was launched and then itself substantially upgraded, the ED upgrade following late in 1993.) With this sort of example it should be noted that the focus of the discussion has shifted away from 'practice makes perfect' at the assembly stage, back to engineering—getting the product design right and its assembly idiot-proof via more extensive work at prototype and pre-production stages. If a product is only released to the public after such investments in extensive preparatory work, one might expect there to be relatively little learning after its launch. However, the investment may be well worthwhile in terms of smaller outlays on production (and on dealing with warranty claims) that will be involved right from the start of the production run, quite apart from the greater customer satisfaction that may be generated.

7.7 Productivity and technical change

Improvements in productivity that are recorded in learning curves often arise without any major breakthrough in the design of physical capital. When engineering advances occur in terms of production methods it is often difficult or impossible to incorporate them into existing items of capital equipment: for example, the Apple Macintoshes on which this book has been produced cannot be upgraded to the latest Power-PC standard. To obtain the advantages of the new technology standard, I must obtain a new machine in which the technology is already *embodied*. Sometimes, the inability of capital items to be moulded like plasticine into new forms embodying the latest technology means that they are immediately discarded when rendered obsolete by the advent of new technology: for example, the slide-rule market suffered a catastrophic blow in 1975 when scientific pocket calculators began to be mass produced. Often, though, new and old vintages of technology are used simultaneously because the market price obtained for their output has not fallen below the average variable costs of operating the old technology. In this section I will explore the impact of new technologies on industrial productivity with the aid of a framework developed in a classic work by an Australian economist, Wilfred Salter (1960).

In competition between firms that own old and new technologies there is a tension between the requirement for new investments to be able to cover both their fixed and variable costs, and the requirement of existing investments, into which resources have already been sunk, to cover their average variable costs. Any margin between average variable costs and price helps to make a contribution to covering costs sunk, for good or bad, in a previous period. However, sunk costs may haunt a firm's management team in so far as the deals done in the past involve a stream of expenses in the present, such as interest payments on debts and fixed-period rental obligations. A firm will be forced into receivership if it cannot generate sufficient revenue to cover its avoidable costs *and* its unavoidable expenses—the sum of which may be called its 'paying-out costs' (see Andrews and Brunner, 1975). When managers are sizing up whether or not to invest in a new technology their attention will therefore centre on whether or not they run an undue risk of bankrupting their businesses because the capacity they create depresses the market price below the level of their expected average paying-out costs. Though their average total costs may be lower, firms with the latest technologies may be the most financially vulnerable in the event of a price war, for those who are producing using old machinery may have long since paid off their debts or had them eroded by inflation: investments are often done on the basis of three- or five-year 'payback period' criteria even though they may potentially have operating lives many times greater.

If managers do get their calculations horribly wrong when making major investments in new plant they may not merely lose control of their businesses but also cause chaos for rival firms who may find themselves competing with whoever buys the assets from the receiver at vastly less than their replacement price. As they guess what sort of price might be possible in the market they may well hope that other players in the market recognize that it is in everyone's interest that they remain solvent. An excellent case in point is the Channel Tunnel: the last thing the cross-Channel ferry operators want in the long run is for the tunnel operators to be forced into receivership by a price war that leaves them unable to service the huge debts incurred during the construction of the tunnel, for the ferry firms have much higher variable costs and would be unable to compete against a debt-free tunnel run by a different company (see the *Economist*, 30 April 1994: 71–2). For simplicity, this game-theoretic aspect of pricing behaviour and investment is absent from the analysis embodied in the Salter-inspired Figure 7.11, which is designed to encapsulate the process of structural change in a competitive industry in which there are quite a few firms competing for a limited volume of business by matching each other's price quotations. I assume that those presently operating are prevented, by the absence of barriers to entry, from engaging in strategies of implicit collusion to raise the price and share the volume of reduced business among themselves. We should note that one form this 'entry' might take is from the reopening of old capacity that presently cannot compete but which has not yet been scrapped and whose owners have ready access to workers who are experienced but presently unemployed.

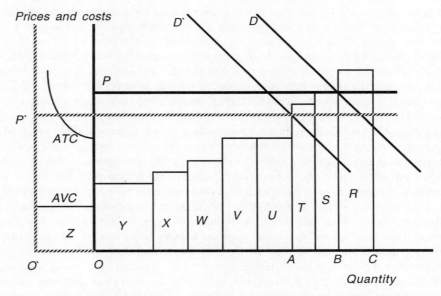

Figure 7.11: Technological progress and supply conditions in a competitive market

In Figure 7.11 it is assumed for simplicity that average variable costs on both old and new technologies are constant. The blocks R to Y on the diagram each show the average variable costs and normal capacity of plants of various vintages that are already in existence. Total capacity is OC in normal circumstances, though each plant may be expected to operate with a margin of slack in normal times (see section 9.6). The various vintages of plant are lined up in order of their average variable costs. Note, however, that some of them might be owned by a single firm that has made investments at different points in time. Demand for the product in question is presently as shown by the demand curve marked D. It should be evident that there is not enough room in the market for all of the plant to be operating. Competitive pressure pushes the price down to OP, which is below the level at which it is viable to operate plant R, and total sales are therefore OB. The latest technology for producing the commodity has capacity and average variable costs shown by the sides of the rectangle labelled Z. If a firm does invest in this technology then the origin on the diagram becomes $O\grave{}$ and, as far as operators of existing plant are concerned, the demand curve in effect shifts to the left by the distance $OO\grave{}$ to $O\grave{}$. But managers will only invest in a 'state-of-the-art' plant if they believe their addition to industry capacity will not drive the price down below average total costs of operating the new plant at its planned normal level of capacity utilization. If this is not the case, then investment in the new technology will be delayed until enough room is created in the market by old technology no longer being serviceable. In the example shown in Figure 7.11 there is enough room to cover the full costs of operating a state-of-the-art plant, even though the addition of its capacity will drive the price down to $P\grave{}$ and force the closure of plants S and T, with quantity settling down at $O\grave{}A$. However, it should be noted that if two firms built type-Z plant, the market would have major problems: there would not be enough room in the market for the new plant and for plants U to Y, and any price war aimed at pushing at least one of U or V from the market would take the price below the level needed to cover the full costs of type-Z plant. These problems of coordinating structural adjustment are examined in sections 10.4 to 10.9.

Salter's framework can also be used for analysing competition between firms operating in economies with different hourly labour costs: it is conceivable that a low-wage economy may be unable to compete effectively against firms in high-wage economies that are using the latest capital equipment. His work also seems to provide a simple but plausible tool for analysing processes of structural adjustment that result in downward movements in short-run industry supply curves as average levels of productivity are raised by investment coming on stream. It gives us a means of seeing how industry supply curves might be upward-sloping even though marginal costs are constant in the normal operating ranges of individual plant, and even though there may be considerable excess capacity in the industry. When an industrial area is depressed and scrap values for old plant are low, it may seem worth holding old plant ready for a possible upturn. This was very well illustrated by the slow processes of structural adjustment to over-capacity in the textile industries of the north of England in the 1950s and 1960s. Until alternative uses were found for old cotton mills and their workforces, mill owners and receivers avoided scrapping old textile plant: they knew that, whenever there was a slight surge of orders and they picked up some of the extra business, they could reopen the mills and re-employ their former workers for a few weeks. This was so even though there were many old mills in existence with similar average variable costs and most of these mills were idle most of the time. With average total costs of best-practice plant lying slightly above the average variable costs of operating the fringe of marginal mills, prices were kept too low for modernization to be viable (see Miles, 1968).

7.8   Corporate culture, productivity and quality

In looking at productivity improvements in the previous two sections, our focus has been on advances that come from incremental learning of better ways of doing things and from progress in engineering science. In this section I want to focus on ways in which productivity may be quite fundamentally dependent on how people in a firm look at the world. A very simple but significant example may be useful to get things started.

Most people nowadays take for granted the idea that products can be made in bulk at a low cost per unit by assembling them from interchangeable, standardized parts that fit together because they have been designed to do just that. If we take this line of thinking a little further, it may lead us to the conclusion that mass-produced products may well have higher quality than those that are made in much smaller volumes by highly skilled crafts-people who are making components without the aid of finely designed moulds and programmed machinery and are thus having to fine-tune components to make them fit together. All this may seem a perfectly reasonable line of thinking, but it is one that may seem startlingly novel to those who normally think of high quality as going hand in hand with low-volume production. However, as Romer (1993: 64) points out '150 years ago people reacted with astonishment and disbelief to the suggestion that goods could be made in this way. British gunsmiths claimed that it was impossible to make a piece of equipment that was as precise as a gun from interchangeable parts'. In those days, the concept of assembly was, as Romer notes, 'a time consuming task performed by skilled fitters whose most important tool was the file that could be used to adjust the shape of the parts that needed to be assembled'. Even in the 1970s, this line of thinking was by no means taken for granted in firms. For example, a report by the Boston Consulting Group (1975) on the demise of the British motorcycle industry noted how, when faced with competition from Japan, producers in the UK retreated up-market, confident in the belief that Japanese motorcycles could not match the quality of their hand-made products. The Japanese firms followed them up-market, applied the same techniques that they had used to produce vast quantities of reliable 50cc to 350cc motorcycles, and produced at a lower cost higher quality 500cc to 1 000cc machines. The problems faced by the British motorcycle manufacturers were compounded by a lack of awareness of the learning curve concept: despite the greater amount of scope for improvements in human operations, they seemed not to be actively looking for ways of meeting learning targets and achieved poorer rates of learning than their Japanese rivals.

Where people in a firm share much knowledge about the firm and assumptions about how the firm operates, about what can and should be done, we may speak of there being a *corporate culture*, a shared view of the world, a particular philosophy for work. Some of a firm's culture may be written down in thick files called 'management manuals', which most people are too busy to read from cover to cover but would be unable to absorb anyway due to bounded rationality. Other aspects of it will be picked up by employees at various

184

initiation sessions as they enter and advance through stages of their careers within the firm. But much of it is tacit knowledge that will be picked up unconsciously over a long period as employees see how things are done and tune into the firm's system of values and practices. A corporate culture is a wonderful device for economizing on time at meetings and for avoiding communications breakdowns, but it also acts as a set of blinkers that may lead a firm to get left behind by competitors who see the changing world differently. Individuals who switch between firms may take a long while to adjust and fit in: initially, their points of reference will be those of the organization they have left and much of what they see may not make sense to them in their new place of employment; if so, their proposals for action may make little sense to their new colleagues.

A considerable literature on corporate cultures exists within disciplines such as social anthropology and management (for example, see Douglas and Wildavsky, 1982; Jelinek, Smircich and Hirsch, eds, 1983; and Lorsch, 1986), but it has received little attention from most economists, who have their own culture in terms of seeing how their subject should proceed (cf. section 4.8). However, there are signs of change here, particularly due to a growing recognition that differences between the performance of Japanese and Western firms involve some fundamental differences in views about how business should be done. Credit for this growth of interest in Japanese business practices is particularly due to Ronald Dore's (1973) book *British Factory–Japanese Factory*. This book makes particularly interesting reading alongside the work of Perry (1970) on student world-views and how they affect learning processes, for the Japanese workers seem to have a less dualistic view of industrial relations than do their British counterparts (cf. section 1.2). In Japan, trade unions and management see each other as necessary and complementary; in the West they tend to be seen by each other as adversaries, 'us' and 'them'. In Japan, a foreman/woman is seen as a member of a team, not as an agent of management, and workers see their loyalty and long-term interests as lying with the firm. Western workers tend to see their interests as allied to those of their trade (electrician, welder, and so on). Overall, Dore's stereotypical Japanese firm had a much more longer-term orientation and was less interested in short-term gain than its Western counterpart was, and it sought to develop long-term trading relationships with customers whilst rewarding workers on the basis of their length of service rather than with a particular rate for a particular kind of job (in a British firm, the latter system resulted in a manual worker typically attaining peak earning at age 25).

Since Dore's pioneering work became widely known, many Western firms have tried to operate increasingly like their Japanese counterparts, but their learning about Japanese ways of doing business has been hindered by the perspectives from which they have tried to make sense of the Japanese philosophy. Two examples may illustrate this point. First, it is often felt that Japanese develop products quickly and cheaply because they are pirating Western products and research. To some extent this is true: it is well known that, for example, Japanese car-makers import batches of luxury German cars and take them to pieces to try to see how they are designed and how fine are the standards of manufacturing tolerances that need to be beaten. However, what is less commonly recognized is that one of the ways that some Japanese firms keep their development costs low is by doing design and manufacturing engineering simultaneously. Teamwork of this kind enables them to avoid many of the redesign costs that tend to be incurred in companies where one set of engineers comes up with a prototype that is a technical success but requires major alterations by another team of engineers because it cannot easily be produced on a large scale due to, say, the inaccessibility of some components. Quality is built into the product right from the outset by thinking ahead about how to make sure that the parts go together only one way, as well as with ease. It is a much more holistic view of engineering and cost control. Secondly, we may note the Just in Time (JIT) method of production which enables Japanese firms to operate with little of their floor-space and finances tied up with components waiting to be fitted together because components are ordered only in small batches to be delivered at a particular time and place. In the West, firms that have adopted JIT have often done so in a heavy-handed way, passing the inventory costs back to their suppliers, who will ultimately need to recover or eliminate these costs if they are to stay in business. What they have tended not to do is focus on reducing inventory levels in the production process *as a whole* by developing better communications with upstream and downstream stages. By contrast, the pioneers of JIT at Toyota saw one of the key advantages in a system of negligible buffering as being the ease with which weak links in the production chain could be identified and addressed. If these weak links proved to be subcontracting suppliers, Toyota would see it in both firms' interests that the subcontractor's problems be sorted out.

Japanese corporate cultures have also illuminated the study of why identical technologies have very different productivity impacts in different country settings. In his 1986 address to the United States Association for the Advancement of Science, Lester Thurow highlighted great differences between experiences of automation in the US and Japan and he linked them to differences in attitudes towards workers and managerial status. (His speech was broadcast widely: my notes were taken from the Australian Broadcasting Corporation's Radio National *Science Show*.) In the US, automation has led to the displacement of very many blue-collar workers. However, moves towards automation coincided with the introduction of new, computer-based management information systems that generated masses more facts and figures to be processed and appraised. Together, these improvements led to a decline in productivity: blue-collar workers were replaced by even more white-collar workers (accountants, clerical staff). Managers in the US have seen the main role of the new production processes as to give them more control over what goes on in the firm. In most cases, office automation has not resulted in managers handling their own paperwork and typing; managers have been reluctant to set about firing their secretarial staff because personal assistants have been seen as status symbols. Moreover, managers have resisted going through the initial period of difficulty entailed in learning to get to grips with word-processing, electronic mail, imaging and other aspects of information technology: they are not used to being trained by staff of lower status, and are often too busy 'fighting fires' to feel able to set time aside to learn anything new.

In Japan, by contrast, the introduction of new technologies has been seen as a way of ensuring the continuing capability of the firm to employ its workers, not as a device to beat the workers down. Thurow notes how the remaining workers on the automated assembly lines at Toyota cease production for the last quarter of an hour of their working day to do their own stock control, having been trained to use the computer facilities that are involved, just as they are responsible for their own quality control. Workers are also given great responsibility in the area of equipment ordering: rather than seeing this as an opportunity for workers to choose a machine which gives them a quiet life, Japanese managers recognize that the workers are the ones who are going to have to live with the machinery and who will have to deal with problems of poor quality caused by any unreliability. The desire to avoid 'us and them' in Japanese firms is strong: all workers in a factory typically eat in the same dining room; there is no such thing as the key to the executive washroom, and all wear the same clothing, regardless of status, when visiting areas in which work clothes are needed. As if all this, plus implicit lifetime employment contracts, were not enough to make workers avoid acting against their employers' interests, Japanese firms also give workers profit-related bonuses akin to those enjoyed by Western executives.

7.9   Flexible specialization

Japan, Italy and West Germany have outclassed the US in terms of their rates of economic growth partly because of how they have chosen to use numerically controlled machines tools and computer-aided manufacturing (CAM) systems. Robot machine tools and stock delivery systems do not need continuity of production to develop speed and accuracy, so it is possible to produce goods to order simply by dialling up the appropriate programme. Small production runs thus do not matter so long as one can spread the fixed costs of design and of programming the CAM system. For example, if the minimum efficient scale of producing a product is 100 000 units a year, a firm using a CAM system may produce a range of, say, four different products of the same broad kind at rates of only 25 000 a year and still stay competitive. It may even enhance its competitive position in so far as each of the products is aimed at a particular market niche: computer-aided design (CAD) may greatly economize on the costs of production engineering for ranges of products that are different on the surface but which share many underlying components.

Piore and Sabel (1984: 16-17) extend this kind of philosophy in looking at alternative corporate responses to competition:

> One—favoured by the American automobile firms—aims at extending the mass-production model. It does so by linking the production facilities and markets of the advanced countries with the fastest-growing third-world countries....
>
> The other major company-level response we call flexible specialization. It is seen in the networks of technologically sophisticated, highly flexible manufacturing firms in central and northwestern Italy. Flexible specialization is a strategy of permanent innovation: accommodation to ceaseless change, rather than an effort to control it. This strategy is based on flexible—multi-use—equipment; skilled workers; and the creation, through politics, of an industrial community that restricts the forms of competition to those favouring innovation. For these reasons, the spread of flexible specialization amounts to a revival of craft forms of production that were emarginated in the first industrial divide.

On their analysis, the trouble for US firms is that they have too little of a craft philosophy to fall back on, having pioneered mass production and the extreme division of labour typified by Henry Ford and the assembly-line system. By contrast, vestiges of craft traditions in Italy, West Germany and Japan make it easier to shift, and to think of shifting, toward flexible specialization and the fat profits that may come from being able to produce 'designer' products and meet needs that others cannot (cf. section 4.3). In these economies plant sizes are relatively small (this does not necessarily mean that companies involved are small, for they may be divisionalized); workers have a wide range of skills and are involved in programming equipment. It was realized that much manufacturing using machine tools involves relatively simple operations that could be taught to microcomputer-driven machines, either by having the machine record the operation or by typing in simple commands. In US firms the philosophy often was that computer-controlled machine tools made sense only in large firms, where they would be programmed by technicians who had a mathematically sophisticated background. They therefore did not rush to produce or purchase the kinds of small machines on which the Japanese had concentrated. When US firms woke up to their potential, Japanese exports of machine tools boomed.

The success of flexible specialization in Italy has been particularly noticeable. It was here that numerically controlled looms were pioneered. Piore and Sabel show how the Prato area of Italy had originally been one in which large integrated textile mills dominated, During the 1930s depression, firms sought to convert fixed to variable costs by laying off workers and selling or renting equipment to them. The former employees then had to bear the risks in the role of dependent subcontractors. To reduce their vulnerability to large firms, they looked to the *impannatore*, whose role it was to keep a watch on currents of fashion as a designer and arranger of distribution, sometimes also as a bulk buyer of raw materials, always searching for new products and processes. Often an individual small firm's design would miss the market for a particular year but because the firm was flexible it would then act as a subcontractor for those who had hit lucky and had an overflow of orders (cf. section 10.7). Vertically integrated firms have all but vanished from the area. The epitome of a company serving in the role of coordinator rather than a producer is Benetton, which subcontracts all of its production and runs its stores around the world on a franchise basis (cf. sections 11.2 and 11.4, and see Jarillo and Stevenson,1991).

All this goes directly against the grain of the ideas of Adam Smith and his famous example of a pin factory as a model of the advantages of specialization: in this factory the task was divided into nearly twenty operations; one person draws out the wire, another straightens it, a third cuts it, a fourth points it, and so on. He justified specialization as follows (1776/1961: 11):

> [The] great increase of the quantity of work which, in consequence of the division of labour the same number of people are capable of performing, is owing to three different circumstances; first, to the increase of dexterity in every particular workman; secondly, to the saving of time which is commonly lost in passing from one species of work to another; and lastly, to the invention of a great number of machines which facilitate and abridge labour, and enable one man to do the work of many.

As Robinson and Eatwell (1973: 16–17) point out, Smith failed to note that a single artisan could draw wire all one day, spend the next day cutting, and so on. Separation of tasks does not necessarily imply specialization by individuals, nor the concentration of workers in a factory-based as opposed to a cottage-based industry.

Smith's arguments about dexterity were to look somewhat questionable as the factory system first developed and went about simplifying processes, deskilling tasks that had once been the pride of artisans who had undertaken long apprenticeships. Marxian economists such as Braverman (1974) have claimed that, in addition to reducing the bargaining power of workers, the deskilling of production alienates them, as it distances them from the final product and deprives them of an overall view of the production process. They become mere cogs in a giant machine, as in Charlie Chaplin's movie *Modern Times*. This does not sound like a recipe for long-run worker commitment in advanced economies where starvation is not the sequel to failing to show up for work or being fired for failing to keep up with the pace of the assembly line. But it has only been relatively recently that companies such as Volvo have pioneered the abandonment of the Fordian production process, encouraging constructive participation and reducing worker boredom by dividing the workplace up into areas in which teams assemble entire vehicles, each individual performing many more tasks than under the production line system.

Nor was Smith's analysis free of contradictions. He actually doubted the dynamic efficiency of the factory system based around specialization of tasks (1776/1961: 303):

> The man whose life is spent in performing a few simple operations, of which the effects too are perhaps, always the same, or very nearly the same, has no occasion to exert his understanding, or to exercise his invention in finding out expedients for removing difficulties which never occur.

Here his work anticipates the behavioural economist's view, that search is a response to perceptions of problems. The kinds of technical progress that emerged might therefore centre not upon problems faced by the workers but by the senior managers: search activities would therefore concentrate much more on financial and marketing issues than on how things could be done better at the manufacturing stage.

To end this section I wish to offer a few other observations about the nature of Japanese business success. The flexibility associated with the use of programmable machine tools contrasts with the potential for instability associated with the close-coupling of production systems associated with their Just in Time approach to stock control. For this strategy to succeed, the machines used in making components must be extremely reliable and the personnel in subcontracting firms must be prepared to be very flexible in the event of a crisis—flexible machinery helps too (cf. Hart, 1940, 1942). The small subcontractors had been drilled into flexibility both with the aid of graduates and advice supplied by their large customers, and by frequent changes in the demands of their customers, who, in the process of catching up, and then staying ahead of their Western rivals, introduced faster model replacement cycles. This aspect of learning by doing—learning to cope with reorganizations—is something that is insufficiently stressed in literature on learning curves.

7.10 The behavioural theory of the firm

As this chapter has moved beyond the standard neoclassical analysis of production, the kinds of topics I have considered and the kinds of sources I have used for discussing them have implicitly taken us more and more in the direction of the view of the firm set out in books by behavioural theorists such as Herbert Simon, Richard Cyert and James March (Cyert and March, 1963; March, 1988; March and Simon, 1958; and Simon, 1945) and evolutionary economists such as Hodgson (1988) and Nelson and Winter (1982). In this section I try to draw some of these threads together by outlining explicitly the essence of the behavioural/evolutionary view. Those interested in reading further on this topic should note that many of the key articles are reprinted in Earl (ed.) (1988a).

The essence of the behavioural approach to the firm is that, prior to constructing theories of economic behaviour that may serve as workable approximations of a complex subject matter, the theorist should study actual decision-making practices in their particular institutional contexts. It is thus no coincidence that two of the three most famous contributors are not usually thought of as economists: Herbert Simon is a professor of computing science and psychology, James March is an organization theorist; only Richard Cyert is an economist with a conventional background. The resulting analysis consequently embodies an interdisciplinary approach, with a great emphasis on organizational factors internal to the firm, instead of the firm being treated as a 'black box' with the focus being purely on external manifestations of its behaviour in response to changes in its external environment. It does not lead behavioural economists to take very seriously the idea that all firms face U-shaped average cost curves (cf. section 8.7; Lester, 1946; Lee, 1985; and Simon, 1986).

It was, in fact, the study of organizational behaviour which led Simon to coin the phrase 'bounded rationality' and propose that, owing to both the scope for information overload and the absence of information which would usefully narrow down the bounds of possibility, decision-makers should be thought of as satisficers r ther than optimizers. Although they can seek to acquire information or aids to handling information, they can never know in advance whether the costs of these strategies will be less than their benefits. Quick action on the basis of a good set of rules of thumb may economize on decision-making inputs and enable a firm to get ahead of rivals that dither because they are always trying to work out what is best with a data set that inevitably is always out of date (this theme is argued at length in Winter, 1964). The limited ability of decision-makers to gather and process information also ensures that they cannot simultaneously be surveying all possible options and implementing decisions. Most staff in firms thus tend to act in a problem-solving manner, rather than engaging in strategic thinking about problems and opportunities that might arise in future. As long as their aspirations seem to be on the way to being met on time, they will leave well alone and concentrate on dealing with problems already at hand. The decision-maker's task can be compared to that of a fire brigade. Many fires that could break out never do, and to keep constant watch on all possible fires would be impossibly costly (see further the paper by Heiner, 1983, which includes some useful parallel discussions relating to hypochondria and behaviour with respect to insurance), so the greatest attention is given to those fires which have already broken out and have passed beyond certain 'conventional' thresholds of danger. However, although modern fire engineering leads to a good idea of the combustibility of certain environments, the smoke of a fire that has already started, and the pressure of time, often make it impossible to assess accurately the nature of the situation and decide on the best means of tackling it.

Since all firms suffer from bounded rationality, satisficing behaviour will not necessarily result in a firm being driven out of a market, unless it sets its targets too low and/or fails to find recipes for matching the performances of its competitors. And even the firm which desires to be at the top of a performance league does not have to be the best in any absolute sense; it merely needs to be able to meet relatively higher levels of attainments than its rivals (the paper by Alchian, 1950, is very good on this theme, even though it predates much of Simon's thinking). An important factor in determining how managers and their workers operate will thus be how vigorously their rivals are competing. In a protected environment that is for some reason difficult to enter, there may be a general lack of pressure for incumbent players to look for better ways of doing things unless one of them judges that there are worthwhile gains to be had from trying harder. As far as the supply of effort is concerned, there may be a kind of kinked curve implied by this sort of thinking: a person may think 'if I try harder, I might get promotion if my rivals don't follow, but if they do I shall have achieved nothing in terms of making myself appear outstanding; however, if I slack off a bit more they will be thankful to see me wrecking my promotion chances but won't necessarily lower themselves to my level'.

Success in meeting aspirations will tend to result in them being raised through time, though there usually seems to be a lag as people wait to see whether they have just enjoyed a freak, non-sustainable over-fulfilment. Recipes for successful search (cf. Hey, 1982) will be called into action by a failure to meet aspirations—at least, they will be so long as search is expected to have an adequate prospect of success. Unsuccessful search for improvements will normally be followed eventually by a lowering of aspirations, though rather non-rational-looking hostile actions indicative of frustration may be observed first when search seems to be failing to come up with any solutions to the problem. In judging whether or not aspirations are 'reasonable', decision-makers will often use their rivals' achievements as points of reference: far from reflecting the state of technology, productivity reflects crowd behaviour.

Behavioural theory highlights the use of hierarchies as devices for economizing on the need to process information, but this is not without its costs. Specialization of functions into different divisions (such as production, sales, stock control, research and development) may enable many potentially wasteful interchanges to be avoided. But it can also result in inconsistent policies: one division may solve its problems at the cost of generating problems for another division. Much the same difficulties can arise due to the lack of an overall perspective when an individual employee or manager is taking a decision. When a decision-maker faces problems on several fronts at once, the common strategy is to rank them in order of importance and then tackle them sequentially ('sequential attention to goals'). The 'solution' to the highest-ranking problems may cause other targets to be compromised still further and, when these are tackled successively, the original problem may reappear.

Although a firm may have its own particular corporate culture, certain internally stated policy goals and, very likely, a publicly espoused 'mission statement', behavioural economists stress that a firm is actually a collection of individuals with their own, disparate *subgoals*. Managers do not all have the same interests as each other at the senior level, any more than they have the same interests as shareholders, middle managers, workers and customers. Many potential clashes of interest are avoided because the divisionalization of the firm via hierarchical methods of organization blinkers people to things that are going on in other parts of the organization which might threaten their interests or lead them to suspect that they, personally, could be getting rather more out of involvement with the firm. Cyert and March (1963) depict the firm as a *coalition* of people with conflicting but also complementary interests: this coalition includes bankers and customers as well as managers, workers and shareholders, in fact anyone who puts in something to the firm expecting to get something out of it. So long as the returns to remaining in the coalition are sufficiently attractive, people will contribute their own inputs which may help generate outputs for others whose goals are different from their own. Rewards to coalition membership may be direct monetary payments or non-pecuniary 'side payments' (for example, 'If you do that for me, I'll do this for you.'), as well as the kinds of emoluments stressed by Williamson (1967) in his *Economics of Discretionary Behavior*, such as expense accounts, fancy office facilities and vehicles, as well as feelings of power that may come from having subordinate staff to whom directives can be given. (Whether subordinates will obey is quite another thing: see Barnard, 1938, for the view that authority is something granted by subordinates, not something that goes automatically with a position of seniority.)

The allocation of payments to coalition members is the result of a bargaining process which is heavily dependent upon the reference points currently being used by coalition members, which may in turn be dependent on conditions in the external environment. It is not bargaining over the division of a fixed cake of outputs but over the disposition of a cake whose size and recipe is also open to question. Bargaining, however, is a costly activity (as is obvious in the area of industrial relations) and is something to be economized upon. Ideally, one would prefer not to be doing it all the time. In a world of environmental turbulence—I mean the competitive environment here, but that may of course be affected by unexpected discoveries of changes in the ecosystem—it will be difficult to anticipate eventualities in advance and haggle over their implications, so scope for new disagreements could continually arise (cf. Shackle's interest in the concept of surprise and his critique of probability: see sections 5.3–5.5). All this might make the scope for keeping a firm intact seem rather limited. Cyert and March (1963) suggest that coalitions stay together by employing the following strategies, separately or in combination: (1) avoiding turbulent environments ('uncertainty avoidance'); (2) trying to ensure that their environments are made less prone to attack from rival coalitions, for example, they may lobby for protective tariffs ('a negotiated environment'); (3) taking up *organizational slack* when the going gets tougher.

The concept of organizational slack begins with the idea that something which disappoints some coalition members or makes them consider moving elsewhere does not *have* to result in them removing their inputs (and thereby disappointing remaining coalition members). It may be possible to keep them loyal if other coalition members are prepared to give up some of their potential claims on the firm's outputs or are prepared to increase their inputs to increase the size or quality of the firm's outputs. So long as there is a difference between the net benefits that individuals receive from being attached to a particular firm and the next best net benefits they think could get from moving elsewhere (their 'transfer earnings'), slack exists in the sense meant by Cyert and March. It does not exist in this sense as a result of a collective policy decision taken by the coalition as a group. Rather it exists because individuals who have access to private or specialist knowledge (for example, about just how tough they will let things get before quitting, or about scope for productivity improvements which would, if implemented, inconvenience them somewhat) have hitherto demanded and succeeded in obtaining bigger returns from other coalition members than the bare minimum they require to meet their aspirations. If the other coalition members knew this they would not have been so generous and would have realized that they were setting their own aspirations needlessly low. Organizational slack tends to grow in good times, as aspirations lag behind attainment levels, so, in bad times, when some aspirations are failing to be met, the firm's outputs or input burdens can be redistributed to keep members participating—for example, shareholders may accept lower dividends without selling their shares and taking their money elsewhere, or workers may agree to higher hourly output rates and a speeded-up production line.

Before we move on to consider what this implies for discussions of efficiency, it is probably useful to add a few comments to what has already been said (in section 3.1) about the relationship between satisficing behaviour and the notion of optimization. The behavioural theory of the firm has often been taken as entailing a vision of firms which operate in a fairly sloppy sort of manner, owing to a lack of competition in their external environments. In such circumstances, senior managers may indeed be able to pursue the quiet life by promoting sycophants, and line workers may be able to get away with establishing a leisurely pace of work and making life difficult for any would-be 'ratebusters' (cf. Jones, 1984). However, in a hotly contested environment all of our foregoing arguments still apply: all decision-makers suffer from bounded rationality and knowledge is incomplete and dispersed (see further, section 9.6.4). Competition may be strong inside a firm as well as in its market environment, as 'young men and women in a hurry' try to win promotion by suggesting to their bosses where there might exist scope for improving productivity (Andrews, 1958: 29; see also section 11.7). But the payoffs to such suggestions can only be discovered through experimentation. Even the managers of the best-performing firms in a market will not know how to do the best thing and will be trying to set themselves workable goals. They do not want to waste time trying to achieve the impossible, but they do not know the bounds of what *is* possible. Well-trained executives may debate hotly amongst themselves the wisdom of, for example, sacrificing short-run profits in the interest of a more secure long-run position for the firm.

7.11　The notion of efficiency in economics

The behavioural view of the firm leaves some economists feeling most uneasy about conventional discussions of the notion of efficiency, but without anything particularly general to say in their place (see Cyert and George, 1969, and Earl, 1984: chapter 11). When mainstream economists speak of efficiency they usually mean *allocative efficiency*, which concerns the question of possible losses of consumer surplus in an economy due to relative prices being distorted in the sense that there is a difference between the willingness of the marginal consumer to buy something and the marginal cost of providing it in the cheapest possible way. This line of thinking can be traced back to the work of Dupuit (1844), and subsequent contributions by Ramsey (1927) and Hotelling (1938) on optimal tax systems and marginal cost pricing, that have been influential in shaping policies concerning the regulation of private enterprises and the management of public utilities. It is a view of efficiency that seems difficult to work with in practical terms if one accepts the subjectivist view that marginal costs are not observable because they are the opportunities that people give up in order to do the things they actually do. But most economists who apply it seem to do so in ignorance of this perspective.

Dupuit suggested that a demand curve could be taken as a measure of the marginal utility consumers derived from consuming a particular product, and the area under the demand curve between the origin and the point on the quantity axis signifying the amount consumed could hence be seen as the total utility derived from consuming that amount (the total utility function is obtained using basic calculus by integrating the marginal utility function). The market price paid by the consumer is a sum of money forgone from other uses so, in terms of utility maximization, a person will not pay a particular price for an extra unit of the commodity if greater utility could be obtained by spending the money elsewhere. Dupuit argued that prices should reflect the cost of providing the marginal unit to the marginal consumer: marginal costs would then equal marginal benefits. Figure 7.12 gives an indication of the problem that could arise if prices were pushed above the marginal cost of production. It takes an example from introductory taxation theory. Rising marginal costs at the level of the firm are assumed to lead to a rising supply curve at the level of the market. In the absence of a tax, the market equilibrium is at *F*, with a price at *OB* and a quantity of *OI*. If a per-unit tax is imposed the supply curve shifts upwards by the amount of the tax. The new market equilibrium is at *D* with a price of *OC* and a quantity of *OH* being purchased. The government collects revenue equal to the area *ACDG*, of which *BCDE* comes from consumers, while *ABEG* is borne by producers. The trouble is that there has been a *deadweight loss* of consumer surplus equal to the shaded triangular area *DEF*. The government has not gained this area as revenue and neither have firms gained it as profit; it has simply been lost from the system rather than being redistributed. There has also been a deadweight loss of producer surplus, equal to the triangular area *EFG*.

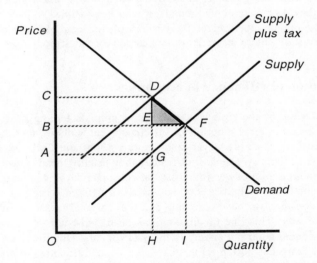

Figure 7.12: Deadweight losses due to the imposition of a tax

Dupuit's particular concern was with socially appropriate systems of charges for bridges and waterways. Owing to their indivisible nature, such items of public infrastructure often have to be constructed with capacities considerably in excess of the volume of traffic that will eventuate even if no charge is made for using them. If this is so, and if the additional user does not cause any deterioration (unlike, say, modern heavy trucks), then the marginal cost to society of an extra person using an uncongested bridge or canal is zero.

The trouble is, if no charges are levied, then the users will not be providing a revenue stream to cover fixed costs such as construction. Any price in excess of zero will result in a deadweight loss of consumer surplus.

The problem raised by Dupuit arises wherever goods are produced under conditions of increasing returns. This is shown in Figure 7.13, which has all the ingredients of a problem of *natural monopoly* even though I have drawn a case where marginal costs are constant (and hence equal to average variable costs), since average total costs continue to fall by the point (Q) at which they cut the product's downward-sloping market demand curve. If the natural monopolist were to set a price of *OS* equal to marginal costs, and hence sell *OL* units of output, a loss equal to *STRM* would be incurred, equal to total fixed costs. If the monopolist were not troubled by fears of another firm trying to stage a raid on its market, and if it did not have to worry about what regulatory authorities might think of its behaviour, then it would be able to maximize its profits in the market by charging a price of *OW* and sell only *OJ*, the output rate at which marginal revenue and marginal costs are equal. It would achieve profits of *VWXY* at the expense of consumers but the latter would suffer a deadweight loss in consumer surplus of *XZQ* compared with the situation at a break-even price of *OU*. Such losses of consumer surplus provide a reason in terms of allocative inefficiency for regulating monopolists, but leave open the question of what price they should be allowed to charge.

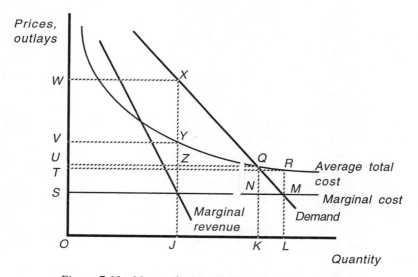

Figure 7.13: Monopolistic pricing and consumer welfare

Dupuit's view was that a strategy of price discrimination might be the answer: in other words, those who enjoyed considerable consumer surplus might somehow be induced to pay a price greater than marginal cost and thereby generate the revenue to cover fixed costs, while those who derived much smaller marginal utility could be charged at marginal cost and hence the resources would not be under-utilized. This sort of pricing method has often been employed by doctors in situations where people who are both poor and sick have neither private insurance nor a welfare state to pay for their health care: a monopolistic medical practice in a small town would tend not to milk the local community for every cent possible but make a reasonable living by charging the rich more to cross-subsidize their treatment of the poor. Another example, perhaps more familiar these days, is the use of 'two-part tariff' systems of charges for regulated public utilities such as electricity or telecommunications: overheads are covered by a fixed charge each year, but there is also a charge which varies depending on the number of units consumed. (Price discrimination is discussed further in section 9.11; recall also the analysis in section 3.4 of the advantages of a two-part tariff system over average-cost pricing in the case of a college dining hall.) However, if consumers cannot be readily divided into groups to which different prices can be charged, an alternative policy is needed to prevent under-utilization of resources.

During the period between the work of Marshall (1890) and Hotelling (1938) there was considerable discussion about the possibility of cutting allocative inefficiency by subsidizing markets in which increasing returns were prevalent. Tax revenue to pay for the subsidies might come from markets where rising marginal cost curves implied that, if regulatory policies limited suppliers to setting prices equal to marginal costs, profits would be made as a result of marginal costs exceeding average costs once output exceeded the rate at which average costs were minimized. If this sort of source did not yield enough revenue other taxes would be needed: ones that did not distort behaviour at the margin because they were charged as a lump sum, rather like a telephone line rental charge in a two-part tariff system. Such taxes might be difficult to contrive in a politically acceptable way. (The hugely unpopular 'poll tax' tried by the Thatcher government in the United Kingdom in the late 1980s is an example of such a tax though, of course, it was not levied for this sort of purpose.) A much more simple proposal was contained in a paper by Ramsey (1927) whose significance was only given due recognition in the early 1980s as part of the 'contestability revolution' in monopoly and oligopoly theory (see section 9.7). Ramsey's work suggested that if a constraint is applied to the total profits of a supplier or group of suppliers a set of prices which just enables this constraint to be met will be Pareto optimal (in other words, it will not be possible for someone to become better off except at someone else's expense). Suppose, then, that we give up trying to contrive an ideal set of taxes and subsidies and recognize that we are in a 'second-best' world in which enterprises have to meet the requirement that their profits are non-negative: if so, the efficient 'Ramsey price' in a market like that illustrated in Figure 7.12 is OU, which will result in sales of OK. This is the configuration at which, at point Q, the average total cost curve intersects the demand curve. The topic of central interest to modern-day market and monopoly regulators has thus become the extent to which market prices are in excess of Ramsey prices, enabling supernormal rates of return to be earned.

This discussion of the concept of allocative efficiency, with its focus on prices and quantities, may seem distant from what the person in the street usually seems to mean by inefficiency, namely, production taking place at costs that are needlessly high due to poor management or work practices. The latter view is quite close to a second kind of efficiency nowadays discussed in the economics literature, namely, X-efficiency. This term is due to Leibenstein (1966, 1976), who suggested that in focusing on deadweight losses of consumer surplus due to relative price distortions, economists were tending to ignore a potentially more significant source of losses to the consumer: losses due to producers using more resources than necessary to produce what they were selling. Calculations of deadweight losses due to prices being set above marginal costs may underestimate how badly consumers are doing, since the recorded 'marginal costs' on which they are based might be needlessly inflated. Likewise, misleading conclusions might be reached about the existence of Ramsey prices: a firm might only be earning normal profits at the price it is charging but its average total costs could be needlessly high due to inflated overhead costs as well as unduly high marginal costs. A naturally monopolistic market or a market which it is difficult to enter is precisely the sort of environment of low competitive pressure in which managers might take a quiet life and their subordinates, too, might be able to work well below their potential in terms of the rate or quality of output they produced.

Leibenstein suggested that X-inefficiency arises for three reasons. First, factor markets are imperfect—which results in the most skilled managers not ending up in the organizations that would benefit most from employing them. Secondly, the production function is imperfectly known. Thirdly, employment contracts are incompletely specified—which enables employees to get away with working less hard than they might if they had agreed to more detailed contracts that offered the same remuneration.

This view of how production may fall short of what might be possible interlocks extensively with behavioural ideas. But some behaviouralists find Leibenstein's work frustrating. For a start, he seemed to write as though the production function is something which is, in principle, capable of being fully spelt out and transmitted from firm to firm as a blueprint. Behaviouralists would point out the impossibility of discovering the best way of using inputs to produce outputs: hence there is no obvious reference point of perfect X-efficiency. There is also the 'tacit knowledge' phenomenon discussed in section 7.2. In raising these issues I would not wish to deny that it may be quite easy for outsiders to identify firms that might be getting more out of their inputs, if only they searched for ways of doing so. Productivity is very much the result of the interplay between the aspirations that managers set themselves, the strength of competition in their environments, which may make these aspirations hard to realize, and the strategies that they use for searching for ways of doing better. Major differences are to be expected between firms that employ different goal-setting procedures, for example in respect of their willingness to hire consultants or obtain outside reference standards by joining databases such as Business Ratios or actually arranging to study how other firms—not normally their own competitors—perform particular kinds of tasks, a practice known as benchmarking. Management theorists often speak of the Not Invented Here philosophy that seems to hold some firms down.

Secondly, Leibenstein fails to realize that employment contracts are left vague because people believe it pays to avoid trying to cover in more detail things that might (but might not) happen (see Loasby, 1976; and section 10.12). Contracts are costly to draw up, so society may gain due to the flexibility that vague contracts give: it often enables corporate coalitions to continue in the face of adversity, instead of factors of production being forced to return to factor markets in search of new employment. More rigidly specified employment contracts might only result in more output if resources are consumed in monitoring the behaviour of employees. Consider, for example, management by objectives, in which the employee negotiates a detailed set of goals with her/his line manager and is then monitored carefully for how well performance matches up to the goals. This certainly has produced higher productivity in many cases. However, one might also note how the increasing concern with 'accountability' is forcing entire organizations to devote considerable time to spelling out their objectives, and to filling in forms stating how far their objectives have been met: all the form-filling may get in the way of going about meeting objectives that may have existed quite adequately inside the heads of members of the organization who were strongly dedicated to their work.

Thirdly, it is by no means clear that X-inefficiency is a bad thing: there is obviously a difference between relatively low productivity that results from ignorance of better modes of organization, and that which results due to workers and managers enjoying a comfortable existence by taking 'on-the-job leisure'. The uptake of organizational slack may keep a corporate coalition intact, but it involves one party's net benefits being transferred, at least in part, to another: is it a good thing, say, for workers to have to work longer hours, or more rapidly, or for lower pay, in order to meet the increased demands of bankers, even if the workers prefer to do so rather than leave the coalition? In Leibenstein's terms, this would be a reduction of X-inefficiency, but it is far from obvious that it is an equitable change.

A third kind of efficiency is *dynamic efficiency*, in other words, how fast the productivity of a collection of resources grows in the long run. The ruthless pursuit of the first two kinds of efficiency may work against the discovery of major sources of productivity improvements from which everyone can benefit. Temporary monopolies may be essential if anyone is to have an incentive to try to develop a new product or process, whilst a rather relaxed working environment (such as a British university in the 1970s in which staff were almost invariably granted tenure of their jobs until retirement age after a short probationary period) might encourage people to work on long-term projects of uncertain returns which occasionally yield fantastic breakthroughs. It is arguable that the short-term orientation of Western firms, occasioned by pressure from the capital market, makes them less likely to thrive in the long run against competition from far-Eastern enterprise.

Behavioural economists are certainly concerned about the ability of the free market to develop new products and processes. The allocation of resources to these tasks is a particularly obvious instance of a problem of bounded rationality, for the returns are intrinsically impossible to specify in advance (see Kay, 1979). To get people to be more innovative, incentives that will promote search might be used. Ones that involve dangling inducements in front of potential innovators may fail to achieve much if they are not noticed by those at whom they are aimed. Measures that increase the competitive pressure to do better sound more promising, so long as they do so without promoting fire-fighting, short-term solutions rather than prompting managers to recognize that in the long run their organizations will only survive if they make initiatives aimed at continually improving their standards a key part of their strategies. However, we should note the dangers of introducing a 'character-building' environment overnight. If managers in firms use rules of thumb as a means of coping with their environments, and if effective rules of thumb cannot be identified the moment their environment changes, firms may find it hard to survive changes that are not introduced gradually unless there is a lot of organizational slack to be taken up within their coalitions. (It is worthwhile to think about what this implies in relation to trade policy, and arguments about the feather-bedding effects of tariffs and quotas. However, attempts to create a 'level playing field' almost overnight may not be particularly wise, for managers may need time to learn a new set of recipes to get their performances on a par with their competitors.) Orderly processes of structural change need some degree of slack permitted by what mainstream economists tend to see as 'market imperfections' (see further, Richardson, 1953; and Hirschman, 1970).

7.12 Essay example: Competitive leadership

Question
'It is out of the constant passing to and fro of industrial leadership that the essence of actual competition arises' (P.W.S. Andrews, 'Industrial analysis in economics', in Wilson and Andrews, eds, 1951, *Oxford Studies in the Price Mechanism*, p. 171). Discuss.

Author's notes
This essay provides an opportunity to call upon a wide range of themes from this chapter, from section 4.3 and from later chapters in this book; Schumpeter (1943) and Downie (1958) are classic theoretical sources, while Klein (1977) contains much useful case material. It would be appropriate to spend the introduction noting how, at first sight, it may seem surprising that there is very much passing of industrial leadership from one firm to another. If one firm gets ahead of its rivals, it appears set to enjoy a virtuous circle of effects. A larger market share may bring economies of large-scale production, and stronger learning effects may come if it can keep its factories consistently busier with orders than its rivals can. If it is actually the pioneer of a particular product, its design may become the generic standard in the market, the model that potential customers typically first think of when they think about the market. A firm which is the leading player in a market may also be able to generate further sales by referring to its leadership in advertisements to risk-averse buyers. It may have its technological leadership nicely tied up in patents that its rivals would find very hard to design their way around (the legal difficulties that Kodak had in trying to break Polaroid's hold on the instant photography market are a good example here). A leader can use a strategy of aggressive pricing to squeeze the profits of its weaker rivals, making it relatively difficult for them to overtake it by investing in product and process innovations, or the leader can aim for a supernormal mark-up and use the proceeds to invest in staying ahead of the opposition. Nonetheless, there are many examples of firms being overtaken in the long run: in the car market, Honda—a company that started as a motorcycle manufacturer after the end of the Second World War—eventually got to topple Ford as the supplier of the most popular car in the US market, but in 1993 the Honda Accord was been beaten back into second place by the Ford Taurus.

The following points/paragraph themes came to my mind on how firms can catch up from way behind seemingly stronger competitors, thereby giving the latter a problem which they may eventually perceive as needing attention:

(a) Followers may be able to learn from leaders' mistakes and enjoy steeper learning curves or learning curves that start out much lower.

(b) Technology is not given: a follower may be more easily able to incorporate new ideas and processes because it is working with a 'clean sheet of paper' and a green-field site for its factory, rather than being constrained by its previous capital accumulation and a workforce that is set in its ways with a corporate culture that is ill-suited to current business conditions. (Note how it is often said that in industrial terms Germany and Japan benefited enormously from having lost the Second World War, and that when Japanese car manufacturers set up factories in the US and UK they deliberately chose to locate them in areas which were *not* thought of as traditional automotive manufacturing centres.)

(c) The would-be leader may find itself better able to offer a suitable product if the pattern of demand changes due to shifts in demographics, income or fashion, etc.

(d) A leader's position may be threatened if rivals come up with new products that better fit in with customer requirements but which are hard for the leader to copy or improve upon.

(e) The leader may have trouble sustaining its performance in the long run, due to difficulties in maintaining its quality of management (cf. Marshall's 1890, 1919 analysis, discussed in section 8.2) or due to managerial disputes arising over the future strategic direction of the firm, or simply due to 'resting on its laurels'. Its larger size could prove a disadvantage if the environment gets more turbulent and senior management are less in touch with the need to change and less able to steer their organizations quickly in new directions.

(f) A rising exchange rate may make it difficult for the leaders to compete against overseas rivals unless it relocates its production offshore or comes up with offsetting innovations.

(g) Organizational changes may provide room for manoeuvre in a company seeking to raise its game: (a) organizational slack may be taken up, with some members of the corporate coalition making sacrifices in preference to allowing the coalition to collapse; (b) organizational innovations (such as a switch to Japanese-style methods or total quality management) may be used to wring more out of existing resources without greater sacrifices being necessary; and (c) some resources may be returned to the marketplace after ways of doing without them have been discovered.

(h) Limited substitutability and outright breaks in the chain of substitution between products (cf. section 4.3) typically mean that some residual market remains for 'also-ran' firms, providing something of a profit and client base from which they can try to innovate their way back to the forefront by the methods described above. If markets were perfectly competitive, a firm which slipped even slightly behind would lose all its customers or profits and have no hope of fighting back (cf. Hirschman, 1970).

(i) Leading firms may have the potential to wipe out competitors completely and yet hold back from doing so for fear of an anti-trust case against them.

(j)   It should not be forgotten that many firms are multi-product operations and a firm that is leading in one area need not be doing particularly well in all of its other areas of interest. If problem areas exist, they may prove a distraction to managers (remember Miller's 7$\pm$2 rule concerning the number of things a person can keep in mind at any one time) with the result that the firm's leading activities start to slip behind due to a lack of attention.

(k)   More generally we should recognize that, in a world of change, decisions will continually have to be taken (including decisions about whether anything new really needs to be done), both by current leaders and by would-be leaders. Boundedly rational managers are to be expected to make some decisions they will live to regret, even if they have been doing rather well of late because their decision rules happened to match rather well the environment in which they had been operating.

7.13   Further questions

1.   Explain how a short-run market supply curve for a competitive industry can be derived from the firms' production functions.

2.   In which circumstances would you expect a subsidy to wage costs to lead to higher employment in existing firms? Distinguish carefully between long-run and short-run effects, and comment on the desirability of such a subsidy.

3.   What determines, in an individual firm, (a) the difference between the average variable (prime) cost of using new equipment and using equipment about to be scrapped, and (b) the age structure of equipment?

4.   'The possession of technical "knowledge" is an attribute of the firm as a whole, as an organized entity, and is not reducible to what any single individual knows, or even to any simple aggregation of the various competences and capabilities of all the various individuals, equipment, and installations of the firm' (Richard Nelson and Sidney Winter, *An Evolutionary Theory of Economic Change*, 1982: 63) How damaging is this claim to the neoclassical theory of the firm? Explain the reasoning behind your verdict.

5.   The Boston Consulting Group suggest that strength of competitive position and large market share go hand in hand. Do you agree?

6.   'The level of industrial concentration, and hence monopoly power must rise in this country if our largest firms are to exploit available economies of scale and compete effectively on world markets.' Discuss.

7.   What are economies of scale? How would you account for the fact that computer prices have fallen but car prices have risen over the past ten years?

8. 'The diversified firm is perfectly consistent with specialization in terms of competence' (Nicolai Foss, *Journal of Evolutionary Economics*, 1993: 134). Discuss.

9. Imagine you are a management consultant advising a manufacturer of heavy duty industrial pumps. You have discovered that the firm appears to have been achieving a 90 per cent learning curve whilst producing a particular model of its industrial pumps. That is to say, its labour input requirements for the marginal unit of output fell by ten per cent each time it doubled its cumulative output. The 100th unit took 100 labour hours to make but the 200th unit only required 90. It has just finished making the 400th unit, which only took about 81 labour hours to produce.

   (a) Find the values of the constants a and b in the firm's learning curve

   $$f(x) = ax^b$$

   where $f(x)$ is the number of labour hours required to produce the marginal unit of output that will bring the total number of units produced up to x. Round the value of a to the nearest whole number and b to two decimal places to simplify subsequent calculations.

   (b) The firm has the possibility of selling a further 400 pumps so long as it charges a competitive price. Given the cost of raw materials and the hourly wage rates that it has to pay, the maximum average cost per additional pump that it could incur in terms of labour would be 75 hours per unit. Would you advise the firm to take up this opportunity and expand its cumulated output of the pump to 800 units? Provide the figures to back up your answer.

10. Give a precise meaning for the phrase 'a firm is producing efficiently'. Discuss the adequacy of competitive pressures in a capitalist economy in causing a firm to be efficient.

11. 'Microeconomic theory focuses on allocative efficiency to the exclusion of other types of efficiencies that, in fact, are much more significant in many instances' (Harvey Leibenstein, *American Economic Review*, 1966: 392). What are these other types of efficiency, and to what extent do studies of the bureaucratic structure of industrial enterprises contribute to our understanding of them?

12. 'It is quite inappropriate to conceive of firm behaviour in terms of deliberate choice from a broad menu of alternatives that some external observer considers to be "available" opportunities for the organization. The menu is not broad but narrow and idiosyncratic; it is built into the firm's routines and most of the "choosing" is also accomplished automatically by those routines' Richard Nelson and Sidney Winter, *An Evolutionary Theory of Economic Change*, 1982: 134). Discuss this statement and its implications.

8 Price and output decisions (1): from Marshall to marginalism

8.1 Introduction

The question of how firms set their prices and rates of output has been one of the core concerns of economics for over a century. In this chapter and in the one that follows it my aim is to present an account of some of the main debates in this area that have preoccupied economists since the publication of Alfred Marshall's *Principles of Economics* in 1890. I also provide practical examples to show the relevance of these debates to decisions in modern-day business. The account of the theoretical debates is more in the nature of a two-part extended essay on the history of economic ideas rather than an attempt to survey the current state of thinking on this topic in the way that one might expect to see in a conventional textbook. There are several reasons for adopting this strategy. First, economists remain divided in their views on pricing behaviour, and current divisions have their roots embedded in the past century of work in this area. Secondly, I wish to correct a misconception that one of the trendy ideas in this area during the 1980s, namely, the theory of contestable markets, actually involved a major breakthrough in thinking: we shall see that this body of thought has much in common with earlier work and yet misses some of its richness. Thirdly, I think that students of economics may learn to think better as intuitive economists when tackling practical problems if they have a feel for the heritage of the subject that comes from working their way through the intellectual struggles that some of the giants of the profession have been involved with, rather than being presented with a sanitized, ready-to-use description of pricing behaviour that glosses over the difficulties that have not been resolved.

From my experience of teaching price theory in this way I know that it involves a considerable intellectual challenge, even though the presentation is not demanding in technical terms. Student readers would probably be wise to take another look at the discussion of Perry's (1970) work on learning processes in section 1.2 before getting into the body of this chapter and keep reminding themselves of it every now and then as they progress through the chapter. For those who are still trying to see the world in terms of black and white certainties and who are taking the view that university teachers are infallible purveyors of the truth, what follows is going to be rather unnerving. We are going to see how some great minds have on occasion misunderstood or been ignorant of each other's arguments and have been prone to forget to look at or to fudge major issues. Having gone through this, we are going to emerge without a general conclusion. Yet we will nonetheless emerge well equipped for tackling practical problems or theoretical essays in this area. The key to making the most of the chapter is to avoid letting a search for a simple *answer* get in the way of learning about pricing and output choices from the *process* of economic discourse.

A summary of the main themes in this chapter is provided at the start of Chapter 9 as a bridge between the two chapters, and you are advised to skip forward to this any time you feel you are losing the thread as you read the present chapter. Although this chapter does not refer to an incredibly large number of scholarly works, its focus on the contributions of particular economists led students to keep asking 'Do we have to learn the names?' when I used the material in lectures. They were rightly worried that some examination questions might require them to know who had voiced a particular idea, yet they seemed to be failing to realize that they might find it far easier to learn the ideas if they learnt 'the names': it is much easier to get a firm grasp of the material if one learns the sequence of key economists and then attaches to each of them their respective theories or critical contributions. Consequently, my answer was, and remains, 'Yes, you do have to learn the names, not least of all because once you have got into the habit of pigeonholing and sequencing ideas you will begin to develop a framework on to which you can hang further ideas and you will cease to think that your lecturers have superhuman memories'. Biographical studies of the key figures are to be found in Eatwell *et al.* (eds) (1987). The first name to remember is that of Alfred Marshall.

8.2   Marshall's evolutionary analysis of the firm

Although Williams (1978) has tried to piece together the origins of the theory of the firm prior to Marshall, it was Marshall who made the first major effort to construct a theory of how firms operate. To understand Marshall's view of pricing it is necessary to have quite a complex appreciation of his theory. Unfortunately, the way that Marshall went about constructing his analysis has resulted in much confusion about the relationship between subsequent neoclassical theories of the firm and Marshall's vision. This confusion has only been drawn to economists' attention relatively recently by the work of, particularly, Loasby (1978, 1989: chapter 4), Levine (1980) and O'Brien (ed.) (1991). The roots of the confusion probably lie in the means by which Marshall (1890/1920, 1919) sought to deal with the basic dilemma he was conscious of as an economic theorist: on the one hand he wanted to capture the rich complexity of real life but recognized the danger that his analysis would become unmanageable; on the other hand, he was fearful that attempts to use mathematics as a means of saying something precise about a subset of relevant features would lead to models that were little more than toys rather than devices which could be used in practical problem solving. As someone who had an intricate knowledge of actual business practices and who was also a skilled mathematician, Marshall ended up trying, somewhat uneasily, to combine both approaches. Subsequent theorists who have focused largely on his graphs and mathematical appendices have tended to miss the subtle richness of his analysis in prose.

It is most important to understand that Marshall was not writing about equilibrium configurations of price, cost and output at the level of the individual firm (even though he often referred to market equilibrium), but about processes of corporate and industrial evolution—and frequently with the aid of biological analogies. In Marshall's analysis, technical progress is continually taking place. New possibilities are emerging, leading to new techniques, processes, products and—the driving force for change—new profit opportunities. This view also applies to Marshall's consumers: they do not start with a given set of wants; wants emerge as the system develops and consumers learn (see Endres, 1991).

Secondly, Marshall's cost curves are fundamentally different from those that are typically drawn in textbooks, since:

(a) They concern costs as managers in firms actually saw them, rather than representing curves which it might be convenient for the economist to draw.

(b) Unlike contributors to the subsequent neoclassical literature, Marshall does not portray the marginal cost concept in terms of the first derivative of a continuously differentiable total cost curve. Rather, he sees it as the cost of switching from one process to another or taking on a new product, the firm's entire output of which is treated as a single unit (1890/1920: 381). As far as the costs of producing individual items of output were concerned, he preferred to speak in terms of 'prime' (or 'direct') costs and 'supplementary' costs, the latter being the contribution to overhead charges. However, he also emphasized that internal information on costs at the margin was lacking and that there were problems in isolating the costs of producing single units of output. What firms could see were average costs, but these changed in a step-like manner with changes of output, and were often moving around due to changes in conditions in input markets.

(c) Marshall's firms had inventory costs and, unlike the single-product firms depicted in later textbooks, produced a variety of products with joint overheads.

(d) Marshall's notion of costs also included marketing costs and other investments in the generation of goodwill.

Strangest of all Marshall's departures in respect of costs is his view of increasing returns and substitutions to economize on costs as factor prices change. When he talks of substitution in favour of a new production combination he regards it not as a movement from one existing isoquant to another, or along an existing production function, but as an event involving an extension and addition to society's repertoire of engineering blueprints. In Marshall's work, 'increasing returns' are the outcome of a process, which is irreversible and takes time and effort; they result from substitution possibilities that are discovered as the rate of production is increased. In subsequent neoclassical analysis, by contrast, they are portrayed as a possibility, available to be selected from a given menu, in which the combination of particular inputs in larger quantities and in the same proportions results in proportionately larger outputs (for the individual firm in the case of internal economies, and for an industry in the case of external ones) (see section 7.2 and Loasby, 1989: 52–3). This difference of approach means that Marshall's long-run average cost curve is more akin to the total cost curves implied by the learning curve notion discussed in section 7.6.

If production methods are not given but result from learning within firms, the question of how firms discover better ways of doing things naturally arises. In considering how firms' cost positions arose, and how they could achieve particular price and output combinations, Marshall paid an unusually large amount of attention to search processes within firms and the quality of management decision-making. He was very interested in developments in cost accounting and in American work on 'scientific management'. A key figure in his analysis is the entrepreneur, whom he sees as forecasting patterns of costs and demands, spotting opportunities for meeting particular wants, improving production processes and ensuring that decisions actually get implemented after they have been reached. Not surprisingly, Marshall was very keen on the idea of business education which, while growing in Germany, was largely absent in Britain at the time he was writing.

A temporary limit to the size of the firm's operations arises due to the entrepreneur's limited capacity to learn, which puts a brake on the discovery of better ways of reducing costs and satisfying customers (see further, section 10.13 and Penrose, 1959). Potential customers would also take a while to learn about the attractions of newer firms. In the early editions of his *Principles*, Marshall's evolutionary analysis was constructed so that human fallibility prevented the entrepreneurial learning process to go so far as to permit giant firms to appear. The long-run equilibrium of the individual firm in his analysis was death (bankruptcy, or voluntary liquidation), even though, at the industry level, falling average costs and prices were to be expected due to the ability of later generations of entrepreneurs to learn from the mistakes of their predecessors, as well as due to the beneficial effects of larger rates of industrial output on the costs of production. as the market grew. In other words, what Marshall had in mind was a kind of 'clogs to clogs in three generations' view of the *life-cycle* of the stereotypical firm. An industry would consist of a changing population of firms in various stages of development, which were thus differently placed in terms of their cost positions and profitability. He used a biological analogy to try to convey this idea (1890/1920: 263):

> [W]e may read a lesson from the young trees of the forest as they struggle upwards through the benumbing shade of their older rivals. Many succumb on the way, and only a few survive; those few become stronger with every year, they get a larger share of light and air with every increase in their height; and seem as though they would grow on forever, and forever become stronger as they grow. But they do not. One tree will last long in full vigour and attain a greater size than another: but sooner or later age tells on them all. Though the taller ones have better access to light and air than their rivals, they gradually lose vitality; and one after another they give place to others, which though of less material strength, have on their side the vigour of youth.

With the aid of this analogy, Marshall argued that *competition would drive industry prices into line with the average costs of the 'representative firm'*. The representative firm was an imaginary construct which involved an averaging out of the characteristics of actual firms in the industry. Industry-wide learning through time would ensure that average costs would fall, leading to corresponding reductions in prices. Contributing to the falling prices through time would be the enlargement of the scale of output which would permit the achievement of 'external economies' via a finer division of activities in the industry (for example, by the emergence of firms that specialize in providing ancillary services) and a larger pool of trained labour. As he noted (1890/1920: 265),

> an increase in the aggregate volume of production will generally increase the size, and therefore the internal economies possessed by such a representative firm;... it will always increase the external economies to which the firm has access; and thus will enable it to manufacture at a less proportionate cost of labour and sacrifice than before.

New firms would start with lower average cost than their predecessors had done and might get to larger sizes if they were operating in larger markets, but they would only be able to progress a limited distance down the long-run average cost curves that they generated before falling into decay themselves. At their peak levels of performance, they would be able to enjoy higher profits than their rivals by virtue of charging much the same price and yet enjoying lower costs of production and marketing.

The 'trees of the forest' analogy might well make sense in a world of family firms, in which success led to a switch of focus away from the firm towards setting up a large country estate, or where later generations of children were either less interested in being involved with the business or less adept at running it. However, Marshall was writing at a time when joint-stock companies were starting to become rather conspicuous by their size. If these firms ran out of an internal capacity to generate management talent or began to suffer from apathy, then their shareholders could vote to have new directors brought in from outside. This possibility opened up a prospect that would have been unsettling to Marshall, given his enthusiasm for capitalism: a firm might go on growing, gaining further increasing returns and then lower its prices, driving smaller firms out of the market and eventually establishing a monopoly for itself. Perhaps, therefore, Marshall was using the wrong kind of biological analogy: more appropriate than 'trees of the forest' might be the analogy of a 'pike in a pond', growing larger by eating small fry.

Marshall's way round the difficulty was to bring organizational considerations to the fore and assert that 'vast joint stock companies often stagnate but do not readily die'. He argued that size distanced shareholders from an appreciation of corporate problems and made it difficult to get new managers appointed and alternative policies implemented. Even a would-be revolutionary manager could have trouble getting progressive ideas accepted:

> A man of restless constructive force, who finds himself on a Board, may urge a reorganization of some parts of the procedure on more advanced lines, or for scrapping some plant that is no longer in the front rank: but he is not unlikely to appeal in vain, if the change would cause much trouble, suggest some criticism of past management, and be of such a nature that its ultimate pecuniary advantage cannot be proved with certainty. As a separate businessman he would probably make the venture ... but the *vis intertiae* of a great company are against him. He can seldom argue the case with numerous scattered shareholders who do not understand the business. He is therefore forced to acquiesce, however unwillingly, in the general opinion, that a company whose capital is almost wholly in the hands of the public must for the greater part adhere rather closely to routine (Marshall, 1919/1923: 317–18).

As other companies caught up with a firm that had hitherto been the industry leader, conflicts between different groups within it might hinder its struggle to remain efficient. It might consequently tend to focus inwards rather than on emerging external threats.

In the 1950s, Marshall's ideas about the inability of firms to keep operating at peak form were extended by some British economists, most notably by Jack Downie in his (1958) book *The Competitive Process* (see also Andrews, 1951: 171–2). The scenario here is of firms jostling for industrial leadership, with costs being reduced in a series of lurches that change profit margins and enable firms to offer their customers better value for money. If they wake up in time to a looming disaster, managers and workers in a fading company may be able to turn it around by finding ways of improving its product range, organizational systems and/or production methods: as the saying goes, 'the fear of hanging concentrates the mind wonderfully'. The rejuvenated firm might once more become a force to be reckoned with. One day, it might even usurp industrial leadership from those firms that had displaced it from dominance and whose managers might now be starting to rest on their laurels or focusing on internal power struggles rather than on external competitive threats. This line of thinking has much in common also with the work of the Americans Cyert and March (1963), on the uptake of organizational slack, and Leibenstein (1966, 1976), on *X*-inefficiency, as discussed in sections 7.10 and 7.11 (see also Earl, 1984).

8.3   Perfect competition and the debate over returns to scale

Marshall's views on the competitive process—with their focus on firms operating in industries in which prices are shaped by the average costs of firms in general and in which individual firms do not appear to have market power—might sound suspiciously like the theory of perfect competition encountered in most introductory textbooks on economics. However, it would be a mistake to believe that Marshall was thinking along the same lines as the theory of the perfectly competitive firm. In fact, it was only after Marshall's death in 1924 that this theory was proposed, and it was the result of a sustained effort to formalize his evolutionary thinking in equilibrium terms. (The term 'perfect competition' actually appears in Edgeworth's (1881: 30–31) work on the contract-curve: a market in which there is an unlimited number of potential suppliers leaves no room for bargaining.) Confusion over the meaning of Marshall's analysis actually started even before the turn of the twentieth century. For example, in reviewing the second edition of Marshall's *Principles*, Edgeworth (1891) both lamented the limited use that Marshall had made of calculus and asked why, if operating according to a law of increasing returns, firms could not get bigger simply by scaling up their uses of inputs and expanding their rates of output. The reason, he suggested, might be limitations to the size of their markets; he made no mention of the dynamic, problem-solving historical processes whereby cost reductions are realized. But he then argued that probably the problem could be ignored since there were few industries that actually enjoyed increasing returns to scale. All this implies that he did not appreciate Marshall's short-run/long-run and static/historical distinctions. Marshall did not believe in short-run increasing returns—on the contrary, he thought that short-run supply prices would tend often to rise with output—but he did believe that in the long run increasing returns were one of the principal driving forces in most sectors of the economy.

Despite taking this view, Marshall (1890/1920: 387–9) gave some thought to what might be implied for government policy if some sectors enjoyed increasing returns and others suffered from decreasing returns. He explored the likely impacts of taxes and subsidies on consumer surplus in a way that is related to the section 7.11 discussion of allocative efficiency and the views of Dupuit (1844) and Ramsey (1927) on the relationship between marginal costs and prices. He suggested that society might gain if it subsidized industries characterized by increasing returns and taxed industries characterized by decreasing returns. In the former case the rise in consumer surplus due to lower prices could exceed the cost of the bounty paid to the industry, whereas in the latter case the proceeds from a tax might be greater than the loss of consumer surplus due to price increases. This sort of thinking evoked a sharp critical response from John Clapham (1922), the leading economic historian of the day, who accused economists of creating theoretical 'boxes' that were empty of any empirical content. Economists seemed to Clapham to be writing abstractly about industries with increasing, constant or decreasing returns; yet they were never seen in practice to classify, say, coal as subject to diminishing returns or the hat industry as subject to increasing returns.

Now, the material in the previous section should lead us not to be surprised that Marshall, despite his wealth of knowledge about British industry, did not classify industries in a manner that would enable his policy suggestion to be implemented. In his evolutionary view, increasing returns or, at worse, constant returns applied to virtually all sectors in the long run: normally, expansions in output were sooner or later associated with falling prices. In the Marshallian view of returns to scale, the time period and the precise definition of the industry would affect the box in which it would be placed: for example, an industry that had been a long way down a learning curve associated with a particular technology might now be approximated as having constant returns, but if a technological breakthrough occurred it might enter a phase of rapid learning and output expansion. (An example from the second half of the twentieth century would be the transition in the electronics industry from tubes/valves to transistors and subsequently to integrated circuits.) This was hardly a convenient view for the emerging welfare economists such as Arthur Pigou, Marshall's successor at Cambridge, who wanted a clear statement of the 'given' possibilities of input/output combinations available to each industry. In the inter-war years, these economists looked for a static, snapshot view of firms and rapidly forgot that Marshall saw economic activity as a historical process unfolding like a movie.

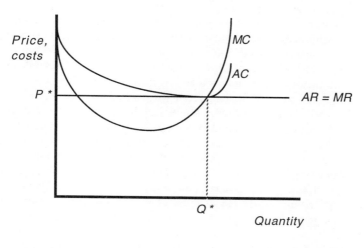

MC	= marginal cost	MR	= marginal revenue
AC	= average cost	AR	= average revenue
P*	= market-determined price	Q*	= equilibrium output

Figure 8.1: Long-run equilibrium of a perfectly competitive firm

209

A major role in switching the focus of the analysis of the firm from dynamic to static mode was played by Piero Sraffa (1925, 1926). In complete contrast to Clapham's concern with empirical tractability, Sraffa criticized a *static* interpretation of Marshallian thinking with respect merely to its logical consistency. The competitive firm was supposed to have no influence over the market price of its outputs or its inputs; it could buy as much of each input as it wished to buy at the going price, and could sell as much of its output as it wished to sell at the going price. Hence such a firm appears to have a horizontal demand curve for its outputs, even though the market demand curve may be downward sloping. If the market price is above average total costs, entry will occur and push the price down. Sraffa (1925) demonstrated (in Italian: the first exposition in English seems to be Pigou, 1928) that for an equilibrium to exist, perfectly competitive firms have to possess U-shaped average cost and marginal cost curves, as shown in Figure 8.1. However, having devised the diagram that has become so famous, Sraffa promptly argued that the theory of the competitive firm would only be logically coherent if restricted to situations in which there were constant returns to scale; yet, if this were done, its scale of output would then be undetermined as it would have both a horizontal demand curve *and* a horizontal average cost curve.

The logical difficulties associated with U-shaped cost curves arose as follows. On the one hand, cost curves that were upward sloping along their *whole* length were incompatible with any kind of equilibrium since 'competition would tend to make every firm infinitely small and the number of firms infinitely large'—as new, smaller-scale producers entered the market, each firm would have 'to reduce its own production to reduce its costs' (Sraffa, 1925, translated by Roncaglia and Eatwell). On the other hand however, if firms enjoy continuously increasing returns in the non-Marshallian sense of having *immediate* access to a falling average cost curve, and yet can sell as much as they wish at the going price, there can be no equilibrium: every increase in output implies a higher profit margin. Clearly, if the competitive firm faces a horizontal demand curve for its output, it eventually needs an upward-sloping cost curve to put a limit to the rate of production that it wishes to undertake.

The sources of such an upward slope are far less clear. If the firm is able to duplicate in physical terms all factors of production, then it is difficult to see why it should not at least enjoy constant returns to scale for engineering reasons. The only way a doubling of all inputs should involve doubling of output with a higher average cost is if, in purchasing more inputs, the firm bids up their prices against itself. This would normally be excluded by the assumption that the firm is so small a buyer of factors of production that it is a price-taker in factor markets. However, a bidding up of factor prices might not be inconceivable, particularly if factor supplies (most obviously labour) are localized and the firm's demands for factors start getting significant in relation to the total demand for them. However, this way of producing a rising cost curve cannot be allowed into a partial equilibrium method of analysis since that approach requires that the positions of an individual firm's cost curves are independent of its demand curve and it assumes that all other prices, including input prices, remain given for alternative possible choices of output and price. If the firm's choice of output affects input prices this could impact upon the costs of firms in other industries and, via its impact on factor incomes, on the demands for products. With demands for and costs of other products changing, their prices might be changing too, so the assumption of other output prices remaining the same would be questionable.

Sraffa's (1926) preferred way of salvaging the partial equilibrium analysis of prices and outputs was to move in the direction of treating firms as monopolists and abandon the idea of the perfectly competitive firm. Instead of portraying firms as facing horizontal demand curves, Sraffa thought they might be better depicted as finding it difficult to expand their sales at a given price—in other words, as if they each had their own downward-sloping demand curves. (The difficulties he had in mind were rather different from Marshall's views about the long-run activity of building up a reputation and thereby generating customer goodwill: Sraffa was talking about *given* downward-sloping demand functions, not ones whose positions firms might be able to move via their marketing efforts.) This was the approach taken by his Cambridge colleague Joan Robinson in her 1933 book *The Economics of Imperfect Competition*. It rehabilitated increasing returns as compatible with the equilibrium of the firm, but did so within a partial equilibrium framework.

The monopoly route was, however, insufficiently rigorous for Hicks, who saw the interconnections between markets that threatened partial equilibrium analysis as being the sort of thing that a general equilibrium approach to modelling an economic system might hope to capture. This was what Hicks (1939) eventually tried to achieve. In general equilibrium analysis one focuses on how the system would look *after all the interconnections have been sorted out via relative price adjustments*. As long as demand curves are nicely downward sloping and firms do run into rising average costs, it seems like there is a prospect that a set of prices will exist which ensures that no one can improve their situation by producing or consuming more or less of any products. But the 'rising cost of inputs' argument might not guarantee a rising cost curve if, in engineering terms, firms faced production functions that exhibited increasing returns to a sufficient degree to offset the rising costs of getting inputs to produce more. (For example, suppose a doubling of all inputs increases outputs by three-fold but only pushes up unit input prices by ten per cent: total costs have risen by 2.2 times against an increase in output of 3 times, so average costs have fallen.)

Hicks (1939: 83–5) asked himself if he could deal with increasing returns in his general equilibrium analysis and concluded, with obvious alarm, that they posed a threat to the possibility of the system ever finding a set of prices that cleared all the markets. Suppose the system is disturbed such that a demand curve in one market moves to the right. If marginal costs of production are falling, the increase in demand may result in a fall in price in that market. The income effects generated by this fall in price may then result in other rightward shifts of demand curves, further income effects and so on. Hicks (1939: 84) decided that he would have to assume that marginal costs 'do generally increase with output at the point of equilibrium (diminishing marginal costs being rare)', and he went on to say (p. 85) that 'We must be aware, however, that we are taking a dangerous step, and probably limiting to a serious extent the problems with which our subsequent analysis will be fitted to deal. Personally, however, I doubt if most of the problems we shall have to exclude for this reason are capable of much useful analysis by the methods of economic theory.' Yet what he had excluded was Marshall's (and, before him, Adam Smith's) view of how economic growth might be driven by falling costs associated with increases in the scale of production. This view had latterly been propounded by Allyn Young (1928). However, Young's contribution to the debate was cut tragically short when, in 1929 at the age of 52, he died of pneumonia in an epidemic of influenza. It was only many years later that Young's line of thinking was used by Nicholas Kaldor (1972) in an attempt to rekindle the debate about the inadequacies of the theory of perfect competition and, as he put it, 'The irrelevance of equilibrium economics'.

An alternative way of getting cost curves to rise was to appeal to the likelihood that some fixed factor would get in the way of the pursuit of economies of scale: perhaps one could not simply scale up all inputs by the same amount. One possibility that was suggested came from Austin Robinson (Joan Robinson's husband) (1931, 1934) and Nicholas Kaldor (1934): limitations in the capacity of management to cope with a larger scale of production might set in beyond some point, even though initially there might be managerial economies to be had from scaling up the firm's use of other factors of production. Communications difficulties might mean that a doubling of the size of the management team as other inputs were doubled would result in average costs tending to rise. But Kaldor found this solution problematic—at least in respect of an equilibrium analysis of the firm. Managers are needed to handle problems as and when they arise, but there is no need for management in a world of equilibrium. If we are to appeal to managerial coordination problems as a limit to the size of the firm, our story must concern economic environments in a state of flux. Of course, this view would not have troubled Marshall, given his emphasis on management's role in shaping the performance of a firm. (We return to the question of managerial coordination Chapters 10 and 11, where modern approaches to the question of what limits the size and scope of firms are considered.)

Before Kaldor, Hicks and the Robinsons made their contributions, Lionel Robbins had helped set the scene for them through his criticisms of Marshall's idea of a representative firm. In 1928 Robbins suggested that there would be considerable practical difficulties in the way of recognizing a typical firm, representative of an industry, in practice. A rather odd reaction to this was that Robinson and others chose to assume that firms in a market would have *identical* costs, and forgot all about Marshall's entrepreneurs and their search of methods of reducing costs. In Marshall's work, differences in average costs amongst firms had been analysed in terms of differences in managerial competence and stage of corporate development, rather than merely in terms of size; and Marshall had been able to analyse the dynamic behaviour of industries without imposing any requirement that firms should all be the same. The new work was static in nature: one had to have a long-run solution of equilibrium and this precluded any recognition that firms could keep reshaping their cost conditions and in doing so change the amount of competitive pressure felt by their rivals. Unit costs came to be seen solely as a function of size, and size was seen as determining the ability of a firm to exploit its customers and suppliers via its monopolistic and monopsonistic practices. The competition policies of many governments soon came to be based on this way of looking at things.

Sight had been completely lost of the informational role of Marshall's (1890) notion of the representative firm. In Marshall's analysis, potential market participants would look at average industry conditions—which they might approximate with reference to a particular firm—to help themselves judge whether they might profitably enter the market and displace weaker performers. The alertness of entrepreneurs, in turn, ensured that prices would tend to be kept down to the average costs of such reference-point firms, so the consumer would not end up being exploited. On the contrary, the pressure of competition would help promote innovative practices that would reduce average costs of surviving firms. In reality, firms nowadays do make such comparisons of themselves with rivals by subscribing to data-base services (such as the Centre for Inter-firm Comparisons, or Business Ratios) that provide them with information about how they stand relative to top, average and bottom practice in return for information about their own positions.

8.4   Exam post-mortem: Cost-curve dialogue

Question

Many textbook discussions of the economics of the firm portray firms as if their marginal costs of production rise as they expand their rates of output. But quite a few economists believe that this is an unwise way of viewing firms, and believe it would be more appropriate to assume that marginal costs are constant or fall as output is increased. You are asked to write a conversational dialogue between two imaginary economists representing these points of view (Professor Rising and Professor Falling), in which they try to convince each other to change their opinions on this issue and point out the analytical significance of holding their preferred view rather than that of their opponent.

Examiner's report

The class had been warned to expect an opportunity to answer one question by way of a dialogue. I had stressed that a good dialogue is often easier to write than a good essay, since (a) there is less need to worry about structure, for it can flow or change course much as a conversation would, and (b) the very nature of a dialogue reduces the risk that one will forget to discuss an issue from several points of view. I had suggested that examples of my own use of dialogues (in Earl, 1983b) might be examined before the examination; these had been inspired by ones in Hofstadter (1979). The dialogues that emerged in the examination often wasted a lot of time in getting started (quite often there were needless scene-setting remarks about two economists meeting in a bar, with many 'Hello' and 'Good evening' kinds of introductions) and then spent far too much time on one or two points, such as diminishing marginal productivity versus learning curves. In general, there seemed to be a failure to realize that in this case the structure of the actual debates from the 1920s and 1930s about the shapes of cost curves (sections 8.2 and 8.3) could have provided a model for an answer.

   Two main technical weaknesses were in evidence. First, there was a tendency to forget that the question was about the possibility of falling *marginal* costs and to write instead about why higher rates of output would result in falling average costs. Here, comments implicitly concerned reductions in average total costs coming from falls in average *fixed* costs achieved when higher rates of sales enable capacity to be operated more intensively. These reductions—which Chandler (1990: 24) calls 'economies of speed'—can, and often do, occur with constant marginal costs. Secondly, there was often a failure to be clear on the difference between falling marginal costs as represented by a learning curve (marginal costs falling with cumulated output through time) and a conventional marginal cost curve (which refers to marginal costs achievable at a particular rate of output in a particular period of time). The concept of diminishing marginal productivity proved difficult to explain clearly, probably because students were forgetting to make clear whether they were talking about the short run (when marginal costs might rise as more workers were put to work on a given set of capital equipment) or the long run (when the possibility of proportionate expansions in the use of all factors should mean that there is no engineering reason for diminishing marginal productivity). Few papers managed to grapple with both physical productivity issues and pecuniary ones, such as the significance of factor supply elasticities, but at least rather more considered scope for using a 'divide and rule' type of organizational structure as a possible means for stopping marginal costs from rising due to great pursuit of subgoals in larger, more complex organizations (see section 11.7). One paper usefully raised Hart's (1940, 1942) concern with the tradeoff between specialization and flexibility: potential reductions in marginal costs might be shunned by growing firms if they would only be possible via commitments to substantial fixed capital items which could not easily be adapted for producing something else in the event that demand fell (see section 7.2).

Economies of scale were often mentioned as a basis for falling marginal costs, but there was little attempt to explain how they arose (one paper did mention Adam Smith's (1776) pin factory example, but no one discussed factors such as economies of increased dimensions, which could have been explained very quickly with reference to the number of square metres of, say, steel required to build a cube-shaped container with a one cubic metre capacity versus a rectangular container with a two cubic metre capacity). Without any explanation of how economies of scale might come about, claims that marginal costs tended to fall because of increasing returns to scale seemed to me to look rather tautological.

8.5   Imperfect and monopolistic competition: the same or different?

In 1933 Joan Robinson published her *Economics of Imperfect Competition* in the United Kingdom and Edward Chamberlin published his *Theory of Monopolistic Competition* in the United States. Both works were offered as alternatives to the theory of perfect competition. When applied to markets where there are no barriers to entry, both works involve equilibrium solutions in which a downward-sloping demand curve for an individual firm is tangential to the downward-sloping portion of the firm's average cost curve. It is perhaps unsurprising, therefore, that the two works are often treated as proposing essentially the same ideas. Joan Robinson herself claimed that her analysis of imperfect competition was basically the same as Chamberlin's theory of monopolistic competition. Chamberlin, by contrast, spent much of his academic career attempting to demonstrate that they were different. In this section I integrate my own readings of these classic works with the perspectives of Loasby (1971, 1976: chapter 10), Romney Robinson (1969) and Skinner (1983), to highlight the differences as well as the similarities between them. But, before I proceed to do this, I will outline the typical textbook summary of these substantial books into a pair of diagrams, Figures 8.2 and 8.3.

Figure 8.2 presents a short-run equilibrium analysis in which supernormal profits are being earned, which is also a long-run solution if there are barriers to the entry of additional producers. The firm represented in the diagram may be either a sizeable producer of a homogeneous product (such as steel sheeting for car bodies, or sulphuric acid) or a producer of a particular differentiated product that is sold in competition with somewhat similar products offered by rival firms. It enjoys falling average total costs of production, but will only be able to expand its sales by lowering the price of its product. Extra sales then come partly at the expense of other firms and partly because lower prices for this sort of product encourage more people to buy it. Anywhere along the demand curve between *E* and *G* will enable the firm to break even; its problem is to select the price and quantity combination that will enable it to maximize its profits.

If the firm's demand (average revenue) curve is downward sloping so, too, is its marginal revenue curve. Beyond a certain point (where the marginal revenue curve intersects the quantity axis) extra sales result in negative marginal revenues: in other words, total revenue will start falling. But before this point is reached marginal revenue will begin to fall below marginal costs, resulting in a seemingly unnecessary sacrifice of potential profits. If the firm sets a price of *OD* and makes only *OM* units available to the market it will be producing at the rate of output at which its marginal revenue equals its marginal cost. This will give it the highest supernormal profit available, namely, the area *CDFK*.

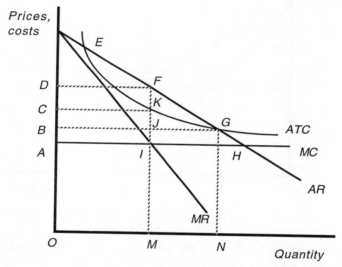

Figure 8.2: Short-run equilibrium of an imperfectly/monopolistically competitive firm

It will be evident that consumers are failing to get prices that are as low or quantities of output that are as high as would be possible without the firm incurring a loss. Compared with the situation in which prices were set at only *OB* and outputs of *ON* were made available, there is a deadweight loss of consumer surplus equal to the area of the triangle *GJF* as well as a transfer of *BDFJ* away from consumers.

Figure 8.3 shows what is often called the 'tangency solution', the long-run equilibrium of the firm when other firms can enter the market in response to the lure of the supernormal profits that it earns in the short run. In long-run equilibrium no one wishes to enter or leave the market. The attempts of new entrants to sell more output in the market cause prices in the industry to fall. Demand curves for individual firms shift to the left until average total costs and average revenues are equal and there is no longer an incentive to enter the market. For mathematical reasons, *OL*, the rate of output at which average total cost curve is tangential to its new average revenue curve, is also the rate of output at which the new marginal revenue curve for the firm cuts its marginal cost curve. At this point, price is *OD`*. Consumers are now able to purchase the products more cheaply but they are buying from an industry which appears to be characterized by more firms, each of whom is operating with spare capacity. Had the incumbent firms not been initially so greedy in setting their prices—for example, had they set prices at *OB* to equalize average total costs and average revenues—there would have been neither the supernormal profits of the short run nor the waste of resources in the idle capacity of the long run.

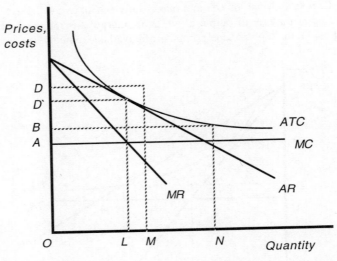

Figure 8.3: Long-run equilibrium of an imperfectly/monopolistically competitive firm

This welfare analysis has had a significant impact on competition policy in many countries. The theory suggests that, even where several 'imperfectly competitive' firms already dominate an industry, action is likely to be necessary to prevent overcharging and the restriction of output by existing firms if entry by other suppliers is difficult. If entry to an industry seems easy, a tax on employment may be used to raise break-even output levels and hence discourage a wasteful use of resources in excess capacity. (Such was the thinking behind the Selective Employment Tax introduced in the United Kingdom in 1966, at a time when it was felt desirable to shift resources from the service sector to manufacturing. When applied to such service firms as retailers, the tax was supposed to have the advantage that it would not be passed on in higher prices. The argument here rested on the idea that, in retail firms, workers may normally be seen as an overhead expense and therefore the tax on employment would not raise marginal costs—see Kaldor, 1980: chapter 6.)

Having considered the conventional wisdom produced by distilling these two famous contributions into a single way of thinking, we may move on to look more closely at their differences. Although they may have ended up with similar long-run equilibrium solutions, their origins are very different. Joan Robinson started with Sraffa's falling cost curve problem, saying that 'Mr. Sraffa's article must be regarded as the fount from which my work flows, for the chief aim of this book is to attempt to carry out his pregnant suggestion that the whole of the theory of value should be treated in terms of monopoly analysis' (1933/1969: xiii). With the benefit of hindsight, however, she claimed in the preface to her second edition that she had been trying to model a real-world situation that represented an empirical anomaly for Pigou's theory of the perfectly competitive firm. She notes that, in Pigou's theory, 'The optimum size of firm, with minimum average cost, is always tending to be established.... Here we were, in a deep slump, and this is what we were being asked to believe.... Imperfect competition came in to explain the fact, in the world around us, that more or less all plants were working part time' (1933/1969: v–vi).

Robinson's 'depression story' is rather difficult to reconcile with her claim in the first edition that 'In general I have endeavoured to build on foundations laid by Marshall and Professor Pigou' (p. viii): Marshall's (1890) evolutionary analysis certainly did not suggest that the optimum size of firm, with minimum average cost, was always tending to be established. When listening to her lectures in the mid-1970s I formed the impression that she wanted to convince her audience that the whole analysis was a kind of intellectual spoof that misfired: she seemed to be saying that it was an attempt to show that if one tried to use the theoretical tools of free-market neoclassical economics in a logically consistent manner, the results would be at odds with believing that markets delivered the best thing for consumers and that workers were paid their marginal value products. Perhaps we are nearer the appropriate explanation of how the book came about when we see her write (1933/1969: vi) about how her colleague Richard Kahn's discovery—that where two average curves are tangential, the corresponding marginal curves cut at the same abscissa—'took on a kind of fascination for its own sake'. Certainly it is with her book that the abstract, formal model of the firm really gets of the ground.

Chamberlin's book was based on his 1927 Harvard Ph.D. thesis, so could not really have been shaped by Sraffa's work and, despite his supervisor having been Allyn Young, he was little interested in making increasing returns a focal issue. In fact, he almost invariably drew his average costs curves as if they eventually turned upwards. His equilibrium focused on a downward-sloping portion of the average cost curve of a firm merely because this was the way things *had* to be given that he started with the proposition that individual firms had their own demand curves, like little monopolists. This starting point in his theory came from his interest in a controversy that had been going on in the United States concerning railroad rates and price discrimination. Where railway users faced a choice of routes and alternative transport modes, the rival products were similar (in that they all involved transportation) yet were sufficiently different for their suppliers to have some discretion over the market prices they charged. Consequently much of his book is concerned with the competitive implications of product differentiation. This is a major contrast with Robinson's work, for most of her analysis proceeds as if firms in an industry are producing identical products and as if brand loyalty amongst consumers is the result of misinformation or irrationality. Loasby (1976: 179) is overdoing it somewhat to suggest that Robinson never had differentiation in mind, but certainly she usually treated differentiation as spurious, involving a waste of resources in advertising and too many producers, each operating with excess capacity.

Chamberlin's interest in differentiated products led him to regard not merely price but also the product itself and its marketing package as policy variables. (The discussion in section 2.9 might usefully be reviewed at this juncture.) This meant that he had to recognize the interdependence of a firm's cost and demand curves. He proceeded as if the firm separated out its price, product and marketing choices—an assumption that often might be quite realistic given the complexity of the problem. For example, managers could consider the impact on the firm's profits of a particular design change, with the price left unchanged. This thought-experiment could be performed at each possible price, so that the best position could be found. It could then be performed with other redesign strategies, or with other strategies involving different marketing methods. These strategies would shift the demand curve about in different ways, and the cost curve likewise. The firm's task was to find the best policy mix.

Whereas Joan Robinson's analysis is dominated by marginal cost and revenue curves, they only appear in four of Chamberlin's many diagrams, though his theoretical solutions necessarily imply Robinsonian marginal equalities. Chamberlin seemed to have had in mind a vision of managers performing a kind of iterative experiment in terms of average costs and revenues, until they stumbled upon the best solution. But such an iteration would involve a good deal of complex conjecturing about market conditions (see also the next two paragraphs) and Chamberlin suggests (1933/1962: 105) that 'businessmen may set their prices with reference to costs rather than to demand, aiming at ordinary rather than maximum profits and more or less taking it for granted that they will continue to enjoy about their usual share of the total business'. This sounds remarkably like the view of pricing that was later to emerge in the non-marginalist 'mark-up pricing' literature (see section 9.6), or behavioural views on satisficing approaches to pricing.

A central feature of Chamberlin's view of the business manager's decision problem was the mutual interdependence of firms: unaware of its use by a German economist in 1914, Chamberlin believed himself to have invented the term 'oligopoly,' and much of his book is spent trying to deal with it. By contrast, Joan Robinson (1933/1969: 21) openly dodged the issue of group interactions: 'The demand curve for the individual firm may be conceived to show the full effect upon the sales of that firm which results from any change in the price which it charges, whether it causes a change in the prices charged by others or not. It is not our purpose to consider this question in detail.' As she later recalled, this 'was a shameless fudge [to make it possible to apply marginalist ideas].... I treated the conditions of demand as being unchanged for an indefinitely long period and I assumed that experiments with prices would leave no traces in market conditions' (1933/1969: vi).

By dodging both the oligopoly issue and the question of product differentiation, Joan Robinson could generate determinate solutions and maintain the concept of 'the industry' (for example, imagine large producers of unbranded sulphuric acid: they would comprise the sulphuric acid industry). Chamberlin had to live with a less precise view of industry and was severely criticized by Triffin (1940) for doing so. Triffin argued that if the elasticity of substitution between 'similar' products is imperfect, their sellers can pursue independent pricing policies: each firm thus is like a miniature industry capable of analysis in isolation.

Chamberlin set out his discussion in terms of alternative scenarios involving large or small groups of firms, in the latter case emphasizing oligopolistic interdependence. His view was that if there were many producers then the effects of a price cut by an individual firm *might* not be noticed by other firms, since these effects might be dispersed, even if, in total, the price-cutting firm picked up quite a few sales. In this situation the firm would have some discretion in the price it charged (so long as it was not fearful that other firms would start noticing how well it was doing and consider copying its policies). However, Chamberlin was prepared to recognize that the 'large group case' might be of limited relevance owing to 'chain effects': there might be lots of fairly similar firms dispersed geographically, so that the brunt of an individual firm's price cut might be borne by those nearby; the latter might then start taking a careful look at their neighbours' behaviour to find out whether someone had been slyly cutting prices. (Competition in petrol retailing provides a useful illustration of this phenomenon.)

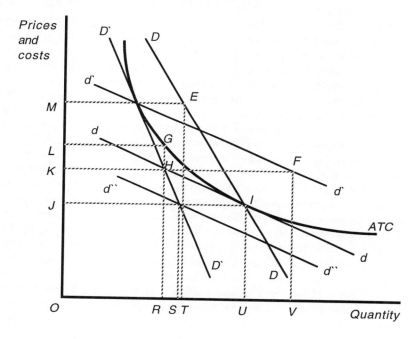

Figure 8.4: Chamberlin's equilibrium solution for a member of a 'small' group of oligopolistic competitors

For situations of recognized interdependence, Chamberlin's graphical analysis was very distinctive but unfortunately too complex to appeal to writers of introductory textbooks. He includes (1933/1962: 90–93) an out-of-equilibrium analysis that recognizes the possibility that excessive entry may take place if greedy pricing generates supernormal profits for existing producers; this analysis is the subject of Figure 8.4 and involves a price war of attrition on the way to an equilibrium price and rate of output. (It is a good analysis to read in preparation for the discussion of coordination problems in Chapter 10.) The analysis proceeds 'as if' all of the rival firms enjoy the same cost curves and, if they charge the same price, equal shares of the total market. This assumption enables Chamberlin to introduce in a simple way his idea that each firm has a 'fractional part of the market' demand curve, which is labelled in upper case as DD in the situation of eventual equilibrium. The more firms there are in the market, the steeper will be the slopes of their DD curves and the further to the left they will lie. (For example, take the case of a simple linear market demand curve $P = 15 - 0.0167Q$. If the price is 10, then total market demand will be 300 units, and if the price is 8, then total market demand will be 420 units in the time period in question. If there are 10 firms in the market then, at a price of 10, they will each sell 30 units and, if the price is 8, they will each sell 42 units: in this case their DD curves have the equation $P = 15 - 0.167Q$. If there are 15 firms in the market and the price is 10, they will each sell 20 units, whereas if the price is 8, they will each sell 28 units: in this case their DD curves have the equation $P = 15 - 0.25Q$.) To keep Figure 8.4 relatively uncluttered, let us suppose that the initial price and quantity configuration at E (price OM and quantity OT) is also a point on DD: this implies that there will be the same number of firms at the end of the story as at the beginning. The trouble with the initial position E is that it cannot be an equilibrium since the price is greater than average total costs. New producers will be attracted into the market, pushing DD to the left.

Now suppose the number of firms entering is such that the typical firm's new 'fractional part of the market' demand curve becomes $D`D`$, tangential to the average total cost curve. If consumers were to choose randomly between each of the would-be suppliers at price OM, there would be room in the market for all of the firms to break even, but at a much reduced rate of capacity utilization compared with the initial situation. This outcome is unlikely to be an equilibrium, either, if each firm feels tempted by the thought of what might happen if it cut its prices and its rivals did not. In this case, it would steal extra sales from its rivals (who, as already noted, *might* not even notice if each only lost a few units) as well as picking up sales from people who otherwise would not have purchased the product. The relevant demand curve seems not to be $D`D`$ but $d`d`$. If a price of OK is tried, each firm that offers to sell at this price may expect to end up at point F, achieving sales of OV units, but if everyone charges this price, whether aggressively or as a follower, then each firm will actually end up at point H: sales per firm will be only OR and each firm will lose LG per unit, giving total losses per firm of $LGHK$. Note here that the price level OK was chosen purely for the sake of illustration: *any* reduction below OM would have produced losses if widely adopted. The losses will be an inducement to engage in further price cutting.

From the standpoint of point H, a firm may imagine that if it cut its price to OJ and were not followed by its rivals it would move down the curve dd to point I, sell OU units and just about break even. The trouble is, if everyone sets out to do this, they will each end up selling only OS units. Further price cuts, to move along $d``d``$, will make losses even worse (they appear to guarantee losses, even if other firms do not act similarly, since $d``d``$ lies below ATC) unless they result in some of the firms quitting the market, leaving a viable space for those that remain. (If all the firms really are identical, it is by no means clear why any particular firm should leave: the price war turns from a game of Prisoner's Dilemma into a game of Chicken! See further, sections 5.9 and 10.9.) As firms quit the market the sales of those that remain will rise until equilibrium is reached with dd and average total costs tangential, intersected by DD.

8.6   Technical exercise: Monopoly and perfect competition

Question (i)
Suppose that the demand curve for an industry's product is given by

$$P = 36 - Q$$

where P is price and Q is quantity. Assume that the industry contains a single monopolistic firm with total costs (C) given by

$$C = 9 + Q^2.$$

Find the quantity of product that the firm will produce and the price it will charge.

Solution
Total revenue = PQ = $36Q + Q^2$. Differentiate the total revenue function to obtain the marginal revenue function. This gives $MR = 36 - 2Q$. (Note that the marginal revenue function slopes downwards at twice the rate of the demand curve.) A monopolist is predicted to set prices by finding the price and quantity at which marginal revenue equals marginal cost. The total cost function can be differentiated to find the marginal cost function, $MC = 2Q$. Setting $MC = MR$ gives $2Q = 36 - 2Q$. Hence $4Q = 36$, so $Q = 9$. *The firm will sell 9 units by setting a price equal to $36 - 9 = 27$.*
   A technically superior answer will provide a check of the second-order conditions to ensure that profits are indeed being maximized with the marginal revenue curve cutting the marginal cost curve from above. Differentiating $MR = 36 - 2Q$ gives $dMR/dQ = -2$. Differentiating $MC = 2Q$ gives $dMC/dQ = 2$. The marginal cost curve is indeed rising and being cut by a marginal revenue curve that falls as quantity increases. If the marginal cost curve were falling and doing so at a rate faster than the marginal revenue curve, then profits could be increased by increasing sales beyond the quantity at which $MC = MR$. However, though marginal cost curves may sometimes fall over part of their length, it would be surprising to find them falling without limit as this would imply that marginal costs eventually became negative! In the case here, we do not have a U-shaped marginal cost curve: marginal costs start rising right from the outset, and the curve begins at the origin. It may further be noted that total fixed costs are 9 and that profits are total revenue minus total costs, in other words, $PQ - C = 27\,(9) - [9 + 9^2] = 243 - 90 = 153$. This can be checked by noting that average total costs are $(9 + Q^2)/Q$ and when Q is 9, average costs are $90/9 = 10$. The profit margin is $27 - 10 = 17$ and 17 times $9 = 153$. Figure 8.5 presents a graphical perspective on the calculations for this question.

Question (ii)
Assume now that the industry becomes perfectly competitive and that there is free entry of firms with cost functions identical to that of the monopolistic firm. Find the new equilibrium quantity and determine how many firms the industry will contain.

Calculations

The equilibrium condition for firms in a perfectly competitive industry is that $MC = AC = MR = AR = P$. The combination of fixed costs of 9 (giving an average fixed cost function of $AFC = 9/Q$) and a marginal cost function $MC = 2Q$ (implying an average variable cost function of $AVC = Q$), gives each firm an average cost function which is U-shaped: eventually the rising average variable cost curve overwhelms the downward path of average total costs that the falling average fixed cost function (a rectangular hyperbola) is tending to generate. ATC is simply total costs divided by Q so $ATC = (9 + Q^2)/Q$ (as noted under (i)) and ATC are minimized when $ATC = MC$. This occurs when $(9 + Q^2)/Q = 2Q$. From this we get $9 + Q^2 = 2Q^2$ and hence we get $Q^2 = 9$, so for each firm the equilibrium quantity is $Q = 3$. When $Q = 3$, $MC = ATC = 6$. (Note, when $Q = 2$, $ATC = 6.5$ and when $Q = 4$, $ATC = 6.25$.) When $Q = 3$ the ATC function is neither rising nor falling: its slope is horizontal, so we can check this result by differentiating the ATC function (using the quotient rule) to get $dATC/dQ = (Q^2 - 9)/Q^2 = 0$ and noting that $dATC/dQ = 0$ when $Q = 3$. (Note that when $Q = 2$, $dATC/dQ = -5/4$, implying that ATC is falling, and when $Q = 4$, $dATC/dQ = 7/16$ implying that ATC is rising.) Alternatively, note that $AFC = AVC = 3$ and ATC equals $3 + 3 = 6$; beyond $Q = 3$, $AVC > AFC$ so ATC must be rising.

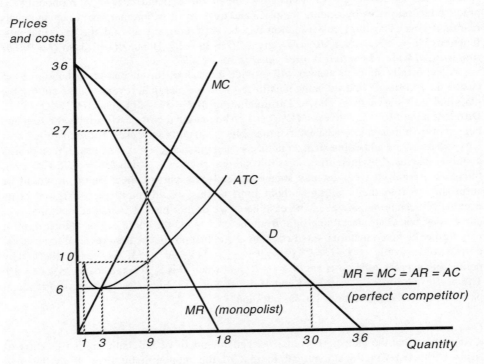

Figure 8.5: Graphical summary of calculations in monopoly and perfect competition exercise

Prospects of profit will cause firms to continue to enter the market until the price equals the minimum average variable cost, that is until $P = 6$. When $P = 6$, *total* sales in the market will be given by $6 = 36 - Q$, so Q will be 30. Thus *in equilibrium there will be 10 firms each with sales of 3 units at a price of 6 per unit.* (A common mistake at this stage is to fail to notice that the reduction in market price pushes up the total sales in the market from 9 to 30: students tend to conclude the end result would be three firms each selling three units.)

Question (iii)
Discuss the economic significance of the two cases for the understanding of the behaviour of firms in market economies.

Author's notes
A real-world monopolist might take steps to try to ensure that it did not encourage entry or encourage potential customers to devise substitutes. For example (like OPEC, as interpreted by Wilson, 1979—see section 9.8), it might set lower prices and not attempt to maximize short-run profits. However, in this example the rising cost curve makes it difficult to come up with an entry-preventing price strategy. If the monopolist were to set prices at 6 to make it pointless for anyone to enter, then the monopolist would be selling 30 but making huge losses (*ATC* are 30.3 at $Q = 30$). In many real-world cases, monopolistic advantages arise initially because average cost curves keep falling until they cut the industry demand curve.

The final equilibrium is also dependent on rising marginal cost curves pulling up the average cost curve of the firms. In reality, the evidence on whether average variable cost curves actually do turn upwards or are downward sloping is rather mixed (see Lee, 1985). As far as pure theory is concerned, it is difficult to explain logically why a small firm should have an optimal equilibrium rate of output: operations can be duplicated to avoid diminishing returns (yet in engineering terms increasing returns seem likely), and a small firm should not find itself driving its input costs up as it bids for more inputs.

Although the mathematics tell us how many firms could survive in this market, they do not tell us anything about the process by which the right number of firms might get established. If more than ten firms try to enter prices will be depressed below 6 and each firm will make losses. Nonetheless, so long as the market price is above the minimum average variable cost that can be achieved, there may be more than ten firms operating in the market at a loss for a long period, for they do not make their losses worse by continuing to operate (any revenue in excess of variable costs is at least something towards covering their fixed costs). In the real world, as we shall see in Chapter 10, coordination problems are considerable if markets lack barriers to entry. An example would be what has happened in passenger aviation markets following deregulation: see section 10.5. Free entry may not be such a wise state of affairs to promote if coordination problems are possible.

In our numerical example, the cost and demand functions are well known and the perfect competition assumption in part (ii) means that any would-be entrant can produce on terms as attractive as incumbent producers. In the real world competitive processes are complicated by uncertainties about costs and by learning curves. Also, it is common for a variety of production technologies of different vintages to be employed by different firms all competing in the same market with different profit margins. In the long run what tends to happen is not that the remaining firms end up using identical technologies but that yet newer technologies are devised and equilibrium is not attained, but productivity keeps rising. The perfect competition example must also be assuming that products are not differentiated. This might be acceptable as an approximation for some industries but not for others.

In defence of such models of competitive behaviour it might be said that they are only intended as rough approximations to give a rough feel of what happens in practice. In reality, even if managers do not know their actual demand and cost curves, they might find similar sorts of profit-maximizing positions by trial and error and with no formal reference to marginal revenues and marginal costs.

8.7 Early criticism and defence of marginalism

The theories of imperfect and monopolistic competition soon came under fire in both the United Kingdom and United States as a result of survey-based research about actual business practices, published by Robert Hall and Charles Hitch (1939/1951), and by Richard Lester (1946). The former questioned 38 businesses (33 of which were manufacturers); the latter based his article on 58 replies. The limited data sets, and the fact that the data were based on questionnaires and interviews, led to pretty savage dismissals of both contributions by committed marginalists, most notably Austin Robinson (1939) and Fritz Machlup (1946). It was claimed that the data were unlikely to be particularly reliable. It was also suggested that it would not matter for economists if, in practice, managers had no idea what their marginal costs and revenues were, so long as they seemed to act 'as if' they did by behaving in accordance with the predictions of marginalist theories.

There are several reasons why we might wish to side more with Hall, Hitch and Lester than with the defenders of marginalist thinking. First, as Morgenstern (1963) argues in his book *On the Accuracy of Economic Observations*, the claim that businessmen will bias their answers either to conceal things from investigators or to tell them what they think they would like to hear might equally well be used against the supposedly 'objective' data that mainstream economists happily use in their empirical work: all officially published statistics are supplied by people in response to requests for information. Secondly, even were the empirical material, however gathered, consistent with marginalist analysis, we should not forget that there may be other theories that are also consistent with the data in the time period in question and which would also be consistent with data obtained in other time periods during which the marginalist theories fared less well; past performance of a particular theory is not a good reason for shutting one's mind to alternative points of view. In any case, it is not obvious from the data that these economists gathered that it makes much sense to represent firms 'as if' they behave in accordance with marginalist principles.

Lester's work focused on employment decisions and how they related to costs. It is as much a critique of short-run applications of neoclassical production theory as it is of marginalist models of firms' price and output decisions. As Lester (1946: 72) says,

> The present author's interviews with business men indicate that most entrepreneurs do not tend to think in terms of marginal variable cost. The heads of manufacturing concerns hiring, say, 50 or more workers consider such a procedure both unnecessary and impractical because (1) they

seem convinced that their profits increase as the rate of operations rises, at least until full plant capacity is reached—they have no faith in the validity of U-shaped marginal variable cost curves unless, perhaps, overtime pay is involved; (2) they consider repeated shifts in the size of a plant's working force, or in its equipment, with changes in the relative costs of different productive factors to be impractical, their adjustments to cost changes taking most frequently the form of product shifts that require little, if any, alteration in equipment; and (3) they see the extreme difficulties of calculating marginal variable costs and the marginal productivity of factors, especially in multi-process industries and under present accounting methods. In thinking about employment in their firm, therefore, they tend to emphasize current and prospective demand for their products and the full-crew requirements for their existing facilities, rather than the current level of wage rates.

Given that Lester also stressed that with many technologies firms found it difficult to vary their workforces as they changed their rates of output we probably need to reinterpret his conclusion that firms seemed to be operating 'at decreasing unit variable costs all along the scale between 70 and 100 per cent of plant capacity'. If hiring cannot be adjusted with output, then what we are really saying is that line workers should not really be classed among the firm's variable costs; rather, they may (to use the terminology suggested by Oi, 1962) be thought of as 'quasi fixed factors.'

Lester also makes us think carefully about the practical difficulties that firms would have in trying to discover what their marginal costs were by means of *experimentation*, particularly if they were multi-process businesses, performing a variety of operations in different cost centres as the products pass through the firm in various stages of completion. His findings might be read to imply that a firm initially appraises its likely demand prospects and sees what sort of technology will be appropriate for dealing with them in a profitable manner. With the firm's technology thereby chosen, its level of costs per unit of output is then largely driven by its scale of output, not by changes in wages, at least not until the machinery wears out and replacements have to be appraised. Higher wages will tend to result not in reductions of output (unless the firm has to abandon production of the product in question)—only 1 in 11 firms mentioned this—but by 'better management practices and increased sales efforts'. Such a response is very much in keeping with the satisficing/problem-solving view of the firm subsequently proposed by Cyert and March (1963) and Simon (1945, 1976, 1986) (see section 7.10).

Hall and Hitch were driven by their findings to a radical critique of Robinson's and Chamberlin's work on pricing—a critique which in some respects harked back to Marshall's view that prices are determined by the average costs of the representative firm. They (1939/1951: 112–13) pointed out that

The most striking feature of the answers was the number of firms which apparently do not aim, in their pricing policy, at what appeared to us to be the maximization of profits by the equation of marginal revenue and marginal costs. In a few cases this can be explained by the fact that the entrepreneurs are thinking of long-run profits, and in terms of long-run demand and cost curves, even in the short run, rather than of immediate profits.... This is expressed to some extent by the phrase commonly used in describing their policy—'taking goodwill into account.' But the larger part of the explanation, we think, is that they are thinking in altogether different terms; that in pricing they try to apply a rule of thumb which we shall call 'full cost', and that maximum profits, if they result at all from the application of this rule, do so as an accidental (or possibly evolutionary) by-product.

An overwhelming majority of entrepreneurs thought that a price based on full average cost (including a conventional allowance for profit) was the 'right' price, the one which 'ought' to be charged.....

   [To determine full-cost prices], prime (or 'direct') cost per unit is taken as the base, a percentage addition is made to cover overheads (or 'oncost', or 'indirect' cost), and a further conventional addition (frequently 10 per cent) is made for profit. Selling costs commonly and interest on capital rarely are included in overheads; when not so included they are allowed for in the addition for profits.

In addition to the idea that a price 'ought' to be worked out in this way, Hall and Hitch suggested six further reasons for the non-marginalist practice: (1) Producers cannot know their demand or marginal revenue curves, either because they are unclear about consumer preferences or because they operate in an oligopolistic market and are unsure of how their competitors would respond to price changes; (2) they fear that competitors would tend to copy their price cuts if they departed from full-cost pricing; (3) they fear that competitors will tend not to match their price increases; (4) as a group, firms in a market judge that the price elasticity of demand for the product will not make a price cut worthwhile; (5) they fear that even if all current producers raised their prices in tandem, the policy would be undermined by new entrants in the long run; (6) changes in prices cannot be effected without cost, particularly to sales personnel and consumers who would find frequent gyrations of prices inconvenient.

   As Lee (1984) has since shown, the full-cost analysis of how prices were set involved a fundamentally different view of how pricing should be modelled. Hall and Hitch found that the firms they studied set their prices well in advance of production, planning to maintain them for a particular period of time (in, for example, their catalogues and price lists). This period was neither the usual 'short period'—since similar prices were to be charged for transactions occurring through time—nor the usual 'long period'—since prices were set in relation to the costs of using an existing production set-up and not all factors were assumed to be variable. Prices thus determined differ from the usual 'market-clearing prices' of supply and demand theory. In the usual analysis a 'market price' is defined and simultaneously determined by a specific exchange of a particular amount of a commodity at a particular point in time, in relation to the costs actually incurred. Hall and Hitch had specific market prices that were common to many *sequential* exchanges involving different buyers and sellers and quantities of the commodity being exchanged. These market prices are not affected by the *actual* costs associated with any specific exchange during the pricing period—whether total costs or marginal costs. There was no *functional* relationship, direct or indirect, between price, cost and actual output.

   Hall and Hitch did not seem to realize that what they had been told represented such a big break with the supply and demand philosophy. As we shall see in the next section, they clung to marginalist thinking when trying to combine some of their empirical discoveries with the concept of a kinked demand curve in order to explain price stability in the face of sales fluctuations—a widely observed phenomenon that was problematic for Robinson's theory and also for other approaches embodying a comparative statics, supply and demand-based equilibrium analysis (neither a collusive oligopoly or a price leadership situation offered reasons why one might expect stable market prices). It makes no sense to use a marginal revenue/marginal cost analysis of kinked demand curves to explain price stability if the full-cost analysis of preset prices suggests that prices are not related to the specific costs and output associated with an exchange. And other economists, not used to drawing a distinction between trade during a pricing period and exchanges in a short period where a firm confronts a particular group of customers and sets a price for the particular transaction, did not see the break either. Instead they queried the full-cost pricing concept, saying that full costs would vary with the rate of output and hence should be associated with varying prices; or they simply said that Hall and Hitch had shown, by marginalist means, why prices were stable in the face of fluctuating demand, but had not explained how prices originally came to be set.

8.8 Kinked demand curves

According to Spengler (1965), the idea of a kinked demand curve originated with Hayes (1928), who based his thinking on two themes: one is nowadays known as 'sticker shock' and involves buyers resisting paying higher prices because they are used to paying a 'customary price' (curve *DD`* in Figure 8.6), the other is an alleged tendency of buyers to judge quality by price, which would result in a backward-bending demand curve (*DD``*). However, as Reid (1981) emphasizes in his book on the kinked demand curve literature, neither Hayes nor Joan Robinson (who in her 1933 book noted the possibility of kinked demand and cost curves) sought to use such a curve formally to explain price stickiness in the face of changing economic circumstances. The recognition by Hall and Hitch (1939) that kinked demand curves might help explain why prices were not changed if demand conditions changed coincided with Paul Sweezy's (1939) realization that kinked demand curves could be used to provide a microeconomic perspective on why wage reductions in times of high unemployment could fail to dissuade employers from reducing their workforces in the face of reduced sales.

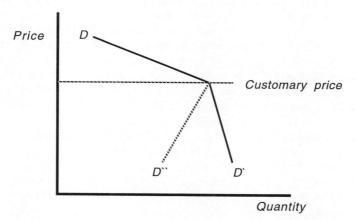

Figure 8.6: The kinked demand curves proposed by Hayes (1928)

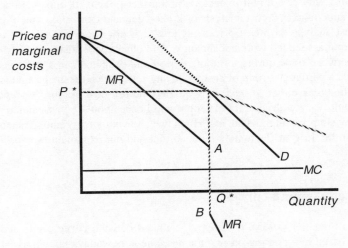

Figure 8.7: The kinked demand curve and price stickiness

The arguments of Hall, Hitch and Sweezy may be summarized with reference to Figure 8.7. They begin with the firm incurring an exogenous shock which changes (usually: reduces) its rate of sales to Q^*. The question then arises as to whether it would be profitable to make any change in prices. A reduction in orders might also result in managers threatening to lay off some workers: if so, the question arises as to whether offers to work for less would prevent these threats from being carried out by permitting price cuts on a sufficient sale to restore sales to their former level, or whether wage reductions would merely lead to an increase in profits at the expense of the workers. The firm is then assumed to take the view that a price cut would be followed, whereas a price increase would generate extra sales for rivals and would therefore tend not to be followed. The market demand curve could thus be perfectly conventional and yet each firm might act as if it faced a kinked demand curve which, by implication, had a discontinuity in its marginal revenue curve directly below the kink. This discontinuity is shown by *AB* in Figure 8.7. The curve is drawn on the assumption that a price already exists (*P**), and the kink is at that price level. *If* marginal costs were in the range of the discontinuity (*they need not be*), then the firm would be maximizing profits at the existing price. It will be evident from Figure 8.7 that quite a wide range of changes in sales (leftward or rightward movements in the curve) or movements of marginal costs might be accommodated with no change in price.

These authors were aware of possible exceptions: (1) price leadership, in which there was a generally recognized first-mover when market conditions changed, and firms would copy the leader; (2) secret price cutting in times of depression, or even overt price cutting by desperate firms who believed they might gain some room for manoeuvre before others followed (they might keep their creditors at bay a while longer, and possibly even pick up some longer-term business from customers who defect from rivals, even if the price reduction is not sustained). These effects would tend to smooth out the kink.

Efroymson (1943, 1955) discussed an alternative possibility: a 'reflex kink', in which the lower part of the curve bends away from the origin, as is shown in Figure 8.8. He suggests that this might arise in boom times when firms are aware of capacity shortages. A price increase does not lead customers to shift to rivals for rival firms are having a hard enough time satisfying existing orders, whereas a price cut will not be followed since rivals have a surplus of customers. With a reflex kink, the existing price (*P**) is, locally, a profit *minimum,* as is shown by the shaded opportunity loss areas either side of the discontinuity in the marginal revenue curve: to the left of *Q**, marginal costs are above marginal revenue so profits can be increased by cutting output back towards the *MC/MR* intersection: to the right, marginal cost is below marginal revenue, so profits can be increased by increasing output towards the rate implied by the *MC/MR* intersection. To know which way the firm might be most likely to jump we need detailed information about how it sees its cost and revenue curves: in the case shown in Figure 8.8, the firm has more to gain by cutting its price and increasing sales beyond *Q**.

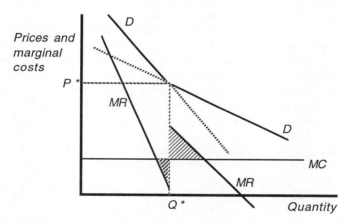

Figure 8.8: Unstable equilibrium with a reflex kinked demand curve

The appeal of the kinked demand curve analysis of oligopoly as a teaching set-piece may help to explain how it has become and remained very popular in textbooks (see Stigler, 1978) despite some heated debates about its empirical content. 'Subjective' testing with the aid of questionnaires tends to support the kinked demand curve idea, but there has been a heated debate over studies involving 'objective' testing, particularly between Stigler (1947) and Efroymson (1955). Part of this dispute is over the assumptions involved. Stigler did not look at what firms claimed to believe, rather at what he felt they ought to have believed about the market they were operating in. He suggested that decision-makers would have reason to believe in a kink if they raise their prices and see that their new prices are not matched by their rivals, and if their price cuts are followed by rivals. So, Stigler suggested, we should look at history and see what basis it gives for holding such beliefs. Efroymson, on the other hand, argued that only if a firm did *not* believe in a kink would it attempt a unilateral price increase, so objective evidence of a kink actually implies a mistake. Firms which believe in the existence of a kink in their demand curves will not change price in normal times, so to find out their beliefs observation will not be enough; we must ask them about their beliefs.

As an example, consider the case of the US cigarette industry 1918–34, with three major players. At the start, American Tobacco raised the price of Lucky Strikes from $6.00 to $7.50 per thousand and the rivals maintained their prices. American Tobacco's sales fell by a third in a month and they revoked the price increase. On the Stigler view, this implies a belief in the kink; on the Efroymson view it indicates that American Tobacco did not actually believe they faced a kink. In subsequent history in this market, price increases or decreases were followed after a very short period regardless of who initiated the price change. Stigler took this evidence as suggesting that they therefore did not believe in a kink. By contrast, Efroymson argued that the firms would not have forgotten what happened in the previous period, his implication being that, having been convinced of the existence of a kink by American Tobacco's expensive experience, the firms subsequently took steps to circumvent it by overt or covert collusion.

We should not be surprised to find that Efroymson also took issue with Stigler about predictions of kinked demand curve theory. Efroymson's view is complex: a reflex kink in boom times, a standard kink in 'normal' times, and desperate price wars in depressed times. It is only in normal times that price stability is expected in oligopolies that do not have price leaders. Stigler, however, compared degrees of price stickiness in different types of markets over an entire business cycle. In comparing differences in flexibility in different types of markets he also looked at list prices, not the prices that were actually used in transactions—rather a strange strategy given that off-list selling could be common (and could be more common at some points in the business cycle than in others). Efroymson also castigated Stigler for writing as if the kinked demand curve analysis is the only way of explaining sticky oligopoly prices, when many other facts might be impinging on what firms were doing (including the costs of changing prices, or fear of government intervention) which might apply equally to all market types and thus make non-dominant oligopolies operate in a similar manner to monopolies and dominant-firm oligopolies.

Stigler's (1982) review of Reid's book tells us a good deal about how he personally operated as an economist. Of Reid's rather pro-Efroymson stance he said that

> It is difficult to understand his approach except on the assumption that a proposed theory is presumed innocent until shown guilty. This is the precise opposite of the presumption I would use: namely, that a new hypothesis has to explain some things presently unexplained in order to be useful (Stigler, 1982: 204).

This is a highly conservative approach to analysis: keep with what we have got as a theory so long as it works. Such a maxim does not admit the possibility that other models that also work may be better equipped to explain future situations in which orthodox models find it unexpectedly hard to cope. Oddly enough, he seems actually to be assuming that the sorts of models he prefers have been proved innocent, but that is simply not possible in a world where the future is not guaranteed to be the same as the past.

Stigler notes that the kinked demand curve theory of oligopoly is little used in the research literature on oligopoly and industrial organization, despite its popularity in undergraduate teaching. He argues (1982: 204) that this neglect by the profession must be due in some part to the decline of interest in the phenomenon of rigid prices: studies of transaction prices have done a little, and strong inflation a lot, to reduce interest in price rigidity. But I believe that at least as large a reason for the neglect is the sterility of the theory: even at its seldom best it is silent about almost everything in oligopoly behaviour that an economist is interested in.

Although Stigler may have been correct if he meant that kinked demand curve notions have not been applied by most economists to other aspects of oligopoly, it should be understood that this is not because it would make no sense to try to do so: the same themes used in explaining price rigidity might well be applied to make sense of absences of both advertising wars and ruthless quality competition.

8.9 An alternative view of the economics of price cutting in response to reduced sales

The kinked demand curve is just one way of explaining why firms may decide not to change their prices if their sales have fallen due to factors such as a general downturn in their market, or their competitors offering more attractive prices or products. As Schendel and Balastra (1969) and Shaw and Sutton (1976: 130–41) have pointed out, even from conventional marginalist analysis it can be shown that a discrete price cut will only increase the firm's profits if the following condition holds:

$$\frac{(P_0 + P_1)}{(Q_0 + Q_1)} \times \frac{(Q_1 - Q_0)}{(P_0 - P_1)} > \frac{0.5\,(P_0 + P_1)}{0.5\,(P_0 + P_1) - Average\ Variable\ Costs}$$

The left-hand side of the inequality is simply the formula for the product's arc elasticity of demand with respect to price changes. It should be observed from the inequality that the bigger average variable costs are, the bigger the elasticity must also be for a price cut to be worth making. The formula assumes that average variable costs (often also called prime or direct costs) do not vary with output; in other words, it assumes that the marginal cost curve is horizontal. However, when doing a pricing case study a careful check on the wisdom of this assumption should always be undertaken: on the one hand, the expected sales increase might be so great as to require production at a rate higher than the firm can undertake unless it goes on to overtime working or introduces another shift; on the other hand, a large increase in production might bring opportunities for obtaining quantity discounts on bought-in components. It should also be noted that if one has all the information required to make use of this inequality—in other words, if one has the old and the proposed price, the average variable costs and the existing and expected rates of sales—then it is possible to calculate directly the impact on the firm's profits by working out the change in variable costs and the change in revenue and comparing the two figures; there is no need for the formula. Even so, the right-hand side may give a very quick guide as to the sort of elasticity needed and if no guess has yet been made about the likely increase in sales, an implausibly huge figure for the required elasticity will save the bother of arguing the case for expecting a particular figure.

Suppose a firm so far has been selling a product at $5 500, based on average total costs of $5 000 at its target rate of output, which gives it a 10 per cent mark-up. Further suppose that its average variable costs are $4 000. Since its sales have fallen well below its target rate, it is considering cutting its price to $5 200. In this case, the average of old and new prices is $5 350 and the required elasticity figure is $5 350/($5 350 – $4 000), which is 3.96. If the expected elasticity of demand is less than about 4, the firm is best not to cut its price, despite the disappointing sales performance. The firm would be better advised to look at other ways of increasing its sales, such as improving its distribution system, spending more on promotion, or changing the product. However if the estimated arc elasticity of demand is 4 or more, it is likely that the product is a close substitute for others: with a figure of 4, what we are saying is that a $300 cut in price (a 5.45 per cent cut in price) would increase sales by 21.8 per cent. Such a big response is something that should be checked for its compatibility with the firm's capacity position: could it actually produce this much more output? (As a working rule of thumb, we may feel safe to assume that target rates of output in 'normal' times are about 90 per cent of maximum possible sustainable output—for a historical perspective on excess capacity, see Steindl, 1952: 4–8.) If other products are indeed close substitutes it is likely that *their* producers would have similar price elasticities of demand, so it would be profitable for them (if their cost situations are similar) to retaliate and, in doing so, they would recover their earlier market shares. This 'retaliation' example is much as in the kinked demand curve case.

However, in a 'close substitutes' situation, in which the 'no retaliation' elasticity looked sufficiently large, price cuts might be profitable if competitors could not cut their prices far as a response without finding themselves unable to cover their average variable costs. Even if they could cover their variable costs whilst matching the price cut they might soon be forced out of the market altogether if they could no longer cover their average total costs and if they could avoid many of their fixed costs by ceasing production (avoidable fixed costs include overhead staff whose employment actually necessitates current payouts, rather than sums of money long since sunk as might be the case with capital items).

The message thus far is that, even according to orthodox marginalist thinking, price changes will not be worthwhile as a means of reacting to changes in market conditions, and we can reach such a conclusion without necessarily invoking the kinked demand curve idea with its discontinuous marginal revenue function. But we should not forget that price cuts can misfire for a variety of reasons even if retaliation is not provoked. In markets for durable products where secondhand sales and trade-ins are common, firms may be afraid that they will lose goodwill if recent customers become annoyed to find themselves suffering capital losses due to the price of new products having been reduced. This may be one reason why, for example, importers of prestige motor cars in Australia and New Zealand tend to avoid price cuts and instead increase product specification if the value of the $A or $NZ increases or tariffs are reduced. Price cuts may also be taken as a signal for further price cuts, leading to the postponement of purchases (Andrews, 1958: 38), or they may be taken as implying desperation on the part of the firm and (a) provoke an inquisition by the firm's creditors, (b) tempt would-be buyers into trying to bargain for even lower prices, or (c) tempt healthy opponents into investing in a price war to drive the firm out of the market even though they will make short-term losses in trying to do this. Finally, if people without experience in the market are judging quality by price (Scitovsky, 1945), then the price cut may discourage sales.

Before leaving this topic, a few words of advice to students tackling pricing case studies seem to be in order. When doing case study work where a possible price cut is the focus of the question, you will often be given information not merely about the firm in question but also about the rivals in the same market. You should look at this information carefully before jumping to conclusions about the likelihood of retaliation. If your firm is assumed likely to pick up X units of extra sales at the expense of rivals, rather than from market growth, you will need to ask how much of these units are likely to come from each of the opponents, for this will affect whether the opponents will find it profitable to cut prices themselves by way of retaliation. Always discuss the wisdom of the assumed gain. To do this you will need to look at the firms' existing relative market shares and any information you have about the reasons for these differences in market share. (Material from Chapters 2–4 on consumer behaviour and decision-making in general may be helpful here.) Having made suggestions about which firms are likely to lose which amounts of sales, you then have P_0 for when you calculate whether it would make sense for these victims of the price cut to retaliate, and you can use their *initial* sales rates, to which they would be trying to return, as the P_1 for these firms. But beware of taking last year's relative sales positions as a guide to what this year's might be like if your firm does not disturb things by changing its price: last year's situation need not have been an equilibrium one; perhaps the market is in a state of transition due to new products and learning about them by buyers not taking place instantaneously (learning by producers may also be affecting cost curves of firms at different rates depending on differences in the quality of their management and differences in their accumulated experience in producing the products in question).

8.10 Case study: 'Black Engineering'

Background and Question
(Adapted from a University of Stirling examination paper devised by Richard W. Shaw.)
Black Engineering Ltd produces a range of six machine tools and currently (1992) has an annual turnover of nearly $24 million. The management is considering a proposal to reduce the price for one of its machine tools from $6 600 to $6 300. You are asked to write a report for the Board of Directors, including a recommendation, on this proposal.

Four firms produce the type of machine tool under consideration. Black Engineering, which currently has a 22.5 per cent market share, has suffered a decline of 2.5 percentage points over the last year. The market leader, White Engineering, holds a 40 per cent market share which has remained unchanged for several years. White Engineering has an overall turnover for all its products of nearly $90 million per year. A third firm, Blue Engineering , which now has a 12.5 per cent market share has, like Black Engineering, seen its share decline by 2.5 per cent of the overall market over the last year. Blue Engineering has an overall turnover for all its products of around $18 million. Finally, Green Engineering, with an overall turnover of around $36 million, holds a 25 per cent share of the market. About a year ago, Green Engineering introduced a new version of the machine tool on to the market and apparently as a result of this Green's share of the market has jumped from 20 to 25 per cent in this period. Previous to this disturbance the market shares of the four firms had remained stable since the mid-1980s.

Executives at Black Engineering believe that their production and selling costs are similar to those of Blue Engineering. However, they believe that the new Green Engineering tool has given that company a modest cost advantage, and also that the larger scale of White Engineering's operations gives the market leader a cost advantage. The current estimated costs for Black Engineering and its competitors are as follows:

	Black Engineering & Blue Engineering tool	Green Engineering new tool	White Engineering tool
	$ per unit	$ per unit	$ per unit
Bought-in materials	3 000	3 000	3 000
Direct labour	1 020	960	900
Other variable costs	300	300	300
Product fixed costs, inc. depreciation and selling costs	780	690	660
Allocated company overheads	600	600	600
Total	5 460	5 700	5 550

Up to the end of 1990 the price charged by Black, Blue and Green (for its old model) for their machine tools had been identical at $6 000. The market leader, White, charged the slightly higher price of $6 600. The operating costs of the machine tools produced by all four firms were thought to be more or less identical: the main costs being the labour cost of the operator (approximately $30 000 per year) and power costs (approximately $1 500 per year). Indeed there was probably little to choose between the products offered by the four firms: each product had a five-year life and all did a very adequate job. All firms offered a maintenance contract with very similar terms based on their experience of the need for repairs. The differences in market share for the four firms were thought mainly to reflect White Engineering's position as the first firm to market such an engineering tool over fifteen years ago, together with its reputation as the market leader for this product and some other machine tools.

This stable position was disturbed by the introduction of Green's new model. Green's sales representatives claim that their new model offers an eight-year life. Further, it is noticeably quieter and marginally easier to handle than the rival products. In recognition of these advantages Green set a price of $7 200 for their new product when it was introduced at the beginning of 1991. Around the same time White Engineering increased the price of its existing product to $7 200, blaming cost-inflation pressures. Both Black and Blue had followed White's lead and raised their prices to $6 600.

A disturbing feature of the market at the moment is the decline in sales of machine tools. After growing rapidly in the early 1980s the market for the engineering tool being considered had stabilized at sales of around 10 000 units per year. However, in 1991, presumably reflecting the pressures imposed by the recession on the engineering industry, the total market had declined to approximately 8 000 units. In current economic circumstances there seems little prospect of any recovery for the next year or two. Not only does this mean that there is excess capacity in the industry but also the burden of overheads has become heavier. In these circumstances executives at Black Engineering are considering a proposal to reduce the price of their machine tool to $6 300. The marketing director believes that such action should at least restore the firm's 25 per cent market share and most probably raise its share by five percentage points to 27.5 per cent.

Author's notes
It would be most unwise to try to reach a conclusion on this question on the basis of a simple kinked demand curve analysis which involved no use of the figures that have been supplied. Instead, use can be made of material from section 8.9.

From the market share figures and the total market size of 8 000 units we can infer that Black's sales are 1 800 units, against 3 200 for White, 1 000 for Blue and 2 000 for Green. If the total market stays at 8 000 units a 25 per cent share is 2 000 units and a 27.5 per cent share is 2 200 units. Black's average variable costs can be calculated by adding together the firm's per unit outlays on bought-in materials, direct labour and other variable costs ($3 000 + $1 020 + $300 = $4 320). For the price cut to be profitable, the required price elasticity of demand for Black's version of the machine tool is

$$\frac{0.5\,(6\,600 + 6\,300)}{0.5\,(6\,600 + 6\,300) - 4\,320} = \frac{6\,450}{2\,850} = 3.03.$$

However, if the price cut only brought a 25 per cent market share for Black, the elasticity is only

$$\frac{(6\,600 + 6\,300)}{(2\,000 + 1\,800)} \times \frac{(2\,000 - 1\,800)}{(6\,000 - 6\,300)} = 2.26.$$

In this case the price cut would appear to reduce profits. (Sure enough, we find that profits would fall by $144 000 since costs would rise by $864 000 but revenue would only rise by $12 600 000 (in other words, $6 300 times 2 000) *less* $11 180 000 (in other words, $6 600 times 1 800), which is $720 000.) With a 27.5 per cent share of the market Black's implied elasticity of demand would be

$$\frac{(6\,600 + 6\,300)}{(2\,200 + 1\,800)} \times \frac{(2\,200 - 1\,800)}{(6\,000 - 6\,300)} = 4.3.$$

In this case, which is the marketing director's more optimistic expectation, the price cut would indeed appear to increase Black's profits. (Costs would rise by $1 728 000 but an extra $1 980 000 of revenue would be achieved, leading to a $252 000 increase in profits.)

We need to consider critically the suggested possibility of a 400 unit increase in sales in a static market where the demand for the product is a derived demand, dependent on the state of business. Extra sales are thus going to be conquest business, but at whose expense? Probably none will be gained from Green, since the Green tool is excellent value for money owing to its life of eight years rather than the five years offered by its rivals. (In the absence of discounting, it would be worth paying for the Green tool up to 1.6 times the price being charged by Black and Blue for their products. Discounting would reduce this figure somewhat.) Some sales might be won from White, for the widened price differential should overcome in the minds of some buyers the more favourable image that White has. Potentially a large increase in sales might come at the expense of Blue, whose products are seen, by those buyers who make comparisons, as identical to those of Black.

In my first scenario, I will assume that considerable substitution takes place in favour of Black, so much so that Black initially seems on target to pick up 400 extra sales from both White and Blue. We need then to consider whether or nor it would be profitable for either of them to retaliate.

The loss of sales to Black means that, at a price of $7 200, White's initial sales rate will become 2 800. If White retaliates by restoring the price difference and charging $6 900 this should bring White's sales rate back to 3 200. In this case, the implied price elasticity of demand for White's machine tool is

$$\frac{(7\,200 + 6\,900)}{(3\,200 + 2\,800)} \times \frac{(3\,200 - 2\,800)}{(7\,200 - 6\,900)} = 3.13$$

The required elasticity is

$$\frac{0.5\,(7\,200 + 6\,900)}{0.5\,(7\,200 + 6\,900) - 4\,200} = \frac{7\,050}{2\,850} = 2.47$$

In this situation, White would be expected to retaliate.

Like Black, Blue needs an elasticity of demand greater than 3.03 for a retaliatory price cut to be profitable. A loss of 400 sales would mean a base quantity of only 600 for Blue, at a price of $6 600. Cutting Blue's price to $6 300 should restore the sales rate to 1 000 units. Here, the implied elasticity of demand for Blue's product is

$$\frac{(6\,600 + 6\,300)}{(1\,000 + 600)} \times \frac{(1\,000 - 600)}{(6\,600 - 6\,300)} = 10.75$$

Blue would certainly be expected to retaliate.

In this scenario, the only gain that Black might hope to achieve would be that due to it being able to hold on to some of the extra sales despite White and Blue matching its price cut. As 'first-mover', Black might hope to achieve an effect of this kind. However, it would need to be on a considerable scale to leave Black with higher profits: remember that even if the net increase in sales is a 2.5 per cent gain in market share (the marketing director's pessimistic scenario), profits are reduced.

For a second scenario, I assume that the tendencies of buyers to substitute are much less marked and that initially Black appears to be on course only to win 400 extra sales, with 200 coming from White and 200 from Blue. Once again, the question of retaliation must be addressed. The implied elasticity for White is now

$$\frac{(7\,200 + 6\,900)}{(3\,200 + 3\,800)} \times \frac{(3\,200 - 3\,000)}{(7\,200 - 6\,900)} = 1.52$$

In this situation White would not be expected to retaliate. For Blue, the implied elasticity is now

$$\frac{(6\,600 + 6\,300)}{(1\,000 + 800)} \times \frac{(1\,000 - 800)}{(6\,600 - 6\,300)} = 4.78$$

Therefore, Blue would still be expected to find it profitable to retaliate. In this scenario it would appear that Black only gets a net increase in sales of 200 units. This is the same figure as in the marketing director's pessimistic guess and it leaves Black with reduced profits.

The calculations so far considered both lead to the price cut not seeming to be a wise move, but they have been undertaken on the assumption that Green's sales are fixed. Given the merits of Green's product, we should really be rather worried about the possibility that Green's sales may grow *regardless* of what Black does to its price. Users of this type of machine tool are likely to switch in favour of the Green product as word gets around about the remarkable value that it offers due to its longer lifespan. This would imply that Black's annual sales rate of 1 800 units is unlikely to be maintained if it leaves its price at $6 600; worse still, for Black to win 2 200 units in sales would involve putting White and Blue under even greater pressure to retaliate.

We obviously need to begin considering if there are any bounds on the rate at which defections to Green might occur. Green is limited in how many it can sell by its production capacity. If the new machines involve similar production efforts to the old model then Green's capacity limit might be inferred from a knowledge of how much it could produce in the past. When the market was not in recession, total market sales were 10 000 per annum and Green used to have only 20 per cent of the market, that is, sales of 2 000 units annually. This is the same as the rate for the new product with a 25 per cent share of the depressed market. We might infer that Green is already working pretty close to capacity. If the 'normal' target for capacity utilization is 90 per cent of 'flat-out' capacity Green might be able to expand production by no more than about 200 to 250 units a year—unless it has new investment coming on stream or can cut production of other lines (which might not be a profitable thing to do) or can at least divert spare resources from these other areas of its operations. As far as the last option is concerned, it can be noted that sales of 2 000 units at $7 200 each imply a revenue for Green of $14 400 000, which is 40 per cent of its total turnover of $36 million. Perhaps, then, Green might indeed have rather more surplus capacity that it can turn to the production of its successful new product, so long as its other resources are not specific to its other lines.

In these circumstances an attractive strategy for Black may be to work out a deal with Green to produce the Green product under licence, before either White or Blue does so. The Green product with White's reputation attached to it would be a very powerful force in this market. If Green proved to be uncooperative (as a ploy for establishing itself as market leader in place of White), then Black might be wiser to consider trying to copy Green's product as closely as possible without infringing any patents that applied to it and with a view to coming up with something even better. It might be noted that Black is much more dependent on this market as a proportion of its total business. It would be in a very precarious position if, by one means or another, Green got together with White and Blue with a view to denying Black access to the new technology. The logistics and legality of such a coalition might be discussed at length, along with a variety of takeover and merger scenarios.

8.11 Case study: 'The Parker retail gun'

Background (devised by Susan A. Shaw)
The development of supermarket and large store trading was accompanied by the need for convenient and speedier means of price marking of individual items for sale. In the late 1960s the first retail 'guns' became available—that is to say, hand held metal guns which stamp from a continuous roll a small sticky label marked with a price which can be set by the user. As Appendix 1 shows, sales of these guns grew steadily during the 1970s. In the early 1980s the market was expected to continue to grow at about 10 per cent per annum, particularly through increased sales to smaller shop units, where penetration had hitherto been relatively low. The life of the guns obviously depends on the extent of their use and on how carefully they are used but they last with average use (about 2 000 labels per week) for about four years. Labels have to be made specially for each make of gun.

In this case study your focus of attention is the state of the retail gun market in the United Kingdom in 1980 and after, in particular on the entry strategy of the Parker company. Parker were planning in autumn 1980 to launch a retail gun early in 1981. At the time they employed 150 people and manufactured a range of different types of office equipment, such as stapling machine and filing cabinets; they had not previously attempted to operate in the retail gun market.

By 1980, the retail gun market in the United Kingdom was dominated by one supplier, the Rallis company, who marketed and distributed the Preco retail gun which they imported under licence as the sole distributor for the French-based Preco company. Rallis held distributorships for a number of imported products, mainly in the field of weighing equipment. They were selling direct to large accounts but used supply houses as intermediaries for other sales. Their turnover in 1979 was £4 million. The Preco gun was efficient and reliable, though it was rumoured that Rallis's managers had been annoyed by communications difficulties in dealing with the French company and were likely to press for some changes in their contract with Preco if the contract were renewed in mid-1981. By

1980, Rallis were selling the Preco guns at £19 per unit. It was believed that their sales were relatively unresponsive to price changes over a wide band around this price. Labels for use with the gun also had to be provided for customers and Parker's contacts had said that these were being produced relatively cheaply by one of the large manufacturers of paper products, who sold them to users at £0.10 per thousand and paid Rallis £10 000 per annum for the manufacturing rights.

Parker had overcome the patent on the Preco gun by adopting a simplified design and a changed label shape. The potential problems of manufacture were also circumvented by subcontracting out the production of the components and then merely assembling the finished products themselves. Parker already had idle floor space and small tools so the set-up costs were minimal. The result was a simple but sturdy gun, light to hold, with a convenient and speedy re-inking process. Parker felt they had developed a product which would be attractive to customers. The supply of labels seemed to present no problems, for they had made arrangements with a paper products manufacturing firm who would sell the labels, paying a royalty of £0.05 per thousand to Parker in return for sole manufacturing rights.

In launching their gun, Parker planned to spend £10 000 on advertisements in *The Grocer* and *Supermarketing*. They intended to use the same direct sales methods that they used for their other products and were confident that existing sales staff could handle the product as it was complementary to their existing product range. However, by autumn 1980 they had not yet decided the price for the gun. They were considering either £21, £19 or £17. Whatever price they chose would have to remain fixed for the remainder of 1981 since it is customary to set prices for this sort of product at the annual trade fair which is held in January each year, and for these prices to remain in force for the entire year. As far as their pricing and marketing strategy was concerned, they were trying to make a plan for the next three years, that is to say, for 1981–83 inclusive.

Parker had the capacity to produce about 15 000 guns a year. Their estimated outlays based on an output of 15 000 are given in Appendix 3. Comparison with the costs of Preco and Rallis was difficult because the details of their trading arrangement were not known. Preco had a very large plant in France and were exporting from it to a number of countries. It was however known that Preco fixed the price of the gun in the United Kingdom and, at a rough guess, due to rises in the value of Sterling in 1980, the direct costs of the Preco gun to Rallis and Preco must have been very similar to the direct costs of Parker.

Questions (no special knowledge of the United Kingdom is needed)

1. Which pricing strategy would you have recommended Parker to adopt, and why?

2. In the light of relevant theoretical literature and any hindsight you have on retailing innovations, comment on the wisdom of Parker's attempt to diversify into the production and marketing of retail guns.

Price and output decisions (1): from Marshall to marginalism

Appendix 1: UK sales volumes for the Preco gun

1970	10 000
1971	13 700
1972	15 200
1973	16 700
1974	18 600
1975	20 700
1976	24 400
1977	28 700
1978	33 800
1979	35 600
1980	39 600

Appendix 2: Estimates of the percentage of the market that Parker will gain at various prices

	Year		
Parker price	1981	1982	1983
£21 (higher than Rallis)	10%	15%	20%
£19 (equal to Rallis)	15%	20%	25%
£17 (lower than Rallis)	20%	25%	30%

Appendix 3: Costs of Parker retail gun manufacture and sale at an output of 15 000 per annum (in £s)

Manufacturing costs

Materials	105 000
Direct labour	90 000
Other direct costs	15 000
Factory overheads*	5 000
Depreciation	2 400

Other costs

Administration^	6 200
Advertising	10 000
Other selling expenses^	5 200

*   Factory overheads are allocated on the basis of a product's direct labour costs as a percentage of company direct labour costs.

^   Administration and other selling expenses are allocated to products on the basis of each product's sales revenue as a percentage of total company sales.

Author's notes

The numbers on this case study are very easy to work out, if you accept the underlying assumptions. In the calculations below, I assume that the same price is charged in each year, but the question of a dynamic pricing strategy could also be addressed (for example, one which involved an introductory low price to get the product better known). A 10 per cent growth rate for the market gives the following figures, assuming (and this may not be true) that the Preco gun accounted for *all* of the sales in the market before 1981:

	1981	1982	1983
Total Market	43 560	47 916	52 708
Parker's sales at £21	4 356	7 184	10 542
Parker's sales at £19	6 534	9 583	13 177
Parker's sales at £17	8 712	11 979	15 812

Parker's expected revenues (£)

	1981	1982	1983
At £21 price	91 476	150 864	221 382
At £19 price	124 146	182 077	250 363
At £17 price	148 104	203 643	268 811

Parker's cost figures are based on 15 000 units a year. Obviously, in the absence of learning effects which increased their effective capacity, they would not be able to meet projected sales at £17 per gun in 1983 without incurring the costs of making further investments or cutting back on other lines of production. Total fixed costs comprise £5 000 (factory overheads) + £2 400 (depreciation) + £6 200 (administration) + £10 000 (advertising) + £5 200 (other selling expenses). One might want to query the two footnotes about how some of these figures are assigned to the retail gun project. For example, if 'overheads' really are overheads then they cannot be pinned down as being anything particularly to do with the retail gun activities. However, since other firms may use this accountants' way of assessing fixed costs in a multiple product firm, then it may be useful to treat fixed costs as in the data in order to get an idea of how the typical firm might see the rate of return in this line of business. The alternative strategy in doing the calculations would be to look purely at the impact of variable costs and revenue changes on net revenues under different scenarios; if this is done, the same conclusion should result. In my calculations I adopted the former route, which means that the fixed costs sum to £28 800. At 15 000 units per annum total variable costs comprise £105 000 (materials) + £90 000 (direct labour) + £15 000 (other direct costs) which gives an average variable cost figure of £14 per unit. Total costs for the forecasts of sales at the various prices are as follows (£):

	1981	1982	1983
At £21 per gun	89 784	129 376	176 388
At £19 per gun	120 276	162 962	213 278
At £17 per gun	150 768	195 506	250 168

After subtracting total costs from their respective total revenues, the following profit (loss) picture emerges:

	1981	1982	1983	Total
At £21 per gun	1 692	21 488	44 994	68 174
At £19 per gun	3 870	19 115	37 085	60 070
At £17 per gun	(2 664)	8 137	18 643	24 116

But it would be most unwise to suggest a price of £21 per gun, even if one accepted all of the assumptions about sales potential. It is vital to remember to consider the revenues that Parker stands to make from its deal with the supplier of labels. Each gun, over its four-year lifetime, will dispense around 416 000 labels. Therefore, on each gun Parker hopes to earn about £20.80 in label royalties. Given that the revenues from the labels are so high in relation to the gun prices, it should seem intuitively obvious that the strategy which will maximize profits, if one accepts the assumptions, is to charge the lowest of the three prices, in other words £17 (or perhaps an even lower price). This is indeed the case if one does the calculations. In undiscounted form, the royalties associated with the hypothesized gun sales in each of the years are as follows (ideally one should do discounting of these figures to find present values):

(£)	1981	1982	1983
Guns sold at £21	90 604.80	149 427.20	219 273.60
Guns sold at £19	135 907.20	199 326.40	274 081.60
Guns sold at £17	181 209.60	249 163.20	328 889.60

When profits on labels are added to profits on the guns themselves the following figures for total profits emerge (£):

	1981	1982	1983	Total
Guns sold at £21	92 296.80	170 915.20	264 267.60	527 479.60
Guns sold at £19	139 777.20	216 441.40	311 166.60	705 751.20
Guns sold at £17	178 545.60	256 300.20	347 532.60	782 378.40

With such a conclusion implied by the figures we should now consider the assumptions underlying them and begin to ask questions. The hindsight one might have could concern the take-off of barcoding in supermarkets, which would be potentially a very serious threat to the market for retail guns in the long run. In fact, the problem is not particularly acute over the timespan of this case study, as supermarkets in the United Kingdom were relatively slow to adopt barcoding and scanning at checkouts (the technology was quite rarely in evidence even in 1984), and in any case the small stores would have provided some kind of residual market for years to come (though one would want to ask how big this would be likely to be). On the basis of the figures suggested, it seems a worthwhile venture, given that set-up costs are minimal: if one accepted the figures it could be seen as a quick hit and run raid on the market as it reached its peak (see section 9.7). However, given that it looks like this to Parker, one might well note the scope for a 'Richardson Problem' of too many firms coming to the same conclusion (see section 10.4). The move by Parker can be discussed very nicely in relation to the work of Moss (1981) on the 'focusing effects' of idle capacity leading to diversification into related areas (see sections 7.4 and 11.6). It seems a diversification strategy that the company is well equipped to handle in manufacturing terms, for pricing guns have a lot in common with Parker's existing products, such as stapling machines. But Parker may by no means be the only firm in this kind of situation.

Marketing is where we can raise bigger doubts, in particular the question of whether Parker's direct sales methods will work in this new context. There is an implicit suggestion of sales synergy (cf. section 7.4): 'existing sales staff could handle the product as it was complementary to their existing product range'. (Perhaps Rallis has stronger sales synergy, being mainly concerned with weighing machines, if these include the kinds that shops will tend to buy.) However, it also seems that the market is likely to be more dispersed than their usual office equipment market: after all they only employ 150 people and yet we are talking in terms of thousands of guns (probably thousands per member of the selling staff); we are also told that the growth is coming from increased sales to smaller shop units. Direct selling—which we may assume to involve Parker in sending out representatives around the country to deal with the buyers—might work with large-scale sales of office equipment, but if the bulk of new custom is to come from small shops, it may be better for Parker to concentrate the efforts of their selling staff on getting the guns stocked by the wholesalers from which smaller stores buy their equipment. (Note that Rallis only tries direct selling with its larger accounts, but for smaller sales uses intermediaries.) It may well be that the smaller stores who are now coming into the market will form the bulk of Parker's potential customers. For users who already have pricing guns and are needing replacements, there may well be a goodwill element working in favour of Rallis's gun, given that people have to learn how to use it (and this may hold even if Parker's gun is easier to use, once mastered).

Since so much of the profit comes from label royalties, a price war with Rallis would not necessarily render the venture pointless for Parker, though a cut in the price below £14 per unit (the average variable cost) would be quite a problem: with the main profit coming from labels it is not an immediate flow and Parker, a small company, could find it more difficult than Preco to absorb initial losses. (It would be possible to do a present value calculation for the profits and costs.) Could Preco/Rallis get away with a predatory pricing battle? Parker might look rather shaky if they took Rallis to a restrictive practices court, given that they themselves are trying to make much of their profit from a monopoly arrangement over label supplies (IBM is an example of a company having the latter sort of trouble on a much bigger scale: they fought for years in the US courts over their monopoly of computer punchcards—see Sobel, 1981.) The possibility of a price war could be complicated still further by movements in the exchange rate: if Sterling rose even further against the French Franc, then Preco could afford an even lower price. But would a price war be likely, anyway? Calculations can be made of the sales losses that the Preco gun could suffer under alternative Parker pricing strategies. (It should be recalled that we are told that Parker and Preco/Rallis incur the same direct costs per gun at the current exchange rate) Possible financial implications of a price war for Rallis can then be explored. For a price cut from £19 to £17 to be profitable, the arc elasticity of demand for the Preco gun must be greater than 4.5. Given the size of the Rallis/Preco market share relative to that which Parker expects to get, it should come as no surprise to discover that it would not pay Rallis to match Parker if they sold the gun at £17. Even if a matching price cut took *all* of Parker's business away in this market (which is not very likely), the arc elasticities of demand turn out to be far too small for the retaliatory price cut to improve Rallis's profits: for 1981, the figure is 1.99, for 1982 it is 2.57 and for 1983 it is 3.05.

It is probably wise to consider the possibility that Parker's profit expectations could be seriously eroded by nasty surprises on the labels front. One possibility is that a pirate supplier of labels could appear and sell the labels via the wholesale network for these kinds of products. Another is that Parker's sales forecasts for its retail gun will turn out to be grossly over-optimistic owing to Rallis labels being very much cheaper than Parker labels, hence making the costs of using a Rallis gun much less over its lifetime. As a pointer to this possibility it should be noted that, although we are not told how much Parker's labels will cost, we are told that Rallis only receives £10 000 for manufacturing rights for all of its labels, and the maker of labels is producing vastly more than Parker's manufacturer will expect to produce.

One would have expected Rallis to have used some kind of tender/auction arrangement to extract the potential monopoly profit from the supplier of labels, and that the potential monopoly producers of labels would have considered the scope for production of pirate labels when striking their deal with Rallis (so their labels may not be priced via an 'marginal cost equals marginal revenue' rule; indeed, Rallis may have dictated the price of labels with a view to shaping the sales of the Preco gun). If Rallis has only extracted this figure, so much less than Parker expect to get from their £0.05 per thousand royalty, then we might expect that the production and distribution costs of labels would amount to more than £0.05 per thousand given that their selling price is £0.10 per thousand. If so, Parker-type labels are going to have to cost much more than those for the Preco gun. Hence the Parker gun could turn out much more expensive overall, even if priced at a discount. However, it might be argued that small shopkeepers may fail to look very carefully at the extra cost of the labels over a long period and that, given the role of inexperienced, causal staff in shops, a gun which was very simple to use could pay for itself in terms of time saved even if it used more expensive labels (but in this connection note again my earlier remarks about goodwill). I would want to have further information on label prices before coming to any strong conclusions about the pricing strategy: otherwise, one feels inclined to recommend charging above £17 and renegotiating the labels deal (if this is possible without penalty).

Finally, if Rallis are annoyed with the communications problems they have been having with their French suppliers, and if their contract is up for renewal, then one possibility to be considered is for Parker to try to get the contract to supply Rallis, rather than trying to crack the market. However, the big problem is that Parker would have nowhere near enough capacity to supply all of Rallis's needs and there would then be the risk that Preco would find another UK distributor.

8.12   Further questions

1. Discuss Marshall's notion of the representative firm.

2. Examine the view that 'barriers to entry are a necessary but not a sufficient condition for supernormal profits, while oligopolistic interdependence is neither a necessary nor a sufficient condition'.

3. Joan Robinson often remarked that she had never been able to grasp the nature of the distinction between *imperfect* and *monopolistic* competition to which Professor Chamberlin attached much importance. Is there any real difference between the two approaches? Justify your answer.

4. Under what circumstances is it likely to be profitable for a firm to cut prices?

5. Does the theory of the kinked demand curve give any real insight into the behaviour of oligopoly firms?

6. Write a conversational dialogue between a person attempting to argue a case for restrictions on shop trading hours and a person who believes firms should be free to open whenever they wish to do so. The conversation should take the form of reasoned discussions rather than mere assertions by either side. You are not required to let either party score a convincing victory but neither are you debarred from doing so.

7. Discuss the proposition that any plausible theory of the growth of individual firms must carry the implication of continually increasing industrial concentration over time.

8. 'Empirical studies which have emphasized the role of market structure in determining business behaviour and performance have placed the cart before the horse. It is business behaviour and performance which determine market structure.' Discuss.

10 'If the function of the orthodox [neoclassical theory] of consumer behaviour is to justify the notion of negatively inclined demand curves, the function of the orthodox [neoclassical] theory of the firm is to justify the notion of positively inclined supply curves' Mark Blaug, 1980, *The Methodology of Economics*: 175). How well does neoclassical economics function in these roles?

11. Consider the costs and benefits to society of a policy of making no attempt to prevent industries from becoming dominated by monopolistic producers.

12. Discuss the applicability of the kinked demand curve analysis of oligopoly to the tobacco industry in the light of the following quotation:

> America's tobacco industry is used both to unpopularity and to a declining domestic market. But tobacco companies have been consoled by their profitability and by the notion

that the decline in smoking, at about 3% a year, was gradual. Now both ideas are being undermined. The process began on April 2nd 1993, known as Marlboro Friday, when Philip Morris slashed the prices of its flagship brand to stem competition from cheap rivals. As other price cuts followed, the industry's operating profits almost halved (*The Economist*, 30 April 1994: 73).

9 Price and output decisions (2): modern variations on Marshall and marginalism

9.1 Introduction and summary of the story so far

During the latter part of Chapter 8, when discussing the Hall and Hitch critique of imperfect and monopolistic competition, I commented briefly that their thinking overlapped somewhat with Marshall's ideas. Even in the first half century of price theory, signs were appearing that D.H. Robertson (1956: 81) may have been right to characterize the evolution of ideas in the following terms:

> Now as I have often pointed out to my students, some of whom have been brought up in sporting circles, high-brow opinion is like a hunted hare; if you stand in the same place, or nearly the same place, it can be relied upon to come round to you in a circle.

Robertson certainly believed his analogy applied to the theory of the firm in the period 1890–1939 (see his letter to P.W.S. Andrews, reprinted in Andrews, 1993: 116–17). We shall see much more of this sort of thing during the course of this chapter as I consider some of the significant contributions from the second half century of price theory. This will be in contrast to what is found in standard microeconomics texts, which consider little more than marginalist ideas from the inter-war period and ignore similarities between ideas from the 1890s and the 1990s. Before we proceed any further, though, it is probably useful to recap on the story so far:

1890–1923: Marshall's historical, evolutionary view of the firm
- Industry tends to be pretty competitive.
- Prices based on average costs of representative firm in the industry.
- Costs fall in the long run due to economies of larger-scale production, technical progress and learning in general.
- Customers take a while to cultivate.
- Success and competitiveness of firm varies through time due to variations in quality and commitment of management.
- Big companies with many shareholders may get too bureaucratic to stay competitive—until things get so bad that there is a major shake-up.

1920s: attempts to present a logically consistent non-historical view of the firm ran into trouble
- Initially, the assumption was that firms faced 'given' prices in product and factor markets: this was formalized as the theory of perfect competition by Pigou (1928) after

the work of Sraffa (1925, 1926).
- But Sraffa posed a logical puzzle, too: why should cost curves ever rise if unlimited factor supplies were available; couldn't firms merely scale up existing production methods and at least keep their average costs constant?
- Sraffa suggested that perhaps the solution lay in assuming that firms did not face given prices but, like monopolists, had demand curves of their own that were downward sloping, implying some discretion in pricing.

Early 1930s: managerial factors considered once again as a limit to the firm
- A suggestion that managerial problems might cause cost curves to turn up as firms get bigger (E.A.G. Robinson, 1931, 1934).
- But management deal with surprises so they have no role in a theory of the firm dealing with static market conditions (Kaldor, 1934).

J. Robinson (1933): the theory imperfect competition
- Falling cost curves are compatible with equilibrium if demand curve falling too.
- Capitalism is seen by her as greedy, inefficient, producing with excess capacity as a result of monopolistic tendencies of firms attracting other firms into market until average costs and revenue equated (tangency solution).
- Fudged aside oligopolistic issues.

Chamberlin (1933): the theory of monopolistic competition
- Firms are best seen as having their own downward-sloping demand curves, which is compatible with equilibrium in a position when their cost curves are falling too.
- Product differentiation may be the source of downward-sloping demand curves for firms.
- Profit maximization could involve finding the quantity at which $MC = MR$, but firms might be able to find optimal profits by comparing different price, total cost and sales scenarios (just like modern managers can do with spreadsheets).
- If it gets too complicated to work out maximum profits, firms may base prices on average costs—sounds rather like Marshall except Chamberlin assumed firms were identical, and had no life-cycle view of costs.
- Product is a variable.
- Marketing expenditure is a variable too.
- Different types of oligopoly are recognized: if only a few producers, interdependence would be obvious.
- If there is a large number of firms, price cuts might not be so conspicuous and therefore not invite retaliation.
- But even with large number of firms, price cuts might be provocative if they took sales from neighbours, rather than from across the market as a whole.

Lester (1946) and Hall and Hitch (1939) case studies
- Cast doubt on the idea that firms use marginalist methods to decide how much to produce, how many workers to hire and how to set prices.
- Hall and Hitch were told that prices were based on full costs—calculations made with

respect to a longish planning period during which there might be ups and downs in daily/weekly rates of sales.

- This suggests prices are not set to 'clear markets' as in supply and demand analysis.
- This involves no mention of setting $MC = MR$ to choose the price: it is much more like Marshall's view.
- Explanations of why prices were set like this included not only difficulties in discovering marginal costs and revenues, but also thoughts about competitive response.
- Likely competitive responses were seen to imply a kinked demand curve; prices would not be changed in response to short-run changes in sales—price stickiness was explained with reference to kinked demand curves moving left or right on diagram, each with kinks at the 'full-cost'-based price.
- However, the reason why it wouldn't make sense to change prices was argued in marginalist terms: the marginal revenue curve would have a gap through which marginal cost curve might cut.
- In a depressed state of business, with sales below break-even level at the full-cost price, firms might behave differently and risk starting a price war, from which they could gain a temporary improvement in their profits.

9.2 Pricing of pioneering products and new brands

In the two case studies considered at the end of Chapter 8 the pricing question was complicated not merely by oligopolistic concerns but also by the presence of improvements in product designs. Some case studies and practical problems will concern a yet more tricky issue: the pricing of revolutionary new products. Little was written on this issue until shortly after the Second World War, when it attracted the attention of Joel Dean (beginning with his 1950 paper). Despite Dean's many subsequent contributions, new product pricing is normally glossed over in microeconomics texts, in contrast to those on managerial economics (a recommended example of the latter is Douglas, 1987: chapter 11). It is useful to explore the relationship between pricing and product life-cycles at this stage—not merely because of the historical timing of Dean's work but also because, depending on how they are priced, new commodities will, to a greater or lesser extent, reduce sales of existing products and raise the 'profitable price cuts' question raised at the end of Chapter 8. Before we look at the pricing of new commodities, it is worth noting that price changes actually may impact in four areas: (1) the attraction of new users, (2) the conversion of customers from rivals, (3) the expansion of the volume of business with existing customers, and (4) the retention of existing buyers' patronage. To make a very obvious point: a zero price (for example, a free sample) may be effective with (1) but it hardly helps (3).

A new brand will not be filling a void but will be taking its place within an established price structure. Its price, seen with reference to existing brands' prices, will not merely tell buyers its cost, but also something about its worth (see section 4.3 on the role of budget ranges as screening devices). This may be especially important if the product is a consumable complement to a high-value item of equipment: two of the classic marketing examples of sales increases that followed price increases concern items which were complementary to high-value products (car polish, and ink for fountain pens) where a poor grade brand could be a very expensive mistake (ruined paintwork; a clogged pen).

The pricing of 'new products' may seem a more open question than the pricing of new brands, as maturity is often missing from the market in three senses: (a) it may not yet be clear which technology will become the industry standard; (b) consumers may have not yet taken on the basic idea—for example, when home computers were introduced, the point of having one was unclear—nor acquired the ability competently to discriminate between rival firms' products; and (c) market shares and price structures are more likely to be made unstable by aggressive rivalry between competitors because of the stronger possibility of significant 'first-mover advantages' (in other words, those who instigate competitive battles may keep some of the market that they initially steal from their rivals even if the rivals later emulate their policies: see further, Klein, 1977). However, the product is unlikely to be completely 'new'. In many cases, it will simply represent a new way of producing particular outcomes, so there may be scope for estimating the maximum that buyers might be prepared to pay for it—in other words, what its superiority is worth to them. In making such estimates, it should not be forgotten that buyers may be reluctant to switch to new techniques unless they meet particular rate-of-return or payback-period targets (industrial buyers are the group most likely to think in these terms, and we would expect their targets to be more demanding the more rapid the pace of technical change seems to be). It may be wise to focus, in promotional material, primarily on the rate of return, rather than on the price (which might look a bit of a 'rip-off'). An example here concerns the new generation of energy-saving 'mini-tube' lights which cost vastly more than traditional light bulbs but eventually pay for themselves in terms of reduced energy use.

With consumer products, price sensitivity may be gauged by using different prices in comparable test-marketing experiments. Econometric investigations involving methods such as the 'hedonic pricing technique' may also provide clues about the worth that consumers place on particular product characteristics, though, as we saw in section 3.6, it is debatable whether such studies yield information about willingness to pay or about the costs that firms incur when building particular characteristics into their products.

Dean's primary focus was on the strategic choice a firm selling a pioneering product has to make between 'skimming pricing' and 'penetration pricing' (intermediate strategies are, of course, possible). The aim of a skimming strategy is to achieve the maximum contribution to profit in the shortest possible time by charging the highest price that the market will bear (and usually combining this with heavy promotional expenditure). This strategy is akin to that assumed in the economics of imperfect competition and may be a wise policy if:

(a) Few competitors exist at the moment and consumers are very sensitive to promotional information about the worth of the new product.

(b) There is scope for market segmentation/price discrimination (for example, commercial users of Apple Macintosh computers are charged a far higher price than educational users, and the selling message to commercial users is slanted very heavily in terms of the savings of valuable staff time that Macintoshes permit via their user-friendly operating system).

(c) Short-term profits help the firm build up reserves for promoting its product against competitors who are attracted into the market. When it is difficult to anticipate ultimate rates of sales or scope for reducing costs, the pursuit of current profits looks less risky.

(d) The firm has a limited sales force and its distribution channels are not well developed.

Penetration pricing involves using 'low' initial prices as a wedge to build up an early mass market, where:

(a) One is aiming to discourage entry, which otherwise seems very likely.
(b) There are major unit cost economies in production and/or distribution on a large scale.
(c) The product's sales seem very price sensitive, even at an early stage in its life-cycle.
(d) There is no 'elite' market of pioneering buyers who are prepared to pay a premium for the latest and the best.

As a means of discouraging entry, a penetration price may not be very successful if the total sales potential is enormous and entry is relatively easy. And it is certainly unwise if one's distribution channels simply cannot cope with a rush of demand. This approach to pricing has much in common with normal cost theory and contestability theory, discussed later in this chapter (see sections 9.6 and 9.7)

Two points often ignored in discussions on this topic need be be made before we move on to the next section. First, cognitive dissonance theory (discussed earlier in section 4.7) should lead us to recognize dangers in using introductory 'low' prices for durable products: consumer resistance may be considerable when 'proper' prices are later established. A refusal to buy at the higher price is a means whereby the consumer avoids having seemingly made a mistake by not buying at the lower introductory price. Consumers who wish to avoid confessing to themselves that they would now be better off had they taken advantage of the introductory price would be expected to cook up all manner of arguments for buying substitute brands which they otherwise would not have preferred. Secondly, the sales success of one firm's new model may provoke retaliation from its affected rivals not in the form of price cuts but in the form of a bringing forward of their new models—albeit at some risk in terms of quality control.

9.3 Essay example: Cellular phone prices

Question
Why is is reasonable to expect a fall in the price of mobile telephones over the next few years? What factors might limit the extent of the fall?

Author's notes
This question offers a good opportunity to display a knowledge of and integrate a variety of topics, including: product life-cycle theory, production theory, learning curves, the uptake of organizational slack under the pressure of competition, and heightened competition due to the pressure of entry. It would be very unwise indeed to try to do an answer in which one

simply drew some supply and demand curves and showed how combinations of movements of them might produce falling prices.

This is a product in a fairly early stage of its life-cycle, and reasons why sales may be expected to grow should definitely be raised. However, logic probably dictates that the first major paragraphs of a good answer concentrate on showing how an increase in demand might result in falling costs of production which could lead to lower prices; later paragraphs on why demand might increase could then take this effect for granted. This is an essay where the reader's task can be made easier if, at the outset, a unifying theme can be outlined: in this case the unifying theme could be that prices of products produced by strongly competing electronics companies would tend to be linked to their unit costs, and these costs would be reduced by anything which increased sales. In other words, this is going to be a modern version of Marshall's (1890) analysis, or of Adam Smith's (1776) thinking on the division of labour being limited by the size of the market: it is a 'virtuous circle' story (cf. section 8.2). Since this line of argument is going to rely on the power of competition to push prices down, it would be wise initially to acknowledge that, in the early stages of the market, competition might not be as fierce as later, and manufacturers would tend to charge premium prices for their products, using the fat profit margins to try to recoup their research and development expenditures (this 'skimming' strategy is common to many product life-cycles (see section 9.2): initially a new product is priced so highly that it is purchased only by those who can comfortably afford it and/or who insist on having the best—for example, the US military, in the case of many pioneering electronics products). As know-how begins to escape about the technology of the products, competition hots up and prices move closer in line with costs, which may themselves be falling.

Cost reductions would come from several areas. First, economies may be obtained from producing on a larger scale to cope with growing demand. In terms of a given mix of factors, economies of scale are rather hard to explain; changes in production set-ups usually occur if the volume of production is increased, so that advantage can be taken of indivisibilities of one kind or another (some mechanization techniques may only make sense for very large rates of output, for example; specialized machinery may likewise be worth investing in only if the rate of production is very substantial). We can anticipate that bigger production runs will enable fixed costs (for example, of research and development, or of moulds for components) to be spread across more units, and that costs of buying components will be reduced not merely because large runs of components will be produced at lower unit costs but also because there may be economies of scale in transacting (fixing up deals) with suppliers.

Secondly, we may expect marginal costs to fall steadily (albeit at a decreasing rate) due to learning effects on the part of workers involved with the manufacture of these products. Automation of some processes may limit the extent for traditional kinds of learning on assembly lines, by installation and servicing of equipment (programming computerized tools, for example) may benefit from 'learning by doing'. It might be worth drawing a learning curve diagram at this stage, and to put a few hypothetical figures on it, because one could then argue that the extent of the cost reduction in the next few years will depend on how far down the curves producers have already progressed (see section 7.6).

Further cost savings may come if production is moved to lower wage economies to be carried out under licence or by subsidiaries of firms in high-wage economies, for example from Japan to Malaysia. This is something that is only done once the product gets relatively well established: early on, technology transfer may be a rather dangerous thing to allow in case company secrets leak out to a licensee company. At an early stage it may also be harder to make the product with great reliability unless this is carried out close to head office and research laboratories, where workers are more experienced and where problems can be ironed out more quickly (see section 11.12).

Fourthly, it is well worth discussing the potential for cost reductions to be achieved via improvements in the design of cellular phones. At this stage one can start noting that cost-saving improvements may be supplemented by improvements that increase demand for phones by making them more attractive to users. Radio telephones have been around for a long while, but early models were limited by their bulk, their power demands, and the inability of the airwaves to cope with large numbers of users at any one time. Mobile phones have only become as cheap as they are right now because of the development of the cellular system and miniaturization of components. Power supply improvements enable portable phones to be used for longer periods without needing to have their batteries recharged. Of course, in facing this sort of question, one may have little idea of the technical aspects of these phones (I don't have much idea myself); however, precedents could be cited from general knowledge (such as pocket calculators), or reference could be made to relevant corporate biographies such as Akio Morita's (1987) book about the Sony company, which provides excellent examples of how, in electronics generally, cost savings are achieved via miniaturization during the life of products—what Sony achieved with tape recorders might likewise be achieved with these types of products.

Finally under the heading of sources of cost reduction, there is probably some payoff to be had by suggesting that, if this market does appear to be potentially a very profitable one, too much production capacity might end up being created, so that, until demand catches up, there may be very vigorous price competition—precedents for this include the production of micro computers and compact discs a few years after their launch (cf. sections 10.4 to 10.7). Not only may excess capacity give rise to keen pricing, in the sense that prices below full costs (or below average total costs) are charged, but poor financial returns may lead firms to search (note the allusion to the decision cycle idea, and to Simon's work) for ways of improving their profitability and general competitiveness. Organizational shake-ups, in other words, may lead to cost reductions (cf. section 7.11). A discussion of this need not be inconsistent with earlier discussions about cost reduction through learning effects and so on. It is possible that, during the initial take-off of the product, when competition may not have been so cut-throat, the producers were too busy concentrating on improving the product and getting market acceptance to have time to keep their minds on ways of improving their organizational methods as their activities expanded in size (cf. sections 10.12 and 11.7). Hesitancy among would-be producers could obviously limit the effects discussed in this paragraph.

In moving on to the question of why demand might expand and drive along the cost-reduction process, one might begin by noting how television advertisements for these products in the recession of the early 1990s concentrated on why on earth anyone might want a mobile phone, particularly in time of depressed business. In other words, we have a case of a product which people may be failing to perceive as a solution to their problems because they lack experience in using it, and because they have not seen many other people using it either. This is a classic problem in the early stages of launching a complex consumer durable, but once people get the idea of the situations in which this product will earn its keep, information spreads like a contagious disease. (The disease analogy is raised in a review by Prais, 1973, of Ironmonger's 1972 book on the demand for new commodities. Ironmonger's work is very much a priority-based, characteristics-based analysis of demand consistent with the analysis in sections 4.2 and 4.3. However, Prais suggested that it might be wise to look at the information-transmission process instead of focusing largely on product demands growing as people moved down their want hierarchies and as better products appeared.) As it is itself a communications device, the cellular phone is particularly likely to generate these 'demonstration effects' because people using a normal phone to contact someone who is using one of them will either realize via the nature of the conversation that the person is mobile, or will learn to infer this by the distinctive number. By interacting with users, one starts to see the benefits of having such a phone. If price reductions do occur, this reduces the risk associated with buying a product that one might end up not using very much.

A second paragraph on the growth of demand could comment further on the role of technical progress in enhancing the product's appeal: reductions in size and power consumption might point the way to a world in which everyone walking around has such a phone on their wrists. Somewhat bridging between this paragraph and the previous one might be a point concerning perceptions about the quality of communication using radio-based phones. People may believe that their conversations will be less clear than with conventional phones owing to scope for interference (for example due to high buildings blocking radio signals); these beliefs may or may not be well founded but could hold back demand until people start thinking that the quality must be getting 'good enough' due to technical progress or as a result of seeing these products being used and/or engaging in calls with other people who are already using them.

Thirdly, it might be worth commenting on what a rise in economic confidence could do to the demand for cellular phones. Although, in depressed times, pioneering business users might see them as devices to give themselves a competitive edge over their rivals, it may take a major economic recovery before people feel it is worth investing in them for more general use. Income effects might be discussed in relation to the luxury of having a mobile phone: the place of such a phone might also be discussed in relation to the hierarchy of needs idea—it is hardly going to look like a necessity.

Having discussed how limited confidence may restrain demand growth and in doing so hold back a virtuous circle of cost reductions, it would be helpful to end by considering factors limiting these processes. Various points might be made here to demonstrate a good grasp of the competitive process. Firstly, the demand for this product will be dependent not merely on its price as a piece of hardware but also on the price of complementary products (such as charges for using it) and substitute products. Improvements in public call boxes (such as cardphones that reduce the incidence of vandalism at public phones and make payment more convenient for longer calls) in conjunction with the availability of increasingly cheap paging devices might rather reduce the appeal of cellular phones. Secondly there is the question of the stigma associated with the pioneering use of cellular phones by yuppies in the mid-1980s: people may resist them because they do not want to be branded as posers—after all, these are rather conspicuous items of consumption. (I recall a tale about two magnates of the entertainment business in Britain at the time when older types of radio phones were being pioneered in cars. One of them was outdone by the other in terms of being first to get one in his car and had a car-phone installed within a few days of this humiliation. When he rang his rival to say he was now just as well equipped, the rival's chauffeur said 'I'm afraid he's busy on the *other* line, will you hold on?'.) On the other hand, one night want to argue that positive conspicuous consumption effects will outweigh these stigma effects—as a tool of social competition, a cellular phone may give one the edge, just as it gives, say, an estate agent or travelling sales representative a competitive edge. Thirdly, it might be argued that although people may come to recognize the benefits of having this sort of phone, the cumulating effects on reduced costs and prices associated with rising sales might be held back as a result of people speculating that prices will fall even further if they wait a while longer.

9.4 Sales revenue maximization

During the 1950s economists began to realize that the introduction of downward-sloping demand curves at the level of the individual firm opened up, in some circumstances, an area of theoretical discretion for managers. This area lies between the firm's demand curve and its best-practice average total cost curve, including all points on the demand curve between the break-even rates of output. Two conditions are required for such discretion to be available in practice to managers who wish to do something other than maximize their firm's profits. First, entry into the market in question must be somewhat difficult, so that the tangency solution depicted in Figure 8.3 in the previous chapter is not forced upon them. Secondly, shareholders must be dispersed and prevented by information costs from coming together, and takeover raiders (whether alternative management teams within the firm, or other companies) must face similar problems in usurping the power of an existing management team. If these conditions are present, then a management team might try to pursue policies that suit themselves but conflict with shareholder interests. In such circumstances the theories of imperfect and monopolistic competition provided an opening for economists seeking to deal with the implications of a growing phenomenon that had been highlighted by the empirical work of Berle and Means (1932), namely, that firms are often run by salaried managers with limited shareholdings.

During our discussions of costs in Chapter 7 we encountered one kind of departure from profit-maximizing behaviour in imperfectly competitive markets, namely, X-inefficiency or organizational slack. If such slack existed, the firm's reported costs could be in excess of those that it might be able to achieve: its actual cost function might be tangential to its demand curve or might cut it between the break-even quantities implied by its hypothetical best-practice average total cost curve. Such a situation might be one in which not just the managers but also the workers are, as Cyert and March (1963) would put it, pursuing their own subgoals, and in which managers are benefiting in different ways from the policies that get selected. An alternative way of looking at managerial discretion is to assume that members of a management team act as a unified group and are successful in ensuring that their firms operate without X-inefficiency but choose a point other than the profit-maximizing point on their firm's demand curve. Such an analytical strategy is exemplified by the contribution of Baumol (1958/1971: 1959), which I will now consider, mindful of the critical analysis of his work by Loasby (1989: chapter 7).

Baumol was actually driven to propose his theory less by published empirical work on the so-called divorce between ownership and control, than by his own experiences as an economic consultant. He found that it was difficult to get managers to take up his policy recommendations if they had a harmful effect on sales, even if they were supposed to have a beneficial effect on profits. Instead, it seemed that managers were interested in expanding the turnover of their firms—in other words, they might be seen as sales revenue maximizers. (Although he is quite careful to point out that he does not mean that managers were interested in maximizing the number of units sold, some textbook treatments describe the model in terms of sales or market-share maximization, subject to a profit constraint: contrast Baumol, 1958/1971: 254, and Douglas, 1987: 374.) Baumol soon realized that he could apply the standard deterministic modelling techniques of neoclassical economics to the study of ways by which such a goal might be met. The abandonment of profit maximization did not mean that one had nothing to say about what firms might do.

Baumol presented his model as one which was supposed to apply to oligopolistic firms, but he never maintained that all such firms have this objective. Rather, he suggested that some of those which he encountered had objectives other than profit maximization which could reasonably be approximated in terms of a desire to maximize sales revenue.

Rather like Joan Robinson, Baumol was forced to fudge when dealing with oligopoly, for his formal model-building activities required a determinate demand curve. He suggested that sales revenue maximization might seem less provocative to a firm's rivals than would the aggressive pursuit of maximum profits—but since the sales revenue-seeking policy will cause greater damage to rivals' sales, the reverse sounds more likely. He also appealed to organizational complexity as a further justification for neglecting interdependence, his suggestion being that it may prevent managers from noticing the interdependence of their firm with others, or may allow them to avoid treating it as their responsibility. To give such a role to complexity is, of course, rather at odds with a model that treats managers as if they *all* want to maximize sales revenue and *know* how to do so (Baumol's is not a satisficing analysis, nor, unlike subsequent behavioural approaches to the firm, does it portray the firm as a coalition of competing interest groups).

At first sight it seems easy to see a basis for treating sales revenue as a proxy variable for the interests of management: more sales will be sought by managers whose interest really lies in the number of their subordinate staff (if they have empire-building goals) and bonuses that go with higher values of sales. However, this justification gives rise to a paradox: despite their assumed interest in staff sizes, Baumol's managers keep their staff usage down to the minimum necessary to maximize sales revenue: his firms have the same cost curves as they would have if they were profit-maximizing firms. The managers are assumed to have a kind of semi-lexicographic way of operating: their first priority is not sales revenue maximization but, rather, to meet a minimum profit figure in order (a) to finance investments that will be necessary to provide the capacity for supplying sales revenue-maximizing rates of output in future periods; and (b) to pay shareholders high enough dividends to keep them from getting together to fire the management team.

The two panels of Figure 9.1 illustrate how alternative pricing policies may impact upon a firm's sales revenue and profits. A standard downward-sloping linear demand curve shown in the upper panel of Figure 9.1 is associated with a total revenue function that is an inverted parabola of the kind shown in the lower panel. Total fixed costs are shown as *OY* and marginal costs (and by implication, average variable costs) are taken as constant, giving rise to a total cost function that is linear, starting from *Y*. Break-even rates of sales are at the prices that generate sales figures of *OA* and *OE*. Profits are maximized at a price *OU* and at sales rate of *OB*, which is the rate at which the slopes of the total cost and total revenue functions are identical, implying that marginal costs and marginal revenue are equal.

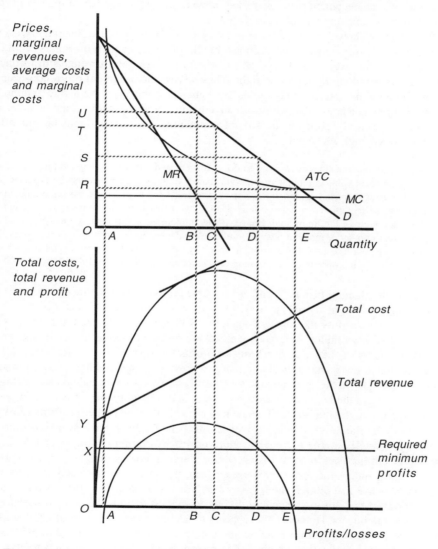

Figure 9.1: Revenue, price and profit implications of alternative managerial goals

Managers who believe they face such a demand curve will maximize their sales revenue if they choose the price and quantity configuration where marginal revenue is zero, that is to say, where the marginal revenue curve cuts the quantity axis, which is the quantity at which the total revenue curve for the demand curve will have its peak. In the case shown, sales revenue is maximized at price *OT* and sales rate *OC* units, which involves a lower price than the profit-maximizing sales rate. Here, sales revenue maximization is unconstrained by the perceived minimum profit requirement (*OX*), though this would be a constraint for a management team interested in maximizing the number of units sold (they would have to be content with sales of *OD* units).

The situation shown in Figure 9.1 is not the end of the story, since Baumol argued that if the minimum profit requirement is not a binding constraint then managers would set about spending the 'excess' profits on advertising to increase sales revenue still further by pushing the demand curve out to the right. Thus he saw the minimum profit constraint as always binding in his model, though in order to guarantee this result he had to assume that the marginal revenue associated with extra advertising is always positive (and he noted that this is not necessarily going to be so, since potential customers might be put off by excessive advertising). As he put it,

> I assume, as most businessmen seem to do, that increased advertising expenditure can always increase physical volume, though after a point sharply diminishing returns may be expected to set in. This means that total revenue must vary with advertising in precisely the same manner. For unlike a price reduction a *ceteris paribus* rise in advertising expenditure involves no change in the market value of the items sold. Hence, while an increase in physical volume produced by a price reduction may or may not increase dollar sales, depending on whether demand is elastic or inelastic, an increase in volume brought about by added advertising outlay must always be accompanied by a proportionate increase in total revenue (Baumol, 1958/1971: 260).

The fact that the Baumol firm is 'spending' possible profits on volume-increasing price cuts or advertising campaigns means that it will be expected to behave differently from a profit-maximizing firm when its environment changes. (Note that Baumol, like Chamberlin, keeps these two policy variables separate to make his analysis manageable.) In the profit-maximizing theory, a change in overheads or profits taxation does not affect the price and quantity at which marginal revenue and marginal cost are equal and hence does not affect corporate behaviour in the short run: the firm merely suffers from (or enjoys) lower (higher) post-tax profits. (In the long run, however, changes in profitability may affect the number of firms competing in the industry and hence it is possible that the earlier profit margins may be restored.) In Baumol's model, however, the firm facing higher profits taxation or overhead costs will be able to generate more profits by cutting its output and raising its price and/or cutting back on advertising whose marginal cost is in excess of its marginal revenue. Thus, unlike the profit-maximizing firm, the sales revenue maximizer makes a short-run response that 'shifts' the increased cost or tax burden on to the customer. Some investigations of tax-shifting behaviour do indeed suggest that increases in corporation tax are passed on to buyers. However, this appears to take place with the sort of lag that seems to be rather inconsistent with the optimizing nature of behaviour postulated in the Baumol model and more in line with the notion of a problem-solving uptake of organizational slack as managers find they are short of sufficient profits (see Coutts *et al.*, 1978).

9.5 Essay example: The case for abandoning the assumption of profit maximization

Question
'It is organizational complexity rather than market imperfections that justifies abandoning the assumption of profit maximization.' Discuss.

Author's notes
The question of when one abandons an assumption such as profit maximization cannot be dealt with properly without some reference to issues of method. The statement under discussion says nothing about the predictive adequacy of a theory of the firm based around this assumption. It might be asked whether or not any empirical challenges have been mounted in this area. The trouble is, there are several theories of the firm based around this assumption, theories that vary according to the assumptions that are made in respect of market structure (perfect competition, imperfect and monopolistic competition, monopoly, competitive oligopoly) and the time horizon over which it makes sense to try to maximize profits (for a long-run view, for example, see the work of Marshall and of Andrews discussed in sections 8.2 and 9.6, respectively). As we have seen, in the case of Baumol's sales revenue maximization theory, the original impetus towards its development was Baumol's experiences as a consultant which made him aware that some managers seemed more interested in expanding turnover than profits. In respect of organizational complexity as referred to in the statement, it might be worthwhile to refer to the work of Leibenstein (1966, 1976) who raises empirical evidence to support his X-inefficiency idea and suggests that firms are failing to achieve maximum profits (see section 7.11).

A more extensive set of arguments might be constructed with reference to the *a priori* appeal of profit maximization. The market imperfections theme can be raised with respect to Baumol's sales revenue maximization theory, which is based on the *twin* requirements of imperfect product markets (to give a downward-sloping demand curve) *and* an imperfect capital market (to give the management team the chance to sacrifice shareholder earnings by choosing somewhere other than the profit-maximizing point on their downward-sloping demand curve). Baumol's theory is a neat theoretical creation, but the wisdom of building an analysis around this pair of imperfections can be explored. The logic of assuming an imperfect product market can be challenged from the standpoint of Andrews's normal cost analysis (section 9.6) and Baumol's own later work on contestable markets (section 9.7), though management might hope to enjoy discretion in markets which were characterized by forms of complexity that made entry difficult in technological terms or made it difficult for consumers to size up where the best deals were to be had (again, see section 9.7).

Points can be made both for and against theorists such as Baumol as far as capital market imperfections are concerned. One line of inquiry to explore is whether or not the fear of takeovers is likely to motivate managers to maximize profits. Here, one could begin with Alchian's (1950) observation that a management team may only need to be relatively fit, not the fittest in an absolute sense, in order to survive. On the empirical side, the work of Singh (1971, 1975) is relevant: he found that while managers in taken-over companies faced a significant chance of being fired within a year or two of a take-over, the best way for most size groups of companies to avoid being taken over was not to become more profitable but to become bigger, even if this came at the expense of profits. Working against the threat of takeovers are the costs that would-be raiders may face if they are to organize a bid (this is easier for a corporate raider to do than for a dispersed group of disaffected shareholders), and uncertainty about the quality of the assets that are being purchased. However, we might also note that many managers may be rather disinclined to harm profitability because they have substantial shareholdings (in pecuniary terms, if not as a percentage of total shares) as a result of being tied to remuneration packages that include stock-options, or because their pay is directly related to financial results. Finally, on this theme, it could be pointed out that even if the stock market were rather weak as a forum for concentrating managers' minds on the pursuit of profits, there are still many firms around that are dominated by individual owner-entrepreneurs. It may even be the case that, by virtue of their insulation from external capital markets, such firms end up setting about undertaking major innovations involving long-run risks in the pursuit of profits (from which further internal growth might be financed)—risks which they would have had found it difficult to pursue if they had to keep their minds on next quarter's results. A well-known example here is the hugely profitable float-glass process pioneered by the Pilkington company in the face of great scepticism about its technical feasibility.

After raising complexity in product and capital markets as the root cause of their tendencies, if any, to provide room for managerial discretion, it could be conceded that organizational complexity may make it difficult for senior managers to know where and how they might improve the profits performance of their firms. Examples may be given in relation to specialized workers being able to 'pull the wool' over the eyes of their colleagues by exploiting their information advantages, and this line of argument could be extended to encompass the organizational slack concept of Cyert and March (see section 7.10). However, it might also be pointed out that bounded rationality arising from cognitive restrictions on the ability of senior managers to size up problems and handle information may provide a perfectly reasonable basis for doubting whether profit maximization is possible, even if they are profit *seekers* by inclination or as a result of contractual inducements. In other words, it is one thing to have one's decision biased by a misleading supply of information, but an altogether different thing to have it biased by the kinds of decision rules that one uses for coping with ignorance, perceived uncertainty or a potentially overwhelming volume of paperwork.

9.6 Normal cost analysis

Having seen how the work on imperfect and monopolistic competition opened up scope for the development of theories in which firms were not assumed to maximize profits, we may now turn to explore rival lines of inquiry that emerged from the criticisms of the work of Robinson and Chamberlin. In this section I discuss an alternative view of pricing developed at Oxford by Philip Andrews (1949a, 1949b, 1950, 1964, 1993) with some assistance from Elizabeth Brunner (Brunner, 1952; Andrews and Brunner, 1975). Parts of my discussion are extracted from an epilogue chapter that I wrote for the 1993 collection of Andrews's work, a collection which includes as its introduction a valuable biographical essay on Andrews by Fred Lee. Andrews's 'normal cost' theory is closely related to the non-marginalist 'full-cost' view of pricing suggested by Hall and Hitch (1939), so it would be wise to review section 8.6 before proceeding further. Though based on empirical research and cogently argued, this approach to pricing failed to achieve acceptance by most economists after initially receiving a very confused reception—and no wonder, for it is an analysis of pricing which does without demand curves or any reference to the notion of marginal equalization.

9.6.1 Andrews's approach to price theory

Like Marshall, Andrews was not content to engage in armchair theorizing. Instead, he (1951: 172) urged the abandonment of the concept of static equilibrium and observed that the alternative patterns of analysis 'will have to be built up out of empirical studies, just as Marshallian concepts were largely informed by their founder's studies of historical processes. No amount of spinning-out of logical chains of analysis based upon static concepts will help in this task.' He obtained a wealth of knowledge of the operations of firms through a succession of case study projects, consultancies and business history works and this played a vital part in the formation of his broader theoretical picture of the working of businesses.

At a time when economics was starting to get more technical, Andrews produced an analysis in prose, that outlined the situational complexities with which businessmen saw themselves as having to cope, and which then proceeded to make its theoretical contribution by uncovering the decision rules that it would be reasonable to use in such situations. The parallels with Cyert and March (1963) should seem obvious when Andrews's work is characterized in this manner, and it was in precisely these terms that, in his obituary note, Farrell (1971) outlined the approach to theorizing that Andrews adopted. For Andrews, the complexities of the business environment were not matters that he felt it appropriate to deal with in asides. Rather, as Farrell (1971: 11) put it, they became 'sources of illumination and the true basis of an incisive theory ... [which was] at once simple and amazingly sophisticated'. Andrews noticed that entrepreneurs usually recognized the presence of few actual, but many potential producers of their products. When deciding what prices to put in their catalogues, they were mindful of the scope for frequent changes in rates of orders, in input prices and in prices of substitutes, factors which implied considerable costs in calculating optimal prices, particularly since firms typically produced, or could consider starting to produce, many products. As Farrell (1971: 12) observed, Andrews concluded that 'the firm must keep in step both with its existing competitors' prices and with that which would render its product attractive to new entrants. So long as the optimal technique did not change, the normal cost rule gave an accurate answer [for pricing problems].'

Andrews's normal cost pricing rule envisaged a firm as setting its prices with reference to actual and potential competitors' costs of invading its market, with the firm's knowledge both of its own cost structure and of its standing relative to its rivals being used to gauge a safe, but not unduly cautious, price. He saw tendencies towards implicit collusion among incumbent firms as being countered by this awareness of scope for *cross-entry*—that is to say, incursions into its territory by established firms from other markets, on the basis of similarities in terms of skills and capital equipment (cf. the Parker retail gun case study in section 8.11). The theory dispenses with both downward-sloping marginal revenue curves and upward-sloping marginal cost curves. With respect to the former, Andrews stressed that customers would not keep coming if the firm set unduly high prices and induced rival suppliers to enter swiftly with better terms, so demand curves were not pertinent to pricing planning, even though sales estimates at normal cost prices would affect the capacity expansion plans of the firm. As far as costs were concerned, Andrews's fieldwork had convinced him that firms' cost curves did not turn up as they increased their rates of output. (In the short run, firms would generally be planning to have some spare capacity in order to be able to satisfy unexpected increases in orders without having to ration regular customers, so even here they would not normally be working with an upward-sloping cost curve.) In short, his behavioural methodology had led him to reject the idea of the optimal size of firm and end up with an analysis in which the current size of a firm depended on its success in marketing and selling and in obtaining access to finance to construct capacity to deliver goods in the quantities for which it could drum up orders.

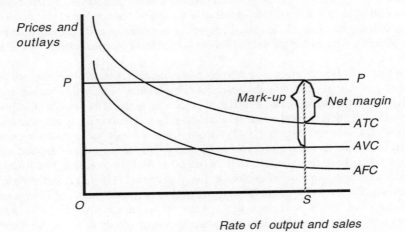

Figure 9.2: The 'normal cost' approach to pricing

Before moving on to examine in more detail the thinking behind the normal cost philosophy we may consider Figure 9.2 as an attempt to sum it up in graphical form. *OS* represents the firm's sales target. The price it charges, *OP*, is formed by adding a mark-up to *AVC*, its average variable costs. The firm's average total costs (*ATC*) are the sum of *AVC* and *AFC*, its average fixed costs, and its planned net margin is the difference between *ATC* and *OP* at *OS*. The horizontal line *PP is not a horizontal demand curve* of the kind found in the theory of the perfectly competitive firm. It simply represents the firm's average revenue possibilities at the price *OP*, but whether actual sales are equal to the target *OS* will depend on how successful the firm is in marketing its product relative to its rivals, on stochastic factors and on the general state of demand.

Because firms typically operate with a margin of slack and are concerned about keeping the goodwill of their customers, changes in the strength of orders will normally lead to changes in their rates of output and/or stockholding levels, rather than in the prices that they charge. When increases in the rate of inflation are associated with buoyant market conditions, this approach to pricing sees them as arising because of changes in normal costs and in the risk of entry. Booming conditions in final product markets may be associated with shortages in factor markets and hence an inflation of factor costs. These are most likely to be passed forward into higher prices if they are expected not to reverse later in the business cycle, which is more likely for wages than for primary commodity inputs. Incumbent firms may be expected to be less afraid of cross-entry by established producers if business conditions generally are booming. Here, managers are more likely to be preoccupied with the task of meeting orders in their regular markets by bringing new investment projects on stream at their scheduled times—in contrast to periods of slack business when excess capacity due to a lack of orders will tend to concentrate managers' minds on the possibility that they might try to break into related lines of activity (Moss, 1981). Consequently existing producers in each industry may perceive that they can charge higher margins and exploit inelastic market-level demand conditions without provoking cross-entry. Once the boom comes to an end these firms would then absorb further cost increases and allow their margins to shrink back to 'normal' levels. The main factor working against such policies of engaging in implicit collusion and 'making hay while the sun shines' is that a condition of *general* overheating is rare, particularly in economies open to competition from overseas producers; there will usually be some firms, somewhere, on the lookout for ways of making use of spare potential by carving new markets for themselves.

9.6.2 Andrews and Brunner versus the marginalists

It is hard to avoid making comparisons between this view of pricing and the work of Robinson and Chamberlin, but economists have often missed the gist of Andrews's thinking as they have done so. Compare Figure 9.2 with Figure 8.2 in the previous chapter. It might be tempting to argue that, if the Andrewsian firm is to be maximizing its profits, then the mark-up shown on Figure 9.2 must correspond to the distance *FI* on Figure 8.2 (cf. Douglas, 1987: 414). But this would completely miss the point that firms think ahead and worry about the possibility of entry. To be sure, a modern-day follower of Andrews would concede that it may not be unreasonable to recognize that managers may believe that their firms face downward-sloping short-run demand curves. However, when one attempts to estimate what these might look like and then note at which point on them prices are being set, it becomes evident that often firms are actually setting prices which imply negative marginal revenues—in other words, their behaviour is inconsistent with the theory of imperfect competition. Andrews's former colleague, Tom Wilson (1979) has even argued this for the case of the OPEC oil cartel: it made sense for the oil exporting countries to moderate their monopolistic demands in case they damaged their markets in the long run by encouraging substitution into technologies that used less oil or in case higher prices for oil sparked off a world-wide recession.

It would be rather less of an error to suggest that Andrews was advocating something corresponding to prices being set at *OB* in Figure 8.2 (in other words, where the short-run average revenue curve cuts the average total cost curve), with the average total cost curve being thought of as including the normal rate of return on capital. But this suggestion misses the fact that Andrews is looking at pricing behaviour in non-market-clearing terms. Prices are seen in neoclassical economics as market-clearing devices, that ensure a balance between the amounts producers are willing to supply and the amounts customers wish to demand. This view may be a reasonable way of portraying the workings of markets for primary commodities—so long as due account is taken of the roles that speculators may play as buyers and sellers in these markets. However, Andrews is suggesting that producers of manufactured goods and services may be seen as setting prices for their products and then waiting to see how many customers are attracted by their terms. In markets where buyers call for tenders, a would-be seller either wins the contract or loses out to a rival bidder who offers a more competitive bid. In other cases the seller does the calling and stands willing to supply as many or as few units as buyers come forward to make purchases at the marked price. Faced with uncertainty about their selling environments, managers tend to set themselves sales targets that seem both reasonable, given the knowledge that they do have, and likely to provide an adequate return. If unexpectedly few buyers show up, selling efforts will be increased and/or marketing campaigns given a rethink; attention might also be given to modifying the product as a means of solving the problem. If sales figures are pleasantly surprising, decision-makers will have to work out whether they have been setting their sights too low, or whether they are dealing merely with a temporary spurt in the market.

It is also worth commenting on the relationship between Figure 9.2 and diagrams used to encapsulate Baumol's (1958) sales revenue-maximizing analysis of the firm. If we were to recast Figure 9.2 in terms of lines representing total costs and total revenue, the revenue line would not be an inverted-parabola as in Figure 9.1 but would be a straight line beginning at the origin, whose slope was dependent on the price that was being charged. Beyond the break-even rate of sales, the total revenue line is above the total cost line, so that sales revenue maximization and profit maximization amount to the same thing: the more the firm sells at the market-preserving price, the more profits it earns. It should therefore be no wonder that Andrews (1964) was rather unimpressed by Baumol's model.

Whereas Joan Robinson was keen to write as if all buyers were rather poorly informed consumers who would be prone to be taken in by attempts of firms to raise prices on the basis of appeal to product differentiation that had little objective basis, Andrews and Brunner noticed that the vast majority of trade involves intermediate stages of production and is actually carried out between firms. Compared with ordinary consumers, corporate purchasing officers might be expected to bring a good deal of expertise to the business of buying intermediate products—though empirical work by Cunningham and White (1974) suggests that it may not always be wise to make this assumption. However, Andrews and Brunner also warn against jumping to the conclusion that boundedly rational individuals will necessarily end up getting a bad deal even if search and experimentation are costly activities. Buyers make their choices in a social world, so reputations have a big role to play in determining which firms they will approach as possible suppliers. Even if many consumers do not bother to search carefully (cf. section 4.1 and Olshavsky and Granbois, 1979), products are likely to be made available at normal cost prices by firms who see that by undermining any attempts at policies of explicit or implicit collusion they may pick those buyers who do take the trouble to search around to find good deals: these may be only, say, ten per cent of the market, but ten per cent may be quite enough to generate a satisfactory return. From this line of argument (originally suggested to Andrews by Neville Ward-Perkins, then one of his undergraduate students), Andrews and Brunner appear to conclude that sooner or later firms in general will be forced to cut their prices to offer similar value for money to firms that follow the normal cost rule. We might, I think, be wiser to recognize that in some cases markets will be populated by firms that are, taken as a group, employing a variety of pricing strategies: some may be using the normal cost rule, while others may be aiming to milk poorly informed buyers in a manner akin to Joan Robinson's vision of their behaviour. If different consumers have different search costs and search rules and if they move in different social groupings, it would appear unwise to predict that competitive pressures will always eliminate price dispersions (see further, Salop and Stiglitz, 1977; and Phlips, 1988).

Even when theorists have been prepared to assume that buyers are well informed, they have not always found it immediately obvious that potential competition is likely often to be a very powerful force limiting the prices that firms can charge: new businesses starting from scratch may have a hard time getting established, particularly if a sizeable investment in capital and marketing is required to get production and sales volumes up to the minimum efficient scale of output. However, in the vision of Andrews and Brunner it appears that a much more powerful threat comes from well-established firms on the lookout for markets which they can enter on the basis of their established know how and capital investments. Such a basis for entry, if strong, would mean that few costs would have to be sunk in an experimental foray into a market where existing suppliers seemed to be incompetent or to be pushing their luck. In the limit, a firm might be able to engage in 'cross-entry' by using its existing sales force and capital equipment, both of which might otherwise be underemployed, and have no need to invest in anything except for advertisements and working capital. An inability to duplicate exactly what is already being offered need not be a barrier: entry can often be achieved by offering a product that can be shown to be differentiated in ways that make it superior in some respects to what is already available (for example, greater reliability and the convenience of electric starting helped Japanese motorcycle firms break into the British market). If existing producers in a market are looking out for expansionary opportunities elsewhere, we might expect them to be well aware of the possibility that raiders from other markets might find it attractive to invade their own territory.

Normal cost analysis leads to a totally different view of the presence of surplus capacity from that proposed by Joan Robinson. Such capacity plays a key role in a firm's attempts to cultivate goodwill relationships with customers. Whereas neoclassical views on pricing seem to treat firms and their customers as engaging in one-off encounters, the Oxford view of Steindl (1952), as well as of Hall and Hitch, and Andrews and Brunner, comes close to the marketing literature in its concern with 're-buys'. A customer lost today is a customer who might have returned time and time again for many years to come, but who may now deal with a rival firm. A customer gained today is potentially a customer for years to come. Hence it is likely to appear profitable to firms to operate with some spare capacity even when the markets in which they operate are not in a state of depression. If new customers arrive on the scene, firms with spare capacity can service them without having to disappoint their regular clientele. In other words, incomplete capacity utilization in normal times may often represent an investment aimed at building up goodwill, though naturally the scale of such investments is limited by the costs of maintaining a margin of slack. In boom times waiting lists may have to be used to ration supplies. However, so long as a firm does not find its waiting lists getting longer than those of its rivals, it should be possible for an individual supplier to acquire further goodwill even despite not being able to satisfy new customers on the spot. Price stability permitted by changes in rates of capacity utilization helps discourage search on the part of existing clients.

In the absence of goodwill relationships, the market shares of competing oligopolistic firms would be totally indeterminate in cases where they were supplying similar products and consumers were well informed: the situation is the same as with Sraffa's (1925) portrayal of a perfectly competitive firm under constant returns to scale. One could, of course, close either analysis by introducing an element of randomness, and this might well be a reasonable approximation in some cases. It should be remembered that the population of buyers in a market will usually be changing through time due to geographical movements, changes in tastes, age and income. Hence at any moment there is likely to be a fringe of inexperienced buyers who might be more than usually likely to make an initial purchase at random (for example, with the aid of Yellow Pages listings) if they do not rely upon familiar brand names or the advice of their friends when deciding which suppliers they might rely upon.

To end this subsection, some remarks about resale price maintenance (RPM) appear to be in order. RPM is a practice which involves manufacturers dictating to retailers the price at which they should sell the product to their customers. If manufacturers find that their instructions are being disobeyed they may refuse to supply further stock to the offending retailers, if it is legal to do so (often such a refusal would be illegal, but it may be possible to pretend to the authorities that one is having supply problems). Now, RPM may appear superficially inconsistent with the normal cost philosophy: it sounds suspiciously like an activity that involves gross margins being raised without regard to the damage that this might do to the firm's sales in the long run. Firms whose pricing policies appear to involve something approaching greedy RPM often find themselves facing competition from discounters.

Compared with marginalist thinking, normal cost theory leads one to take a more open-minded view of what may be going on in such situations (contrast Andrews and Friday, 1960, with Borts, 1961). A careful examination *may* reveal that the discounters are able to enter because they are riding piggyback on the dealers who are following the pricing recommendations of manufacturers who are taking a longer-term perspective on how to build up their markets and are focusing on non-price competition as the means to this end. (The italics are added to remind readers that one is not guaranteed to come to a conclusion that comes out in favour of RPM; careful case-specific analysis should always be conducted.) In the case of durables, such as cars, electrical appliances and bicycles, the complexity of the products, and their long operating lives, means that retailers who can offer expert sales advice and after-sales service will be preferred as distribution outlets by manufacturers. A franchise arrangement between manufacturer and retailer is commonly used as a device for controlling quality of the retailer's services and hence to build up goodwill and long-run brand loyalty (see further section 11.4). This means it can be inappropriate for economists to focus on the individual transaction between customer and retailer. For example, an approved car dealer makes money not merely from the initial sale but from servicing the vehicle. If the after-sales service is seen as high quality, the chances of continuing the relationship via a trade-in and repurchase of the same brand may be increased: brand loyalty may thus be generated as customer and retailer get to know each other better. Brand-loyal customers may keep buying the same brand on the basis of the after-sales service even if their insights into the product itself are rather limited despite the best attempts of sales staff to open their eyes to what it can do (recall here the critique of consumer theory by Olshavsky and Granbois, 1979, and note that market research by motor manufacturers has confirmed that many non-enthusiast buyers of cars make their choices with very little knowledge of technical differences between products). Each loyal customer may be an excellent source of word of mouth advertising; disaffected customers may be even more powerful publicists of a negative kind. Hence, as far as manufacturers and retailers are concerned, quality control in the retail environment is a key ingredient of business success.

Now, if retailing is a highly competitive business (as we might expect it to be given the ease of finding premises for rent), then discounting will only be possible at the cost of leaving off some of the services that a non-discounter might provide, particularly before-sales advice and after-sales service. Buyers may be able to get these services by going to full-price retailers but not actually buying the product from them, so in the long run the full-price retailers will have trouble making adequate profits from their shops. The lack of attachments between retail showrooms and after-sales service may mean that the full-price retailers do not even get a lot of business in terms of after-sales service: consumers might go to firms that specialize in offering repair services for a variety of brands. Such a situation does not have the makings of a market equilibrium even though consumers seem to be benefiting in the short run. In the absence of protection against discounters, retail franchise holders are likely to be less willing to invest in brand-specific items for displaying and servicing the products. Nor will they be prepared to hold in stock a wide enough range of spare parts to keep customers happy by providing them with rapid repair services. (Discount 'quick fit' service centres keep their prices down by concentrating on a limited range of repair/replacement services that are frequently in demand.) If, in the long run, the 'full service/full price' retailers are driven out of business, then customers *may* feel uneasy about purchasing products that require careful explanation, demonstration and back-up. If so, rival discounters may then start to compete more on a non-price basis, recognizing that it is in their mutual interests to develop alliances with manufacturers and follow their recommendations and standards of service—until someone upsets the market by starting the discounting/piggyback cycle once again. An exception might be where customers get increasingly familiar with the products because of their widespread use or are attracted to manufacturers who can demonstrate in their advertisements that they have succeeded in developing simpler, more reliable products.

9.6.3 Strategic and tactical extensions of normal cost analysis
In this subsection I explore some of the subtleties involved in employing the normal cost philosophy in markets that are in something of a state of flux and where potential competition may be expected to take some time to materialize. It may be useful to re-read section 9.2 on new product pricing before going any further. In an important sense, new product pricing is concerned with managing the time profile of sales: people who are holding back from buying today might be customers in the future, but they might be captured by other firms.

A related perspective on pricing is central to work by economists who have focused their attention on large, growth-oriented corporations—Eichner (1973, 1976) called them 'megacorps'—run by management teams that are confident of their capacities to undertake major investments in diversification. The retained profits of megacorps provide a means for financing research and development and the purchase of new plant and machinery without incurring the underwriting fees charged by merchant banks or the risk of embarrassment associated with the flotation of a new issue in an unpredictable stock market. Alternatively, they may be used to finance portfolio investment or takeover raids against other firms. The management team of a megacorp may therefore be expected to consider the impact of their pricing decisions on the volume of funds that will be available for investment, and here they are likely to recognize an important tradeoff.

Such managers will not expect their firms to suffer an immediate catastrophic loss of market goodwill if they set prices somewhat above 'normal cost' levels. Although some sales may be lost quite quickly to existing rivals if the latter do not follow suit, this kind of substitution will be limited in so far as products are differentiated in 'non-price' terms and prices are not taken outside the budget ranges of target customers. Although cross-entry may be provoked, new producers may take a considerable period of time to accumulate the additional physical and intellectual resources needed to produce comparable outputs and build up market credibility, even if, in broad terms, the market into which the latter are moving is rather similar to their original area of interest. (An obvious example is how, after its initial diversification into car manufacturing, away from a dependence on motorcycle manufacturing, the Honda company took practically a quarter of a century to come anywhere near to posing a serious threat to European manufacturers of prestige motorcars.) In these situations the costs of attempting to keep competitors out of their markets indefinitely may be judged to be unduly substantial in terms of forgone shorter-term profits, particularly since such costs might be incurred without even producing the desired result. Managers may therefore decide to risk reductions in the long-run sales of their existing products by pricing them so as to generate larger profit flows in the short run.

How far the management team of a megacorp will try to push up its profit margin will depend upon the time horizons that its members keep in view: if the firm will become a likely takeover target or be unable to raise external funds from its bankers unless it can demonstrate strong profitability right now, its top managers will be more likely to risk damaging the long-run prospects of its current products by greedy short-run pricing.

The dynamic nature of the market environments in which such pricing choices have to be made ensures that these decisions are hazardous: the timing of competitive entry and the magnitude of an entrant's threat cannot be known in advance with certainty; nor can strategists be sure that the higher profits that their firms earn in the short run on their existing products will be sufficient to enable them to carve a secure position for their firms further down the track. If entry is more rapid than expected, incumbent producers may not have had sufficient time to plough their supernormal profits back into superior new products, more cost-effective production processes, or portfolios of financial assets that give them security against would-be takeover raiders.

My colleague John Wood (1992) has suggested a further variation on this strategic theme, which is thoroughly Andrewsian in its focus on the irreversible damage that a firm may do to its long-run position if it is greedy in the short run. Like Eichner, Wood recognizes that 'skimming' pricing may be tempting if entry is not expected to be immediate. However, firms that practise this strategy may then find that the supernormal profits they were hoping to achieve are then captured by suppliers of factors of production, such as workers or landowners. The fact that the firms are failing to earn unduly high rates of return does not mean that any competition that they expected to materialize at some stage in the future now will not do so, for rival sources of supply may not have to incur the inflated production costs because they are buying their factors in geographically segmented markets. If the interlopers break into the market by offering a lower price, the original suppliers may then experience major difficulties if they cannot renegotiate their factor supply arrangements on less generous terms. (For example, consider a situation in which the advent of Chilean supplies of Kiwifruit pushes down the world price of this product. New Zealand growers may have locked themselves into substantial bank loans to finance the purchase of land for their Kiwifruit farms, land whose price they had been able to bid up because they were making so much money from a skimming price strategy. The price of New Zealand land suitable for growing the crop may now fall, but this will wipe out part of the growers' collateral, not their debts.)

Moving on to a rather shorter-term tactical focus, we may note that in some lines of business managers have frequently to weigh up whether to make a deal with a potential customer today or instead hold out for a rather better deal in the near future. Such a dilemma arises in two kinds of situations. The first is when firms cannot replace used-up inventories instantly and without cost. An obvious instance of this concerns the pricing of used cars, even though the ease of entry and exit makes the used-car market appear hotly contested. If a dealer lowers the price of a vehicle today it may be possible to clinch the sale and free up scarce space and working capital. But if replacement stock with good potential profitability is not being offered as a trade-in or cannot immediately be found in the wholesale market, it may be better to lose today's potential customer to a rival. Tomorrow it may be possible to sell the vehicle to a person who is less inclined to haggle and/or has a more marketable trade-in to offer, or who has missed out on the broadly similar product that today's lost customer has purchased from a rival car yard.

Secondly we must consider the predicament of firms operating in an industry that suffers from patterns of demand that are so erratic as to deter incumbent firms from investing in enough capacity to satisfy peak demand levels. This case can be illustrated with reference to the construction industry (see Andrews and Brunner, 1975: chapter 5). Building firms typically put in tenders for more work than they can handle, expecting only to win a proportion of the contracts. How low they will go in making any bid for a contract is constrained by their perceptions of their own opportunity costs: if they win a particular tender battle, they forgo the use of the committed resources from servicing other contracts which might be won at a later date. When they place their bids, they cannot be sure how low they need to go to win, for they usually cannot be sure quite how desperate their rivals are to get the business: the opportunity costs of their rivals are private, subjective constructs. (It should perhaps be added that although the cheapest tender will normally win, a firm that *is* known to be *really* desperate for business could fail to get a contract despite promising to undercut all other tenders: the customer might justifiably fear that this firm could be forced into liquidation before the job is finished.)

It is in the nature of the construction industry that jobs are typically non-standardized, one-off tasks. A building firm that is not adaptable will rapidly go out of business owing to the thinness of demand for narrowly defined kinds of work (a thin market is one in which the supply of or demand for the product arises on an erratic basis through time). However, many firms will pick up experience and equipment which suits them particularly well for certain kinds of jobs, for example, concreting rather than bricklaying. Hence although firms in the industry are normally able to undertake a great variety of contracts, they will be keener to win some contracts than others, just as used-car dealers are not normally confined to selling a particular model of used car and yet nonetheless prefer to trade in a particular part of the market. If a building firm is finding a lack of work in its preferred area it can try to get contracts for other kinds of work, but if its managers take the view that their preferred kind of contract is likely to emerge before too long, then they would be foolish to tie up its resources elsewhere for very far into the future unless they do so on exceptionally good terms. In putting in bids for the jobs that are currently available, they may specify higher prices than they would quote if they took a more pessimistic view of future prospects and were keener to win these contracts. If rivals are also taking the view that better contracts will be available in future for firms that have the capacity to handle them, they may likewise put in tenders that reflect these opportunity costs and the firm in question may still stand a chance of winning enough of these contracts to fill its order books.

In the latter case we do not have the pure form of 'normal cost' pricing discussed in section 9.6.1, for prices will move around as incumbents' opportunity costs change with the strength of demand, failing to cover full costs (in the accounting sense, meaning financial outlays) in depressed times and entailing supernormal margins in peak periods. Nonetheless, if incumbent firms wish to discourage cross-entry they must not allow their long-run earnings to rise above the opportunity costs of would-be rivals. The same is true for the earlier case illustrated with reference to the used-car market.

9.6.4 The compatibility of strong competition and organizational slack

Andrews disliked intensely any suggestion that firms do not engage in maximizing behaviour and that members of corporate coalitions can often get away with the pursuit of their own sub-goals. His views on the role of organizational zealots and the power of competition from potential producers led him to take issue with the work of Cyert and March (1963), despite his own essentially behavioural methodology. He misconstrued their view of 'organizational slack' as pertaining to something which arose in situations where competition was lacking—situations that his fieldwork suggested to him were the exception rather than the norm—and where there was no need to strive to take high quality decisions. He intensely disliked satisficing as a concept (see Andrews and Brunner, 1975: 1, where he described theorizing along such lines as 'evading economic analysis').

But despite these attacks, and his emphasis on the long-run power of competition, it is clear from his work that, like Cyert and March, Andrews certainly did not believe that firms always operate on some objectively given cost curve. Rather, like Marshall (1890) and Downie (1958), his view of competitive processes stresses problem-induced discoveries:

> The very ups and downs of the trade cycle contribute their own element making for the increased efficiency of business over time, but the individual business will also get its share of minor setbacks. Something always remains from the enforced ideas of economy and novelty to which business men are driven by such forces. Innovation and the rest of such factors will mean that the

forces of competition ... will cause the level of the normal-cost price always to fall (Andrews, 1951: 172).

Sometimes ... the whole of the top echelon become ineffectual, especially when they are but complementary to a particular personality and decline in effectiveness with him. In this case powerful pressures build up from below and are reinforced by outside competitive pressures in the ordinary sense.... However much 'fat' its previous success may have built up against just such a winter, in the end the process of exhaustion becomes obvious and rejuvenation is enforced (Andrews, 1958: 29).

Within a firm whose potential is being squandered by some staff, the pressures for change come from promotion-hungry staff seeking to demonstrate their capabilities to those to whom their ineffectual colleagues report. Andrews (1958) calls this the process of 'internal competition': an underlying assumption here is that, in the long run, it does not pay competent, ambitious staff to be sycophantic 'yes-people' because a firm that cannot adapt to keep pace with rivals will either go bankrupt or get taken over in the long run. Further discussions of the process of search and the uptake of slack are found in Andrews and Brunner (1975: 158) where one can see that Andrews had his own jargon phrase— 'plasticity of costs'—for organizational slack and did believe it had some bearing on the determination of costing margins.

The important point to note is that, in a world of private information and bounded rationality, vigorous competition and slack can both exist. Normal cost theory does not require firms to have identical profit margins, merely to set prices according to the conjectured opportunity costs of potential producers of similar products. Likewise, the theory of internal competition does not require people in identical job slots to put in an identical performance to that which would be offered by those by whom they could be replaced; they merely have to offer what their superiors will conjecture to be the opportunity cost output. Firms or individual members of such entities that enjoy informational advantages may certainly consider the possibility that they could achieve for their efforts short-run returns that are in excess of their transfer earnings. But few decision-makers in such situations would regard themselves as facing well-defined downward-sloping 'demand functions' for their outputs. Rather, they would normally bear in mind the strong possibility that any conspicuous abnormally high returns they earn, or costs they impose upon others, may constitute an incentive for others to acquire similar skills and bid away their quasi-rents, or design a substitute with which to replace output from them.

To the extent that agents sometimes set out to achieve supernormal returns that prove unsustainable in the long run, this may be due to them having made poor conjectures about what would be sufficiently moderate a demand as to preserve their positions for the future, or it may arise because they prefer to discount distant returns somewhat and accordingly have chosen to exploit their temporary advantage in full recognition of the risk of encouraging entry. This analysis would imply an accord with the view of Littlechild (1981) that there is no reason to condemn abnormally high short-run earnings as *necessarily* implying a loss of consumer surplus. Without the lure of such earnings, agents may not have bothered to invest in the know-how from which these earnings were derived: deviations from normal rates of return are often part of the dynamic by which the competitive process progressively reduces costs.

9.7 Contestable markets and idiosyncratic products

Scholars of Andrews's work have been suffering acutely from feelings of *déjà vu* in recent years, feelings made all the more troubling by thoughts that what they were seeing was rather more insightful in its original Andrewsian guise. The source of such feelings is the proliferation of research on the 'contestability' approach to industrial structure, associated particularly with the contribution of Baumol, Panzar and Willig (1982).

According to Baumol's summary article (1982: 2), the key theme in this new work is that

> in the limiting case of perfect contestability, oligopolistic structure and behavior are freed entirely from their previous dependence on the conjectural variations of *incumbents* and, instead, these are generally determined uniquely and, in a manner that is tractable analytically, by the pressures of *potential* competition to which Bain has directed our attention so tellingly (italics in original).

As we saw in the previous section, the emphasis on the power of potential competition is the foundation of the work of Andrews and Brunner. Their thinking predates that of Bain.

If Baumol and his associates are to be said to have made an important addition to Andrews's line of thought, it must only be their emphasis that the *perfectly* contestable market is one in which *both* entry *and* exit are costless, there being no sunk costs. An absence of sunk costs entails a situation in which a market has been entered either without any investment expenditure being necessary, or where an entrant is certain that investments can be recouped in full by selling the assets for a price that equals their original purchase price. In such a market, the ability to exit without having made any capital commitment guarantees freedom of entry, and the fear of hit-and-run raids concentrates incumbents' minds wonderfully against the idea of pursuing socially undesirable pricing policies. If sunk costs are zero, would-be raiders do not have to worry about the kinds of retaliatory measures that incumbents might implement, for if the raiders find they cannot make a normal profit they can simply exit. Baumol *et al.*'s argument is that if incumbents realize this, then they will set their prices so as to stop the raiders from wanting to enter in the first place. Hence, whether there is one firm or a multitude of firms actually operating in it at any time, a perfectly contestable market never offers the incumbent(s) more than the normal rate of profit. It is a market in which 'Ramsey prices' prevail (see section 7.11).

Baumol and his colleagues have succeeded in capturing the imagination of industrial economists where Andrews failed, despite (or because of?) the fact that the 'new' exposition concentrates on the theoretical ideal in a highly formal manner. Tom Wilson (one of Andrews's colleagues at Oxford in the 1940s) has described the formal theory as 'another exercise in comparative statics, with all the problems of inadequate information, risk, and uncertainty largely ignored' (1984: 227). Goodwill, a concept central to Andrews' analysis of the determination of market share, figures nowhere in Baumol *et al.*'s treatise. Nor, indeed, would we expect to find a logical place for it in the first 370 pages, since the concept concerns the empirically significant phenomenon of repeat business and it is only on page 371 that their analysis is broadened to take account of the passage of time. Since they lack the goodwill factor to provide a limit to the size of the firm (it is only a short-run restraint in Andrews's process analysis), Baumol *et al.* (1982: 113) note that their 'powerful analysis of the number of firms that minimizes industry costs' was 'made possible by the assumption that average costs first decline, achieve their minimum and then rise'. In fact, it would appear from Lee's (1985) painstaking survey of empirical studies that it is unwise to make generalizations, for the evidence differs quite markedly depending on which market one is examining. For example, *consistently upward-sloping* cost functions tend to be observed in markets where firms have accumulated a range of machines of different vintages, the older ones of which cost more to run—see section 7.7 on Salter's (1960) classic 'vintage model' of how technological improvements affect the behaviour of firm and industry costs through time. There, the cost curves of *neither* Baumol *et al. nor* Andrews and Brunner would be correct, though their conclusions might be.

Followers of the Andrews and Brunner analysis do not take very seriously the idea of a *perfectly* contestable market in which there are no sunk costs and both entry and exit are costless. In this hypothetical situation, which contestability theorists have suggested might be a not unrealistic 'as if' way of viewing many markets, the ability of firms to stage costless 'hit-and-run' raids concentrates incumbents' minds wonderfully against any temptation they might have to pursue socially undesirable pricing policies. Prices then become parameters that incumbents have to live with, rather than discretionary variables chosen in the light of sometimes imperfect judgements about the likely behaviour of other firms (for a detailed appraisal of the contestability literature, see Davies and Lee, 1988). Throughout this book it should be understood that, although I may speak of markets as 'hotly contested', I do not have in mind a state of perfect contestability as a reference point. Exit is hardly likely to be costless if entry involves expenditure on new physical equipment—assets will only be perfectly marketable if they are not at all idiosyncratic. Almost any situation in which marketing costs have to be incurred also violates the costless exit condition—advertisements are a particularly obvious example of an expense which is non-recoverable when a firm abandons operations in a market. A debatable exception—suggested by one of my students, Mark Devlin—is where the advertisements have been used to build up a recognized brand name which has a market value because of the goodwill that is attached to it. The difficulty here is that it is by no means obvious that a popular brand name is going to have a market value if, despite having built up this goodwill, the raider has found it uneconomic to stay in the market. For example, the incumbents might have engaged in a predatory price-cutting strategy, taking temporary losses themselves, to teach the raider *and any other would-be raiders* a lesson about their greater staying power; after the raider had ceased operating in the market, the incumbents could then restore prices to their previous levels. Such practices may be of doubtful legality, but bankrupt entrepreneurs may experience difficulties fighting for redress in the courts.

Marketing considerations actually receive serious attention in the Andrews-inspired analysis of corporate behaviour. The notion of perfect contestability would be more acceptable if formal contracts between buyers and sellers could be specified in detail and then enforced without significant costs being involved by parties on either side. Doubts about standards of service would thereby be eliminated. In reality, of course, transaction costs of this kind are often difficult to ignore and with some products it is intrinsically difficult to set out in very much detail what is going to be delivered. The most extreme cases arise in markets for information: a fully specified contract would include all the information that the customer was hoping to purchase by signing the contract, so there would be a danger that the customer might be able to make off with the information after inspecting the contract without having to go as far as signing it. Other obvious examples are markets where creative skills and investments in research are involved, such as the advertising industry (see Earl, 1991) and architecture: a client must either sign a rather vague contract and then let the chosen supplier get to work on the details, or be prepared to face up to the higher prices that would be involved if it insisted on being able to choose between fully specified advertising strategies. In the latter situation, the higher prices would be due to the risk premium that firms would require given the uncertainty over whether they would actually win the contract after putting in all the work.

There is a parallel here with defence contracting, which sometimes does involve governments choosing between fully developed systems, and the designs that are tendered unsuccessfully may never get into production. If a government wishes to avoid compensating would-be defence contractors for the uncertainties involved in up-front expenditures on research, the alternative is to sign up for something that is only partially designed and then pay the additional bills involved in getting it fully ready for use. Then the question of who should bear the costs of unexpected cost over-runs arises: if the government agrees to pick up the tab in the form of a payment involving a mark-up on outlays, careful attention to keeping costs under control is less likely to be the order of the day once the contract has been signed. However, even with such an arrangement the deal might not be as bad as all that for the customer, for the prospect of winning such a cosy environment ought to mean that the initial tendering battle is particularly keenly fought (for further discussions in this area, see Arrow, 1962).

In markets where buyers cannot be certain of the quality of what they are agreeing to purchase, firms do not merely have to decide how much to invest in physical equipment. To ensure that their physical equipment does not run at disastrously low rates of capacity utilization they must also make decisions about the kind of investment to make in research and development and in marketing in order *to overcome any doubts* that potential buyers have about their products and standards of service. For any hypothetical combination of physical and marketing investments, the key question is therefore whether a price that covered the full costs of development, production and marketing would be likely to be low enough to generate the sales volumes required for profits targets to be met.

Marketing costs do not arise only when firms seek to enter markets or expand their interests in their existing markets by launching new products. Attempts to build up market share as an addition to previous attainments may also prove very costly unless the market population is changing and/or incumbents enrage their regulars by letting their standards slip below satisfactory levels, thereby provoking them to search for a better source of supply. Certainly, as Andrews emphasized in his analysis of goodwill, some degree of flux is to be expected in markets, even in the absence of changing macroeconomic conditions, but if new customers or disaffected former clients of rival producers are not to arrive on a purely random or socially-driven basis, marketing expenses will obviously be necessary. To build up sales still further will require an investment in marketing to overcome goodwill relationships that exist between incumbent firms and those buyers who would otherwise see no point in changing their purchasing routines. These relationships, which figure nowhere in Baumol *et al.*'s (1982) treatise on contestable markets, may be seen as implicit contracts that emerge as alternatives to fully-specified contracts that would be too costly to construct. If buyers are satisfied, they will tend to return on future occasions even if there are other firms claiming to offer an identical deal. They thereby avoid the risk of paying the same price for what might turn out to be an inferior non-price deal with an untried alternative supplier, and if they are recognized as 'regulars' they may get preferential treatment on occasions when they are in urgent need of supplies. The risks associated with a disappointing standard of quality or service may be such that a 'better the devil you know' consideration will not just keep buyers away from alternative suppliers who quote an identical price; it may also deter them from switching to unknown suppliers that are offering cheaper deals.

9.8   Essay example: Generalizations about pricing

Question

'[I]t clearly seems impossible to replace the old text-book slogans with any simple generalizations. A debate which consists in defending or attacking "principles", such as the "full-cost principle", "the marginal principle" or the "normal-cost principle", and trying to fit all types of situations into one system is obviously foredoomed to futility' (Joan Robinson, 'Imperfect competition revisited', *Economic Journal*, **63**, December 1953: 590). Discuss.

Author's notes

It may be easier to understand what Joan Robinson was getting at if you take a look at the date of her article. She is writing on the twentieth anniversary of the publication of her (1933) book *The Economics of Imperfect Competition*. At that time a heated debate was going on about the merits of the full cost and normal cost pricing ideas of economists from Oxford University. The 1939 Hall and Hitch article on business behaviour, in which both the kinked demand curve and full cost analyses were proposed, was republished in 1951 in a book edited by Tom Wilson and Philip Andrews, entitled *Oxford Studies in the Price Mechanism*. Andrews's own book *Manufacturing Business*, appeared in 1949 and was accompanied by several articles. What seemed to be going on in the profession was that the marginalists were trying to say that the mark-up-oriented approaches could not explain all pricing situations, and that situations described by the Oxford economists as consistent with their own approach could be rationalized in terms of marginalist thinking. Andrews and Brunner, meanwhile, were working on ways of extending the range of their analysis, by applying normal cost ideas not just to manufacturing but also to retailing. This tendency of economists both to search for general theories and to try to absorb allegedly anomalous phenomena into their own ways of viewing their world has carried on in this area of economics ever since. For example, when reviewing Andrews's and Brunner's 1975 book *Studies in Pricing*, Pickering (1976: 622) complained that they had not constructed a 'sufficiently general model of oligopoly'. The latest instalment of the debate is to be found in the winter 1990–91 issue of the *Journal of Post Keynesian Economics*, involving Langlois (for the marginalists) and Lee and Mongin (for the normal cost school), with myself appealing for a willingness to recognize that different models may be applicable in different contexts—my own paper includes the Joan Robinson quotation in its introduction.

A useful starting point for this essay might be to note that economists, like managers in the real world, have to cope with complexity and that very often they seem to try to cope by building general models. When a new model is proposed, a common reaction is to try to absorb it into their existing way of viewing things. Given sufficient ingenuity, it may be possible to force every pricing situation into a single model of price-setting: rather as Procrustes, in classical mythology, was able to make his guests fit his guestroom bed perfectly by stretching them or chopping bits off their bodies! But before one sets about trying to do so, two questions appear worth asking. First, is it easier to work with several models and adopt a 'horses for courses' approach to making sense of pricing behaviour, rather than to go through great difficulties in order to force everything into one's single perspective? Second, may there be dangers of viewing the world from one kind of perspective, even if it is convenient to do so? In the next chapter we will see how G.B. Richardson's work on economic coordination leads to the conclusion that market imperfections, so called, may help the system to function in an orderly manner: policies aimed at removing imperfections to make the real world more like the ideal world of neoclassical economics may thus give us cause for concern. Perhaps the same situation arises in respect of competition policies where pricing methods are at issue.

As far as Joan Robinson's general claim is concerned, it would be convenient to be able to identify situations which it would be impossible to reconcile with well-known pricing rules. Consider first the theory of monopolistic/imperfect competition. Suppose a short-run demand curve can be conjectured for firms in a particular real-world industry. If prices are set in order just to sell the quantity at which marginal revenue is equal to marginal cost, then we should not expect to find firms setting prices on inelastic portions of their demand curves (where marginal revenues are negative). But this is precisely what Tom Wilson (1979) suggested was going on in the oil industry in the late 1970s: members of the OPEC cartel seemed to be setting prices far lower than those which would have maximized their profits at that time. He proposed plausible reasons about why they were doing this: fears about switches to substitutes or the damage that high oil prices might do to world prosperity and hence the demand for oil.

Now, Wilson's example can tend to provoke two reactions from one-model theorists (if they don't simply ignore it). The normal cost school can feel smug that their views seem to hold up *even* in the case of a market in which a cartel at times has had a lot of influence over prices. However, the marginalists might then feel inclined to say that Wilson is not doing their position justice: a forward-looking manager would consider tradeoffs between profits today and profits tomorrow. Some technique which recognized this tradeoff, also recognizing that managers might have preferences over a dollar today versus a dollar in the future, might be the unifying rule for pricing. As was noted in section 9.6.3, a theory based on this idea was published by Eichner (1973, 1976), who believed himself to be writing in a *non*-marginalist manner. But the technique that is needed might be much more complex than anything which we have covered and more complex than even that which Eichner proposed, given the inter-relations between today's price, tomorrow's entry, learning by customers, and so on (cf. section 7.6). But it might be something which can be modelled: in fact, I think the tool known as 'dynamic programming' is what one would have to use. Perhaps we should think of all managers 'as if they are dynamic programmers'. The analysis would admit as special cases: on the one hand, perfectly contestable markets, where entry is instantaneous and incumbents cannot for a moment charge prices in excess of those which yield a normal profit; and on the other hand, completely closed monopoly markets, where even the possibility of designing substitutes in the long run is ruled out. But it would only be as good at the numbers that went into it: if there were great uncertainty about the relationships involved, we might begin to doubt that managers would bother to use it or even act 'as if' they used it.

To ensure a fair and balanced argument, we also should try to consider examples that would be inconvenient for mark-up/normal cost types of theories of pricing. It is not impossible to find different prices being charged for the same product, even after adjustments have been made for different distances for the customer from the supplier, or differences in product characteristics. Should we then say that this reflects a lack of willingness to search on the part of buyers, with some players exploiting customer ignorance and getting away with it? This may sound like bad news for the normal cost approach, and it is certainly what one observes in some markets, such as insurance, which is why insurance brokers exist. Those insurance companies that charge high prices seem to be judging that it is better to seek to make money by milking those who do not search around very much, whereas those who set lower prices may have a different view. Even the presence of insurance brokers may fail to make the situation strongly contestable because people may be unwilling to use them as sources of information if they fear that they will be getting biased advice.

When challenged in this sort of way, the normal cost theorist might well argue that it would be a mistake to jump to the conclusion that normal cost theory does not apply to such a market. Firstly, it may be that we are not looking at an equilibrium situation but, rather, one in which some players are making different assessments of what kind of price it is safe to charge to stay in business in the long run, with some of these assessments being incorrect. We should bear in mind that normal costs are subjective phenomena: managers' guesses about the cost structures of their actual and potential rivals relative to their own influence the kinds of mark-ups that they will wish to apply. It is not unknown for firms to go broke by setting their prices needlessly low, particularly if people start judging quality by price (customers in a sense may be doing a sort of normal cost analysis of their own, in the belief that 'you get what you pay for'—cf. the discussion of hedonic prices in section 3.6). Secondly, the economist may have failed to standardize for more subjective aspects of the product, which make it harder for would-be producers to work out whether or not a raid will be successful (this also may promote judging quality by price). Thirdly, it may be that we are looking at multi-product firms as if they are single product firms. Perhaps they are using a loss-leader in an attempt to win business (e.g. cheaper car insurance, in the hope that they can sell their clients more expensive house insurance). The key thing is whether their overall pricing strategy seems to involve setting prices as if their markets were to some degree protected from competition. One sign of this may be whether or not they seem to adjust their prices with the general strength of business or simply adjust the number of units that they sell, so long as the market situation stays within 'normal' bounds.

If price adjustments are indeed observed in line with changes in the state of demand, one might still rescue the non-marginalist approach by saying that the general framework is not one of simple mark-ups (though in general the average profit margin must not be so high as to attract entry) but one in which the rule is: base your price on a figure slightly less than that at which you think it would be attractive for a competitor to offer output, bearing in mind that your competitors' opportunity costs may change with the state of trade, and that in some situations you would prefer not to offer the product at such a price yourself given the chance of possibly winning more lucrative orders elsewhere. As we saw in section 9.6.3, this is rather how Andrews saw the building trade.

Should we feel comfortable with such ways of trying to handle anomalies in order to hang on to a particular broad view of pricing? Probably what we are clinging to in these cases is a vision of (a) managers thinking about the benefits of making small adjustments, tradeoffs, and (b) managers constantly worrying about competition. One can see the appeal of the former to economists in general, yet the long-run pricing version of it seems so complex as to be in danger of missing the methods by which managers in practice try to cope with limited computational capabilities and irreducible uncertainties.

In respect of the latter, we end up with a very subjective view of pricing (which may make testing the ideas difficult: we may explain everything, rather like astrology ...) and are in danger of underplaying the length of time that can sometimes pass before entry takes place. An important factor affecting the kind of strategy that managers pursue may be the sorts of time horizons with which they are working: if payments (or superannuation entitlements) depend on results being achieved right now, the temptation to discount the future rather heavily may be rather great. If so, risks may be taken with regard to extracting high profit margins—risks that managers taking a longer view would not dare to take. If we assume, as the normal cost school tend to assume, that fairly swift entry is normally expected and that managers therefore have to think in terms of how to protect their future markets via their current pricing, we may fail to argue that there is a need for policies aimed at promoting a longer-run orientation amongst managers. The success of Japanese business in invading the markets of Western firms might have been rather less had such policies been promoted in Western nations; for there is a major difference of focus between Japanese managers who think ten years ahead and Western managers who are concerned with the next quarter's profit figures. On the other hand, we should not ignore the dangers of a world-view which sees all pricing in marginalist terms, seeing firms as mini-monopolies: it was no accident that Andrews ended up being hired to speak in defence of firms taken to court under monopolies legislation. If the threat of potential competition is substantial, perhaps we should not be so worried that a merger, by reducing the number of incumbent firms, might lead to higher prices. What appears to be necessary is analysis on a case-by-case basis.

9.9 Essay example: Retail pricing in theory and practice

Question

Discuss the problems involved in using *either* conventional marginalist approaches to the theory of the firm *or* models built around the mark-up pricing idea to analyse the pricing behaviour of firms in the retailing industry.

Price and output decisions (2): modern variations on Marshall and marginalism

Like the question examined in section 1.6, this is a question about the adequacy of either of these *theories* as means of making sense of pricing policies used in the business of retailing. Effective answers will therefore concentrate on raising instances of how observed retail pricing policies seem inconsistent with what the chosen theory leads one to expect, or how characteristics of the retailing environment lead one to doubt that the chosen theory is likely to be applicable. The task of appraising theories is rather like that of appraising the design for an aeroplane: we may say 'It doesn't fly very well'. (It may have crashed!) Or we may say 'It looks unlikely that it will fly, given the assumptions its designers are making'.

Since this is an invitation merely to discuss the problems involved in using one of these theories in this context, it would be perfectly in order to raise what seem on the surface to be difficulties for the theory chosen as the subject for the discussion and then go on to show how the theoretical framework is actually perfectly well equipped for dealing with problems.

Though this essay is an either/or type of question, I find it hard to see how anyone could do it well without being on top of both of these theories of pricing behaviour. For example, if one is following the view of mark-up pricing discussed in section 9.6—namely, Andrews's 'normal cost' analysis—then it should be emphasized that this view of price-setting makes no reference to demand curves, merely to expected sales at a price that the price-setter feels it will be safe to charge, given that too high a mark-up may encourage other firms to invade the market. This implies that we should not be seeing firms as apparently setting their prices as if they feel they have a demand curve on which they can choose a higher price or a lower one depending on what will have the best impact on current profits. In terms of short-run demand curves that might exist, Andrews-style pricing decisions may entail prices being set that imply negative marginal revenues for the shop (these would be inconsistent with marginalist analysis). In other words, the firm would prefer higher prices but is afraid of trying to achieve them. The set of existing retail suppliers of the product(s) in question may all prefer higher prices and, if the threat of entry seemed smaller, might follow a price leader to higher price levels, but otherwise they dare not seek to raise their prices. The oligopoly issue thus is absolutely central to the mark-up approach, but some recognition of how it is supposed *not* to produce the sort of behaviour that one would expect in conditions of imperfect competition is needed if one goes searching for potential anomalies. To explain what mark-up theory leads one not to expect is easier if *reference* is made to the rival approach. But what is not required in an answer to this question is the systematic setting out of one theory followed by the systematic setting out of another. Reference to the other theory is in order merely as a rhetorical device.

This question offers an opportunity to display awareness of the relationship between retailers and manufacturers, and of the intermediating role of wholesalers. Manufacturers may be suggesting prices and retailers may be following their suggestions. The prices retailers pay to manufacturers are often the retailers' only variable costs, unless their staff receive commissions on how much they sell. Differences in standards of service are thus to be expected to result in differences in the sort of mark-up that is necessary if a firm is to find it viable to stay in or enter retailing: huge mark-ups on average variable costs may be entirely consistent with very hotly contested retail trading if substantial fixed costs are incurred in presenting the store and staffing it to a high standard.

In terms of potential empirical anomalies, it is probably easier to do the essay for the case of the mark-up approach. The marginalist approach does not actually lead us to expect very much in particular. It is consistent with firms charging similar prices for similar products, but also with them exploiting any monopoly power they believe they have and hence charging different prices from each other. With the mark-up approach an obvious possible problem is the existence of situations in which identical products are selling for different prices: this sounds inconsistent with Andrews's view that competition forces prices into line with the costs of potential entrants. But this may be less of a problem than it first seems: (a) firms may have different ideas of what price is safe to charge and some could be very expensively wrong (note the amount of exit in retailing); (b) the products may not actually be identical, as standards of service offered by retailers may differ in the minds of the consumers; and (c) stores may be selling a range of products and using a mark-up approach on average but experimenting with loss-leader strategies as a way of getting customers to come into their stores.

On the question of whether the theory seems likely to apply in this context, the assumptive structure of the marginalist approach leads it to entail a big 'as if' commitment if we use it, though more so in some parts of retailing than others. In the case of supermarkets the sheer number of products involved (tens of thousands of different products, many of which are close substitutes for each other) makes it rather hard to conceive of managers weighing up the pros and cons of a slightly higher price for this versus a slightly lower price for that, to maximize their overall profits. We might expect them largely to follow the manufacturers' recommendations about what price should be charged, which then pushes the question back to how the manufacturers might recommend prices for their rather smaller ranges of products, mindful of their competitive positions.

In many areas of retailing entry is so easy that one can doubt whether managers would be likely to act as if they had downward-sloping demand curves (note that the tangency solutions for the equilibrium of the firm in imperfect and monopolistic competition do assume easy entry; what is at issue is the rationality of acting without regard to the likelihood of entry). At this stage a perceptive student will discuss reasons for easy entry, point to evidence of retail turnover (vacant stores), and discuss also the ease of exit (note the assisting role of liquidator discount stores). Sectors of retailing where entry is rather difficult are bad news, potentially, for the mark-up approach but are perfectly OK for marginalism. A good essay may be expected to discuss differences in entry ease amongst different areas of retailing, and recognize how such differences can be used in debating whether the theory chosen has a problem or not. Does the existence of monopoly franchises in a given town suggest that monopolistic practices (involving pricing with reference to marginal costs and marginal revenue) are likely? It is wise to bear in mind here that the retailer may have to do what the manufacturer wants in order to maintain the franchise, so once again the question falls back to what makes sense for the manufacturer. The possibility of non-franchised dealers appearing might also be considered, if one is looking for an Andrews-style critique of marginalism in this area. In the case of imported items, it may be possible for such a dealer to obtain supplies at close to the ex-factory price by developing contacts with a less scrupulous franchised dealer overseas. (Being party to this strategy of parallel importing will not harm the overseas dealer's profits so long as the manufacturer does not discover the source of the apparent sales success and take back the franchise rights.) The debate over resale price maintenance, mentioned at the end of section 9.6.2, is relevant here.

In marking this essay I would reward the effective use of case studies or personal shopping experience (it would be preferable to see one area of retailing being contrasted with another): for example, one might note differences between pricing strategies of corner stores and supermarkets and consider whether these are problematic for either of the theoretical approaches.

9.10   Exam post-mortem: The contestability *revolution*?

Question

Do you agree with the claim that the theory of contestable markets proposed by Baumol and his colleagues represents a revolutionary breakthrough in the analysis of oligopolistic competition? Justify your answer.

Examiner's report

This was a popular question that was frequently handled disastrously. What I hoped to see were attempts to show that, although the theory of contestable markets takes a very different view of competition from that which underpinned much of the literature of industrial economics and many laws on competitive practices, the theory has similar implications to the earlier normal cost analysis of Andrews (1949a, 1949b) and Brunner (1952) and even to Marshall's thinking as long ago as 1890. Quite what conclusion were reached would then depend on how 'revolutionary breakthrough' had been defined: certainly, Baumol and his colleagues have had a far greater and much more instantaneous impact on policy than Andrews and Brunner did.

This question demonstrated just how poor members of the class were at pigeonholing ideas for use in an exam, how they were prone to dive into an answer without first asking themselves if they were about to use the appropriate material. In the lectures I had been careful to draw their attention to the way that Baumol's thinking had changed between his 1958 model of the sales revenue maximizing firm and his 1980s work on contestability. Some students ignored Baumol's work altogether, despite it being mentioned in the wording of the question. Many of this group wrote about the kinked demand curve (only one of them made any attempt to integrate this theory with ideas about the effects of easy entry). Others muddled together the two Baumol theories or tried to answer the question in terms of the sales revenue maximization theory. In almost all cases, there was a complete failure to bring in the work of Andrews and Brunner and thereby deal with the 'revolutionary' aspect of the question.

As for those who tried to talk about the appropriate Baumol contribution, many revealed major confusion on the role of 'hit-and-run raiders' in contestability theory. It might have been argued that Baumol's most important advance over Andrews and Brunner was that he showed how easy exit was a precondition for a powerful entry threat. However, the class largely missed this point and commonly said that the raiders rush in *and* rush out of a market if it seems easy to make money by doing so. The impression I got was that the class thought that raiders would enter *planning to quit* once they had made a satisfactory return, which is a complete misunderstanding of the significance of easy exit. The answers should have said that the ability to quit a market without leaving behind any sunk investments means that raiders would not be worried in the slightest by suggestions that incumbent firms might invest in predatory retaliation to force raiders out of the market. This being the case, incumbents can expect raiders to arrive should they charge prices in excess of the opportunity costs of would-be raiders.

In commenting on how revolutionary the contestability analysis is, hardly anybody took the line that Baumol and his colleagues were greatly overestimating the ease of exit because they were failing to recognize the non-recoverable nature of marketing expenditures. Nor did anyone recite the point that incumbents may only believe in a threat of entry once they have seen it actually materialize as a result of themselves being unduly greedy in their pricing.

9.11   Price discrimination and product bundling

In this section I am going to discuss some further pricing practices that have received considerable attention from a marginalist standpoint since the works of Robinson and Chamberlin appeared in the 1930s, but which need also to be examined in relation to the contestability and normal cost analyses. First, we will consider price discrimination, the policy of charging different prices to different consumers even though they are purchasing essentially the same product. Several types of price discrimination have been identified:

(a) *First-degree price discrimination* is said to occur when the supplier succeeds in charging each buyer the maximum that they would be prepared to pay. In other words, no consumer surplus (the difference between what people have to pay and the maximum that they would have been willing to pay, if that were necessary) is enjoyed. Examples of this are rather difficult to find—not surprisingly, since we do not normally tell sellers the maximum amount we are prepared to pay, in case we can get away with pleading poverty and paying less. Frank (1991: 395) suggests that some mail-order companies try to come quite close by sending out catalogues with different price lists in them, the price list depending on the typical income levels of the suburb (in New York, Park Avenue would have much higher prices listed than, say, the Bronx). Otherwise, his closest example to perfect price discrimination is the canny bargaining behaviour in bazaars in the Middle East, where the merchant haggles with customers on an individual basis.

Charity fund raisers using modern direct marketing techniques may adopt rather similar strategies when trying to extract as much as possible from their unwitting donors. The recipient of a letter about a typical mailed charity fund-raising appeal is faced with a series of boxes to tick, each of which contains a suggested amount for the gift. If one gives $50 rather than $10, $20, $75 or $100, it is likely that future fund-raising letters will involve a set of boxes that start with higher figures and work up to even higher figures, to try to push the donor into giving more. The computer-based letters can be customized time and again to suit what is known about potential donors. (The psychology involved here is worth thinking about: some people may be using a decision rule which, up to some maximum figure, involves them in ticking the middle box, so that they can tell themselves they are not being particularly mean; others might always try to make themselves feel good, up to a point, by ticking the box with the biggest value.)

(b) *Second-degree price discrimination* is defined differently by different economists. Frank (1991: 395), for example, defines it as a situation in which the seller offers discounts on marginal units. This is common with electricity companies in the United States: one might be billed at 10 cents per kilowatt hour for the first 300 hours that one uses, 8 cents for the next 700, and 5 cents per kilowatt hour for all quantities over 1 000 (cf. Figure 3.6 in Chapter 3 of this book). This strategy obviously is an imperfect way of extracting the maximum from the consumer for each unit sold, but it may nonetheless come quite close to eliminating most consumer surplus. Note that with this sort of system each buyer faces the same price structure; there is no attempt to tailor the rate structure to take account of elasticity differences between buyers.

Douglas (1987: 395), by contrast, defines second-degree discrimination as a strategy which involves changing the price of a given product through time: if you are prepared to wait longer, you may get the product more cheaply than someone who wants it urgently. The market for recorded music is a good example of this. 'Full-price' classical recordings are often reissued on 'mid-price' and, eventually, 'budget-price' labels (for example, Deutsche Grammophon recordings after a decade may end up on the DG Privilege series, and after perhaps two decades may resurface on the Heliodor label). A variation on this theme is to repackage a couple of recordings in a two-for-one deal.

Frank also has such strategies in mind, but he notes some more subtle variations used to conceal what is really going on, and puts them under the heading of the '"hurdle" model of price discrimination'. Here, the hurdle refers to some contrived inconvenience that the buyer must suffer in order to get the lower price. For example, the characteristics of the cheap product may be altered slightly to deter the buyers whose upper limits are greater. With books, for example, second-degree discrimination (Douglas-style) often involves the lower price only being available later on when a paperback edition is launched. The premium price will be paid by people who want the latest book, or are prepared to pay for durability (as libraries might) or who simply like the better quality feel of a hardback. The difference in hardback and paperback book prices is normally out of all proportion to their differences in cost of production. Shop-soiled products are another way of attracting the more reluctant/poorer customer: slightly damaged whitegoods may be sold for considerably less than pristine examples, even though the latter may soon end up scratched in normal use. Frank also notes the use of rebates that may be available if one is prepared to accumulate packaging labels and go to the bother of mailing them to the manufacturer, or the case of supersave and standby airline tickets where 'special conditions apply' clauses are the price that one must pay (usually in the form of inflexibility or uncertainty) for getting the seat for less.

(c) *Third-degree price discrimination* is said to occur when a given product is sold for different prices in different markets, higher prices being charged in markets where the demand is less sensitive to price. Economics textbooks are an obvious example: the Prentice-Hall International Student Edition of Douglas (1987) is not available to students in the United States (who have to content themselves with the hardback but have enough money to do so), and it is probably sold for less in poor countries than in the UK, Australia or New Zealand. This sort of behaviour by publishers is not the result of their benevolence: as Frank (1991: 392) says about the pricing of his own text, 'The price that maximizes profits in the US market would discourage most Third World students from buying'.

Normally such pricing strategies are analysed in marginalist terms and, as Reed and Bates (1990) have recently pointed out, many textbooks involve technical faults over matters as basic as defining the marginal revenue curve associated with adding up the demand curves for different markets in which the price-discriminating firm operates. (The common errors are made in the texts by Douglas, 1987, and Frank, 1991, referred to in this section.) Simple linear demand curves are normally assumed, as in Figure 9.3. When their respective marginal revenue curves are correctly added together horizontally the result is an overall marginal curve resembling the marginal revenue curve associated with the reflex kinked demand curve in Efroymson's (1943, 1955) analysis of oligopoly firms operating in a booming market (compare the third panel of Figure 9.3 with Figure 8.8).

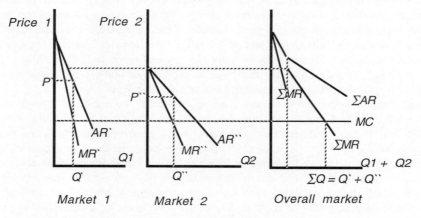

Figure 9.3: A price-discriminating monopolist selling in two markets

A price-discriminating monopolist will maximize its profits by producing the output (ΣQ) at which its marginal costs are equal to the overall marginal revenue function. As far as the prices and quantities in each of its markets are concerned, they are found by taking the marginal cost figure at the point at which $MC = \Sigma MR$ and finding, in each market, the price whose marginal revenue is equal to this marginal cost figure, hence $P`$, $Q`$ and $P``$, $Q``$. (Note: most texts draw upward-sloping marginal cost curves, in contrast to the horizontal marginal cost curve that I have drawn. Evidently, if marginal costs are constant—as is more likely in practice—the price-discriminating monopolist can simply find the price and quantity combinations at which $MC = MR$ separately for each market, without having to add up the marginal revenue curves.)

It should be noted that price-discrimination policies will founder if people who have access to cheaper supplies are in a position to resell them to those who would otherwise be excluded from them. Such behaviour, which is known as arbitrage, would tend to eliminate price differences between markets or customers. Geographical mobility may also make things tricky for would-be price discriminators, unless they can get away with restrictive strategies. For example, to get away with charging higher prices for cars in the United Kingdom than in other European Community countries, manufacturers tend to make it known that those who visit the European mainland to bring back a personal import may experience difficulty in finding a right-hand drive model or a British dealer who is willing to carry out any warranty work.

In general, price discrimination sounds at first sight most unlike the sort of situation that would fit into the sort of highly competitive vision of capitalism suggested by Andrews: we have just been speaking of price-discriminating monopolists and measures by which arbitrage may be hindered. However, I imagine that he would have pointed out that firms which earn supernormal profits by practising it will soon find their markets invaded by others firms. Here we might note how rampant price discrimination is in the airline business and how entrants devised discriminatory strategies of their own as devices to help them get a foothold in this business. Returning to the UK/EC car market example, I would point out that it is no accident that the UK was selected by the Japanese as their first European market in the early 1970s: the British drove on the same side of the road as the Japanese and, better still, the incumbent manufacturers were trying to charge them excessive prices.

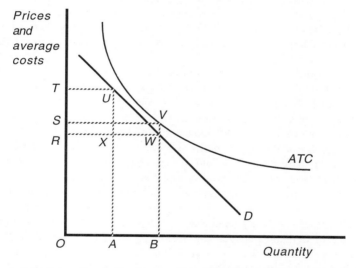

Figure 9.4: Price discrimination as a way of making a firm's market viable

An extension of the competitive perspective on price discrimination leads to an interesting possibility depicted in Figure 9.4. Here we have a case of a product that cannot be sold profitably without price discrimination taking place, for the firm's average total cost curve lies to the right of its perceived demand curve. If the firm were to sell at a price of *OR* it would achieve sales of *OB* and incur losses equal to *RSVW*. However, if it can segment its customers into two groups it may earn sufficient extra revenue from the up-market group to cover the losses incurred in selling to those who are less willing or able to pay for its product. For example, it may sell *OA* units at a price of *OT* and *AB* units at a price of *OR*: if the area *RTUX* is greater than or equal to *RSVW*, then it will not make losses. The diagram does not allow us to determine precisely which set of prices it will pay to charge in the long run. But we can at least say that an unduly greedy mix of prices may attract competition and push the demand curve even further to the left.

In the case of publishing, we should note that publishers are likely to set their prices with a view to the competitors that may emerge if they are too greedy; for what matters as far as potential competitors are concerned is the total profit from a particular book, not its earnings in a particular market. If one publisher starts out by pricing very high in affluent markets and very low in poor ones and does unexpectedly well, would-be copycat publishers may find that they can only offer viable books if they, too, adopt a highly skewed pricing strategy: if they sell more expensively in the less affluent market they will be unlikely to win sales, so the key issue is whether they can profitably undercut the pioneer in the affluent market. The overall demand for this sort of book *may* be such that even if they picked up more sales by undercutting the original supplier in the affluent market their overall earnings would seem too low to make entry worthwhile. Thus although a book may sell with a tiny margin in some markets, it would be unwise to jump to the conclusion that it could sell for anywhere near this price in all markets. Publishers could actually be setting different mark-ups in different markets, using higher mark-ups from more affluent markets as a means of covering the set-up costs of publishing their books and only earning a normal rate of return on their invested capital. These themes should be kept in mind as I conclude this section by considering three further variations on the price-discrimination theme.

(d) *Quantity discounts* are somewhat similar to second-degree price discrimination as defined by Frank. However, in markets where close substitutes exist they may involve a rather different underlying story based on differences in marketing/transaction costs rather than on differences in willingness to pay. Consider the market for new cars: why do fleet purchasers get a better deal than individuals? Certainly, if a major buyer does switch to a rival supplier, the firm that loses the business will have a major chunk of capacity to fill by other means. Such spare capacity would not automatically be filled by buyers displaced from rivals if the latter ran into capacity constraints and raised their prices or created waiting lists. But it is altogether too simplistic to suggest that the car manufacturer may give better deals to large buyers simply because of the possibility of having spare capacity to fill.

Economists might normally make sense of these discounts in terms of differences in price elasticity of demand between the various customer groups. It might cost a car manufacturer less in terms of the expected value of lost revenue to have a satisfactory chance of winning a contract with a fleet buyer, than it would cost if prices were subsequently cut to increase sales to individuals to offset the loss of the fleet order.

An alternative way of looking at the issue is in terms of transaction costs, the costs of making a deal happen. The costs associated with fixing up a single fleet deal involving several thousand vehicles may be much less than those involved in selling the same number of vehicles to individual buyers. More finely aimed advertising media can be used, and fewer hours of staff time are likely to be involved with a fleet deal, even if greater effort is lavished on wooing an individual fleet buyer. (With this type of product we should not ignore the possibility that fleet sales may actually serve as a marketing device in respect of sales to individual customers: for example, people who learn to drive in a particular car may then purchase one of their own. This marketing role may be worth paying for via lower prices, if they are necessary to clinch the contract.) Inventory costs may also be lower, not merely because fewer demonstrators will be needed but also as a result of the fleet buyer making a forward purchase of a standardized product, rather than expecting on-the-spot choices of a range of specifications. By forming a buying collective, a group of individuals could in principle set about trying to reduce many of these costs for the manufacturer, but to do this would obviously involve *them* in other kinds of transaction costs.

(e) *Product bundling* is the term applied where a supplier tries to extract more from some consumers by lumping products together. For example, a car manufacturer may sell a number of levels of specification for a particular model, but their differences in price may be entirely out of proportion to the differences in costs of production. The aim is to exploit the more up-market buyer's lower price sensitivity. It may be left open to the less well-off buyer to come pretty close to a higher-level model by going to the trouble of adding options to a more basic variant. However, in some cases 'optioning up to higher specification' may actually be more costly because the firm judges it can make more money by selling a sub-set of the extra features with a fat mark-up.

Whether or not such a strategy actually will necessarily result in monopolistic profits is debatable. As with third-degree price discrimination in the market for textbooks, we must not forget that the overall earnings from a particular activity are what will determine whether or not it is profitable to undertake. Without the high margins on higher specification models, a manufacturer might not find it viable to offer more basic models at the sorts of prices that are observed. (Figure 9.4 can be seen as a simplified illustration of this point.)

Product bundling has also been used as a device for discouraging customers from thinking about whether they might be wise to shop around and assemble what they want from a variety of suppliers (possibly even doing some of the work themselves). An example of this is the advertising industry, where until recently it was quite common for advertisers to purchase an entire campaign—creative inputs, advertisement production, and booking of media space—via an advertising agency whose fee was specified in terms of a fraction of the total expenditure on media space. This style of operation has recently been undermined by the arrival of specialists that concentrate on offering particular services and enable advertisers to see that they may save money by using a range of suppliers (see Earl, 1991). Set menu meals in restaurants are another example of a bundled product with an informational rationale. Customers may resist paying a well-defined price for a soup or dessert dish, but a set menu meal frames their choice in a somewhat different way, taking the focus away from the cost of a marginal dish to whether or not the total price of the meal falls within their budget range. The set menu meal will normally work out less expensive than one assembled with more freedom of choice from separate dishes, but it may prove effective for getting customers to increase their total spending in a way that increases the profits of the restaurant since (a) they may otherwise choose, say, only two courses; and (b) by providing them with an additional course for relatively small addition to the total cost the chef is likely to get economies in producing a particular three-course meal set menu if it is a popular choice. For other examples of bundling strategies, see Adams and Yellen (1976) and Cready (1991).

(f) *Block booking* is a variation on product bundling that has been common in the film distribution business (though it is now illegal in some countries) and in the market for advertising slots. (Beware: the same phrase is sometimes used to mean the same thing as a quantity discount—as in the case of a package holiday firm that pre-purchases blocks of seating in airlines, seats at theatres, rooms in hotels, and so on.) For example, cinemas might find that they would have to agree to show a particular movie company's 'B-grade' movies if they were to be allowed to put on its 'A-grade' films. Likewise, advertisers may find that they can only purchase, say, television time if they also purchase space in the same media conglomerate's newspapers. Following Stigler (1968) (discussed by Phlips (1981: 156–7), we may consider two advertisers who are trying to reach somewhat different audiences and therefore value differently the outlets of a particular media company. Assume, for simplicity, that buyers can only purchase one unit of each service. Given their assessments of the payoffs to placing their advertising dollars with rival media organizations, the two advertisers rate as follows the maximum worth to them of the media company's products:

A would pay at most $8 000 for a TV slot *and* $2 500 for a full page in a newspaper;

B would pay at most $7 000 for a TV slot *and* $3 000 for a full page in a newspaper.

Now, if the media company is to sell its TV and newspaper spaces separately, and if it cannot charge the buyers different prices for the same services, it must price its TV slots at $7 000 and newspaper pages at $2 500. Higher prices would entail a failure to sell newspaper space to A and failure to sell TV time to B. Its total revenue from these two clients would be $19 000. However, if it block-booked these clients, insisting that they could only buy TV and newspaper space as a bundle, for a cost of $10 000 each, it would make an extra $1 000.

9.12 Exam post-mortem: The pricing of books

Question
In the light of a careful consideration of the nature of the products involved, discuss whether marginalist or 'full cost'/'normal cost'/'mark-up' theories of pricing behaviour are most likely to be the best guides to understanding pricing decisions in the book-publishing industry.

Examiner's report
Some perfectly competent expositions of the rival theories of pricing scored very badly because they had nothing to say about how the peculiarities of the book-publishing industry might affect one's expectations about the pricing methods that would be used in this context. Most students were so busy regurgitating the theories with the aid of carefully drawn diagrams that they did not pause and note that there was no request for expositions of either theory. It would have been perfectly in order to spend the introduction setting out the key features of the rival theories in summary form, and then spend the rest of the answer

considering the characteristics of this business area that seemed to point one way or another as regards the sort of pricing strategy that publishers would be expected to adopt. Many of the theory regurgitations actually failed to get across the key philosophical difference between the two approaches to pricing, namely, whether prices are set as if a (temporary) monopoly demand curve exists for the product in question, with output being restricted accordingly to clear the market, or whether worries about the power of competition are such that prices are based on costs, with mark-ups set low enough to deter potential suppliers from offering rival products. It was common for answers to lack any discussion of how mark-ups might be set.

As a group, the class actually managed to pick up most of the significant features of this business area. The trouble was that, individually, students each tended to spot only a single significant feature and in many cases then had no idea of what its implications might be.

For example, one student mentioned that books have copyright protection, but then did not go on to suggest that this might give a publisher a monopoly for the duration of the copyright, a situation that might be expected to promote a marginalist strategy of 'charging what the market would bear' without any fear of competition. Still less did this student put a counter view that publishers have to worry about competition from very similar products, despite their copyrights (for example, one neoclassical microeconomics text can be very similar to another without any breach of copyright arising).

Another student mentioned that books often exhibit bell-shaped sales profiles through time as they go through their product life-cycles, but did not try to suggest that perhaps different approaches to pricing might apply at different stages—for example, one might suggest that publishers would possibly use a marginalist approach when a book is new and lacks rivals, but then switch to a mark-up approach to secure the market in the long run, once the initial set-up costs have been recouped. The common policy of a hardback-only strategy when a book is launched could have been used to back up such a suggestion.

Many other answers recalled the use of books as an example in lectures on price discrimination but then they failed to consider this issue with reference to the product life-cycle, dwelling instead on the different prices that firms charged for their books in different markets. Since the conventional expositions of price discrimination are set out in marginalist terms, students simply regurgitated the marginalist price-discrimination diagrams and concluded that normal cost pricing made no sense in such cases. They failed to remember that I had pointed out that price-discrimination strategies might be constrained by publishers' worries about the long-term damage that could be done to their markets by attempts to undercut them if they were unduly greedy in the short run (see section 9.12).

Some of the better answers highlighted the uncertainties involved in the business of publishing and the sheer number of books in many publishers' catalogues. On this basis they plausibly argued that a rule-of-thumb approach seemed plausible. Others recognized that publishers' pricing decisions might be rather bound up with their ability to win authors. The latter issue is complicated by the related questions of how unique the book in question happens to be, and what goals are being aimed at by authors. For example, academic authors may receive the main payoff from their books (if these are not textbooks) via the good that these do to their reputations and hence their promotion rates. They therefore might be rather keen to have their ideas spread widely and in print for a long while, and hence be keen to see pricing strategies rather akin to those suggested in normal cost analysis; they would not be happy to have to sign up with publishers known to prefer to set high prices based on short-run monopolistic considerations if this would mean that very few of their books were sold, albeit with high margins.

To the extent that an author has a unique talent and is keen to make money, the idiosyncratic nature of the product *may* enable worries about the appearance of substitutes to be swept aside and prices to be set with reference to marginal costs and the price elasticity of demand. However, it might be argued, from everyday experience, that the works of top-earning authors, like those superstar musicians, do not seem usually to be priced differently from those of their less highly regarded rivals: a 'best seller' might be characterized as a work which sells an unusually large number of units in a particular price band and its price might be set on the basis of a conventional mark-up on average variable costs. Either way, however, much of the monopoly earnings might be captured by the author if the author's literary agent auctions the work to the highest bidder prior to publication.

One final point seems worthy of attention: no one considered the role of the bookseller in determining the prices of books to the consumer or legal restraints on booksellers in respect of where they can source their stock; everyone wrote as if book prices were set by the publishers and that each book had just one publisher. In international publishing, territories are often partitioned between publishers in the author's contract, whilst in some countries publishers can legally refuse to supply stock to booksellers whom they find discounting their products. Both of these factors have been argued by some commentators to enhance scope for monopolistic policies on the part of publishers, yet they have also been argued to benefit consumers in the long run (for example, discounting of best sellers in supermarkets could drive specialist bookstores out of business and make it harder for buyers to obtain a wide range of books: cf. Andrews, 1993; Andrews and Friday, 1960).

9.13 Essay example: Pricing and the multi-product firm

Question
'Pricing decisions for products with (a) common costs and (b) related demand must be made jointly for all the products involved.' Discuss.

Author's notes
This is a question where it is reasonably easy to explain why jointness causes problems for pricing decisions but where it is difficult to find economists tending to provide neat answers. Note that the question does not stress solving the problem; rather, it seems initially to make one focus on the existence of a problem. Therefore I would expect students to be rewarded generously for creative thinking about how to solve the problem.

A straightforward way to begin this essay would be to note that most textbook discussions of pricing are set out as though firms produce a single final product, whereas in practice the typical firm has a *range* of products to sell. Indeed a shop is a very obvious example of a firm selling many products from within the same premises. Demand for items stocked by a particular shop may be inter-related in the same way as it is for the firm that supplies a particular range of products to stock: a low price for sales of a lower-grade product may win customers not merely from other lower-grade brands but also from that brand of higher-grade product. Some product demands may also be related because items are complementary in the sense that they are used together (the Parker retail gun case study in section 8.11 is a good illustration of this, but one can suggest many other examples, such as skis and ski jackets, or ingredients for a meal). An interesting example of complementary demands having very serious implications for long-run pricing strategies is that of Apple Macintosh computers. They were sold as high-margin products initially on the basis that they were easier to use and could save valuable time at a greater rate than rival computers such as IBM/MS-DOS-based PCs. Software developers focused their efforts on developing programs for PCs, not Macintoshes; lack of software in turn limited further the attractiveness of high-priced Macintoshes even in the business market despite the fact that the user-friendly Macintosh operating system had advantages in terms of its ability to save valuable time. Some PC software companies gave their software away in order to help get customers hooked on PCs and then become buyers of their more expensive products. One can go so far as to say that products that are unrelated in terms of their characteristics and that are produced by different manufacturers (for example, petrol, bread, newspapers and chocolate bars) may nonetheless have related demands as far as the retailer is concerned if they can all be bought at the same time (hence the use of 'specials' to lure customers into a particular petrol station shop).

If one sees pricing from the standpoint of Chamberlin's (1933) theory of monopolistic competition, it may seem that a multi-product firm faces a very complex pricing problem, a further layer of complexity on top of the choice of optimal mix of price/advertising/product-design that exists at the level of the individual product: the task seems to be to choose the optimal set of prices given that, instead of a single demand curve, one has a set of simultaneous equations relating demand curves and marginal revenue curves and possibly also a matrix of inter-related cost functions. (A matrix method of finding the best set of prices is likely to be necessary.) However, the task of pricing product ranges might be simplified somewhat if looked at from the standpoint of Andrews's (1949a, 1949b) normal cost theory of pricing which makes no reference to demand curves and instead focuses on the costs of potential competitors and what these imply for the size of mark-up that can be charged without doing damage to one's market in the long run. This simplification is more difficult to justify if potential producers seem likely to enter with entire product ranges of their own, but that is rather unusual (for example, it took Honda almost two decades to move from producing mainly mini-cars to offering a range including luxury executive vehicles, and it took Toyota even longer to go to the very top of the market and develop its Lexus brand to challenge Mercedes and Cadillac).

On the cost side, there are a variety of ways in which costs may be difficult to disentangle across products. One example that may involve both fixed and variable costs is where production involves by-products (slaughterhouses may end up with hides and the basis for blood and bone fertiliser, as well as meat products from the animals they murder). Though a business may be worth starting on the basis of one product alone, the marketability of its by-products may mean that the original product has to be sold at a lower price to keep competitors out of the market in the long run. Other kinds of shared costs are fixed costs of developing components that can be used in a several different products, a common brand name, a common set of production facilities, a common distribution system and a single, coordinating head office (see section 7.4).

In some cases we may only have common overhead costs to worry about, rather than shared variable costs. Here, it should be noted that theories of pricing covered in this course do not make overhead costs play a major role in the price-determination process. Rather the focus is on variable costs or marginal costs. In the case of monopolistic/imperfect competition theory, the rule is find the quantity at which marginal revenue equals marginal cost and then find the price at which precisely that quantity will be bought. In the case of theories of mark-up pricing (such as Andrews's normal cost analysis), the mark-up is usually thought of as being added to average variable costs (often known also as direct costs and which, if constant, are equal to marginal costs) at some 'normal' level of output. In both cases the difference between price and average variable costs leaves a margin from which the firm may hope to cover its overhead costs. A multi-product firm may cover its overheads from the 'contribution margins' on each of the products it sells, taken together. If it is finding its overheads very easy to cover and is making supernormal profits, such a firm may attract competing suppliers into some of its markets. Fear of this, or actual entry of competition, may make the firm lower its contribution margins. The argument here is exactly the same as with single-product firms except that we cannot readily say anything about equilibrium or break-even points for any individual product market that the firm might be involved with unless the firm somehow decides to allocate a portion of its fixed costs to each of its activities despite them being inter-linked. Overhead allocations may not make sense from an economic point of view, but they may be quite common in practice based on simple decision rules: one rule might be to divide overheads up among product markets on the basis of the fraction of the firm's sales in each of its markets in the previous year.

If actual and potential competitors in particular markets were known to be prone to use similar rules of thumb for allocating overheads, the problem of working out a safe competitive price would be simplified. Otherwise the threat of cross-entry seems to make the appropriate mark-up size difficult to judge: the trouble is, cross-entry by firms that are diversifying across market boundaries is inherently likely to involve common costs; however, potential cross-entrants might come from quite a range of product areas (fax machines might be produced by photocopier manufacturers and by computer printer manufacturers) and they might be weighing up a variety of possible directions in which to move to make the most of opportunities that involve shared costs (should a photocopier maker diversify into computer printers rather than, or as well as, fax machines?). They may not be able to move in lots of possible directions simultaneously without making a mess of things.

These types of lines of argument could be applied in relation to retailing. As is pointed out in sections 8.5 and 9.9, it is common in retailing for variable costs simply to be the cost of buying in stock from the manufacturer (new car sales would be different, for commissions tend to be paid to successful sales staff, whereas shop assistants will not be paid more for checking out more). The task for the retailer may be simplified by manufacturers suggesting a 'recommended retail price' (RRP) and the difference between this and the price paid by the shop is the gross margin. If the shop follows the manufacturer's advice, attention is taken away from the pricing question as long as the manufacturer is aware of competitive conditions and other retailers follow the RRP. Instead, the question then becomes one of whether enough can be sold to justify stocking the product, given the scarce space and working capital taken up by unsold stocks of the product. But many retailers of course do depart from RRPs, at least on some items, with a view to luring customers into their shops rather than their rivals' ones: 'loss-leaders' are a classic example of inter-related product pricing. Here, though, the overall price of the shop's offerings (the 'basketful' of its goods, as Andrews put it), taken together must not be high enough to exceed prices quoted by actual and potential long-run competitors.

9.14 Conclusion

Although a century of research on theories of pricing behaviour has failed to result in a consensus among economists, I nonetheless think lessons can be drawn from the debates that they have engaged in. First, it could be a mistake to try to absorb lines of thinking from one framework into another, as part of a search for a general model. 'Absorptionist' work may, however, be useful in so far as it adds to our knowledge of the limitations of our theories: for example, the attempts of Langlois (1989a, 1989b) to use questions about inventory policy to bridge between normal cost and marginalist thinking ought to make normal cost theorists recognize that they may have been all too ready to assume that the pace of production can easily be varied. (A price-setting, quantity-taking firm is going to have problems if the rate of purchase is persistently less than its rate of output: if there are costs to changing that rate of output, it may find itself torn between spoiling the market by cutting prices or incurring the costs of piling up inventories.) Instead of looking for general models, we should try to keep in mind the kinds of context in which particular models may be relatively safe to use (see Earl, 1990–91, and sections 9.9 and 9.12).

Secondly, neoclassical economists have given insufficient attention to the implications of the fact that pricing is an inherently speculative activity where errors in sizing up the likely behaviour of rivals may turn out to be very expensive. Unlike work in the Marshallian tradition, the modern neoclassical literature, with its tendency to portray markets as very highly contestable, does not force us to keep in mind ways in which the irreversible nature of time may affect the kinds of pricing strategies that entrepreneurs will find appealing. In thinking about which theories to use in which contexts we should always ask ourselves whether we are dealing with situations in which re-buys matter, whether there are likely to be advantages to being the first to cut prices or otherwise change one's marketing mix, and whether overly arrogant pricing stances by incumbents may provoke market invasions that lead consumers to change their non-price demands in the light of experience with the somewhat different products offered by interlopers.

Finally, we should follow Scitovsky (1950, 1985, 1990) in seeing that the main source of market power is ignorance: firms can earn supernormal profits if would-be rivals have difficulty in copying their production processes or signalling to potential customers that their products offer comparable or superior value for money to that provided by established brands. However, would-be innovators may opt not to try to turn their visions into production realities unless they believe they face a good enough prospect of being able to obtain profit-generating knowledge advantages that will take time to erode.

9.15 Further questions

1. What do you consider the best theory of oligopoly available, and why?

2. 'A *planned* and deliberate reserve of excess capacity is at all times held by most producers, and with good reason from their point of view. But part of it, at least, is waste from the point of view of the community' (Josef Steindl, *Maturity and Stagnation in American Capitalism*, 1952: 10). Discuss.

3. Imagine that you work as an economic advisor to an airline. Members of the airline's Board of Directors have been considering trying to reduce confusion amongst potential customers by offering a single standard of service and a single price on each route, in place of a mass of special deals and special conditions. You are invited to write a memorandum to the Board in which you present a critical appraisal of these proposals.

4. A common jest amongst historians of economic thought is that 'It's all in Marshall'. In the context of the economics of industries and firms, do you see Marshall's ideas as horribly out of date or years ahead of their time? Explain your answer.

5. 'With the growth of big business, competition becomes more vigorous, not less.' Discuss.

6. Outline the conditions for a perfectly contestable market. What advantages has contestable market theory over standard industrial organization theory? Discuss the applicability of the theory to almost contestable markets.

7. Do you agree with P.W.S. Andrews's claim that management-oriented theories of the firm are simply ways of evading economic analysis by treating each firm as a monopolist? Justify your answer.

8. What role, if any, have demand factors to play in the determination of industrial prices?

9. 'The major failing of theories of mark-up pricing is that there is no adequate theory of what determines the mark-up.' Discuss.

10. Are Shackle's theory of choice under uncertainty and Andrews's 'competitive oligopoly' theory of the firm fundamentally incompatible or ripe for integration? Justify your answer.

11. 'In practice business managers regard oligopolistic interdependence not as a peculiarly intractable problem but rather as one among many aspects of uncertainty about the future outcomes of alternative strategies.' Discuss.

12. Since it is often difficult to get information about the demand for proposed innovative products, does this mean that prices should be set on the basis of costs?

13. Suppose it has been found that motor cars (both British and foreign models) are cheaper in all European countries than in Britain, and that many British buyers are going to some other European country to buy new cars. Under what conditions will a pricing policy on this lead to profits being maximized?

14. A chapter in a recent book (*The Growth of Global Business: New Strategies*, 1992, edited by J. Clegg *et al.*) includes the following information about pricing quotations for renting cars and hiring accountants:

Renting a group A car in London, per week (July 1991, in £UK)		Hiring an accountant in Dublin, per hour (1990, in £IR)	
Hertz	214	Partner, international firm	90
Avis	199	Manager, international firm	60
Budget	203	Partner, local firm	40
Thrifty	147	Manager, local firm	30
Acton	147		
Express	140		
East London	150		
Team Cars	150		

You are invited to discuss these differences in pricing quotations in the light of relevant economic theory. Note that Hertz, Avis, Budget and Thrifty rental car operations are to be found in many countries, often based around franchising arrangements. It is therefore probably wise to read section 11.4 or better still see Dnes (1992: 131–51) for case studies of Avis and Budget, rather than treating this simply as an opportunity for applying material from price theory.

15. In what circumstances would you expect entry to be likely in an oligopolistic market?

16. When and why might a monopolist charge two different prices to consumers? What would be the effect on prices and quantities sold in each of these markets of an outward shift in the demand of *one* of those two groups of consumers.

17. 'It does not matter whether we think the corporation should maximize the welfare of its stockholders, or of its management, or of its workers, or of some combination of these; the truth is that it cannot *maximize* anything.' Discuss.

18. Technical Exercise: Executive Remuneration and Shareholder Interests.

Read the background information below and then answer the questions that follow it.

Background
The questions concern a relatively small manufacturer of a particular kind of machine, operating in a stable, inflation-free market environment. On the production side the firm

is doing things the best it can, but shareholders have been disappointed by the levels of profits that have been made in the past few years. The shareholders have taken the view that this performance is due to inappropriate price and output decisions having been made, rather than needlessly high unit production costs due to poor work practices. A new management team of five executives has been appointed, and each will receive basic pay of $40 000 per year. Total fixed costs, including these basic executive salaries, are expected to be $880 000 per year. From past experience, the executives reckon that the firm faces demand and average variable cost functions that are linear. For example, last year, the firm sold 900 units of the machine tool at a price per unit of $2 000, and average variable costs were $800; the year before last the previous management team had experimented with a price of $1 720 and sold 1 000 units, with average variable costs being recorded at $780.

Debate is now raging between the major shareholders and the executives about the payment of bonuses to each executive, which will depend on the performance the company achieves. The shareholders are insisting that the executives should only be given a bonus on the condition that net profits of $100 000 per year are left over, after payments of bonuses and any corporate taxes, so as to provide sufficient funds for replacing equipment and paying dividends to shareholders. Presently, there are no profits taxes to pay. Three proposals have been tabled:

(a) Each executive will be paid a bonus of ten per cent of gross profits (that is, ten per cent of total revenue minus all costs except executive bonuses), so long as net profits after corporate taxes and bonus payments are no less than $100 000.

(b) Each executive will be given a bonus of two per cent of sales revenue, so long as this leaves enough to pay corporate taxes (if any) and provide net profits of at least $100 000.

(c) Each executive is to get a bonus of $40 per unit sold by the firm, so long as net profits are at least $100 000 after bonuses and corporation taxes have been paid.

Questions
(1) How would you rank these proposals from the standpoint of (i) the shareholders, and (ii) the executives? Provide calculations to back up your answers, and show the effects that different executive bonus schemes would have on the price and output decisions.

(2) Suppose that a profits tax is introduced at a rate of twenty per cent, and which applies to profits that remain after executive bonuses have been paid. This means that profits remaining after executive bonuses and other expenses have been paid will have to be $125 000 if net profits of $100 000 are to be left over. What implications would this profits tax have for your rankings of the three proposals? Again, back up your answers.

Note: these questions assume the firm can only produce whole units of output and that it charges prices in dollars and cents only (no fractions of cents).

(3) The background to these questions makes no mention of the marginal revenue products generated by these executives. Briefly discuss the usefulness of marginal productivity theory as a means to understanding the determination of the remuneration of executives.

Author's note

Sometimes, when I have set this question, students have used spreadsheet methods, or simple trial and error, to find their answers. The question does require calculations to be provided: this should be seen as a requirement that the problem is set up in mathematical terms and solutions then derived from the model that has been worked out. To use a spreadsheet strikes me as dodging quite a lot of this task, given that quite elementary mathematics is all that is needed to set up the various functions and find key points.

10 The coordination of economic activities

10.1 Introduction

Over twenty years ago, Professor Frank Hahn (1970), a leading general equilibrium economist, highlighted in a keynote lecture how little progress he and his colleagues had made in modelling plausible processes by which the forces of supply and demand might eventually produce a situation of general equilibrium in which no one could see a way of improving her/his allocation of resources by trying to strike a new set of deals. His verdict was that 'the most intellectually exciting question in our subject remains: Is it true that the pursuit of private interests produces not chaos but coherence, and if so, how is it done?' (Hahn, 1970: 1). He was, of course, alluding to Adam Smith's (1776) path-breaking attempts to make sense of the workings of decentralized economic systems almost two centuries before. In 1776 Smith had written of 'the invisible hand of the price mechanism' serving to guide resources into markets where people had a need for them, and away from markets where they were no longer required. The market itself supposedly provided signals which would point individuals in the right direction so that their decisions would not all turn out to be horribly inconsistent despite being taken independently. This viewpoint has been accepted as gospel by many politicians and economic think-tanks, despite the contrary view held by many socialists that the signalling mechanism is defective and that therefore there needs to be some degree of economic planning by the authorities, accompanied by the use of economic directives to push resources into particular activities. Hahn appeared to be saying that economic theory had provided no basis for believing that the free market is the ideal institutional arrangement for ensuring that resources are not wasted.

This was a pretty dramatic confession, and within three years Hahn was defending himself and his fellow general equilibrium theorists against charges that they were dealing with fairyland constructions that bore no resemblance to the real world (Hahn, 1973a, 1973b; see also the critical examination of his arguments by Coddington, 1975b). In this chapter I explore the nature of the problem of coordinating behaviour in economic systems that was troubling Hahn. I also consider some possible solutions which turn out to provide foundations for much recent work on the economics of corporate strategy. The coordination problem is barely addressed in conventional microeconomics texts: indeed, once it is recognized, grave question marks arise about the very notion of 'the supply function' that is so central to neoclassical economics. We begin with the broad vision that underlies the work of Hahn and similarly-minded theorists.

10.2 General equilibrium analysis

General equilibrium theory focuses both on the individual decision-maker and the role of the individual in the workings of the broader system. Decision-makers are often referred to in this work as 'economic agents': this needless use of the word 'agent' as a piece of jargon should not be confused with the use of the word to refer to a person or organization—such as a travel agent or real estate agent—who has agreed to try to do something on behalf of someone else (the person commissioning the task is known as the 'principal'). Each individual at any point in time is assumed to have a set of preferences, a set of technological opportunities and an endowment of wealth (including personal skills). An individual in possession of these pieces of information and facing these constraints ought to be able to work out what s/he would want to buy and sell if particular sets of relative prices prevailed in the economy. In other words, there will exist supply and demand functions at the level of the individual. If we aggregate these across all the individuals and adjust relative prices until supplies and demands balance in all markets we appear able to discover the conditions for equilibrium across the entire economy. If the set of 'market-clearing' relative prices were known by all members of the economy, and if everyone traded only at this set of relative prices, supply and demand would balance and people would be making the best of available information about technological possibilities.

This seems such a reasonable way of viewing things until one asks: 'How might the right set of prices be discovered?' and 'Supposing the right set of prices were not easily discovered, what might happen then—what if people were trading on the basis of an incorrect set of prices, would the system get out of control?'. Hahn's fellow general equilibrium theorists were very good at specifying the conditions for equilibrium, but less capable of saying how an equilibrium might be achieved in the first place. Back in the last part of the nineteenth century, the early general equilibrium theorists—in particular Edgeworth and Walras—were well aware of precisely the same problem and told various stories about how it might be imagined to be dealt with. Much inspiration was drawn from looking at auctions and the workings of commodity markets, but the stories were essentially intended as thought-provoking fiction, not as close approximations to what goes on generally in markets.

One solution, raised by Edgeworth (1881), involved imagining that people would shop around and when they believed they had found a pretty good deal they would make a *provisional* contract to accept it. At that stage, however, no money would change hands, rather as nowadays one might get a used-car dealer to put a particular vehicle 'on hold until tomorrow morning' without even putting down a deposit. (A rather similar transaction from the real world is the purchase of an *option* to buy or sell something at a later date at a particular price. Here, as with deals involving non-refundable deposits, a fee is involved and, if the buyer decides not to exercise the option, a loss will be incurred unless someone else is willing to buy it for an amount at least equal to its purchase price.) They would continue searching, trying to find a better deal. Each time they discovered something that appeared to be a better deal, they would cancel the seemingly inferior previous provisional contract and replace it with another provisional contract encompassing the better deal. This process of 'recontracting' would go on, and on, and on, until no one was discovering better deals, either as a buyer or seller. Once that situation were pronounced to exist, the contracts made with respect to it would be declared binding and people would go off and deliver or receive the goods referred to in the contracts. One obvious problem is that this search for a better deal could go on for ever; related to it is the fact that if people are busy searching for deals, they can't be involved in production or consumption. In the real world, therefore, people tend to trade at prices which may be far from perfect, merely to enable themselves to get on with their lives, or they employ intermediary agents (such as insurance brokers and travel agents) to find them better deals, by virtue of their specialized knowledge of particular markets. A second problem is that of deciding that the time has come to firm up the contracts: we appear to need some central auctioneer who senses that there is no room for improvement and orders people to settle their deals at a particular set of relative prices.

Walras (1874) also explored the auction analogy but seems further to have been inspired by the workings of the Paris commodity and stock markets. There, expert traders would be assembled together, much shouting would go on, and yet within a few minutes the price for, say, tin or wool would emerge. No one was overseeing the system and yet it appeared to be able to grope its way towards a balance of supply and demand. Why not think of markets in general 'as if' they behaved like these markets? Given the chaos that occurs from time to time in such markets is often far greater that is observed elsewhere, this might be rather unwise.

We might also be wary of extending the stock market analogy to the economy at large on the basis of its greater complexity and decentralization. Much of the time these types of markets are trading existing assets, not current output (the trade in new share issues is tiny compared with that in existing shares), and they appear to exhibit major problems of instability from time to time when their focus *is* on current production such as agricultural or mineral outputs (the problems of the tin exchange in London, and problems encountered by attempts to stabilize wool prices are conspicuous recent examples). With commodity exchanges, the traders are only dealing with a limited range of standardized products: the variety of shares and other financial titles traded is tiny compared with the range of products bought and sold (remember: a typical supermarket may have more than 10 000 different products on offer on its shelves). The items that modern consumers buy are the outputs of production systems employing many thousands of distinct inputs, which are themselves outputs of other input-using systems (cf. Sraffa, 1960). This input/output problem has a time dimension. At one extreme there is the question that the Just In Time approach to stock management presumes can be coped with: is this morning's set of outputs suitable as inputs for this afternoon's production plan? At the other there are investment decisions with very long gestation periods: a major chemicals plant or power station may take years to come on stream. How can a chemicals company be confident that the parts will show up for finishing the plant or that the market for its output will exist? Will enough skilled workers have been trained?

If we had access to information about technologies, preferences and wealth constraints in the system, it would in principle be possible to run a giant 'input–output model' and discover a set of relative prices that would promote a growth in supply in various areas through time to match up in the best possible way with preferences to consume through time and to do particular kinds of jobs. The authorities could then tell enterprise managers what to produce and reward them for delivering the goods. Instead of fumbling its way to the right set of prices for each period, the centrally directed economy could go straight there, without wasting resources along the way.

In a sense, this is what the Russians tried to do, though heroic aggregations and simplifications had to be made to cope with insufficient information or computing power. Shortages often resulted because of shortages elsewhere due to breakdowns, corruption, apathy or simple miscalculations. The French with their Planning Commission have fared rather better, and so too have the Japanese with MITI. In both of these cases the profit motive is driving the firms along, but where they choose to go comes from getting together and working out priority areas for investment, with (in the French case) banks being directed to put money into particular areas and make it difficult to obtain in unfavoured areas. Attempts by other countries to emulate such methods of 'indicative planning' have sometimes provided evidence that voluntary adherence to the plan is insufficient to avoid coordination fiascos: in the UK in the 1960s, the electricity suppliers acted in accordance with the government's growth targets but few other managers believed them. The result was a massive surplus of electricity-generating capacity and, subsequently, overcapacity in the firms that had geared themselves up to supply power station turbines and suchlike and suddenly found their orders curtailed (see Richardson, 1969).

If we don't have coordination being achieved by centralized free trading or by the government getting parties together to work out coordinated strategies, how do investment decisions get taken, such that society does not waste opportunities? Some economists assign a key role here to entrepreneurs, the subject of the next section. Others assume the existence of suitable supply functions, oblivious of the logical problems of doing so. These problems will be revealed in section 10.4.

10.3 The role of the entrepreneur

For well over two centuries the role of the entrepreneur has received attention from economists who have been interested in the way in which economic activity is coordinated. However, the discussion in this section will be brief: for further reading, I would recommend Casson (1982), Ricketts (1987: chapter 3) and the articles reproduced in Casson (ed.) (1990). Much of this literature, particularly that produced by behavioural economists, has emerged from attempts to uncover what makes an entrepreneur, in order that policy measures may be designed to promote entrepreneurship. Some of this work has tended to stress the role of psychological and sociopolitical factors, taking for granted literature on the role of entrepreneurs in society which focuses more on the coordination issue.

Right from the start, with the work of Cantillon in 1755, the literature on entrepreneurship has highlighted the uncertainty with which entrepreneurs choose to contend. Cantillon portrayed an entrepreneur (or 'undertaker' in Cantillon's own terms) as someone who buys something at a known price in the hope of realizing a gain by selling it at a higher price. The trouble was, and remains, that 'These Undertakers can never know how great will be the demand in their City, nor how long their customers will buy of them since their rivals will try all sorts of means to attract customers from them. All this causes so much uncertainty among these Undertakers that every day one sees some of them become bankrupt' (Cantillon, 1755, reprinted in Casson, ed., 1990: 7). Frank Knight (1921) similarly focused on the uncertain future price that the entrepreneur is prepared to confront at the same time as taking on definite legal obligations. The lure of profit is the attraction of a difference between costs and expected revenue that is greater than that imagined for using one's resources in an alternative activity, but not everyone is prepared to take the risk that actual revenue will fail to match up with a stream of payment obligations. Thus Knight sees entrepreneurs as people with an unusual willingness to tolerate uncertainty and shoulder risks.

Subsequent work in psychology helps us explain why some people are willing to take on the role of entrepreneur. For example, personal construct psychology (Kelly, 1955) suggests that the way in which we size up ('construe') how well we are likely to cope with various situations affects the kinds of situations in which we are willing to place ourselves. Thus we might expect entrepreneurs either to be oblivious to the risks that they are running, so that they are not paralysed by anxiety, or to see themselves as well able to cope with any problems that might arise as a result of embarking on particular ventures. Blinkered optimism does not sound like the basis for good economic coordination. Fortunately, empirical work by Gilad (1986) does indeed find that people who become entrepreneurs tend to believe that they can control events by their own actions; in other words, they have an 'internal locus of control'. This work also highlights the need of role models for entrepreneurs when forming their theories about what they will be able to handle. A rather similar finding seems implied in studies of patterns of business start-ups in the UK undertaken by Johnson and Cathcart (1979). It seems that small businesses tended not to appear so frequently in areas dominated by large firms, compared with areas in which there was a tradition of small enterprise. This finding makes sense not merely because in the latter areas it will be easier to find suitable premises to rent. It also seems likely that, compared with someone working on an assembly line in a giant factory, a person working in a small firm can get a broad idea of the whole business and thus be much more easily able to imagine running a business in that geographical area.

The 'Austrian School' of economists has a long tradition of focusing on the entrepreneur as someone who helps match society's capabilities and wants by being especially *alert* to opportunities (see particularly Kirzner, 1973, 1979, and Caldwell and Boehm (eds), 1992). From this perspective, entrepreneur are seen as coordinating agents whose reward for noticing gaps in the market may be the earning of temporary monopoly profits until others wake up to what they are doing and how they are doing it and then step in (or appear likely to step in) to contest the market (see Littlechild, 1978, 1981). Closely related to the Austrian view is the thinking of George Shackle (1988), who portrays entrepreneurs as people endowed with particularly *creative imaginations*. The entrepreneur is not just responding to a stimulus but is forming new hypotheses about where money might be made, an activity that typically involves taking a number of existing notions and fitting them together in new ways (cf. the writing on creativity by Koestler, 1975). Examples of this include the development of Rollerblades, which merge aspects of rollerskates and ice skates—obvious to most people, but only with hindsight!—and the fact that Henry Ford's idea to make cheap cars via mass production on an assembly line involved the recognition that meatpackers in Chicago were getting low costs by using a moving line when taking cattle to pieces and that he could get the same results in automotive manufacturing by reversing this technique. Gilad's (1986) research is also relevant here. He suggests that one reason why many entrepreneurs come from politically troubled areas may be that political fragmentation promotes debate about alternative ways of thinking: people who are used to debating ideas and policies with others may be less likely to take the business environment as given.

In their keenness to emphasize the benefits of entrepreneurial alertness, Austrians have not always seemed particularly alert themselves to scope for error that arises if opportunities are seen through a fog of uncertainty. Moreover, though members of the Austrian School often quote Shackle's work approvingly, they seem not to realize just how big a difference there is between seeing entrepreneurs as: (a) agents who help economic systems more rapidly towards equilibrium positions implied by pre-existing underlying preferences, endowments and technologies; and (b) agents who develop new products and production methods, creating a new road for the economy to go down (see Buchanan and Vanberg, 1991). Shackle's focus on creativity provides a somewhat subversive bridge away from the Austrian faith in the entrepreneur as someone who helps reduce the incidence of missed opportunities, towards the evolutionary vision of Joseph Schumpeter (1943). The disruptive role of *novelty* in the struggle between firms is stressed in Schumpeter's work: he portrays the entrepreneur as an innovator who overturned tried and trusted conventions by producing something new or new production methods. On this view, the entrepreneur is a disequilibrating agent in the economy, whose experiments upset the established order and change the data of the system. Schumpeter coined the phrase 'creative destruction' to summarize the process whereby technological change is induced by entrepreneurs reacting with yet further new ideas to the damage done to their businesses by rivals who have rendered their existing products or processes obsolete (cf. section 7.12).

10.4 Richardson's critique of supply and demand

The standard story of how the 'invisible hand of the market' results in an appropriate mix of goods being produced may be stereotyped as follows. If prices rise, people will turn their attention to buying relatively cheaper products, so sales of the newly expensive product will fall. This gives us downward-sloping demand curves. For firms to produce more of a product, they will need to obtain inputs. If the economy is fully employed, or if there are structural bottlenecks, firms will only be able to obtain resources by bidding them away from other users. So expansions of output will involve extra costs. This being so, firms will only wish to expand their rates of output if they expect to get a higher price per unit than they currently receive. From this basic line of thought upward-sloping supply curves emerge. Where supply and demand curves intersect is a price/quantity combination at which there is no incentive to enter or leave the market or change one's level of capacity.

Profit incentives (that is, *anticipated* excesses of revenue over expenditure compared with what is seen as likely from other markets) will attract people to switch into producing for markets where supply is insufficient. Extra output will push down prices of output. Extra demand for inputs will raise input prices. The incentive for further entry is diminished as we move closer to the supply/demand intersection. In the input-producing industries, similar processes will be at work and similarly in the industries producing inputs for the input industries, and so on. Given a stable set of preferences for consumption goods, and an unchanging technology for production, supply and demand might eventually come into balance across the whole economy without any government direction being necessary.

Richardson (1956, 1959, 1960/1990) raised some problems with this basic story (a useful guide to Richardson's work has been provided by Loasby, 1989: chapter 6). He posed the question of how a firm might decide whether to enter (or expand capacity in) a market where it can see, currently, an excess of goods demanded over goods supplied, or if it anticipates growth in demand in a market that is presently in balance. Its scope for profit depends not merely on it being right about demand for the product. It must guess who else is going to produce it (in other words, the level of competitive investment) and whether the supply of inputs will actually be available at viable prices—which depends on *complementary* investment in input industries. All the other firms thinking of entering face the same problem. If no one enters, the existing producers may make fat profits, whilst consumer surplus is much smaller than it might have been. If lots of new capacity is created, huge losses could result—either because the product is produced in such large quantities that it can only be sold at knockdown prices, or because a deficiency of input supplies means that many new plants cannot produce at all. From this standpoint, investment decisions seem to have much in common with the Chicken game discussed in section 5.9.

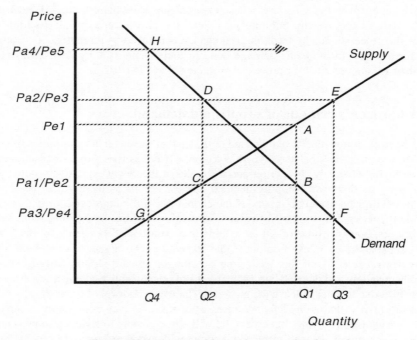

Figure 10.1: An unstable, explosive 'cobweb' cycle

The problem raised by Richardson is the basis of a set-piece diagram from introductory economics, known as the 'cobweb model' (because of the diagram's appearance) or 'hog cycle' (because of its ability to approximate what is often observed in the pig market). Depending on the relative slopes of the supply and demand curves, convergence, regular oscillations or unstable behaviour can be modelled in terms of the cobweb diagram. Figure 10.1 is an example of the third kind. The story begins at A with the producers expecting a price of $Pe1$ and producing $Q1$, only to find that the price they can get for this output is $Pa1$, on the demand curve at point B. They assume this price to continue in period 2 and cut back their output to $Q2$, at point C on the industry supply curve. Much to their surprise, great excess demand results and the market-clearing price shoots up to $Pa2$, at point D on the market demand curve. The producers then jump to the conclusion that this price will prevail in period 3, so they expand their output to $Q3$, at point E on the industry supply curve, only to find that the market clearing price is $Pa3$, at point F on the demand curve, and so on. The cobweb model is typically outlined to show the power of elementary supply and demand theory, not just in the pig market but in other 'boom–bust' agricultural markets and in the construction industry. From Richardson's standpoint, however, what it really does is to expose serious logical difficulties with the notion of a supply curve.

Most economists seem to have managed to ignore this problem by concentrating on current production decisions, rather than on the informational requirements for a rational investment decision. In stories about perfect competition, the individual producer is cast as being so small in relation to the total market as to be unable to affect total output, and hence price. But many small producers simultaneously adding a little to each of their outputs may produce a major change in total output. Of course, if they do so without making extra investments, the losses incurred due to a rather lower price emerging may not be catastrophic (cf. section 9.7 on the theory of contestable markets). The presumption seems to be that, sooner or later, they will get it right and develop 'rational expectations' (see Muth, 1961). But where investments are necessary, resource misallocations on the way to finding an equilibrium may be very expensive in terms of either wasted capacity or demand being unmet due to hesitancy on the part of would-be producers). Producers may, individually, be unable to affect current prices in a supposedly 'perfect' market (which, as Arrow, 1959, realized, itself begs the question of who actually sets prices if all producers are price-takers), but current prices are not what they need to know to take their investment decisions. What they want to know are what prices are actually going to be in the future. The trouble is, for most products, such future prices do not exist in the present: one must try to guess what the other players are going to do, as they, meanwhile, are trying to guess what one is going to do. If the parties do not communicate, there seems to be no basis on which to form rational expectations.

10.5 Essay example: Deregulation in aviation and financial services

Question
In the mid-1980s governments in a number of countries deregulated their airline and financial services industries, promising consumers benefits in the form of lower prices and superior standards of service. However, the most conspicuous sequel to deregulation in these industries has been major instability, with many firms running into financial crises. You are invited to consider both the promised benefits and the sequel to deregulation in the light of relevant theoretical material.

Author's notes

This is a wide-ranging question, but one perhaps best considered at this juncture to draw attention to the possible relevance of Richardson's concerns about entry coordination to those involved in formulating industrial policy. It would be possible to do a considerable amount of research on problems associated with structural changes in both of these industries: to this end, *The Economist* would be a very useful source, particularly for those whose libraries take the excellent index to *The Economist* (the cover story 'Too many airlines' on 19 October 1991 is a particularly helpful piece). In this set of notes I only use a few illustrative examples: my aim is to show how someone might try to cope with this sort of question if forced to improvise on it in an examination context with only the minimum of information about the details of these industries.

A good answer should both show reasonable range in terms of the kinds of economic ideas raised to make sense of the 'before' and 'after' situations, and display some attempts at deeper analysis in a few chosen areas. Diagrams contrasting monopolistic competition price and output choices with those in a hotly contested environment (where normal cost/mark-up pricing might be expected) could be used quite effectively: the better ones would show higher cost curves for the regulated scenario and discuss this in terms of incentives and problem of X-inefficiency (cf. section 7.11). As ever, when undertaking an industry case study, students ought to engage in a careful consideration of the nature of these industries, both in respect of their products and production processes, focusing on the ease/difficulty of copying what another player is doing.

A useful starting point for dealing with this question is to consider the types of regulations that had tended to characterize these industries. Since these differed between countries (as has the extent of deregulation) the main thing to start with is enough background knowledge to put together a broad picture. In the case of financial services, it would be necessary to know that regulations included rules concerning:

(i)   Freedom to enter particular geographical markets (for example, foreign banks were often barred, or could only enter via some kind of joint venture or by setting up something other than a bank, such as a finance company specializing in making hire purchase available).
(ii) The composition of portfolios in terms of types of assets and/or liabilities.
(iii) The areas in which institutions could lend (building societies may not have been able to lend on anything but housing).
(iv) Rates of interest that could be offered on particular accounts.
(v)   Diversifications of activities often were not allowed.

In the case of airlines, rules precluded free entry, particularly on main city-pair routes. Access to terminal facilities was often controlled by incumbent players with the blessing of the authorities. Fares were sometimes controlled by authorities.

These sorts of regulations did not necessarily eliminate competition between firms (unless they created monopolies), but economists were sometimes concerned about the form that they led competition to take. For example, if price competition were ruled out via interest rate controls, banks could seek to win market share at each other's expense via forms of non-price competition, such as offering more branches which were often operating with much surplus capacity (which might lead to a bidding up of prices for prime commercial property), bundling services together ('no account fees' is another way of saying 'higher rates of interest on deposits').

However, economic theory does lead one to doubt that these regulated markets would necessarily provide services as cheaply as might be possible. These are markets where attempts at non-price competition are often easily copied if they seem to be successful. For example, a new type of account may merely involve a bit of staff briefing and computer software to operate it for customers. The main sunk cost will be in selling the account to the public. If the efforts of one bank to sell a particular kind of product lead to general customer awareness of the advantages of that product, the rival banks can piggy-back into this market niche probably without spending nearly so much in advertising as the pioneer had to. In this sort of situation, it only pays to pioneer a new kind of financial service if (a) there are major first-mover advantages (that is, you keep a lot of the business that initially you win, even though rivals match your product), or (b) the volume of new business is so great, and comes without costs in terms of losses from other accounts, that the bank is better off even if its rivals do quite rapidly copy it. Perhaps credit cards are an example here, in so far as they encouraged people who would not normally seek a bank loan to start using credit (it is interesting to note that possible psychological reasons for the success of credit cards have been discussed in relation to cognitive dissonance theory by Maital, 1982, and Etzioni, 1986, 1988).

To the extent that entry is made difficult, incumbent firms will tend to be setting prices with reference to each other, rather than with reference to the opportunity costs of would-be entrants. A situation of price-leadership may emerge, in which all incumbents recognize the disadvantages of aggressive competition and collude implicitly by following one of their number in changing prices or introducing innovations. Higher prices or poorer standards of service may thus be suffered by consumers, compared with what they might hope to enjoy in a more contestable environment. The profits from operating like this may not appear so large as to attract the attention of the authorities if the lack of competitive pressure causes banks or airlines not to bother to seek ways of cutting costs and, indeed, encourages management or employees to push their luck in respect of salaries, staff purchases and an attractive working environment (in relation to this, Australian students might recall that a very disruptive dispute involving Australian pilots in the late 1980s centred upon the desire of management to increase the number of 'stick hours' that pilots would have to work, and reduce the number of staff per plane, in the run-up to deregulation). In other words, here is an opportunity for an essay to use the ideas of Cyert and March (1963) in relation to organizational slack or Leibenstein (1966, 1976) on *X*-inefficiency (cf. section 7.11).

When turning to consider behaviour in a deregulated environment, one might begin by noting that it is debatable whether these types of industries are ones in which a constant high pressure of work is a good thing: these are markets where mistakes can be very costly indeed. We may not have had plane crashes due to aircrews having to work more intensively or for longer hours, but perhaps some of the financial crashes have some of their roots in poor judgement coming as a result of excessive work pressure (consider the stereotypical yuppie lifestyle, that results in rapid burnout). This can be related to discussions concerning bounded rationality in Chapter 2 and section 4.1.

If entry is made easy in legal terms, there is scope for a major coordination problem if entry is also easy in economic terms, as we saw in section 10.4. It may indeed have been unfortunate that deregulation occurred at a time when the theory of contestable markets was becoming all the rage, for most people seemed to be ignoring the marketing side of entry, and the fact that advertising costs, and the costs of staff whose main role is to sell the services, cannot be recovered if a decision is made to exit. Aviation was often characterized as highly contestable owing to the fact that airliners are obviously mobile capital and could often be leased rather than it being necessary to have all the cash to buy them up-front (Australasian students might note that much of Ansett's turnover nowadays comes from leasing planes to other airlines). Banking, likewise, appears to be easy to enter in terms of physical requirements: offices can be rented, joint venture arrangements can be started up (for example, foreign banks can get local insurance companies to act as their agents). If incumbent firms have been taking it easy, and if entry looks easy for these sorts of reasons, there is a major risk of too many firms clamouring for business.

To win or to keep business in a more hotly contested market, it may seem desirable to seek to give oneself a competitive edge by investing in something that the rivals don't yet offer—in other words, make the market one in which the capital requirements are greater, change consumer perceptions of what constitutes adequate service so that the market is less contestable. But if many try to do this, all could get their fingers burnt. For example, competition between banks is not necessarily such a brilliant idea where new technologies are involved: autoteller machines and electronic funds transfer at point of sale (EFTPOS) may have taken off at less expense if banks had not initially tried to set up rival systems as a way to appeal for new business. Major banks often found that smaller institutions could get in on the cheap by forming consortia, or by joining up with rival banks seeking to spread the costs of their investments, so in the end it may not have resulted in much of a way of keeping the smaller players down. Likewise, in aviation, competition in terms of fancier services and better planes is great if the others don't follow, but if all try, there may be a flooded market for older aircraft (and hence catastrophic secondhand values) and low returns to the investments. (Possibly some firms were hoping to get first-mover advantages on the basis of aircraft manufacturers often having long waiting lists for their products.) In short, quality competition can be just as fruitless as price competition: if it seems to be working and can be copied, a quality improvement is just as likely to be copied as a price cut is, so long as the elasticities are suitable (cf. section 8.9).

The contestability literature not only seemed to forget the sunk costs of marketing (which may be very considerable for airlines who are not fronted by gifted self-publicists such as Richard Branson or Nicki Lauda), but also the human capital requirements for easy entry—and so, too, did some of the entrants. Decision rules that work well in one environment may be poor performers elsewhere. This is most easily discussed in respect of banking diversification (lots of banks and insurance companies ended up with weak investment bank divisions, or paid far too much when trying to get into real estate agency businesses by buying up existing operators). It proved hard to find enough competent staff to deal with expanding volumes of business, and staff did not always cope well in new territories. For example, a major part of the Bank of New Zealand's enormous losses came from its operations in Australia. The *Australian Financial Review* (9 March 1989), argues that BNZ got into trouble by trying to emulate the aggressive New Zealand entrepreneurs such as Ron Brierley, Bruce Judge and Allan Hawkins when they seemed to be taking the rest of the world by storm. *With no experience* of a major property and sharemarket downturn, the bank's officers seem to have paid little attention to the debt-servicing capacity of its borrowers and lent heavily on the basis of the perceived value of property and equity investments.

A peculiarity of financial services is that success may require the supplier to know quite a lot about the client, and to be able to keep a close eye on that client's financial behaviour. This may be difficult to achieve if institutions start competing aggressively with each other and customers get into the habit of switching between institutions on the basis of small differences rather than developing long-term relationships with them. Note also that if banks try to attract funds by offering higher returns, they will need to charge borrowers more in order to be able to pay their depositors interest: this may push them into dealing with more risky clients. For further reading on the dangers of applying simple-minded treatments of contestability theory to the financial services sector, see Davis (1988, 1990).

10.6 The Arrow–Debreu solution

Before considering Richardson's own thoughts on how economies cope in practice (in so far as they do cope) with the problem that he raised—which may for shorthand be called 'the Richardson problem', in his honour—I will outline a different, utterly impractical view that captured the attention of some economists around the time Richardson was writing, associated with the work of Nobel Prize winners Arrow (with Debreu, 1954) and Debreu (1959) (see also Arrow and Hahn, 1971). The tale that I am about to recount is so patently unrealistic that it ought to make you think carefully about the costs involved in using markets and thereby prime you up for later in the chapter, where the discussion centres upon the economics of alternative institutional arrangements for coping with transaction costs. If the Arrow–Debreu analysis only has this effect, we might say that its contribution to our understanding of how the world copes with the coordination problem is 'akin to the contribution of flatness to mountaineering' (Coddington, 1975b: 553).

In the sophisticated Arrow–Debreu view of general equilibrium analysis, goods are carefully defined, not merely with respect to their characteristics but also with respect to the 'state of the world' in which they are to be delivered. The latter aspect leads to the phrase 'contingent commodities' to describe goods defined in this way. Sets of prices are assumed to exist with respect to these precisely defined goods, and because goods are so precisely defined, information about prices is the only additional information that people need to possess about them to make their decisions about which goods to buy and sell (cf. section 3.2 and Kay, 1984: 1–3). People are assumed to have in mind lists of all possible states of the world that might come about. They are assumed to be able to attach probabilities to each of these states and to know how they would feel about taking delivery of goods in each of these states (or about having to honour contracts in which they had agreed to deliver particular kinds of labour services in particular states of the world). For example, a house in a low-lying area will seem much less worth having if the greenhouse effect occurs in a big way, whereas certain kinds of crop strains would be very attractive.

Given these preferences and conjectures, people are assumed to be willing to put in bids for the purchase or sale of commodities defined in this 'contingent' manner, their bids reflecting not merely the utilities associated with the possible states of nature but also how likely they believe them to be. For example, I might think the greenhouse effect is most unlikely and therefore sell many hours of my labour time as a labourer working on building up coastal defences to deal with it, if and only if it materializes to a particular degree. By entering into the contract I get purchasing power, but I only have to undertake the labouring if the greenhouse effect occurs to the specified degree. The purchasing power can be used to pay for consumption goods which will only be delivered in the event that particular states of the world eventuate. It might be that I believe a new ice age is on the way and order lots of warm clothing with the money received from agreeing to work as a labourer in a world suffering from the greenhouse effect. If the ice age does not materialize and the greenhouse effect does, then I will have to do the labouring but will only receive those consumption goods whose delivery specifies 'if and only if the greenhouse effect has raised the sea level by X centimetres'.

The Arrow–Debreu tale assumes that trade in commodities all takes place prior to any production, with no contracts being finalized until a set of prices has emerged which balances offers to buy and sell for all commodities. A coordinator ('The Auctioneer') calls for bids at a trial set of possible prices (for example, on a system of computer screens linked to a central processor). Where supply exceeds demand, prices are reduced, and vice versa. Once the right set of prices has been discovered, the contracts are finalized for all time and production is then able to begin. People do not know precisely what they are going to be producing or consuming at any point in the future, for they do not know how the future is going to turn out, but they do know exactly what they will be doing in the event of a particular state of nature occurring at a particular point in time.

It is easy to offer reasons why economic activity is not in general organized as in the Arrow–Debreu story:

(a) The auction process, whereby the set of relative prices is discovered which will ensure all markets clear, could run into major difficulties if any of the production technologies exhibit increasing returns (which are bad news for upward-sloping supply functions).

(b) Technical progress and the preferences of yet-to-be-born people cannot be built into the set of contracts.

(c) It will be impossible to take account of all the states of nature that *could* arise. If people fail to imagine events that occur (which is very likely, with bounded rationality limiting their power of imagination), they may end up being surprised by totally unexpected situations not allowed for in the contracts (cf. Shackle's work on uncertainty, discussed in section 5.4).

(d) Very many states of nature that worry decision-makers will never actually eventuate, so the contracts would often be redundant. This is no worry if there are zero costs of drawing up contracts, but in reality it may pay people to leave the deals that they do somewhat vague (and hope to get by with some give and take—cf. the idea of organizational slack discussed in section 7.10) or use short-term contracts and return to the market on successive occasions to draw up relatively simple contracts based on greater information (such as whether the greenhouse effect is occurring and at what rate), rather than trying to sort out everything by a once and for all auction. Instead of ordering things in advance, people save their money, often not knowing with any great degree of certainty when they will spend it and what they will spend it on. In doing this—in exercising a preference for liquidity—they are not merely doing something which calls into question the practical relevance of neoclassical consumer theory to understanding saving behaviour (see Richardson 1960/1990: 159–72). They are also helping to generate macroeconomic problems. An act of saving depresses demand today without signalling to producers the lines of production in which they ought to be investing to deliver output in future (Keynes, 1936: 210).

(e) Things take time to produce, so production may have to start before it is known which state of the world will prevail, or consumers will have to receive things with a lag, by which time the state of the world could be very different. (In reality, of course, such time lags mean that entrepreneurs have to guess how the world is going to look and start producing in advance of receiving orders).

(f) States of the world may be very difficult to decide upon yet differences may be very significant to disagreeing parties, so contracts could turn out to be inoperable. In effect, the Arrow–Debreu system is a world in which every event is insured against, but we all know of problems insurance companies have with their clients over decisions about what has happened, even with attempts to make things precise via long contracts containing much 'fine print'.

(g) Contracts are costly to enforce, yet default in one contract could cause defaults by other contractors if there were no way of arranging alternative sources of supply because markets were no longer open having already supposedly arranged the full employment of resources.

In the Arrow–Debreu world there is none of the economic uncertainty upon which speculators often thrive: the forward contracts essentially cover uncertainties about how useful or unattractive things/tasks will be in the future, not uncertainties about relative prices or the preferences and investment decisions of others. There is no buying of goods or titles to goods with a view not to their use but with an eye to their possible exchange value in the future. (In practice, much trade in futures markets is done purely on a speculative basis with players not expecting actually to take delivery of or supply the commodities because they expect to resell the title to them to someone else for a profit before the delivery date.) It should also be noticed that uncertainties of one kind breed uncertainties of other kinds. Technological uncertainty is a disincentive for firms to make long-term hiring contracts with workers (unless they can make the contracts rather vague and are assured of an expanding market in the long-term—as Japanese firms seem to have been until recently). This means that workers will face uncertain incomes and be even less inclined to order goods far into the future than they would have been given their fears about the possible obsolescence of the things that they might order. The absence of futures markets for final output in turn militates against long-term hiring contracts or orders for inputs of non-human factors of production, and so on.

10.7 Real-world solutions to the Richardson problem

Richardson suggests that excess entry is in practice limited by what most economists would call market imperfections. These factors may include the following (not all of which are to be found in Richardson's work):

(a) the lack of awareness of potential profit opportunities by potential producers (cf. Shackle and Kirzner on entrepreneurship as discussed in section 10.4);

(b) the lack of ability to act upon perceived profit opportunities, due to inappropriate skills, supplies of finance and other resources (in other words, inadequate knowledge of the production function or inelastic factor markets);

(c) communication between firms via trade associations and leaks to the trade press about their plans—in other words, coordination is facilitated by the 'voice mechanism';

(d) observations of each other's investment behaviour (like (c), this is easier the fewer the number of actual and potential participants—cf. sections 9.6 and 9.7);

(e) fears concerning the difficulties of picking up customer goodwill even if one charges a lower price than established firms (cf. the earlier notes on idiosyncratic products and how they make less credible the threat of market entry);

(f) industrial espionage;

(g) entry-deterring pricing policies undertaken by existing firms who collude tacitly over the rates at which they expand their capacities (again, cf. sections 9.6 and 9.7).

These arguments go against the grain of the conventional view that consumers probably benefit from production *not* being concentrated in the hands of a few firms and from firms taking their decisions without collusion. In a world of ignorance and uncertainty, perfect competition is by no means the ideal market structure. If there are only a few firms involved in an industry, and if entry is difficult, then firms may find it easier to work out what each is planning; consequently resources may not be wasted in over capacity and wants won't go unsatisfied because firms have been too scared to invest. This kind of perspective suggests also that sometimes industrial espionage might be quite a good thing (though I don't recall seeing Richardson going so far as to say this).

As far as the question of complementary investment is concerned, Richardson (1972) draws attention to a variety of practical strategies used as devices by which firms try to guarantee their input supplies (possibly at the risk of forgoing access to cheaper, but uncertain, sources that do in the event actually materialize). These strategies include:

(a) making forward purchase orders, though not always as tightly binding as the kinds of deals imagined by modern-day general equilibrium theorists: for example, for many years Japanese purchasers of iron ore signed contracts which specified how much ore they would take over the next five years, but not precisely when they would take it, which gave them a lot of flexibility;

(b) vertical integration (if in doubt, do it yourself!). Interestingly enough, though officially not allowed, this was a common response of enterprises in the former USSR to the failure of supplies to materialize, for without inputs managers could not meet the production targets on which their bonuses depended;

(c) taking partial ownership of potential suppliers, in order to influence their policies;

(d) developing close relationships with suppliers who seem sufficiently trustworthy to inform of one's investment plans. The suppliers keep one's secrets and expect that they will find it in their long-run interests to expand their own capacity to suit their customers. A firm that encourages complementary investment by another and then tries to 'rip it off' by some devious strategy will run into problems of supply in the long run if it develops a bad reputation because word gets around about its opportunistic behaviour. The message here is that competition works because it encourages people to act cooperatively, and cooperation thrives on competition (see further, Foss, 1994).

Later in this chapter and in Chapter 11 we will be looking at the arguments that have been put forward trying to explain how firms may come to choose between different strategies of these kinds.

Richardson-like thinking by other economists

As I have stressed elsewhere in this book, Marshall (1890, 1919) made much of the fact that resource allocation takes place in a world where knowledge required for decision-making is incomplete and dispersed, both within markets and within firms. He was really wrestling with problems of oligopolistic coordination rather than constructing something which is either a fumbling, non-rigorous attempt at modelling perfect competition or a foreshadowing of the economics of imperfect competition. Within markets, he emphasized the role of contacts and special expertise in aiding coordination (see Loasby, 1978). For example, he noted that, in a small country town, the number of traders will be small, with a good idea of each other's behaviour tendencies, so they may also have a good idea of what might be the appropriate price. That is, coordination is facilitated by fewness of traders, with personal contact and regularity in dealings with particular suppliers, not the anonymity and large numbers of perfect competition. He also noted that large firms may be advantaged by the number of contacts they can have round the world, for these will enable them to pick up information more rapidly. The growth of firms may thus be good for welfare in so far as it aids coordination. The parallels with Richardson's views should be obvious, even though the country town market situations Marshall described a century ago may be rather different from the world of modern-day business.

An unusually Richardson-like analysis of the problem of investment coordination characterizes the work on capacity expansion and contraction of the famous economist-turned-business strategist Michael Porter in his famous 1980 best-seller *Competitive Strategy*. Unlike authors of most texts in his area, Porter pays less attention to the mechanics of discounted cashflow or internal rate of return calculations than to the problems of finding the numbers to put into them.

Porter presents the firm's capacity expansion decision as involving six stages: (1) determine the firm's options for the size and type of capacity additions (firms will only take seriously a particular scale of investment and a limited range of technologies); (2) assess possible future demand and costs; (3) assess possible technological changes and obsolescence; (4) predict capacity additions by each competitor based on the competitor's expectations about the industry; (5) add the figures from (4) to one's own plans to determine the supply and demand balance for the industry and resulting industry prices and costs; (6) determine expected cash flows from the capacity addition.

Any detailed consideration of the cash flow calculations would be complicated by the uncertainties involved in all of the numbers: we are not dealing with well-defined cost and demand curves but ranges of possibilities that involve rival sets of assumptions or *scenarios*. Market research may enable one to narrow down the bounds of possible demand in the market as a whole, and preferences for one's product relative to rival offerings, if these are known. New products present a particular headache: how rapidly will demand switch in their favour? In the 1980s, for example, firms in the recorded music industry were surprised by the rate at which customers moved from vinyl records to CDs. But, as will be clear from what I have said already, it is stage (4) that is really problematic.

Porter sees carefully contrived corporate *announcements* as the main way of avoiding coordination disasters: the voice mechanism, yet again. One route would be to keep the firm's expansion plans a closely guarded secret, whilst publicly saying that one doesn't believe the prospects for the market are very good—the hope is that others will be deterred by these sentiments. Alternatively, one should try to make preemptive announcements of investment plans to frighten away the opposition. Preemptive strategies limit the room remaining for later investors in the market. Porter is careful to warn that this strategy could result in over-capacity warfare unless the conditions are right: competitors must be willing to back down (they might not be if they have better staying power and longer time horizons); the preemptive move must be signalled before competitors make their investment decisions; the firms must have credibility as one which could be undertaking investment of the kind that is being announced; the announced capacity expansion must be judged to be large by competitors and to involve economies of scale relative to the total market.

In my own work (Earl, 1992c), I have taken the view that predicting the direction and style of corporate investments is less difficult if one has an idea of the management philosophies of the companies in question. I draw a parallel between scientific behaviour and management. To avoid questioning everything all the time, a scientist copes with life by using a *method*, a set of basic principles and rules for how and how not to behave when building theories and facing up to results (most economists treat every problem of choice as a question of constrained optimization, for example). If we know a scientist's method we can predict her/his behaviour reasonably well. Corporate philosophies are often revealed via press interviews with managers and statements in annual reports, as part of the process of preemption that Porter advocates. They may also be inferred from studying past decisions

314

and identifying consistent business themes. However, recent corporate behaviour may not always seem *obviously* consistent with past actions, despite there being no change in corporate philosophy: there may nonetheless be method in apparent madness.

10.8 Exam post-mortem: Investment interdependence

Question

'Whether an individual firm's investment decision has a satisfactory payoff depends upon the investment decisions of other firms, as well as upon what consumers decide to buy.' Discuss this statement and its implications for business and public policy.

Examiner's report

This question was set as an invitation to make use of material covered in sections 10.3 to 10.7. I had hoped that it would seem obvious enough that investment returns depend on whether or not consumers opt to buy a product, so that those who attempted the question might comment no more than briefly on the role of market research and how changes in tastes and fashions might prove inconvenient to entrepreneurs. Alas, this often did not happen: many students waffled endlessly about the prediction of consumer demand, or about elasticity and substitution, without moving on to consider the less straightforward aspect of the statement, namely, the impact of investment decisions of other firms.

Of those who bothered to write about the interdependence of corporate decisions, very few actually wrote about the Richardson problem. Instead, most wrote about interdependent *pricing* strategies and regurgitated at length on the kinked demand curve. Some wrote about hit-and-run raiders in a manner that seemed more suited to the question reviewed in section 9.10 and which ignored the fact that if entry and exit really involve no sunk costs then in a sense a hit-and-run raid does not involve an investment decision.

The answers that got as far as the Richardson problem were often marred by a failure to discuss not merely competitive investment but also complementary investment, and/or by a failure to say anything about matters of policy, such as what Richardson's perspective might imply for government stances towards horizontal or vertical mergers. Although the reading list had included material on indicative planning which would have been very useful for this question, nothing on this theme was in evidence. At the level of corporate policy, there was a tendency for Porter's contributions concerning preemptive investment signalling to be forgotten.

Some of the answers that ignored Richardson's work managed nonetheless to work fairly effectively because they took the question as an opportunity to write about Schumpeter's analysis of entrepreneurship in terms of a never-ending process of creative destruction. It was also argued that firms could enhance the payoffs from their investments if they could learn from the mistakes made by others. Another line of argument which *could* have worked was the possibility that firms may harm each other's returns in so far as they try to foist incompatible versions of a product on to a public that then decides to buy none of them until it becomes clear which one will dominate (the failure of both attempts to establish a technology standard for quadraphonic hi-fi systems would have been an excellent example of this and it had been mentioned in lectures: cf. section 5.9).

10.9 Endgames: quitting versus hanging on

The Richardson problem also arises in product markets that are in trouble, where incumbents face the basic problem of coping where there is little prospect for reestablishing consumption at its former high levels, a situation which may include the possibility of a prolonged period of industry-wide excess capacity. The product life-cycle literature has rather presumed that all industries decline in the same way. It suggests that as a market shrinks buyer loyalties disappear, the cross-elasticity of demand rises, products become less differentiated, prices fall closer to costs and marginal, smaller plants are shut down. The competitive structure evolves into oligopoly. The primary reasons suggested for the decline are: (a) technological obsolescence; (b) competing products have become better advertised or upgraded; (c) fashions or cultural values are changing; (d) the product is no longer needed; (e) the product is 'sick' (prone to unreliability, for example). In this section my discussion draws on the rather more carefully considered work of Harrigan (1980), which is an excellent source of case studies, and Porter (1980: chapter 12).

Five endgame strategies have typically been proposed:

(a) *Harvesting* or *milking* is most commonly recommended. The firm reduces investment flows to the activity to generate higher cash flows from the business, followed ultimately by divestiture (this is essentially strategy (2) in the numerical examples used in Earl, 1984: 86–90). This relies on the possibility of neglecting assets without them immediately becoming unusable (like not servicing a car at recommended intervals). The cash generated is funnelled rapidly into new activities.

(b) *Divest now.* Before the earning value of assets falls to low the firm sells them to rivals or even sells them for scrap with the proceeds being invested elsewhere (this is the same as strategy (1) in the numerical examples in Earl, 1984: 86–90). The key thing here is to be ahead of the market in recognizing the down-turn, for the market for assets may deteriorate very suddenly once the endgame gets going (another case for investing in more general purpose assets, as discussed in section 7.9).

(c) *Shrink selectively.* The firm repositions itself into segments of the market that are likely to be enduring and attempts to build up customer loyalties in these segments.

(d) *Increase the firm's commitment to the market.* The idea here is that the firm may be able to dominate in the business of selling to remaining pockets of demand (so long as some do exist).

(e) *Hold Investment Level.* The firm does not seek to dominate the residual market but seeks to match competition by investing in cost-reducing technologies.

Firms may differ in their choices of endgame strategies not merely because they have different perceptions of the situation but for a variety of other factors which I will now consider, drawing heavily on Harrigan (1980) and Porter (1980).

Strategic needs of the corporation

(a) Linked activities may be difficult to shed without raising the unit costs of other lines of production or reducing the demand for other products in the firm's portfolio. For example, if firms produce ranges of products and only one segment of the market declines it may be unwise to pull out of it because this will have adverse effects on demand for other products in the range and make distributors less willing to stock one's products (cf. the discussion of synergy/economies of scope in section 7.4). The very act of closing down a particular operation may have adverse repercussions on the firm's image, unless the firm has acquired the declining activity as part of a larger merger that was aimed merely at getting control of some viable assets.

(b) Single–product businesses are more likely stay in the market simply because managers cannot divest to nowhere without abolishing their own jobs and they may not be confident that they can get a strong position in an alternative line of business. Such firms are more likely to try to sell themselves to a stronger rival or spoil the market with a bitter endgame war.

(c) The internal politics of a vertically integrated firm may make such a firm prone to stay on and fight. Internal customers may be able to exert pressure for continued access to input supplies on advantageous terms, with the politics possibly detracting from the economist's advice that opportunity costs should not be forgotten. Internal suppliers may in the past have been able to negotiate advantageous terms by not passing on the full benefits of vertical integration but may now be prepared to give these up (an example of the uptake of organizational slack), giving the firm a new-found edge over its less integrated rivals.

(d) Managers may prefer not to have to make a spectacular withdrawal from an activity because they will then have to write down asset values in making their annual report. Managers may also find it psychologically easier to let their firms incur a succession of little losses than make a big admission of failure by scrapping assets before they are worn out. The size of the loss will be greater the more vertically integrated is the firm's involvement with the product—production and distribution with the aid of subcontractors may still involve firms in a major write-down of assets if they withdraw, but each will only have a relatively small error to report.

Demand characteristics

If a decline has been brought about by technical change, there is far less prospect for revitalization than if there has been a possibly temporary switch in fashion or demographic structure. The excess capacity problem is most likely to be acute when firms are not sure what long-term demand looks like. If they *were* all convinced, they could choose to leave or stay on the basis of their relative strength, etc. Chances of keeping customers may be enhanced if they face considerable switching costs. For example, when transistors appeared, manufacturers of electronic goods could not immediately cease using valves ('receiving tubes'), for their products had to be redesigned, and in some applications it took a long while for the benefits of transistors to become realizable without costs being incurred in

317

other dimensions—as in the case of amplifiers for rock bands, where the transistor amplifiers could not initially reproduce the smooth distortion sound of overdriven valve amplifiers.

Structural traits of the industry
(a) If the product is differentiated the chances of avoiding a disastrous price war are higher. If the product is not differentiable, victory may be expected to go to the lowest-cost producer. Differentiation may be due more to efforts of intermediaries than endgame producer; if so, continued support from intermediary must be assured.

(b) Buyers will differ in their bargaining power. If there are only a few main buyers they may be able to exert stronger pressure on the firm, making it less worthwhile to stay in the market.

(c) Indifferent suppliers (whose attitudes may reflect more attractive sales prospects elsewhere) could exacerbate problems of firms: why should such suppliers bother to invest, rather than divest themselves of their commitment to the market? Committed suppliers, on the other hand, can help endgame players (and themselves) to find it worthwhile to stay in the business by offering higher quality, faster delivery and being willing to build in distinguishing attributes.

(d) High capital intensity will mean that bigger losses have to be reported by management teams that pull out, the more so the less depreciated the assets are. Furthermore, the lower the ratio between average variable costs and the average of original and reduced prices, the less elastic demand has to be for a price cut to be profitable, so price wars become more likely if the declining industry uses a capital-intensive technology. If the assets are not particularly specific to making the product in question, then managers should be expected to be more willing to pull out; however, if reinvestment requirements are low, they may be much more inclined to engage in a harvesting strategy.

(e) It may be more worthwhile to stay on in the market if products are differentiated and if the firms in the industry have a history of recognizing their interdependence, or not spoiling the market by price wars, and if participant firms have other interests besides the declining business. By contrast, there will be scope for chaos if firms with big plants seek to invade the market segments of other groups in order to use up spare capacity.

Internal strengths relative to rivals
Before deciding whether to quit, firms are likely to examine whether their unit costs are lower owing to their choices of technology and management methods, and whether they have advantages that may enable them to get ahead in the endgame. For example, one very useful engineering skill is in repairing assets and/or making them less specific. Marketing skills may be particularly necessary if one is to build a commanding position in a particular niche; however, one should not forget the opportunity costs of one's marketing

talents—they might otherwise be employed in selling in a new area. Financial strength may also play a vital role in determining who the survivors will be in the market: to what extent are competitors burdened with debts, and could they be pushed into bankruptcy without an unduly long price war? Debt interest and repayments are among the 'paying out' costs which firms must cover if they are to stay in business, and a firm which has borrowed to invest in a more capital-intensive technology may be unable to withstand a price war for long, despite having lower average variable costs. (However, following bankruptcy, that firm might be run by a receiver and be in a better position to make life difficult for others remaining in the the market.)

Different combinations of these factors are shown by Harrigan to have different implications for investment decisions. Increased investment would be worth considering seriously if the firm is either (i) quite cost efficient, or (ii) clearly identified as the industry leader, or (iii) sells a branded, well-accepted product and has other corporate strengths, in an industry with (i) relatively low exist barriers, (ii) few maverick competitors and (iii) a low rate of technological change by users of the product. However, one would not expect it to be wise to engage in a strategy of shrinking selectively if the declining products are undifferentiated—unless this shrinking meant closing down in sequence different vintages of marginal plant of a multi-plant business (see section 7.7). Nor would such a strategy make much sense even if the firm in question enjoyed some strengths and the market had some long-run residual prospects but the industry was characterized by (i) relatively high fixed costs, capital-intensive technologies or high exit barriers; (ii) there are maverick competitors prone to engage in cut-throat competition; or (iii) the product is developing a 'commodity' status (as with small portable televisions which are little differentiated nowadays in terms of price or performance). In such circumstances the outlook for profitable competition is not good and harvesting would make more sense. A strategy of holding investment level might well make sense if the firm is likely to be serving a residual market of loyal customers; possesses competitive strengths; has strategic reasons for wanting to stay in the business and yet wishes to avoid potential conflict with another deeply committed rival by seeking dominance.

10.10 Essay example: Price instability

Question

How would you explain the observation that prices of primary products tend to be more unstable than prices of manufactured goods and services?

Author's notes

This question has often proved popular with students but they have tended to score poorly on it due to a failure to make sufficient use of economic theory in their answers. I would expect the person in the street to be able to talk about disruptions that might affect *many primary producers simultaneously*—for example, the damage that a harsh winter or a drought might do to the activities of sheep farmers, coffee plantations, orchards and vineyards. Such a point is well worth making, with an emphasis on the need for the disaster to affect a substantial part of the production process, but it should not be spun out to form the entire essay. Instead, essays should ideally spend some time comparing and contrasting the two types of industries in search of characteristics that may help explain the observation.

A useful starting point is the issue of product differentiation and how it relates to price elasticity of demand. Primary products tend not to be differentiated; instead they tend to be sold as standardized products of particular grades (for example, wheat of a particular variety, or wool fibre whose strands do not exceed a particular thickness). If a supplier does not match the price offered by other suppliers it will be difficult to achieve any sales at all. In the event of an excess of supply over demand suppliers will thus find it necessary to follow price reductions initiated by the most desperate suppliers. By contrast, for manufactured goods and services, limited substitution between the products offered by rival firms may mean that, if one supplier cuts its prices in the face of reduced demand, the others may not suffer a catastrophic loss of sales if they do not follow suit. This point might be related to material on non-compensatory decision rules from sections 4.2 and 4.3. It might be worth thinking of primary products as somewhat like the case of perfect competition and manufactured ones as being approximated by imperfect or monopolistic competition.

Secondly, there is the question of whether or not mismatches between flows of output and sales can be dealt with easily by adjustments in inventory levels. Primary products may be expensive to store due to their bulk relative to their value, or due to their perishability. Once produced, primary output will tend, therefore, to be sold for whatever it will fetch. It is typically not going to make sense for an individual primary producer to destroy output in a bid to raise its price, for the individual producer is only contributing a minute amount of the world supply. Manufacturing firms may find it far easier to turn output rates up and down as sales go up and down: once a crop is planted, by contrast, it keeps growing and will be worth keeping growing so long as the costs of bringing it to harvest are less than the expected revenue.

With agricultural products, producers often have to take their planting decisions simultaneously for biological reasons. Their land may be suited for growing a variety of crops. The producers are geographically dispersed. Each producer tends to be a small player relative to the total market: this may arise because (a) as farms get bigger, internal coordination problems increase, along with risks of theft of stock or crops—though less so in this age of light aircraft, cellular phones and radios; (b) the take-over of farming by giant corporate operators may be limited in so far as lifestyle factors making farming a family business mean that corporate farming has trouble competing with family farmers who are happy to work for relatively low returns; (c) even large corporate farms may be small players on a world scale. Taken together, these factors make it difficult for individual producers to guess who else will be planting the crops that they are thinking of planting that season. Matters are very different in oligopolistic industries where firms can take measures to study their rivals and can seek to frighten off rivals by preemptive announcements about their investment policies. The work of Richardson and Porter, discussed in sections 10.4 and 10.7 is highly relevant here. The simultaneity problem is present in some manufacturing sectors, such as the fashion goods part of textiles and clothing. However, it is less acute in so far as firms that come up with designs that turn out to be difficult to sell are able to reduce production of these items and act as subcontractors for firms that have hit lucky. As is noted in section 7.9, this practice is found in the Italian fashion industry.

In the light of the formula discussed in section 8.9 on the economics of cutting prices, it should seem worthwhile to consider the structure of costs in these industries. The ratio of fixed costs to total costs may be much higher in primary products: if so, this increases the distance that prices can be reduced without the producers quitting this line of business. Once the fixed costs have been incurred they are likely to be non-recoverable sunk costs. A mine is a great example of a sunk cost, for if it proves unsuccessful it will be difficult to get any money to pay for the machinery that has been installed or the labour time involved in digging it; likewise, once a crop has been planted the farmer cannot dig up the seed and resell it. By contrast, a numerically controlled machine tool may have quite a good secondhand value because it is versatile and small enough to be moved from one factory to another (technical progress is the main thing tending to make it difficult to sell such equipment for prices that are not wildly different from their purchase prices less an allowance for their physical depreciation). The manufacturing industries that seem more prone to price instability tend to be ones such as the chemicals industry that involve high fixed costs relative to total costs.

It would be wise to examine the relationship between primary products and manufacturing activities. In industries where in normal times the price of primary inputs is insignificant in relation to total production costs, a major increase or decrease in primary product prices can occur without making a big percentage difference to the manufacturers' total costs. A particularly extreme example would be the brewing industry (see Neale, 1970: 486–91, which is an excellent source on this essay generally). The price inelasticity of demand for beer has made it a popular target for governments seeking to raise tax revenues. If the hop harvest fails, brewers will bid up hop prices dramatically if alternative sources of supply are not available. By contrast a glut of hops will lead to a collapse in their prices as a few cents off the price of a litre of beer will not provoke an increase in consumption on a scale sufficient to use up all the hops. Another interesting case is the meat-processing industry in New Zealand, whose most innovative producer, the Fortex Company, collapsed spectacularly during 1994. The desire of Fortex managers to keep their expensive factories running, to generate at least something towards their fixed costs, led them to try to outbid rivals to get supplies of animals at a time when available stock was falling in New Zealand following two severe winters and a longer-term switch of grazing land towards forestry. Unfortunately, their output prices were constrained by export prices, except in so far as their innovative product differentiation could give them premium prices. They could not easily seek supplies of live animals from overseas. Because their plants were the most modern they had the biggest debt burden but also the biggest room for bidding up the price of their inputs. This may have been profitable for those farmers who sold stock to them *and* ultimately got paid for it, but it did not enable the company to service its debts sufficiently to keep the banks happy. Though the less innovative firms with higher variable costs and lower debt burdens initially benefited from the demise of Fortex, their longer-term positions would be challenged if the Fortex plants were reopened after being sold by the Fortex receivers at prices well below their replacement costs (there is a parallel with the discussion of the economics of the Channel Tunnel, in section 7.7).

The uncertainties about supply conditions for primary products and their standardized nature make them ideal vehicles for speculation. In terms of classical theories of speculation, this should smooth out prices if the goods in question can be stored: speculators buy in a glut and keep up prices higher than they otherwise would have been, and then sell in times of shortage, pushing prices down somewhat. However, there are other theories of speculation which suggest that speculation tends to be destabilizing: speculators may make more money by guessing what other speculators are up to and trying always to be holding the commodity (or financial asset) whose price is about to go up most rapidly. This is a topic that should be raised with caution, however, because primary products are by no means the only ones to have speculative factors affecting their prices: other examples from recent years include real estate, works of art and exotic sports cars—all of which are products where rates of output tend to be difficult to change quickly.

There is much scope in this essay for relating these sorts of ideas to material in Chapters 8 and 9 on theories of pricing behaviour. At a bare minimum I would hope to see some discussions of how the kinked demand curve might be applied to manufacturing (in contrast to perfect competition for primary products). Kinked demand curve ideas can be used to explain prices not being changed not just when demand conditions change but also when marginal cost conditions change. I would also hope to see attempts being made to discuss mark-up pricing theory, particularly Andrews's normal cost analysis as a theory of pricing which can readily explain a failure of prices to be changed when sales rates vary: 'normal costs' are often taken to refer to typical costs or producing at the target rate of capacity utilization, so prices would not be affected by fluctuating raw materials costs.

10.11 Problem-solving institutions

This section is a bridging one in which I introduce New Institutional Economics (NIE), also known as transaction cost economics (TCE), a rather different approach to the firm that is not discussed in conventional microeconomics texts. It is an approach that has developed out of inquiries into the problems of economic coordination and the role that social and legal institutions such as firms, markets, customary dealings, contractual obligations and communications networks play in helping to made them manageable. Given this focus, we should not be surprised that it turns out to be closely related to the means by which the Richardson problem is in practice made less formidable, so readers should review section 10.7 before going further into this section. It involves an emphasis on interconnections between activities—such as the multi-stage nature of production and distribution processes associated with a particular product, or diversification into partially related areas—and on how the difficulties that managers face in coping with these interconnections may be affected by choices about which ones to avoid, which ones to handle in-house, which ones to subcontract and which ones to handle via collaborative arrangements with other organizations. The key theme is that economic organization is a reflection of perceptions about the opportunity costs of *different ways of arranging and implementing deals* to get things done. In other words, it is a reflection of anticipated *transaction costs*, the costs of finding potential trading partners, bargaining with them, drawing up contracts, monitoring their implementation and, if necessary, using legal processes or other means to obtain redress. An institution in this context is a potentially durable or already well-established way of getting things done: General Motors and Toyota are both institutions but they produce a different mix of products using different arrangements (for example, General

Motors makes more of its inputs in-house, whereas Toyota relies a lot on networks of subcontractors); the McDonald's fast food franchising system is an institution that is distinctively different from a unique, up-market owner-operated restaurant; in the context of consumer economics, marriage is an institution, an alternative not merely to cohabitation but also to using housekeeping services, escort agencies, and so on, to produce particular end results. Habitual and customary modes of conduct are, in this sense, institutions every bit as much as established practices and structures that have legal foundations.

An appreciation of how transaction costs affect these choices provides a powerful perspective for making sense of the existence of greatly differing firms that we see around us. For example, international differences in business practices and modes of organization may, from this standpoint, be seen as reflecting cultural differences on the extent to which managers in different organizations are prepared to trust each other's claims about their commitments. Compared with Japan, America seems a very untrusting, lawyer-dominated society, so it is readily understandable why US managers may be less inclined to do business on the basis of relatively informal yet longstanding relationships between firms and instead end up handling in-house many of the activities that their Japanese counterparts tend to put out to subcontractors.

One of the best ways to tune into the strengths and weaknesses of NIE is to read about it alongside business history material, where real-life transactions can be examined. I would particularly recommend delving into Karl Sabbagh's (1989) book *Skyscraper*, which is based on a Channel Four UK documentary television series about the construction of a major building in New York City. It is a fascinating source of information on coordination problems in the construction industry and how they are dealt with. It includes, for example, not merely detailed discussions of relationships between subcontractors and the construction management company but also a case of the use of 'hostages' which is worth recounting here to give a flavour of the kinds of things we will be looking at in the remainder of this book. Put simply, the hostage idea entails one firm allowing its client a claim on it which will only be relinquished once the task has been performed. It may make an *offer* of a hostage in order to give the client an added reason to believe that the deal is likely to be properly implemented and hence deter the client from offering a lower price as an insurance device (cf. the discussion of the economics of self-control, in section 4.7), or the client may suggest taking a hostage if the firm seems unwilling to move on the price. There is obviously an element of this in deals where it is agreed that payments will be made in instalments as work progresses. Often, in such arrangements, both parties have a hostage aimed at reducing the riskiness of the transaction, for the supplier can threaten not to complete the undertaking if the customer fails to pay up, and the customer can refuse to pay if the work is not done according to specification. In Sabbagh's example, the hostages were floors, actually called 'hostage floors', held by the city authorities. He quotes one of the managers as follows: "'To make sure that the developer does what he says he's going to do, tenants are not allowed to occupy those floors until we get signed off by the Transit Authority for the subway and city planning for the plaza. So I have ten floors in the middle part of the building which are held hostage until we can get the TA to sign off on their five floors and city planning to sign off on their five floors'" (Sabbagh, 1989: 30).

Such problem-solving arrangements would be utterly unnecessary in a world in which legal redress could be obtained in a costless manner in the event that a deal were not adequately implemented. The need for them would also be much reduced if people could be relied upon to set higher moral standards for their own conduct and were not inclined to act in an *opportunistic* manner—in other words, if they were not inclined to pursue their self-interest guilefully by exploiting contractual ambiguities and information advantages that they have over those with whom they are dealing. The more that people are willing to behave in a devious manner, the more likely it is that exchange and specialization will collapse in a flood of lawyers' bills and that social order will degenerate into the 'law of the jungle'. Even members of a notoriously opportunistic group such as the Mafia (whose interests in the supply of Italian stone facings happen to figure in the coordination problems and transaction costs involved in the building project described by Sabbagh, 1989: 186–90) build their lives around certain 'do' and 'don't' rules.

This subtle way of looking at the economics of the firm has grown in popularity over the past twenty years and a considerable body of NIE/TCE literature now exists. The title of this section actually comes from a useful review article by Loasby (1990a) on some of the significant books in this area. Textbook treatments remain rare: Ricketts (1987) and Milgrom and Roberts (1992) are noteworthy contributions at this level. However, much of the relevant professional literature is quite accessible as a result of its non-technical nature: I particularly recommend the work of Kay (1984), Coase (1988), Hodgson (1988), Pitelis (1991) and Williamson and Winter (eds) (1991). The last of these is a book based on the entire Spring 1988 issue of the *Journal of Law, Economics and Organization*, which is a fiftieth anniversary retrospective on the article by Coase (1937) that triggered the literature in this area. Williamson (1975, 1985) is one of the other key contributors—the 'hostage' and 'opportunism' concepts both come from his work, for example—but though he also manages to get by without mathematics or intricate diagrams his jargon-ridden style requires great patience at times. If you do take a look at Williamson or Coase in the original you should do so mindful of the fact that some of their ideas have lately been subject to considerable criticism (see, for example, Dietrich, 1991, 1994; Kay, 1992; Foss, 1993; Pitelis, ed., 1993).

One particular line of weakness of Williamson's work is already implied in the discussion above where reference was made to the Mafia and the rules that shape their behaviour. Although the transaction cost literature is allied to behavioural economics by virtue of its focus on problems that arise from information and complexity, often in the context of a firm seen as an organization (rather than as a 'black box' as in neoclassical theory), the transaction cost research programme as set out by Williamson adheres to the neoclassical view that people should be seen as selfish individuals who will act deviously if the price is right. This is in contrast to the work of Etzioni (1988) and ideas about lexicographic choice discussed in Chapters 3 and 4. Of course, in defence of Williamson's line of thinking it may be pointed out that most moral codes leave *some* room for discretion on the part of those who choose to adhere to them. Within these bounds, they may succumb to temptations to exploit contractual ambiguities to improve their own positions at the expense of other parties. However, the reluctance of people to allow agents to perform services for them need not have anything to do with worries that opportunistic behaviour will take place as the service is being undertaken, when it may be difficult to monitor what they are doing. Rather, a would-be principal's anxiety might stem from a fear that the agent lacks sufficient *competence* to deliver a satisfactory outcome and will be unable—as distinct from unwilling—to offer adequate compensation for making a mess of things. Either way, it might make sense to engage in 'do it yourself', but Williamson's focus is only on the opportunism-based scenario (see section 11.2 and Foss, 1993).

In the rest of this chapter, and in Chapter 11, I will be attempting to present an introduction to New Institutional/transaction cost economics, taking account of many of the recent critical contributions and attempting as far as possible to integrate transaction cost ideas with elements from evolutionary approaches to the firm (such as Penrose, 1959, and Nelson and Winter, 1982) which provided a good deal of inspiration for the critics.

10.12 The rationale of firms and markets

The use of the word 'rationale' in the singular form in the heading of this section might come as a puzzle to some readers: if we think of firms and markets as different economic institutions, should we seriously expect them to have the same rationale? In this section, my task is to show how both firms and markets emerge as coordination-assisting devices because of the presence of transaction costs, broadly defined. Though the application of New Institutional thinking to making sense of markets is relatively recent (in Hodgson, 1988, chapter 8), it seems more logical to explore it prior to Coase's (1937) classic analysis of the nature of the firm.

Advantages of market-based transactions over non-market exchanges
Hodgson (1988: 174) defines the market as 'a set of social institutions in which a large number of commodity exchanges of a specific type regularly take place, and to some extent are facilitated and structured by those institutions'. He sees the market partly as consisting of mechanisms that facilitate contractual agreements and the exchange of property rights by helping both to 'regulate and establish a consensus over prices and, more generally, to communicate information regarding products, prices, quantities, potential buyers and potential sellers'. To illustrate what may be involved here, we can think of the institutions that make up the used-car market. Even as relatively casual observers we may note the following.

(a) Motor vehicle dealers tend to group themselves together in particular geographical concentrations or along particular main highways. This would have come as no surprise to Marshall (1890, 1919), for it is an example of a phenomenon he highlighted long ago and which consequently is now known as a 'Marshallian district' (for a useful examination of how Marshall's thinking relates to modern theories of industrial organization, see You and Wilkinson, 1994). Clustering of rival firms makes it easier for potential customers to do comparison shopping, so although the dealers may have to keep a very close eye on the prices of their rivals (whose closeness makes this easier), this will tend to compensate handsomely in terms of increased sales for any reduction in profit margins associated with not opting to set up as the sole dealer in a particular suburb. Firms in a Marshallian district are also likely to benefit from easier access to information about the quality of potential personnel, so personnel have an incentive to try to build up good reputations by doing their best rather than acting opportunistically:

that way, personnel may become sought after by other group members. Put simply: word gets around more easily, for good or bad, within a more confined space. Customers thus have reason to expect more consistent standards of service if they shop with members of the group. Finally, we should note the likelihood that Marshallian group members and their customers will benefit from 'external economies of scale' in the form of access to cheaper ancillary services since the concentration of business permits greater division of labour (in the car market this would include the presence of firms that specialize in providing particular kinds of mechanical reconditioning services and valet services). Porter (1990) has extended this line of thinking to suggest that clustering may also have implications for relative competitive strengths of nations.

(b) Although used-car dealers in some countries are required to be licensed by law, such dealers tend in any case to set up voluntary trade associations so as to differentiate between members and non-members and hence try to signal which firms can be trusted. Those who fail to keep to the associations' standards of fair and honest dealing will have their memberships revoked.

(c) Publications are available that specialize in providing guide prices for trade-in, private sale, auction sale and dealer sales of particular models.

(d) Newspaper advertisements provide a forum through which potential buyers and sellers can seek to communicate with each other.

(e) Dealers nowadays are able to offer quite extensive warranties on pre-owned vehicles, whilst motoring associations offer, as a regular service, advice on the state of vehicles being considered for purchase.

(f) Although, for many days or months, there may be no one actively looking around for certain relatively rare, idiosyncratic vehicles, dealers tend to hold out for marked prices for considerable periods rather than trying to turn over such stock as soon as possible. This helps potential buyers have a clearer picture of what they might reasonably be expecting to get if they were later wishing to resell such vehicles (see further, Earl, 1995b).

Such a market certainly is not a perfect one: there is still room for taking up time in searching, and in haggling over the cost of changing from one vehicle to another, and still considerable risks due to asymmetries in the information held by buyers (including dealers, at trade-in time) and sellers.

In the absence of such institutions, however, the task of switching from one car to another one would on most occasions be highly traumatic. Individuals would lose the economies of communication that newspaper advertisements bring, and might have to cover vast distances as they sought to find someone who wanted to do a deal with them direct. (We might think of an analogy here in terms of the problem that rare whales have in finding mates if there is no specific area of ocean to which they automatically gravitate to form pairs and no introduction agency of the kind that some humans use to find partners.) And they would have little idea of what constituted a reasonable price that it might be hard to improve upon (note how markets serve in this cognitive role). People who had access to working capital and could easily rent a site from which to operate would not unnaturally start thinking of setting up as dealers or purveyors and transmitters of information if they judged that others might be willing to pay to avoid all this uncertainty and hassle, and that there were economies to be had in specializing in knowing about buyers, sellers, prices and products.

It is hard to see a limit to the operations of markets in terms of decreasing returns to scale. The only ones that come to my mind are congestion and the possibility that market institutions for quality control might start running into difficulties if the market that they served got so large as to be difficult to monitor owing to a shortage of skilled monitoring personnel and difficulties in coordinating standards amongst them. Financial markets in the late 1980s might have been characterized as being overstretched in this sense (certainly, fraud investigators fought hard to keep abreast of some of the devious practices that often lay behind the financial collapses that occurred in this period). However, it might be argued that this was more of a problem associated with the pace of growth rather than a static diseconomy of scale (cf. the discussion of Penrose's work on the dynamic restraints on firm growth, in section 10.13). At the other end of the spectrum from market failure due to excessive size is the possibility that markets will not come into existence at all: for some specialized, heterogeneous products, we may predict that markets will fail to emerge because trade is so infrequent that informational economies could never be obtained. In such cases, individual buyers and sellers would find each other through word of mouth or by haphazard personal contacts.

Finally, it seems that the work of economists such as Andrews (1949b) and Marshall (1890) on long-run pricing behaviour may point us to a rather paradoxical view of the nature of marketing. If a buyer uses a market and concludes a deal with a particular seller, the seller is very likely hoping to win repeat business. If the seller markets the product so convincingly as to win the buyer's goodwill, the buyer may abandon using the market, at least for a time, in subsequent transactions: instead of gathering information with the aid of market institutions, the buyer may simply engage in regular exchanges with the customary supplier. Perhaps, then, the role of marketing is to deter the use of markets and to promote direct exchange between buyers and the seller who is undertaking the marketing activities.

The nature of the firm

Though it may seem natural to try to explain the existence of firms as institutions in technological terms (cf. the discussion of the work of Moss, 1981, at the end of this section), NIE/TCE focuses instead on the role of transaction costs. The starting point is to notice that production takes time and involves a sequence of actions each one of which is intended to add value to the product in question. In principle, each identifiable stage in such a process could be undertaken by a separate firm and that firm might even be a one-person business. For example, although a worker on a vehicle assembly line is normally an employee of a car company, such a person could work in the same physical factory, producing the same physical outputs, under very different legal arrangements. Rather than receiving a wage, the worker could have bought the right to use the particular part of the production line during a specified part of the week, and could be buying partly finished vehicles from fellow workers on the immediately preceding stage in the production process. The worker could then add on components which s/he had purchased from another company, before passing the value-added vehicles on to the next worker on the line in exchange for a previously agreed sum. Quality control at each stage could be monitored by another party, rather as the Automobile Association does inspections of used cars for would-be buyers. In this arrangement, the worker's income before tax is the revenue s/he receives from selling the more-value-added vehicles less the cost of buying time on the production line, components to be fitted and the less-value-added vehicles, along with the costs of fixing up these deals and ensuring that everything went according to contract in terms of quality control.

The physical capital in the hypothetical example just given does not even have to be owned by a single firm that is selling rights of access to self-employed workers: it could be owned by a consortium. Alternatively, rather than renting rights of access, the workers themselves might have formed a consortium to buy the physical capital, agreeing through a somewhat complex contract what their rights of access would be and how shares in the consortium could be disposed of when individuals wanted to pull out (cf. timeshare holiday apartments). In short, huge production systems do not necessarily go hand in hand with big business, even though often they do in practice (cf. Kay, 1983a). So what is the rationale for the firm? This was the question that Coase posed and sought to answer in his seminal 1937 paper.

There is no role for the firm as an institution in the imaginary 'contingent contracts' world proposed by Arrow and Debreu—long after after Coase had written his paper—as a means of solving the problem of economic coordination (see section 10.6). There, one could have huge factories with complex production technologies, that were sometimes prone to breaking down or needing to be re-jigged to produce a changed mix of outputs. But these would not be firms as we know them. There would be no people taking decisions about which outputs should be produced, who should be promoted, who should attend to breakdowns and how, and so on. Managers and organizational hierarchies would be conspicuous by their absence. All the changes in the activities of any production system would be implemented according to contingent clauses in the contracts by which the factors of production had agreed to participate in the system in question. If the state of the world were specified, they would know exactly what their obligations were.

A rationale for the firm becomes apparent once we recognize the problems likely to arise if attempts are made to arrange production via a system of contingent contracts. These contracts will entail major costs for the parties involved in setting them up, some of which might be avoided by other methods of doing business. For example, there will be masses of redundant clauses, since only one state of the world out of many conceivable states will actually prevail at any one time. Such contracts may prevent access to new technologies that were not envisaged at the time of drawing up the contract ('If I knew then what I know now, I'd have....'). To economize on the costs of having redundancy in long-term contracts, or on risks of commitment to an outmoded technology, one can make short-term contingent contracts. But then there may be major problems due to having frequently to return to the negotiation table. An extreme example would be where an entrepreneur hired workers by hour-long contracts that specified precisely what they would do for the hour in question. Production would have to stop at the end of each hour. Worse still, even such short-term contracts could generate disastrous results if unanticipated states of the world eventuated, especially in a highly integrated plant using explosive or toxic substances. An alternative to using such contracts is to arrange production with the aid of *loosely specified* contracts, and use *managers to decide what should be done* and to give instructions as to which policies should be implemented as and when the need arises. The management team serves as a coordinating device to reduce the tendency for members of the organization to take inconsistent decisions about the appropriate course of action: managers decide how events are going to be interpreted by the firm as a whole and what the appropriate set of responses should be, given that interpretation. The loosely specified contracts that bind the members of the firm together may specify termination conditions but unless either side wishes to bring them into play the arrangement will persist without a need to keep returning to the market to renegotiate terms.

Though Coase wrote about the internal operations of a firm in hierarchical terms, hierarchy is by no means essential to the analysis he offered. Non-hierarchical types of firms obviously exist, such as the one-person firm, partnerships that employ no subordinates, or cooperative, worker-managed firms. Members of non-hierarchical firms can operate on a collegial basis, getting together at meetings to work out collectively what they should do, without having to sign any new contracts among themselves. However, it is easy to see that there may be advantages in terms of person-hours spent on decision-making to limit the extent of internal democracy and delegate some decisions to individuals or representative committees. Teams of workers, who had capital to pool together in a firm, *might* hire bosses to enable them to spend less time on managerial issues even though in practice groups of workers find it difficult to raise capital and it is normally management teams that hire workers. The single-person firm is obviously somewhat problematic to discuss as a coordinating device, but it seem quite easy to make sense of with reference to problems associated with using markets to get things done. A person who opts to be self-employed may prefer to be her/his own boss and opt to participate in product markets repeatedly to make a living, rather than to be an employee and be subject to inflexible working hours or a succession of short-term jobs. (The last point is really saying that people may opt to become self-employed due to a failure of the labour market as a device for matching them up with employers with whom they can establish a stable relationship.) Such a person may choose to work behind the legal front of a one-person firm in so far as this has advantages in terms of tax treatment and marketing.

An employee's contract of work leaves scope for that worker (or manager) to try to behave in her/his own interest at the expense of whoever has done the hiring, for it will not specify precisely what the employee is supposed to do. Such behaviour may be possible due to ignorance on the part of the hirer about the standard of work that is being performed or how well it relates to the hirer's interests. If information relevant to a transaction exists somewhere in the economic system but is not available to one of the parties to the transaction, Williamson (1975, 1985) would say that a state of *information impactedness* prevails. Following Williamson, a person who guilefully exploits someone else's ignorance in this sort of way is said in the TCE literature to be acting with *opportunism*. This is an example of a *principal-agent problem* (the entity requesting the service is the principal, the entity performing the service is the agent), which can also arise between one firm and another, or between a firm acting as an agent supposedly on behalf of a customer: in each case, the person putting up the money may be rather worried about being 'taken for a ride' because the agent faces some kind of conflict of interest.

But the vagueness that opens the way for opportunistic behaviour (what Cyert and March, 1963, would call devious 'subgoal pursuit') may have advantages for employers. This is because the agent hired may have acquired specialist knowledge as a result of past experience in her/his line of employment, knowledge which the hirer does not posses. If employers specify precise production targets on the basis of what they *do* know about the production technology, then they may needlessly forgo the opportunity to obtain output that employees would otherwise willingly deliver on the basis of their own more advanced knowledge. If an employee's output slips below the rate that the hirer knows an inexperienced employee could achieve, s/he will be in trouble, but s/he must also worry about competition from other experienced workers with similar 'idiosyncratic knowledge'. This worry will mean s/he may end up performing beyond the minimum level of output that the hirer would tolerate, given the sum that is being paid for the output. The result of the vagueness of contracts by which parties are tied to a firm is thus that 'organizational slack' (which we have discussed earlier in section 7.10 in relation to the work of Cyert and March) may exist.

Teamwork is an obvious area where problems would be likely to arise if attempts were made to specify production inputs (that is, what the worker can expect to have at her disposal when doing her job) and outputs for individuals. We have a problem of indecomposability: marginal products cannot be identified (as Alchian and Demsetz, 1972, pointed out). However, the existence of such problems does not mean that production necessarily has to be arranged by the principal via loosely specified contracts: an entire whole team might be hired according to a complex contingent contract, and the team members could then argue amongst themselves over whether they were doing their jobs well enough and what should be their share of the proceeds.

The discussion so far leaves us with a rather fuzzy view of the nature of a firm. Jensen and Meckling (1976) have taken the contractual perspective so far as to suggest that a firm is simply an artificial legal construct comprising a 'nexus of contracts' between principals and agents. They end up finding it very difficult to distinguish what is inside a firm from what is outside a firm, rather as Cyert and March (1963) suggest we should see the firm as a coalition that includes not merely managers, workers and shareholders, but also bankers, suppliers and customers. All this has been very unsettling for economists who were sympathetic to Coase's starting point, the idea that economists should recognize and be able to explain the nature of the boundaries of firms given the fact that some economic activities involve transfers of commodities and money in markets *between* firms and others involve operations being undertaken in some sense *inside* firms. If a firm is just a legal fiction based around a nexus of contracts, does it make sense to speak of a firm having a corporate strategy? This is a major worry given that the transaction cost literature has been developed very much with a view to making sense of choices concerning the set of activities to bring inside the boundaries of a firm (see Chapter 11). Matters get worse for those who like to think in dualistic, 'black and white' terms once it is pointed out that markets exist inside some firms: internal labour markets, internal capital markets and internal product markets where prices are negotiated and charged for transfers between divisions (see section 11.7).

If we think back to the discussion of the work of Perry (1970) in section 1.2 on alternative ways of thinking, we may find the fuzziness of the contractual view of the firm less worrying. I share Fourie's (1989) view that we can get closer to the essence of a firm by focusing on the *durability* and flexibility of the nexus of contractual relationships which give it a legal status, particularly if we note that through time members of a firm will build up expertise and capacity to work as teams which cannot easily be conveyed to newcomers as elements of complex contracts whereby they are admitted to a firm. As an ongoing legal entity, a firm is, in a sense, greater than the sum of its parts; it is something that could not simply be cloned afresh by assembling a group of outsiders with similar paper qualifications and presenting them with a corporate management manual and set of technology blueprints (cf. the discussions of tacit knowledge and corporate culture in sections 7.2 and 7.8). A particular firm is defined not merely by the contracts that bind its members together through time but also by who those members happen to be and the experiences they have had. This is a holistic, non-reductionist view of the firm (cf. the critique of reductionism in Kay, 1979). As for the issue of whether a nexus of contracts can meaningfully be said to have a strategy, the obvious point to make is that it is not a firm as a whole, such as General Motors or Sony, that devises and undertakes to implement a strategy; rather, this is done by the management team—the team is, if you like, the firm's brain. The particular nexus of contracts that comprises, say, Sony did not primarily happen as a result of a myriad of uncoordinated actions. It was, for the most part, assembled through the efforts of the management team choosing to hire particular personnel and take control of capital assets and seeking to build up relationships with customers and suppliers of finance and inputs. Through time, contracts and personnel come and go and the activities of the firm may change focus, but, as a whole, it can still meaningfully be said to be the same firm because significant resources and contracts remain part of it for long periods as it evolves.

Once these points have been made the idea that we should be able to think about what is inside and outside a firm in a dualistic manner becomes less compelling. Against the dualistic perspective we may line up the following observations. First, there is obviously a spectrum of specificity along which contracts can be located. Some people have more complex employment contracts than others, even though they are members of the same firm and it is not unknown (particularly in universities) for people on a succession of short-term contracts actually to have a more durable relationship with their employers than those whose contracts are open-ended and involve long resignation notice periods. Certainly some contracts between firms or between firms and individuals may be quite tightly specified: for example, in the early 1990s there was a major legal battle over an office block in Auckland that arose out of the unwillingness of a property company to pay a construction company supposedly on the ground that some of the ceilings were a few inches lower than specified. (The interest in the ceiling height clause looked somewhat opportunistic, given that a glut of office space had appeared in the city while the building work was going on.) Yet many contracts involve very little detail, as in the case of a typical customer's contract with a taxi-cab firm: when I say 'Take me to the airport', I may be aware of the flag-fall charge and the rate per kilometre but I leave it to the driver to determine the route and speed. This gives the driver the ability to use expert knowledge of traffic conditions and cope with surprises to get me there sooner, but also it opens up the possibility that I will be taken on a needlessly circuitous route. Many contracts have an implicit side to them based on conventions about reasonable behaviour: these sound closer to the 'firm' end of the firm/market spectrum.

Much business is done without any formal contract at all, with terms being negotiated only after a service had been carried out. Hybrid payment arrangements should also be noted. An obvious example is where a waiter is an employee of a restaurant but who receives a large part of his or her income from tips: this may make good sense to the restauranteur if it is difficult to monitor closely the standard of service provided by the waiter. A related dimension that makes it difficult to decide which side of the boundaries of the firm a deal lies is the extent to which a contract involves repeat business. Where relational contracting or goodwill are in evidence we may feel happier about the suggestion by Cyert and March (1963) that we should see suppliers and customers as if they are members of the firm: someone who takes a taxi from a particular firm to work every day is much more intimately involved with the cab company than is a passenger who is obviously a tourist at the end of a disappointing holiday in an unfamiliar city.

As far as a firm's sources of finance are concerned, we have a spectrum of commitment to the firm as an ongoing institution, a spectrum recognized by an order of entitlements to repayment in the event that the firm is wound up. Owners of five-year debentures sold on financial markets have a well-defined relationship with the firm that issued the debentures, but not an intimate one. How intimate the relationship is between the firm and its bankers can vary greatly: there is a world of difference between a one-off loan for a specific period and a relationship that includes the flexibility of overdraft finance and/or involves bank representation on the board of the firm. Shareholders stand at the end of the queue of creditors and have no specific rights to dividend payments. Like employees, shareholders have an open-ended contractual link to the firm: they do not continually *have* to make new deals in financial markets, though they can trade in their shares when they want, just like a worker can give notice to quit.

The various contractual/knowledge-based perspectives on industrial organization that I have been attempting to integrate in this section are by no means the only body of thought that has been proposed recently to explain the division of labour among firms: another one stresses technological factors. Drawing much inspiration from the work of the business historian Alfred Chandler (whose 1977 book on the rise of big business in the United States is called *The Visible Hand*, to highlight the role of management rather than market forces as a coordinating device), Scott Moss (1981) downplays the difficulties of drawing up and enforcing workable contracts in a world in which people may be inclined to act with opportunism; instead he argues that the key role in determining the boundaries of a firm is played by technological factors. Oddly enough, given that he lists the work of Penrose (1959) as an influence, he does not raise the question of whether contracting difficulties might arise from worries about competence as well as/instead of opportunism.

Moss highlights technological factors because he finds it hard to see how firms can exchange goods if these are perishable, bulky and non-standardized. Certainly a lack of product standardization makes it difficult to achieve economies of scale in marketing, and may deter intermediaries from holding stocks on a speculative basis. Producers may therefore tend to engage in a policy of building to order or selling on their own behalf. But really this problem is an informational one: the idiosyncrasy of the product means that special expertise is required to sell it. To use many intermediaries to handle an idiosyncratic product may not be desirable because of the lack of economies of scale in training them about the product's features, but this need not preclude a specialist firm being contracted to act as sole selling agent, instead of the producing firm doing the selling itself. Transaction cost economists such as Williamson (1975) would stress that there could then be the risk that an external monopolistic selling agent could hold the producer to ransom once the start-up costs of acquiring the idiosyncratic selling know-how had been incurred, for the producer would then recognize that alternative selling agents could not match the cost position of the 'first-mover'. Moreover, a seller who had made such a commitment might also fear being held to ransom by the producer on occasions when production considerations made this seem a sharp move. These mutual fears about a bilateral bargaining problem *could* mean that a market deal between a producer and seller was rejected in favour of bringing the two together in the one firm where the incentives to behave with opportunism were reduced. Those who take a broader view than Williamson of the origins of contracting problems would note, however, that if both parties recognize they are 'in the same boat', each may also recognize that it makes no sense to torpedo the other. In the latter view, a reluctance to use intermediaries in marketing may better be explained in terms of the desire to economize on costs of getting the manufacturer's message across to the selling agent.

Similar arguments can be made with respect to the claims of Moss about perishability. His favourite example concerns the production of sheet steel, which has to be rolled from hot steel slabs. Any disruption which allows the hot steel to cool down involves considerable reheating costs, but any disruption in the supply of hot steel slabs to a rolling mill may also involve major costs in terms of down-time or lost customer goodwill due to a failure to deliver. If both sides feel inclined to exploit any contractual vagueness, and if contractual vagueness is expensive to eliminate by the design of the contract or if it is difficult to police whether parties are acting in accordance with the contract, then the combining of hot steel and rolling interests in a single firm may seem an attractive way of ensuring that sheet steel gets produced in a profitable manner. If costs of drawing up and enforcing contracts were negligible, the perishability of hot steel and costs of down-time/goodwill losses would not have any bearing upon industrial organization and choices of strategy.

The idea that markets may fail because bulky goods cannot easily be passed from firm to firm misses the point that it may be adequate if just ownership titles change hands: for example, the immobility of houses may well account for the lack of used house yards similar to those for used cars, but legal complexity and the difficulties of guarding dispersed, unoccupied properties against squatters and vandals look more likely candidates as barriers to the existence of 'used house dealers' who accept housing trade-ins: rather, we have estate agents who bring buyers and sellers together but do not take title to properties while they are on the market. In so far as bulk (and perishability) makes it imperative that the various stages of production are located in close physical proximity, one would have thought pressures for bringing different stages of production under a common ownership umbrella would be reduced, for there would be greater scope for parties to a deal to observe each other's behaviour.

The message I hope you will take from this section into the remainder of the book and beyond is that, in interpreting and criticizing strategic decisions of companies, the essential thing to be able to do is to consider different legal ways of participating in the lines of business that the companies are involved in and then examine creatively differences in the kinds of risks that they entail. There are no necessarily right answers but we can try to argue carefully about which risks should have been taken seriously, and why. Even if NIE/TCE leaves us feeling we cannot be very precise about what we mean by a firm, we can at least use this kind of economics to see things in the world of business that we might otherwise not have noticed.

10.13 Limits to corporate growth

If we follow Coase (1937) and see the firm as arising out of transactional difficulties associated with using the market as an efficient coordination device in a world of uncertainty, complexity, ignorance and surprises, the question of what determines the size of a firm naturally arises: how many activities will be *internalized* within its legal boundaries? The answer that Coase himself provided was simple: a person hiring factors of production will only make use of loose contracts and managerial hierarchies in so far as the marginal benefits of, as he put it, 'superseding the market' seem to exceed the marginal costs of using market-based means of coordination. The costs of trying to use management systems rather than price signals to direct production include:

(a) The costs of paying for the managers (or, in less hierarchical organizations, committees of workers) who decide what should be done, costs which have to be incurred if what has to be done is not spelt out in advance in contingent contracts.

(b) The costs of measures to cut down shirking and other opportunistic actions by agents, for example by paying for monitoring of work. Even then, as Loasby (1976) points out, it is not clear whether the person doing the monitoring is doing a good job: to hire a third person to check the monitor does not remove this problem. Moreover, auditing is by no means a cheap service for which to pay.

(c) The risks of finding oneself stuck with outmoded capital equipment if one tries to economize on the costs of arranging leasing/rental deals by buying capital items for oneself. Even when a firm is trying to sell up-to-date items of machinery as a result of a change in its production plans, it is likely to discover that the secondhand market may be far from perfect if the machinery is highly specific rather than general purpose in nature (cf. the idea that idiosyncrasy is a barrier to contestability, discussed in section 9.7).

Changes in perceptions of these costs and risks may result in management teams opting to change the set of activities that their firms undertake. So, too, may learning by human factors of production. For example, as managers get better in their roles as decision-makers and coordinators, they will be able to take on more and more tasks without making a mess of things, and they are likely to be under pressure to do so from promotion-hungry staff who try to demonstrate their competence by coming up with proposals for ways of cutting costs or for new lines of activity (see Andrews, 1958). (However, like workers in general, they may prefer to shirk somewhat, rather than to use this ability to the full, if they have doubts about being able to reap higher rewards as a result of success in persuading their bosses to follow their suggestions.) At any moment, however, there will be a tradeoff between time spent in (a) managing existing activities; (b) dreaming up and debating the potential merits of new schemes; and (c) setting about implementing activities that get approved. Attempts to grow very rapidly may thus be at the cost of difficulties due to insufficient attention being given to established activities. Managers may then feel a need to allow their firms to digest all the activities that have been internalized. This managerial constraint on growth can only partially be overcome by taking on extra managers, for managers take time to learn to function effectively as a team and should not be expected to get familiar with their new firm's culture overnight (see Penrose, 1959, Marris, 1964 and, for an out-of-equilibrium adaptation of Marris, see Earl, 1984: 7–16). Growth by merger and takeover may allow the teamwork constraint to be relaxed somewhat, but there may be scope for difficulties if the merging teams think very differently and feel intense rivalries.

Although learning within a firm adds to its potential output, it is not intrinsically the case that the firm must take on new activities and, if necessary, bring yet more members into the coalition to make best use of spare capacity in the existing pool of resources. Spare capacity can be returned to the market: for example, managers could work fewer hours in the firm in question and spend the rest of the week as independent consultants. Machines or spare factory space could be rented out to other producers. One thing which is likely to deter such choices is the costs of arranging deals with new users of resources, compared with the costs of taking on new activities. Another factor may be the impossibility of keeping corporate secrets within the firm: senior management may end up helping rivals in the course of their consultancy activities. (Note how Japanese firms offer extensive social facilities to their workers to try to prevent them from mixing socially with employees of rival firms to whom they might accidentally leak confidential information about their employer.) A technology licence may let the licensee laugh all the way to the bank after it has developed a related product on the basis of know-how picked up through the licensing deal (see section 11.12). Thus it may be in the interests of shareholders that firms they own move into new areas and get bigger through time, rather returning spare resources to the market on every occasion that these become available.

There are several kinds of spare resources that a firm may come to possess through learning. I do not mean merely that associated with the learning curve concept, in other words, the ability of a firm to produce a given output in a shorter time than hitherto (which liberates machinery and the time of workers and managers), but also the gathering of knowledge that may have extensive ranges of potential applicability, in relation to product development, production methods and marketing. Even brand names and trade marks enjoy spare capacity in so far as they can be used successfully as signals of quality of new activities. But contracting problems may often mean that it is more attractive to try to increase earnings by using the resources oneself rather than letting others pay for having access to them.

The kinds of spare resources just discussed open up potential for achieving 'synergy'/'economies of scope' (see section 7.4). It should be recognized that although synergy results from doing things together rather than separately, it is not inherently the case that it can only be achieved if the related things are in the charge of one management team. This is despite the fact that many mergers of firms are often justified with reference to opportunities for synergy. As Kay (1982) points out, *synergy can be traded* so long as all parties to the potential deal feel that they are getting a fair return and do not feel vulnerable to opportunistic actions by those with whom they seek to trade synergy (if you stand to lose little by acting with opportunism but potentially have much to gain from doing so, you may find other firms rather unwilling to trade synergy with you). Internalization may also be preferred where there are fears that the would-be purchaser of synergistic benefits may not have the competence to realize the synergistic potential and might even inadvertently harm the firm whose resources it was utilizing.

More synergy trading takes place than most economists (even Kay himself) seem to realize. Indeed, quite complex synergy trading networks can be identified. The Porsche car firm earns a lot through engineering consultancy work for more down-market automotive firms, rather than trying to use its engineering talents as a basis for breaking into the market for less exotic vehicles. It also lets *some* of its clients make use of its brand image as part of these deals (for example, some SEAT cars have been badged as having 'System Porsche' engines, but I doubt that Lada, one of its most recent clients, will be allowed to do this, even for an additional fee, given Lada's lowly image!). Porsche also has had Volkswagen-Audi assemble its cheaper models to contract, often using many Volkswagen-Audi components; it has even acted as an assembler of some of Mercedes-Benz's more specialized sedans. It is quite common in retailing for a firm with a good product that lacks a well-established market reputation to have its product sold as an own-brand offering of an established company: it thereby saves some of the costs of marketing, whilst the brand-name firm saves the costs of designing and setting up production of the item in question. Harley Davidson makes a lot of money by selling the rights to use its brand name on products such as clothing and cigarettes (Wheelen and Hunger, 1989: 466–7); Kodak sells as '35mm Kodak cameras' products made by Chinon Industries, Inc. in Japan (Assael, 1990: 51). But note that brand-name synergy has its limits: Harley Davidson films and Kodak leather jackets and cigarettes might not be such bright ideas. Technology licensing deals are also common: for example, Mitsubishi licenses its 'silent shaft' engine technology to Porsche, saving the latter from the need to develop an alternative way of overcoming engine vibrations that does not breach Mitsubishi's patent. Entire products may be produced under licence, with or without components being supplied by the licenser firm: for example, before the Mitsubishi Motor Company set up its New Zealand subsidiary, it initially achieved a market presence in New Zealand by allowing Todd Motors, a leading new vehicle dealer, to assemble kits of its cars—there is not, after all, a particularly major difference in terms of skills needed to run a successful large smash repairs operation and a small-scale new vehicle assembly operation.

10.14 Conclusion

In this chapter we began with the problem of how the decisions of different firms might be reconciled with one another under uncertainty in order to avoid chaos and an inefficient use of resources. In answering this question we moved gradually towards an institutional view of the nature of firms, and of the questions we can ask about firms. This new view sees the limits to the size of a firm as being determined by the limited powers of coordination recognized presently by its management team and their perceptions of the costs of involving other parties in the processes of production and distribution. This is a refreshingly broad perspective compared with the traditional approach to the firm which focuses on price/quantity choices or choices of optimal (or satisfactory) production technique, and which encourages us to see the optimal size of firm in respect of a U-shaped cost curve for a single product. It also appears to go some way beyond the work of Andrews (1949b, 1993), who tended to see managers as typically being able to expand capacity slightly ahead of their 'normal' sales projections and who hence portrayed the limit to the size of the firm only in terms of its limited ability to pick up customer goodwill in the various markets in which it is operating.

At least Andrews got a good way towards asking the sorts of questions that interest the New Institutional economists. He emphasized that firms run the risk of losing business to their customers if the latter engage in *vertical integration* and that firms face further competitive pressures from established operators in other lines of business who are looking out for new activities in which to *diversify* in order put their spare human and physical resources to use. Both of these topics are examined from the transaction cost standpoint in the next chapter. Neoclassical contestability theorists have likewise encouraged us to focus on these sources of competitive pressure, but in a more extreme way, due to their lack of interest in the goodwill phenomenon. In a perfectly contestable market, the Richardson problem would be acute due to ease of entry, but it would not matter because of the ease of exit. In the real world, exit problems mean that the Richardson problem is potentially very significant, but informational barriers to entry often limit the extent to which costs are mistakenly sunk in the overbuilding of capacity.

10.15   Further questions

1.   'To the extent that modern capitalism appears to produce economic coherence rather than chaos, this is more the result of the "visible hand" of corporate management rather than the workings of the "invisible hand" of the price mechanism.' Discuss.

2.   'In view of the fact that while economists treat the price mechanism as a coordinating instrument they also admit the coordinating function of the "entrepreneur", it is surely important to inquire why coordination is the work of the price mechanism in one case and of the entrepreneur in another' (Ronald Coase, *Economica*, 1937: 389). Discuss.

3.   'There was little realization [in the model of the perfectly competitive economy] that the elements which had been banished as "imperfections" were necessary, in some measure, for the provision of adequate information, that an unequal distribution of knowledge and the existence of "frictional" restraints were required to make the system work' (George Richardson, *Economic Journal*, 1959: 32). Discuss.

4.   'The mechanics of making a capacity expansion in the traditional capital budgeting sense are quite straightforward—any finance textbook will supply the details. Future cash flows resulting from the new capacity are forecasted and discounted to weight

them against the cash outflows required for the investment. The resulting net present value ranks the capacity addition against the other investment projects available to the firm.'

'However, this simplicity masks an extremely subtle decision-making problem' (Michael Porter, *Competitive Strategy*, 1980: 325).

To which problem is Porter alluding? Does it have any solutions?

5. Discuss the view that we need not worry about the probable exhaustion of natural resources such as oil because the price mechanism will ensure that these resources are optimally utilized.

6. 'The often-heard claim that uncertainty cannot be satisfactorily incorporated into General Equilibrium Theory is completely false. All that is required is the replacement of the concept of a commodity by the concept of a contingent commodity.' Discuss.

7. 'The reason for creating a planned economy is that the market is unable to give effect to individual preferences.' Discuss.

8. Forward markets for labour and manufactured products are conspicuously absent in present-day economies. Why? What are the implications for economic theory and policy?

9. 'The firm is dead: long live the firm!' (A. Alchian and S. Woodward, *Journal of Economic Literature*, 1988: 65). Discuss.

10. 'The most significant implication of the rise of the giant corporation is not the potential social and economic abuse of monopoly power but the potential gains to be had from easier inter-firm planning, and the replacement of the market mechanism by the internal administrative machinery of the largest firms.' Discuss.

11. Discuss the claim that 'For the full understanding of the boundaries of the firm we really need a more thoroughgoing economic micro-analysis of knowledge, one that can adequately handle "the tacit dimension", in Polanyi's apt phrase' (Nicolai Foss, *Journal of Evolutionary Economics*, 1993: 142).

12. In his book *The Emergent Firm* Neil Kay observed that 'The Reagan administration in its first year advocated the market mechanism as the ideal system of economic organization and encouraged corporate merger to achieve economies and an advantageous competitive position' (1984: 203). Kay then claimed that these were inconsistent policies. Do you agree? Explain your reasoning.

13. 'It cannot be denied that there is something scandalous in the spectacle of so many people refining the analyses of economic states which they give no reason to suppose will ever, or have ever, come about. It is probably also dangerous' (Frank Hahn,

Econometrica, 1970: 1). What, then, has General Equilibrium Theory to offer as a contribution to the understanding of how the real-world economy operates?

14. 'Planning and information agreements between leading producers and the government are needed to facilitate investment co-ordination in oligopolistic industries. These should be reinforced by the abandonment of the present competition policy assumption that information agreements in general are against the public interest.' Discuss.

15. 'The elements which limit the size of firms in practice are very largely dynamic elements; it is therefore not surprising that static theory has had so much trouble over the matter' (John Hicks, *Value and Capital*, 1939: 200). Discuss.

16. 'In orthodox economics the market is regarded as a kind of state of nature, the natural medium through which individual traders interact, existing before and independently of social institutions. From this viewpoint we are not impelled to raise the question as to why markets exist. In contrast, if markets are regarded as either planned or spontaneous social institutions the question is raised as to why they evolve, survive and spread throughout the modern world' (Geoffrey Hodgson, *Economics and Institutions*, 1988: 178). Attempt to provide an answer to the question that Hodgson raises.

17. Write an essay on the economics of *either* timeshare holiday accommodation *or* temporary employment agencies.

18. What do you understand by the term 'equilibrium' in the context of the economics of firms and industries? Examine the factors that hinder and the attainment of equilibrium states in firms and industries.

19. One aspect of the durability of firms as institutions is the immobility of many of their employees. Examine factors likely to deter workers from seeking to move between firms. What policies can you suggest to enhance inter-firm labour mobility? What might be the consequences of greater inter-firm labour mobility?

11 Economics of corporate strategy and structure

11.1 Introduction

In this chapter I develop ideas introduced in sections 10.11–10.13 to investigate why firms may end up producing distinctive mixes of products and how they go about organizing their activities, both internally and in terms of their relationships with other business organizations. At the outset, it is helpful to have some notion of strategy in mind. I like Jay Lorsch's (1986: 95) definition of a firm's strategy as

> the decisions taken over time by top managers, which, when understood as a whole, reveal the goals they are seeking and the means used to reach these goals. Such a definition of strategy is different from common business use of the term in that it does not refer to an explicit plan. In fact, by my definition strategy may be implicit as well as explicit.

To some extent, this view of strategy overlaps with the concept of corporate culture, which embraces wider sets of shared beliefs about how members of a particular firm should see relationships within the firm and what they should see as appropriate modes of conduct (see section 7.8). Lorsch argues at length that changes of strategy can be difficult to implement if they are inconsistent with an existing corporate culture. For example, a firm that historically has been committed to quality in both strategic and cultural terms could have difficulties in adopting a strategy involving expansion into lower-cost markets: obsessive attention to detail on the part of workers could result in poor productivity without the end results in terms of finish and fit even being noticed by budget-conscious customers. Many of the core ideas of a firm's strategy are likely to be so ingrained that they are rarely stated explicitly: it is unlikely that Ford executives ever pause to ask themselves why they are in the car and truck business, but their company's recent moves into satellite telecommunications clearly imply that their corporate philosophy has become something rather more complex than Henry Ford's vision of providing a basic car for the typical US family, and to making it affordable by standardization and assembly-line methods.

The noun 'strategy' takes us to the adjective 'strategic'. But in orthodox microeconomics no distinction is drawn between strategic and tactical decisions. Neil Kay (1982: 52) pioneered building the distinction into an analysis of corporate evolution and industrial economics. He adapted the writing of the nineteenth-century military thinker Von Clausewitz to distinguish between these two types of decisions in a business context:

> The conduct of war (business) is the formation and conduct of the fighting (competition). If this fighting (competition) was a single act, there would be no necessity for any further subdivision, but the fight is composed of a greater or less number of single acts, complete in themselves, which we call combats (product market rivalries). From this arises the totally different activities, that of the *formation* and *conduct* of these single combats in themselves, and the combination of

them with one another, with a view to the ultimate object of the war (competition). The first is called *tactics*, the other *strategy* (italics in original).

Kay's view is consistent with that of Lorsch: note how Lorsch is concerned with understanding a sequence of decisions 'as a whole'. By contrast, the standard theory of the firm is concerned with the formation and conduct of single combats—in other words, with tactics. It proceeds as if firms either do not produce multiple products or as if one can safely treat each of their many activities in isolation, only comparing them in terms of required rates of return. The need to consider activities in groups arises if individual activities are, or can be, linked together via some common factor or spill-over effect, in other words, if there is potential for synergy.

The distinction between strategic and tactical decisions is less clear cut than it might initially appear. Is pricing tactical? Not always, as the concept of a loss leader shows. Many firms have to be wary of the danger that keen pricing for one product may cannibalize sales of other models in their catalogues—see further section 9.13. Is product design tactical? Frequently no, for product ranges achieve sales synergy via common features in their appearance (images), and are often designed to make the most of shared components (vehicle makers can create new products by, as they say, 'dipping into their parts bins' and coming up with new combinations).

Although it is tempting to say every choice is strategic in a multi-activity firm, strategies certainly do not involve fully fleshed out plans that take account of all the possible inter-relationships between activities. Some potential for synergy is often sacrificed because because of the management costs that would be required to realize it. Bounded rationality makes delegation and specialization necessary: strategists cannot know everything there is to know about all the activities their firms undertake, and organizations in which everyone consults with everyone else before any decision gets taken are likely to produce chaos. Universities provide a good example of this: much of the potential for integration between, say, business subjects such as economics, marketing and finance is left for students to achieve themselves even though in principle it would be possible for lecturers to get together and coordinate their teaching more closely so that repetition would be minimized and students would have conceptual linkages drawn to their attention. It should also be noticed that even where overlaps between activities are exploited by a firm, the limited abilities of management to gather together corporate resources and handle change means that new activities will be added sequentially, contingent upon circumstances that have unfolded (which may not have been anticipated). In other words, choosing a strategy involves choosing between rival *programmes* of action (for example, 'We'll move further up-market...'), and the *order* in which things will be done if things work out as expected (such as, 'First we'll revamp our top-range models...').

11.2   Vertical integration

Many strategic decisions involve questions about how how far a firm should internalize activities that are involved in producing and distributing a particular product to which it is to some extent already committed. Vertical integration is said to occur whenever a firm is involved in successive stages of a multi-stage nature of production and distribution process. Forward vertical integration involves taking on activities nearer to the final customer end (for example, setting up one's own distribution network), whereas backward vertical integration involves taking on earlier stages (for example, a steel firm starting to mine its own iron ore). Strategic decisions about vertical integration frequently focus on increasing the number of stages undertaken by the firm in question, but sometimes firms choose to scale down the extent to which they engage in 'do it yourself' and opt to rely increasingly on external suppliers and downstream purchasers. In such cases, we would say that vertical disintegration is going on.

It is hard to think of products where there is no scope for varying the extent of vertical integration, because all production takes time and outputs need to be marketed. At each stage in a production process inputs are transformed into outputs with the aim of adding value. The process of adding value takes time and involves the progressive transformation of inputs into different physical and perceptual forms as well as their physical relocation. It normally involves the use of capital items manufactured in previous periods and workers who have previously been trained. Each stage in any sequence of this kind potentially could in principle be undertaken by different legal entities such as firms, individuals or government institutions. For example, a supermarket or hospital does not intrinsically have to bake its own bread (though some do) any more than a bakery has to grow its own flour, train its own staff or build its own ovens and delivery trucks. Nor do households necessarily have to buy their bread ready made rather than buying flour and yeast and turning it into bread themselves. Some do, some don't. In this section I explore economic theories of why vertical integration decisions get taken in the ways that they do. An extensive literature exists on this topic: a survey article by Casson (1984) provides a useful theoretical guide, while Harrigan (1983) provides an excellent set of case studies.

11.2.1 Varieties of vertical integration

At the outset it is necessary to note that economists used to see vertical integration in dualistic, black and white terms: a yes or no answer would be given to the question of whether an activity was integrated. Nowadays, however, many economists see vertical integration in a much more subtle way, and have begun to consider a variety of forms that it can take.

Taper integration is where a firm is involved in a number of stages in a sequential production process but only produces some of the output of a particular stage or stages in-house, with the rest of the output at the stage in question being supplied by outside contractors. This provides a means whereby a firm can improve its bargaining position—not merely because it is partly insulated against strike threats but also because, if a firm can assume that its own costs are indicative of those of its suppliers, it is better placed to understand how far it can bid for lower prices. Some stages in a firm's activities might be undertaken entirely in-house, while the degree of taper integration might vary between production stages that involve a mixture of in-house and subcontracted output. For example, a record company may make 70 per cent of its CDs in its own plants but may have the rest produced from its masters by other firms with CD manufacturing capacity. It might record only half the albums in its own studios but do all of its CD mastering itself.

Quasi-integration is a fuzzy concept that means, simply, 'almost' vertical integration: it denotes ambiguity in the boundaries between vertically related firms. The term has been applied to a very wide range of phenomena including cooperative ventures, minority equity investments, the provisions of loans and loan guarantees or pre-purchase credits by one company for another that supplies its components, and the tendency of firms to form customary trading relationships. The quasi-integration phenomenon was identified by Blois (1972) and Richardson (1972) and we have already noted its role in the process by which complementary investments are coordinated (see section 10.7; see further, section 11.11). Ricketts (1987) also includes under this heading situations in which firms own some of the machinery used by downstream or upstream contractors, or train the staff employed by contractors. Some department stores have up-market crockery or perfume counters which are, in effect, manufacturer's stores within the department stores. Another phenomenon that might be classed as quasi-integration is the fact that although firms such as Qantas and Singapore Airlines do not manufacture their own airliners, they partially control the quality of those that Boeing make for them by having their own engineers on site in Boeing's Seattle factory to watch how their particular aircraft are put together.

The literature on quasi-integration often makes its difference from arm's-length contracting clearer by distinguishing between interactions based purely around *property rights* assigned by contracts, and *obligational* contractual relations based around trust and loyalty rather than specific contractual commitments. Quasi-integration involving the use of, say, a one-way minority shareholding to gain preferential treatment from a particular firm has elements of both arm's-length contracting and internalization and is not strongly focused on the development of trust: the shareholding may even have a somewhat menacing role. Quasi-integration involving a purely obligational contracting relationship may have neither a contract to spell out the long-term nature of the relationship in terms of flows of outputs and payments nor any ownership claims. In formal legal terms this kind of quasi-integration is nothing more than a series of short-term contracts, but in practice one party serves the other more like a loyal employee on a long-term contract. An example of this is where trading partners do business with each other time and time again even though they have no stakes in each other's assets and have not—unlike, say, singer George Michael and Sony—signed a long-term commitment to stick together. Such relationships should not be seen as altruistic or as necessarily based around the 'better the Devil you know' principle for coping with uncertainty. In many cases the underlying motivation for a customer giving repeat business to a particular supplier may be to encourage the supplier to become more willing to make specific investments for produce goods on the customer's behalf, instead of producing them at somewhat greater cost using general-purpose equipment. Relationships between authors and publishers quite often have this form, though some publishers ask their authors to sign contracts in which publication of one book is dependent on the author agreeing to give the publisher first refusal of the author's next work: if the publisher seems to be competent at promotion and distribution first time around, the author may sign up again in order to encourage the publisher to invest more heavily in her/his work on the expectation of having future works to publish. Other examples of obligational contracting include clothing retailers such as Marks and Spencer and Benetton who repeatedly buy their goods from the same trusted suppliers, and the Fiat car company whose new factory for its Punto model is surrounded by the factories established by dozens of independent smaller firms that supply Punto components on a Just in Time basis and whose investments depend for their profitability on the success of the Punto model. Some useful case study investigations contrasting the use of simple subcontracting and quasi-integration strategies in Britain and Japan are Sako (1992) and Thoburn and Takashima (1992). Compared with British firms, the Japanese ones tend more frequently to be found engaging in obligational contractual relationships, rather than arm's-length trading.

Franchising is an arrangement in which one party—the franchisee—signs an agreement to undertake to pay particular fees, carry out particular investments and perform a particular set of operations as specified by another party—the franchiser—in return for particular rights of protection against suppliers of duplicate products and for the right to be the claimant on profits remaining after contractual obligations have been met. This is very common in distribution: for example, before a car retailer can obtain supplies of new Ford cars from Ford factories, the retailer must have been allowed by Ford to sign up as an Approved Ford Dealer; once approved, the retailer's premises will have to be presented and stocked in a manner acceptable to Ford and particular standards of service and rates of sales will have to be met. Closely related to franchising and taper integration is *production under licence*, whereby one manufacturer provides blueprints (and often, components) to allow another firm to make clones of its products for sale in a particular market in return for the payment of specified royalty fees. An example here is Fisher and Paykel, a New Zealand-based whitegoods manufacturer, which makes Kelvinator refrigerators under licence and thereby economizes on costs of developing its own designs. The 'Kelvinator by Fisher and Paykel' refrigerators are then sold in franchised dealerships, whose franchise contracts prohibit them from selling the products of imported rivals such as AEG, but without competition from imported Kelvinators produced by the licenser firm. Franchising and licensing relationships greatly blur the issue of what we mean by vertical integration. In formal terms these relationships may be so heavily structured by the terms of a contract that they seem the antithesis of internalization. Yet the nature of the contracts makes these relationships more like an internalized command systems than a normal kind of interaction between supplier and customer. If I buy some paint from a hardware store I can use it how I wish in respect of my own property, and I am not obliged to read the instructions. By contrast, if I am running a franchised hardware store then I must run it in a particular way in order to continue to have access to supplies of paint, and so on, that the franchiser uses its considerable buying power to obtain on attractive terms. Franchisees and licensees may be running legally independent businesses but their relationships with their respective franchisers and licensers are hierarchical, like those between workers and bosses (see further, sections 11.4, 11.5 and 11.12). It should also be noted that these relationships are often part of a taper integration strategy: most franchisers run a few of their own branch operations as well as putting most out to franchise, using the former for experimenting with new ideas and as benchmarks for their franchisees' performance standards.

11.2.2 *Transactional difficulties as a basis for vertical integration*
It should not seem surprising that some firms studiously avoid strategies involving the internalization of vertically related activities: other firms often have trouble making them work. For one thing, vertical integration is something that it is difficult to explain in terms

of attempts to obtain synergy, for the knowledge and capital requirements of different levels of production are often markedly different. Vertical integration also lays a firm open to being taken advantage of by the suppliers it internalizes (since they will then have a captive market inside the firm) and it may leave the firm vulnerable in the event that the demand for the downstream product falls. The latter fear is why, for example, Levi-Strauss choose to make denim clothes but have opted not to make denim cloth. Given these potential hazards we need to consider what potential gains might lead firms to engage in vertical integration. The answer in terms of New Institutional Economics lies in the difficulties of using the market to obtain deliveries (or sales) of what one wants, when one wants it. This should come as no surprise, given what was said in the previous chapter, where many examples actually concerned vertical integration. (If demand for denim clothes rises and Levi-Strauss cannot call upon a large enough committed clientele of denim cloth suppliers, they might be regretting not having their own cloth manufacturing capacity.) Inter-firm transacting may be avoided due to four main kinds of transactional difficulties:

(i) *The impossibility of finding a trading partner who has a similar view of the end-product's market prospects.* This is particularly likely in the case of pioneering products. An entrepreneur may opt for a 'do it yourself' strategy because upstream suppliers feel it is too dangerous to invest in equipment specific to the entrepreneur's requirements or because potential downstream users or distributors are utterly unwilling to get involved due to their inability to see sufficient demand for the end product (see Silver, 1984). The problem here is one that originates with bounded rationality and uncertainty: you may have a great idea but be unable to articulate it convincingly to anybody else whom you would like to get involved in getting it turned into a viable production scheme.

(ii) *Costs involved in communicating one's requirements clearly to potential suppliers of goods and services.* Internalization of an activity may eliminate a stage in the process of communicating the specification of a task. A very simple example of this is the process of getting a letter typed: I may be a slower typist than my secretary, but for non-standard letters it will be quicker for me to do the typing myself rather than dictate the letter and check that it has been typed correctly, given the difficulties I may have in expressing myself in an intelligible way (cf. the concept of tacit knowledge). More generally we can note that if a subcontractor is used to perform a particular task, a manager in the firm requiring the service must explain to a manager of the subcontracting firm what is required, and the latter will then need to communicate that to the workers. So long as broadly similar types of work frequently need to be done, it may be far less risky and costly in terms of managerial time to hire the necessary workers and equipment and then give the instructions directly. That way, there will be fewer people involved and hence fewer opportunities for the message to become scrambled. This possible consequence of internalization might be called 'communications synergy'.

(iii) *The impossibility of designing contracts that provide for full compensation in the event of incompetence on the part of a supplier or a distributor.* Take for example a firm that makes switches for a wide range of customers. One of these might be a manufacturer of luxury motor cars, that deals with dozens of small component suppliers. The loss of that contract, due to the switches turning out to be unreliable, might not be ruinous to the switch manufacturer whereas electrical gremlins could be disastrous for the car-maker's market goodwill. The switch manufacturer might be genuinely sorry for embarrassment that lapses of quality cause but totally unclear how much compensation should be paid—see, however, point (iv) below. If sales of the car in question are tumbling it may be difficult to ascertain the extent to which this is due to electrical gremlins caused by the switch supplier's poor quality control. Though complaints may be received from disgruntled customers, the voice mechanism is unlikely to be completely effective and it will be difficult to establish how many potential buyers were deterred by tales they heard at, say, cocktail parties concerning experience with these gremlins. One possible solution is for the car-maker to internalize component manufacturing wherever incompetence is experienced or feared, but quasi-integration might be sufficient. If the car maker concentrates its component sourcing with a small range of companies with good track records it gives each supplier a major incentive to make sure there are no lapses of quality: not merely is there much business at stake with this firm but prospects for sales to others could be severely dented by news that it had lost such a large chunk of business due to unreliability.

(iv) *Scope for opportunistic behaviour on the part of the firm supplying inputs or being supplied with outputs.* This difficulty may often go hand in hand with anxieties about incompetence: a supplier that lets a firm down may not have done this deliberately to serve own interests but, once approached by the firm's lawyers, it may try to pass the buck by exploiting ambiguities in the situation. The structure of some transactions may inherently offer scope for opportunism, as in cases where an agent acting on behalf of a principal faces a conflict of interest. Consider the predicament of a publishing firm that uses an intermediary to distribute its books in overseas markets. If that intermediary is part of another publishing firm that produces rival products, then it has to trade off the earnings it can make from pushing its client's products to the best of its ability, against the earnings it can make from concentrating on pushing its own products at the expense of those of its client. The intermediary could try to explain away poor sales of the client's books with reference to the difficulties of selling in this market, difficulties which it knows better than the client. How could the publisher prove otherwise, thousands of miles away from the scene? If the publishing firm is aware of these risks, it is likely to consider the pros and cons of some transactional alternatives. For example, making commission contingent on the distributor selling a minimum number of books may look a bit better to the publisher than a sum per book, so long as a distributor can be found who will accept such a deal. Something which might produce an even better selling effort would be a deal in which the distributor actually bought a minimum number of books for resale from the publisher. Yet another strategy for the publisher to consider is, of course, vertical integration, which would involve setting up a distribution network from scratch or taking over an incumbent firm. This option might well be blocked by imperfections in the capital market and the limited capabilities of the firm's management team. Otherwise, though, it might look attractive since those involved in the distribution side would know that if they failed to work effectively they would be helping rival firms at the expense of their own employers. There would be some incentive for all employees to pull together and follow management's exhortations, even where the latter could find it difficult to prevent shirking by the former within the compass of their loosely-specified contracts of employment. But it might not escape the attention of those involved in distribution that they had something of a captive market, unlike that enjoyed by an external contractor, so they could feel able to take things more easily without their employers deciding to write off the sunk costs of their investments in distribution. Worse still, if there were economies of scale in distribution, it could be difficult to find an outside market for any surplus capacity owing to a lack of faith on the part of would-be clients. So even if in-house distribution employees could be expected to do their best, the questionable services of outside contractors might look preferable to the unit costs of avoiding the market. Vertical integration, in short, is not a sure-fire way of disposing of risks of opportunism. No wonder 'some firms do, but some firms don't!'.

11.2.3 Transactional perspectives on Porter's analysis of vertical integration

To try to help you get into 'thinking transactionally' about vertical integration, I will now take from the work of the famous business strategist Michael Porter (1980: chapter 14) a long list of factors that he suggests promote vertical integration and look at them from this standpoint. Although Porter himself is not writing from the transaction cost perspective it turns out that the factors on his list reduce to problems of information and principal-agent difficulties that are likely to be expensive to overcome via detailed contracts.

(a) *Volume of throughput is greater than the minimum efficient scale of production.* If a firm's needs are less than minimum efficient scale vertical integration forces it either to incur higher unit costs or finds itself having to sell surplus output to its competitors, with considerable scope for market failure due to (fears of) opportunism. Taper integration provides a neat way of dealing with indivisibilities (for example when one's requirements are between one and two times the minimum efficient scale of production).

(b) *Economies of internal control and coordination.* Porter lists things that are difficult to deal with in contracts, such as scheduling, reacting to emergencies, and he notes implicitly that internalization changes the structure of incentives in a situation where contracts cannot specify everything or are expensive to enforce ('more trust can be placed on an insider to keep the needs of its sister unit in mind', whereas 'external suppliers are not so motivated to deliver punctually'). The development and production engineering of new products may be cheaper to coordinate without so much risk of a loss of secret information. Getting subcontractors to make components may also result in loss of secrets, for example, concerning specifications and manufacturing tolerances.

(c) *Economies of information.* A problem with using independent distributors, for example, is that they may adjust their stock levels as demand changes, thereby not transmitting information back up the system about the change. However, Porter fails to consider the possibility of trading information when he talks about spreading the fixed costs of monitoring the end market and predicting supply over all parts of an integrated firm.

(d) *Economies of avoiding the market.* Here Porter (1980: 304) is taking a rather narrow view of the importance of transaction costs:

> By integrating the firm can potentially save on some of the selling, price shopping, negotiating and transaction costs of market transactions. Although there will usually be some negotiating in internal transactions its cost should not be nearly as great as that of selling to or purchasing from outside parties. No sales force and no marketing or purchasing departments are needed. Moreover, advertising is unnecessary as are other marketing costs.

(e) *Economies of stable relationships.* Removal of the risk of being dropped by customers will encourage internalized supplier to 'tune' its product more specifically for the user. Note here, however, the possible use of long-term contracts, or quasi-integration, as alternative means towards this end.

(f) *Vertical integration as a 'Tap into Technology' that is crucial to the base business.* For example, 'Many mainframe/mini computer firms have engaged in backward integration to get a better understanding of semi-conductor technology'. The problem that is promoting vertical integration here is either the existence of barriers—secrecy or tacit knowledge—to purchasing such an understanding 'off the shelf', or an expectation that creative thinking may occur as a result of a firm's personnel being involved at both levels. Novel ideas and fully specified contracts do not go together.

(g) *Assurance of supply and demand.* This is basically the same argument considered in earlier discussions in relation to risks of disruptions. It relates also to fears of the market not having enough capacity due to effects of the Richardson problem, which would not arise in a world of forward contracting.

(h) *Offset bargaining power.* If there is no effective choice of alternative trading partner the market provides no way of countering rip-off activities. Opportunistic inclinations of monopolistic suppliers might not be restrained by their customers merely threatening to internalize the activity if monopolists do not judge their customers competent enough to carry out their threats. The transaction cost literature portrays bargaining problems as prone to lead to internalization even if a buyer initially has a large number of potential suppliers among which to choose. Potential traders may realize that whoever gets the initial contract may end up in a curious bargaining position when the contract comes up for renewal. On the one hand, the 'first-mover' may have inside knowledge against which inexperienced would-be contractors cannot compete. If a firm anticipates running into this sort of situation it may be inclined to engage in vertical integration to internalize the first-mover's advantage. On the other hand, the firm may have trouble finding willing suppliers because *its* bargaining power after the first round is seen as unduly great in prospect: if a successful subcontractor has to make commitments to specific capital investments, it could be vulnerable if the customer company threatened to go elsewhere. These difficulties could be avoided if long-term contingent contracts between customer and supplier could be used in place of a series of short-term contracts. However, these might be seen as difficult to construct and unduly likely to fail owing to opportunistic behaviour in the face of ambiguities about which state of the world had eventuated (see section 10.6).

(i) *Enhanced ability to differentiate.* Vertical integration may give 'better control of channels of distribution in order to offer superior service or provide opportunities for differentiation through in-house manufacture of proprietary components' (under licence?). If contracts with outsiders were fully specified and things were done to order this would not provide a rationale for vertical integration.

(j) *Elevate mobility/entry barriers.* Note, though, that if transaction costs were lower, this could be done without vertical integration, via a series of long-term contracts with suppliers and distributors.

(k) *Use a vertical integration strategy to enter a higher return business.* This involves putting more of one's eggs in the same basket and seems ultimately to reduce to a response to deficiencies in the capital market: an alternative would be to give the funds back to shareholders as dividends, and leave it up to them whether or not to place the money with established firms in these lucrative upstream or downstream areas.

(l) *Defend against foreclosure* (in other words, against integration by others). This seems to reduce to the sorts of issues raised under earlier headings, such as assurance of supply.

11.2.4 *Vertical integration and the product life-cycle*

To end this discussion I would like to emphasize that it is unwise to assume that the extent of vertical integration will remain constant through the life-cycle of the end product. However, theorists have been divided about the relationship between vertical integration and product life-cycles. Morris Silver (1984) argues that, when technologies are uncertain and rapidly evolving, improved coordination is possible if different stages of production take place within a single firm. A more important possibility is that technological breakthroughs can be kept secret from competitors if knowledge relating to them is not traded to other firms involved in different levels of the production process and who might collaborate with a third party or integrate themselves to produce a rival product. However, as knowledge of the basis of a successful line of business begins to seep out, strategists may decide upon a disintegration strategy, selling off or closing down some of their operations and increasingly making use of outside contractors.

A rather different conclusion is reached by Kathryn Harrigan (1983), even though she also focuses on problems of knowledge and uncertainty. She recognizes that early in the life of a product vertical integration could be seen as a means to reduce customer uncertainties by undertaking risks that no other supplier or distributor would perform or by creating a new way of reaching the customer. However, she contends that in most cases specialized suppliers are better suited to do these things for the firm *until* uncertainties concerning market acceptance of the product and its viability are resolved. In this way the firm avoids putting too many of its eggs in the one basket.

Harrigan argues that, in general, predictability of an industry promotes vertical integration (this seems a bit odd from the standpoint of transaction cost theory, since stability means there should be few changes to have to write into contracts and customary dealing relationships can be built up). Early on, joint ventures are a way of enabling risks to be spread. As a product takes off, taper integration lets firms keep abreast of what is going on in the market, within parameters that are now relatively established. Integration is less hazardous once demand is expected to last longer than the depreciation life of the physical capital. In an established industry vertical integration may be increased as highly specialized production methods tend to require guaranteed throughput if an acceptable rate of return is going to be achieved. If the product seems to be coming to the end of its life it may pay to get out of some stages of the upstream production process both to dispose of assets before it is too late and to be able to get a better deal from desperate suppliers. It may be possible to gain an edge in an endgame by integrating forward to get a better control over factors affecting customer loyalty and more immediate access to market intelligence, but the risks of increasing commitment to a dying market should be obvious.

Whatever the life-cycle stage a product is in, we should recognize that factors internal to firms that produce it may affect their propensity to engage in vertical integration. Divisions may avoid buying from rival sister units for opportunistic reasons, even though it would help the operations of the company as a whole (cf. section 11.7).

11.3   Essay example: The international removals business

Question
The firms involved in the international removals business differ greatly in terms of the extent to which they make vertical integration central to their strategies. Some rely heavily on the use of specialist subcontractors; others have removal depots all around the world and even own the ships upon which containers of household effects are transported. Sometimes strategies of a single firm even differ from country to country: for example, in one country they may own their own trucks and employ the staff who do the packing and unpacking, whereas in another country the warehouse may make use of subcontracted teams who use their own vehicles painted in the livery of the company to whom they are subcontracted. To what extent does the transaction cost analysis of corporate strategies help us to make sense of such diverse choices?

Author's notes
I set this question, and hoped to be able to work out an answer, as someone who has several times been a customer in this market, first moving from Scotland to Tasmania and then across the Tasman Sea to Christchurch in New Zealand. Each time, I talked with staff from the firms with whom I dealt and discovered how different were the strategies involved. I was interested to see just how close were the quotations of the well-known firms from whom I sought estimates; it had also been interesting, between the two moves, to hear of the troubles—including difficulties in obtaining redress when a dispute arose—that friends and

colleagues had encountered when dealing with similar moves whilst trying not to pay the prices quoted by the well-known firms and hence using less well-known operators. These snippets of information colour both the question and the notes that follow.

This is a significant product for consumers: changing countries is a very expensive activity and many people have great psychological commitments to the contents of their homes. Costs of an unfortunate choice of removalist may be considerable, such as damage to possessions (note that insurance contracts may leave room for debate about compensation and will not normally compensate for the inconvenience that damage causes) or delays in arrival (which may cause chaos for a family trying to decide what to do about renting/ buying a home and the timing of completion dates for house purchase deals). This seems to imply that a major focus should be the issue of *quality control*.

The types of people who move internationally may do so more than once, and move in social circles comprising people with international experience of moving. If consumers have heard about disasters that have befallen others, or have had bad experiences themselves, then they may well be aware that a major problem area is likely to be over the issue of who is to blame. If one is dealing with a variety of firms, each acting as agents for the firm that handles the first stage of the move, they may all be inclined to blame each other for poor results. Consumers may therefore feel happier to deal with a firm that can point to its own international network of subsidiaries or franchises or some other form of corporate network (Pickfords, for example, is a group of independent but linked firms). International brand names may count for a lot for picking up customers and any errors may get talked about resulting in many lost sales, so well-known companies have a stronger incentive to maintain excellent quality control. Internalization may be a means of reducing the chance of errors by getting participants in a move to recognize the damage that lax work can do for the company's long-term prospects. Possibly the chance for error is reduced by having internal coordination within the one firm whose workers have a common philosophy and which enjoys an integrated information system.

People using the services of these companies may be able to group them on the basis of their likely non-price performance, as a result of reading their brochures, talking with friends, picking up signals from Yellow Pages (are they members of the appropriate trade association?). This gives them scope for opportunistic behaviour when getting quotations if their new employers are to pay the bills. If they work on the presumption that internationally well-known brand names are more reliable but are likely to be more expensive, they may choose to get quotations only from firms that they perceive to be roughly identical in non-price terms and then be forced by their employers to use the rule 'choose the cheapest'. This sort of behaviour would mean that success could depend crucially on being able to achieve lower costs than one's rivals.

Vertical integration strategies pose a dilemma here: owing to the vagaries of patterns of trade and directions in which people wish to move, it may sometimes be cheapest to make use of outside contractors (such as shipping lines) who are bidding against each other for business rather than having money tied up in capital which is infrequently used. The best quotation may come from a firm whose managers are experts at shopping around and who develop a good idea of which contractors they can rely upon to build up a good reputation. On other occasions it may seem far better to be vertically integrated. For example, in respect of my trans-Tasman move I was informed that the Ansett Transport Group in

351

Australia owns Union Bulkships as well as Ansett Wridgeways International Removals, whereas Downard Pickfords in Australia does not run its own shipping services. Pickfords might find themselves wanting to get container space across the Tasman Sea and find that they are dealing with a shipping line owned by a major competitor. However, Pickfords has a Christchurch affiliate whereas Ansett uses local firms. Ansett is less likely than Pickfords to be able to get repeat business when someone whom it has moved across the Tasman Sea wishes to move elsewhere.

Different sizes of markets may affect companies' choices about how to organize their affairs in different parts of the world. In a small, erratic market, it may seem attractive to try to pass risks of shortages of business on to subcontractors and pay them fees on a piece-rate basis and for the amount of use made of their trucks, whilst having employees share the packing work with them to ensure quality control. In this situation one might worry about the subcontractor being tempted, after a while, to go it alone in the removals business (particularly on domestic removals, if not internationally) on the basis of insights acquired from working with another firm. Some transaction costs theorists might argue that on frequently requested removals runs there will be economies to be had from bringing all the business within one firm, but against this one might argue that experience should make it easier to work out relatively standardized arrangements with subcontractors who have turned out to be reliable. So long as the flow of business seems mutually beneficial, each end of the chain has good reason for expecting the other party not to act with opportunism.

Since this is a business where there are potentially lots of different ways of achieving delivery, and since not everybody may be able to get their employers to pay risk premiums that may go with having an international firm doing the moving, we probably shouldn't be surprised that there exists a cheaper part of the market based around mainly local small removalists in different countries who trade with each other and whose worry is more about re-buy business from other removalists than from customers (because of their lack of an international brand name). Their main problem is building up a suitable information network, but we should expect specialist freight-forwarding agencies to exist to help them get together.

11.4   Franchising: a case study of McDonald's economics

Franchising was pioneered by Singer Sewing Machine Company as a way of taking the risk out of building a distribution system by getting local investors to lay out most of the capital. Further major contributions came from General Motors during the inter-war period in order to assist the automobile's take-off as an item of mass consumption financed by hire purchase (see Sloan, 1965). For a fee, the franchiser firm shares with inexperienced regional operators its investment in developing a production and distribution system. Franchises also benefit in many cases from operating and marketing economies associated with being part of a larger system. Franchising can thus appear to be a relatively risk-free way of getting started in business that looks especially appealing to those who have lost their jobs and want to use their redundancy cheques to start a business of their own—though sometimes, of course, the small investor's risk is actually substantial because the franchiser has not developed the system well enough to ensure that everyone involved wins. McDonald's is the most famous example; others include Benetton, The Body Shop, Coca Cola, Tie Rack, Sock Shop, Kentucky Fried Chicken, leading car-rental companies such as Avis and Budget and many new vehicle dealerships. It is also to be found in petrol retailing, car exhaust and brake repairs, carpet cleaning, hardware stores (Mitre 10 in Australia and New Zealand), and real estate agencies (Century 21, for example). Even university education is sometimes organized internationally on a franchise basis. Although franchising is a common form of economic organization it has received surprisingly little attention in the economics literature. The text by Ricketts (1987) is one of the few to discuss it, and draws heavily on a paper by Rubin (1978). Recently Dnes (1992) has provided an invaluable set of case studies of franchising strategies. In this section, however, I explore the success of McDonald's and use Australian examples to show how the McDonald's empire has been expanded on an international basis. My main additional source is Love's (1986) book on McDonald's and articles in the *Weekend Australian* (8–9 November 1986, on Love's book; and 8–9 October 1988: 30, an article by Adam Shand called 'The Fast Food Route to Riches').

Franchise operations have a great appeal to a mobile public that has trouble distinguishing between good, bad and indifferent suppliers of particular kinds of products. Busy shoppers may be prepared to pay a premium price to economize on search costs and cut down the risk of a poor product. A successful franchise arrangement ensures that whichever branch a consumer happens to visit the quality of the product and standard of service can be taken for granted. Not only may this uniformity enable a higher price to be charged (as a no-risk premium), but also the costs of bringing the product to the customer are kept down by the great purchasing economies which the mother company can engage in on behalf of its franchisees: its bargaining clout may be considerable in respect of advertising media buying or the purchase of raw materials, packaging items and so on. A heavy investment in perfecting the product and advertising campaigns may be spread very widely.

The statistics for McDonald's are quite staggering: the chain captures 17 per cent of all restaurant visits in the United States and 7.3 per cent of all money spent by Americans eating out (19.5 per cent of the $45 billion fast-food market in the United States), is the largest US purchaser of beef, and purchases 7.5 per cent of the entire US potato crop for its US outlets, spending $400 million a year on promotion. The 412 McDonald's franchises in Australia achieved a turnover of $450 million in 1987. Finding the best frying temperature for each frying vat and the best potato (which turned out to be a 3-week cured No. 1 Idaho Russet) did not come cheaply—in attempting to optimize the quality of its French fries, the McDonald's company spent $3 million on research and development.

Such demand and cost conditions may appear to make owning a franchise like having a licence to print money, especially since the success rate of new franchisees in well-established systems is remarkably high. (In the first 17 years of McDonald's operations in Australia, only three were forced to close.) Not surprisingly, therefore, the best franchises are difficult to get. In Australia McDonald's only interviews 25 of the thousands of unsolicited applicants it gets each year, and only gives ten new licences annually. Successful interviewees are required to possess entrepreneurial initiative and be highly self-motivated and be able to raise almost $1 million in capital, of which at least 45 per cent must not be borrowed. This $1 million does not cover the cost of the sites, which the franchisees rent from McDonald's. It is there to cover a security deposit, the signs, furniture, kitchen equipment and starting inventory. (To keep entry easy for potential good managers, however, a leasing arrangement was developed whereby all the furniture and equipment could be leased from the company. About half of new operators enter this way.) Despite these entry costs, some franchisees actually operate several sites. McDonald's only owns 245 of its units. By way of comparison, Kentucky Fried Chicken is cheaper to join (about $600 000 in Australia) but has only recently entered the individual franchising arena: until 1987, all KFC operations in Australia were owned by KFC itself (270) or were franchised to large firms (Collins Food, Queensland, had 51, Competitive Foods in Western Australia had 25). In its overseas operations McDonald's outlets are set up in a variety of ways, varying from country to country. Most commonly, a joint venture is formed in which McDonald's and a local entrepreneur each put up half the funds. Individual branches then may be franchised by the local joint venture company, along the same lines as with the US parent operation.

The terms and policing of the contract, every bit as much as the nature of the product, determine how well a franchising operation operates. Quality control is the most important thing to be able to ensure, for just as a good experience in McDonald's in the US may make an American visit McDonald's when overseas as a tourist, so a bad experience in one McDonald's outlet may lead a consumer to boycott every one s/he encounters. If high demand and low costs were assured, there would be a risk that franchisees might be tempted to take a 'quiet life' attitude to their activities, ignoring the fact that a few lost sales to them could have many damaging repercussions elsewhere. The franchiser has to decide how best to motivate its franchisees. Interestingly enough, however, in Japan it was found that there was absolutely fanatical attention to the detail of the McDonald's manual: Japanese McDonald's operators and their staff didn't have to have procedures drummed into them by repeated visits of inspectors from head office.

Before Ray Kroc devised the McDonald's system in 1955, most franchisers used financial pressure to motivate their franchisees. One route was to assess the likely profits to be made from a well-run operation and then demand this amount as the fee for the franchise. The disadvantage here was that it greatly raised the initial capital requirements, and was likely to deter applicants who were not confident of the accuracy of the franchiser's assessments and aware that the franchising field is littered with ventures that made money only for the franchisers. The alternative route, favoured by many of McDonald's initial rivals, was to charge exorbitant prices for the inputs that the franchisee had to purchase from the franchiser, rather than passing on benefits that the franchiser had obtained from buying wholesale. This policy was prone to backfire as well, for the franchisees would tend to try to get round the onerous input prices by covertly getting inputs from other sources (which might not be up to the same standards). Once the franchisee began to get experience of dealing with other bodies there would also be a temptation to try going it alone with a similar kind of product. It is interesting to note that, with some franchising operations, the emphasis on charging steeply for inputs has come about partly because the founding firm was originally an input supplier. (The losses of Burger Chef in the 1970s seem to be related to this conflict of interests. It had been owned by a manufacturer of restaurant kitchen equipment, and the strategy of the restaurant division was constrained by the interests of its equipment division. At a time when the public turned towards grilled hamburgers, Burger Chef continued to concentrate on broiled ones because its parent firm sold broilers.)

Ray Kroc's philosophy was fundamentally different, both from his leading rivals and from the McDonald brothers themselves. Kroc came across the McDonald brothers while he was working as a travelling salesman who had the selling rights of the multi-mixers that were used in the McDonald's kitchen. He rapidly became aware of the deficiencies of the brothers' strategy. Having worked out the logistics of fast food and developed a clean, family image by making the pristine state of their kitchens visible to consumers, the McDonald brothers were content to take things easy; they were not empire builders and disliked travelling to establish new branches. They only embarked upon franchising at first in a very half-hearted way. They sold their first franchise for a one-time $1 000, which gave the buyer the right to use their name and their 'arches' symbol, a 15-page description of their fast-food method and the design of their restaurant, and a week's worth of expertise. The brothers therefore had no continuing revenue from each franchise and no incentive to develop the product or take other measures to ensure the franchisee's success. The result was a lack of product uniformity, and sloppy, dirty stores that tarnished the brand name. Even despite the low franchise price, the concept became a subject for piracy: the McDonald brothers warmly welcomed visitors, but in any case, the very nature of their glass-walled kitchens made their operations easy for outsiders to study.

Kroc's philosophy was that the best way to make McDonald's a lot of money was by making sure McDonald's had an incentive to help its franchisees make their own fortunes. (This is a kind of self-control strategy reminiscent of some of the examples discussed in relation to household behaviour in section 4.7.) Instead of going for a quick profit up-front, Kroc decided to look towards the longer-term potential of the market. The incentive was to be provided by charging only a small initial fee, with the bulk of earnings to come from a percentage of sales levy. At a time (1955) when franchise fees of $50 000 were not unknown, Kroc decided to charge a mere $950, making the bulk of the firm's money from a 1.9 per cent royalty on sales (now it charges a 3 per cent service fee; most other chains charge 4 per cent). By the mid-1980s the basic fee was still only $10 000. While its fees were low, the degree of control McDonald's had over its franchisees was unprecedented. To make the company stand out from its rivals Kroc ensured that its standards of product quality and service uniformity reached new heights, and he achieved this by specifying in great detail how a franchise was to run and by monitoring operations: the modern manual runs to over 600 pages. Consultants from the mother company make contact on a weekly basis, and breaches of rules are not tolerated. A bizarre example of this attitude to business was reported by Bernard Levin in *The Times*, 9 March 1989 (p. 16): Mr Tony Maslin, the deputy manager of the Oxford (UK) McDonald's was fired for swapping his lunchtime hamburger for a lunchtime pizza from a female employee of Pizzaland next door (by lunchtime, he was sick and tired of hamburgers and she had a similar attitude towards pizzas). It transpired that the McDonald's handbook decrees that staff may not give the food away. Mr Maslin said he could see nothing in it to prevent exchanges of food, but the McDonald's lawyer declared that the swap amounted to gross misconduct.

McDonald's use of roving inspectors to guarantee that the franchise manual is followed to the letter is in sharp contrast to the findings of Dnes (1992) in his wide range of franchising case studies. In most of the systems studied by Dnes, franchising had been preferred by the franchiser as a means of geographical expansion because it was seen as a way of getting commitment to high quality with minimal monitoring costs. These entrepreneurs reasoned that if they developed by internal expansion they could run into problems of motivating salaried managers of distant branches to ensure that everything was done exactly as the management manual specified. Franchisees would have a much more serious commitment to sticking to their instructions because their own money was at stake and they would benefit personally if they increased the profitability of their operations. Franchisees in these systems had relatively infrequent contact with their respective franchisers. The more 'laid back' monitoring philosophy of many of the franchises studied by Dnes was accompanied by franchise manuals that were much less complex than the gigantic McDonald's manual and left much more room for discretion. Instead of focusing right down to the minutiae of daily operations, these franchise agreements concentrated on the economies of promotion and input-purchasing, and on the role of the franchiser as an agent who could keep abreast of technological improvements and pass the knowledge on to franchises. The picture one is left with as a result is that a McDonald's franchise is so constrained in contractual terms that it is barely a firm in the sense proposed by Coase (1937) and outlined in section 10.12.

Although McDonald's does not tolerate franchisees interfering with the menu, head office does encourage initiatives from the franchisees. With overseas expansion, standardization became more difficult to enforce at arm's length, and it was found important to offer more freedom in order to attract overseas participation, because of doubts about the transferability of an American philosophy to a different culture. Local menus and store designs would tend to appear as operators found it a struggle to persuade locals that American tastes were the thing to have. However, McDonald's always took the view that if they changed to fit in with local cuisine they would lose their identity. Therefore they sought, over the long run, to bring their overseas partners around to this way of thinking. As it turns out, they have actually been more successful at changing local eating habits than changing their menus to fit in with existing ones.

A further difference that is crucial in the McDonald's strategy is that the company sells franchises for individual stores, not for territories. Many franchising operations sought to make quick money by selling territorial franchises which were then resold several times in smaller and smaller units. The unfortunate store operators would then have to pay a fraction of sales revenues to each tier in this regional network—no wonder they often decided to quit and go it alone.

McDonald's leases its sites to its franchisees on a twenty year basis, with the contract set up so that any violation of the franchise is a violation of the site lease too. This might be seen as opening up scope for the same sort of conflict of interest that arises in franchising operations where the franchising firm forces its clients to take its ice-cream mixes, burger broilers or whatever. However, the McDonald's contract is cunningly designed so that its franchisees do not feel they are being exploited. The amount of rent they have to pay depends on how well they are doing. If they are not doing very well they only pay a base fee, but after a particular point they must then pay 8.5 per cent of sales as rent (originally 5 per cent). Anything which helps sales helps rental earnings. Originally it leased sites from property owners who were prepared to build McDonald's restaurant units and then leased them to its franchisees on a mark-up of 40 per cent, but then the company started purchasing land and building stores, until in 1982 it became the world's largest owner of retail real estate. The vast bulk of its earnings now come, formally speaking, from rentals, not as payment for supplying the concept. Originally McDonald's had trouble raising the funds to purchase sites but got round this by demanding a security bond from its franchisees, which was then used as a down-payment.

Though McDonald's acts as an input purchaser for its franchisees, the philosophy is that service charges cover its activities as an intermediary activity, and all the benefits from input price reductions are to be passed on to the franchisees. As Kroc once put it, 'No one could accuse us of taking kickbacks, commissions or anything of that kind unless he wanted to face about a million-dollar slander suit, because I would throw one at him in a split second.... Our operators know which side their bread is buttered on. And the result is that they are cooperative. When you find a good selfish reason for people to cooperate with you, you are pretty sure of their cooperation' (Love, 1986). By contrast, many rival franchisers found that their alternative approach resulted in them facing exclusive supply litigation from their disgruntled franchisees. This should not be taken to imply that McDonald's has kept itself out of the courtrooms: its tough policies have resulted in many challenges from disgruntled franchisees, but the verdicts have invariably entailed victory for McDonald's and sometimes new legal precedents have been set.

11.5 Exam post-mortem: Real estate and optometry franchising

Background

Franchising is an increasingly popular business strategy. Two examples of markets in which franchising is becoming popular as a way of organising economic activity are as follows:

(a) Real estate selling and renting. (Note that an estate agent is engaged by the *seller of* a house to act on his/her behalf to find a buyer. No commission is paid by the buyer. The fee paid by the seller is based on a sliding scale according to the price realized for the property. In some countries the industry is regulated and the fee scale is an industry-wide one, applying to all estate agents, whether franchise members or not.)

(b) Following the deregulation of the optometry industry in the United Kingdom in the 1980s, franchised eye-care centres appeared there. These offer eye-testing services and deal in sight correction and protection products such as spectacles, contact lenses and their associated products, and sunglasses. The leading optometry franchises offer to supply *most* prescriptions of spectacles within an hour of two. The spectacles supplied on this basis are made up in the stores, whereas in the pre-franchising era prescriptions were sent by optometrists to manufacturers of lenses and frames and it would take a week or two for the finished product to be delivered, even where the prescription and frame might be a common one.

Questions (both carry the same weight)

(i) Noting the similarities and differences between the businesses of selling houses and eye care, discuss reasons why franchising may have proved attractive in these two markets.

(ii) Discuss what the contracts between franchisers and franchisees might cover in the case of *either* the real estate business *or* the optometry business. For whichever of the two cases you choose note how the design of the contract might affect the success of the arrangement.

Examiner's report

This was a very popular question but many answers were remarkably superficial and some regurgitated on franchising in general whilst saying nothing about estate agencies and optometrists in particular. A really first-class answer had to make clear that these high-involvement businesses differ considerably from well-known franchising systems used for retailing low-involvement products such as fast food. There were no such answers; having correctly pointed out that a franchise is commonly used as a device for convincing customers of uniform quality standards, most answers stopped short of considering alternative devices for achieving this end or other roles that franchising might be expected to serve. Not a single answer noted that at first sight both of these lines of business are ones in which the basic role of franchising needs to be questioned.

Whereas tourists can visit a Pizza Hut in, say, the United Kingdom and expect to receive exactly the same product as would be served up in a Pizza Hut in New Zealand, real estate agents act as intermediaries in a market for products whose very lack of standardization makes buying and selling without opportunity loss a decidedly problematic task. The extent to which a franchiser might hope to standardize selling methods might be expected to be rather limited once the real estate agent has moved beyond the initial presentation of advertisements, offices and initial interviews with prospective purchasers. To be sure, clients on both sides of the market want to have some way of assuring quality of service: sellers would be distressed to hear that their agents were annoying buyers by trying to misrepresent houses to them or taking them to see properties which in no way matched the buyers' stated requirements. In principle, some form of registration or licensing by a professional real estate institute can be used as a guarantee of service, and in most countries such professional associations, *as well as* real estate franchising, are very much in evidence. As far as optometry is concerned, the costs of poor service may be considerable but clients may in principle check that their optometrists have appropriate professional credentials and, sure enough, these are usually displayed prominently in optometry stores.

A neat way to look at the real estate business would have been to suggest that it sets far less demanding professional standards than optometry does, in which case there could still be a role for franchising as a device for controlling quality: indeed, surveys of public opinion appear to rate estate agents as little better than politicians and used-car dealers. An unreliable estate agent may, in a social setting, lead to word spreading as if all agents associated with a particular franchise are hopeless or opportunistic. The franchiser company thus has a strong incentive to monitor the standards of its franchisees. Although the average house owner undertakes the major event of moving home every seven years or so, memories of what happened last time are still likely to be vivid. The act of moving house may often involve geographical movements into new territory, so it might be expected that people selling a house through one franchise that has impressed them in the past when they were buyers now look around to find another branch of the franchise in the area to which they are moving. In this sense, the role of the franchise as a branding device may indeed be as in the fast-food business, but students who tried this line of argument tended to make the point without relating the infrequency of use of the market, the likely vividness of a brand name in this context (it may be easier to recall the estate agent brand rather than the agent who served one so well some years ago), and the fact that buyers are often also selling.

In the case of optometry the professional standards of optometrists may be less of an issue than the ability to get a fast delivery of the prescription that the optometrist has recommended. Herein lie problems of judgement. If spectacles produce headaches, is it the fault of the manufacturer or the optometrist that prescribed them? Were the spectacles really necessary in the first place? There was much scope for drawing attention to principal-agent problems and trying to see what bearing franchising had on them, but no one spotted this. I would have been far happier to see discussions that came to no definite conclusion in this area than no discussion at all. Amongst other things, it could have been noted that a vertically integrated franchise arrangement makes a problem the fault of the franchise, period, so the incentives for optometrists to make sure they buy into an excellent production system are strong, as are the incentives for the franchisers to choose carefully the optometry professionals whom they sign up as franchisees. However, prescribing and dispensing do not have to be carried out by a single firm and customers might be rather uneasy about the conflict of interest facing an optometrist who stood to make more money by recommending (a new set of) spectacles than by advising the client that all was in order. This might suggest that 'fast glasses' franchises might merely involve dispensing (which is, I believe, all they are allowed to cover in some countries, such as Australia), but this would then remove the principal-agent problem at the cost of taking away from customers the opportunity to reduce transaction costs by engaging in one-stop shopping.

One difference between the two lines of business that received little attention was that, unlike real estate franchising, the optometry case involved a method of bringing to a wide market a production technology that had required some careful working out (the stock control logistics seem quite mind-boggling if prescriptions and demands for frames are nonstandardized: note that there is not a promise to supply *all* orders in an hour or two). In principle, this coverage could have been achieved via a multi-branch expansion by the firm that pioneered it, but this would have involved major capital requirements compared with a franchise arrangement (one good paper that mentioned this also noted that a system of franchised owner–manager operations might generate more staff motivation than one built around a set of subsidiary branch operations). It might also have been noted that the technology could have been licensed on its own, to optometry stores that then adopted their own styles as retailers. Students tended to concentrate on the possible role of identical corporate logos, shop layouts, 'scripts' for reception staff, and so on, whilst forgetting to consider alternative ways that the investment in technology might have been exploited. Even then, around half forgot to discuss the economies of scale effects that a franchise can achieve in areas such as advertising its single brand name, or through bargaining power with suppliers of spectacle frames and suchlike. Of those who did talk about economies of bulk purchasing many failed to note the belief of McDonald's mastermind Ray Kroc that many franchisers undermine their operations by failing to pass these savings on to their franchisees and instead using the later as a captive market.

In general, discussions of optometry could have stressed the newness of the fast glasses service and related it to lecture material on first-mover advantages. One might imagine that people used to slow service in this area would have worries about standards where the service is speeded up. This being so, it may be worth paying to share one's trading name with that of a firm which develops an early reputation for combining speed and accuracy in the dispensing of spectacles. Otherwise, one could well imagine optometrists simply signing up for the technology and then supplying the hardware speedily under their own established names: no one pointed out that goodwill might well be lost if long-time customers of an optometrist feel that their trusted purveyor of a professional service has been swallowed up by some faceless corporation.

The question of the nature of the contract and how it might affect the operation's success was dealt with in a very superficial manner, with a major tendency for students to forget that the contract involves two parties. Most students concentrated on specifying styles of operation and the need for some kind of monitoring system; many forgot to suggest that the franchiser might run staff training programmes. Few took as their starting point Ray Kroc's philosophy that the way for a franchiser to make a lot of money was to find ways of enabling the franchisees to make a lot of money and then take a slice of this in the form of a turnover-based royalty (in a real estate franchise, this might involve, say, ten per cent of takings being paid to the franchiser). Rather, there was a tendency not to discuss financial aspects at all.

Although the lectures had noted how territorial problems and piracy often lay behind the failure of franchising systems, few answers tried to raise these issues. It would have been easy to build a discussion around the possible vulnerability of territory-based real estate agencies in periods when the housing market is depressed: on the one hand, unlike a franchisee, an independent real estate agency can seek to maintain its business by broadening its territory across a wider range of suburbs; on the other hand, to the extent that agents do not abandon their franchises and try to go it alone, the predominance of franchising in this market helps to limit mutually destructive competition for territory during such periods. With the fast glasses production process, an additional point to make would be the possibility that patent protection of the process (an unlikely aspect of real estate agencies) might reduce the risk of piracy by former franchisers acting in conjunction with other spectacle suppliers.

11.6   Diversification

Though neoclassical production theory does set out marginal conditions concerning the optimal mix of products that a firm might produce (see section 7.4), mainstream economics has typically focused on firms as if they are only involved in the production of a single product. This attitude towards multi-product firms is perhaps a tacit recognition that marginalist equilibrium analysis is unlikely to be a very helpful way of approximating processes by which firms come to diversify their ranges of interests through time by committing themselves to new activities and resources. Corporate growth tends to be an evolving, problem-solving activity in which actual or anticipated unused capacity of one kind—in terms of machinery or managerial and other human resources—leads to lumpy investments being made in other kinds of capacity, which result in new imbalances becoming apparent (see sections 7.4 and 10.13, which were based on Penrose, 1959, and

Moss, 1981; also note the discussions of the power of potential competition in sections 9.6 and 9.7). Acts of diversification may include the kinds of internalization decisions considered in section 11.2, which concerned vertical relationships between stages of a particular production and distribution processes. However, the term is more frequently employed in respect of investments that are not based around forward and backward integration in respect of final product markets to which the firm is already committed. An evolving firm's managers aim to draw on competitive advantages that they and their firms have already built up, not by replicating their operations in markets that are already saturated but using them as a basis for a competitive head start in markets that have some kind of horizontal relationship—something in common—with something that the firm has hitherto been doing. For example, diversification from publishing academic books into publishing novels, or into magazines and newspapers, and from print media into electronic media involves the use of shared business themes concerning the gathering, packaging and marketing of information: a firm with interests in these areas makes sense in terms of economies of scope or potential for synergy. We can similarly make sense of a firm that diversifies from sugar production into building-board manufacture once we know that the board is made of sugar cane residue, so long as we can see reasons why the cane by-product might be difficult to sell to a firm that already has expertise and a brand reputation in the building products market. By contrast, diversification straight from academic book publishing into the manufacture of musical instruments appears to involve no common thread, so we should be rather surprised to encounter a company that had grown in this way. In this section I explore the economics of diversification somewhat further with the aid of Neil Kay's (1982, 1984) work, which is built around the theme that many firms undergo dramatic transformations, often at great cost in terms of borrowing on international capital markets, because the ways in which their management teams seek to exploit their existing resource bases are shaped by a desire to avoid 'putting too many eggs in too few baskets'.

When a firm seeks to use up scope for achieving both production and marketing synergy by increasing its range of activities, the least demanding strategy in terms of the pressure it places on management and on the firm's financial resources will be one which involves producing additional products that are similar to those it already makes and which sell in much the same markets. If the firm's planners feel that they are not operating in an environment prone to 'muggings'—Kay's use of the word in this context means nasty surprises such as technological innovations and adverse changes in tastes or in government policy—then they are likely to feel under considerable competitive pressure to adopt this strategy. If the firm spreads its talents across a variety of fields, it risks being undercut by rivals that are ruthlessly pursuing economies of scale and scope. However, Kay predicts that if the planners believe their firm's environment is one in which catastrophic muggings are likely, they will probably hedge their bets by choosing a strategy that makes only a limited use of potential synergy links between activities. They might therefore undertake investments which realize potential for production synergy but involve making a commitment to a new kind of market, and/or which expand their firm's range of offerings in its existing market but require it to acquire new kinds of production equipment and managerial know-how.

A memorable example consistent with Kay's analysis is the Kaman Corporation, which initially developed a high degree of expertise in manufacturing parts for military helicopters

361

from lightweight 'composite' materials. Its operations were vulnerable to cutbacks in defence budgets in the event that the Cold War came to an end. The firm's management hedged against this by using their expertise in a totally new context, the manufacture of the Ovation range of round-backed acoustic guitars. This could have been a costly distraction from achieving peak performance as a defence contractor but, given that the defence business seemed dangerous, the diversification made sense: if the innovative guitars succeeded, as indeed they did, existing instrument makers would have a hard time copying them, as indeed they have. Note that Kaman might have avoided the need to develop new kinds of manufacturing expertise, establish the Ovation brand name and develop distribution links if it licensed its technology or sold ready-moulded composite guitar bodies to a firm such as Fender, Gibson or Martin, that was already established as a leader in the premium-quality guitar market. It is interesting to conjecture from the standpoint of transaction cost economics why they did not adopt this strategy: perhaps the established manufacturers were not convinced that expensive plastic-backed guitars would find a market; if the new guitars did not succeed it might be difficult to discover whether this was due to opportunistic behaviour by the technology licensee, such as backpedalling on promoting them because of the damage their success would do to investments already made in respect of traditional guitars; perhaps there were fears that the licensees might discover that the technology could be applied to yet other new areas, not covered by the licensing deal; and so on.

Hedging strategies often involve a diversifying firm taking over other firms and then achieving the various synergies by policies of rationalization. This route has the advantage of giving the firm access to established markets, equipment and managerial expertise. It is also a way for the management team to make the position of their firm less vulnerable almost overnight, so long as the acquired resources can be digested without too much trouble (which often is not the case: see Earl, 1984: 184–7) and have not been purchased at an inflated price with borrowed funds, leaving the firm with a dangerous gearing ratio.

Centred as it is on fears concerning the possible sudden truncation of the life-cycles of products and/or production processes, Kay's hedging analysis is something of a departure from the conventional finance theorist's approach to diversification. In the orthodox analysis, the various activities in which the firm is involved are assumed to be prone to exhibit some variance in their earnings through time but they are not portrayed as likely to suffer a terminal downturn or, in the case of new products, to die in their infancy. Rather, the idea is that corporate earnings and cashflows can be smoothed out by putting together a diversified portfolio of activities that are not expected simultaneously to go through temporary bad patches.

This analysis of corporate evolution prompts an important question: whose interests are these kinds of corporate diversifications actually intended to serve? Their appeal to shareholders is not immediately obvious. If shareholders wish to insure themselves against erratic earnings and/or the possible failure of some companies whose shares they own, they can do so by buying diversified portfolios for themselves. Given this, they might be expected to be interested in new or established firms that are trying to reap the advantages of specialization. When managers of such companies generate higher profits than they feel they need to reinvest to maintain an acceptable rate of return in their existing line of business, they can dispose of surplus earnings without diversifying by distributing them to shareholders as dividends. The shareholders can then use these dividends as they choose. If shareholders do not wish to use dividends to finance consumption, they can either place them on the money market or use them to buy small shareholdings in other companies. Alternatively, they can choose to invest in specialized companies that tend to retain their surplus earnings but which use them to fund portfolio investment on behalf of their shareholders—*not* to satisfy the shareholders' hedging and/or earnings-smoothing motives, but to help them to reduce their tax liabilities (if marginal tax rates on dividends are higher than on capital gains) and give them indirect access to economies of scale in making deposits or buying shares. (The latter only became important in economies such as the UK in the 'Big Bang' of the late 1980s when fixed-rate commissions on share purchases were abolished.)

Given the scope for shareholders to hedge by portfolio investment, the appeal of companies that are diversifying in the manner predicted by Kay would seem to originate from the costs of returning corporate resources to factor markets and assembling resources into smoothly operating firms. Brand-new firms may have all sorts of strategic advantages because they are specialized around a carefully chosen set of competences and new equipment, but all sorts of costs must be incurred to put such a firm together—such as costs of raising finance and initial problems of coordination whilst team skills and a corporate culture are being established. When an established, synergy-based firm goes bankrupt after suffering a catastrophic mugging the dispersion of its resources involves the dissipation of reputations attached to team skills, destruction of corporate capital in the form of tacit knowledge, and payments to receivers. An established hedging firm that is more likely to remain in existence in the long run may not reach the same peaks as firms that ruthlessly pursue synergy but it may nonetheless seem 'greater than the sum of its parts' because it economizes on start-up and break-up costs; the crucial thing is that it does not seem to be hedging so far that it is insufficiently competitive in any of its product markets and therefore seems unduly likely to cease being a going concern.

Hedging and earnings-smoothing diversification strategies may also be in the interests of teams of senior managers, enabling diversified firms to attract such staff whilst offering less generous terms than specialized firms. But here, too, the basis for such strategies is initially open to question. This is so even though, for a senior manager of a specialized company, the price of a catastrophic mugging in its product market is likely to be the need to find a new job, and despite the possibility that this may also be the price of being a manager in a specialized firm which just goes through a temporary bad spell: an imperfectly informed stock market may undervalue the firm's assets and prompt a successful takeover raid, leading to changes being made in respect of senior personnel. Such managers would be justifiably afraid of losing their jobs, given that they could expect to find themselves competing for alternative positions against others who still had high-ranking positions and would not be asked to explain why their firms failed or why they were 'let go' during a post-takeover rationalization. A well-conceived strategy of diversification reduces the likelihood that a firm will suffer a major setback to its overall earnings unless there is a general downturn in activity. Hence it is a means by which managers can try to make their positions less vulnerable. However, such a strategy also has its risks, for things may go badly wrong as the managers move into unfamiliar territory, so it is by no means the natural solution to their problem.

In principle, senior managers might conceivably hedge their employment bets in turbulent market environments by dividing their working weeks between several firms, as sometimes happens with non-executive board members and 'blue-collar' operatives. In practice, however, employers would be likely to be wary of increasing the sizes of their management teams by hiring senior staff on a part-time, job-sharing basis: this policy could open up considerable scope for managerial confusion unless staff sharing a particular role spent a lot of time making detailed records or briefing each other about what had happened on their latest shift; worse still, a company could suffer as a result of opportunistic behaviour by managers whose loyalties were divided between the various (possibly competing) companies between which they divided their time.

Alternatively, a management team might concentrate on extracting an impressive performance from a specialized set of activities in the hope that they could later raise new funds to tide them through a temporary bad patch or to finance the development and marketing of a new product if they are unlucky enough to be hit by a catastrophic mugging in their present product market. However, they are likely to encounter a problem similar to that which leads those screening job applicants to be biased in favour of those who are presently employed. If the company seeking to raise money is a specialized one that has just suffered catastrophic mugging in its product market, potential suppliers of funds are likely to experience difficulties in deciding whether the company's current misfortunes are the result of bad luck or a lack of foresight on the part of management. Were the latter the case, the company might be one to avoid, for though its management team may profess to be basing their proposals on specialized knowledge they may also be tending to see potential costs and revenues through rose-tinted spectacles. A similar problem arises in respect of companies that are performing poorly at present despite being involved with products whose life-cycles have not entered an obvious stage of terminal decline. Faced with uncertainties about management capabilities, those with funds may prefer to steer clear of such companies and concentrate on ones that are making less grand claims about the potential of their investment plans but which are not presently in difficulties. In other situations the problem may be that it is difficult to raise venture capital on the open market without giving too much of one's plans away to potential competitors. By borrowing from bankers instead of raising equity capital managers could achieve greater confidentiality, but this has a cost in the form of higher risks of bankruptcy because interest payments are rather harder to suspend than equity dividends in times of crisis.

Since diversification internalizes part of the capital market it provides a means by which a management team can sidestep the need to persuade sceptical new sources to provide funds (or the cost of persuading a merchant bank of doing the persuading on their behalf) and preserve secrecy without taking on additional gearing risks. A diversified firm is able, in the language of strategic marketing theory, to 'milk' its mature 'cash cows' to fund the development and marketing of cash-hungry new products, some of which may take off, turning from 'question marks' into 'star performers'. Management's task is to make sure that enough stars appear and get turned into new cash cows as older cash cows and some question marks turn into 'dogs' and have to be liquidated. If they succeed at this, they can escape a forced return to the labour market (see Earl, 1984: chapter 1).

We must not forget the other strategy by which senior managers can avoid the risks of losing their jobs and the costs of going to the capital market to raise funds each time they run into trouble. As noted earlier, if a specialized firm is earning profits in excess of those required for investment in its existing area of interest, it can use the surplus for portfolio investment rather than paying out larger dividends or diversifying into unfamiliar territory. Then, when it subsequently finds itself needing to change direction or deal with a temporary cashflow problem, it can liquidate some of these investments. Most firms do practise this policy on a limited scale, though few are inclined to accumulate huge mountains of cash because the possibility of achieving higher returns on equities or physical investment may make those that do so seem attractive takeover targets. Their reluctance to use surplus funds to accumulate substantial minority equity investments 'for a rainy day' is probably partly because shares have unpredictable values and (much less importantly) because transaction costs must be incurred to dispose of the shares when the rainy day comes. But they may also fear that they could be seen as potential majority shareholders by the companies whose shares they purchase and thereby invite retaliatory corporate acquisitions of their own shares.

It is interesting here to note that in Japan unique institutional circumstances have actually led giant companies to make extensive use of equity holdings as pools of reserve assets. Prior to 1945, the Japanese business scene was dominated by a handful of giant conglomerates—the Zaibatsi—that owned about 40 per cent of industry. These firms were broken up by the occupying forces. In their places have emerged loose industrial groupings of related firms that are not formally tied under a particular corporate holding company but which nonetheless see themselves as sharing risks with each other (as in the case of Mitsubishi Manufacturing and the Mitsubishi Bank, which are nowadays separate companies). The share ownership structure involved in these groupings is one that probably would be deemed illegal if practised elsewhere, for 70 per cent of Japanese shareholdings involve one firm owning shares in another and many of the cross-shareholdings are highly incestuous in nature. This unusual concentration of ownership makes it very difficult for outsiders to engineer takeover raids via open market purchases of shares, so management can get on with the business of overseeing the development and marketing of better products without having to worry about short-term profitability. In effect, the companies diversify by holding shares in each other, rather than by diversifying in product markets. When a company needs funds for a major restructuring it sells some of its shares to other companies in its ownership nexus, usually via direct negotiation rather than by placing them on the general market. In this way a Japanese firm can try to conquer its overseas rivals by doing particular things really well and then regrouping to invest in something new if its product comes to the end of its life-cycle or other producers catch up and the going gets too tough.

11.7   Internal markets and organizational structure

Although much of this chapter has been focused on strategic decisions to internalize certain activities that might otherwise have been performed by one firm on behalf of another, activities being internalized by strategic decisions, it should be noted that in a number of key areas internalization does not actually result in the total replacement of markets but, rather, their subdivision and partial confinement within the firm in question.

(a) *An internal product market*. Divisions of a firm will trade goods and services with each other at internal 'transfer prices' that are the result of negotiation between divisions and may even be the subjects of contested bidding processes. For example, Vauxhall and Opel, the European branches of General Motors, purchase some of their engines from General Motors subsidiaries in Brazil and Australia. Changes in exchange rates may impact on the relative profitability of divisions in ways that depend on agreements concerning transfer prices: when the Australian dollar fell sharply against European currencies in 1986 this was a windfall gain for Vauxhall and Opel since General Motors–Holden had agreed to supply 'Family II' series engines at prices denominated in Australian dollars. It is common for head offices of multinational firms to set up transfer pricing structures that ensure most of their profits are made in countries that have low rates of corporate tax.

(b) *An internal capital market*. This typically comprises an individual or a committee whose role is to decide on the relative merits of competing proposals for the allocation of funds to the various activities in which the firm has, or might have, an interest. Such a market has considerable potential to function more effectively than external capital markets. This may help further to explain why large diversified firms may appeal to small shareholders even though they are aware they may face considerable personal costs if ever they feel dissatisfied with a management team's performance and wish to initiate moves to call an extraordinary general meeting and/or get a large assembly of similarly disaffected shareholders together to vote in a new board. By purchasing shares in a limited number of diversified companies, individuals do not necessarily achieve any increase in their ability to influence the performance of the companies in which they have a stake. However, they may choose to purchase shares in firms whose incumbent management teams have reputations for being able to extract superior performances from their assets.

(c) *An internal labour market*. Decisions have to be taken about who to promote, demote or move sideways in the light of relative competitive strengths of existing employees and changes in the direction taken by the company's operations. The management of internal labour markets can have a major role to play in determining the value of a firm's stock of human capital. A worker who has been working in a particular position for several years is likely to have higher productivity than a freshly hired worker would be able to achieve, since much knowledge of the corporate culture and tacit knowledge about the task are picked up 'on the job'. It can therefore be costly to lose an experienced worker due to a failure to offer internal opportunities on a par with those offered by rivals. Promotion opportunities within an internal labour market often play a valuable role in deterring workers from going back into the external labour market. If workers are aware that there are several rungs ahead on the promotion ladder which are not open to external competition they have a stronger incentive to demonstrate to their superiors their skills and willingness to work hard. Promotion to the next rung may be valued not merely for the rewards it brings directly but also because it is seen as a prerequisite for promotion to the level beyond. The practice of filling vacancies by internal promotion often makes sense in any case due to the tasks having firm-specific aspects: for example, someone who has been a line worker in a factory may be better qualified to be a supervisor on that particular line than someone who has been working in another firm. By limiting the extent to which vacant positions are filled from the external labour market, a management team signals to workers that commitment to the organization is valued and at the same time eliminates costs of screening external applicants. (For further discussions of internal labour markets and processes of internal competition, see Andrews, 1958; Doeringer and Piore, 1971; and Milgrom and Roberts, 1992: chapter 11.)

Although some internal markets may be as hotly contested as external markets, we should also recognize scope for collusion between different interest groups on internal committees, just as we would look out for potential for collusive behaviour in market-based transactions. By forming coalitions, empire-building division heads may be able to exert majority voting power at meetings. In dividing up a firm into manageable units there is scope both to avoid unnecessary paperwork and efforts involved in arranging/attending meetings, and to reduce the incidence of opportunism. The difficulties entailed in devising a satisfactory structure are the subject of the rest of this section.

Bounded rationality normally dictates that the division of labour within a firm involves the creation of some kind of hierarchical system. Typically, we may expect a 'top-down' process of resource allocation, in the light of flows of information and proposals sent up by lower-level personnel. The firm is divided into divisions to which particular responsibilities are given, along with budget limits. Each division, in turn, normally is divided up in a hierarchical manner, with particular personnel made responsible to particular senior staff who report to and take orders from the divisional head. Senior staff may have a broad picture of what is going on in the firm, but it will lack focus compared with what is seen by junior staff in the much narrower areas in which they specialize.

In some organizations the hierarchy takes a very strict ('mechanistic') form: if a person wishes to communicate with someone else elsewhere in the division, or in another division, information may have to be routed upwards until it reaches a high enough apex in the organizational structure such that an individual with responsibility for both areas of interest can route it down to the other party. This vertical system has the virtue of enabling the coordinator at each apex in the hierarchy to have a clearer picture of what is going on in her/his area of responsibility than would be possible if a subordinate simply bypassed normal channels and went directly to the person with whom they wished to deal. Scope for confusion is likely to be reduced. However, an organization which is so formal as to preclude lateral relationships will not be able to deal rapidly with problems whose ramifications spread far and wide—as one would expect them to do if strategies are built around synergy themes.

Less formal ('organic') organizational structures not only give members the opportunity to interact laterally as well as vertically. They may also give members greater freedom with respect to what they do with their resources rather than stipulating ways in which budgets may be used and insisting that any significant decisions (for example, concerning equipment purchases) have to be approved at high levels. Informal organizations also make extensive use of *ad hoc* committees and working parties which are often short-lived and aim to deal with particular pressing issues by bringing together people from different areas of expertise, and with different backgrounds and (from a formal organization perspective) status. They do not draw a fine line between those who think and take decisions (managers, the firm's brains) and those who take orders (workers, the firm's hands). Technological complexity is also contributing to the breakdown of formal organizations. Specialists in fields that senior staff know little about are no longer merely consulted by executives who reserve the right to take decisions; increasingly, they take decisions themselves in direct consultation with the workers and ground-level technicians (see Toffler, 1970)). Executives pretty well have to take their recommendations because they cannot query them without calling in yet more advisors.

Regardless of how formal their hierarchical structures are, firms typically assign their personnel to particular levels and departments with flows of responsibility. Economists were little interested in how firms were divided up internally until Alfred Chandler (1962) hypothesized that changes in corporate structures follow changes in strategies in a problem-solving, cyclical manner, with the typical firm going through four 'chapters' of evolution:

(1) The initial growth and accumulation of resources.
(2) Rationalization of the use of resources and the development of an integrated, functionally-based organizational structure.
(3) Expansion into new markets in an attempt to ensure the continuing full employment of corporate resources.
(4) The development of a new multi-divisional structure based on product or regional divisions to facilitate the continued mobilization of resources in the face of both short-term changes in market demands and long-term trends.

The cyclical nature of Chandler's story is very much a consequence of bounded rationality on the part of entrepreneurs and managers. Initially a firm's operations may be on a small enough scale for the founding entrepreneur not to be forced by coordination problems to focus on matters of organization. The focus is on raising finance, getting the product right and building up a market presence. With an increase in the scale of operations and the development of a range of related products, it gets progressively more difficult for a single individual to be able to serve as a coordinator and increasingly worthwhile to assign particular specialized tasks to groups of staff that report to a departmental head who in turn reports to the chief executive. Figure 11.1 shows the kind of structure that emerges in this second chapter, which is nowadays known as U-form (unitary) structure. In so far as the firm's growth has been based around the pursuit of economies of scope this sort of structure seems to make perfect sense: each department can concentrate on achieving a particular synergy effect. However, it is inherently difficult for the chief executive to decide which products and departments are performing well, the more so the more products that the firm is involved with and the more decisions the chief executive needs to take. Shared production systems, research and development costs and common distribution systems make it unclear whether any product should be discontinued: it may be possible to identify variable costs but even if these exceed the product's price it might be dangerous to discontinue it because its sales generate sales for other products in the firm's range of offerings. (Claims about jointness in demand are often used as a basis for continuing to produce a 'flagship model' despite recording a loss on every unit sold; they also provide the classic 'feeder route' justification for subsidizing branch lines in railway networks.) The chief executive is very dependent on advice from departmental heads, who may serve on the executive committee as well as standing to gain or lose resources depending on the strategic decisions that get taken. Each departmental head will be prone to blame heads of other departments, either opportunistically or because of looking at the world from a departmental point of view—for example, the head of marketing may claim that sales could be improved by a bigger allocation of resources to marketing, whereas the head of research might believe that the products would sell themselves if they were more up to date in design.

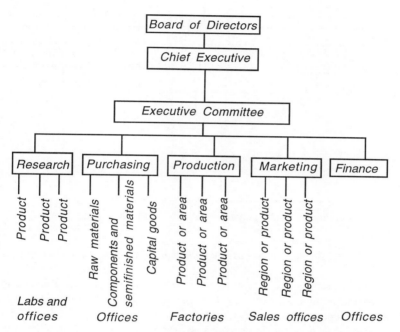

Figure 11.1: A U-form (functionally-based) corporate structure

Many firms that have made the transition from the third to the fourth of Chandler's four chapters in the evolution of a modern diversified corporation stretched the U-form structure beyond its efficient scale of operation. In three of the four pioneering cases that he studied, growth led to a crisis of profitability that led some staff to question the wisdom of a functionally-based structure; only in the fourth case did managers anticipate they would run into difficulties if they did not come up with an organizational structure that meshed better with their strategy. In the absence of an innovative alternative organizational design, these companies might have been forced to downsize to avoid being selected out of existence by competitive pressures. The solution proposed and eventually accepted within General Motors, Du Pont, Standard Oil and Sears Roebuck was the multi-divisional (M-form) structure, a hypothetical example of which is shown in Figure 11.2.

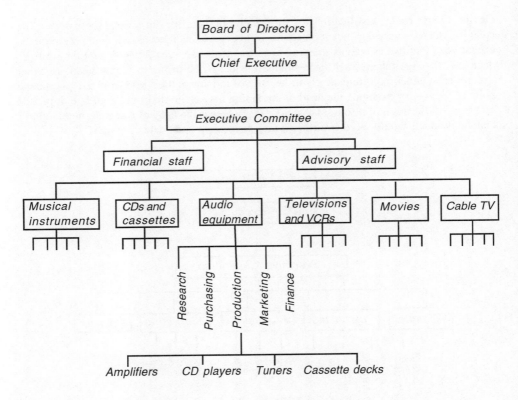

Figure 11.2: M-Form structure of a hypothetical audio-visual entertainments firm

The essence of such a structure in its pure form is that the firm is divided into a set of miniature U-form companies each of which handles a particular product line or market territory as an independent profit centre. Head office concentrates on providing advice to the divisions and making strategic decisions about relative investment funding and rates of expansion of the divisions. In addition to providing performance data on their existing operations, divisions may be required to submit major proposals for approval by head office. The divisional delegations might lobby in favour of their pet projects or against proposals being suggested to them by head office, but they do not have the power to decide which projects are given the go-ahead. Top management at head office will listen to cases made in the lobbying process, seek expert advice from their strategic planning staff at head office, and then decide which course of action is going to be allowed. They can do this in a dispassionate way since they will not be the ones who administer the policies that are selected, unlike a divisional head who is unlikely to propose, say, a major scaling down of her/his empire. To enhance their divisions' prospects for growth and long-term survival the divisional heads need to be able to come up with projects that will appeal to head office, as well as a solid record of performance. On this basis, they can appeal to lower-level divisional staff for innovative ideas and a commitment to raising productivity: they must all pull together, for their competitors are not merely other firms in their product markets but other divisions competing for scarce corporate resources. In short, the M-form structure is designed to deter opportunism and promote X-efficiency. Once this structure was adopted by some firms, competitive pressures became greater still for other firms whose strategic thinking was running ahead of their awareness of the limitations of a U-form structure.

Alert readers may have noticed some difficulties with the rosy picture I have just painted of the M-form structure—difficulties that make it doubtful whether Chandler's fourth 'chapter' is the end of the story of the interplay of corporate strategy and structure. One obvious feature is an additional layer of highly paid senior managers and advisory staff, the price of getting lower-level personnel to behave in the interests of the company as a whole. The profit-centres/'divide and rule' philosophy on which the M-form system is based may promote an obsession in the divisions with delivering results that can be measured immediately in terms of the indicators used by head office for deciding on funding allocations between the divisions. It is inherently difficult to demonstrate how much worse the firm's performance would be if this layer were done away with in favour of, say, a more consensus-based, Japanese-style approach to resource allocation in which personnel are open to changes that benefit the company as a whole because they believe they have a career-long commitment to the company (cf. Kono, 1984, and the discussions in sections 7.1 and 7.8).

Secondly, the supposedly dispassionate nature of the strategic decision-makers may be questioned. Some attempts at introducing M-form structures have tried to economize on the costs of strategic decision-making by having divisional heads serving on key strategic committees. This may not be so foolish as it sounds, even though it violates the key idea that those who make funding allocations should not be the same people as those who put the funds to work on a daily basis (what is known in public service applications of M-form thinking as the 'funder–provider split'). Though divisional heads may naturally be inclined to try to defend and extend their empires, they have a much clearer idea of the resources they are working with and may be much closer to their customers. The arguments they put forward *may* be entirely sincere, not opportunistic. In any case, even if members of head office committees are not involved in administering the outcomes of strategic decision-making, they will be looking at proposals in terms of world-views that are products of where they have spent earlier parts of their careers.

Finally, but perhaps most importantly, it may be noted that there is a fundamental conflict between building a strategy around economies of scope and implementing it with the aid of a structure that works on a 'divide and rule' philosophy. A firm which adopts an M-form structure may unwittingly sacrifice synergy and actually promote behaviour which damages its overall long-run performance. Consider the hypothetical firm shown in Figure 11.2, which is loosely inspired by the activity mix of the Sony Corporation in the early 1990s. The firm has interests in complementary hardware and software products of two kinds. Television manufacture and marketing is different from the manufacture and marketing of movies and videos, so it makes sense to allocate them to separate operating divisions. This is so even though the firm's head office may have made a strategic decision as a producer of, primarily, audiovisual hardware to diversify into the related software as a means of enhancing its prospects for creating new technology standards. If the firm develops a new audio-playback technology, its audio software and hardware divisions both

371

stand to benefit from it success, so they have an incentive to cooperate. So far, so good, and a similar point may be made in respect of a new video format. Division of hardware production into audio and video groups is, however, questionable if they use similar components and technologies, and are marketed through the same distribution channels under the same brand name. However, if they are merged into a single division their size may be so disproportionately great that they can attract an undue amount of attention from head office. In this age of the music video we can hardly overlook the possibility that recording artists signed with this company would have dealings with both software divisions. Artists and head office might both prefer a coordinated marketing strategy for audio and video products that maximized their total earnings, whereas the video division might be keen to pursue policies to steal business from the audio division, and vice versa. The instrument division might perform better if the recording division concentrated on promoting artists that used its equipment and would probably prefer that artists signed to the firms label were put under pressure to use and hence promote its instruments, but this might go directly against the interests of the recording division (for example, the instruments division might specialize in making electric guitars, whereas the recording division is concentrating on the new market for 'unplugged' acoustic rock music).

This type of conflict is due to an acute case of what Simon (1969) labels as the problem of 'indecomposability', and it is explored at greater length in Kay (1982, 1984) and Earl (1984). It is particularly prone to arise for companies whose operations are both multinational and multi-product. Some firms have tried to deal with it by developing a matrix structure in which middle managers are subordinate to several senior managers, but this often turns out to be too complicated as well as enabling subordinates to play off their superiors against each other. A more practical solution is for divisions to trade with each other, with the division having the biggest commitment to a particular shared function being the one that acts as a subcontractor to the others. An example here is the Ford Motor Company which, in mid-1994, restructured itself in a second attempt to make the concept of 'the world car' work successfully: put simply, Ford US was given responsibility for developing large, rear-wheel-drive cars and utility vehicles whereas Ford Europe was placed in charge of smaller cars with front-wheel drive. The idea is to achieve economies in areas such as research and development, component sourcing, tooling and production, by eliminating the practice of having parallel ranges of technically dissimilar products in different parts of the world. Ford US and Ford Europe will be trading designs and finished products: they will doubtless haggle with each other over transfer prices but all the time recognizing that they both need to support each other. However, if tastes are not globally standardized, there remains a risk that the US and European divisions will each be tempted to design their products with their eyes primarily on their local markets and the products will then need extensive modification to fit in with requirements of customers elsewhere.

11.8   Exam post-mortem: Shareholders and diversification

Question
'Since the capital market offers shareholders all the opportunities for diversification which they need, shareholders' interests provide no case for a firm's diversification.' Discuss.

Examiner's report

Material from section 11.6 would have been sufficient as a basis for tackling this question, but surprisingly many students tried to answer it as if I had never discussed diversification from a transaction cost standpoint. For example, some—I presume they were accountancy students—wrote about the legal obligations of managers to serve shareholders' interests. These answers seemed remarkably naive, given all that had been said in the lectures about the difficulties of proving what was going on in a firm, and why, and about the consequent scope for opportunistic behaviour and organizational slack. Those that did try to suggest that managers were diversifying in their own interests (to guard against the risk of losing their jobs in the event of a failure in a major product market) often forgot to consider barriers that managers might encounter if they tried to hedge by other means (for example, difficulties in working part-time for several firms) or the danger that they might increase their chances of running into trouble by moving into new territory. However, some who did talk about the hazards of diversification did so without making clear why anybody, whether shareholders or managers, would favour it as a strategy.

All too often, diversification was discussed only with respect to a hedging motive, rather than as a means for making use of existing corporate resources. Consequently, there was a widespread failure to discuss how potential problems in trading synergy or in returning surplus resources to the market might lead managers to internalize new activities in the interests both of themselves and of the shareholders. Those who discussed hedging often completely failed to see the point of the quotation, namely, that shareholders can themselves diversify by purchasing shares in a variety of specialized firms even if no diversified ones exist. When the diversified firm was portrayed as an internal capital market, answers sometimes stopped short of explaining how a multi-divisional internal structure might be a far more powerful incentive system than an external capital market and that shareholders might therefore be keen to own stakes in firms organized in this sort of way.

11.9   Essay example: Conglomerates and competition

Question

Does the trend towards increasingly diversified 'conglomerate' firms imply that the economy is getting less or more competitive? Justify your answer.

Author's notes

Background reading for this essay might begin with chapter 5 of Utton (1982). However, plenty of material from the present book can be used to handle it from first principles so long as one knows what is meant by the term 'conglomerate' in the business sense. The *Concise Oxford Dictionary* defines a conglomerate as a 'group or corporation formed by the merging of unrelated firms'. This is how economists normally define conglomerates, too, so any essay which does not dwell on the implication of having firms consisting of (relatively) unrelated activities is really missing the point. It would be wise to make clear at the outset what would be taken as evidence of greater competition going on in an economy. The creation of extra capacity, new products and cost-cutting that leads to better products and/or lower prices may be noted. So, too, might reduced profit margins resulting from keener pricing. It would be perfectly in order to talk about the difficulties of detecting competition: for example, does uniform pricing suggest strong competition or collusion? The answer is not clear.

It would also be in order to take issue with the premise that the trend is towards increasingly diversified conglomerates: note the demise of some of the famous conglomerates of recent years and the fragmentation of conglomerates via management buyouts or sales of subsidiaries to firms in related lines of business. In economies such as Australia, where banks lost huge sums that they had lent to conglomerates in the 1980s, there have been suggestions that interest rates for borrowers were pushed up as banks attempted to increase their profits to compensate for bad-debt writeoffs and thus restore their balance sheets to health. This in turn has made investment funding expensive for other firms and made it more difficult for them to compete against overseas rivals.

The dictionary definition also highlights the tendency of these firms to be put together via mergers (more often hostile takeovers than willing marriages) rather than by investment in new assets in areas unrelated to what the firm has previously been doing. Compared with the latter ways of achieving corporate growth, the conglomerate route does not add new capacity to the economy and thus produces a less competitive situation than if the funds were used to buy new equipment or develop new products and processes. To the extent that conglomerates are being put together on the basis of borrowed money their activities may be crowding out the investment plans of firms that would have been seeking to grow by raising external finance to purchase new assets. But this is not necessarily the case: it is conceivable that those who sell their shares to a conglomerate may put the money they thereby receive into investment schemes that do involve the creation of new capacity, processes or products. It may not merely be a kind of financial crowding out that conglomerates produce: a lot of good brainpower may be tied up in such firms, focusing on which companies to buy and sell—in other words, engaging in paper-shuffling rather than genuine enterprise.

Designers of competition policy have tended to focus less on the effects of conglomerate growth on resource availability and more on whether or not conglomerates may be able to get up to mischief in the marketplace. Traditionally, merger policies focused on concentration ratios and how mergers might affect them (in other words, how much of the market was held by the top few firms) or whether mergers involving vertical integration might give the merging firms an unfair advantage over their less integrated rivals (for example, by cornering a source of raw materials or a distribution network). Conglomerates, by the unrelated nature of their activities, do not seem to pose these sorts of threats. Nonetheless, there have been fears that a conglomerate might be able to engage in predatory pricing policies in some of its markets if it could cross-subsidize an aggressive price war from its operations in other markets. This might even involve selling products at prices below average variable costs of production as an investment in a future monopoly position. Incumbent firms that did not have such 'deep pockets' to dig into would be driven out of the market and potential raiders would be frightened off by the example of what happened to the incumbents, unless they could enter without incurring sunk costs.

This sort of argument should ideally be subjected to careful scrutiny (though perhaps not too much should be expected by instructors, since the standard of argument in the literature is often weak here). It begs several questions, including the following.

(a) What is assumed to be going on in the conglomerate's other areas of business whilst it is engaging in predatory cross-subsidization? Is it not possible that the conglomerate would be wary of such a strategy if it involved letting its other lines of business slip back (for example, due to not investing profits in new products or processes, or due to entry being provoked by attempts to milk these markets)? To get this story up and running we seem to require a previous success in obtaining a monopoly market that can be used as a source of funds, or a strategy by the monopolist for milking some of its operations prior to selling them to an unsuspecting buyer.

(b) What kind of impact on morale, and hence on productivity, does this sort of strategy have for the divisions whose funds are being used to finance the predatory strategy?

(c) Utton notes that some authors have asked whether this sort of ploy could work as conglomerates got very common, because they would end up battling with each other; consequently, some kind of tacit collusion might develop in which they divided up competitive battlegrounds amongst themselves, avoiding competition in most markets.

This discussion ought to lead to a recognition that other would-be predators may be deterred from aggressive pricing moves if they are competing with firms that are parts of conglomerates. The consumer does not get the benefit of keener pricing in the short run, but may not have to contend with monopolists in the long run.

The ways in which conglomerates are formed and operate may have implications for the operations of firms in terms of motivation and the time horizons over which decisions are focused. The concept of internal competition is relevant here (see section 11.7). Conglomerate management teams have an opportunity to develop an internal capital market based around an M-form structure that is free of complications associated with linkages between activities. Poor performers may be threatened with being sold off (possibly in bits) or starved of funds. These threats may, like the fear of hanging, concentrate minds of managers and workers in these divisions wonderfully. But if performance is measured in a very short-term way, risk-taking with a view to the long run may be penalized. This could result in divisions of the conglomerate being less inclined to innovate and feeling more inclined to risk long-run raids on their markets (by setting their prices rather as assumed in theories of imperfect competition instead of on the basis of normal costs) in order to make their current performances look adequate. Much the same kinds of pressures may arise in firms that are potential victims of conglomerate raiders: management may get obsessed with making their balance sheets look good so that their companies do not seem worth buying up and restructuring.

The role of a conglomerate head office as a device for promoting restructuring can be considered. Often a conglomerate singles out a victim firm in the belief that it can improve the performance of the firm's assets, whether by improving motivation, management or marketing, or by simply selling off surplus assets and firing surplus workers. This role may or may not have beneficial effects on competition, depending on the extent to which the conglomerate is adopting a short-term strategy. Allegations about 'asset stripping' are not uncommon in relation to conglomerate behaviour, but it may well be that a taken-over company is not simply being milked, but is instead being relieved of organizational slack that the external capital market had allowed to develop (cf. section 7.10 and Hope, 1976).

Attention can usefully be devoted to the theme of the benefits and risks of unrelated diversifications versus the pursuit of economies of scale and scope (cf. section 11.6). A large firm need not be a conglomerate; indeed, the pure conglomerate with no common threads to link its activities is a very rare beast in empirical terms. A radically diversified conglomerate is likely to find itself in a weak competitive position because it is doing battle with firms whose interests are concentrated in relatively few markets and which are seeking to exploit synergy between related activities. This may give them cost or marketing advantages over the conglomerate. Even in respect of the internal capital market aspect of a conglomerate it should be noticed that managers are likely to be better able to make accurate judgements about efficiency and the allocation of investment funds if they specialize in a few sectors and acquire expert knowledge of them (N.M. Kay, 1993: 251). Thus we might say that competitive pressure would be rather stronger if, instead of putting together conglomerates, the so-called entrepreneurs that created them had put together companies that were much more integrated. On the other hand, perhaps the theoretical advantages of specialization and synergy-oriented strategies are reduced in practice if linkages between activities make it difficult to make credible threats to axe individual activities that contribute little to profits when considered on their own.

Overall, it is by no means clear what sort of conclusion should be reached. I would not penalize students who came to no particular ultimate verdict so long as they made clear the difficulties in the way of reaching a yes/no type of answer. Were this essay being written as a term paper rather than as an examination answer, I would hope to be able to reward some students for their willingness to dig up and integrate relevant case study material.

11.10 Case study: The 1986 Daimler-Benz mergers

Background
Through a quick-fire series of acquisitions, Daimler-Benz, a manufacturer of trucks and high-technology up-market cars, became West Germany's biggest industrial company during 1986, with interests ranging from aerospace to household electrical goods. The basis for the acquisitions was a cash mountain built up from export-fuelled profits. Daimler-Benz—a company traditionally noted for attempting to do a few things well, and for pioneering the introduction of advances in automotive engineering (such as fuel-injection systems and anti-lock braking)—diversified dramatically by purchasing controlling stakes in the AEG electrical and electronics group (which had been pulled back from the brink of bankruptcy in 1982 via a strategy that sought to cut down on low-profit household goods and build up sales of more lucrative professional equipment), the Dornier aerospace concern, and engine-maker MTU.

Questions

(1) What do you think was the key motive behind Daimler-Benz's buying spree? What

alternative means of achieving this goal do you think Daimler-Benz's corporate planners would have been wise to consider, and why do you think they would have rejected such alternatives in favour of the merger strategy actually adopted?

(2) Would the absence of its cash mountain (for example, if the US dollar, and hence Benz export earnings, had not been so strong in 1984–85) necessarily have stood in the way of Daimler-Benz's growth strategy? Do you think Daimler-Benz would have been more likely to engage in even more acquisitions in the period in question if it had had an even bigger cash mountain at its disposal? In both cases, justify your reasoning.

(3) How should Daimler-Benz organize its vastly expanded empire to get the best out of these acquisitions, while ensuring that top management does not lose its grip on the core vehicles business? In answering, be sure to consider a number of alternative structures and explain why you are advocating a particular structure and rejecting the alternatives.

Author's notes

Hindsight is an advantage in answering these questions. The *Economist* has some useful articles on what has happened since these mergers were undertaken (for example, the 10 March 1990 issue reported news of discussions between Daimler-Benz and the Japanese conglomerate Mitsubishi concerning possible joint ventures, and the 14 May 1991 issue presented a critique of the firm's diversification strategy). However, these notes were written to show what might have been said in an essay in 1986 without the luxury of such information, by someone who had both grasped material in this book and done a little research on the competitive process in the motor industry.

(1) The achievement of synergy is a likely candidate as the underlying motive for this series of mergers. First, bear in mind that Mercedes-Benz cars have been at the forefront of technological innovations for a long period (see Perrow, 1970: 167–70), and increasing competitive pressures from Japan and their local rival BMW have been pushing them further and further in this direction. Involvement with both electronics and aircraft manufacturing may provide them with a head-start over their rivals in terms of the development of exotic materials, new electronic gadgetry (an up-market car is a very heavy user already of electronic entertainment systems and numerous electric motors for things such as windows, door locking, sunroof opening, heating fans, seat adjustment, and more and more electronics are being built into cars in respect of engine management systems, self-diagnosis/tuning, cruise controls and, in the not so distant future, computer-based navigation systems using satellites and compact discs) and improvements in aerodynamics and braking. On paper, at least, the links with Dornier and AEG make much sense. Ownership of AEG, if AEG is intended to become (or is already) a components supplier, may give Benz greater ability to ensure its demanding quality control standards are met (though there are risks of staff at AEG feeling they now have a 'captive internal market').

Benz would by no means be the first into the cars-plus-aircraft business. Saab in Sweden have for a long while been exploiting their dual involvement when selling their cars, via glossy advertisements in business magazines, so one can see marketing synergy potential too: even if manufacturing and research and development synergies are not all that strong in practice, customers may believe they are and prefer to buy cars from firms that claim their products benefit from aerospace technology. Soon after this set of mergers took place, a similar thing happened in the UK, between British Aerospace and the Rover Group, though many people argued that British Aerospace's main motive was to get hold of the Rover Group's accumulated tax losses. One might well suggest that this sort of financial synergy could be operating here too, given the comments about AEG being pulled back from the brink of bankruptcy. It may also be the case that Daimler-Benz and Dornier have been major markets for AEG's professional equipment for their factories: here, too, the takeover of AEG might be portrayed in terms of vertical integration.

We are not told what kinds of engines MTU produce but we might make some convenient guesses. If they are a maker of engines for military vehicles and marine uses, one might expect manufacturing synergy and/or research and development synergy links with, particularly, Benz's truck interests. But perhaps they make aviation engines that might be used in Dornier aircraft.

There are obvious potential marketing synergy links associated with the high prestige of the Mercedes-Benz brand name: advertisements for AEG consumer products might be (and in fact subsequently were) tailored so as to make explicit reference to the fact that AEG is part of the Benz group. Even if there were no production, research or operating synergies from the change of ownership, at least an illusion could be created which would have been impossible without the merger. It should be noted that, in this strategy, quality control is critical: if the car business suffers from falling standards, the poor image will rub off on to other of its product lines, and vice versa, once customers are aware that Benz is involved in its diverse activities.

In commenting on alternative transactional methods for trying to reach these synergy goals it is easy to highlight scope for market failure: for a start, tax losses are not marketable as such; secondly, in a high-technology context, a strategy of getting outside firms to do work on a consultancy basis carries the risk that the knowledge may end up in rival firms (for example, in BMW's cars). However, one can note that in the past Benz has used outside sources, for example, in pioneering fuel-injection systems; reference may also be made to the success of Porsche as a company doing engineering consultancy work for many of its rivals (cf. section 10.13). Although it would be difficult to claim truthfully that AEG electrical goods were produced by the makers of Mercedes-Benz vehicles without AEG actually having been taken over, an alternative would have been for AEG to make products as a subcontractor for sale under the Mercedes-Benz brand name. Here one could foresee potential for things to go wrong: in addition to possible bargaining problems over the transfer price of the products between AEG and Daimler-Benz, there might be image problems if the Mercedes-Benz brand name got rather too widely used (once it started appearing on toasters and vacuum cleaners its prestige gloss in the car market might fade). In the engine business vertical integration is by no means a natural way of arranging things: Boeing, after all, does not make its own aircraft engines, while Ford and the Rover Group have had Peugeot supply diesel engines for some of their cars. So a discussion of what sorts of market failure could provoke internalization is needed.

Finally, it seems worth considering a possible hedging motive for the mergers. A hint is given that Benz is very heavily reliant on the North American market. In the mid-1980s the firm benefited from the strength of the US dollar relative to the Deutschmark. A fall in the value of the dollar could prove very bad news for Benz profits (precisely such a fall did in fact take place in the years following the flurry of acquisitions). The increasing threat from BMW (and the anticipated threat from up-market brands conspicuously being established by Japanese producers Honda [Accura], Toyota [Lexus] and Nissan [Infiniti]) might also make Daimler-Benz think about not having too many eggs in the vehicles basket. Once again, alternative forms of insurance could be considered by the Daimler-Benz management team, such as to use their cash mountain for portfolio investment.

(2) On the question of alternative methods of finance, it is essential to consider the possibility of the firm raising external funds to finance the mergers, either via issues of debentures (with the risks of fixed interest charges) or equities, or financing the mergers via share exchanges. Knowledge of the peculiarities of the German financial system might lead one to be in a position to comment on the possibility of the venture being financed by loans from a consortium of German banks, who would keep an eye on things by ensuring they had strong board representation. The question of how the existing shareholders might react to the dilution of their control also needs to be considered: much would have depended on whether there was a strong concentration of ownership in the hands of a few family groups. Here, a reading of Marris (1964) would pay off in terms of usable material.

It is possible to appeal to Penrose (1959) and the wider material on corporate learning on the issue of whether even more mergers would have made sense (see sections 7.6, 7.8 and 10.13). The acquisitions strategy really is a huge undertaking, with great scope for corporate indigestion. Research on the car industry reveals that matters were worse than one might realize from the question, since Benz had undertaken a major model-revamping of its cars during this period and had run into unprecedented criticism for poor quality control.

(3) This is a classic case of an indecomposable company which does not neatly fit into either an M-form or a U-form stereotype of structure owing to the pronounced synergy links that we are arguing may underlie the strategy (cf. section 11.7). There are no easy, flawless answers. If the preservation of secrecy of high technologies is a key motive for merging, then it may not be particularly necessary to integrate the activities of the various firms: Dornier or AEG could do subcontracting work on Mercedes-Benz cars and be paid an internal transfer price, with head office in a position to stop them from doing outside consultancy work for rivals. But of course, there might be risks with such a form of organization due to the incentive for Dornier and AEG to undermine the car operations in order to get more resources allocated to their own primary areas of interest (they might be rather slow coming up with the finished consultancy goods, and say the delay was unavoidable). These risks might point in the direction of a form of organization in which Daimler-Benz had a number of in-house design consultancy companies (an aerodynamics facility and a microelectronics facility, for example), each overseen by boards composed of representatives from the client companies within the Daimler-Benz group. In discussing this possibility, many points could be made concerning the divided loyalties of people who plan and allocate resources and yet spend some of their time administering projects. It is rather hard to see how vehicle interests could not end up being rather over-represented at board level. On the other hand, attention could easily get diverted away from the core vehicles

business by problems in other areas about which vehicle builders knew little: how are car-makers to make sense of what is going on if AEG once again finds itself in trouble?

It does not seem necessary to integrate the selling arms of these different lines of business, since they will operate through rather different distribution channels. However, there would seem to be sense in centralizing the marketing *planning* by pooling skills of representatives from the various arms of the firm, and perhaps even creating a centralized in-house advertising division (rather than using outside agencies: cf. Earl, 1991). There may be gains to be had from separating out cars from trucks and buses, and combining the engine-manufacturing operations of trucks and buses with MTU products. But even so, one would still expect internal trade between the car division and other engine-using groups in terms of advances in engine technology.

11.11   Joint ventures and other cooperative strategies

A quarter of a century ago, it would have seemed natural to see cooperation between firms as anti-competitive, as synonymous with collusive behaviour aimed at raising prices. Nowadays, however, business economists devote considerable attention to more benign kinds of cooperative behaviour among firms. A flavour of some of this work has been provided in earlier sections of this book, where I have considered phenomena such as relational contracting (section 10.12), the trading of synergy (section 10.13), quasi-integration, franchising and licensing (section 11.2), and noted how fuzzy they make the boundaries of the modern firm. The kinds of cooperative behaviour so far considered essentially concern pre-specified flows of information or physical goods and services. In this section, by contrast, my primary focus is on joint ventures between firms, which are embodied in contractual relationships that leave unspecified many decisions about resource flows between the trading partners. Some joint ventures are based around the development and production of particular products, with much reciprocal visiting of each other's works by executives and engineers. Others are based around the creation of a jointly owned company, such as an export-marketing company to act on behalf of two firms whose product ranges are complementary. Such ventures are run like conventional multi-shareholder firms except that all of the key decisions are taken by representatives of the partners and profits are paid out to the partners in proportion to the stakes they have invested (normally a two-company joint venture will involve a 50:50 ownership split, with any initial imbalance in the assets that are pooled being offset by cash payment). Joint ventures have become increasingly popular both as means of solving business problems and as subjects for research: a comprehensive and reader-friendly source is Contractor and Lorange (eds) (1988), which focuses particularly on international joint ventures.

When viewed from the standpoint of New Institutional Economics, joint ventures do not have an immediately obvious rationale. More conspicuous are potential problems, for a joint venture is an exceedingly complex institution that it is unwise to see as a simple hybrid located along a spectrum which has market transacting at one end and internalization at the other. Neil Kay (1991: 140) draws attention to three major difficulties:

First, joint ventures typically involve significant bargaining costs in negotiating and policing agreements. Second they involve a dual system of parental control of the child, with duplication of monitoring effect and potential for confusion and conflict in directing the venture. Third, intellectual property and other intangible assets may be appropriated by partners taking advantage of the degree of intimacy such collaboration involves. This latter type of loss may be regarded as a redistribution of gains rather than a straightforward deadweight loss, as in the first two cases. However, incorporating allowances for 'leaky' intangible assets is notoriously difficult to achieve in contracts and so all three sources of costs may discourage joint ventures.

The likely significance of these difficulties will vary depending on the type of joint venture. Some involve two companies getting together to pursue a single objective: once resources have been committed to a joint venture of this kind, it pays the partners to cooperate as much as possible towards using them to meet the common objective even though they get only a fraction of the total returns. Other joint ventures involve the exploitation of complementary capabilities for mutual benefit: you have one skill, I have another, so we get together to do things that neither of us could perform so successfully on our own. Here, incentives to act with opportunism are much stronger. I will want to try to get as much out of you whilst giving you as little insight as possible into my distinctive capability, and vice versa. Many joint ventures involve a mix of both kinds of objectives: for example, they may involve the development of competing products that have some major components in common and which are contributed by both partners, with other elements that are distinctive to one partner's product but engineered with some assistance from the other, and the remainder designed and produced independently (as with the Honda Legend/Rover 800 executive cars).

Partners are particularly likely to become tempted to act selfishly if the joint venture is designed to deal only with a temporary problem and has a finite lifespan. Both may hope that they can avoid future joint ventures by learning enough about each other's distinctive capabilities during the life of the initial agreement. Early on, they may be uncertain whether it might lead to further joint ventures and so cooperate conspicuously, to show each other why future deals might be worth considering. This will encourage reciprocal cooperation. However, if they eventually conclude that in all likelihood this will be a one-off affair they may begin to distance themselves from each other, making self-fulfilling their predictions about the relationship's limited longevity (see further, John Kay, 1993: 151–4).

One alternative to a joint venture is market contracting, for parties to pay each other for goods delivered and services rendered. Many pairs of companies do indeed set up reciprocal trading relationships that involve far more integration in engineering and/or marketing terms than is achieved in many joint ventures. This is well illustrated by two partnerships entered into by General Motors–Holden to cope with changes in the rules of the game in the Australian car market in the mid-1980s, namely the introduction of lead-free petrol and local content/import duty rules which were related to the annual sales of particular car designs. Initially, Holden supplied four-cylinder engines and body panel pressings to Nissan to use in the Australian version of the Nissan Pulsar and bought back Holden-badged Pulsars for sale through its dealer network; Holden also bought six-cylinder engines and gearboxes from Nissan for use in its larger cars. No joint-venture company was involved. Subsequently, Holden did not renew these contracts but instead formed a joint-venture company with Toyota Australia. To be sure, the joint-venture company did slim down and modernize the vehicle assembly operations that it inherited, but the resulting ranges of

Holden and Toyota cars involved nothing more than 'badge engineering'. In principle, Holden could have purchased Toyota Corollas straight from Toyota for sale as Holden Novas, just as it had purchased Nissan Pulsars to sell as Holden Astras. In practice, however, constraints on market contracting led the firm to prefer to go through considerable transaction costs to set up the joint venture with Toyota.

Legal frameworks are one set of constraints that may favour joint ventures over simple contracting. In the Holden/Toyota case, the joint venture permitted the joint determination of the prices of their products to maximize total profits, on which the parent companies had a 50:50 claim. This enabled them to make the most of subtle specification differences to position the badge-engineered products slightly differently so as to guard against excessive price competition between their dealer franchises. As independent companies, they would have been unable to do this without falling foul of Australian competition law. They would in any case have been less likely to end up maximizing joint profits if their assets were not pooled together: for example what was good for profits of the Holden Commodore, also sold as a Toyota Lexcen, might not be good for profits of the slightly smaller Toyota Camry, also sold as a Holden Apollo. (Even with the joint venture this problem remains to some extent, since the joint-venture firm buys inputs from both multinational parent firms: see further, Earl, 1992b.)

In cases where forward or backward integration is the subject of a joint-venture agreement, the obvious question is why one of the firms does not internalize this stage of production outright and then sell some of the good or service in question to the other firm. Central to this type of case is a minimum efficient scale of production that is in excess of the requirements of either party taken separately but less than their joint requirements. In the light of the book distribution example at the end of section 11.2.2, it should be obvious that there is a potential principal-agent problem here due to conflicts of interest. Whoever acts as the supplier of the upstream or downstream service has to supply a competitor. Occasions might arise in which it paid the supplier to leave the competitor in the lurch (for example, a major surge of orders for the internalizing firm's own product) or suited the competitor to switch, or threaten to switch, to another supplier (perhaps an overseas one, following a rise in the value of the domestic currency), leaving the supplier with spare capacity that it was difficult to turn to other uses.

It would be costly to use market contracting in place of a joint venture that called upon the resources of several firms to develop a new product, for the fact that the project is moving into uncharted territory makes it impossible to specify in advance precisely what will need to be contributed by each firm at a particular point. Each time a short-term contract had been implemented and the parameters of the project had been more clearly defined the firms would have to get back to the negotiation table to draw up a contract for the next stage. By contrast, a single joint-venture contract to cover an entire project enables engineers and designers from the partner companies to concentrate on solving problems as the need arises, within frames of reference agreed at the outset. Even though particular broad areas of responsibility may be assigned, it will not be specified precisely who will be doing what at a particular time, so problems encountered during the development phase will be thrashed out as and when they arise. The argument here is exactly the same as used by Coase (1937) in his analysis of the reasons why firms come into existence.

Where a joint venture might involve a mutual exchange of capabilities between a pair of firms achieved through exchanges of personnel and teamwork involving personnel from both companies, the market-based alternative would be for the supplying firm's employees to write the relevant knowledge down and for the receiving firm to pay a fee for it. Knowledge may be bartered without any money changing hands if the two firms place identical values on the information. Unfortunately, a variety of difficulties arise here. First, note that, for a buyer of information, the problem is knowing whether it is worth the price being asked for it; this is something that can only be known for sure by looking at it before paying. The problem for the seller of information is that the buyer may take a look at the information, absorb it and then claim that it is not worth buying. This is known as the 'Arrow paradox', after Arrow (1971: 74). Where a technology can be written down and patented the Arrow paradox ceases to be a worry since although the technology can be freely examined, it cannot be used without payment of a fee acceptable to the owner of the patent. However, the tacit knowledge problem may get in the way of this, leading to a preference for strategies based around joint ventures as means of allowing a two-way osmosis of different organizational capabilities (cf. Hennart, 1988; and Kogut, 1988). This line of thinking may be developed as follows.

If personal knowledge were easy to write down or otherwise transfer between organizations, the supplying firm's employees would be open to offers from rival companies that wanted to purchase their expertise by hiring them and having them start work before they had a chance to write down a record of their know-how for their original employers. The reality often is that knowledge takes time to transmit and it is difficult to know precisely when or how much of the message got through. When knowledge is difficult to articulate and grasp, it may be very unclear quite what will be required to pass it on to another party. If the buyer pays a fixed fee up-front, the supplier (teacher) has an incentive to be slack and blame the buyer (pupil) for any difficulties, whereas the buyer may hope to get a cheaper deal by misrepresenting its starting point in terms of knowledge and capacity to absorb further knowledge. If the supplier of knowledge does so on an hourly basis there is an incentive to deliver slowly and for the buyer to push to move on to the next piece of information despite having only a weak grasp of the prerequisite stages. Even if there is a mutual coincidence of wants and capabilities, this is not a good atmosphere for generating confidence that the outcome of attempts to trade know-how will be mutually beneficial. (This use of the word 'atmosphere' is due to Williamson, 1975; a more colloquial way of saying the same thing would be 'vibes', as in 'bad vibes'.) A very different atmosphere is likely to arise if two firms get together in a joint venture that involves a common objective which will not be met unless there is a two-way flow of capabilities. Knowledge is transmitted by a process of osmosis in the course of teamwork focused on solving particular problems, rather than by formal attempts to convey specific skills, in which different personnel in each firm play the roles of teacher and student. This approach to swapping capabilities by getting the partner firms' personnel to work together allows for both sides to make creative contributions as they work together, so although one side may have more to offer than the other in their areas of recognized excellence both sides may learn. Furthermore, the fact that they focus on solving problems related directly to the common objective means they will waste little time trying to teach each other things that they already know. A concrete example may help make the point clearer: there is a profound difference between, say, on the one hand, Honda bartering its 'guide to engine and powertrain engineering' for Rover's 'guide to how to make car interiors spacious and opulent', and, on the other hand, Honda and Rover agreeing to contribute equally to a pair of executive sedans based around jointly designed components, with Honda leading the powertrain team and Rover leading the bodyshell and interiors teams.

Another alternative to a joint-venture strategy is for the prospective partners to merge their resources into a single company, so long as this is not vetoed by the regulatory authorities because they are concerned about increased prospects for market manipulation by vertical integration or monopolistic market power. The merger strategy has a variety of problems of its own. The proposed joint venture might involve a relatively small part of each firm's assets, so the merger solution would be rather like using a sledge hammer to crack a walnut. After merging, the management teams would have to address much bigger questions of resource allocation across the merged unit as a whole, including the extent to which it made sense to integrate operations that may have been based around very different corporate cultures. Once a merger has led to the integration of the assets of the merging firms, it may be very difficult to dissolve if difficulties develop: there is a parallel here between corporate relationships and human relationships, with mergers being analogous to marriage and joint ventures analogous to dating. It should also be noted that many firms nowadays are not thinking of individual corporate alliances but rather, networks of strategic alliances, each one set up with a view to solving a particular problem. Many of these alliances may be small enough so as not to provoke large-scale competitive retaliation. If each of these alliances were replaced by a merger, the resulting corporate giants might be unwieldy as well as unpalatable to the regulatory authorities.

Although these kinds of considerations may lead companies sometimes to favour joint ventures to meet particular objectives and to favour full internalization or arm's-length marketing contracting on other occasions, it seems that in some inter-company relationships these three types of strategies may be pursued sequentially in a lexical manner that begins with licensing, progresses to joint ventures of increasing intimacy and ultimately goes on to merger. The licensing arrangement allows the licenser to test how well the licensee can match its own production standards and get a better idea of the licensee's capabilities to offer something that the licenser needs. If this exercise in 'testing the water' is sufficiently encouraging, joint ventures enable the companies to learn more about each other both in terms of of capabilities and willingness to cooperate with enthusiasm rather than opportunism. The more that personnel from the two firms work with each other, the more that a unified tacit knowledge set and a team spirit may be created. In other words, instead of knowledge of different kinds merely being transferred between the firms through participation in successive ventures, new knowledge is developed that is specific to the firms as a whole, just as happens within individual firms as they evolve. If so, merger may be seen as a way of cementing the situation with, by this stage, relatively little cost but with potential for further improvements in productivity due to the change in atmosphere—rather as in relationships between couples which progress from cautious dating through to greater trust and mutual fascination, which leads to cohabitation and, ultimately to marriage. In some cases an improved atmosphere and greater commitment may be generated simply by an exchange of partial shareholdings, rather than by a full-scale merger: an example here is the growing bonding between Honda and Rover prior to the somewhat opportunistic 1994 sale of Rover to BMW by British Aerospace (see Earl, 1992b).

11.12   Multinational enterprise

Much of the literature on joint ventures has emerged as an offshoot of a slightly earlier explosion of research on multinational firms, much of which has focused on transaction costs and comparative institutional analysis. A particularly useful recent source is Pitelis and Sugden (eds) (1991). Kay (1983b) presents a convenient review article on some of the books that have appeared in this area. Among the most useful sources in terms of combining theoretical and case study materials are Rugman (ed.) (1982), Casson (1986) and Casson (ed.) (1983). A good empirical survey has been provided by Vonortas (1990). The discussion in this section is particularly inspired by Galbraith and Kay (1986), which overlaps with Kay (1984).

The existence of firms that have subsidiaries in countries other than those in which they were originally set up is something that we should not take for granted. Many firms choose to get by without such subsidiaries even though they are keen to see their products reaching an international public. There is much that might deter firms from setting up overseas operations.

(a) The overseas markets may be ones in which patterns of tastes are very different, so it might be better to leave to others the task of marketing one's product in these markets, rather than investing in overseas operations and ending up losing a great deal.

(b) The legal environment may be very different, and so too the sociopolitical setting in which business has to be done (in some countries, corruption is the norm and getting proposals past bureaucrats may be very difficult without paying bribes or having connections with people in high places). Local contractors may know better how to cope.

(c) The culture of the workplace may be very different from what one's management are used to.

(d) It may be difficult to monitor overseas subsidiaries at great distance without committing a lot of time from staff based at head office.

(e) There may be substantial economies of scale in producing in a single plant.

Given these factors, it is perhaps not surprising that many firms, if they are thinking of having overseas operations in the long run, prefer to go through a gradual process of familiarization with the countries in question. This can be achieved by developing some kind of collaborative strategy with local firms (Kay, 1991).

All this begs the question of why a firm should consider having overseas operations in the first place. An alternative strategy is to export the products, and use agents in the overseas country to market one's goods in that market. This, of course, raises the possibility of principal-agent problems: how can an exporter be sure that the agent is doing a good job, especially if the agent acts for other firms that produce products which compete with one's own? A second difficulty is that the local agents may not have the same kind of long-term staying power as a manufacturer. (For example, in the late 1980s, some car-importing franchises in Australia were taken over by overseas manufacturers whose sales there had declined after they increased their prices because of the collapse of the Australian dollar. An alternative strategy, though, might have been for the manufacturers to act as sources of capital to keep the local distributors in business.) Such fears may provide a rationale for setting up an overseas subsidiary for distribution purposes, but that still leaves open the question of why firms may go to the trouble of setting up overseas production facilities.

Exporting may be made difficult by trade policies of overseas governments that are, for example, interested in developing manufacturing bases of their own. Exporting may have to be made very difficult indeed before it starts making sense to have one's products made on a small scale in the overseas market, unless, of course, set-up costs can be avoided because there exists spare capacity in these markets which can be adapted to make one's products. But overseas production can occur without it being undertaken by the company that has developed the product. An overseas firm can either be contracted to make the product on one's behalf (for example, for many years, Nissan Australia used spare capacity to assemble kits of Volvo cars for Volvo's Australian distribution branch to sell in that market), or it can be allowed to make the product under licence. In this way, risks of commitment to production facilities can be avoided.

A firm which allows another firm in another country to have access to its designs does, however, run the risk that the other firms will make off with some of its know-how. This is particularly likely where the know-how is not product-specific—in other words, where it can be used in another product that was not mentioned in the contract and possibly not even have been conceived of at the time. This is a big danger in the early stages of development of a technology when all the spinoffs have yet to be worked out. Producers of advanced products are likely to feel far happier about letting other firms access their designs towards the latter stages of the product life-cycle—unless piracy seems likely. The hazards of technology licensing may take decades to be felt. For example, in the course of discussing how British Leyland (now the BMW-owned Rover Group) got itself the path to recovery by producing Honda cars under licence, Sir Michael Edwardes, a former head of British Leyland, points out in his autobiography (1983: 201–2) that

> In the early 1930s the Austin Motor Company [later part of British Leyland] gave Datsun a licence to produce a car in Japan.... In the early 1950s Datsun obtained another licence to build, from parts supplied by Austin, the A40 Somerset. This deal helped to get the Japanese motor industry off the ground....
>
> Looking back at the history of Austin it is intriguing to see that the little Austin 7 acted as a catalyst in the development of more than one motor manufacturer in the late 1920s and 1930s. It was built under licence in Germany by the Dixi company which became part of the motorcycle organisation, Bayerische Motoren Werke AG—and the Austin 7 thus became the first BMW car. It was also assembled in a part of the Peugeot factory in France as the 'Rosengart' and appeared in the United States as the 'Bantam', also assembled locally.

As a latter-day counterpart of this sort of example it is interesting to note the role of outside expertise in the setting up of the Korean car business. It received a great boost by being able to attract top management talent in the form of frustrated executives formerly employed in the UK car industry, and initially merely assembled kits under licence. But increasing proportions of inputs have been locally made and new models have involved more and more Korean design inputs. The Korean firms initially enjoyed very close relationships with overseas manufacturers—Daewoo with General Motors, Hyundai with Mitsubishi—including minority shareholdings. Daewoo was even allowed to sell an Opel Kadett-based model through General Motors dealerships in some countries, badged as a Pontiac Lemans. General Motors executives said in interviews in the late 1980s that they believed that although the Korean producers would get better and better at making cars, they expected their own firms to be able to stay ahead. However, at the start of 1992, shortly after a new Kadett was introduced in Europe, General Motors sold its Daewoo shareholding and in 1993 Mitsubishi began to distance itself from Hyundai as the latter introduced its first home-grown engines.

The rationale for setting up an overseas subsidiary thus lies in perceptions of potential for some kind of market failure, such as the possible leakage of technology secrets in the course of trade between firms. The work of Casson and Rugman was much inspired by Coase (1937) and the subsequent literature on transaction costs. However, in 1960, an American radical economist, Stephen Hymer, sought in his doctoral dissertation (published in 1976) to portray the multinational firm as a device for extracting monopoly returns in a world of imperfect markets. The implication was that such firms might well offer little to the economies in which they invested, but might take much from them in the form of investment inducements. To prevent the escape of knowledge into the local community, they would ensure that key positions were filled by expatriate employees from the head office and would concentrate on adding value in low technology areas.

The anti-multinational view might be extended in a rather different way: such firms can be seen as having overseas operations as means of exerting bargaining power over their workers. The threat may be that 'if you don't agree to our terms, we shall close this plant and source our products from elsewhere in our corporate empire, such as one of our low wage plants'. On the other hand, we might see the strategy from the company's point of view as a means of insuring itself against the risk of being mugged by opportunistic workers in one country.

Discussions about the role of overseas subsidiaries as devices by which a firm may avoid putting all its eggs in the one basket might be extended beyond the labour market. By being involved in a range of countries one may reduce the risk of loss due to political change (for example, nationalization by a left-wing government). Similarly, a downturn in business in one country may not do so much damage to one's overall operations if one has operations in many markets. But all of these arguments need to be viewed critically: labour market risks can be hedged against by having contracting relationships with overseas firms, and losses due to events such as political upheaval may be avoided by not having assets overseas in the first place. Firms that export can hedge by exporting to a number of markets or by diversifying the products they make and sell in their domestic markets. We are thus driven back to the question of what advantages overseas investment has to offer over exporting or the use of contracting relationships with overseas firms.

In addition to the suggestion that fears of know-how loss and of being let down by agents promote overseas investment, the issue of quality control and market signalling receives much attention in the modern literature. It may be difficult to guarantee quality in a market where the product is being supplied by a firm that is acting as one's agent.

Investments in quality assurance facilities *may* seem to be necessary if quality cannot be guaranteed via the contract or by having one's inspectors present. For example, Honda spent a fortune in the UK on a predelivery inspection plant, to iron out bugs in vehicles assembled on its behalf by Rover, but Honda subsequently extended its investments in the UK to include a local assembly plant of its own, in which Rover took a partial shareholding (see Earl, 1992b). It may even seem necessary to 'do it oneself' in terms of production and/or distribution to guarantee the integrity of one's brand name. The banana industry is a classic example of this. Though bananas are not a high-technology product, they are perishable and easily damaged during harvesting and shipping. Damage is difficult to detect without peeling them, so consumers will choose in favour of trustworthy brands. Vertical integration of growing, shipping and distribution is therefore used to promote a commitment to quality (Hennart, 1991: 91–2; Casson, ed., 1983).

In financial services markets and other sectors where client confidentiality is required (such as advertising) a multinational that can claim not to rely on agents may be in a stronger position when it comes to winning clients: prospective clients may recognize that it has an incentive to be more careful about the information it is using because any leak may be directly traceable to it, rather than possibly be arising from any number of outside contractors. In these types of markets it has also been hoped that multinational clients would tend to wish to use multinational suppliers of services purely for reasons of having had satisfactory experiences with them in other countries. If franchise arrangements or joint ventures cannot be worked out—custom-designed products like advertising campaigns can hardly be franchised like Pizza Hut or Budget car rentals—overseas subsidiaries may be necessary to win business from companies that are themselves expanding overseas. However, attempts to diversify overseas in these lines of business via mergers and takeovers have not always been particularly successful: some banks have bought dud banks, and advertising agencies have not always been able to convince head offices that their quality standards are uniform—this is hardly surprising, given the creative aspect of advertising— and that clients would therefore benefit from imposing from head office a directive that the entire company deals with a particular supplier of services (see Earl, 1991).

11.13   Essay example: Transaction costs and tourism

Question
Examine the economic organization of the international tourism industry in the light of the recent theoretical contributions that highlight the role of transaction costs in shaping choices between different ways of getting things done.

Author's notes
To tackle this assignment there is no need to spend a long while obtaining detailed empirical material. To get started it is merely necessary to take a careful look at aspects of this industry that should readily stand out from a careful reading of brochures of travel firms and from thoughtful observations from personal experience—such as: scope to buy tickets at both travel agents and at high street offices of major airlines; international hotel chains such as Sheraton, Hilton and Holiday Inn; ownership of resorts and surface transport

operations by airlines such as Ansett; international car-rental firms which sometimes have local franchisees rather than owning their local operations; tour operators who can provide fly-drive holidays in Europe for little more than the price other firms charge for a return air ticket; arguments about the extent of Japanese ownership of resorts in Australasia and Hawaii, and so on. Research on the international hotel business by Dunning and McQueen (1981) is especially useful as further reading. This is an assignment for which I would hope that instructors would reward creative thinking: the question is not one for which *the* right answer exists; rather, it is an opportunity for people to show whether they can analyse economic organization from the transaction cost standpoint.

With this sort of question it is wise to begin by thinking about the nature of the product and characteristics of the buyers. This may lead to ideas such as the following about the sorts of transactional difficulties that may arise and the pros and cons of ideas about possible ways of dealing with them.

(1) We are dealing with a service industry, which renders the list of alternatives to multinational investment smaller than usual: export of these services is not possible in the way that export of goods manufactured in a home-base factory is possible. So the choice of methods for being involved comes down to (a) selling one's know-how to local operators (either as a consultant or via a franchise arrangement; (b) obtaining management contracts to run local assets (such as a contract to run a particular hotel investment as, say, a Hilton Hotel, for the next twenty years); (c) purchasing assets overseas and having local firms or other multinationals manage them; or (d) purchasing assets overseas and then managing them oneself. Intermediate strategies might also be envisaged, for example, where the running of an overseas asset is franchised to local operators but their staff are trained by the firm that sells the franchise.

Different hazards arise with each of these different strategies. With (a) there is the possibility of the franchisees making off with more than the franchiser bargained for (for example, using the know-how obtained from running a franchised car-hire firm as a means of setting up a rival, independent firm. This will be difficult in so far as there are advantages to being an incumbent (such as an international brand name, or established bargaining power with suppliers of vehicles).

With (b) the length of the contract may prove problematic if one decides that the market is not such a good one to be in after all; there may also be difficulties involved in keeping secret the key to one's managerial advantages, as key staff may be paid 'golden hellos' as inducements to get them to defect to rival enterprises. Again, though, there is the question of barriers to entry on the marketing side (if a hotel does not already have a reputation on a par with hotels from which it seeks to steal both market and staff, how can it make itself attractive?).

With (c) what we really have is property investment, not investment in service provision as such, and the investor is at the mercy of the contractor: on the one hand the local contractor may have superior local know-how but on the other hand there is the risk that it will not be used to good effect. The question of the terms of the contract is central to sorting out incentives here: the right to run the hotel might be auctioned, with the hotel owner allowing the successful bidder the right to do whatever is seen fit (within specified bounds) to the hotel. Alternatively, the hotel owner might pay the management team in terms of a royalty per room filled per night, and keep all the profits remaining after the management team's expenses and royalties have been deducted (the expenses might turn out rather high, in this case!), or some kind of profit-sharing joint venture might be worked out.

With (d) aside from the risk of staff defecting, the main hazard is that of not knowing the territory and consequently ending up with poor rates of capacity utilization. (It may be possible to keep staff loyal by offering them the prospect of promotion and generally filling senior vacancies from within rather than by making recourse to the external labour market.

(2) This is an 'experience good', in other words, one which cannot properly be assessed until after it has been consumed. How, then, is the consumer to be able to choose? One method is to avoid making contracts until one reaches the place in which one wants to stay, and then check out the local rental car firms, hotels and so on. But this may mean that the traveller needs a longer time in the place to incur these transaction costs and then get on with the business or pleasure that is the purpose of the trip; possibly all the local services might be fully booked, anyway, if one does not book up in advance. Here it should be noted that the role of experience is complicated in many cases by the fact that the paid-for services are consumed jointly with the environmental attractions of a particular locality and tourists (unlike business travellers) may prefer to limit their forward bookings in order to be able to pass swiftly through places that they do not find appealing and linger instead at places they discover to be particularly attractive. Even so, they may still be reluctant to spend a lot of time choosing on the spot which suppliers of travel services to use.

A second strategy is to choose something familiar, in other words, to rely on a brand name whose products one has experienced already and hope that these products are standardized (Sheraton Hotels, Avis car rental, etc.). Providers of geographically wide-ranging branded services are therefore likely to have a competitive advantage over localized firms: they may be expected to enjoy economies of scale in advertising and find it possible to incur higher fixed costs—and hence provide better services—due to their higher occupancy rates. Unbranded firms may thus have to depend heavily on their reputations being spread by word of mouth or on the possibility that travellers will make use of information published in directories by companies seeking to fill this informational gap in the market.

Thirdly, travellers may rely upon the advice of travel agents. However, travel agents may face major conflicts of interest, that may worry either the travellers or the suppliers of travel services. Normally when fixing up travel, one does not pay commission to the travel agent in any explicit sense: one simply pays for the services that the agent has fixed up. The agent then keeps an unspecified part of the proceeds, how much depending on the deal that the agent has done with the supplier of the service. Someone seeking advice on good deals overseas at the budget end of the market may find that travel agents do not have many products that they feel inclined to recommend, because it is not worth their while to do so if they can make better commission from acting for up-market suppliers. Of course, to induce the agents to recommend cheaper sources of a travel service, a supplier could offer similar commissions to those offered by more up-market ones, but even this—or an even bigger fee—may not be enough to get the agent to make a recommendation. The problem is that travel agents, like their clients, face an information problem: they may not be confident about the quality of the product but they are likely to be wary of risking the loss of customer goodwill. In other words, not all failures by travel agents to suggest cheaper accommodation should be put down to opportunism, the guileful use of information that the other party does not have.

Given this, it is no wonder that cheaper, owner-operated motels have tended to form themselves into franchise-like networks (such as Budget Motels, Best Western, and Flag Inns) that try to get economies of scale in promotion and the advantages of a shared brand name that gives signals about the quality of service to those who have stayed previously with a network member. Those whose standards fall too low are requested to leave the network; those whose standards are way above the network's norm ought to find it profitable to join a more prestigious group, so customer expectations should not be inflated unrealistically either. Networks nearer the bottom of the middle of the market do not seem to bother with using travel agents to show their brochures to potential customers and arrange bookings. This is hardly surprising given the convention that the price of a motel room to the traveller is the same regardless of how it is booked. At the bottom end of the market the slice that a travel agent would need to be offered in commission might be so great that it would seem better to run a bigger risk of not having a room occupied at all. (Note that a forward booking by an agent takes away most of the profit margin and ties up the room for the night in question; it might have been possible to fill it anyway from passing trade.)

Anyone who deals frequently with a travel agency will probably have noticed that the staff are often away on 'holidays' provided by suppliers of travel services. These are worth commenting on: from one standpoint they might seem to be a device to bias recommendations, but from another they are means by which the travel agents get to know more about some of the products in respect of which they are acting as an intermediary. Some kind of bias is certainly likely to result: the travel agents reduce their risks by limiting their recommendations to products they know well; the trouble is, there are only so many products they can try out on behalf of future customers.

Travellers who think agents may be giving biased advice because of the commission they stand to make may feel happier if they (the travellers) pay a fee to an independent travel consultant for advice about what to book up, given their requirements, and for doing the booking. However, it still is not obvious how they can be sure that the advice is impartial (unless there is some legal framework in place, rather as occurs with investment advisory services in many countries, where anyone caught accepting kickbacks may lose the right to call themselves an independent investment advisor). Also there is the problem of the travel agent not being particularly industrious if the fee is not based on the quality of the advice (the traveller faces difficulties in judging its quality: even after the trip has been undertaken the traveller may still be unclear what the alternatives might have been like).

The conflict of interest problem also arises when an agent handles rival suppliers of very similar services such as air travel: they run the risk that the agent may 'push' one of their competitors' products because a better commission is the reward for making a sale. This may lead to suppliers bidding against each other for the agent's favour or adopting other strategies to reduce the conflict of interest. An alternative strategy is to engage in vertical integration and provide one's own retail outlets, specializing in one's own product. Here, customers are not under any illusions that they are being given impartial advice, but if they are satisfied with the brand of service from prior experience they may feel they can get a better deal by doing it directly rather than by using an agent—especially if they are suspicious of agents. Normally companies that engage in vertical integration in these markets do so in a taper integration manner, mixing the use of their own retail outlets with the use of agents. Quite often they end up acting as agents for other parties (an international airline may have a 'preferred' domestic carrier or car-hire company) on a reciprocal basis. There is usually only a single preferred partner, so the provider of the other service does not have to worry about a conflict of interest; instead, the customer then has to worry about whether the recommended combination of products is the best value for money, given his/her goals as a traveller. In other cases, firms in this industry actually may feel they can exert more control over the situation by engaging in internalization (for example, the franchiser companies for Avis car-rental operations and Sheraton Hotels were at one time both part of the communications multinational ITT; Ansett Airlines owns the Hayman Island resort off Australia's Queensland coast, while its rival Qantas Airlines owns the Dunk Island resort). If customers are worried about this sort of arrangement, they may prefer to get travel fixed up via a travel agent, which has different problems.

(3) Note that we have introduced the idea of a bundle of products being what the consumer is typically buying. Brand-name bundling may have synergistic benefits: if you think Ansett air travel is good, you might also have high expectations of an Ansett-owned resort, or an Ansett all-inclusive holiday. A package deal reduces transaction costs for the buyer or for the travel agent, but the costs of fixing up standardized holidays are then largely borne by the tour operator under whose brand name the packages are sold. Tour operators often will have no operating interests in any part of the package holidays that they sell. Their on-site representation serves merely to ensure that customers pass smoothly from one stage to the next and that suppliers are delivering the services as promised. The rationale for tour operators seems to be that they can get economies of making large-scale forward bookings with suppliers of travel services and grouping them together in standardized bundles. Suppliers may prefer a large booking as this reduces their contract-forming costs and enables them to make more forceful commitments when fixing up their own supplies of inputs. The tour operator may then be the one that shoulders the risk of being unable to resell at a satisfactory profit all the seats, rooms and so on, that have been booked in advance (cf. section 9.11).

(4) We are dealing with a population of mobile buyers, usually from affluent nations. Although they may be going to unfamiliar territories it is perhaps the firms based in affluent nations who stand a bigger chance of knowing what services to provide, even if they do not know the overseas markets very well. Japanese tourists may prefer to sign up for holidays with Japanese owned and managed overseas resorts because they feel their expectations are more likely to be met. However, if the culture of a suitably Japanese resort can be written down in the form of a contract that can be enforced without undue cost, such arrangements ought not to be necessary. But there may be dangers that the knowledge may seep out.

As a general concluding point it may be worthwhile to emphasize that the different types of risks that different types of customers and suppliers may perceive open up the possibility that a range of different ways of organizing the delivery of travel services may all be profitable to offer.

11.14   Case study: The rise and fall of Filofax in Japan

Background

(Based on material in *The Economist* on 12 November 1988, 30 September 1989 and 17 February 1990.)

In 1984, the small, one-product British firm Filofax found that its 63-year old speciality—a leather-bound loose-leaf diary/'personal organizer' with a collection of printed sheets for various notes, facts and guides—had suddenly become a sought-after product in Western economies. Although the Filofax company had spent nothing on advertising, the Filofax product was becoming something without which no self-respecting yuppie would wish to be seen. To get into the Japanese market, Filofax signed an exclusive distribution deal with Apex International, which rapidly found 300 retailers for Filofax binders and loose-leaf sheets. Apex spent heavily on magazine advertisements featuring as Filofax users movie star Diane Keaton and movie director Steven Spielberg.

Filofax sales soared, from a value of £681 000 in 1983 to £14.7 million in 1988. Its Japanese market went from a mere 10 million Yen in 1984 to ¥800 million in 1987, at which time Apex was selling Filofaxes at ¥36 000 apiece. The huge difference between production costs and the market price had been slow to attract competitors in the United Kingdom but in Japan this was not the case: by late 1988, thirty rival products were being offered in the Japanese market, many of which were of better quality than the original but only one-third of the price.

Apex did not fight back by cutting the price, one reported reason being that it did not wish to alienate those who had already bought the product. Instead, it used the benefits of the rising Yen (which made imports from the United Kingdom cheaper) to do four things. First, Apex spent about ¥1 200 on a smart box to differentiate the product, on the basis that the Japanese buyer is typically impressed by top quality packaging and presentation, and had all paper refills repackaged in more expensive plastic bags (bearing the Filofax name) on their arrival in Japan. Secondly, Apex sent out display cases costing ¥1 million to the 50 smartest sales outlets. Thirdly, instead of supplying the leather binder and refills separately, it began to offer binders complete with five refill packs and 100 different sample note sheets. Fourthly, it set up a Goldcard club supplying information to members in a bid to turn the product from an item of stationery into a lifestyle component.

Apex's policies appeared to be very successful and caused Filofax to start rethinking its promotion methods in Western markets where it handled its own distribution. In Japan the Filofax became market leader in terms of sales turnover despite selling as a price that was half as much again as its chief competitor, Bindex. (Bindex was the biggest volume seller with five per cent of the two million unit market in 1988, a market that was, at that time, forecast to grow to between 2.5 and 3 million units in 1989.) Apex was planning to open a Filofax English Language School, and to offer Filofaxes with crocodile skin coverings—the latter being a bid to appeal to women, who had so far largely resisted the personal organizer fad.

Such innovative policies caused some observers to suggest that Filofax was in danger of finding that Apex had turned from being its collaborator to become its competitor in the Japanese market. The only lever Filofax had was its trademark. Filofax turned down an offer from Apex to purchase the company outright but agreed to let Apex make, for the Japanese market, a more down-market 'Stylofax' product. By late 1988, Stylofax was already outselling Filofax.

1989 saw a dramatic turnaround in the performance of the Filofax company. It moved from healthy profits to a £554 000 pretax loss for the first half of the 1989–90 financial year, with an expected full-year loss of a million pounds. Filofax sales fell by 20 per cent as times grew hard for some yuppies and as others, who were still doing well, started spending their money on electronic organizers and portable telephones. Filofax tentatively began to diversify away from its single product by producing a business briefcase but appeared to reckon that it did not have the resources or expertise to put its brand name on a collection of unrelated products. Its main survival strategy therefore was to concentrate on broadening its market by advertising in ways aimed at appealing to (a) senior executives, who had previously been deterred by its faddishness, and (b) busy mothers. Filofax also sought to build up its long-term market by offering entry-level products for students. These products included a registration card with which Filofax hoped to keep track of users as their careers progressed and to target them for mail promotions of new Filofax products such as student examination guides and miniaturized business directories.

Question
Write a critical appraisal of the marketing strategies adopted by the Filofax company from 1983 to 1990.

Author's notes
It would be most unwise to try to tackle this question on the basis that case study work requires nothing more than the rearrangement of the material that is provided in the case, under the Strengths, Weaknesses, Opportunities and Threats (SWOT) headings. Nothing could be further from the truth, even though this sort of approach is promoted by many American marketing texts. Instead, try to work on the basis that marks are awarded for the insight that is added to the material, in terms of the use of theoretical analysis to make sense of what happened and as a basis for critical comment. Some of the material in the case may well be worth questioning, even though it comes from a respected publication such as *The Economist*.

The analysis should begin with an examination of the Filofax product, its market and production process. You cannot hope to go on to do a successful SWOT analysis until you have done this. The examination will help you decide whether the manufacturers have any sustainable competitive advantages that will enable them to keep ahead of potential rivals and preserve their market positions in the long run. The identification of these advantages, if there are any, will have implications for the way in which Filofax should have chosen to operate. If the situation looks pretty grim for the long run, this, too, will have implications with respect to the wisdom of the strategy that the firm adopted. It may well be the case that a strategy of going for as much profit as possible in the short run makes perfect sense, even if it encourages entry by lower-cost producers who would have appeared anyway, sooner or later (cf. sections 9.6 and 9.10).

The Filofax product is yet another example of an experience good, whose worth is difficult to assess in advance of purchase, especially if people are used to making do with alternative information/time management systems. In order to make sense of the product life-cycle embodied in this case, you should consider the attributes of the product in relation to alternative technologies: consider what it is that a Filofax enables its owner to produce (cf. section 3.6). The pre-Filofax technology involves the use of diaries, address books and so on, which involve a lot of redundant paper and cannot be recycled. A Filofax can save time on up-dating that otherwise has to be undertaken at the start of each year when last year's diaries become obsolete. It is a much more flexible system for people whose personal environments change a good deal during each year. The wisdom of targeting users who may not have a good deal of information to manage is questionable (busy mothers may be rather borderline as potential buyers, while senior executives will often have their information and time management done for them by their secretaries).

These aspects are carried over into electronic personal organizers, where the throwaway element is reduced yet further by advanced programming and the lack of need for refills; worse still, for Filofax, these new products include calculator facilities, spelling and thesaurus capabilities and so on. As the prices of the appropriate sorts of microchips fall further, the attractions of Filofaxes in functional terms will fade: this is something the company should have been anticipating in the mid-1980s, even at the time sales of its own product took off in a big way. Limitations to the rate of decline of the Filofax may come from the fact that electronic personal organizers are also experience goods: potential users may find them intimidating because of their complexity—do not forget the significance of bounded rationality—and may be anxious about the possible loss of all their data due to system failure, battery wearout or whatever—something they would not suffer with a Filofax, with which they have hard copy. (One would have thought it quite simple to remove the anxiety of potential buyers by designing the organizers to allow periodic data dumps from them on to personal computers or tape cassettes.)

Though easily seen as a convenient means to the end of improving control over one's life (cf. Earl, 1986: 92–101), a Filofax was also a status symbol, used publicly in the process of fixing up appointments: one can argue that it symbolizes how expensive a person's time is, how busy that person is, regardless of how expensive it is as a product. (Its public use may help it hold out against electronic substitutes where the scope for embarrassment in the hands of an inexperienced user might be rather large!) The more expensive variants add to this image, in so far as onlookers are aware of relative prices, but only so long as the user is not ripe for being judged as someone who has got more money than sense, given the availability of cheaper and possibly better products. This leads to the question of the wisdom of the pricing strategy adopted on behalf of Filofax by its Japanese agent. By keeping its price way above its rivals, did Apex reduce the probability that people would actually make comparisons with cheaper substitutes and discover that they were actually better despite their lower prices, or did it encourage people to search for something cheaper?

We cannot come to a clear-cut answer to this question, but we might obtain some clues by considering the buying process. In the case of the United Kingdom, where no advertising was being done, purchases would largely arise as a result of a *demonstration effect*: as a result of people seeing others using a Filofax or hearing about one via references to yuppie lifestyles in the media. These occasions would see the brand name of the product being used as the name of the class of product, which might result in people going shopping for a Filofax, rather than for a Filofax-type product. This equating of brand and generic names may be one of the company's main advantages. However, given the sorts of prices that were being charged, and the possible difficulties of distinguishing the real thing from close copies, one really should raise questions about the long-run viability of the market position that was being aimed for, even if new technologies had not appeared, and even despite the fact that the Japanese buyers were 'taken in' by packaging and in-store promotions. To prevent people from seeing the alternatives would require that these were not stocked in similar outlets, or that they could *credibly* be packaged as superior if sold alongside cheaper clones.

The question of the product's durability should not be overlooked: this is a product that generates on-going business via the refills. Once a customer has invested in the complete package we may observe what neoclassical economists would regard as non-rational behaviour in the form of a failure to treat sunk costs as sunk (cf. section 4.7): people may in fact be reluctant to switch to the newer technology and make their Filofaxes redundant. If the basic product lasts a long time, and if there are difficulties for onlookers in distinguishing different grades of it, then one might question the stated basis for Apex's reluctance to lower prices, namely that 'it did not wish to alienate those who had already bought the product'. These people will be out of the market for the durable part of the product for quite a while, and may not even notice that prices have fallen unless they have a reason to gather price information or observe the prices in advertisements/hear about what friends had paid (here, recall the discussion of cognitive dissonance theory in section 4.7 in relation to post-purchase information-gathering biases). The worries about alienating people who had already bought Filofaxes would be much more justifiable if the Filofax product were part of a wider range of products with the same brand name, but it was actually only as part of the strategy of *not* lowering prices that Apex started to broaden the Filofax idea. Perhaps of more concern is the risk that price cuts would encourage expectations of further price cuts in the minds of those who were considering buying—if, that is, they were aware of the previous price as a result of advertising about price cuts. Unless Apex actually decided to move substantially down-market, advertisements mentioning price cuts would be rather difficult to reconcile with ongoing attempts to portray the product in terms of premium quality.

Following this consideration of the product's attributes, one might question the extent to which Filofax sales really were being lost to portable phones in 1989: these serve somewhat different needs. Also their likely purchasers, at the pioneer/take-off stage of market growth, might be consumers who already had Filofaxes from some years before, having at that stage been pioneers in the market. In general the problem with the yuppie market need not have been that the average yuppie was not doing so well, but that the market of new yuppies had shrunk, so producers were left with a market segment that was already largely saturated.

In manufacturing terms we have a rather simple, low-technology item whose basic design is easy to duplicate and whose production requirements should not prove a barrier to entry by rivals from a variety of areas (cf. sections 9.6 and 9.7). Examples of potential competitors that could be suggested include producers of stationery equipment, such as ring binders (they are likely to be more familiar with working in plastic than leather, but this is a factor which will make it easy for them to produce down-market versions) or wallets and briefcases. Note, however, that the Filofax company seemed somewhat sceptical of the closeness of alternatives even such as briefcases to its area of expertise: possibly this is why it found itself facing so many rivals. Stationery suppliers who have specialized in the production of consumables (in other words, the paper refills) might consider finding subcontractors to make the binders for them. The prospect of finding suppliers in low-wage economies seems rather strong. For Filofax to compete against these in quality terms it must be able to keep hold of the upper end of the market by virtue of offering a superior finish. The case material suggests that it was failing to do so. There is scope for innovation by changing the binding material (as with crocodile skin) or by changing the contents of the refills to give the product new uses, but such changes would be easy for others to follow unless they were patentable (this is unlikely, and for a small company like Filofax, the costs of enforcement in the courts might be prohibitive if any patents were challenged, particularly overseas).

Summing up so far, the long-term prospects for Filofax to continue selling the sorts of volumes that it had sold at its peak do not seem good, though perhaps there will be enough of a residual market (people with more money than sense/impressed by fancy packaging) to enable it to return to its pre-fad sort of position: small volume, high price. Possibly it will enhance these prospects by developing ties with specialist distributors/branders such as Dunhill and Cartier, and getting involved with producing other leather-based products under their brand names. But the question is focusing on the past, not the future. The foregoing discussions give a basis for considering the possibility that it was perfectly rational to adopt a skimming/milking strategy, as intimated at the end of the second paragraph of these notes (see also section 10.9). To know if this was what Filofax were up to, though, we would need more information about the extent to which they made investments in new capacity that was specific to this product, and quite how the losses occurred in 1989–90.

A sign that Filofax were not thinking in this way could be their failure to *license* the manufacture of the product in Japan, via Apex, and thereby reap returns for higher sales without having to do any capacity expansion of their own. Here it should be noted that when this case was set in an examination, some students suggested that Filofax should have *franchised* its product's manufacture. This is a misunderstanding of franchising, which is largely concerned with distribution of a standardized product and usually only includes manufacturing if the product has to be made on the spot (as with fast food), or is a service. Since distributional skills for the Japanese market were what Filofax appeared to lack, franchising by Filofax would make no sense, even though production licensing might be rational (except that Filofax was not ahead on quality, either, so it would not be in a position to charge for its know-how), and even though Apex might have found it worthwhile to franchise distribution rights to particular stores, using its knowledge of how to promote products in Japan. So, perhaps all Filofax would really have been fit to license was the brand name. But whether they licensed the brand name or a complete blueprint, they could have generated a royalty income and avoided committing themselves to extra capacity.

In deciding whether the company really were engaging in a deliberate 'milking' strategy, it would also be useful to know what the company did with the profits made during the years that sales were doing very well: the company can be criticized for seeming to have done nothing decisive by way of research and development to provide a basis for their future profitability (the briefcase venture sounds rather half-hearted). In general one probably can feel justified in wondering to what extent strategic planning was really going on for most of the period, given the 'all eggs in one basket' kind of operation that they were running and the failure to look for related lines of activity at an early stage and for ways of exploiting the brand name over other products (cf. sections 10.13 and 11.4 to 11.6). Furthermore, the product lines into which they decided to diversify, whilst also being information-related, actually involve few obvious manufacturing similarities (that is, little prospect of production synergy). This sort of move might make better sense if Filofax engaged in a joint venture with firms involved in directory publishing. There is scope here to use material from section 11.11 as a basis for discussing the problems of arranging such a venture, in terms of the distribution of benefits, incentive effects and the possible use of cross-shareholdings as means for reducing conflicts between the partners.

Distribution and promotion methods used by Apex in Japan were to some extent copied by Filofax in the United Kingdom. It may be premature to suggest this was a good thing, and to criticize Filofax both for not adopting these methods in the UK before, and for failing to engage in any advertising at all prior to the take-off of the product. It is probably wiser to consider the transferability of marketing strategies between different cultures before jumping to that conclusion. For example, European consumers may be far less impressed than the Japanese with lavish packaging. Also, the kinds of circumstances in which Japanese purchases were made might be rather different. Detailed knowledge of cultural rituals is required before conclusions can be reached about the international applicability of any given strategy. Students doing courses in Japanese studies might be in a position to impress with a detailed discussion of the Japanese attitudes towards gift-giving at particular stages of an individual's life, relating to events such as graduation; these could be contrasted with Western culture. This could have implications for the wisdom of particular choices of media for advertising: for example, if Filofaxes might be bought as graduation presents in Japan but as tools for work by those already in employment in the West, then magazines with a broad (but well-educated) readership, rather than business magazines, might make better sense in Japan than in the West. The wisdom of using Diane Keaton and Steven Spielberg to endorse the product might be queried: would either be familiar in Japan? The latter, after all, is a director, so his picture might mean little and fail to catch the eye of readers.

Though Filofax's historic lack of spending on advertising is surprising, it could be argued that, once Filofaxes had started to catch on, it is far from obvious that the company needed to spend heavily on advertising in the yuppie market. The products would tend to sell themselves because of their visible use as part of the yuppie lifestyle. However, for people outside such a social network who might nonetheless have been potential customers, the concept of a Filofax may well have been a mystery that some advertising could have overcome.

Although the question concerns Filofax, not Apex, the policies of Apex should be criticized in so far as they raise doubts about the wisdom of Filofax's decision to start the relationship with Apex. It does seem a rather curious sort of deal. Cost savings could surely have been achieved if Filofax had done its original packaging for Japanese sales to Apex's specifications, rather than leaving it to Apex to repackage its products. Of far greater concern is the principal-agent problem that arises once Apex starts getting involved in production of its own (cf. section 11.2): to what extent does Apex have an interest in selling Filofaxes if it can sell Stylofaxes? And was not Apex coming pretty close to stealing the Filofax brand name by choosing a pretty similar-sounding word which might not conjure up a different image in Japan in the way that it might to an English-speaking buyer?

This issue should be considered further in relation to market segmentation. If the two products were appealing to different clientele, they might not be substitutes for each other; if so, then the conflicts of interest might only be tending to arise due to Apex's limited managerial attention being diverted away from the task of handling Filofaxes—recall the discussion in section 10.13 of the work of Penrose (1959) on managerial limits to the growth of firms, as well as the issue of bounded rationality more generally. When this case was used in an examination students commonly assumed that the Stylofax product did actually harm Filofax sales in Japan. It should be noted that at no point does the case material say this happened. Even in the absence of market segmentation, we can argue that, with many fad-type products, the appearance of competition actually does existing lines no harm, because it raises the public's awareness of the product. In other words, we should not think of competitive rivalry taking place with respect to a *static* demand curve for personal organizers in general.

Given the 'fad' nature of the product one might want to suggest that it could be difficult to know how strong the sales growth would have been if Apex had not gone about promoting it in the way that it did. The crucial thing was that Filofaxes got stocked in the right kinds of stores in Japan and in prominent places in those stores. This was something that Filofax on its own would have had great trouble doing, given its lack of contacts in the Japanese market (which is notorious for being based on connections between firms). An alternative to an exclusive distribution deal would have been to sign contracts with a number of distributors, whom it could then have played off against each other. However, the exclusive deal at least ensured that Apex did not land up trying to run policies that contradicted those of another distributor and did not lose any benefits of its efforts, so the incentive to do well on behalf of Filofax was strong until it came up with its own product. As far as scope for playing distributors off against each other is concerned, Filofax seemed to have little leverage aside from its brand name: if it dumped Apex, the latter could easily find Japanese manufacturers of clones of the product, whilst Filofax would be faced with the immediate need to find some other wholesaler to ensure that it did not lose the goodwill of the retailers.

We are not told about the extent (if any) to which Filofax tried to engage in a policy of market segmentation in Britain by producing down-market versions of its product, and thereby forestall entry by importers or new UK producers. There, it obviously would have faced a dilemma, for if it did not segment its market in this way it might lose out in the long run, whereas if it did so it could reduce the credibility of its up-market model. Although adding down-market models to its range might have seemed better in the long run (either way, the credibility problem arises), we should not forget that if Filofax were worried about the existence of the market in the long run, it would not be wise to embark on capacity expansion on a grand scale. A policy of staying at the top end of the market is thus understandable.

11.15   Exam post-mortem: Reasons for multinationals

Question

'The growth of multinational enterprises is neither as natural nor obvious as might appear from superficial observation' (Neil Kay, 1984, *The Emergent Firm*). Discuss this view and the theoretical rationale for the existence and growth of such firms.

Examiner's report

This question was often quite well done, on the basis of the material presented in section 11.12. I was pleased to see that some students tried to illustrate their arguments not only by referring to cases such as Austin, Sony and Filofax which I had mentioned in lectures but also ones from their own reading or local knowledge (for example, the Malaysian car industry). However, one answer fell down badly because it consisted of a copious supply of examples with no theoretical framework. Another fared poorly because it consisted of no more than an attempt to regurgitate material from a tutorial essay on transactions costs and tourism (section 11.13).

Many of the weak answers missed the transaction cost perspective altogether and simply concentrated on writing about the advantages of cheap labour. Some of those that tried to give a transaction cost perspective forgot to point out the difficulties that may be encountered if a firm sets up an overseas subsidiary; others wrote about these difficulties but not about why, despite them, firms might bother to set up overseas operations. One attempt wasted much time by talking about conglomerates without relating them to question: a conglomerate need not be a multinational, even though some are.

11.16   Conclusion

It is appropriate that the subject matter of this chapter has been left to the end of the book. The open-ended analysis is very unlike the kind of economics covered in introductory economics. My focus has been on the rich array of ways in which economic activities are arranged between and inside firms, and I have repeatedly considered how strategic choices may depend very much on creative thinking about what could go wrong if particular commitments are made. Strategic choices in a world of uncertainty and ambiguity seem more like experiments that ask questions rather than the optimal solutions to well-defined questions. At any one time it is common for a given product to be produced by firms that have very different resource bases and views of the world and are hence involved in different systems of vertical relationships and producing different mixes of products.

Though many of the economists who have made contributions in the areas covered in this chapter were originally inspired by the work of Williamson (1975), much that has been presented here is implicitly at odds with some of his key themes. Williamson maintains that internalization is promoted by bounded rationality (which limits the extent to which people can use contracts to guard themselves against surprises), opportunism (which means that promises about fair and equitable future conduct cannot be relied upon) and asset specificity (which means that, if a trading partner does turn out to be opportunistic, assets cannot easily be switched to alternative uses). In his analysis all three features have to be present for

400

internalization to be preferred over market-based arrangements. However, at various points in this chapter it has actually been a lack of asset specificity that seemed to promote internalization, given fears of opportunistic behaviour and limitations on the construction and enforcement of complete contracts: diversification is based around the transferability of investments between product market activities, and multinational subsidiaries have a rationale as devices to present the escape of know-how that is potentially applicable to areas other than those in which it is presently being applied (see further, Neil Kay, 1992, 1993). Williamson's thesis is more illuminating in respect of vertical relationships, though subsequent theorizing in areas such as quasi-integration and franchising has emphasized the ability of transactors to see that in the long run it often pays not to be labelled as an opportunist: exchange is promoted by differences in skills and barriers to the acquisition of new capabilities; those who develop reputations for foul play may find no one is prepared to play with them and end up themselves having to undertake tasks that they are relatively ill-equipped to handle.

For anyone who has studied the material in this text and in readings recommended to accompany it, the objective measure of what has been gained in the process is likely to be the kind of examination grade attained at the end of the programme of study of which it formed a part. However, another pointer is the acuteness of the expert eye that the reader may have developed for making sense of consumer and industrial markets and the behaviour of firms and other organizations. It can be very satisfying to be able to look at the behaviour of individuals and firms and observe and present a case why, on the basis of theoretical material discussed in this book, particular decisions are likely to be successes or failures, or why particular decisions have been taken. In due course, one can usually check the correctness of one's conjectures by keeping track of the fortunes of the companies in question in the business press. Students who can achieve this degree of expertise—who can make critical appraisals of corporate strategies and tactics and who can see in decisions things of which the ordinary mortal is oblivious—are well on the way to being competent to take significant business decisions or enter the high-flying world of the management consultant. But they should not get carried away with the power of their recently acquired know-how, for every topic covered in this text can be explored in greater depth and academics are doing precisely that in most cases. Hence I hope that I have not merely assisted my readers to develop an expert eye but also a lasting desire to keep reading in this area. If I have succeeded in fostering this desire I may, with luck, have left some readers wondering where to begin the next stage of their reading to begin the sharpening of their powers of insight. I can think of no better starting point than John Kay's perceptive but very readable 1993 book *Foundations of Corporate Success*. But I would add a reminder: the classic works from earlier generations of economist are always worth reading, and re-reading. As with major works of literature, it is often possible to see more subtle layers of thinking in classics of economics each time one reads them. Even parts of this book are likely to be open to fresh interpretations second or third time around.

11.17   Further questions

1.   Rate each of the following products on a scale ranging from one (most unlikely) to ten

(wouldn't be at all surprising) with respect to whether or not you would expect to see the company that developed them being willing to use licensing and/or franchising arrangements to get them manufactured and/or distributed:

(a) a mobile carpet-cleaning service
(b) fax machines and photocopiers
(c) television rental services
(d) luxury cars
(e) washing machines and other 'white goods'
(f) passenger airline services

Justify your ratings in terms of relevant economic theory.

2. Write an essay on the economic issues that you would expect to underlie decisions about vertical integration taken by firms that insure motor vehicles and buildings against accidental damage.

3. What factors should be considered by a manufacturer when deciding how to distribute a low-volume specialist foodstuff?

4. 'The choice of distribution system does not depend on issues of transport and handling costs alone.' Discuss.

5. Outline and account for the major variations in the structure of management systems in large-scale firms.

6. Discuss the difficulties involved in using capital budgeting methods such as discounted cash-flow analysis in the context of vertical integration decisions.

7. Joint ventures between firms have become increasingly common in recent years. Examine their likely merits and problems as alternatives to inter-firm contracting or mergers between firms. Do you think joint ventures are more likely to be relatively short-lived 'affairs' between companies than preludes to corporate 'marriages'? Explain your reasoning.

8. Discuss, with reference to one or more actual large-company examples, the problems involved in designing an effective organizational structure.

9. What light do economic theories of corporate structures shed on the problem of designing effective organizational structures in systems of higher education?

10. Discuss, with reference to actual business examples, whether Neil Kay's theoretical extensions of transaction cost analyses of the firm are more usefully seen as prescriptive rather than descriptive contributions.

11. Margins taken by wholesale intermediaries on some goods are over 20 per cent of final selling price. Why then might manufacturers sell through them rather than absorbing this margin themselves?

12. In what ways, if any, do large, modern corporations behave differently from the traditional, small 'family firm'?

13. In the light of recent theories of business strategy and industrial organization, discuss the characteristics of the recorded music business that might lead to its outputs being produced by multi-product, multinational enterprises such as EMI or Sony.

14. Why do manufacturers of nationally known brands of consumer durables such as cars, camera and hi-fi equipment often only allow a limited number of retail outlets (sometimes one per locality) to stock their products, whereas producers of nationally known brands of related consumables such as petrol, film and audio cassettes often go to great lengths to ensure that their products are widely stocked?

15. 'Joint ventures are often, though not exclusively, created due to competitive motives, either between partners or relative to other firms. Herein lies the irony, namely, that the competitive conditions that motivate the creation of a joint venture may also be responsible for its termination' (Bruce Kogut, in F.J. Contractor and P. Lorange, eds, *Cooperative Strategies in International Business*, 1988: 169). Discuss with reference to recent economic theorizing about the nature of cooperative business strategies.

16. 'Joint ventures are much more likely to succeed if they are perceived as a preliminary to more intimate co-operation than as finite activities' (John Kay, *Foundations of Corporate Success*, 1993: 38). Discuss.

17. 'The existence of hierarchy must imply a highly asymmetrical view of cooperation and one which must mean a generally Pareto inefficient outcome. It is perfectly reasonable to argue that efficiency depends on cooperation, but it is equally reasonable to argue that cooperation by all parties necessitates a democratic organizational structure, not a hierarchical one' (Keith Cowling, reviewing Miller, 1992, in the *Economic Journal*, September 1993: 1362). Discuss.

18. Critically appraise the corporate strategy adopted over the past decade by a large company of your choice.

Bibliography

Note: Figures in brackets at the end of each entry refer to the pages on which the work is cited in the text.

Adams, W.J. and Yellen, J.L. (1976) 'Commodity bundling and the burden of monopoly', *Quarterly Journal of Economics*, **92**, 475–98 (287).

Akerlof, G.A. (1970) 'The market for 'lemons': quality uncertainty and the market mechanism', *Quarterly Journal of Economics*, **84**, 488–500 (138).

----- and Dickens, W.T. (1982) 'The economic consequences of cognitive dissonance', *American Economic Review*, **72**, 307–19 (92–3).

Albanese, P. (ed.) (1988) *Psychological Foundations of Economic Behavior*, New York, Praeger (64, 88).

Alchian, A.A. (1950) 'Uncertainty, evolution and economic theory', *Journal of Political Economy*, **58**, 211–22 (190, 259).

----- and Demsetz, H. (1972) 'Production, information costs, and economic organisation', *American Economic Review*, **62**, 777–95 (330).

----- and Woodward, S. (1988) 'The firm is dead: long live the firm', *Journal of Economic Literature*, **26**, 65–79 (338).

Allais, M. (1953) 'Le comportement de l'homme rationnel devant le risque; critique des postulats et axiomes de l'école Americaine', *Econometrica*, **21**, 503–46 (108).

Anand, P. (1982) 'How to be right without being rational (the von Neumann and Morgenstern way)', *Oxford Agrarian Studies*, **11**, 158–72 (72).

----- (1987) 'Are the preference axioms really rational?', *Theory and Decision*, **23**, 189–214 (36).

Andrews, P.W.S. (1949a) 'A reconsideration of the theory of the individual business', *Oxford Economic Papers*, **1** (new series), 54–89 (reprinted in Andrews, 1993, and Earl, ed., 1988a) (260, 281, 291).

----- (1949b) *Manufacturing Business*, London, Macmillan (260, 275, 281, 291, 327, 337).

----- (1950) 'Some aspects of competition in retail trade', *Oxford Economic Papers*, **2** (new series), 138–75 (reprinted in Andrews, 1993) (260).

----- (1951) 'Industrial analysis in economics', in Wilson, T. and Andrews, P.W.S. (eds) (1951) (reprinted in Andrews, 1993) (199, 207, 261, 271).

----- (1958) 'Competition in the modern economy', reprinted from G. Sell (ed.) *Competitive Aspects of Oil Operations*, London, Institute of Petroleum (reprinted in Andrews, 1993) (193, 232, 271, 334, 367).

----- (1964) *On Competition in Economic Theory*, London, Macmillan (260, 264).

----- (1993) *The Economics of Competitive Enterprise: Selected Essays of P.W.S. Andrews* (edited by F.S. Lee and P.E. Earl), Aldershot, Edward Elgar (247, 260, 290, 337).

----- and Brunner, E. (1975) *Studies in Pricing*, London, Macmillan (181, 260, 269–71, 275).

----- and Friday, F.A. (1960) *Fair Trade*, London, Macmillan (partly reprinted in Andrews,

1993) (266, 290).

Ansoff, H.I. (1968) *Corporate Strategy*, Harmondsworth, Penguin Books (175).

Arestis, P. and Sawyer, M. (1994) *The Elgar Companion to Radical Political Economy*, Aldershot, Edward Elgar (12–13).

Arrow, K.J. (1959) 'Towards a theory of price adjustment', in Abramowitz, M. *et al.* (eds) *The Allocation of Economics Resources*, Stanford, CA, Stanford University Press (305).

----- (1962) 'Economic welfare and the allocation of resources for invention', in *The Rate and Direction of Inventive Activity*, National Bureau of Economic Research, Princeton, NJ, Princeton University Press (274).

----- (1971) *Essays in the Theory of Risk Bearing*, Chicago, Markham (383).

----- and Debreu, G. (1954) 'Existence of an equilibrium for a competitive economy', *Econometrica*, **22**, 265–90 (309).

----- and Hahn, F.H. (1971) *General Competitive Analysis*, San Francisco, Oliver & Boyd (309).

Arthur, W.B. (1989) 'Competing technologies, increasing returns, and lock-in by historical events', *Economic Journal*, **99**, 116–31 (147).

----- (1993) 'Pandora's marketplace', *New Scientist* (Supplement), 6 February, 6–8 (147).

Assael, H. (1990) *Marketing: Principles and Strategy*, Hinsdale, IL, Dryden Press (336).

Barnard, C. (1938) *The Functions of the Executive*, Cambridge, MA, Harvard University Press (192).

Baumol, W.J. (1958) 'On the theory of oligopoly', *Economica*, **25**, 187–98 (page references to reprint in Archibald, G.C., ed., 1971, *Theory of the Firm*, Harmondsworth, Penguin Books) (256, 258, 264, 281).

----- (1959) *Business Behavior, Value and Growth*, New York, Harcourt Brace & World, Inc. (256).

----- (1982) 'Contestable markets: an uprising in the theory of industrial structure', *American Economic Review*, **72**, 1–13 (272, 281).

-----, Panzar, J.C. and Willig, R.D. (1982) *Contestable Markets and the Theory of Industrial Structure*, San Diego, Harcourt Brace Jovanovich (272–4, 281).

----- and Quandt, R.E. (1964) 'Rules of thumb and optimally imperfect decisions', *American Economic Review*, **54**, 23–46 (70).

Baxter, J.L. (1993) *Behavioural Foundations of Economics*, London, Macmillan/New York, NY, St Martin's Press (67).

Becker, G.S. (1965) 'A theory of the allocation of time', *Economic Journal*, **75**, 493–517 (53).

Berle, A.A. and Means, G.C. (1932) *The Modern Corporation and Private Property*, New York, Harcourt, Brace & World, Inc. (255).

Berlyne, D. (1960) *Conflict, Arousal and Curiosity*, New York, McGraw-Hill (88).

----- (1971) *Aesthetics and Psychobiology*, New York, Appleton-Century-Croft (88).

Bettman, J. (1979) *An Information Processing Theory of Consumer Choice*, Reading, MA, Addison-Wesley (67).

Blatt, J.M. (1983) *Dynamic Economic Systems: A Post-Keynesian Approach*, Armonk, NY, M.E. Sharpe, Inc./Brighton, Wheatsheaf (111–12).

Blaug, M. (1980) *The Methodology of Economics*, Cambridge, Cambridge University Press (62, 245).

Blois, K.J. (1972) 'Vertical quasi-integration', *Journal of Industrial Economics*, **20**, 253–71 (343).

Borch, K. (1968) *The Economics of Uncertainty*, Princeton, Princeton University Press (40).

----- (1973) 'The place of uncertainty in the theories of the Austrian school', in Hicks, J.R. and Weber, W. (eds) (1973) *Carl Menger and the Austrian School of Economics*, Oxford, Oxford University Press (136).

Borts, G. (1961) 'The recent controversy over resale price maintenance', *Journal of the Royal Statistical Society*, **124** (General), 244–9 (266).

Boston Consulting Group (1975) *Strategy Alternatives for the British Motorcycle Industry*, House of Commons Paper 532, London, HMSO (184).

Braverman, H. (1974) *Labor and Monopoly Capital*, New York, Monthly Review Press (188).

Brooks, M.A. (1988) 'Toward a behavioral analysis of public economics', in Earl (ed.) (1988b) (29, 128).

Brown, C.V. (1983) *Taxation and the Incentive to Work*, Oxford, Oxford University Press (44).

Brunner, E. (1952) 'Competition and the theory of the firm' (Parts I and II), *Economia Internazionale*, **5**, 508–23, 729–45 (260, 281).

Buchanan, J.M. and Thirlby, G.F. (eds) (1973) *LSE Essays on Cost*, London, LSE/Weidenfeld & Nicolson (156).

----- and Vanberg, V.J. (1991) 'The market as a creative process', *Economics and Philosophy*, **7**, 167–86 (121, 303).

Caldwell, B.J. (1982) *Beyond Positivism*, London, George Allen & Unwin (62, 95).

----- and Boehm, S. (eds) (1992) *Austrian Economics: Tensions and New Directions*, Boston, Kluwer Academic Press (302).

Cantillon, R. (1755) *Essay on the Nature of Trade* (English version edited by H. Higgs, 1931, London, Macmillan, partially reprinted in Casson, ed., 1990) (301).

Carter, C.F. (1953) 'A revised theory of expectations', *Economic Journal*, **63**, 811–20 (reprinted in Earl, ed., 1988a) (126).

Casson, M. (1982) *The Entrepreneur: An Economic Theory*, Oxford, Martin Robertson (127, 301).

----- (ed.) (1983) *The Growth of International Business*, London, George Allen & Unwin (385, 388).

----- (1984) 'The theory of vertical integration: a survey and synthesis', *Journal of Economic Studies*, **11**, 3–43 (342).

----- (1986) 'Contractual arrangements for technology transfer: new evidence from business history', *Business History*, **28**, 5–35 (reprinted in Earl, ed., 1988a) (385).

----- (ed.) (1990) *Entrepreneurship*, Aldershot, Edward Elgar (301)

Chamberlin, E.H. (1933) *The Theory of Monopolistic Competition*, Cambridge, MA, Harvard University Press (page references to 8th edn, 1962) (xii, 214, 217–20, 248, 291).

Chandler, A.D. (1962) *Strategy and Structure*, Cambridge, MA, MIT Press (368).

----- (1977) *The Visible Hand: The Managerial Revolution in American Business*, Cambridge, MA, Belknap Press/Harvard University Press (332).

----- (1990) *Scale and Scope: The Dynamics of Industrial Capitalism*, Cambridge, MA, Belknap Press/Harvard University Press (175, 213).

Clapham, J.H. (1922) 'On empty economic boxes', *Economic Journal*, **32**, 305–14 (209).

Clegg, J., Cox, H., and Ietto-Gillies, G. (eds) (1992) *The Growth of Global Business: New Strategies*, London, Routledge (295).

Coase, R.H. (1937) 'The nature of the firm', *Economica*, **4** (new series), 386–405 (152, 324–325, 328, 334, 337, 356, 382, 387).

----- (1988) *The Firm, the Market and the Law*, Chicago, University of Chicago Press (324).

Coddington, A. (1975a) 'Creaking semaphore and beyond: review of G.L.S. Shackle's *Epistemics and Economics*', *British Journal for the Philosophy of Science*, **26**, 151–63 (33).

----- (1975b) 'The rationale of general equilibrium theory', *Economic Inquiry*, **13**, 539–58 (11, 298, 309).

Contractor, F.J. and Lorange, P. (eds) (1988) *Cooperative Strategies in International Business*, Lexington, MA, D.C. Heath (380, 403).

Court, A.T. (1939) 'Hedonic price indexes with automotive examples', in *The Dynamics of Automobile Demand*, New York, General Motors Corporation (59–60).

Coutts, K.J., Godley, W.A.H. and Nordhaus, W.D. (1978) *Industrial Pricing in the United Kingdom*, Cambridge, Cambridge University Press (258).

Cready, W.M. (1991) 'Premium bundling', *Economic Inquiry*, **29**, 173–9 (287).

Cross, J.G. (1965) 'A theory of the bargaining process', *American Economic Review*, **55**, 67–94 (133).

Cunningham, M.T. and White, J.G. (1974) 'The behaviour of industrial buyers in their search for machine tools', *Journal of Management Studies*, **11**, 114–28 (reprinted in Earl, ed., 1988a) (264).

Cyert, R.M. and George, K.D. (1969) 'Competition, growth and efficiency', *Economic Journal*, **79**, 23–41 (reprinted in Earl, ed., 1988a) (193).

----- and March, J.G. (1963) *A Behavioral Theory of the Firm*, Englewood Cliffs, NJ, Prentice-Hall (145, 189, 191–92, 208, 225, 255, 261, 270, 307, 330, 332).

Davies, J.E. and Lee, F.S. (1988) 'A post Keynesian appraisal of the contestability criterion', *Journal of Post Keynesian Economics*, **11**, 3–25 (273).

Davis, E.P. (1988) 'Industrial structure and dynamics of financial markets; the primary eurobond market', Bank of England Discussion Papers, No. 35 (309).

----- (1990) 'An industrial approach to financial instability', Bank of England Discussion Papers, No. 50 (309).

Day, R.H. (1967) 'Profits, learning and the convergence of satisficing to marginalism', *Quarterly Journal of Economics*, **81**, 302–11 (reprinted in Earl, ed., 1988a) (71).

Dean, J. (1950) 'Pricing policies for new products', *Harvard Business Review*, **28** (November–December) (249–50).

Debreu, G. (1959) *Theory of Value*, New Haven, CT, Cowles Foundation (309).

Department of Prices and Consumer Protection (1978) 'Economies of scale and learning effects', *A Review of Monopolies and Mergers Policy*, Appendix C (Cmnd 7198),

London, HMSO, reprinted in L. Wagner (ed.) (1981) *Readings in Applied Microeconomics* (2nd edn), Oxford, Oxford University Press (178).

Dietrich, M. (1991) 'Firms, markets and transaction cost economics', *Scottish Journal of Political Economy*, **38**, 41–57 (324).

----- (1994) *Transaction Cost Economics and Beyond: Toward a New Economics of the Firm*, London, Routledge (324).

Dnes, A.W. (1992) *Franchising: A Case Study Approach*, Avebury, Aldershot (295, 353, 355).

Dobb, M.H. (1969) *Welfare Economics and the Economics of Socialism*, Cambridge, Cambridge University Press (48).

Doeringer, P.B. and Piore, M.J. (1971) *Internal Labor Markets and Manpower Analysis*, Lexington, MA., D.C. Heath (2nd edn, 1985, Armonk, NY, M.E. Sharpe, Inc.) (367).

Dore, R. (1973) *British Factory–Japanese Factory: Origins of National Diversity in Industrial Relations*, London, George Allen & Unwin (185).

Dorfman, R., Samuelson, P. and Solow, R. (1958) *Linear Programming and Economic Analysis*, New York, McGraw-Hill (172).

Douglas, E. (1987) *Managerial Economics* (3rd edn), Englewood Cliffs, NJ, Prentice-Hall (52, 249, 256, 263, 283–4).

Douglas, M. and Wildavsky, A. (1982) *Risk and Culture*, Berkeley, CA, University of California Press (185).

Downie, J. (1958) *The Competitive Process*, London, Duckworth (199, 207, 270).

Doyle, P. and Fenwick, I. (1975) '"Are goods goods?: some further evidence": a comment', *Applied Economics*, **7**, 93–8 (53).

Drakopoulos, S. (1990) 'The implicit psychology of the theory of the rational consumer: an interpretation', *Australian Economic Papers*, **29**, 182–98 (40).

----- (1992) 'Psychological thresholds, demand and price rigidity', *Manchester School*, **40**, 152–68 (39, 71).

----- (1994) 'Hierarchical choice in economics', *Journal of Economic Surveys* (forthcoming) (41).

Dunn, R. (1987) *The Possibility of Weakness of Will*, Indianapolis, IN, Hackett (93).

Dunning, J. and McQueen, M. (1981) 'The eclectic theory of the multinational enterprise: a case study of the international hotel industry', *Managerial and Decision Economics*, **2**, 197–210 (reprinted in Rugman, ed., 1982) (389).

Dupuit, J. (1844) 'On the measurement of the utility of public works', *Annales des Ponts et Chausées*, 2nd series, **8**, English translation by R.H. Barback in *International Economic Papers*, **2** (1952), 83–110, reprinted in Munby, D. (ed.) (1968) *Transport*, Harmondsworth, Penguin Books (193–5, 208).

Earl, P.E. (1983a) 'A behavioral theory of economists' behavior', in Eichner, A.S. (ed.) (1983) (94).

----- (1983b) *The Economic Imagination*, Brighton, Wheatsheaf (67, 118, 213).

----- (1984) *The Corporate Imagination*, Brighton, Wheatsheaf (92, 193, 208, 316, 335, 362, 364, 372).

----- (1986) *Lifestyle Economics*, Brighton, Wheatsheaf (41, 61, 67, 72, 118–19, 395).

----- (ed.) (1988a) *Behavioural Economics*, Aldershot, Edward Elgar (12, 67, 110, 190).

----- (ed.) (1988b) *Psychological Economics: Development, Tensions, Prospects*, Boston, MA, Kluwer (88, 94).

----- (1990) 'Economics and psychology: a survey', *Economic Journal*, **100**, 718–55 (88).

----- (1990–91) 'Normal cost versus marginalist models of pricing: a behavioral perspective', *Journal of Post Keynesian Economics*, **13**, 264–81 (293).

----- (1991) 'Principal-agent problems and structural change in the advertising industry', *Prometheus*, **9**, 274–95 (274, 287, 380, 388).

----- (1992a) 'On the complementarity of economic applications of cognitive dissonance theory and personal construct psychology', in Lea *et al.* (eds) (1992) (92, 126).

----- (1992b) 'The evolution of cooperative strategies: three automotive industry case studies', *Human Systems Management*, **11**, 89–100 (382, 384, 388).

----- (1992c) 'Scientific research programmes and the prediction of corporate behaviour', *Cyprus Journal of Economics*, **5**, 75–95 (314).

----- (1995a) 'Cognitive development of students and strategies for bringing indeterminacy into the economics classroom', in Boehm, S., Frowen, S.F. and Pheby, J. (eds) *Economics as the Art of Thought: Essays in Memory of G.L.S. Shackle*, London, Routledge (7).

----- (1995b) 'Liquidity preference, marketability and pricing', in Dow, S.C. and Hillard, J. (eds) *Keynes, Knowledge and Uncertainty*, Aldershot, Edward Elgar (120, 132, 326).

----- and Kay, N.M. (1985) 'How economists can accept Shackle's critique of economic doctrines without arguing themselves out of their jobs', *Journal of Economic Studies*, **12**, 34–48 (reprinted in Earl, ed., 1988a) (71).

Eaton, B.C. and Eaton, D. (1991) *Microeconomics* (2nd edn), New York, W.H. Freeman (4).

Eatwell, J., Milgate, M. and Newman, P. (eds) (1987) *The New Palgrave: A Dictionary of Economics*, London, Macmillan (12, 204).

Edgeworth, F.Y. (1881) *Mathematical Psychics*, London, C. Kegan Paul & Co. (127, 208, 299)

----- (1891) 'Review of *Principles of Economics* (2nd edn) by A. Marshall', *Economic Journal*, **1**, 611–17 (208).

----- (1925) 'On the determinateness of economic equilibrium', in his *Papers Relating to Political Economy*, London, Macmillan, 113–19 (reprinted in Ricketts, ed., 1988) (127).

Edwardes, M. (1983) *Back from the Brink*, London, Collins (386).

Efroymson, C.W. (1943) 'A note on the kinked demand curve', *American Economic Review*, **33**, 98–109 (228, 284).

----- (1955) 'The kinked demand curve reconsidered', *Quarterly Journal of Economics*, **69**, 119–36 (228–30, 284).

Eichner, A.S. (1973) 'A theory of the determination of the mark-up under oligopoly', *Economic Journal*, **83**, 1184–2000 (268, 276).

----- (1976) *The Megacorp and Oligopoly*, Cambridge, Cambridge University Press (reissued 1980, White Plains, NY, M.E. Sharpe, Inc.) (268, 276).

----- (ed.) (1983)*Why Economics is not yet a Science*, Armonk, NY, M.E. Sharpe, Inc./London, Macmillan (62, 96).

Elster, J. (1983) *Sour Grapes: Studies in the Subversion of Rationality*, Cambridge,

Cambridge University Press (92).

----- (1984) *Ulysses and the Sirens*, Cambridge, Cambridge University Press (71, 93).

----- (1989) *Nuts and Bolts for the Social Sciences*, Cambridge, Cambridge University Press (91, 127, 131).

Endres, A.M. (1991) 'Marshall's analysis of economising behaviour with particular reference to the consumer', *European Economic Review*, **35**, 333–41 (204).

Engel, J.F., Blackwell, R.D. and Miniard, P.W. (1986) *Consumer Behavior* (5th edn), Hinsdale, IL, Dryden Press (29).

Etzioni, A. (1986) 'The case for a multiple utility conception', *Economics and Philosophy*, **2**, 159–83 (307).

----- (1988) *The Moral Dimension: Toward a New Economics*, New York, Free Press (40, 63, 67–8, 70, 72, 307, 324).

Farrell, M.J. (1971) 'Phillip Andrews and Manufacturing Business', *Journal of Industrial Economics*, **20**, 10–13 (261).

Festinger, F. (1957) *A Theory of Cognitive Dissonance*, New York, Harper & Row (92–3).

Fishbein, M.A. and Ajzen, I. (1975) *Belief, Attitude, Intention and Behavior: An Introduction to Theory and Research*, Reading, MA, Addison-Wesley (72–3).

Fisher, F.M., Griliches, Z. and Kaysen, C. (1962) 'The costs of automobile model changes since 1949', *Journal of Political Economy*, **70**, 433–51 (60).

Ford, J.L. (1987) *Economic Choice under Uncertainty: A Perspective Theory Approach*, Aldershot, Edward Elgar (110).

Foss, N.J. (1993) 'Theories of the firm: contractual and competence perspectives', *Journal of Evolutionary Economics*, **3**, 127–44 (202, 324–5, 338).

----- (1994) 'Cooperation is competition: George Richardson on coordination and interfirm relations', *British Review of Economic Issues*, **16**, 25–49 (313).

Fourie, F.C. v. N. (1989) 'The nature of firms and markets: do transactions approaches help?', *South African Journal of Economics*, **57**, 142–60 (331)

Frank, R. (1991) *Microeconomics and Behavior*, New York, McGraw-Hill (ix, 4, 33, 67, 104, 106, 119, 282–6).

Friedman, M. (1953) *The Methodology of Positive Economics*, Chicago, University of Chicago Press (62).

Frowen, S.F. (ed.) (1990) *Unknowledge and Choice in Economics*, London, Macmillan (contains Hey, 1985; Loasby 1990b; Wiseman and Littlechild, 1990).

Gabor, A. and Grainger, C.W.J. (1966) 'Price as an indicator of quality: report on an inquiry', *Economica*, **33**, 43–70 (78).

Galbraith, C.S. and Kay, N.M. (1986) 'Towards a theory of multinational enterprise', *Journal of Economic Behavior and Organization*, **7**, 3–19 (reprinted in Earl, ed., 1988a) (385).

Gilad, B. (1986) 'Entrepreneurial decision making: some behavioral considerations', in Gilad, B. and Kaish, S. (eds) (1986), volume A (302).

----- and Kaish, S. (eds) (1986) *Handbook of Behavioral Economics*, Greenwich, CT, JAI Press (67).

Gimpl, M.L. and Dakin, S.R. (1984) 'Management and magic', *California Management*

Review, **27**, 125–36 (reprinted in Earl, ed., 1988a) (125).

Godet, M. (1987) *Scenarios and Strategic Management*, London, Butterworths (121).

Gorman, W.M. (1956) 'A possible technique for analysing the quality differential in the egg market', mimeographed (52).

Green, H.A.J. (1976) *Consumer Theory* (rev. edn), London, Macmillan (54).

Grunert, K.G. and Olander, F. (eds) (1989) *Understanding Economic Behaviour*, Dordrecht, Kluwer (88).

Hahn, F.H. (1970) 'Some adjustment problems', *Econometrica*, **38**, 1–17 (298, 338).

----- (1973a) 'The winter of our discontent', *Economica*, **60**, 322–30 (11, 298).

----- (1973b) *On the Notion of Equilibrium in Economics*, Cambridge, Cambridge University Press (298).

Haines, G.H., jr (1975) 'Commentary on Ratchford "The new economic theory of consumer behavior: an interpretive essay"', *Journal of Consumer Research*, **2**, 77–8 (54).

Hall, R.L. and Hitch, C.J. (1939) 'Price theory and business behaviour', *Oxford Economic Papers*, **2**, 12–45 (page references to reprint in Wilson and Andrews, eds, 1951) (224–8, 261, 275).

Hanson, P. (1987) *The Joy of Stress*, London, Pan Books (89).

Harcourt, G.C. (1972) *Some Cambridge Controversies in the Theory of Capital*, Cambridge, Cambridge University Press (166).

Harrigan, K.R. (1980) *Strategies for Declining Businesses*, Lexington, MA, Lexington Books (316).

----- (1983) *Strategies for Vertical Integration*, Lexington, MA, Lexington Books (342, 349).

Hart, A.G. (1940) *Anticipations, Uncertainty and Dynamic Planning*, Chicago, University of Chicago Press (168, 189, 214).

----- (1942) 'Risk, uncertainty and the unprofitability of compounding probabilities', in Lange, O., McIntyre, F. and Yntema, T.O. (eds), *Studies in Mathematical Economics and Econometrics*, Chicago, University of Chicago Press (168, 189, 214).

Hawkins, D.I., Coney, K.A. and Best, R.J. (1980) *Consumer Behavior*, Dallas, Business Publications, Inc. (72).

Hayes, H.G. (1928) *Our Economic System*, New York, Holt (227).

Heiner, R.A. (1983) 'The origin of predictable behavior', *American Economic Review*, **73**, 560–93 (190).

Hennart, J.-F. (1988) 'A transaction costs theory of equity joint ventures', *Strategic Management Journal*, **9**, 361–74 (383).

----- (1991) 'The transaction cost theory of the multinational enterprise', in Pitelis and Sugden (eds) (1991) (388).

Hey, J.D. (1982) 'Search for rules for search', *Journal of Economic Behavior and Organization*, **3**, 65–81 (reprinted in Earl, ed., 1988a) (70, 191).

----- (1985) 'The possibility of possibility', *Journal of Economic Studies*, **12**, 70–88 (reprinted in Frowen, ed., 1990) (113)

Hicks, J.R. (1939) *Value and Capital*, Oxford, Oxford University Press (page references to second edition, 1946) (28, 34, 39, 62–3, 106, 211, 339).

----- (1976) 'Some questions of time in economics', in Tang, A., Westfield, F.M. and

Worley, J.S. (eds) (1976) *Evolution, Welfare, and Time in Economics: Essays in Honor of Nicholas Georgescu-Roegen*, Lexington, MA, Lexington Books (99).

----- and Allen, R.G.D. (1934) 'A reconsideration of the theory of value, parts I and II', *Economica,* **1,** 52–76, 196–217 (28, 34).

Hirschman, A.O. (1970) *Exit, Voice, and Loyalty: Responses to Decline in Firms, Organizations, and States*, New York, Norton (151, 199–200).

Hoch, S.J. (1984) 'Hypothesis testing and consumer behavior: "if it works don't mess with it"', in Kinnear, T.C. (ed.) *Advances in Consumer Research 11*, Ann Arbor, MI, Association for Consumer Research (68).

Hodgson, G.M. (1988) *Economics and Institutions*, Oxford, Polity Press (189, 324–5, 339).

-----, Samuels, W.J. and Tool, M. (1994) *The Elgar Companion to Institutional and Evolutionary Economics*, Aldershot, Edward Elgar (12).

Hofstadter, D. (1979) *Godel, Escher, Bach: An Eternal Golden Braid*, Brighton, Harvester Press (31, 213).

Hogarth, R.M. and Makridakis, S. (1981) 'Forecasting and planning: an evaluation', *Management Science*, **27,** 115–37 (reprinted in Earl, ed., 1988a) (90).

----- and Reder, M.W. (eds) (1987) *Rational Choice: The Contrast between Economics and Psychology*, Chicago, University of Chicago Press (88).

Hope, M. (1976) 'On being taken over by Slater Walker', *Journal of Industrial Economics*, **24,** 163–79 (376).

Hotelling, H. (1938) 'The general welfare in relation to problems of taxation and railway and utility rates', *Econometrica,* **6,** 242–69 (193, 196).

Houthakker, H.S. (1952) 'Changes in quantities and qualities consumed', *Review of Economic Studies,* **19,** 155–63 (52).

----- and Taylor, L.D. (1970) *Consumer Demand in the United States: Analysis and Projections* (2nd edn), Cambridge, MA, Harvard University Press (63).

Hurrell, J.J., Murphy, L.R., Sauter, S.L. and Cooper, C.L. (eds) (1988) *Occupational Stress: Issues and Developments in Research*, New York, Taylor & Francis (89).

Hymer, S.H. (1960) *The International Operations of National Firms: A Study of Direct Investment*, MIT doctoral dissertation, published in 1976, Cambridge, MA, MIT Press (387).

Ironmonger, D.S. (1972) *New Commodities and Consumer Behaviour*, Cambridge, Cambridge University Press (254).

Jarillo, J.C. and Stevenson, H.H. (1991) 'Co-operative strategies: the payoffs and the pitfalls', *Long Range Planning*, **24,** 64–70 (188).

Jefferson, M. (1983) 'Economic uncertainty and business decision-making', in Wiseman, J. (ed.) *Beyond Positive Economics?* London, Macmillan (121–4).

Jelinek, M., Smircich, L. and Hirsch, P. (eds) (1983) 'Organizational culture' (special issue), *Administrative Science Quarterly*, **28,** 331–499 (185).

Jensen, M.C. and Meckling, W.H. (1976) 'Theory of the firm: managerial behaviour, agency ownership structure', *Journal of Financial Economics*, **3,** 305–60 (330).

Johnson, P.S. and Cathcart, D.G. (1979) 'The founders of new manufacturing firms: a note on the size of their "incubator" plants', *Journal of Industrial Economics*, **28,** 219–24 (reprinted in Casson, ed., 1990) (302).

Jones, S.R.G. (1984) *The Economics of Conformism*, Oxford, Blackwell (193).

Kahneman, D. and Tversky, A. (1979) 'Prospect theory: an analysis of decision under risk', *Econometrica*, **47**, 263–91 (reprinted in Earl, ed., 1988a) (108–11).

Kaldor, N. (1934) 'The equilibrium of the firm', *Economic Journal*, **44**, 60–76 (212, 248).

----- (1972) 'The irrelevance of equilibrium economics', *Economic Journal*, **82**, 1237–55 (147, 211).

----- (1980) *Reports on Taxation 1: Papers Relating to the United Kingdom*, London, Duckworth (216).

Katouzian, H. (1980) *Ideology and Method in Economics*, London, Macmillan (62).

Katzner, D.W. (1970) *Static Demand Theory*, London, Collier-Macmillan (54).

Kay, J. (1993) *Foundations of Corporate Success*, Oxford, Oxford University Press (136, 138–40, 143, 381, 401, 403).

Kay, N.M. (1979) *The Innovating Firm*, London, Macmillan (148, 198, 331).

----- (1982) *The Evolving Firm*, London, Macmillan (335–6, 340–41, 361, 372).

----- (1983a) 'Optimal size of firm as a problem in transaction costs and property rights', *Journal of Economic Studies*, **10**, 29–41 (328).

----- (1983b) 'Review article: multinational enterprise', *Scottish Journal of Political Economy*, **30**, 304–12 (385).

----- (1984) *The Emergent Firm*, London, Macmillan (158, 309, 324, 338, 361, 372, 385, 400).

----- (1991) 'Multinational enterprise as strategic choice: some transaction cost perspectives', in Pitelis and Sugden (eds) (1991) (380, 385).

----- (1992) 'Markets, false hierarchies and the evolution of the modern corporation', *Journal of Economic Behavior and Organization*, **17**, 315–33 (324, 401).

----- (1993) 'Markets, false hierarchies and the role of asset specificity', in Pitelis (ed.) (1993) (376, 401).

Keller, M. (1989) *Rude Awakening: The Rise, Fall and Struggle for Recovery of General Motors*, New York, Morrow (167).

Kelly, G.A. (1955) *The Psychology of Personal Constructs*, New York, Norton (70, 302).

Keynes, J.M. (1936 *The General Theory of Employment, Interest and Money*, London, Macmillan, (311).

----- (1937) 'The general theory of employment', *Quarterly Journal of Economics*, **51**, 209–23 (126).

Kirzner, I.M. (1973) *Competition and Entrepreneurship*, Chicago, University of Chicago Press (302).

----- (1979) *Perception, Opportunity and Profit*, Chicago, University of Chicago Press (302).

Klein, B.H. (1977) *Dynamic Economics*, Cambridge, MA, Harvard University Press (199, 250).

Knight, F.H. (1921) *Risk, Uncertainty and Profit*, Boston, MA, Houghton Mifflin (112, 301).

Koestler, A. (1975) *The Act of Creation*, London, Picador Books (302).

Kogut, B. (1988) 'Joint ventures: theoretical and empirical perspectives', *Strategic*

Management Journal, **9**, 319–22 (383).

Kono, T. (1984) *Strategy and Structure of Japanese Enterprises*, London, Macmillan/ Armonk, NY, M.E. Sharpe, Inc. (371).

Kornai, J. (1971) *Anti-Equilibrium*, Amsterdam, North-Holland (11, 39, 71).

Lakatos, I. (1970) 'Falsification and the methodology of scientific research programmes', in Lakatos, I. and Musgrave, A. (eds) *Criticism and the Growth of Knowledge*, London, Cambridge University Press (94).

Lancaster, K.J. (1966a) 'A new approach to consumer theory', *Journal of Political Economy*, **74**, 132–57 (34, 53).

----- (1966b) 'Change and innovation in the technology of consumption', *American Economic Review*, **56**, May, 14–23 (34, 53).

----- (1971) *Consumer Demand: A New Approach*, New York, Columbia University Press (34, 53, 61).

Lane, R. (1991) *The Market Experience*, Cambridge, Cambridge University Press (67, 88).

Langlois, C. (1989a) 'A model with target inventory and markup with empirical testing using automobile-industry data', *Journal of Economic Behavior and Organization*, **11**, 47–74 (293).

----- (1989b) 'Markup pricing versus marginalism: a controversy revisited', *Journal of Post Keynesian Economics*, **12**, 127–51 (293).

Latsis, S.J. (1972) 'Situational determinism in economics', *British Journal for the Philosophy of Science*, **25**, 207–45 (150).

----- (ed.) (1976) *Method and Appraisal in Economics*, Cambridge, Cambridge University Press (94).

Lavoie, M. (1992) 'Towards a new research programme for post-Keynesianism and neo-Ricardianism', *Review of Political Economy*, **4**, 37–78 (94).

Lea, S.E.G., Tarpy, R.M. and Webley, P. (1987) *The Individual in the Economy*, Cambridge, Cambridge University Press (42, 88).

-----, Webley, P. and Young, B. (eds) (1992) *New Directions in Economic Psychology*, Aldershot, Edward Elgar (88).

Lee, F.S. (1984) 'Full cost pricing: a new wine in a new bottle', *Australian Economic Papers*, **23**, 151–66 (226).

----- (1985) 'Post Keynesian view of average direct costs: critical evaluation of the theory and the empirical evidence', *Journal of Post Keynesian Economics*, **8**, 158–72 (190, 223, 273).

-----, Mongin, P., Earl, P.E. and Langlois, C. (1990–91) 'Symposium on the marginalist controversy and price theory', *Journal of Post Keynesian Economics*, **13**, 233–92 (275).

Leibenstein, H. (1966) 'Allocative efficiency vs. "X-efficiency"', *American Economic Review*, **56**, 392–415 (196–8, 202, 208, 259, 307).

----- (1976) *Beyond Economic Man*, Cambridge, MA, Harvard University Press (96, 196, 208, 259, 307).

Lester, R.A.(1946) 'Shortcomings of marginal analysis for wage-employment problems', *American Economic Review*, **36**, 63–82 (190, 224–5, 248).

Levi, I. (1986) *Hard Choices*, Cambridge, Cambridge University Press (72).

Levine, A. (1980) 'Increasing returns, the competitive model and the enigma that was

Alfred Marshall', *Scottish Journal of Political Economy*, **27**, 260–75 (204).

Linder, S.B. (1970) *The Harried Leisure Class*, New York, Columbia University Press (23).

Lipsey, R.G. and Rosenbluth, G. (1971) 'A contribution to the new theory of demand: a rehabilitation of the Giffen good', *Canadian Journal of Economics*, **4**, 131–63 (57).

Littlechild, S.C. (1978) *The Fallacy of the Mixed Economy*, London, Institute of Economic Affairs (156–7, 302).

----- (1981) 'Misleading calculations of the social costs of monopoly power', *Economic Journal*, **91**, 348–64 (271, 302).

Loasby, B.J. (1967) 'Management economics and the theory of the firm', *Journal of Industrial Economics*, **15**, 165–76 (reprinted in Earl, ed., 1988a) (150).

----- (1971) 'Hypothesis and paradigm in the theory of the firm', *Economic Journal*, **81**, 863–85 (214).

----- (1976) *Choice, Complexity, and Ignorance*, Cambridge, Cambridge University Press (29, 168, 197, 214, 217, 334).

----- (1978) 'Whatever happened to Marshall's theory of value?', *Scottish Journal of Political Economy*, **25**, 1–12 (52, 204, 313).

----- (1982) 'The entrepreneur in economic theory', *Scottish Journal of Political Economy*, **29**, 235–45 (166).

----- (1989) *The Mind and Method of the Economist*, Aldershot, Edward Elgar (204–5, 256, 304).

----- (1990a) 'Review article: problem-solving institutions', *Scottish Journal of Political Economy*, **37**, 197–201 (324).

----- (1990b) 'The use of scenarios in business planning', in Frowen (ed.) (1990) (121, 123).

Loomes, G. and Sugden, R. (1982) 'Regret Theory: an alternative theory of rational choice under uncertainty', *Economic Journal*, **92**, 805–24 (111).

Lorsch, J. (1986) 'Managing culture: the invisible barrier to strategic change', *California Management Review*, **28**, 95–109 (reprinted in Earl, ed., 1988a) (185, 340–41).

Love, J.F. (1986) *McDonald's: Behind the Arches*, New York, Bantam Books (353, 357).

Lussier, D.A. and Olshavsky, R.W. (1979) 'Task complexity and contingent processing in brand choice', *Journal of Consumer Research*, **6**, 154–65 (72).

Lux, K. and Lutz, M. (1986) 'Economic psychology: the humanistic perspective', in MacFadyen, A.J. and MacFadyen, H.W. (eds) (1986) (42).

MacFadyen, A.J. and MacFadyen, H.W. (eds) (1986) *Economic Psychology: Intersections in Theory and Application*, Amsterdam, North-Holland (88).

Machlup, F. (1946) 'Marginal analysis and empirical research', *American Economic Review*, **36**, 519–34 (224).

Maital, S. (1982) *Minds, Markets and Money*, New York, Basic Books (125, 307).

March, J.G. (1988) *Decisions and Organizations*, Oxford, Blackwell (69–70, 189).

----- and Simon, H.A. (1958) *Organizations*, New York, Wiley (189).

Marris, R.L. (1964) *The Economic Theory of 'Managerial' Capitalism*, London, Macmillan (335, 379).

Marschak, J. (1968) 'The economics of inquiring, communicating, deciding', *American Economic Review*, **58** (supplement), 1–18 (30).

Marshall, A. (1890) *Principles of Economics*, London, Macmillan (page references to 8th edn, 1920) (xii, 53, 178, 196, 200, 203–9, 212, 217, 247, 252, 270, 281, 313, 325, 327).

----- (1919) *Industry and Trade*, London, Macmillan (page references to 4th edn, 1923) (200, 204, 207, 247, 313, 325).

Maslow, A. (1954) *Motivation and Personality*, New York, Harper & Row (41–2).

Mason, R. (1989) *Robert Giffen and the Giffen Paradox*, Oxford, Philip Allan (49).

McCloskey, D. (1990) *If You're So Smart: The Narrative of Economic Expertise*, Chicago, University of Chicago Press (125).

McKern, R.B. and Lowenthal, G.C. (eds) (1985) *Limits to Prediction*, Sydney, Australian Professional Publications (121).

McQueen, D. (1994) 'On rereading Samuelson I: A teacher's perspective', *Challenge*, March/April, 39–45 (143).

Middleton, E. (1986) 'Some testable implications of a preference for subjective novelty', *Kyklos*, **39**, 397–418 (88).

Miles, C. (1968) *Lancashire Textiles: A Case Study of Industrial Change*, Cambridge, Cambridge University Press/NIESR (184).

Milgrom, P. and Roberts, J. (1992) *Economics, Organization and Management*, Englewood Cliffs, NJ, Prentice-Hall (324, 367).

Miller, G.A. (1956) 'The magic number seven plus or minus two: some limits on our capacity for processing information', *Psychological Review*, **63**, 81–97 (30).

Miller, G.J. (1992) *Managerial Dilemmas: The Political Economy of Hierarchy*, Cambridge, Cambridge University Press (403).

Morgenstern, O. (1963) *On the Accuracy of Economic Observations*, Princeton, NJ, Princeton University Press (224).

Morita, A. (1987) *Made in Japan: Akio Morita and Sony*, London, Collins (139, 144, 253).

Moss, S.J. (1981) *An Economic Theory of Business Strategy*, Oxford, Martin Robertson (174, 243, 263, 327, 332–3, 361).

Muellbauer, J. (1974) 'Household production theory, quality, and the "hedonic technique"', *American Economic Review*, 64, 977–94 (60).

Muth, J. (1961) 'Rational expectations and the theory of price movements', *Econometrica*, **29**, 315–35 (305).

Muth, R.F. (1966) 'Household production and consumer demand functions', *Econometrica*, **34**, 699–708 (53–4).

Neale, A. (1960) *The Antitrust Laws of the U.S.A.: A Study of Competition Enforced by Law* (2nd edn, 1970), Cambridge, NIESR/Cambridge University Press (321).

Nelson, R.R. and Winter, S.G. (1982) *An Evolutionary Theory of Economic Change*, Cambridge, MA, Harvard University Press (167, 189, 201–2, 325).

Nisbett, R.E. and Ross, L. (1980) *Human Inference: Strategies and Shortcomings of Social Judgment*, Englewood Cliffs, NJ, Prentice-Hall (91).

O'Brien, D.P. (ed.) (1990) 'Special issue on Marshall: the *Principles* centenary', *Scottish Journal of Political Economy*, **37**, 2–84 (204).

Oi, W.Y. (1962) 'Labor as a quasi-fixed factor', *Journal of Political Economy*, **70**, 538–55 (225).

Olshavsky, R.W. and Granbois, D.H. (1979) 'Consumer decision making—fact or fiction?',

Journal of Consumer Research, **6**, 93–100 (reprinted in Earl, 1988a) (69, 72–3, 75, 126, 264, 267).

Pardini, A. and Katzev, R.D. (1986) 'Applying full-cycle psychology in consumer marketing: the defusing objections technique', *Journal of Economic Psychology*, **7**, 87–94 (135).

Payne, J.W. (1976) 'Task complexity and contingent processing in decision making: an information search and protocol analysis', *Organizational Behaviour and Human Performance*, **16**, 336–87 (72).

Peacock, A. (1976) 'Review of T. Scitovsky's *The Joyless Economy*', *Journal of Economic Literature*, **14**, 1278–80 (90).

Penrose, E.T. (1959) *The Theory of the Growth of the Firm* (2nd edn, 1980), Oxford, Blackwell (154, 206, 325, 332, 335, 360, 379, 399).

Perrow, C. (1970) *Organizational Analysis: A Sociological View*, London, Tavistock (377).

Perry, W.G., jr (1970) *Forms of Intellectual and Ethical Development in the College Years: A Scheme*, New York, Holt, Rinehart & Winston (xiii, 7–8, 22–3, 123, 185, 203, 330–31).

----- (1981) 'Cognitive and ethical growth: the making of meaning', in Chickering, A. (ed.) *The Modern American College*, San Francisco: Jossey-Bass (xiii, 7–8).

----- (1985) 'Different worlds in the same classroom', *On Teaching and Learning: The Journal of the Harvard–Danforth Center*, **1**, 1–17 (xiii, 7–8).

Pheby, J. (1988) *Methodology and Economics: A Critical Introduction*, London, Macmillan (62).

Phlips, L. (1981) *The Economics of Price Discrimination*, Cambridge, Cambridge University Press (288).

----- (1988) *The Economics of Imperfect Information*, Cambridge, Cambridge University Press (265).

Pickering, J.F. (1976) 'P.W.S. Andrews's and E. Brunner's *Studies in Pricing*: review', *Economic Journal*, **86**, 621–2 (275).

-----, Harrison, J.A., Hebden, J.J., Isherwood, B.C. and Cohen, C.D. (1973) 'Are goods goods? Some empirical evidence', *Applied Economics*, **5**, 1–18 (53).

Pigou, A.C. (1928) 'An analysis of supply', *Economic Journal*, **38**, 238–57 (210, 247).

Piore, M.J. and Sabel, C.F. (1984) *The Second Industrial Divide: Possibilities for Prosperity*, New York, Basic Books (187–8).

Pirsig, R.M. (1974) *Zen and the Art of Motorcycle Maintenance*, London, Bodley Head (15).

Pitelis, C.N. (1991) *Market and Non-Market Hierarchies*, Oxford, Blackwell (324).

----- (ed.) (1993) *Transaction Costs, Markets and Hierarchies*, Oxford, Blackwell (324).

----- and Sugden, R. (eds) (1991) *The Nature of the Transnational Firm*, London, Routledge (385).

Polanyi, M. (1958) *Personal Knowledge*, London, Routledge & Kegan Paul (167).

Porter, M.E. (1980) *Competitive Strategy: Techniques for Analysing Industries and Competitors*, New York, Free Press (314, 316, 338, 347–8).

----- (1990) *The Competitive Advantage of Nations*, London, Macmillan (326).

Prais, S.J. (1973) 'Review of D.S. Ironmonger's *New Commodities and Consumer Behaviour*', *Economic Journal*, **83**, 578–80 (254).

Ramsey, F.P. (1927) 'A contribution to the theory of taxation', *Economic Journal*, **37**, 47–61 (193, 196, 208).

Ratchford, B.T. (1975) 'The new economic theory of consumer behavior: an interpretive essay', *Journal of Consumer Research*, **2**, 65–75 (54, 61).

Reed, G.V. and Bates, J.M. (1990) 'Some deficiencies often found in the textbook analysis of the monopolist discriminating between two markets', *Scottish Journal of Political Economy*, **37**, 386–95 (284).

Reid, G.C. (1981) *The Kinked Demand Curve Analysis of Oligopoly*, Edinburgh, Edinburgh University Press (227).

Remenyi, J.V. (1979) 'Core demi-core interaction: toward a general theory of disciplinary and subdisciplinary growth', *History of Political Economy*, **11**, 30–63 (94).

Richards, L. (1985) *Having Families: Marriage, Parenthood and Social Pressures in Australia*, Ringwood, Victoria, Penguin (69).

Richardson, G.B. (1953) 'Imperfect knowledge and economic efficiency, *Oxford Economic Papers*, **5**, 136–56 (199).

----- (1956) 'Demand and supply reconsidered', *Oxford Economic Papers*, **8**, 113–26 (304).

----- (1959) 'Equilibrium, expectations and information', *Economic Journal*, **69**, 223–37 (reprinted in Earl, ed., 1988a) (304, 337).

----- (1960) *Information and Investment*, Oxford, Clarendon Press (2nd edn, 1990) (304, 311).

----- (1969) *The Future of the Heavy Electrical Plant Industry*, London, BEEMA (137, 301).

----- (1972) 'The organisation of industry', *Economic Journal*, **82**, 883–96 (reprinted in Earl, ed., 1988a, and Richardson, 1960/1990) (312, 343).

Ricketts, M. (1987) *The Economics of Business Enterprise: New Approaches to the Theory of the Firm*, Brighton, Wheatsheaf (ix, 301, 324, 343, 353).

----- (ed.) (1988) *Neoclassical Microeconomics*, Aldershot, Edward Elgar (12).

Robbins, L.C. (1928) 'The representative firm', *Economic Journal*, **38**, 387–404 (212).

Robertson, D.H. (1956) *Economic Commentaries*, London, Staples Press (247).

Robinson, E.A.G. (1931) *The Structure of Competitive Industry*, London, Nisbet (212, 248).

----- (1934) 'The problem of management and the size of the firm', *Economic Journal*, **44**, 242–57 (212, 248).

----- (1939) '*Oxford Economic Papers*: review', *Economic Journal*, **49**, 538–43 (229).

Robinson, J.V. (1933) *The Economics of Imperfect Competition*, London, Macmillan (page references to 2nd edn, 1969) (211–12, 214–18, 227, 248, 275).

----- (1953) 'Imperfect competition revisited', *Economic Journal*, **63**, 579–93 (275).

----- and Eatwell, J.L. (1973) *An Introduction to Modern Economics*, New York, McGraw-Hill (188).

Robinson, R. (1969) *Edward H. Chamberlin*, New York, Columbia University Press (214).

Romer, P. (1993) 'Ideas and things', in 'The Future Surveyed', supplement to *The Economist*, 11–17 September, 64–8 (184).

Rosen, S. (1974) 'Hedonic prices and implicit markets', *Journal of Political Economy*, **82**, 34–53 (58).

Roy, A.D. (1952) 'Safety first and the holding of assets', *Econometrica*, **20**, 431–49 (112).

Rubin, P.H. (1978) 'The Theory of the Firm and the Structure of the Franchise Contract',

Journal of Law and Economics, **21**, 223–33 (353).

Rugman, A. (ed.) (1982) *New Theories of the Multinational Enterprise*, London, Croom Helm (385).

Ryan, M.J. and Bonfield, E.H. (1975) 'The Fishbein extended model and consumer behavior', *Journal of Consumer Research*, **2**, 118–36 (72).

Sabbagh, K. (1989) *Skyscraper: The Making of a Building*, London, Macmillan/Channel Four Television (323–4).

Sako, M. (1992) *Prices, Quality and Trust: Inter-firm Relations in Britain and Japan*, Cambridge, Cambridge University Press (344).

Salop, S.C. and Stiglitz, J.E. (1977) 'Bargains and ripoffs: a model of monopolistically competitive price dispersion, *Review of Economic Studies*, **44**, 493–510 (265).

Salter, W.E.G. (1960) *Productivity and Technical Change*, Cambridge, Cambridge University Press (181, 273).

Schendel, D.E. and Balastra, P. (1969) 'Rational behaviour and gasoline price wars', *Applied Economics*, **1**, 89–101 (231).

Schoemaker, P.J.H. (1991) 'When and how to use scenario planning: a heuristic approach with illustration', *Journal of Forecasting*, **10**, 549–64 (121).

Schumacher, E.F. (1973) *Small is Beautiful: A Study of Economics as if People Mattered*, London, Blond & Briggs (166).

Schumpeter, J.A. (1943) *Capitalism, Socialism and Democracy*, London, Unwin University Books (new edition published by Routledge, London, 1994) (149, 199, 303).

Scitovsky, T. (1945) 'Some consequences of the habit of judging quality by price', *Review of Economic Studies*, **12**, 100–105 (78, 233).

----- (1950) 'Ignorance as a source of oligopoly power', *American Economic Review*, **40**, May, 48–53 (293).

----- (1971) *Welfare and Competition* (2nd edn), London, George Allen & Unwin (170).

----- (1976) *The Joyless Economy*, New York, Oxford University Press (88, 90).

----- (1985) 'Pricetakers' plenty: a neglected benefit of capitalism, *Kyklos*, **38**, 517–36 (293).

----- (1986) *Human Desire and Economic Satisfaction*, Brighton, Wheatsheaf (88).

----- (1990) 'The benefits of asymmetric markets', *Journal of Economic Perspectives*, **4**, 135–48 (293).

Shackle, G.L.S. (1949) *Expectation in Economics*, Cambridge, Cambridge University Press (2nd edn, 1952) (112, 131, 142).

----- (1958) *Time in Economics*, Amsterdam, North-Holland (112, 114).

----- (1970) *Expectation, Enterprise and Profit*, London, George Allen & Unwin (112, 143).

----- (1979) *Imagination and the Nature of Choice*, Edinburgh, Edinburgh University Press (112).

----- (1988) *Business, Time and Thought* (ed. S.F. Frowen), London, Macmillan (302).

Shaw, R.W. and Sutton, C.J. (1976) *Industry and Competition: Industrial Case Studies*, London, Macmillan (231).

Silver, M. (1984) *Enterprise and the Scope of the Firm: The Role of Vertical Integration*, Oxford, Blackwell (345, 349).

Simon, H.A. (1945) *Administrative Behavior*, New York, Free Press (189, 225).

----- (1957) *Models of Man*, New York, Wiley (28, 31).

----- (1959) 'Theories of decision-making in economics and behavioral sciences', *American Economic Review*, **49**, 253–83 (reprinted in Earl, ed., 1988a) (28, 71, 125).

----- (1969) *The Sciences of the Artificial*, Cambridge, MA, MIT Press (68, 168, 372).

----- (1976) 'From substantive to procedural rationality', in Latsis, S.J. (ed.) (1976) (31, 225).

----- (1983) *Reason in Human Affairs*, Oxford, Blackwell (111).

----- (1986) 'The failure of armchair economics', interview in *Challenge*, **29**, 18–25 (190, 225).

----- (1992) *Models of my Life*, New York, NY, Basic Books (67, 100).

Singh, A. (1971) *Take-overs: Their Relevance to the Stock Market and the Theory of the Firm*, Cambridge, Cambridge University Press (259).

----- (1975) 'Take-overs, economic natural selection, and the theory of the firm: evidence from the postwar United Kingdom experience', *Economic Journal*, **85**, 497–515 (259).

Skinner, A.S. (1979) 'Adam Smith: an aspect of modern economics?', *Scottish Journal of Political Economy*, **26**, 109–26 (95).

----- (1983) 'E.H. Chamberlin: the origins and development of monopolistic competition', *Journal of Economic Studies*, **10**, 52–67 (214).

Sloan, A.P., jr (1965) *My Years with General Motors*, London, Sidgwick & Jackson (80, 144, 352).

Smith, A. (1776) *An Inquiry into the Nature and Causes of the Wealth of Nations* (E. Cannan, ed.) (1961), London, Methuen (188–9, 214, 252, 298).

Sobel, R. (1981) *I.B.M.: Colossus in Transition*, New York, Times Books (243).

Spengler, J.J. (1965) 'Kinked demand curves: by whom used first?', *Southern Economic Journal*, **32**, 81–4 (227).

Sraffa, P. (1925) Sulle relazioni fra costo e quantita prodotta', *Annali di Economia*, **2**, 277–328 (210–11, 248, 266).

----- (1926) 'The laws of returns under competitive conditions', *Economic Journal*, **36**, 535–50 (210, 248).

----- (1960) *Production of Commodities by Means of Commodities*, Cambridge, Cambridge University Press (300).

Staw, B.M. and Ross, J. (1989) 'Understanding behavior in escalation situations', *Science*, **246**, 13 October, 216–20 (92).

Steedman, I. (1982) 'The empirical importance of joint production', University of Manchester Economics Discussion Paper No. 31/*Proceedings of Colloque: Production Jointe et Capital Fixe*, Nanterre (172).

Steinbruner, J.D. (1974) *The Cybernetic Theory of Decision*, Princeton, NJ, Princeton University Press (92, 113).

Steindl, J. (1952) *Maturity and Stagnation in American Capitalism*, New York, Monthly Review Press (232, 265, 294).

Stewart, A. and Stewart, V. (1981) *Business Applications of Repertory Grid Analysis*, New York, McGraw-Hill (61).

Stigler, G.J. (1939) 'Production and distribution in the short run', *Journal of Political Economy*, **47**, 305–27 (168).

----- (1947) 'The kinky oligopoly demand curve and rigid prices', *Journal of Political*

Economy, **55**, 432–47 (229).

----- (1968) 'A note on block booking', in his collection *The Organization of Industry*, Homewood, IL, Irwin (288).

----- (1978) 'The literature of economics: the case of the kinked oligopoly demand curve', *Economic Inquiry*, **16**, 185–204 (229).

----- (1982) 'Review of G.C. Reid *The Kinked Demand Curve Analysis of Oligopoly*', *Economic Journal*, **92**, 203–4 (230).

Strotz, R.H. (1957) 'The empirical implications of a utility tree', *Econometrica*, **25**, 269–80 (54).

Sweezy, P.M. (1939) 'Demand under conditions of oligopoly', *Journal of Political Economy*, **47**, 568–73 (227–8).

Taylor, B. and Wills, G. (eds) (1969) *Pricing Strategy*, London, Staples (78).

Thaler, R. (1980) 'Toward a positive theory of consumer choice', *Journal of Economic Behavior and Organization*, **1**, 39–60 (reprinted in Earl, ed., 1988a) (90, 93–4, 100, 110, 119).

----- and Shefrin, H.M. (1981) 'An economic theory of self control', *Journal of Political Economy*, **89**, 396–406 (93).

Thoburn, J.T. and Takashima, M. (1992) *Industrial Subcontracting in the UK and Japan*, Aldershot, Avebury (344).

Tirole, J. (1988) *Theory of Industrial Organization*, Cambridge, MA, MIT Press (104).

Toffler, A. (1970) *Future Shock*, London, Bodley Head (368).

Triffin, R. (1940) *Monopolistic Competition and General Equilibrium Theory*, Cambridge, MA, Harvard University Press (218).

Tversky, A. (1969) 'Intransitivity of preferences', *Psychological Review*, **76**, 31–48 (72).

----- (1972) 'Elimination by aspects: a theory of choice', *Psychological Review*, **79**, 281–99 (72).

----- and Kahneman, D. (1981) 'The framing of decisions and the psychology of choice', *Science*, **211**, 453–8 (91, 109).

Utton, M.A. (1982) *The Political Economy of Big Business*, Oxford, Martin Robertson (373).

van Raaij, W.F., van Veldhoven, G.M. and Warneryd, K.-E. (eds) (1988) *Handbook of Economic Psychology*, Dordrecht, Kluwer Academic Publishers (88).

von Neumann, J. and Morgenstern, O. (1944) *The Theory of Games and Economic Behavior*, Princeton, NJ, Princeton University Press (105, 108, 136).

Vonortas, N.S. (1990) 'Emerging patterns of multinational enterprise operations in developed market economies: evidence and policy', *Review of Political Economy*, **2**, 188–220 (385).

Walras, L. (1874) *Elēments d'ēconomie politique pure*, Lausanne, L. Corbas (translated by W. Jaffe and published as *Elements of Pure Economics*, London, Allen & Unwin, 1954) (300).

Waterman, D.A. and Newell, A. (1971) 'Protocol analysis as a task for artificial intelligence', *Artificial Intelligence*, **2**, 285–318 (81).

Watts, M. and Gaston, N. (1982) 'The "reswitching" of consumption bundles: a parallel to the capital controversies', *Journal of Post Keynesian Economics*, **5**, 281–8 (56).

Wheelen, T.L. and Hunger, J.D. (1989) *Strategic Management and Business Policy* (3rd edn), Reading, MA, Addison-Wesley (16, 336).

Williams, P.L. (1978) *The Emergence of the Theory of the Firm*, London, Macmillan (204).

Williamson, O.E. (1967) *The Economics of Discretionary Behavior*, Englewood Cliffs, NJ, Prentice-Hall (192).

----- (1975) *Markets and Hierarchies*, New York, Free Press (xiii, 158, 324, 329, 333, 383, 400–401).

----- (1985) *The Economic Institutions of Capitalism*, New York, Free Press (xiii, 158, 324, 329).

----- and Winter, S.G. (eds) (1991) *The Nature of the Firm: Origins, Evolution and Development*, Oxford, Oxford University Press (324).

Wilson, T. (1979) 'The price of oil: a case of negative marginal revenue?', *Journal of Industrial Economics*, **27**, 301–16 (223, 263, 276).

----- (1984) *Inflation, Unemployment, and the Market*, Oxford, Clarendon Press (272).

----- and Andrews, P.W.S. (eds) (1951) *Oxford Studies in the Price Mechanism*, Oxford, Oxford University Press (199, 275).

Winter, S.G., jr (1964) 'Economic "natural selection" and the theory of the firm', *Yale Economic Essays*, **4**, 224–72 (reprinted in Earl, ed., 1988a) (190).

Wiseman, J. and Littlechild, S.C. (1990) 'Crusoe's kingdom: cost, choice and political economy', in Frowen, S.F. (ed.) (1990) (156).

Wood, J.W. (1992) 'The costly consequences of protection and other devices for raising returns', paper presented to the Economic Society of Australia (Queensland), Inc. Conference, 1–4 September, Gold Coast (268).

You, Y.-I. and Wilkinson, F. (1994) 'Competition and co-operation: toward understanding industrial districts', *Review of Political Economy*, **6**, 259–78 (325).

Young, A. (1928) 'Increasing returns and economic progress', *Economic Journal*, **38**, 527–42 (211).

Index

Accountability, 157–8, 198
Addiction, 64–5, 89
Advertising, 65, 86, 88, 92–3, 157, 199, 217, 231, 239–40, 253, 258, 265, 286–8, 307, 316, 326, 353, 378, 380, 388, 393–8
Agenda of possible options, 70
Agents, 16, 18, 290, 299–300, 308, 325, 330, 351, 385
Airports, 121–2
Allais paradox, 108
Altruism, 66, 127, 343
Anxiety, 88–9, 125, 325, 346, 395
Arbitrage, 284
Arousal, 88–9
Arrow paradox, 383
Artificial intelligence, 67
Ascendancy function, 115
Aspiration levels, 33, 71–9, 114, 118, 128–31, 148–9, 184, 190–93, 197, 264
Asset stripping, 375
Assumption/Axioms, 28, 36–42, 62, 71, 100, 167–8, 218–19, 229, 240, 242, 248, 259–60, 272, 278, 280
Atmosphere, 383–4
Auctions, 244, 290, 299–300, 389
Auditing, 156, 334
Austrian School of Economists, 302–3
Automation, 186, 252
Availability bias, 91
Aviation industry, 285, 305–9, 343, 376–80, 389, 402
Axiom of Archimedes, 40, 45, 63, 112

Badge engineering, 381–2
Bankruptcy, 181–2, 206, 269, 273, 319, 363
Bargaining, 127–36, 141, 143, 157, 188, 192, 208, 282, 317, 333, 342, 348, 353, 359, 378, 380
Barter, 383
Battle of the Sexes, 138
Benchmarking, 197, 344
Behavioural economics, 28, 63, 67–101 *passim*, 110, 128–31, 145–54 *passim*, 168, 189–93, 197, 218, 256, 261, 270–71, 324

Black box, 150, 158, 190, 324
Block booking, 288
Bottlenecks, 174, 303
Boundaries of the firm, 145
Brands, 126, 141, 149–50, 175–6, 249–50, 292, 335, 352, 358–9, 388–9, 392–9, 403
  brand loyalty, 3, 99, 101, 266–7, 390
Break-even analysis, 120, 292
Brewing industry, 321
Budgets, 42, 54, 57–8, 68, 77–9, 249, 268, 340, 367
Bundling, 287, 307, 392
Burnout, 307
Business history, 144, 175, 332

Capabilities, 381–4, 401
Capacity, 179, 225, 232, 237, 239, 240, 303–5, 373, 397
  constraints, 25, 120, 172–4, 232, 237
  excess/spare/surplus, 17, 25, 120, 137, 174, 176, 181–4, 194, 216, 238, 248 253, 262, 265, 294, 306, 316–19, 335, 347, 360, 382, 386
  expansion, 304, 312–14, 337–8, 374
Capital, 166, 181–3, 199, 207, 214–15, 226, 232, 269, 328, 342, 345, 364
Car market, 37, 76–84, 91, 132–3, 147, 175–6, 180–81, 186–9, 199–200, 266–70, 285–6, 291, 295, 325–6, 336, 340, 343–6, 352–3, 372, 376–86, 403
Case study method, ix, 16–18, 353
Catastrophe, 176, 181, 361–3
Certainty effect, 108
Channel Tunnel, 182, 322
Characteristics theory of demand, 52–60, 62, 72–99 *passim*, 104–5, 140, 142, 161, 254
Chicken game, 139–40, 220, 304
Choice matrix, 72, 76, 81, 86, 97
Cigarettes, 64, 93, 230, 245–6
Cobweb model, 304–5
Cognitive dissonance, 92–3, 96, 123, 251, 307, 396
Collaboration, 176, 322, 380–87, 394
Collusion, 22, 182, 226, 262–4, 312, 367, 375,

380

Commitment, 93–4, 140, 384

Competence, xiv, 168, 176, 201–2, 212, 250, 265, 271, 324–5, 332, 335, 343, 345–8, 381–4

Competition, 187, 193, 199–200, 207, 271, 294, 319, 360, 373–6, 393–4, 403

   foreign, 16, 200, 263, 374

   imperfect, 144–5, 211, 214–18, 245–8, 250, 259, 276, 279–80, 320, 375

   internal, 191, 197, 271, 366–72, 375

   monopolistic, 144, 214–22, 245–8, 259, 276, 280, 291, 306, 320

   non-price, 16, 58–61, 77–88, 149, 267, 306–7, 351

   perfect, 144, 200, 208–12, 221–3, 248, 259, 262, 312, 320, 337

   policy, 212, 216, 276, 382, 384

   potential, 16–17, 261–74, 278, 292–3, 361, 364, 374, 396–7

   pressure of, 196–8, 202, 361, 371, 376–7

   price, 16, 77–8, 149, 231, 246, 253, 266–7, 306–8, 382

   quality, 231, 308

   social, 255

   technological, 148–50, 181–3

Competitive advantage, 361–2, 394

Complementarity, 54, 138–9, 154, 249, 291, 380

Completeness, 36–7

Complexity, 16–18, 27, 31–2, 68–9, 72–6, 99–100, 110–11, 121, 134, 147, 155, 168, 204, 217, 256, 259–61, 266–7, 276, 291, 300–301, 324, 328, 334, 395

Computer-aided design (CAD), 187

Computer aided manufacturing (CAM), 187

Computer industry, 138–9, 143, 181

Concentration, 245

Confidence, 254

Conflict of interest, 329, 346, 354, 364, 382, 391–2

Conglomerates, 154, 373–6

Conspicuous consumption, 78, 254–5

Constraints, 42–50, 94

   piecewise linear, 43

Construction industry, 137, 269–70, 278, 323, 331

Consultants, 197, 335–6, 378–9, 389

Consumer surplus, 193–6, 208, 215, 271, 282–3

Contestability, 17, 141, 193, 196, 203, 251, 259, 272–4, 277, 281–2, 293–4, 305–9, 334, 337, 366–7

Contingent commodity, 37, 309

Continuity, 40, 65

Contract curve, 128

Contracts, 145, 151, 153, 157, 238, 244, 269–70, 343–8, 360, 381–4, 392, 399

   ambiguities in, 197, 324

   complex, 328, 331

   contingent claims, 309–10, 328–9, 334, 348–9

   defaults in respect of, 311

   employment, 135, 151–2, 157, 177, 187, 197, 329, 331, 343, 347

   implicit, 187, 275

   long-term, 17, 311, 348

   management, 389

   nexus of, 330–31

   provisional, 299

   short-term, 311, 328–9, 343, 382

   specificity of, 135, 151–2, 154, 177, 197, 273–5, 311, 329–34, 347–9, 382

Contribution margin, 174, 292

Conventions, 139, 299, 323

Convexity, 37–9, 127

Cooperative behaviour, 137, 313, 343, 372, 380–84, 403

Coordination, 31, 138–40, 151–2, 158, 185, 212, 223, 276, 298–335 *passim*, 339, 343, 347, 349, 351, 367, 372

Copyright protection, 289

Core ideas, 71, 91–3, 340

Corner solution, 45–6, 60, 63–4

Costs, 17, 303

   average/full, 163, 195–7, 205–7, 210, 212, 214–23, 247, 255

   bargaining, 127, 323

   common, 21

   curves, 205

   direct, 205, 226, 231, 240, 243

   enforcement, 311, 392, 397

   fixed, 2, 56, 120, 165, 175, 181–3, 188, 195, 213, 221, 232, 241, 252, 291, 319, 321

   hiring, 151, 154, 367

   information, 255

   inventory, 186, 205, 287

   joint/common, 290–93

   managerial, 334, 341

   marginal, 25, 50, 60, 120, 146, 157, 163,

171–2, 194–5, 205, 210–30, 244, 248–9, 252, 261, 276, 284, 292, 322, 334
marketing, 157, 205, 273–5, 286
monitoring, 323, 334, 348, 355–6, 380–81, 385
opportunity, 43, 92, 156–7, 176, 269–71, 278, 307, 321
overhead, 197, 205 213, 216, 233, 240, 258, 292
paying out, 181
prime, 201, 205, 226, 231
production, 157–8
redesign, 185–6
reductions in, 206–7, 252
replacement, 322
retraining, 120
search, 153, 353
selling, 234
start-up, 153, 243, 332, 363, 386
sunk (non-recoverable), 14, 17, 147, 175, 181–2, 265, 272–4, 282, 307–8, 321, 347, 374, 396
switching, 318
total, 163, 176, 205, 221, 226
transaction, 157–8, 273, 286–7, 309, 322–35 *passim*, 345–9, 362, 373, 380–92 *passim*, 400, 402
U-shaped cost curve, 190, 210, 221–5, 273, 337
variable, 120, 163–5, 179, 181–4, 188, 201, 225, 231–7, 262, 279, 292, 318, 321, 374
Craft work, 184–8
Creativity, 113, 121, 123, 141, 143, 302–3, 334, 348, 383–4, 388, 400
Credibility, 103, 140, 143, 147, 268, 376, 396, 399
Cross-subsidization, 369, 374–5
Crowding out, 374
Culture, 301, 356, 398
corporate, 184–6, 191, 200, 323, 335, 340, 385, 392

Data mining, 95
Deadweight loss, 194–7, 215, 381
Decision cycle, 29–30, 67–71, 96, 174, 253
Decision rules, 67–100 *passim*, 140–41, 157, 201, 261, 278, 282, 292, 308, 324, 351
additive differences, 73, 76, 83–4, 86–7, 112
characteristic filtering, 74–7, 82, 86, 112

compensatory, 72–7, 83–4, 86–7, 97, 141
conjunctive, 74, 77, 80, 82–4, 97
contingent, 7, 83, 86
disjunctive, 74, 78, 82, 84, 86
elimination by aspects, 74, 76, 80, 86, 88
hybrid, 75–6, 86, 112
lexicographic, 74–5, 80, 324
non-compensatory, 74–8, 83, 99–100, 141, 320
polymorphous, 73, 76–7, 86
unweighted averaging, 73, 86
Decomposability, 54, 68, 168
Defence industry, 274
Deliberation, 70, 73
Demand,
complementary, 22, 54, 249, 371–2
cross-elasticity of, 54, 316
in declining industries, 317
income elasticity of, 79
price elasticity of, 18, 226, 231–7, 244, 276, 286, 290, 317, 320
related, 21, 290–293
Demand curves, 23, 148, 193–4, 256–8, 261, 279
downward-sloping, 195, 210–11, 214–21, 245, 248, 255, 259, 271
fractional part of the market, 219–20
horizontal, 210–11, 262
kinked, 20, 226–30, 245, 249, 315, 322
Demonstration effect, 96, 254, 395
Deregulation, 305–9
Deskilling, 188–9
Diminishing marginal productivity/returns, 20, 59, 159, 213–14, 258
Diminishing marginal utility, 34, 106
Discontinuities, 65, 77, 166, 228–9
Discounted cashflow analysis, 314, 337
Distribution systems, 18, 103, 249, 251, 342–7, 352, 361–2, 372, 385–6, 393–8, 402–3
Diversification, 168, 175–6, 202, 239, 243, 268, 292, 306–8, 322, 337, 360–80, 388, 394, 398, 401
Dividends, 362–4
Division of labour, 252, 326
Dualism, 9, 330–31, 342
Durables, 58, 180, 266–7, 396, 403

Econometrics, 121, 159, 250
Economic growth, 211
Economic rent, 24

Economies of increased dimensions, 161, 214

Economies of scale, 139, 147, 161–3, 177, 201, 208–15, 248, 252, 314, 332, 347, 361, 363, 376, 385–6, 390

  external, 205–6, 326

Economies of scope: *see* synergy

Economies of speed, 213

Edgeworth Box, 127–8, 143

Efficiency, 174, 193–8, 202, 206–7, 248, 270, 336, 376

  allocative, 193–6, 202, 208

  dynamic, 198

  minimum efficient scale of production, 153, 347, 382

  Pareto, 127–8, 196, 403

  X-efficiency, 177, 196–8, 208, 255, 259, 306–7, 371

Endgames, 316–19

Engineering, 159–61, 185–6, 347, 376, 381

Entrepreneurship, 114, 158, 162, 205, 212, 225–6, 261, 273, 301–3, 311–12, 315, 329, 337, 345, 355, 368, 376

Entry/Exit, 17, 219–23, 226, 248–51, 255, 267, 277–82, 292, 295, 303, 306–9, 312–14, 337, 375, 393–4, 399

  barriers to, 1, 153, 182, 191, 214, 223, 259, 318–19, 337, 349, 389

  costless, 272–4

  cross-, 262–5, 268, 292

  excessive, 219, 223

Environment, 16, 42, 191–2

Envy, 66

Equilibrium, 28, 32, 35–46, 60, 147, 150, 174, 204–6, 214–24, 248, 267, 339, 360

  comparative static, 145–6, 209, 226, 261

  general, 211, 298, 301, 309–10, 338–9

  multiple equilibria, 39

  partial equilibrium method, 210–11

  Nash equilibria, 143

  stability of, 65, 145–6, 300

Essay technique, 12–15

Estate agents, 299, 308, 353, 357–60

Ethics, 40–42, 324

Exchange, 323

Exchange rate, 17, 200, 232, 243–4, 366, 377, 379, 382, 386, 393

Excitement, 88–90

Expectations, xii, 71–2, 91, 111, 152, 244, 396

  rational, 305

Expected utility theory, 104–13 *passim*, 118–19, 141

Experience, 167, 176, 233, 244, 253, 266, 270, 330, 351, 354, 366

  experience good, 24, 37, 80, 126, 390–92, 395

Experimentation, 14, 71, 99, 108–9, 125, 146, 148–50, 193, 217, 225, 265, 280, 344, 400

Evolutionary analysis, 145–8, 174, 177, 189, 204, 209, 217, 226, 247, 303, 325, 331, 360, 368–9

Fashion goods, 26, 65, 96, 174, 316–17, 321, 393–5, 399

Filofax, 393–9

Finance, 332

Financial services, 305–9, 388

Fire-fighting behaviour, 186, 190, 198

Firm,

  as a coalition, 191–2, 198

  boundaries/size of, 210–12, 272, 328–37, 360, 367–80

  life-cycle of, 206

  managerial theories of, 255–8

  multi-product, 360, 372

  nature of, 325–32, 382

  optimum size of, 217

  representative, 206, 212, 225, 245

First-mover advantages, 147, 250, 307–8, 333, 348, 359–60

Flexibility, 122, 152, 168, 187–9, 214, 283, 313, 331

Framing effect, 90–91, 100, 109, 132, 287

Franchising, 141, 152–3, 175, 266–7, 280, 295, 344, 351–60, 380, 385, 388–92, 397, 401–2

Free disposal, 40–42, 165

Funder–provider split, 371

Gambling, 105, 108–11

  fair gamble, 105–6

  gambler preference map, 116–17

Games, 31, 104, 127, 136–42, 182, 220, 304

Gearing ratio, 362

Giffen good, 48–9, 57–8

Goodwill, 205, 211, 225, 232, 243–4, 262, 265–8, 272–4, 327, 332, 337, 360, 391, 399

Greenhouse effect, 143, 309–11

Guarantees/warranties, 103, 138, 285, 326

Habits, 33, 63, 100, 323, 356
Hedging, 126, 361–4, 373, 378–9, 387
Heuristics (see also decision rules), 68
Hierarchies,
    of decision-makers, 139, 329
    of firms, 344
    of problems, 68
    of wants, 41–2, 58, 77, 254
    organizational, 191, 328–9, 334, 344, 367–8, 403
Hit-and-run raid, 243, 273–4, 281–2
Home economics, 27
Hostages, 323–4
Housing market, 51, 96–8, 357–60

Ignorance, 31–3, 124–6, 198, 277, 293, 329, 334
Image, 378
Imagination, 113, 121, 310
Income,
    changes in, 33, 46, 78
    effect, 47–50, 57, 63, 211, 254
    real, 45–51
Income consumption curve, 46–7
Incumbent producers, 216, 223, 262–3, 268, 270, 272–4, 277, 293, 306–7, 346, 374
Indecomposability, 330, 372, 379
Indeterminacy, 127
Indifference curves, 23, 35–57 *passim*, 69, 98–9, 106, 115, 127–31, 159
Indivisibilities, 58–9, 99, 161, 172–5, 194, 252, 347, 360
Induction, 28
Industry,
    concentration of, 201, 374
    espionage in, 312
    leadership, 199–201, 207
    operational definition of, 54, 218
    structure, 272
Inferior good, 46–8, 78–9
Infinite regress, 31, 70–71
Inflation, 182, 262
Information, 29–33, 37, 67–75, 78, 86, 91–2, 95–8, 132, 140–41, 145, 148, 157–8, 191–3, 260, 272, 294, 300, 309, 324–9, 333, 337, 347–8, 361–3, 380, 389–90
    agreements, 339
    asymmetric, 324, 326
    confidential/secret, 153, 253, 335, 345–9, 364, 387–9
    impactedness, 329
    market for, 273–4, 383
    misinformation, 217
    overload, 190
    private, 271
    promotional, 251
    technology, 186
Innovation, 2, 37, 147, 187, 198–200, 239, 260, 270, 293–4, 303, 307, 397
Input–output model, 300
Instability, 303–9
Institutions, 143, 309, 322–3, 325, 339
Insurance, 106–8, 112, 142, 190, 196, 277, 308, 311, 362–4, 379, 387, 402
    brokers, 300, 277
    excess, 108
Integration, 329, 341, 376, 380–81, 384
    backward, 342, 361, 382
    forward, 342, 361, 382
    quasi-, 343–8, 380, 401
    taper, 342, 344, 347, 350, 392
    vertical, ix, 188, 312–13, 317, 322, 337, 341–52, 361, 374, 378, 388, 391, 402
Interdependence, 136–42, 171–4, 218–20, 248, 256, 294, 304
Interest rates, 306, 374
Intermediaries, 279, 299, 332–3, 346, 358, 403
Internalization, xi, 326–37, 341–9, 351, 361, 364–5, 378, 380–84, 400–401
Intolerance, 40, 76, 98
Inventories, 186, 269, 287, 293, 320
Investment, 31, 103, 120–22, 140, 153, 172, 174, 181–3, 199, 205, 232, 241, 265, 268, 272, 300–301, 304–16, 319, 338, 343, 359–61, 370, 374, 397
    competitive, 304
    complementary, 304, 312, 343
    consumer, 396
    overseas, 385–9
    portfolio, 362–3
    property, 389
Invisible hand, 298, 303, 337
Involvement, 69, 74–5, 100, 119–20, 358
Irreversibility, 103, 119–20, 140, 146–7, 205, 268, 293
Isocost lines, 147, 159, 162–3, 169–70
Iso-profit lines, 173–4
Isoquants, 147, 159–63, 169–70, 205
Iso-revenue lines, 170–71

Japanese business, 185–9, 199–20, 311, 335, 344, 365, 371, 393–9
Job-sharing, 364
Joint ventures, 124, 308, 350, 354, 380–85, 388, 403
Judgements, 71, 91, 150, 273, 364, 376
Just in Time (JIT), 175, 177, 186, 189, 344

Knowledge, 154, 167, 184, 193, 197, 261, 264, 293, 299, 308, 312–13, 330, 335, 345, 349, 378, 383–4, 387
    idiosyncratic/specialist, 192, 201, 330, 364, 376, 384
    tacit, 167, 185, 197, 338, 345, 348, 363, 366, 383

Labour mobility, 339
Learning, 33, 139, 149, 177, 241, 247
    by customers, 180, 204, 233, 243
    by entrepreneurs, 301
    by students, 7–11, 19, 22, 203
    curve, 17, 80, 177–81, 184, 189, 199, 202, 205, 213, 223, 233, 251–2, 327
    within firms, 184–5, 334–5, 379
Leasing, 308, 334, 356
Licensing, 139, 238, 252–3, 335, 344, 362, 380, 386, 399, 402
Linear programming, 172–4
Linkages, 154, 174–6, 317, 322, 341, 361–2
Liquidity, 17, 311
Loss-leader, 277, 280, 292, 341
Loyalty, 185, 343

Mafia, 324
Management, 157–8, 167, 186–7, 191–3, 196–200, 212, 247
    buyouts, 374
    by objectives, 197
    information systems, 186, 351
    manuals, 184
    public utility, 157, 193
    scientific, 205
    team, 181, 255–60, 268, 329–35, 346, 363–6, 384
Marginal product, 163–5, 225, 297, 330
Marginal rate of substitution, 44, 60
    constant, 38, 60
    diminishing, 34, 48, 64
Marginal revenue, 146, 215–17, 221–30, 244,

248–9, 257–8, 261, 276, 279, 284
Marginal utility theory, 23–5, 193–6
Marginalism, 71, 218, 224–7, 232, 248–9, 266, 275–81, 284, 288–90, 293, 360
Marketing, 18, 29, 37, 53, 67–9, 72, 101–2, 149, 177, 217–18, 238–9, 243, 248–50, 261, 264, 274–5, 286, 308, 327, 332–3, 352, 361, 369, 371, 377–81, 389
    direct, 282–3
    export, 380, 385, 393–8
    mix, 293
    strategic, 364
Markets, 144, 149, 298–301, 325–33
    capital, 198, 260, 346, 365–6, 372–6
    captive, 347, 359, 377
    commodity, 264, 300
    factor, 197, 248, 263, 269, 312
    failure of, ix, 327, 329, 333, 345, 378, 387
    forward, 338
    futures, 311–12
    imperfections of, 144, 197, 199, 259–60, 276, 311, 337, 346, 349, 363, 387
    internal, 330–31, 364–6, 375–7
    labour, 329, 338, 364, 387
    leader, 233
    saturation, 396
    segmentation, 250, 399
    share of, 201, 218–22, 272, 275, 306
    stock, 125, 260, 268, 300, 363
    structure, 245, 259
    thin, 270
    wholesale, 269
Marshallian district, 325–6
Mass production, 184, 187–8
McDonald's, 352–7
Meat-processing industry, 291, 321
Megacorp, 268
Mergers, 175, 238, 315, 335–6, 338, 373–80, 384
Merit good, 52
Method, 2–4, 6, 11, 23–6, 62–3, 94–6, 119, 245, 259, 270, 314
Miller's rule, 30, 73, 97, 100, 201
Miniaturization, 253
Mission statement, 191
Money pump, 37
Monopoly, 195–8, 201, 207, 210–12, 216, 221–3, 243–4, 248, 277–8, 280, 285, 290, 294–5, 348, 374–5, 387
    natural, 195, 197

regulation of, 193–6
Monopsony, 212
Monotonicity, 39
Moral dimension of choice, 40, 78
Motivation, 157–8, 177, 347, 354, 374
Motorcycle industry, 80, 184
Mugging, 361–3, 387
Multinational enterprise, 252–3, 366, 372, 385–92, 400–403
Multi-process operations, 225

Natural resources, 338
Needs, 41–2, 396
Negotiation, 127–35, 192, 206, 329, 348, 380–82
Neoclassical economics, 34–64 *passim*, 94, 98–9, 127, 130–31, 140, 145–70 *passim*, 205, 245, 256, 263, 293, 298, 324, 337, 360, 396
New Institutional Economics (NIE), 322–32, 337, 345, 380
Normative economics, 28, 62, 113, 123, 141

Occam's Razor, 28
Oligopoly, 20–22, 31, 145, 177, 196, 218–21, 226, 229–31, 245, 248, 256, 266, 270, 275, 279, 281–2, 294–5, 313, 316, 320, 339
Opportunism, xiv, 324, 329–33, 336, 346–51, 362, 364, 367, 369–73, 381–4, 387, 391, 400–401
Optimality/constrained optimization, 32, 38, 42, 68–70, 88, 145–8, 158, 162, 168–74, 190, 193, 261, 291, 314
Option, 299
Optometrists, 356–60
Organization, 151, 154–5, 324
  industrial, 153, 230, 333
  internal, 145, 151, 207, 259–60, 367–71
  structure of, 158, 177, 213, 367–73, 379–80, 402–3
Organizational slack, 192, 198, 200, 208, 255, 258, 270–71, 307, 310, 317, 330, 373, 376

Patent, 16, 199, 238, 360, 383, 397
Path dependence, 89, 92–3, 147
Payback period, 182
Perishability, 332–3, 388
Piracy, 355, 360, 386
Planning, 298–301, 315, 338–9
Pollution, 172
Portfolio choice, 117, 362–3

Positive economics, 62, 113, 123
Potential surprise theory, 112–19, 123, 134, 141
Prediction, 71, 119–26, 141, 381
Preferences, 33–42, 44, 71, 95, 98, 109, 127, 147, 159, 276, 299–303, 309–10, 338, 385
  cardinal, 34, 47, 58, 106, 159
  changes in, 37–8, 61, 76
  lexicographic, 41–2, 63–4, 129–31, 256
  ordinal, 34, 47, 106
  reversal of, 108
  separable, 54
Prices and pricing, 25, 31, 44–51, 63–4, 77–8, 135, 137–9, 144, 148, 151, 166, 174, 180–84, 193–7, 203, 206–44 *passim*, 247–94 *passim*, 298–309, 315, 319–22, 325, 374, 393–8
  complications caused by jointness, 21–2, 290–93, 341, 382
  customary, 227
  discounting, 266–7
  dispersion of, 265, 295
  'full-cost' theory of, 225–7, 248–9, 260–61
  future, 305
  gambit price, 131–4
  guide price, 326
  hedonic prices analysis, 59–60, 87, 277
  indicator of quality, 61, 227, 233, 277, 323
  input, 210–11
  long-run, 327
  marginal cost pricing, 50–51, 157, 193, 195
  market clearing, 211, 226, 249, 263–4, 289
  mark-up, 218, 260–71, 279–80, 286–94, 322
  natural prices, 312
  normal cost theory of, 145, 177, 260–72, 276–7, 288–93, 322, 375
  penetration, 250–51
  predatory, 243, 273, 374–5
  price-consumption curve, 45
  price discrimination, 135, 195–6, 217, 250, 282–8
  price effect, 47–8, 57
  price-leadership, 226, 228, 230, 279, 307
  price mechanism, 151–2, 298–301, 337–8
  price signals, 298, 314–15, 334
  price-taker, 305
  price war, 16, 181–2, 219–20, 230, 232, 243–4, 249, 318–19
  Ramsey price, 196–7, 272
  reservation price, 107, 132–5

secondhand price, 120, 140, 146, 154, 182–3, 232, 308, 321
 skimming, 250–2, 268–9, 397
 stickiness, 226
 transfer price, 366
Principal, 299, 325
 -agent problem, 330, 346–7, 382, 385
Principle of Gross Substitution, 40, 63, 74
Priorities, 74–7, 83, 98, 149, 254, 301
Prisoner's Dilemma, 136–8, 141, 220
Probabilities, 104–13, 118–19, 134, 141, 309, 395
Problem-solving behaviour, 28–32, 86, 190–91, 225, 258, 360, 380–84
Procedures, 67, 125–6, 131
Producer surplus, 194
Product, 231, 374, 394
 base model, 135
 bundling, 287–8, 307, 392
 by-, 16, 172, 291, 361
 characteristics/attributes of, 16–18, 52–60, 72–88, 95, 250, 320, 394–6
 complementary, 16, 239, 243, 371–2
 differentiation, 1, 214, 217–19, 224, 248, 264–5, 268, 318–20. 349
 idiosyncratic/specialized, 290, 326–7, 332, 334
 intermediate, 264
 joint, 172, 175, 177, 368
 life-cycle, 16, 23, 25, 78–9, 149, 180, 251, 289, 316, 349–50, 362–5, 386, 395
 pioneering, 249–51, 345, 376
 range, 16, 21, 175, 239, 243, 290, 317, 396
 standardized, 320, 322, 332
 transformation curve, 170–71
 uniformity of, 355
Production function, 147, 159–67, 176–7, 197, 201, 205, 312
Productivity, 148–9, 165–7, 181–6, 191–3, 197–8, 223, 340, 366, 370, 375
Professional services, 152–3, 358–60
Profit, 120, 155, 180, 193, 195–6, 204, 207, 221, 228, 231, 235–6, 242–4, 248, 255–8, 279, 285–6, 301–2, 307, 362, 366, 380
 centre, 369–72
 constraint, 147, 256–8
 function, 145
 margin, 78, 174, 199, 207, 210, 268, 271, 277, 292, 374, 403

 maximization, 171–4, 256–60, 295
 motive, 300
 retained, 268
 supernormal, 199, 214–19, 269–71, 292–3
Programmes, 67, 341
Promotion, 393–9
Prospect Theory, 104, 109–12
Protocol analysis, 81
Psychology, 7–8, 28, 30, 33, 34, 38, 64, 67, 70, 72, 88–94, 97, 110, 134, 140, 190, 282, 301–2, 307, 317
Public choice, 29
Publishing industry, 1, 283–5, 288–90, 343, 346–7, 361

Quality, 149, 153, 186, 254, 274–5, 308, 340, 353, 391–3, 396
 control of, 186–7, 251, 266, 327–8, 346, 351–9, 377–9, 387–8
Quantity discounts, 43, 283, 286, 288
Quasi-fixed factors, 225

Randomness, 125–6, 136, 140, 220, 266, 274
Ratebuster, 193
Rationality, 36–8, 73, 100, 136, 217
 bounded, 31–2, 43, 67, 71, 77, 94–5, 101, 110, 117, 121, 123, 145, 148, 167, 184, 190–93, 198, 201, 260, 271, 307, 310, 341, 345, 367–8, 395, 399–400
 global, 30, 32, 67
Rationalization, 362–3, 368
Re-buys, 265, 352
Recipes for success, 68, 190–91
Recontracting, 299
Recorded music industry, 22–6, 138–9, 283, 314, 343, 371–2, 403
Reference point, 73, 109, 114, 116, 185, 191
Reflection effect, 109
Reflexivity, 36–7, 71
Regret Theory, 111
Relational contracting, xii, 152–3, 185, 266–7, 274, 309, 313, 332, 343, 387
Reputation, 95, 132, 139–40, 175–6, 233, 238, 264, 289, 313, 326, 346, 360, 366, 390, 401
Resale price maintenance, 266–7, 281
Research and development (R&D), 148, 167, 177, 191, 198, 368, 398
Research programme, 94–6, 324
Resource-based view of firms, 153–5

Retailing, 175, 216, 218, 238–44, 266–7, 278–81, 292, 343–4

Returns to scale,
constant, 160–61, 210, 266
decreasing, 160–62, 327
increasing, 160–62, 195–6, 205, 208–12, 217, 310

Richardson problem, 243, 309, 315–16, 322, 337, 348

Rip-off, 78, 250

Risk, 18, 33, 99, 103–42 *passim*, 151, 268, 302, 309, 326, 334, 345–51, 361–5, 372, 379, 391–2
risk aversion, 106–9, 142
risk-lover, 106, 109
risk neutrality, 106
risk premium, 274, 352

Routines, 68, 148, 202

Royalties, 239–43, 344, 390

Rules of thumb, 33, 68, 70, 132, 148, 168, 190, 198, 225–6, 232, 289

Safety first principle, 112

Satiation, 39, 44

Satisficing, 32, 68–71, 95, 118, 147–8, 218, 190–93, 225, 256, 270

Saving, 66, 142, 311

Scenario planning, 63, 113, 119–24, 134, 141, 143, 168, 236–8, 241

Search/shopping around, 29, 33, 70–71, 97, 191, 205, 253, 264, 271, 277, 287, 299, 395

Self-control, 64, 93–4, 323

Self-employment, 329

Shareholders, 191–3, 207, 247, 255, 260, 295–6, 330–32, 343, 349, 362–3, 366, 372–3, 379–80

Shell International Petroleum Company, 121–4

Side payments, 192

Signalling, 103, 137, 149, 151–2, 232, 293, 298, 314–15, 387–8

Situational determinism, 150

Skills, 17, 187–9, 197, 262, 381–4

Smoothness, 38

Snob appeal, 78

Social aspects of choice, 24, 66, 69, 73, 75, 78, 95, 126, 141, 191, 254–5, 264–6, 274, 346, 350–51, 393–9

Specialization, 161, 187–9, 191, 202, 214, 252, 287, 323, 326, 341, 350, 361–5, 368, 376, 391, 397

Specificity of assets, 12, 154, 238, 318–19, 334, 343, 345, 348, 382, 397, 400–401

Speculation, 255, 264, 311, 322, 332

Stability/instability, 25, 319–22

Standardization, 184, 340, 352, 356–9, 372

Status, 78, 89, 175, 186–7, 395

Stocks, 262, 269, 292, 332, 399, 403

Strategic planning, 148, 190

Strategy, 18, 174–6, 243, 298, 330, 333–4, 340–42, 345–52, 360–80, 394–403

Stress, 90

Strikes, 133, 179–80

Structural change, 181–4, 199

Subcontracting, 17, 174, 176, 186–8, 238, 321–3, 342–52, 372, 378–9, 397

Subgoal pursuit, 191–2, 214, 255, 330

Subjective expected utility (SEU) theory: *see* Expected utility theory

Subjectivism, 61, 156–7, 269, 277–8

Substitution, 33, 159–60, 166–70, 200, 205, 232, 236, 268, 271, 276, 277, 289, 320, 395
effect, 47–50, 57, 63, 78
elasticity of, 218
marginal technical rate of, 160

Superstition, 125

Supply, elasticity of, 214

Supply and demand theory, 24–6, 120, 144, 226, 245, 298–309 *passim*

Supply curves, 25, 183, 194, 201, 245, 251, 303
kinked, 191

Supply price, 208

Surprise, 112–21, 148, 152, 248, 334, 400

Survey-based research, 224–7

SWOT analysis, 393

Synergy, 16, 21, 154–5, 172, 175, 177, 243, 317, 335, 341, 344–5, 361–3, 368, 371–3, 376–80, 392, 398

Tactics, 340–41

Takeover raiders, 255, 259, 268, 362–5, 374

Tangency solution, 215–16, 220, 248, 255, 280

Targets: *see* aspiration levels

Tariffs, 232, 381, 386

Tastes: *see* preferences

Taxation, 44, 63–6, 193–6, 208, 258–9, 378
corporate, 366
poll tax, 196
Selective Employment Tax, 216

Teamwork, 329–33, 383–4
Technology, 299–300, 378–9
    blueprints of, 167, 197, 205, 331, 344, 397
    changes in, 146–9, 181–3, 186, 199–200, 204,
        242, 247, 250, 303, 310, 316–17, 328,
        349, 356, 361, 380, 386
    embodied, 181
    intermediate, 166
    of consumption, 55–7, 61
    of production, 53–4, 120, 158–66, 191, 328,
        330, 348
    standards, 138–9, 147, 149, 316, 371
    transfer, 253, 386–7, 401
    vintages of, 167, 181–3, 223
Tenders, 137, 269, 274
Tests of adequacy, 72–6
Threshold effect, 38, 71, 190
Tie-break, 74–8, 82, 84, 86, 93, 117
Time, 205, 209, 213, 226, 267, 311, 327
    historical, 146
    horizon, 266–8, 278, 371, 375, 381, 385, 401
    logical, 146, 166
Tipping, 332
Tourism and hospitality industry, 388–92
Trade association, 138, 153, 311, 326, 351, 358
Transfer earnings, 192
Transitivity, 37–8, 74, 87, 91
Travel agents, 300, 390–91
Trial and error, 146, 148, 224
Trust, 313, 323, 343, 347
Turbulence, 71, 192

Two-part tariff, 196

Uncertainty, 31, 33, 43, 61, 70, 75, 88–9, 100,
    103–42 *passim*, 148–9, 153, 192, 198, 223,
    264, 268, 274, 283, 289, 294, 301–5,
    310–11, 322, 334–6, 343–5, 349, 381–4, 400
Universities, 158, 341, 353, 402
Utility function, 106, 109, 145, 159, 193–4
    cardinal, 159
    concave, 106–7, 109
    convex, 106, 109
    linear, 106
Utility maximization, 34
Utility tree, 54, 68, 99

Vacations, 53–8
Vegetarianism, 40–41, 63, 145
Video cassette recorders, 27, 29, 53, 84–8,
    138–9, 147, 370–72
Virtuous circle, 199, 252, 254
Voice mechanism, 151–2, 311, 314, 346

Wages, 166–8, 183, 201, 227–8, 387
Welfare economics, 50–52, 157, 193–8, 215–18,
    102, 127–8, 208–9, 313
Wholesalers, 279, 399, 403
Wishful thinking, 92, 123
World-views, 8–11, 22–3, 91–2, 184–5, 278,
    369, 371

Yuppies, 254, 393–8